IN SEARCH OF EARLY AMERICA

THE WILLIAM & MARY QUARTERLY

1943-1993

The *William and Mary Quarterly,* Third Series, is a publication of the Institute of Early American History and Culture. The Institute is sponsored jointly by the College of William and Mary and the Colonial Williamsburg Foundation.

IN SEARCH OF EARLY AMERICA

CONTENTS

FOREWORD

During my twenty-four years of teaching, commercial publishers have sent me numerous collections of essays purporting to reflect the most important historical scholarship to which graduate and undergraduate students should be exposed as part of their academic experience in advanced courses and surveys. Invariably, these books have left me wondering about the rationale used in selecting the writings they include. Because only a few scholars ever seem to be involved in the assembling of these texts, I have tended to regard such volumes as presenting only a partial view of what constitutes a given field's "most significant" work, and I have often mused about what early Americanists as a whole would identify as the seminal contributions of their peers. At the risk of being labeled a consensus historian, I have to admit that I really wanted a consensus, arrived at democratically. Hence my decision to poll the readership of the *William and Mary Quarterly*.

The articles reprinted in this collection represent a remarkable range of perspectives. The topics, the methodology, and the creative use of varied sources suggest how research and writing about early America have developed during the Institute of Early American History and Culture's first half-century of existence, while the postscripts by the nine living authors remind us of the politics of history. If students in the 1990s are amazed to discover how radical and even unpopular it once was to try to record the experience of the inarticulate or to challenge accepted ways of thinking about the American Revolution, they must also be impressed by the energy and acuity of the debates and the passionate sense of engagement that historians bring to their work.

Juxtaposed with the personal reflections of their authors, these essays offer especially compelling evidence that the study of the past is a challenging and important pursuit worthy of the time, attention, and investment of bright and lively minds. For the generations of students who will be reading this book, that strikes me as the most important point *In Search of Early America* can make.

Ronald Hoffman
Director

INTRODUCTION

The fifty volumes of the Third Series of the *William and Mary Quarterly,* containing some 1,200 articles, testify to the productivity and quality of early American historical studies, for which the *Quarterly* is the primary journal. They make a running report on scholarly interests, highlighted by articles that challenge conventions, advance interpretation, and prompt fresh inquiry. The present editors, mindful of their distinguished predecessors, join the Institute's director in proudly presenting a representation of such articles to mark the semicentennial of the founding of the Institute of Early American History and Culture.

The eleven articles reprinted here constitute an ongoing meditation on the making and meaning of America; postscripts by the nine living authors help bring the act of reflection up to date. Enhanced by afterthought, these texts show historical intelligence in action, at peak form. Here are historians thinking, talking, asking questions, sometimes arguing, continually inventing and reinventing their field of vision.

The collection exhibits certain clusterings. Immediately obvious is a strong tilt toward the eighteenth century; only two essays address the seventeenth—two and a half, allowing for the seventeenth-century origins of Edmund S. Morgan's "Puritan Ethic." This distribution approximates that of the Third Series as a whole. There is also a marked concentration on the American Revolution and the Revolutionary experience, reflecting American historians' concern with their nation's formative moment. A streak of American exceptionalism runs through such essays as those by Perry Miller, whose Puritans are doomed to be "left alone with America"—one of the most memorable exit lines in historical writing—and Gordon S. Wood, whose Revolution is unique in being "peculiarly an affair of the mind." At the same time, several authors take cues from current British scholarship, and two develop explicitly comparative frames of reference—Pauline Maier by noting similarities between English and American mobs; Lois Green Carr and Lorena S. Walsh primarily by noting differences in the conditions of English and American women's lives. As the agenda of early American studies continues to expand in such directions as these, the comparative dimension takes on ever greater importance.

The collection reproduces a striking revision of historical thinking that became visible in the 1960s. It reflects the dominance of intellectual history in the early years of the Third Series and indicates how that genre was refashioning itself as the study of cultural values and ideology. There is a kind of climax in Gordon Wood's 1966 observations about "the predominantly intellectual character" of the Revolution and the "explanative force" of ideas; the "republican synthesis" was already taking shape. Then, just two years later, Jesse Lemisch's "Jack Tar" signaled a change. Thereafter, social history took the lead; many of the social historians' projects focused on people who were relatively disadvantaged, insecure, and inarticulate, as represented here by Lemisch's sailors, Rhys Isaac's Virginia Baptists, Lois Carr and Lorena Walsh's Maryland women, and Alfred F. Young's Boston shoemaker.

In another sense, the appearance of deep change and radical reorientation is illusory. A closer look into these essays suggests that the transition, much trumpeted at the time, was neither very sudden nor very sharp. As early as 1957, in the heyday of intellectual history, Morgan offered an argument and a program for the study of local institutions. A decade later, Wood opened a door—though it seemed to some at the time merely a side door—to a new generation of behavioral historians. On the other side, Lemisch maintained that sailor Jack "had a mind of his own" and envisioned a middle region "between ideology and inertness." The essays by Isaac, Young, and James A. Henretta explore that region— the expansive ground of "mentality"—to locate deeply patterned, pervasive, and persistent constructions of social reality. Rounding the volume's circle, such studies of "consciousness" in relation to social structures, conditions, and experience bring us back to Miller's examination of the Puritan mind under pressure and in flux.

A notable feature of these essays—and, surely, a reason why our subscribers chose them—is that, in one way or another, they started something. Work of this kind justifies the article form by seizing the opportunity to try out a new thought or suggest a fresh approach, to test an innovative method of analysis, to speculate, to take chances—without having to commit to anything as formidable as a book. Such articles are high-risk productions—for their authors and for their editors, too. Such venturesome, valuable pieces are well represented in this selection.

Perry Miller's "Errand," published just months before the second volume of his *New England Mind*, focused the theme of declension (a.k.a. Americanization) in Puritan culture that teased the minds of a subsequent generation or two of scholars. Cecelia Kenyon not only took seriously the long-neglected Antifederalist alternative but also gave a strong post-Progressive push to the study of the "theoretical foundations" and "ideological context of the Constitution." Gordon Wood advertised and advanced the turn to ideology in the study of past politics. Edmund Morgan, as noted, urged systematic inquiry into local communities.

Jesse Lemisch, in the 1960s, gave a working demonstration of how to draw the story of the inarticulate out of traditional sources; with Pauline Maier, he expanded historians' notions of the nature and extent of a political act. Rhys Isaac's dramatic contrasting of the social worlds of gentry and evangelical dissenters underlined emergent interest in popular culture viewed from an ethnographic angle. Lois Carr and Lorena Walsh, frankly committed to asking questions, linked gender, demography, and numbers to blaze "trails in the public records" looking for clues to people who left no written records of their own; their article illustrates the movement of historical attention from New England to the Chesapeake. Grounding the values and attitudes of farm families in the material conditions of their lives, James Henretta focused attention on the emergence of the market economy. Alfred Young's experiment in social biography—the "life history of an ordinary man"—provided a model of its kind. The richly personalized and populated work of Isaac, Young, and Lemisch helped set the pace and standard for a people-centered history. It was a memorable day when Jack Tar came rolling up Broadway into historians' ken. It was another when Brother Waller took his whipping and then "went back singing praise to God" to "preach with a great deal of liberty."

This volume shows historians speaking to each other, among themselves. Much of the conversation runs along familiar lines of shoptalk projecting intentions, exchanging views, and defining positions in the continual negotiation through which scholars establish place and purpose. Kenyon, Morgan, and Wood all talk back to Charles A. Beard. Henretta comes to grips with James T. Lemon and Charles S. Grant. Wood writes a brief for Bernard Bailyn. Carr and Walsh clarify issues and offer agendas for consideration by fellow workers in social history. Footnotes keep the conversation going with the sotto voce exchange of references to others' work that underwrites the scholarly community of discourse. Significantly, footnotes swell with the rise of the new social history: there were vast stores of material to uncover and new methods to perfect for exploiting it; many participants were joining in as the profession boomed in the 1960s and into the 1970s; these cohorts were animated by a powerful commitment to collaborative enterprise for which footnotes served a networking function.

First and last, much of the talk is academic, though all these articles prove, and some prove beyond a doubt, that academic prose is not invariably prosy. People who write for learned periodicals like the *Quarterly* tend naturally to write for people like themselves—scholars, teachers, students, interested nonacademic readers. At the same time, as citizens of the wider world of public affairs, with engagements and obligations that reach beyond the campus, historians sometimes speak past each other, through and beyond their immediate subjects, to bring their thought to bear—more or less critically—on aspects of the larger polity or culture. Thus Cecelia Kenyon's account of the Antifederalists can be read as an attempt to break open the intellectual lockbox of 1950s politics. Lemisch's and Maier's theme of "rioting as political expression" recalls the 1960s, as does Lemisch's poignant surprise that so many jailed seamen "remained Americans" at all. Noteworthy, too, are Morgan's ambivalent thought about the persistence of the Puritan ethic—"perhaps it is not quite dead yet"; Maier's remark that "popular impatience constituted," or was believed to constitute, "an essential force in the maintenance of free institutions," with the reverse twist of her coda; Isaac's invocation of radical communal values; perhaps above all Miller's mordant musings on the angst of a society—the Puritans' or our own—whose best minds know that "something has gone wrong," who "do not know where they are going" or what, as a society, they are.

Although *In Search of Early America* is commemorative in purpose, it deserves to be regarded not as a monument but as a challenge, not as a shrine but as an incentive. The volume represents the achievement of a half-century of early American historical studies, to be sure; equally important, it constitutes a point of departure, as the authors' own postscripts variously recognize and urge. These essays, standing proxy for many of comparable worth in this journal and others, exhibit the historical mind and imagination not only pursuing unfinished business but regularly rewriting the overall agenda. The field of early American history and culture is what it is today because such men and women have developed it—earnestly, skillfully, intelligently. Their best reward will be the constant renewal and expansion—by encompassing a broadening range of cultures and disciplines—of the conversation to which their scholarship has made such signal contributions.

The contents of this book were selected by a poll of subscribers during the fall of 1992 and the winter of 1993. Readers report finding the choosing difficult and rewarding. Asked to pick the "ten most significant" articles (a tenth place tie led to the inclusion of eleven), some expressed a wish to name twenty, thirty, or more. One respondent chose six and wrote, "After these come about twenty more—recent ones—so equal that I cannot select four as superior, so will refrain." More than one reader noted that the ballot list was "a great resource" for reading and research that "provoked serious consideration of where we have been the last fifty years." The editors are grateful to the hundreds of subscribers who devoted time and thought to creating this work.

Balloting was conducted, and the edition produced, under the direction of Ann Gross, managing editor of the *Quarterly*, assisted by Gregory B. Poitras, Catherine Lunt, the journal's staff, and the Institute's editorial apprentices. Catherine Mason and Kelly Thompson of Catalyst Design created the cover and interior design.

Presented in chronological order of publication, the articles appear as originally printed in every substantive respect. Typographical errors, where caught, have been silently corrected. Technical details conform to current *Quarterly* style.

Michael McGiffert
Editor

ERRAND INTO THE WILDERNESS

PERRY MILLER

It was a happy inspiration that led the staff of the John Carter Brown Library to choose as the title of its New England exhibition of 1952 a phrase from Samuel Danforth's election sermon, delivered on May 11, 1670: *A Brief Recognition of New England's Errand into the Wilderness*. It was of course an inspiration, if not of genius at least of talent, for Danforth to invent his title in the first place. But all the election sermons of this period—that is to say, the major expressions of the second generation, which, delivered on these forensic occasions, were in the fullest sense community expression—have interesting titles; a mere listing tells the story of what was happening to the minds and emotions of the New England people: John Higginson's *The Cause of God and His People In New-England* of 1663, William Stoughton's *New England's True Interest, Not to Lie* in 1668, Thomas Shepard's *Eye-Salve* in 1672, Urian Oakes's *New England Pleaded With* in 1673, and, climactically and most explicitly, Increase Mather's *A Discourse Concerning the Danger of Apostasy* in 1677.

All of these show by their title-pages alone—and, as those who have looked into them know, infinitely more by their contents—a deep disquietude. They are troubled utterances, worried, fearful. Something has gone wrong. As in 1662 Wigglesworth already was saying in verse, God has a controversy with New England; He has cause to be angry and to punish it because of its innumerable defections. They say, unanimously, that New England was sent on an errand, and that it has failed.

To our ears these lamentations of the second generation sound strange indeed. We think of the founders as heroic men—of the towering stature of Bradford, Winthrop, and Thomas Hooker—who braved the ocean and the wilderness, who conquered both, and left to their children a goodly heritage. Why then this whimpering?

Some historians suggest that the second and third generations suffered a failure of nerve; they weren't the men their fathers had been, and they knew it. Where the founders could range over the vast body of theology and ecclesiastical polity and produce profound works like the treatises of John Cotton or the subtle psychological analyses of Hooker, or even such a gusty though wrong-headed book as Nathaniel Ward's *Simple Cobler*, let alone such lofty and right-headed

This address by Perry Miller, professor of American Literature at Harvard University, was delivered to the Associates of the John Carter Brown Library at their annual meeting on May 16, 1952, and is printed in the *Quarterly* through the cooperation of that organization. Mr. Miller's essay concerns itself with ideas which will be dealt with more fully in his forthcoming book, *The New England Mind*, volume II.

Ed. Note: This article was originally published in *William and Mary Quarterly*, 3d Ser., X (January 1953), 3–19.

pleas as Roger Williams' *Bloudy Tenent,* all these children could do was tell each other that they were on probation and that their chances of making good did not seem very promising.

Since Puritan intellectuals were thoroughly grounded in grammar and rhetoric, we may be certain that Danforth was fully aware of the ambiguity concealed in his word "errand." It already had taken on the double meaning which it still carries with us. Originally, as the word first took form in English, it meant exclusively a short journey on which an inferior is sent to convey a message or to perform a service for his superior. In that sense we today speak of an "errand-boy"; or the husband says that while in town on his lunch hour, he must run an errand for his wife. But by the end of the Middle Ages, errand developed another connotation: it came to mean the actual business on which the actor goes, the purpose itself, the conscious intention in his mind. In this signification, the runner of the errand is working for himself, is his own boss; the wife, while the husband is away at the office, runs her own errands. Now in the 1660s the problem was: which had New England originally been—an errand-boy or a doer of errands? In which sense had it failed? Had it been despatched for a further purpose, or was it an end in itself? Or had it fallen short not only in one or the other, but in both of the meanings? If so, it was indeed a tragedy, in the primitive sense of a fall from a mighty designation.

If the children were in grave doubt as to which had been the original errand—if, in fact, those of the founders who lived into the later period and who might have set their progeny to rights found themselves wondering and confused—there is little chance of our answering clearly. Of course, there is no problem about Plymouth Colony. That is the charm about Plymouth: its clarity. The Pilgrims, as we have learned to call them, were reluctant voyagers; they had never wanted to leave England, but had been obliged to depart because the authorities made life impossible for Separatists. They could, naturally, have stayed at home, had they given up being Separatists, but that idea simply did not occur to them. Yet they did not go to Holland as though on an errand; neither can we extract the notion of a mission out of the reasons which, as Bradford tells us, persuaded them to leave Leyden for "Virginia." The war with Spain was about to be resumed, and the economic threat was ominous; their migration was not so much an errand as a shrewd forecast, a plan to get out while the getting was good, lest, should they stay, they would be "intrapped or surrounded by their enemies, so as they should neither be able to fight nor flie." True, once the decision was taken, they congratulated themselves that they might become a means for propagating the gospel in remote parts of the world, and thus of serving as stepping-stones to others in the performance of this great work; nevertheless, the substance of their decision was that they "thought it better to dislodge betimes to some place of better advantage and less danger, if any such could be found." The great hymn that Bradford, looking back in his old age, chanted about the landfall is one of the greatest passages, if not the very greatest, in all New England's literature; yet it does not resound with the sense of a mission accomplished—instead, it vibrates with the sorrow and exultation of suffering, the sheer endurance, the pain and the anguish, with the somberness of death faced unflinchingly:

> May not and ought not the children of these fathers rightly say: Our fathers were Englishmen which came over this great ocean, and were ready to

perish in this wilderness; but they cried unto the Lord, and he heard their voyce, and looked on their adversitie.

We are bound, I think, to see in Bradford's account the prototype of the vast majority of subsequent immigrants—of those Oscar Handlin calls "The Uprooted": they came for better advantage and for less danger, and to give their posterity the opportunity of success.

The Great Migration of 1630 is an entirely other story. True, among the reasons John Winthrop drew up in 1629 to persuade himself and his colleagues that they should commit themselves to the enterprise, the economic motive frankly figures. Wise men thought England was overpopulated and that the poor would have a better chance in the new land. But Massachusetts Bay was not just an organization of immigrants seeking advantage and opportunity. It had a positive sense of mission—either it was sent on an errand or it had its own intention, but in either case the deed was deliberate. It was an act of will, perhaps of willfulness. These Puritans were not driven out of England (thousands of their fellows stayed and fought the Cavaliers)—they went of their own accord.

So, concerning them, we ask the question, why? If we are not altogether clear as to precisely how we should phrase the answer, this is not because they themselves were reticent. They spoke as fully as they knew how, and none more magnificently or cogently than John Winthrop in the midst of the passage itself, when he delivered a lay sermon aboard the flagship *Arbella* and called it *A Modell of Christian Charity*. It distinguishes the motives of this great enterprise from those of Bradford's forlorn retreat, and especially from those of the masses who later have come in quest of advancement. Hence, for the student of New England and of America, it is a fact demanding incessant brooding that John Winthrop selected as the "doctrine" of this discourse, and so as the basic proposition to which, it then seemed to him, the errand was committed, the thesis that God had disposed mankind in a hierarchy of social classes, so that "in all times some must be rich, some poore, some highe and eminent in power and dignitie; others mean and in subjeccion." It is as though, preternaturally sensing what the promise of America might come to signify for the rank and file, Winthrop took the precaution to drive out of their heads any notion that in the wilderness the poor and the mean were ever so to improve themselves as to mount above the rich or the eminent in dignity. Were there any who had signed up under the mistaken impression that such was the purpose of their errand, Winthrop told them that, although other peoples, lesser breeds, might come for wealth or pelf, this migration was specifically dedicated to an avowed end that had nothing to do with incomes. We have entered into an explicit covenant with God, "we have professed to enterprise these accions upon these and these ends"; we have drawn up indentures with the Almighty, wherefore if we succeed and do not let ourselves get diverted into making money, He will reward us. Whereas if we fail, if we "fall to embrace this present world and prosecute our carnall intencions, seeeking great things for our selves and our posterity, the Lord will surely break out in wrathe against us, be revenged of such a periured people and make us knowe the price of the breache of such a Covenant."

Well, what terms were agreed upon in this covenant? Winthrop could say precisely—"It is by a mutuall consent through a specially overruleing providence, and a more then ordinary approbation of the Churches of Christ to seeke out a place of Cohabitation and Consorteshipp under a due forme of Government both civill and ecclesiasticall." If it could be said thus concretely, why should there be any ambiguity? There was no doubt whatsoever as to what Winthrop meant by a due form of ecclesiastical government: he meant the pure Biblical polity set forth in full detail by the New Testament, that method which later generations, in the days of increasing confusion, would settle down to calling Congregational, but which for Winthrop was no denominational peculiarity but the very essence of organized Christianity. What a due form of civil government meant, therefore, became crystal clear: a political regime, possessing power, which would consider its main function to be the setting up, the protecting and preserving of this form of polity. This due form would have, at the very beginning of its list of responsibilities, the duty of suppressing heresy, of subduing or somehow getting rid of dissenters—of being, in short, deliberately, vigorously, and consistently intolerant.

Regarded in this light, the Massachusetts Bay Company came on an errand in the second and later sense of the word: it was, so to speak, on its own business. What it set out to do was the sufficient reason for its setting out. About this Winthrop seems to be perfectly certain as he declares specifically what the due forms will be attempting: the end is to improve our lives to do more service to the Lord, to increase the body of Christ and to preserve our posterity from the corruptions of this evil world, so that they in turn shall work out their salvation under the purity and power of Biblical ordinances. Because the errand was so definable in advance, certain conclusions about the method of conducting it were equally evident: one, obviously, was that those sworn to the covenant should not be allowed to turn aside in a lust for mere physical rewards; but another was, in Winthrop's simple but splendid words, "we must be knitt together in this worke as one man, wee must entertaine each other in brotherly affection," we must actually delight in each other, "always having before our eyes our Commission and community in the worke, our community as members of the same body." This was to say, were the great purpose kept steadily in mind, if all gazed only at it and strove only for it, then social solidarity (within a scheme of fixed and unalterable class distinctions) would be an automatic consequence. A society despatched upon an errand that is its own reward would want no other rewards: it could go forth to possess a land without ever becoming possessed by it; social gradations would remain eternally what God had originally appointed; there would be no internal contention among groups or interests, and though there would be hard work for everybody, prosperity would be bestowed not as a consequence of labor but as a sign of approval upon the mission itself. For once in the history of humanity (with all its sins), there would be a society so dedicated to a holy cause that success would prove innocent and triumph not raise up sinful pride or arrogant dissension.

Or, at least, this would come about if the people did not deal falsely with God, if they would live up to the articles of their bond. If we do not perform these terms, Winthrop warned, we may expect immediate manifestations of divine wrath, we shall perish out of the land we are crossing the sea to possess. And here in the 1660s and 1670s, all the jeremiads (of which Danforth's is one of the most poignant) are castigations of the people for having defaulted on precisely these articles. They recite the long list of afflictions an angry God had rained upon them, surely enough to prove how abysmally they had deserted the covenant:

crop failures, epidemics, grasshoppers, caterpillars, torrid summers, arctic winters, Indian wars, hurricanes, shipwrecks, accidents, and (most grievous of all) unsatisfactory children. The solemn work of the election day, said Stoughton in 1668, is "Foundation-work"—not, that is, to lay a new one, "but to continue, and strengthen, and beautifie, and build upon that which has been laid." It had been laid in the covenant before even a foot was set ashore, and thereon New England should rest. Hence the terms of survival, let alone of prosperity, remained what had first been propounded:

> If we should so frustrate and deceive the Lords Expectations, that his Covenant-interest in us, and the Workings of his Salvation be made to cease, then All were lost indeed; Ruine upon Ruine, Destruction upon Destruction would come, until one stone were not left upon another.

Since so much of the literature after 1660—in fact, just about all of it—dwells on this theme of declension and apostasy, would not the story of New England seem to be simply that of the failure of a mission? Winthrop's dread was realized: posterity had not found their salvation amid pure ordinances but had, despite the ordinances, yielded to the seductions of the good land. Hence distresses were being piled upon them, the slaughter of King Philip's War and now the attack of a profligate King upon the sacred charter. By about 1680, it did in truth seem that shortly no stone would be left upon another, that history would record of New England that the founders had been great men, but that their children and grandchildren progressively deteriorated.

This would certainly seem to be the impression conveyed by the assembled clergy and lay elders who, in 1679, met at Boston in a formal Synod, under the leadership of Increase Mather, and there prepared a report on why the land suffered. The result of their deliberation, published under the title *The Necessity of Reformation,* was the first in what has proved to be a distressingly long succession of investigations into the civic health of Americans, and it is probably the most pessimistic. The land was afflicted, it said, because corruption had proceeded apace; assuredly, if the people did not quickly reform, the last blow would fall and nothing but desolation be left. Into what a moral quagmire this dedicated community had sunk, the Synod did not leave to imagination; it published a long and detailed inventory of sins, crimes, misdemeanors, and nasty habits, which makes, to say the least, interesting reading.

We hear much talk nowadays about corruption, most of it couched in generalized terms. If we ask our current Jeremiahs to descend to particulars, they tell us that the Republic is going on the rocks, or to the dogs, because the wives of politicians aspire to wear mink coats and their husbands take a moderate five-percent cut on certain deals to pay for the garments. The Puritans were devotees of logic, and the verb "methodize" ruled their thinking: When the Synod went to work, it had before it a succession of sermons, such as that of Danforth and the other election-day or fast-day orators, as well as such works as Increase Mather's *A Brief History of the Warr With the Indians,* wherein the decimating conflict with Philip was presented as a revenge upon the people for their transgressions. When the Synod felt obliged to enumerate the enormities of the land so that the people could recognize just how far short of their errand they had fallen, it did not, in the modern manner, assume that regeneration would be accomplished at the next

5

election by turning the rascals out, but it digested this body of literature; it reduced the contents to method. The result is a staggering compendium of iniquity, organized into twelve headings.

First, there was a great and visible decay of godliness. Second, there were several manifestations of pride—contention in the churches, insubordination of inferiors toward superiors, particularly of those inferiors who had, unaccountably, acquired more wealth than their betters, and, finally, a shocking extravagance in attire, especially on the part of these of the meaner sort, who persisted in dressing beyond their means. Third, there were heretics, especially Quakers and Anabaptists. Fourth, a notable increase in swearing and a spreading disposition to sleep at sermons (these two phenomena seemed basically connected). Fifth, the Sabbath was wantonly violated. Sixth, family government had decayed, and fathers no longer kept their sons and daughters from prowling at night. Seventh, instead of the people being knit together as one man in mutual love, they were full of contention, so that lawsuits were on the increase and lawyers were thriving. Under the eighth head, the Synod described the sins of sex and alcohol, thus producing some of the juiciest prose of the period: militia days had become orgies, taverns were crowded; women threw temptation in the way of befuddled men by wearing false locks and displaying naked necks and arms "or, which is more abominable, naked Breasts"; there was "mixed Dancings" along with light behavior and "Company-keeping" with vain persons, wherefore the bastardy rate was rising. In 1672, there was actually an attempt to supply Boston with a brothel (it was suppressed, but the Synod was bearish about the future). Ninth, New Englanders were betraying a marked disposition to tell lies, especially when selling anything. In the tenth place, the business morality of even the most righteous left everything to be desired: the wealthy speculated in land and raised prices excessively; "Day-Labourers and Mechanicks are unreasonable in their demands." In the eleventh place, the people showed no disposition to reform, and in the twelfth, they seemed utterly destitute of civic spirit.

"The things here insisted on," said the Synod, "have been oftentimes mentioned and inculcated by those whom the Lord hath set as Watchmen to the house of Israel." Indeed they had been, and thereafter they continued to be even more inculcated. At the end of the century, the Synod's report was serving as a kind of handbook for preachers: they would take some verse of Isaiah or Jeremiah, set up the doctrine that God avenges the iniquities of a chosen people, and then run down the twelve heads, merely bringing the list up to date by inserting the new and still more depraved practices an ingenious people kept on devising. I suppose that in the whole literature of the world, including the satirists of imperial Rome, there is hardly such another uninhibited and unrelenting documentation of a people's descent into corruption.

I have elsewhere endeavored to argue that, while the social or economic historian may read this literature for its contents—and so construct from the expanding catalogue of denunciations a record of social progress—the cultural anthropologist will look slightly askance at these jeremiads; he will exercise a methodological caution about taking them at face value. If you read them all through, the total effect, curiously enough, is not at all depressing: you come to the paradoxical realization that they do not bespeak a despairing frame of mind. There is something of a ritualistic incantation about them; whatever they may signify in the realm of theology, in that of psychology they are purgations of soul; they do not discourage but actually encourage the community to persist in its heinous conduct. The exhortation to a reformation which never materializes serves as a token payment upon the obligation, and so liberates the debtors. Changes there had to be: adaptations to environment, expansion of the frontier, mansions constructed, commercial adventures undertaken. These activities had not been specifically nominated in the bond Winthrop had framed. They were thrust upon the society by American experience; because they were not only works of necessity but of excitement, they proved irresistible—whether making money, haunting taverns, or committing fornication. Land speculation meant not only wealth but dispersion of the people, and what was to stop the march of settlement? The covenant doctrine preached on the *Arbella* had been formulated in England, where land was not to be had for the taking; its adherents had been utterly oblivious of what the fact of a frontier would do for an imported order, let alone for a European mentality. Hence I suggest that under the guise of this mounting wail of sinfulness, this incessant and never successful cry for repentance, the Puritans launched themselves upon the process of Americanization.

However, there are still more pertinent or more analytical things to be said of this body of expression. If you compare it with the great productions of the founders, you will be struck by the fact that the second and third generations had become oriented toward the social, and only the social, problem; herein they were deeply and profoundly different from their fathers. The finest creations of the founders—the disquisitions of Hooker, Shepard, and Cotton—were written in Europe, or else, if actually penned in the colonies, proceeded from a thoroughly European mentality, upon which the American scene made no impression whatsoever. The most striking example of this imperviousness is the poetry of Anne Bradstreet: she came to Massachusetts at the age of eighteen, already two years married to Simon Bradstreet; there, she says, "I found a new world and new manners, at which my heart rose" in rebellion, but soon convincing herself that it was the way of God, she submitted and joined the Church. She bore Simon eight children, and loved him sincerely, as her most charming poem, addressed to him, reveals:

> If ever two were one, then surely we;
> If ever man were loved by wife, then thee.

After the house burned, she wrote a lament about how her pleasant things in ashes lay and how no more the merriment of guests would sound in the hall; but there is nothing in the poem to suggest that the house stood in North Andover or that the things so tragically consumed were doubly precious because they had been transported across the ocean and were utterly irreplaceable in the wilderness. In between rearing children and keeping house she wrote her poetry; her brother-in-law carried the manuscript to London, and there published it in 1650 under the ambitious title, *The Tenth Muse Lately Sprung Up in America*. But the title is the only thing about the volume which shows any sense of America, and that little merely in order to prove that the plantations had something in the way of European wit and learning, that they had not receded into barbarism. Anne's flowers are English flowers, the birds, English birds, and the landscape is Lincolnshire. So also with the productions of immigrant scholarship: such a learned and acute work as Hooker's *Survey of the Summe Church Discipline,* which is specifically about the regime set up in America, is written entirely within the logical patterns, and out of the religious experience, of Europe; it makes no concession to new and peculiar circumstances.

The titles alone of productions in the next generation show how concentrated have become emotion and attention upon the interest of New England, and none is more revealing than Samuel Danforth's conception of an errand into the wilderness. Instead of being able to compose abstract treatises like those of Hooker upon the soul's preparation, humiliation or exultation, or such a collection of wisdom and theology as John Cotton's *The Way of Life* or Shepard's *The Sound Believer,* these later saints must, over and over again, dwell upon the specific sins of New England, and the more they denounce, the more they must narrow their focus to the provincial problem. If they write upon anything else, it must be about the Half-Way Covenant and its manifold consequences—a development enacted wholly in this country—or else upon their wars with the Indians. Their range is sadly constricted, but every effort, no matter how brief, is addressed to the persistent question: what is the meaning of this society in the wilderness? If it does not mean what Winthrop said it must mean, what under Heaven is it? Who, they are forever asking themselves, who are we?—and sometimes they are on the verge of saying, who the Devil are we, anyway?

This brings us back to the fundamental ambiguity concealed in the word "errand," that *double-entente* of which I am certain Danforth was aware when he published the words that give point to the exhibition. While it was true that, in 1630, the covenant philosophy of a special and peculiar bond lifted the Migration out of the ordinary realm of nature, provided it with a definite mission which might in the secondary sense be called its errand, there was always present in Puritan thinking the suspicion that God's saints are at best inferiors, despatched by their Superior upon particular assignments. Anyone who has run errands for other people, particularly for people of great importance with many things on their minds, such as Army commanders, knows how real is the peril that, by the time he returns with the report of a message delivered or a bridge blown up, the superior may be interested in something else; the situation at headquarters may be entirely changed, and the gallant errand-boy, or the husband who desperately remembered to buy the ribbon, may be told that he is too late. This tragic pattern appears again and again in modern warfare: an agent is dropped by parachute and, after immense hardships, comes back to find that, in the shifting tactical or strategic situation, his contribution is no longer of value. If he gets home in time and his service proves useful, he receives a medal; otherwise, no matter what prodigies he has performed, he may not even be thanked. He has been sent, as the devastating phrase has it, upon a fool's errand, than which there can be a no more shattering blow to self-esteem.

The Great Migration of 1630 felt insured against such treatment from on high by the covenant; nevertheless, the God of the covenant always remained an unpredictable Jehovah, a *Deus Absconditus.* When God promises to abide by stated terms, His word, of course, is to be trusted; but then, what is man that he dare accuse Omnipotence of tergiversation? But if any such apprehension was in Winthrop's mind as he spoke on the *Arbella,* or in the minds of other apologists for the enterprise, they kept it far back and allowed it no utterance. They could stifle the thought, not only because Winthrop and his colleagues believed fully in the covenant, but because they could see in the pattern of history that their errand was not a mere scouting expedition: it was an essential maneuver in the drama of Christendom. The Bay Company was not a battered remnant of suffering Separatists thrown up on a rocky shore; it was an organized task-force of Christians, executing a flank attack on the corruptions of Christendom. These Puritans did not flee to America; they went in order to work out that complete reformation which was not yet accomplished in England and Europe, but which would quickly be accomplished if only the saints back there had a working model to guide them. It is impossible to say that any who sailed from Southampton really expected to lay his bones in the new world; were it to come about—as all in their heart of hearts anticipated—that the forces of righteousness should prevail against Laud and Wentworth, that England after all should turn toward reformation, where else would the distracted country look for leadership except to those who in New England had perfected the ideal polity and who would know how to administer it? This was the large unspoken assumption in the errand of 1630: if the conscious intention were realized, not only would a federated Jehovah bless the new land, but He would bring back these temporary colonials to govern England.

In this respect, therefore, we may say that the Migration was running an errand in the earlier and more primitive sense of the word—performing a job not so much for Jehovah as for history, which was the wisdom of Jehovah expressed through time. Winthrop was aware of this aspect of the mission—fully conscious of it. "For wee must Consider that wee shall be as a Citty upon a Hill, the eies of all people are uppon us." More was at stake than just one little colony. If we deal falsely with God, not only will He descend upon us in wrath, but even more terribly, He will make us "a story and a by-word through the world, wee shall open the mouthes of enemies to speake evill of the wayes of god and all professours for Gods sake." No less than John Milton was New England to justify God's ways to man, though not, like him, in the agony and confusion of defeat but in the confidence of approaching triumph. This errand was being run for the sake of Reformed Christianity; and while the first aim was indeed to realize in America the due form of government, both civil and ecclesiastical, the aim behind that aim was to vindicate the most rigorous ideal of the Reformation, so that ultimately all Europe would imitate New England. If we succeed, Winthrop told his audience, men will say of later plantations, "the lord make it like that of New England." There was an elementary prudence to be observed: Winthrop said that the prayer would arise from subsequent plantations, yet what was England itself but one of God's plantations? In America, he promised, we shall see, or may see, more of God's wisdom, power, and truth "then formerly wee have beene acquainted with." The situation was such that, for the moment, the model had no chance to be exhibited in England; Puritans could talk about it, theorize upon it, but they could not display it, could not prove that it would actually work. But if they had it set up in America—in a bare land, devoid of already established (and corrupt) institutions, empty of bishops and courtiers, where they could start de novo, and the eyes of the world were upon it—and if then it performed just as the saints had predicted of it, the Calvinist internationale would know exactly how to go about completing the already begun but temporarily stalled revolution in Europe.

9

When we look upon the enterprise from this point of view, the psychology of the second and third generations becomes more comprehensible. We realize that the Migration was not sent upon its errand in order to found the United States of America, nor even the New England conscience. Actually, it would not perform its errand even when the colonists did erect a due form of government in church and state: what was further required in order for this mission to be a success was that the eyes of the world be kept fixed upon it in rapt attention. If the rest of the world, or at least of Protestantism, looked elsewhere, or turned to another model, or simply got distracted and forgot about New England, if the new land was left with a polity nobody wanted—then every success in fulfilling the terms of the covenant would become a diabolical measure of failure. If the due form of government were not everywhere to be saluted, what would New England have upon its hands? How give it a name, this victory nobody could utilize? How provide an identity for something conceived under misapprehensions? How could a universal which turned out to be nothing but a provincial particular be called anything but a blunder or an abortion?

If an actor, playing the leading role in the greatest dramatic spectacle of the century, were to attire himself and put on his make-up, rehearse his lines, take a deep breath, and stride onto the stage, only to find the theatre dark and empty, no spotlight working, and himself entirely alone, he would feel as did New England around 1650 or 1660. For in the 1640s, during the Civil Wars, the colonies, so to speak, lost their audience. First of all, there proved to be, deep in the Puritan movement, an irreconcilable split between the Presbyterian and Independent wings, wherefore no one system could be imposed upon England, and so the New England model was unserviceable. Secondly—most horrible to relate—the Independents, who in polity were carrying New England's banner and were supposed, in the schedule of history, to lead England into imitation of the colonial order, betrayed the sacred cause by yielding to the heresy of toleration. They actually welcomed Roger Williams, whom the leaders of the model had kicked out of Massachusetts so that his nonsense about liberty of conscience would not spoil the administrations of charity.

In other words, New England did not lie, did not falter; it made good everything Winthrop demanded—wonderfully good—and then found that its lesson was rejected by those choice spirits for whom the exertion had been made. By casting out Williams, Anne Hutchinson, and the Antinomians, along with an assortment of Gortonists and Anabaptists, into that cesspool then becoming known as Rhode Island, Winthrop, Dudley, and the clerical leaders showed Oliver Cromwell how he should go about governing England. Instead, he developed the utterly absurd theory that as long as a man made a good soldier in the New Model Army, it did not matter whether he was a Calvinist, an Antinomian, an Arminian, an Anabaptist or even—horror of horrors—a Socinian! Year after year, as the circus tours this country, crowds howl with laughter, no matter how many times they have seen the stunt, at the bustle that walks by itself: the clown comes out dressed in a large skirt with a bustle behind; he turns sharply to the left, and the bustle continues blindly and obstinately straight ahead, on the original course. It is funny in a circus, but not in history. There is nothing but tragedy in the realization that one was in the main path of events, and now is sidetracked and disregarded. One is always able, of course, to stand firm on his first resolution, and to condemn the clown of history for taking the wrong turning: yet this is a desolating sort of Stoicism, because it always carries with it the recognition that history will never come back to the predicted path, and that with one's own demise, righteousness must die out of the world.

The most humiliating element in the experience was the way the English brethren turned upon the colonials for precisely their greatest achievement. It must have seemed, for those who came with Winthrop in 1630 and who remembered the clarity and brilliance with which he set forth the conditions of their errand, that the world was turned upside down and inside out when in June, 1645, thirteen leading Independent divines—such men as Goodwin, Owen, Nye, Burroughs, formerly friends and allies of Hooker and Davenport, men who might easily have come to New England and helped extirpate heretics—wrote the General Court that the colony's law banishing Anabaptists was an embarrassment to the Independent cause in England. Opponents were declaring, said these worthies, "that persons of our way, principall and spirit cannot beare with Dissentors from them, but Doe correct, fine, imprison and banish them wherever they have power soe to Doe." There were indeed people in England who admired the severities of Massachusetts, but we assure you, said the Independents, these "are utterly your enemyes and Doe seeke your extirpation from the face of the earth: those who now in power are your friends are quite otherwise minded, and doe professe they are much offended with your proceedings." Thus early commenced that chronic weakness in the foreign policy of Americans, an inability to recognize who in truth constitute their best friends abroad.

We have lately accustomed ourselves to the fact that there does exist a mentality which will take advantage of the liberties allowed by society in order to conspire for the ultimate suppression of those same privileges. The government of Charles I and Archbishop Laud had not, where that danger was concerned, been liberal, but it had been conspicuously inefficient; hence, it did not liquidate the Puritans (although it made halfhearted efforts), nor did it herd them into prison camps. Instead, it generously, even lavishly, gave a group of them a charter to Massachusetts Bay, and obligingly left out the standard clause requiring that the document remain in London, that the grantees keep their office within reach of Whitehall. Winthrop's revolutionaries availed themselves of this liberty to get the charter over-seas, and thus to set up a regime dedicated to the worship of God in the manner they desired—which meant allowing nobody else to worship any other way, especially adherents of Laud and King Charles. All this was perfectly logical and consistent. But what happened to the thought processes of their fellows in England made no sense whatsoever. Out of the New Model Army came the fantastic notion that a party struggling for power should proclaim that, once it captured the state, it would recognize the right of dissenters to disagree and to have their own worship, to hold their own opinions. Oliver Cromwell was so far gone in this idiocy as to become a dictator, in order to impose toleration by force! Amid this shambles, the errand of New England collapsed. There was nobody left at headquarters to whom reports could be sent.

Many a man has done a brave deed, been hailed as a public hero, had honors and ticker-tape heaped upon him—and then had to live, day after day, in the ordinary routine, eating breakfast and brushing his teeth, in what seems protracted anticlimax. A couple may win their way to each other across insuperable obstacles, elope in a blaze of passion and glory—and then have to learn that life is a matter of buying the groceries and getting the laundry done. This sense of the

11

meaning having gone out of life, that all adventures are over, that no great days and no heroism lie ahead, is particularly galling when it falls upon a son whose father once was the public hero or the great lover. He has to put up with the daily routine without ever having known at first hand the thrill of danger or the ecstasy of passion. True, he has his own hardships—clearing rocky pastures, hauling in the cod during a storm, fighting Indians in a swamp—but what are these compared with the magnificence of leading an exodus of saints to found a city on a hill, for the eyes of all the world to behold? He might put up a stout fight against the Indians, and one out of ten of his fellows might perish in the struggle, but the world was no longer interested. He would be reduced to writing accounts of himself and scheming to get a publisher in London, in a desperate effort to tell a heedless world, "Look, I exist!"

His greatest difficulty would be not the stones, storms, and Indians, but the problem of his identity. In something of this sort, I should like to suggest, consists the anxiety and torment that inform productions of the late seventeenth and early eighteenth centuries—and should I say, some thereafter? It appears most clearly in *Magnalia Christi Americana,* the work of that soul most tortured by the problem, Cotton Mather: "I write the Wonders of the Christian Religion, flying from the Depravations of Europe, to the American Strand." Thus he proudly begins, and at once trips over the acknowledgment that the founders had not simply fled from depraved Europe, but had intended to redeem it. And so the book is full of lamentations over the declension of the children, who appear, page after page, in contrast to their mighty progenitors, about as profligate a lot as ever squandered a great inheritance.

And yet, the *Magnalia* is not an abject book; neither are the election sermons abject, nor is the inventory of sins offered by the Synod of 1679. There is bewilderment, confusion, chagrin, but there is no surrender. A task has been assigned upon which the populace are in fact intensely engaged. But they are not sure any more for just whom they are working; they know they are moving, but they do not know where they are going. They seem still to be on an errand, but if they are no longer inferiors sent by the superior forces of the Reformation, to whom they should report, then their errand must be wholly of the second sort, something with a purpose and an intention sufficient unto itself. If so, what is it? If it be not the due form of government, civil and ecclesiastical, that they brought into being, how otherwise can it be described?

The literature of self-condemnation must be read for meanings far below the surface, for meanings of which, we may be so rash as to surmise, the authors were not fully conscious, but by which they were troubled and goaded. They looked in vain to history for an explanation of themselves; more and more it appeared that the meaning was not to be found in theology, even with the help of the covenantal dialectic. Thereupon, these citizens found that they had no other place to search but within themselves—even though, at first sight, that repository appeared to be nothing but a sink of iniquity. Their errand having failed in the first sense of the term, they were left with the second, and required to fill it with meaning by themselves and out of themselves. Having failed to rivet the eyes of the world upon their city on the hill, they were left alone with America.

MEN OF LITTLE FAITH:
THE ANTI-FEDERALISTS ON THE NATURE
OF REPRESENTATIVE GOVERNMENT

CECELIA M. KENYON

One of the gravest defects of the late Charles Beard's economic interpretation of the Constitution is the limited perspective it has encouraged in those who have accepted it, and the block to fruitful investigation of the ideas and institutions of the Revolutionary Age to which it has been conducive. Like many theories influential in both the determination and the interpretation of historical events, Beard's thesis and its implications were never carefully analyzed either by himself or his followers. As a result, its impact on the study of American history produced certain effects not anticipated, which Beard himself must surely have regretted. The economic interpretation employed by him somewhat tentatively as a tool for analysis and research quickly became a methodological stereotype and led to a stereotypical appreciation of the Constitution and of the historical context in which it was created.

Beard's failure—perhaps it was deliberate refusal—to subject his thesis to rigorous analysis or to define it with precision makes it impossible to label him a clear-cut, thorough-going economic determinist. His position was always ambiguous and ambivalent, and in his later years he explicitly repudiated any monistic theory of causation.[1] Nevertheless, the thrust of *An Economic Interpretation of the Constitution* and the effects of its thesis as applied have frequently been those of simple and uncritical commitment to a theory of economic determinism.

Of these effects, the most significant has been a disinclination to explore the theoretical foundations of the Constitution. In the chapter entitled "The Constitution as an Economic Document," Beard presented the structure of the government, particularly the system of separation of powers and checks and balances, as the institutional means chosen by the Founding Fathers to protect their property rights against invasion by democratic majorities.[2] This interpretation, or variations of it, has been widely accepted, though it has been frequently

Miss Kenyon is a member of the Department of Government at Smith College.

Ed. Note: This article was originally published in *William and Mary Quarterly*, 3d Ser., XII (January 1955), 3–43.

[1] A critical and definitive study of Beard as an historian has not yet been done. Interesting commentaries on the ambiguity to be found in Beard's thesis are Max Lerner's "Charles A. Beard," in his *Ideas Are Weapons* (New York, 1939), 161–162, and Richard Hofstadter's "Charles Beard and the Constitution," in *Charles A. Beard: An Appraisal,* edited by Howard K. Beale (University of Kentucky Press, 1954). Hofstadter also cites the different attitudes toward the Constitution and its framers reflected in the Beards' *The Rise of American Civilization* (1927) and their *Basic History of the United States* (1944). Beale's essay in the same collection, "Charles Beard: Historian," recounts in broad terms the shifts in Beard's historiographical thought throughout his career. It is with the Beard of the earlier period that this essay is concerned, for this was the period of his most influential works.

[2] Charles A. Beard, *An Economic Interpretation of the Constitution* (New York, 1913), Ch. VI,

challenged both directly and indirectly.[3] Its tendency is to dispose of the institutional thought of the men who framed the Constitution as ideological response to economic interest. The present essay offers yet another challenge to this position, not by further examination of the Constitution or its authors, but by analysis of the Anti-Federalist position of 1787–1788.

Perhaps because theirs was the losing side, the political thought of the Anti-Federalists has received much less attention than that of the Founding Fathers. Since they fought the adoption of a Constitution which they thought to be aristocratic in origin and intent, and which by Beardian criteria was inherently anti-democratic in structure, there has been some tendency to characterize them as spokesmen of eighteenth-century democracy. But their theory of republican government has never been closely analyzed, nor have the areas of agreement and disagreement between them and the Federalists been carefully defined. It is the purpose of this essay to explore these topics. A very large proportion of the people in 1787–1788 *were* Anti-Federalists, and a knowledge of their ideas and attitudes is essential to an understanding of American political thought in the formative years of the republic.

Implicit in this purpose is the thesis that the ideological context of the Constitution was as important in determining its form as were the economic interests and motivations of its framers, and that the failure of Beard and his followers to examine this context has rendered their interpretation of the Constitution and its origin necessarily partial and unrealistic.

Beard's conclusions rested on two assumptions or arguments. One was that the framers of the Constitution were motivated by their class and perhaps their personal economic interests; a great deal of evidence, drawn from more or less contemporary records, was presented to support this part of the thesis. A second assumption was that the system of separation of powers and checks and balances written into the Constitution was undemocratic. In making this second

14

---

especially 154–164. See also the succinct statement in *The Economic Basis of Politics* (New York, 1922), 66–67: "Under the circumstances the framers of the Constitution relied, not upon direct economic qualification, but upon checks and balances to secure the rights of property—particularly personal property—against the assaults of the farmers and the proletariat." In Charles and Mary Beard's *The Rise of American Civilization* (New York, 1927), the theme is continued: "Almost unanimous was the opinion that democracy was a dangerous thing, to be restrained, not encouraged, by the Constitution, to be given as little voice as possible in the new system, to be hampered by checks and balances." (p. 315; cf. p. 326.) It was this position which the Beards had apparently abandoned by the 1940s. The attitude of *The Republic* (1942), and of *The Basic History* (1944), is one of appreciation of the authors of the Constitution, not condemnation.

[3] In 1936 Maurice Blinkoff published a study of the influence of Beard on American historiography and came to the conclusion that authors of college history textbooks had adopted Beard's views "with virtual unanimity." *The Influence of Charles A. Beard upon American Historiography*, University of Buffalo Studies, XII (May 1936), 36. I have not conducted a comprehensive survey, but it seems to me that Blinkoff's conclusions would probably not be accurate for today.

For challenges to the Beard position, the reader may consult the survey of reviews of *An Economic Interpretation of the Constitution* cited in Blinkoff, as well as some of the selections in the *Amherst Problems in American Civilization* series; Earl Latham, editor, *The Declaration of Independence and the Constitution* (Boston, 1949), though this collection is, in the opinion of the author, biased in favor of the Beard interpretation. See also B. F. Wright, "The Origin of Separation of Powers in America," *Economica*, May 1933; and "The Federalist on the Nature of Political Man," *Ethics*, Vol. LIX, No. 2, Part II (January 1949); and Douglass Adair, "The Tenth Federalist Revisited," *William and Mary Quarterly*, 3d Series, Vol. VIII (January 1951).

assumption Beard was more influenced by the ideas of the Populist and Progressive movements of his own time, I think, than by a study of the political beliefs current in 1787. He was preoccupied in 1913 with his period's interest in reforming the structure of the national government to make it more democratic, which by his standards meant more responsible to simple majority rule. Thus he judged an eighteenth-century frame of government by a twentieth-century political doctrine. The effect was to suggest by implication that the men who in 1787–1788 thought the Constitution aristocratic and antagonistic to popular government thought so for the same reasons as Beard.[4] The evidence shows clearly that their reasons were frequently and substantially different. These differences serve to illuminate the context of the Constitution and to illustrate the evolutionary character of American political thought.

II

At the center of the theoretical expression of Anti-Federalist opposition to increased centralization of power in the national government was the belief that republican government was possible only for a relatively small territory and a relatively small and homogeneous population. James Winthrop of Massachusetts expressed a common belief when he said, "The idea of an uncompounded republick, on an average one thousand miles in length, and eight hundred in breadth, and containing six millions of white inhabitants all reduced to the same standard of morals, of habits, and of laws, is in itself an absurdity, and contrary to the whole experience of mankind."[5] The last part of this statement, at least, was true; history was on the side of the Anti-Federalists. So was the authority of contemporary political thought. The name of Montesquieu carried great weight, and he had taught that republican governments were appropriate for small territories only. He was cited frequently, but his opinion would probably not have been accepted had it not reflected their own experience and inclinations. As colonials they had enjoyed self-government in colony-size packages only and had not sought to extend its operation empire-wise. It is significant that the various proposals for colonial representation in Parliament never grew deep roots during the

---

[4] There is no doubt at all that many of the Anti-Federalists did regard the Constitution as dangerous and aristocratic, and its framers and supporters likewise. They were acutely suspicious of it because of its class origin and were on the lookout for every evidence of bias in favor of the "aristocrats" who framed it. Note, for example, the attitude of Amos Singletary expressed in the Massachusetts ratifying convention: "These lawyers, and men of learning and moneyed men, that talk so finely, and gloss over matters so smoothly, to make us poor illiterate people swallow down the pill, expect to get into Congress themselves; they expect to be managers of this Constitution, and get all the power and all the money into their own hands, and then they will swallow up all us little folks like the great *Leviathan;* yes, just as the whale swallowed up Jonah!" Jonathan Elliot, *The Debates in the Several State Conventions on the Adoption of the Federal Constitution as Recommended by the General Convention at Philadelphia, in 1787,* Second Edition, 5 vols. (Philadelphia, 1896), II, 102. See also reference to this attitude in a letter from Rufus King to James Madison, January 27, 1888. This letter is to be found in the *Documentary History of the Constitution of the United States of America, 1786–1870* (Washington, 1894–1905), 5 vols.; IV, 459. A similar feeling was reported to exist in the New Hampshire convention. See John Langdon to George Washington, February 28, 1788, ibid., 524.

[5] The *Agrippa* Letters in Paul Leicester Ford, *Essays on the Constitution of the United States* (Brooklyn, 1892), 65. See also pp. 91–92.

debate preceding the Revolution. This association of self-government with relatively small geographical units reinforced Montesquieu's doctrine and led to further generalizations. A large republic was impossible, it was argued, because the center of government must necessarily be distant from the people. Their interest would then naturally decrease; and when this happened, "it would not suit the genius of the people to assist in the government," and "Nothing would support the government, in such a case as that, but military coercion."[6] Patrick Henry argued that republican government for a continent was impossible because it was "a work too great for human wisdom."[7]

Associated with the argument regarding size was the assumption that any people who were to govern themselves must be relatively homogeneous in interest, opinion, habits, and mores. The theme was not systematically explored, but it apparently stemmed from the political relativism prevalent at the time,[8] and from the recent experience of conflicts of interest between the colonies and Great Britain, and later between various states and sections of the new confederation.

It is not easy to measure the relative strength of national and state sentiment in either individuals or groups,[9] but it is clear that the Anti-Federalists were conscious of, and emphasized, the cultural diversity of the peoples in the thirteen states. They argued that no one set of laws could operate over such diversity. Said a Southerner, "We see plainly that men who come from New England are different from us."[10] He did not wish to be governed either with or by such men. Neither did the New Englanders wish to share a political roof with Southerners. "The inhabitants of warmer climates are more dissolute in their manners, and less industrious, than in colder countries. A degree of severity is, therefore, necessary with one which would cramp the spirit of the other. . . . It is impossible for one code of laws to suit Georgia and Massachusetts."[11] To place both types of men under the same government would be abhorrent and quite incompatible with the retention of liberty. Either the new government would collapse, or it would endeavor to stamp out diversity and level all citizens to a new uniformity in order to survive. Such was the reasoning of the leading New England publicist, James Winthrop. His indebtedness to Montesquieu is obvious. His failure to grasp the

---

[6] Elliot, IV, 52.

[7] Elliot, III, 164; cf. III, 607 ff.; II, 69, 335; the *Centinel* Letters in John Bach McMaster and Frederick D. Stone, editors, *Pennsylvania and the Federal Constitution, 1787–1788* (Historical Society of Pennsylvania, 1888), 572; R. H. Lee, "Letters of a Federal Farmer," in Paul Leicester Ford, *Pamphlets on the Constitution of the United States* (Brooklyn, 1888), 288; George Clinton, Cato, in Ford, *Essays,* 256 ff.

[8] Political relativism had long been a part of the colonial heritage. Seventeenth-century Puritans, who were sure that God had regulated many aspects of life with remarkable precision, believed that He had left each people considerable freedom in the choice of their form of government. The secularized legacy of this belief prevailed throughout the era of framing state and national constitutions. Fundamental principles derived from natural law were of course universally valid, and certain "political maxims" regarding the structure of the government very nearly so, but the embodiment of these general truths in concrete political forms was necessarily determined by the nature and circumstances of the people involved.

[9] On this subject see John C. Ranney, "The Bases of American Federalism," *William and Mary Quarterly,* Series 3, Vol. III, No. 1 (January 1946).

[10] Elliot, IV, 24.

[11] From the *Agrippa* Letters, Ford, *Essays,* 64.

principles of the new federalism is also clear; for the purposes of this argument, and indeed for almost all of their arguments, he and his colleagues refused to consider the proposed government as one of limited, enumerated powers. They constantly spoke and wrote as if the scope and extent of its powers would be the same as those of the respective state governments, or of a unified national government.[12]

In addition to the absence of cultural homogeneity, the Anti-Federalists emphasized the clash of specific economic and political interests. These were primarily sectional,[13] and were of more acute concern in the South than in the North. In Virginia, for example, George Mason expressed the fear that the power of Congress to regulate commerce might be the South's downfall. In Philadelphia he had argued that this power be exercised by a two-thirds majority, and he now feared that by requiring only a simple majority "to make all commercial and navigation laws, the five southern states (whose produce and circumstances are totally different from those of the eight northern and eastern states) will be ruined."[14] It was also argued in several of the Southern conventions that a majority of the Eastern states might conspire to close the Mississippi,[15] and that they might eventually interfere with the institution of slavery.[16] In New England and the Middle states, there was less feeling that the interests of the entire section were in jeopardy, and therefore less discussion of these concrete issues and their divisive effect. One writer did strike out at the Federalist plea for a transcendent nationalism and repudiated the notion of sacrificing local interests to a presumed general interest as unrealistic and prejudicial to freedom. "It is vain to tell us that we ought to overlook local interests. It is only by protecting local concerns that the interest of the whole is preserved." He went on to say that men entered into society for egoistic rather than altruistic motives, that having once done so, all were bound to contribute equally to the common welfare, and that to call for sacrifices of local interest was to violate this principle of equality and to subvert "the foundation of free government."[17]

There was much to be said for Winthrop's argument. It was an unequivocal statement of the principle that self-interest is the primary bond of political union. It was also an expression of an attitude which has always played a large part in our national politics: a refusal to sacrifice—sometimes even to subordinate—the welfare of a part to that of the whole. Pursuit of an abstract national interest has sometimes proved dangerous, and there was a healthy toughness in the Anti-Federalist insistence on the importance of local interests. But Winthrop skirted around the really difficult questions raised by his argument, which were also inherent in the Anti-Federalist position that the size of the United States and the

17

---

[12] It was this misunderstanding of the proposed new system which Madison attempted to remove in *Federalist* 39.

[13] Curiously enough, the Big-Little State fight, which almost broke up the Convention, played very little part in the ratification debates. And ironically one of the evidences of ideological unity which made the "more perfect union" possible was the similarity of argument put forth by the Anti-Federalists in their respective states.

[14] "Objections," Ford, *Pamphlets,* 331.

[15] Elliot, III, 326.

[16] Elliot, IV, 272–273.

[17] *Agrippa* Letters, Ford, *Essays,* 73.

diversity which existed among them were too great to be consistent with one republican government operating over the whole. No one would deny that a certain amount of unity or consensus is required for the foundation of popular, constitutional government; not very many people—now or in 1787—would go as far as Rousseau and insist on virtually absolute identity of interest and opinion. The Anti-Federalists were surprisingly close to Rousseau and to the notions of republicanism which influenced him, but they were sensible, practical men and did not attempt to define their position precisely. Consequently they left untouched two difficult questions: how much, and what kind of unity is required for the foundation of any republican government, large or small; and how, in the absence of perfect uniformity, are differences of opinion and interest to be resolved?

III

The Anti-Federalist theory of representation was closely allied to the belief that republican government could operate only over a small area. The proposed Constitution provided that the first House of Representatives should consist of sixty-five members, and that afterwards the ratio of representation should not exceed one representative for thirty thousand people. This provision was vigorously criticized and was the chief component of the charge that the Constitution was not sufficiently democratic. The argument was two-fold: first, that sixty-five men could not possibly represent the multiplicity of interests spread throughout so great a country; second, that those most likely to be left out would be of the more democratic or "middling" elements in society. The minority who voted against ratification in the Pennsylvania Convention calculated that the combined quorums of the House and Senate was only twenty-five, and concluded that this number plus the President could not possibly represent "the sense and views of three or four millions of people, diffused over so extensive a territory, comprising such various climates, products, habits, interests, and opinions."[18] This argument, accompanied with the same calculus, was repeated many times during the ratification debate.

Almost all of the leaders of the opposition laid down what they believed to be the requisites of adequate representation, and there is a remarkable similarity in their definitions. George Mason, speaking in the Virginia Convention against giving the central government the power of taxation, based his argument on the inadequacy of representation as measured by his criteria: "To make representation real and actual, the number of representatives ought to be adequate; they ought to mix with the people, think as they think, feel as they feel—ought to be perfectly amenable to them, and thoroughly acquainted with their interest and condition."[19] In his *Letters of a Federal Farmer,* Richard Henry Lee developed the same idea further:

> a full and equal representation is that which possesses the same interests, feelings, opinions, and views the people themselves would were they

---

[18] "Address and Reasons of Dissent of the Minority of the Convention of Pennsylvania to their Constituents," reprinted in McMaster and Stone, *Pennsylvania and the Constitution,* 472.

[19] Elliot, III, 32.

all assembled—a fair representation, therefore, should be so regulated, that every order of men in the community, according to the common course of elections, can have a share in it—in order to allow professional men, merchants, traders, farmers, mechanics, etc. to bring a just proportion of their best informed men respectively into the legislature, the representation must be considerably numerous.[20]

It was the contention of the Anti-Federalists that because of the small size of the House of Representatives, the middle and lower orders in society would not be elected to that body, and that consequently this, the only popular organ of the government, would not be democratic at all. It would, instead, be filled by aristocrats, possibly by military heroes and demagogues.[21] Why should this be? Lee asserted simply that it would be "in the nature of things." Mason seems to have assumed it without any comment or argument. Patrick Henry reasoned that since the candidates would be chosen from large electoral districts rather than from counties, they would not all be known by the electors, and "A common man must ask a man of influence how he is to proceed, and for whom he must vote. The elected, therefore, will be careless of the interest of the electors. It will be a common job to extort the suffrages of the common people for the most influential characters."[22] This argument reflects one of the basic fears of the Anti-Federalists: loss of personal, direct contact with and knowledge of their representatives. They sensed quite accurately that an enlargement of the area of republican government would lead to a more impersonal system, and that the immediate, individual influence of each voter over his representative would be lessened.

The most elaborate explanation of the anticipated results of the electoral process was given by the moderate Anti-Federalist in New York, Melancton Smith. He argued that very few men of the "middling" class would choose to run for Congress, because the office would be "highly elevated and distinguished," the style of living probably "high." Such circumstances would "render the place of a representative not a desirable one to sensible, substantial men, who have been used to walking in the plain and frugal paths of life." Even if such should choose to run for election, they would almost certainly be defeated. In a large electoral district it would be difficult for any but a person of "conspicuous military, popular, civil, or legal talents" to win. The common people were more likely to be divided among themselves than the great, and "There will be scarcely a chance of their uniting in any other but some great man, unless in some popular demagogue, who will probably be destitute of principle. A substantial yeoman, of sense and discernment, will hardly ever be chosen."[23] Consequently, the government would be controlled by the great, would not truly reflect the interests of all groups in the community, and would almost certainly become oppressive.

---

[20] Ford, *Pamphlets,* 288–289.

[21] This idea appeared frequently in Anti-Federalist arguments. See, for example, the "Address and Dissent of the Minority. . . ," McMaster and Stone, *Pennsylvania and the Constitution,* 472, 479; Lee, "Letters of a Federal Farmer," Ford, *Pamphlets,* 295; Elliot, III, 266–267, 426 (George Mason).

[22] Elliot, III, 322.

[23] Elliot, II, 246.

19

Anti-Federalists in Massachusetts were also uneasy about the capacity of the people to elect a legislature which would reflect their opinions and interests. The arguments emphasized geographical as well as class divisions, and expressed the fear and suspicion felt by the western part of the state toward Boston and the other coastal towns. It was predicted that the latter would enjoy a great advantage under the new system, and this prediction was supported by a shrewd analysis in the *Cornelius* Letter:

> The citizens in the seaport towns are numerous; they live compact; their interests are one; there is a constant connection and intercourse between them; they can, on any occasion, centre their votes where they please. This is not the case with those who are in the landed interest; they are scattered far and wide; they have but little intercourse and connection with each other. To concert uniform plans for carrying elections of this kind is entirely out of their way. Hence, their votes if given at all, will be no less scattered than are the local situations of the voters themselves. Wherever the seaport towns agree to centre their votes, there will, of course, be the greatest number. A gentleman in the country therefore, who may aspire after a seat in Congress, or who may wish for a post of profit under the federal government, must form his connections, and unite his interest with those towns. Thus, I conceive, a foundation is laid for throwing the whole power of the federal government into the hands of those who are in the mercantile interest; and for the landed, which is the great interest of this country to lie unrepresented, forlorn and without hope.[24]

20

What the Anti-Federalists feared, in other words, was the superior opportunities for organized voting which they felt to be inherent in the more thickly populated areas. They shared with the authors of *The Federalist* the fear of party and faction in the eighteenth-century American sense of those words. But they also feared, as the preceding analyses show, the essence of party in its modern meaning, i.e., organizing the vote, and they wanted constituencies sufficiently small to render such organization unnecessary.

This belief that larger electoral districts would inevitably be to the advantage of the well-to-do partially explains the almost complete lack of criticism of the indirect election of the Senate and the President. If the "middling" class could not be expected to compete successfully with the upper class in Congressional elections, still less could they do so in state-wide or nation-wide elections. It was a matter where size was of the essence. True representation—undistorted by party organization—could be achieved only where electoral districts were small.

IV

The conception of the representative body as a true and faithful miniature of the people themselves was the projection of an ideal—almost a poetic one. Very few of its proponents thought it could actually be realized. In the Anti-Federalist

[24] The *Cornelius* Letter is reprinted in Samuel Bannister Harding, *The Contest over the Ratification of the Federal Constitution in the State of Massachusetts* (New York, 1896). See pp. 123–124.

attack on the Constitution, it served as a foil for an extraordinary picture of antic-ipated treachery on the part of the representatives to be elected under the proposed government. No distinction was made on the basis of their method of election, whether directly or indirectly by the people. All were regarded as potential tyrants.

This attack stemmed directly from the Anti-Federalist conception of human nature. They shared with their opponents many of the assumptions regarding the nature of man characteristic of American thought in the late eighteenth century. They took for granted that the dominant motive of human behavior was self-interest, and that this drive found its most extreme political expression in an insatiable lust for power. These were precisely the characteristics with which the authors of *The Federalist Papers* were preoccupied.[25] Yet the Anti-Federalists chided the Federalists for their excessive confidence in the future virtue of elected officials, and criticized the Constitution for its failure to provide adequate protec-tion against the operation of these tyrannical drives. There is surely an amusing irony to find the Founding Fathers, who prided themselves on their realism, and who enjoy an enviable reputation for that quality today, taken to task for exces-sive optimism. But they had to meet this charge again and again. Thus Caldwell in the North Carolina Convention found it "remarkable,—that gentlemen, as an answer to every improper part of it [the Constitution], tell us that every thing is to be done by our own representatives, who are to be good men. There is no security that they will be so, or continue to be so."[26] In New York Robert Lansing expressed the same feeling in a passage strikingly reminiscent of the famous paragraph in Madison's *Federalist* 51:

21

> Scruples would be impertinent, arguments would be in vain, checks would be useless, if we were certain our rulers would be good men; but for the virtuous government is not instituted: its object is to restrain and punish vice; and all free constitutions are formed with two views—to deter the governed from crime, and the governors from tyranny.[27]

This and many other similar statements might have been used interchange-ably by either side in the debate, for they symbolized an attitude deeply embed-ded and widely dispersed in the political consciousness of the age. There were frequent references to "the natural lust of power so inherent in man";[28] to "the predominant thirst of dominion which has invariably and uniformly prompted

---

[25] See B. F. Wright, "*The Federalist* on the Nature of Political Man," *Ethics* (January 1949).

[26] Elliot, IV, 187; cf. 203–204, and III, 494. Caldwell's statement is very similar to Madison's comment in *Federalist* 10: "It is in vain to say that enlightened statesmen will be able to adjust these clashing interests, and render them all subservient to the public good. Enlightened states-men will not always be at the helm."

[27] Elliot, II, 295–296. Madison's declaration was this: "But what is government itself, but the greatest of all reflections on human nature? If men were angels, no government would be neces-sary. If angels were to govern men, neither external nor internal controls on government would be necessary. In framing a government which is to be administered by men over men, the great difficulty lies in this: you must first enable the government to control the governed; and in the next place oblige it to control itself."

[28] Mason in Virginia, Elliot, III, 32.

rulers to abuse their power";[29] to "the ambition of man, and his lust for domination";[30] to rulers who would be "men of like passions," having "the same spontaneous inherent thirst for power with ourselves."[31] In Massachusetts, another delegate said, "we ought to be jealous of rulers. All the godly men we read of have failed; nay, he would not trust a 'flock of Moseses.'"[32]

It is to be noted that this dreadful lust for power was regarded as a universal characteristic of the nature of man, which could be controlled but not eradicated. The Anti-Federalists charged that the authors of the Constitution had failed to put up strong enough barriers to block this inevitably corrupting and tyrannical force. They painted a very black picture indeed of what the national representatives might and probably would do with the unchecked power conferred upon them under the provisions of the new Constitution. The "parade of imaginary horribles" has become an honorable and dependable technique of political debate, but the marvelous inventiveness of the Anti-Federalists has rarely been matched. Certainly the best achievements of their contemporary opponents were conspicuously inferior in dramatic quality, as well as incredibly unimaginative in dull adherence to at least a semblance of reality. The anticipated abuses of power, some real, some undoubtedly conjured as ammunition for debate, composed a substantial part of the case against the Constitution, and they must be examined in order to get at the temper and quality of Anti-Federalist thought as well as at its content. Their source was ordinarily a distorted interpretation of some particular clause.

One clause which was believed to lay down a constitutional road to legislative tyranny was Article I, Section 4: "The times, places, and manner of holding elections for senators and representatives, shall be prescribed in each state by the legislature thereof; but the Congress may, at any time, by law, make or alter such regulations, except as to the places of choosing senators." Here was the death clause of republican government. "This clause may destroy representation entirely," said Timothy Bloodworth of North Carolina.[33] If Congress had power to alter the times of elections, Congress might extend its tenure of office from two years to four, six, eight, ten, twenty, "or even for their natural lives."[34] Bloodworth and his colleagues feared the worst. In Massachusetts, where debate over this clause occupied a day and a half, the primary fear was that Congress, by altering the places of election, might rig them so as to interfere with a full and free expression of the people's choice. Pierce suggested that Congress could "direct that the election for Massachusetts shall be held in Boston," and then by pre-election caucus, Boston and the surrounding towns could agree on a ticket "and carry their list by a major vote."[35] In the same state the delegate who would not trust "a flock of Moseses" argued thus: "Suppose the Congress should say that none should be electors but those worth 50 or a £100 sterling; cannot they do it? Yes,

---

[29] Henry in Virginia, ibid., 436.

[30] "Letters of Luther Martin," Ford, *Essays,* 379.

[31] Barrell in Massachusetts, Elliot, II, 159.

[32] White in Massachusetts, Elliot, II, 28.

[33] Elliot, IV, 55.

[34] Elliot, IV, 51–52, 55–56, 62–63, 87–88.

[35] Elliot, II, 22.

said he, they can; and if any lawyer . . . can beat me out of it, I will give him ten guineas."[36] In Virginia, George Mason suggested that Congress might provide that the election in Virginia should be held only in Norfolk County, or even "go farther, and say that the election for all the states might be had in New York."[37] Patrick Henry warned, "According to the mode prescribed, Congress may tell you that they have a right to make the vote of one gentleman go as far as the votes of a hundred poor men."[38]

Any of these acts would have been a flagrant abuse of power, but no more so than that which Mason and others predicted under Article II, Section 2, which gave to the President the power to make treaties with the advice and consent of two-thirds of the senators present. This power was believed to be fraught with danger, particularly among Southerners, who feared that the majority of Northern states might use it to give up American rights of navigation on the Mississippi. The North would not have a two-thirds majority of the entire Senate, of course, but Mason suggested that when a "partial" treaty was involved, the President would not call into session senators from distant states, or those whose interests would be affected adversely, but only those he knew to be in favor of it.[39] His colleague, William Grayson, suggested the similarly treacherous prospect of such a treaty's being rushed through while members from the Southern states were momentarily absent from the floor of the Senate: "If the senators of the Southern States be gone but one hour, a treaty may be made by the rest."[40]

This fear at least had some foundation in fact—there was a conflict of interest between North and South over the Mississippi. It would seem that the fear expressed in North Carolina by Abbott on behalf of "the religious part of the society" was pure fantasy: "It is feared by some people, that, by the power of making treaties, they might make a treaty engaging with foreign powers to adopt the Roman Catholic religion in the United States."[41]

This was not the only provision objected to by "the religious part of the society." They were greatly displeased with the last clause of Article VI, Section 3: "but no religious test shall ever be required as a qualification to any office or public trust under the United States." In the same speech quoted above, Abbott reported, presumably on behalf of his constituents, "The exclusion of religious tests is by many thought dangerous and impolitic." For without such, "They suppose . . . pagans, deists, and Mahometans might obtain offices among us, and that the senators and representatives might all be pagans."[42] David Caldwell thought that the lack of a religious qualification constituted "an invitation for Jews and pagans of every kind to come among us," and that since the Christian religion

[36] Elliot, II, 28.

[37] Elliot, III, 403–404.

[38] Elliot, III, 175. Cf. *Centinel,* McMaster and Stone, *Pennsylvania and the Constitution,* 598, and James Winthrop in the *Agrippa* Letters, Ford, *Essays,* 105.

[39] Elliot, III, 499.

[40] Elliot, III, 502.

[41] Elliot, IV, 191–192. Abbott was not an Anti-Federalist, but was, according to L. I. Trenholme, in *The Ratification of the Federal Constitution in North Carolina* (New York, 1932), something of an independent. See p.178. He voted for ratification.

[42] Elliot, IV, 192.

was acknowledged to be the best for making "good members of society . . . those gentlemen who formed this Constitution should not have given this invitation to Jews and heathens."[43] Federalist James Iredell reported a pamphlet in circulation "in which the author states, as a very serious danger, that the pope of Rome might be elected President."[44] This unwittingly placed fresh ammunition at the disposal of the opposition. An Anti-Federalist admitted that he had not at first perceived this danger and conceded that it was not an immediate one. "But," said he, "let us remember that we form a government for millions not yet in existence. I have not the art of divination. In the course of four or five hundred years, I do not know how it will work. This is most certain, that Papists may occupy that chair, and Mahometans may take it. I see nothing against it. There is a disqualification, I believe, in every state in the Union—it ought to be so in this system."[45]

It is to be noted that these fears were fears of the majority of electors as well as of their elected representatives, and that these statements can hardly be said to glow with the spirit of liberty and tolerance. These beliefs were undoubtedly not shared by all Anti-Federalists, but they would not have been expressed so vigorously in the convention debates had they not represented a sizeable segment of constituent opinion.

Another provision severely and dramatically criticized was that which gave to Congress exclusive jurisdiction over the future site of the national capital and other property to be purchased for forts, arsenals, dockyards, and the like.[46] It was predicted that the ten-mile square area would become an enormous den of tyranny and iniquity. In New York George Clinton warned "that the ten miles square . . . would be the asylum of the base, idle, avaricious and ambitious."[47] In Virginia Patrick Henry pointed out that this provision, combined with the necessary and proper clause, gave Congress a right to pass "any law that may facilitate the execution of their acts," and within the specified area to hang "any man who shall act contrary to their commands . . . without benefit of clergy."[48] George Mason argued that the place would make a perfect lair for hit-and-run tyrants. For if any of the government's "officers, or creatures, should attempt to oppress the people, or should actually perpetuate the blackest deed, he has nothing to do but get into the ten miles square. Why was this dangerous power given?"[49] One man observed that the Constitution did not specify the location of this site, and that therefore

24

[43] Ibid., 199.

[44] Ibid., 195.

[45] Ibid., 215. This quotation transmits a sense of the method of Anti-Federalist debate admirably. A similar statement by Amos Singletary of Massachusetts gives something of the flavor of the thinking done by the honest and pious patriots of the back country, in which opposition to the Constitution was strong: "The Hon. Mr. Singletary thought we were giving up all our privileges, as there was no provision that men in power should have any *religion,* and though he hoped to see Christians, yet by the Constitution, a Papist, or an Infidel, was as eligible as they. It had been said that men had not degenerated; he did not think that men were better now than when men after God's own heart did wickedly. He thought, in this instance, we were giving great power to we know not whom." Elliot, II, 44.

[46] Article I, Section 8.

[47] The *Cato* Letters; reprinted in Ford, *Essays,* 265.

[48] Elliot, III, 436.

[49] Ibid., 431.

Congress was perfectly free to seat itself and the other offices of government in Peking. All in all, a terrible prospect: the Pope as President, operating from a base in Peking, superintending a series of hangings without benefit of clergy! Or worse.

There was no bill of rights in the Constitution. This caused genuine fear for the security of some of the liberties thus left unprotected. The fear itself, though real and well founded, frequently found expression in melodramatically picturesque terms. The Anti-Federalists sometimes mentioned freedom of the press and freedom of conscience,[50] but they were primarily preoccupied with the failure of the Constitution to lay down the precious and venerable common-law rules of criminal procedure. The Constitution guaranteed the right of trial by jury in all criminal cases[51] except impeachment, but it did not list the procedural safeguards associated with that right. There was no specification that the trial should be not merely in the state but in the vicinity where the crime was committed (which was habitually identified with the neighborhood of the accused); there were no provisions made for the selection of the jury or of the procedure to be followed; there were no guarantees of the right to counsel, of the right not to incriminate oneself; there was no prohibition against cruel and unusual punishments. In short, there were few safeguards upon which the citizen accused of crime could rely.[52] Apprehension concerning the latitude left to Congress in this matter was expressed in several conventions;[53] it was Holmes of Massachusetts who painted the most vivid and fearful picture of the possible fate of the unfortunate citizen who ran afoul of federal law. Such an individual might be taken away and tried by strangers far from home; his jury might be handpicked by the sheriff, or hold office for life; there was no guarantee that indictment should be by grand jury only, hence it might be by information of the attorney-general, "in consequence of which the most innocent person in the commonwealth may be . . .

25

[50] The expressed fear that Roman Catholicism might be established by treaty did not reflect any strong belief in religious freedom. It was nothing more than simple anti-Catholicism, as the remarks about the lack of a religious qualification for office-holding clearly indicate. On the other hand, there was some concern expressed in Pennsylvania over the rights of conscientious objectors to military service. See McMaster and Stone, *Pennsylvania and the Constitution,* 480–481.

[51] Article III, Section 2. The Constitution made no provision for jury trial in civil cases because different procedures in the several states had made the formulation of a general method difficult. The Anti-Federalists leaped to the conclusion that the lack of a written guarantee of this right meant certain deprivation of it, and they professed to be thoroughly alarmed. But their primary fear centered around what they regarded as the inadequate guarantees of the right of trial by jury in criminal cases.

[52] If George Washington's word is to be trusted, the actions of the Founding Fathers with respect to trial by jury and a bill of rights did not stem from any sinister motives. In a letter to Lafayette on April 28, 1788, he gave this explanation: "There was not a member of the convention, I believe, who had the least objection to what is contended for by the Advocates for a *Bill of Rights* and *Tryal by Jury.* The first, where the people evidently retained everything which they did not in express terms give up, was considered nugatory. . . . And as to the second, it was only the difficulty of establishing a mode which should not interfere with the fixed modes of any of the States, that induced the Convention to leave it, as a matter of future adjustment." *Documentary History of the Constitution,* Vol. IV, 601–602.

[53] In New York, see Elliot, II, 400; Virginia, III, 523 ff., North Carolina, IV, 143, 150, 154–155.

dragged from his home, his friends, his acquaintance, and confined in prison." "On the whole," said Holmes, "we shall find Congress possessed of powers enabling them to institute judicatories little less inauspicious than a certain tribunal in Spain, which has long been the disgrace of Christendom: I mean that diabolical institution, the *Inquisition*. . . . They are nowhere restrained from inventing the most cruel and unheard-of punishments and annexing them to crimes; and there is no constitutional check on them, but that *racks* and *gibbets* may be amongst the most mild instruments of their discipline."[54]

Should Congress have attempted any of these actions, it would have amounted to a virtual coup d'état and a repudiation of republicanism.[55] The advocates of the Constitution argued that such abuse of power could not reasonably be expected on the part of representatives elected by the people themselves. This argument was not satisfactory to the Anti-Federalists. They reiterated again and again the universal perfidy of man, especially men entrusted with political power, and emphasized the necessity of providing adequate protection against manifestations of human depravity. They charged that the authors and advocates of the Constitution were about to risk their liberties and those of all of the people on the slim possibility that the men to be elected to office in the new government would be, and would always be, good men.[56]

The Federalists also argued that election would serve as a check, since the people could remove unfaithful or unsatisfactory representatives, and since knowledge of this would make the latter refrain from incurring the displeasure of their constituents. This argument was flatly rejected. Patrick Henry stated his position emphatically during the course of his objection to Congressional power of taxation:

> I shall be told in this place, that those who are to tax us are our representatives. To this I answer, that there is no real check to prevent their ruining us. There is no actual responsibility. The only semblance of a check is the negative power of not re-electing them. This, sir, is but a feeble barrier, when their personal interest, their ambition and avarice, come to be put in contrast with the happiness of the people. All checks founded on anything but self-love, will not avail.[57]

In North Carolina the same opinion was expressed in a rather remarkable interchange. Taylor objected to the method of impeachment on the ground that since the House of Representatives drew up the bill of indictment, and the Senate

---

[54] Elliot, II, 109–111.

[55] This method of arguing drove the Federalists to exasperation more than once, as when one delegate in the Virginia Convention, an infrequent speaker, lost patience with Patrick Henry's "bugbears of hobgoblins" and suggested that "If the gentleman does not like this government, let him go and live among the Indians." Elliot, III, 580; cf. 632, 644. Also note the reporter's tongue-in-cheek note on Henry's opposition to the President's power of Commander-in-Chief: "Here Mr. Henry strongly and pathetically expatiated on the probability of the President's enslaving America, and the horrid consequences that must result." Ibid., 60. But Henry, who was so good at this technique himself, attacked it in his opponents. See ibid., 140.

[56] See above, section IV.

[57] Elliot, III, 167; cf. 327.

acted upon it, the members of Congress themselves would be virtually immune to this procedure. Governor Johnston answered that impeachment was not an appropriate remedy for legislative misrule, and that "A representative is answerable to no power but his constituents. He is accountable to no being under heaven but the people who appointed him." To this, Taylor responded simply, "that it now appeared to him in a still worse light than before."[58] Johnston stated one of the great principles of representative government; it merely deepened Taylor's fear of Congress. He and his fellow Anti-Federalists strongly wished for what Madison had referred to as "auxiliary precautions" against possible acts of legislative tyranny.

V

These additional safeguards were of two kinds: more explicit limitations written into the Constitution, and more institutional checks to enforce these limitations.

In recent years the Constitution has been much admired for its brevity, its generality, its freedom from the minutiae which characterized nineteenth-century constitutions. These qualities were feared and not admired by the Anti-Federalists. They wanted detailed explicitness which would confine the discretion of Congressional majorities within narrow boundaries. One critic complained of "a certain darkness, duplicity and studied ambiguity of expression running through the whole Constitution."[59] Another said that "he did not believe there existed a social compact on the face of the earth so vague and so indefinite as the one now on the table."[60] A North Carolinian demanded to know, "Why not use expressions that were clear and unequivocal?"[61] Later, he warned, "Without the most express restrictions, Congress may trample on your rights."[62] Williams of New York expressed the general feeling when he said in that state's convention, "I am, sir, for certainty in the establishment of a constitution which is not only to operate upon us, but upon millions yet unborn."[63] These men wanted everything down in black and white, with no latitude of discretion or interpretation left to their representatives in Congress. It was an attitude which anticipated the later trend toward lengthy constitutions filled with innumerable and minute restrictions on the legislatures.

To no avail did the Federalists argue that if future representatives should indeed prove to be so treacherous and tyrannical as to commit the horrible deeds suggested, then mere guarantees on paper would not stop them for a minute. It is easy to call the Anti-Federalist attitude unrealistic, but to do so is to miss a large part of its significance. Like the Founding Fathers, like all men of their age, they

---

[58] Elliot, IV, 32–34.

[59] Thomas B. Wait to George Thatcher, January 8, 1788, in "The Thatcher Papers," selected from the papers of Hon. George Thatcher, and communicated by Captain Goodwin, U.S.A., *The Historical Magazine,* November and December 1869 (Second Series, Vols. 15–16), No. V, 262.

[60] Elliot, III, 583.

[61] Elliot, IV, 68; cf. 70, 153, 154–155, 168.

[62] Ibid., 167.

[63] Elliot, II, 339.

were great constitutionalists. They were also first-generation republicans, still self-consciously so, and aware that their precious form of government was as yet an experiment and had not proved its capacity for endurance. Its greatest enemy was man's lust for power, and the only thing which could hold this in check, they were convinced, was a carefully written and properly constructed constitution. They placed even greater emphasis on the structure of government than did the Founding Fathers, and refused to take for granted, as the latter did, that the "genius" of the country was republican, and that the behavior of the men to be placed in office would in general be republican also.

The Anti-Federalists wanted a more rigid system of separation of powers, more numerous and more effective checks and balances, than the Founding Fathers had provided.[64] They thought this elementary principle of good government, this "political maxim," had been violated, and that corruption leading to tyranny would be the inevitable result. That the doctrine celebrated by Montesquieu did enjoy the status of "maxim" seems unquestionable. Violation of separation of powers was one of George Mason's major objections to the Constitution.[65] Richard Henry Lee made the same protest,[66] and further lamented that there were no "checks in the formation of the government, to secure the rights of the people against the usurpations of those they appoint to govern."[67] James Monroe said that he could "see no real checks in it."[68] It is no wonder that an obscure member of the Virginia Convention, when he rose with great diffidence to make his only speech, chose safe and familiar ground to cover:

28

> That the legislative, executive, and judicial powers should be separate and distinct, in all free governments, is a political fact so well established, that I presume I shall not be thought arrogant, when I affirm that no country ever did, or ever can, long remain free, where they are blended. All the states have been in this sentiment when they formed their state constitutions, and therefore have guarded against the danger; and every schoolboy in politics must be convinced of the propriety of the observation; and yet, by the proposed plan, the legislative and executive powers are closely united.[69]

In Pennsylvania, whose Revolutionary state constitution had embodied very little of separation of powers, an apparent return to Montesquieu's doctrine led to criticism of the Constitution. In the ratifying convention, one of the amendments submitted had for its purpose "That the legislative, executive, and judicial powers

---

[64] Thus in *The Federalist* 47, Madison felt obliged to defend the Constitution against this charge. This was first pointed out to me by B. F. Wright and was the origin of the present essay. See the discussion in his article "The Federalist on the Nature of Political Man," *Ethics* (January 1949), especially 7 ff.

[65] "Objections of the Hon. George Mason, to the proposed Federal Constitution. Addressed to the Citizens of Virginia." Ford, *Pamphlets,* 330.

[66] "Letters of a Federal Farmer," Ford, *Pamphlets,* 299.

[67] Ibid., 318.

[68] Elliot, III, 219.

[69] Ibid., 608.

be kept separate."[70] In that same state, the leading Anti-Federalist pamphleteer "Centinel," who is believed to have been either George Bryan, a probable co-author of the 1776 Constitution and formerly in sympathy with the ideas of Tom Paine on this subject, or his son Samuel, now expressed himself in the usual manner:

> This mixture of the legislative and executive moreover highly tends to corruption. The chief improvement in government, in modern times, has been the complete separation of the great distinctions of power; placing the *legislative* in different hands from those which hold the executive; and again severing the *judicial* part from the ordinary *administrative*. "When the legislative and executive powers (says Montesquieu) are united in the same person, or in the same body of magistrates, there can be no liberty."[71]

The Anti-Federalists were just as unequivocal about the inadequacy of the Constitution's system of checks and balances. Patrick Henry hit his top form when he took up the matter in Virginia: "There will be no checks, no real balances, in this government. What can avail your specious, imaginary balances, your rope-dancing, chain-rattling, ridiculous ideal checks and contrivances?"[72] Later in the Convention he argued that what checks there were had no practical value at all—for reasons which must cloud his reputation as a spokesman for the masses imbued with the radical spirit of Revolutionary democracy: "To me it appears that there is no check in that government. The President, senators, and representatives, all, immediately or mediately, are the choice of the people."[73] His views were echoed by his colleague, William Grayson.[74]

In New York, Melancton Smith returned to the subject several times, arguing, because there would eventually be corruption in Congress, "It is wise to multiply checks to a greater degree than the present state of things requires."[75] In Massachusetts James Winthrop tied up the concept of separation of powers with checks and balances very neatly. "It is now generally understood that it is for the

29

---

[70] McMaster and Stone, *Pennsylvania and the Constitution,* 423. See also 475–477 for discussion back of this.

[71] McMaster and Stone, *Pennsylvania and the Constitution,* 587.

[72] Elliot, III, 54.

[73] Ibid., 164. He then went on to point out that the British House of Lords constituted a check against both the King and the Commons, and that this check was founded on "self-love," i.e., the desire of the Lords to protect their interests against attack from either of the other two branches of the government. This consideration, he said, prevailed upon him "to pronounce the British government superior, in this respect, to any government that ever was in any country. Compare this with your Congressional checks. . . . Have you a resting-place like the British government? Where is the rock of your salvation? . . . Where are your checks? You have no hereditary nobility—an order of men to whom human eyes can be cast up for relief; for, says the Constitution, there is no title of nobility to be granted. . . . In the British government there are real balances and checks: in this system there are only ideal balances." Ibid., 164–165.

[74] Ibid., 421, 563. Grayson also expressed his preference for a form of government—if there was to be a national government at all—far less popular than the one proposed. He favored one strikingly similar to the plan Hamilton had suggested in Philadelphia, a president and senate elected for life, and a lower house elected for a three-year term. See Elliot, III, 279.

[75] Elliot, II, 259, 315.

security of the people that the powers of the government should be lodged in different branches. By this means publick business will go on when they all agree, and stop when they disagree. The advantage of checks in government is thus manifested where the concurrence of different branches is necessary to the same act."[76]

There can be little doubt that the Anti-Federalists were united in their desire to put more checks on the new government. This was natural, since they greatly feared it. Expressions of the opposite opinion were extremely rare. Rawlins Lowndes in South Carolina remarked casually and without elaboration that it was possible to have too many checks on a government.[77] George Clinton and the Pennsylvanian "Centinel" both warned that a government might become so complex that the people could not understand it,[78] but both men expressed the usual fear of abuse of power,[79] and "Centinel" paid his respects to Montesquieu and explicitly criticized the inadequacy of checks by the President or the House of Representatives on the Senate.[80]

Thus no one, so far as I have been able to discover, attacked the general validity of the system of separation of powers and checks and balances. The Anti-Federalists were staunch disciples of Montesquieu on this subject, and they would have found quite unacceptable J. Allen Smith's dictum that "The system of checks and balances must not be confused with democracy; it is opposed to and cannot be reconciled with the theory of popular government."[81]

Although there was much oratory about the Founding Fathers' deviation from Montesquieu's doctrine, there were surprisingly few proposals for specific alterations in the structure of the new government. Of these, the most important was a change in the relationship between President and Senate. The latter's share in the treaty-making and appointing powers was believed to be a dangerous blending of executive and legislative power which ought to have been avoided. Possibly because of their recent memory of the role of the colonial governor's council, possibly because there was no clear provision in the Constitution for an executive cabinet or council, the Anti-Federalists saw the Senate very much in the latter's role and expected it to play a very active and continuous part in giving advice to the President. This was clearly contrary to the doctrine of the celebrated Montesquieu—at least it seemed so to them.

The result would certainly be some form of joint Presidential-Senatorial tyranny, it was argued, but as to which of the two departments would be the stronger of the "partners in crime," the Anti-Federalists were not agreed. Patrick Henry said that the President, with respect to the treaty-making power, "as distinguished from the Senate, is nothing."[82] Grayson, with the North-South

---

[76] *Agrippa* Letters in Ford, *Essays,* 116.

[77] Elliot, IV, 308–309.

[78] Clinton's *Cato* Letters in Ford, *Essays,* 257; *Centinel* in McMaster and Stone, *Pennsylvania and the Constitution,* 569. "Centinel" expressed a desire for a unicameral legislature.

[79] Clinton in Ford, *Essays,* 261, 266; *Centinel* in McMaster and Stone, *Pennsylvania and the Constitution,* 617.

[80] McMaster and Stone, *Pennsylvania and the Constitution,* 586–587; 475–477.

[81] *The Spirit of American Government* (New York, 1907), 9.

[82] Elliot, III, 353.

division in mind, predicted a quid pro quo alliance between the President and "the seven Eastern states." "He will accommodate himself to their interests in forming treaties, and they will continue him perpetually in office."[83] Mason predicted a "marriage" between the President and Senate: "They will be continually supporting and aiding each other: they will always consider their interest as united. . . . The executive and legislative powers, thus connected, will destroy all balances."[84] "Centinel" of Pennsylvania also feared that the President would not be strong enough to resist pressure from the Senate, and that he would join with them as "the head of the aristocratic junto."[85] Spencer of North Carolina, in support of a remedy in which all of the above men concurred, argued that with an advisory council entirely separate from the legislature, and chosen from the separate states, the President "would have that independence which is necessary to form the intended check upon the acts passed by the legislature before they obtain the sanction of laws."[86]

Although the prevailing opinion thus seemed to be that the President was not strong enough, there were some who believed that he was too strong. George Clinton argued that the extensive powers given to him, combined with his long tenure of office, gave him both "power and time sufficient to ruin his country." Furthermore, since he had no proper council to assist him while the Senate was recessed, he would be without advice, or get it from "minions and favorites"—or "a great council of state will grow out of the principal officers of the great departments, the most dangerous council in a free country."[87]

One man in North Carolina, the only one to the best of my knowledge, departed from the ordinary Anti-Federalist line of attack and criticized the executive veto from a clear majoritarian position. It was Lancaster, who projected the hypothetical case of a bill which passed the House of Representatives unanimously, the Senate by a large majority, was vetoed by the President and returned to the Senate, where it failed to get a two-thirds vote. The House would never see it again, said Mr. Lancaster, and thus, "This is giving a power to the President to overrule fifteen members of the Senate and every member of the House of Representatives."[88]

Except for Lancaster, most Anti-Federalists feared the Senate more than the President, but all feared the two in combination and wanted some checks against them. The separate advisory council for the President was one, and shorter terms and/or compulsory rotation for Senators and President, plus the power of state recall of the former, were others. Direct, popular election of either was *not* proposed.

Since most of the state executives and legislators held office for annual or biennial terms, one would naturally expect the substantially longer tenure of the President and Senate to be severely criticized. There were numerous objections to the six-year term of Senators, some to the four-year term of the President, and a

---

[83] Ibid., 492.

[84] Ibid., 493–494.

[85] McMaster and Stone, *Pennsylvania and the Constitution*, 586.

[86] Elliot, IV, 117–118.

[87] *Cato* Letters, Ford, *Essays*, 261–262.

[88] Elliot, IV, 214.

few to the two-year term of members of the House of Representatives. It is to be noted, however, that there was no serious attempt to shorten the length of term of any of these officers, nor was there any attempt to make the tenure of either the President or the Senate correspond with that of the House. It was agreed that the two houses should "afford a mutual check" on each other,[89] and that the "stability" provided by the Senate "was essential to good government."[90]

The most insistent and repeated criticism was the failure of the Constitution to provide for the compulsory rotation of office for Senators and the President. "Nothing is so essential to the preservation of a republican government as a periodical rotation," said George Mason,[91] and Melancton Smith pronounced it "a very important and truly republican institution."[92] They greatly feared that President and Senators would be perpetually re-elected, and in effect hold office for life. Mason, for example, was quite content for the Senate to serve six years, and the President even eight, but he believed that without rotation, the new government would become "an elective monarchy."[93] The President would be able to perpetuate himself forever, it was assumed, because his election would always be thrown into the House of Representatives. In that body, corruption, intrigue, foreign influence, and above all else, the incumbent's use of his patronage, would make it possible for every man, once elected, to hold office for life. Senators would "hold their office perpetually,"[94] by corrupting their electors, the state legislatures. In New York, where the subject was debated very thoroughly, the Anti-Federalists were challenged to show how such corruption could take place, and continue for life, among a group which was continuously subject to popular election, and which would presumably not be permanent. To this challenge Lansing replied, "It is unnecessary to particularize the numerous ways in which public bodies are accessible to corruption. The poison always finds a channel, and never wants an object."[95] No distinction as to comparative corruptibility was made between national and state representatives.

To Federalist objections that compulsory rotation constituted an abridgment of the people's right to elect whomsoever they wished, Melancton Smith replied impatiently, "What is government itself but a restraint upon the natural rights of the people? What constitution was ever devised that did not operate as a restraint on their natural liberties?"[96] Lansing conceded that rotation placed a restriction on the people's free choice of rulers, but he thought this beneficial: "The rights of the people will be best supported by checking, at a certain point, the current of popular favor, and preventing the establishment of an influence which may leave to elections little more than the form of freedom."[97]

[89] Elliot, II, 308 (Lansing).

[90] Ibid., 309 (Smith).

[91] Elliot, III, 485.

[92] Elliot, II, 310.

[93] Elliot, III, 485.

[94] Elliot, II, 309 (Smith).

[95] Elliot, II, 295.

[96] Ibid., 311.

[97] Ibid., 295. It was in this debate that Lansing made the Madisonian statement quoted above, 20.

The power of recall by state legislatures was associated with compulsory rotation as a means of preventing senatorial abuse of power. Not only would it enforce strict responsibility of senators to their electors, but in so doing it would protect the interests and preserve the sovereignty of the separate states. For these reasons, its adoption was strongly pressed in several of the ratifying conventions. Beyond these reasons, which were primary, recall combined with rotation would have a secondary beneficent result. It would serve to prevent the perpetuation of intra-legislative parties and factions—something which the Anti-Federalists feared quite as much as their opponents. Even if the power of recall should not actually be used, said Lansing, it would "destroy party spirit."[98] When his opponents turned this argument against him, and suggested that factions within the state legislatures might use the power to remove good, honorable, and faithful men from the Senate, the answer was that the legislatures had not abused the power under the Articles of Confederation and would almost certainly not do so in the future, and that even if they did, ample opportunity would be provided for the displaced senator to defend himself. The influence of "ambitious and designing men" would be detected and exposed, and the error easily corrected.[99] A curious "Trust them, trust them not" attitude toward the state legislatures is thus revealed. They could not be trusted to refuse re-election to unfaithful or ambitious senators, though they could be trusted to remove the same and to leave in office all those who deserved well of them and of their constituents.

From this it is clear that the Anti-Federalists were not willing to trust either upper or lower house of the proposed national Congress; neither were they willing to trust their own state legislatures completely, though they had less fear of the latter because these could be kept under closer observation.

The same attitude is indicated by Anti-Federalist reaction to the restrictions placed on state legislatures by Article I, Section 10 of the Constitution, and to the then potential review of both state and national legislation by the Supreme Court.

Of the latter prospect, frequently said to have been one of the great bulwarks erected against the democratic majority, very little was said during the ratification debate. There was no explicit provision for judicial review in the Constitution, and it is probably not possible to prove conclusively whether or not its authors intended the Supreme Court to exercise this power. The evidence suggests that they probably assumed it would. Hamilton's *Federalist* 78 supports this view. The issue was never debated in the state conventions, and there are almost no references to it in any of the Anti-Federalist arguments. Since *Federalist* 78 was published before the Virginia, New York, and North Carolina Conventions met, this lack of discussion is significant and would seem to reflect lack of concern. There was severe criticism of Article III, particularly in Virginia, but it centered around the jurisdiction of the lower federal courts to be established by Congress, not around the Supreme Court. The issue was entirely one of state courts versus federal courts, not of courts versus legislatures.

The single direct reference to judicial review made in the Virginia Convention—at least the only one I have found—suggests that this institution was, or would have been, thoroughly congenial to the Anti-Federalists. The statement was made by Patrick Henry:

[98] Elliot, II, 290.

[99] Ibid., 299.

> Yes, sir, our judges opposed the acts of the legislature. We have this land-mark to guide us. They had fortitude to declare that they were the judiciary, and would oppose unconstitutional acts. Are you sure that your federal judiciary will act thus? Is that judiciary as well constructed, and as independent of the other branches, as our state judiciary? Where are your landmarks in this government? I will be bold to say you cannot find any in it. I take it as the highest encomium on this country, that the acts of the legislature, if unconstitutional, are liable to be opposed by the judiciary.[100]

There was nothing equivocal about Henry's attitude. It elicited no comment. Possibly neither side wished to commit itself; more likely the statement was lost and forgotten after brighter flames had issued from the great orator's fire. What is really significant, however, is the complete absence of debate over judicial review. The Anti-Federalists probed the Constitution for every conceivable threat, explicit or implicit, to their conception of free and popular government. If they had considered judicial review such a threat, they would surely have made the most of it, and particularly after *Federalist* 78 was published.

There was also comparatively little attention given to the restrictions which Article I, Section 10 of the Constitution placed on the state legislatures. Among other things, the states were forbidden to coin money, emit bills of credit, make anything but gold or silver legal tender for the payment of debts, or pass any law impairing the obligations of contracts. These are the provisions which recent historians have emphasized as designed to protect the property of the conservative class against the onslaughts of the radical democratic majority. The Anti-Federalists had very little to say about these provisions. The notation of the New York Convention's action is significant: "The committee then proceded through sections 8, 9, and 10, of this article [I], and the whole of the next, with little or no debate."[101] In Virginia and the Carolinas there was more discussion, but nothing like a full-dress debate, and very little indication of any strong or widespread opposition. In fact, Patrick Henry said that the restrictions were "founded in good principles,"[102] and William Grayson said of the prohibition against paper money, "it is unanimously wished by every one that it should not be objected to."[103] Richard Henry Lee expressed his preference for paper money to be issued by Congress only.[104] Of the few objections or doubts expressed, these were typical. Henry in Virginia and Galloway in North Carolina both expressed a fear that the contract clause might be interpreted to force the states to redeem their respective shares of the depreciated Continental currency and of state securities at face value.[105] Henry was also angry because of the necessary implication that the states were too "depraved" to be trusted with the contracts of their own citizens.[106]

[100] Elliot, III, 325.

[101] Elliot, II, 406.

[102] Elliot, III, 471.

[103] Ibid., 566.

[104] J. C. Ballagh, editor, *The Letters of Richard Henry Lee,* 2 vols. (New York, 1911–1914), 421–422.

[105] Elliot, III, 318–319; IV, 190.

[106] Elliot, III, 156.

With regard to the prohibition of paper money, two men in North Carolina defended the previous state issue as having been a necessary expedient in troublesome times, but did not seem to object to the prohibition of future issues.[107] One man argued against this clause and the supreme law clause on the ground that the effect might be to destroy the paper money already in circulation and thereby create great confusion.[108] His contention was denied.[109] These remarks, none of which expressed direct opposition, were typical. In South Carolina, however, Rawlins Lowndes came out flatly against this restriction, defended the previous issue of paper money and the right of the state to make further issues in the future.[110] His position appears to have been the exception, at least of those which were expressed openly and publicly on the various convention floors.[111]

The response of the Anti-Federalists to these important limitations on the power of the states can accurately be described, I think, as one of overall approbation tempered by some doubts caused by fear that they would be applied retroactively. This attitude is in rather curious contrast with the extremely jealous reaction to other changes in federal-state relations for which the Constitution provided. There were violent objections to federal control over state militia, to Congressional power to tax and to regulate commerce, to the creation of an inferior system of federal courts. All these things brought forth loud cries that the states would be swallowed up by the national government. These important restrictions on the economic powers of the states were received with relative silence. There was apparently very little objection to these limitations on the power of state legislative majorities.

It remains to consider the extent to which the general Anti-Federalist distrust of their representatives, particularly those who were to serve in the national government but also those who served in their state legislatures, reflected also a distrust of the majorities who elected them, that is to say, of the people themselves. The answer is partly wrapped up in the whole complex of ideas constituting the Anti-Federalist conception of republican government, which I shall attempt to draw together in the concluding section of this essay. Some parts of the answer can be put into the record here.

---

[107] Ibid., IV, 88, 169–170.

[108] Ibid., 180, 184–185.

[109] Ibid., 181–185.

[110] Ibid., 289–290.

[111] There appears to have been more opposition to the provisions of Article I, Section 10 expressed outside of the Convention than inside. See Trenholme, *Ratification in North Carolina,* 42, and Clarence E. Miner, *The Ratification of the Federal Constitution in New York,* Studies in History, Economics and Public Law, Vol. XCIV, No. 3, Whole No. 214, Columbia University (New York, 1921), for the extra-Convention debate in New York. It may be that this was one of the subjects the Anti-Federalists preferred not to debate for the official record. See Trenholme, 166–167, for a discussion of the refusal of North Carolina Anti-Federalists to state in the Convention objections to the Constitution being made outside. There was also apparently a similar situation during the Virginia Convention, where the Federalists objected to what was happening "outdoors." See Elliot, III, 237. See also the remarks of Alexander C. Hanson, a member of the Maryland Convention. In discussing these provisions, of which he strongly approved, he wrote, "I have here perhaps touched a string, which secretly draws together many of the foes to the plan." In *Aristides,* "Remarks on the Proposed Plan of a Federal Government," Ford, *Pamphlets,* 243.

The attitude of the Anti-Federalists toward the people as distinguished from their representatives, and toward the general problem of majority rule, was not radically different from that of their opponents. It is a curious and remarkable fact that during the course of this great debate in which the most popular national constitution ever framed was submitted to the public for the most popular mode of ratification yet attempted, there was very little tendency on either side to enthrone "the people" or to defer automatically to their judgment. Neither side showed the slightest inclination to use as its slogan, "Vox populi vox Dei." Rather was the contrary true, and some of the Anti-Federalist expressions of this attitude could easily have fitted into the dark picture of human nature presented in *The Federalist*. Indeed, the speeches and essays of the Anti-Federalists were peculiarly lacking in the great expressions of faith in the people which are to be found in the writings of Jefferson, and even occasionally in *The Federalist* itself. This is partly to be accounted for because their position was a negative one; they attacked the proposed system on the ground that it would be destructive of liberty.

It was therefore perhaps natural that they sometimes expressed fear about what may be called the constituent capacity of the people—the capacity of the people to act wisely in the actual choice of a constitution. They were afraid that the people might not see in the proposed new government all of the dangers and defects which they themselves saw. And there were gloomy comments about lack of stability. Said George Clinton in the New York Convention, "The people, when wearied with their distresses, will in the moment of frenzy, be guilty of the most imprudent and desperate measures. . . . I know the people are too apt to vibrate from one extreme to another. The effects of this disposition are what I wish to guard against."[112] His colleague, Melancton Smith, spoke in a similar vein:

> Fickleness and inconstancy, he said, were characteristic of a free people; and, in framing a constitution for them, it was, perhaps, the most difficult thing to correct this spirit, and guard against the evil effects of it. He was persuaded it could not be altogether prevented without destroying their freedom. . . . This fickle and inconstant spirit was the more dangerous in bringing about changes in the government.[113]

It was "Centinel," author or son of the author of Pennsylvania's revolutionary Constitution, who expressed the gravest doubts about the capacity of the people to make a wise choice in the form of government, and who expounded a kind of Burkeian conservatism as the best guarantor of the people's liberties. In a passage apparently aimed at the prestige given to the proposed Constitution by the support of men like Washington and Franklin, "Centinel" wrote that "the science of government is so abstruse, that few are able to judge for themselves." Without the assistance of those "who are competent to the task of developing the principles of government," the people were "too apt to yield an implicit assent to the opinions of those characters whose abilities are held in the highest esteem, and to those in

[112] Elliot, II, 359.
[113] Elliot, II, 225.

whose integrity and patriotism they can confide." This was dangerous, because such men might easily be dupes, "the instruments of despotism in the hands of the *artful and designing*." "Centinel" then continued:

> If it were not for the stability and attachment which time and habit gives to forms of government, it would be in the power of the enlightened and aspiring few, if they should combine, at any time to destroy the best establishments, and even make the people the instruments of their own subjugation.
> The late revolution having effaced in a great measure all former habits, and the present institutions are so recent, that there exists not that great reluctance to innovation, so remarkable in old communities, and which accords with reason, for the most comprehensive mind cannot foresee the full operation of material changes on civil polity; it is the genius of the common law to resist innovation.[114]

Later in the same series of articles, "Centinel" pronounced "this reluctance to change" as "the greatest security of free governments, and the principal bulwark of liberty."[115] This attitude provides an interesting comparison with the unquestioning assumption in the Federal Convention that the proposed Constitution would be submitted to the people for their verdict, and with the level of popular understanding of political affairs to which the essays of the *Federalist Papers* were addressed.

Serious reservations about the capacity of the people as electors were implicit in several of the arguments noted above. The advocacy of religious qualifications for office-holding indicated a desire to restrict the choice of the electorate to certified Protestants, and the demand for compulsory rotation of senators and President rested on the fear that corruption of both state and national legislatures by the incumbents of those offices could not be prevented by the feeble check of popular election. Perhaps most important was the belief that the people, voting in the large constituencies provided for by the Constitution, would either lose elections to their presumed aristocratic opponents because of the latter's superior capacity for organization, or would themselves let their choice fall on such aristocrats, or be deceived by ambitious and unscrupulous demagogues.

There was no more confidence in the inherent justice of the will of the majority than there was in its electoral capacity. Since the Anti-Federalists were skeptical that constituent opinion would be adequately reflected in the national legislature, they were less inclined than the Federalists to regard the government as the instrument of the people or of the majority. When they did so, there was not the slightest tendency to consider its decisions "right" *because* they were majority decisions. Rather was there always some standard of right and justice, independent of the majority's will, to which that will ought to conform. The Anti-Federalists were perfectly consistent in their conception of political behavior and did not regard a majority as superior to the sum of its parts, that is to say, of

[114] McMaster and Stone, *Pennsylvania and the Constitution,* 566–567.

[115] Ibid., 655. It may be noted that this Burkeian friend of Tom Paine had not undertaken to submit the radical revolutionary Constitution of Pennsylvania to the people of that state for full, free, and deliberate debate, but had rushed its ratification through the legislature with most unseemly haste.

individual men motivated by self-interest and subject to a natural lust for power. There was very little discussion of majority rule and minority rights as fundamental principles of representative government, but the attitude of the Anti-Federalists is, I think, reasonably clear.

They assumed, of course, that in a republican form of government, the majority must rule. But they also assumed that the will of the majority ought to be limited, especially when the "majority" was a legislative one. They demanded a bill of rights, with special emphasis on procedural protections in criminal cases, and vehemently repudiated the somewhat spurious Federalist argument that a bill of rights was not necessary in a government ruled by the people themselves. To this, James Winthrop replied:

> that the sober and industrious part of the community should be defended from the rapacity and violence of the vicious and idle. A bill of rights, therefore, ought to set forth the purposes for which the compact is made, and serves to secure the minority against the usurpation and tyranny of the majority. . . . The experience of all mankind has proved the prevalence of a disposition to use power wantonly. It is therefore as necessary to defend an individual against the majority in a republick as against the king in a monarchy.[116]

The reaction of the Anti-Federalists to the restrictions imposed on state legislative majorities by Article I, Section 10 of the Constitution is also relevant at this point. These provisions were certainly intended to protect the rights of property against legislative invasion by majorities. If there had been any spirit of doctrinaire majoritarianism among the opponents of the Constitution, this would surely have been the occasion to express it, and in quite unequivocal terms. There was very little open criticism of these provisions, none on the grounds that they violated the principle of majority rule or that they were designed to protect the interests of the upper classes.[117] What criticism there was, was expressed largely in terms of practical considerations.

Distrust of majority factions in much the same sense as Madison's was emphatically expressed by the one sector of Anti-Federalism which constituted the most self-conscious minority. Southerners felt keenly the conflict of interest between North and South and were vehemently opposed to surrendering themselves to the majority of the seven Eastern states. One of the reasons for George Mason's refusal to sign the Constitution had been his failure to get adopted a two-thirds majority vote for all laws affecting commerce and navigation. His fears for the South's interests were shared by his fellow Southerners and were frequently expressed in the Convention debates. "It will be a government of a faction," said William Grayson, "and this observation will apply to every part of it; for, having a majority, they may do what they please."[118] Other colleagues in Virginia

---

[116] *Agrippa* Letters, Ford, *Essays,* 117. See also Elliot, III, 499, for a similar statement from William Grayson.

[117] See above, footnote 111, for discussion of the possibility of more criticism expressed outside of the conventions.

[118] Elliot, III, 492.

joined in this distrust of the anticipated Northern majority uniting to oppress the South.[119] In North and South Carolina it was much the same. Bloodworth lamented, "To the north of the Susquehanna there are thirty-six representatives, and to the south of it only twenty-nine. They will always outvote us."[120] In South Carolina, Rawlins Lowndes predicted that "when this new Constitution should be adopted, the sun of the Southern States would set, never to rise again." Why? Because the Eastern states would have a majority in the legislature and would not hesitate to use it—probably to interfere with the slave trade, "because they have none themselves, and therefore want to exclude us from this great advantage."[121]

There was, then, no doctrinaire devotion to majoritarianism. It was assumed that oppression of individuals or of groups might come from majorities of the people themselves as well as from kings or aristocrats.

VI

For a generation the *Economic Interpretation of the Constitution* has exerted a deep and extensive influence over students of American history and government. The conception of the Constitution as the product of a conservative reaction against the ideals of the Revolution has been widely accepted, and Beard's analysis of the document itself commonly followed. According to this interpretation, the Founding Fathers secured their property rights by placing certain restrictions on state legislatures and by setting up a government in which the system of separation of powers, with checks and balances, indirect elections, staggered terms of office, and a national judiciary with the potential power of judicial review, would restrain the force of turbulent, democratic majorities. Surprisingly little attention has been devoted to the Anti-Federalists, but it is implied that they were the true heirs of the Revolutionary tradition—equally devoted to individual liberty and majority rule. The Federalists' desire for strong central government and the Anti-Federalists' fear of such are also considered, but the allegedly undemocratic structure of the national government itself is strongly emphasized. This aspect of the Beard thesis is open to question.

For the objections of the Anti-Federalists were not directed toward the barriers imposed on simple majority rule by the Constitution. Advocates and opponents of ratification may have belonged to different economic classes and been motivated by different economic interests. But they shared a large body of political ideas and attitudes, together with a common heritage of political institutions. For one thing, they shared a profound distrust of man's capacity to use power wisely and well. They believed self-interest to be the dominant motive of political behavior, no matter whether the form of government be republican or monarchical, and they believed in the necessity of constructing political machinery that would restrict the operation of self-interest and prevent men entrusted with political power from abusing it. This was the fundamental assumption of the men who wrote the Constitution, and of those who opposed its adoption, as well.

[119] Ibid., 152, 221–222.

[120] Elliot, IV, 185.

[121] Ibid., 272.

The fundamental issue over which Federalists and Anti-Federalists split was the question whether republican government could be extended to embrace a nation, or whether it must be limited to the comparatively small political and geographical units which the separate American states then constituted. The Anti-Federalists took the latter view; and in a sense they were the conservatives of 1787, and their opponents the radicals.

The Anti-Federalists were clinging to a theory of representative government that was already becoming obsolete, and would have soon become so even had they been successful in preventing the establishment of a national government. Certainly it was a theory which could never have provided the working principles for such a government. For the Anti-Federalists were not only localists, but localists in a way strongly reminiscent of the city-state theory of Rousseau's *Social Contract*. According to that theory, a society capable of being governed in accordance with the General Will had to be limited in size, population, and diversity. The Anti-Federalists had no concept of a General Will comparable to Rousseau's, and they accepted the institution of representation, where he had rejected it. But many of their basic attitudes were similar to his. Like him, they thought republican government subject to limitations of size, population, and diversity; and like him also, they thought the will of the people would very likely be distorted by the process of representation. In fact, their theory of representation and their belief that republican government could not be extended nation-wide were integrally related.

They regarded representation primarily as an institutional substitute for direct democracy and endeavored to restrict its operation to the performance of that function; hence their plea that the legislature should be an exact miniature of the people, containing spokesmen for all classes, all groups, all interests, all opinions, in the community; hence, too, their preference for short legislative terms of office and their inclination, especially in the sphere of state government, to regard representatives as delegates bound by the instructions of constituents rather than as men expected and trusted to exercise independent judgment. This was a natural stage in the development of representative government, but it contained several weaknesses and was, I think, already obsolete in late eighteenth-century America.

Its major weaknesses were closely akin to those of direct democracy itself, for representation of this kind makes difficult the process of genuine deliberation, as well as the reconciliation of diverse interests and opinions. Indeed, it is notable, and I think not accidental, that the body of Anti-Federalist thought as a whole showed little consideration of the necessity for compromise. The Founding Fathers were not democrats, but in their recognition of the role which compromise must play in the process of popular government, they were far more advanced than their opponents.

It is clear, too, that the same factors limiting the size and extent of direct democracies would also be operative in republics where representation is regarded only as a substitute for political participation by the whole people. Within their own frame of reference, the Anti-Federalists were quite right in insisting that republican government would work only in relatively small states, where the population was also small and relatively homogeneous. If there is great diversity among the people, with many interests and many opinions, then all cannot be represented without making the legislature as large and unwieldy as the citizen assemblies of ancient Athens. And if the system does not lend itself readily to compromise and conciliation, then the basis for a working consensus must be considerable homogeneity in the people themselves. In the opinion of the Anti-Federalists, the American people lacked that homogeneity.[122] This Rousseauistic vision of a small, simple, and homogeneous democracy may have been a fine ideal, but it *was* an ideal even then. It was not to be found even in the small states, and none of the Anti-Federalists produced a satisfactory answer to Madison's analysis of the weaknesses inherent in republicanism operating on the small scale preferred by his opponents.

Associated with this theory of representation and its necessary limitation to small-scale republics was the Anti-Federalists' profound distrust of the electoral and representative processes provided for and implied in the proposed Constitution. Their ideal of the legislature as an "exact miniature" of the people envisaged something not unlike the result hoped for by modern proponents of proportional representation. This was impossible to achieve in the national Congress.[123] There would not and could not be enough seats to go around. The constituencies were to be large—the ratio of representatives to population was not to exceed one per thirty thousand—and each representative must therefore represent not one, but many groups among his electors. And whereas Madison saw in this process of "filtering" or consolidating public opinion a virtue, the Anti-Federalists saw in it only danger. They did not think that a Congress thus elected could truly represent the will of the people, and they particularly feared that they themselves, the "middling class," to use Melancton Smith's term, would be left out.

They feared this because they saw clearly that enlarged constituencies would require more pre-election political organization than they believed to be either wise or safe. Much has been written recently about the Founding Fathers' hostility to political parties. It is said that they designed the Constitution, especially separation of powers, in order to counteract the effectiveness of parties.[124] This is partly true, but I think it worth noting that the contemporary opponents of the Constitution feared parties or factions in the Madisonian sense just as much as, and that they feared parties in the modern sense even more than, did Madison himself. They feared and distrusted concerted group action for the purpose of "centering votes" in order to obtain a plurality, because they believed this would distort the automatic or natural expression of the people's will. The necessity of such action in large electoral districts would work to the advantage of the upper classes, who, because of their superior capacity and opportunity for organization of this kind, would elect a disproportionate share of representatives to the Congress. In other words, the Anti-Federalists were acutely aware of the role that

41

---

[122] I do not mean to suggest that the Anti-Federalist attitude concerning homogeneity and what modern social scientists refer to as consensus was hopelessly wrong. A degree of both is necessary for the successful operation of democracy, and the concept itself is an extremely valuable one. I would merely contend that the Federalist estimate of the degree required was both more liberal and more realistic. On the subject of the extent to which the American people were united in tradition, institutions, and ideas in 1787–1788, see Ranney, "Bases of American Federalism."

[123] Nor for that matter, has it been the pattern of representation in state legislatures.

[124] See, e. g., E. E. Schattschneider, *Party Government* (New York, 1942), 4 ff.

organization played in the winning of elections, and they were not willing to accept the "organized" for the "real" majority. Instead they wanted to retain the existing system, where the electoral constituencies were small, and where organization of this kind was relatively unnecessary. Only then could a man vote as he saw fit, confident that the result of the election would reflect the real will of the people as exactly as possible.

Distrust of the electoral process thus combined with the localist feelings of the Anti-Federalists to produce an attitude of profound fear and suspicion toward Congress. That body, it was felt, would be composed of aristocrats and of men elected from far-away places by the unknown peoples of distant states. It would meet at a yet undesignated site hundreds of miles from the homes of most of its constituents, outside the jurisdiction of any particular state, and protected by an army of its own making. When one sees Congress in this light, it is not surprising that the Anti-Federalists were afraid, or that they had little faith in elections as a means of securing responsibility and preventing Congressional tyranny.[125]

Their demand for more limitations on Congressional power was perfectly natural. These were believed to be necessary in any government because of the lust for power and the selfishness in its use which were inherent in the nature of man. They were doubly necessary in a government on a national scale. And so the Anti-Federalists criticized the latitude of power given to Congress under Article I and called for more detailed provisions to limit the scope of Congressional discretion. We are certainly indebted to them for the movement that led to the adoption of the Bill of Rights, though they were more concerned with the traditional common-law rights of procedure in criminal cases than with the provisions of the First Amendment. They were at the same time forerunners of the unfortunate trend in the nineteenth century toward lengthy and cumbersome constitutions filled with minute restrictions upon the various agencies of government, especially the legislative branch. The generality and brevity which made the national Constitution a model of draftsmanship and a viable fundamental law inspired in the Anti-Federalists only fear.

They repeatedly attacked the Constitution for its alleged departure from Montesquieu's doctrine of separation of powers, emphasized the inadequacy of the checks and balances provided within the governmental structure, and lamented the excessive optimism regarding the character and behavior of elective representatives thus revealed in the work of the Founding Fathers. It is significant, in view of the interpretation long and generally accepted by historians, that *no one* expressed the belief that the system of separation of powers and checks and balances had been designed to protect the property rights of the well-to-do. Their positive proposals for remedying the defects in the system were not numerous. They objected to the Senate's share in the appointive and treaty-making powers and called for a separate executive council to advise the President in the performance of these functions. Shorter terms were advocated for President and Congress, though not as frequently or as strongly as required rotation for senators

42

---

[125] It is worth noting again that the abuses of power dwelt upon by the Anti-Federalists were usually extreme ones, almost amounting to a complete subversion of republican government. They did not regard as of any value the Federalists' argument that a desire to be re-elected would serve to keep the representatives in line. The Federalists had no clear idea of politics as a profession, but they were close to such a notion.

and President. No one suggested judicial review of Congressional legislation, though Patrick Henry attacked the Constitution because it did not explicitly provide for this safeguard to popular government.

Had the Constitution been altered to satisfy the major structural changes desired by the Anti-Federalists, the House of Representatives would have been considerably larger; there would have been four rather than three branches of the government; the President would have been limited, as he is now, to two terms in office; the senators would have been similarly limited and also subject to recall by their state governments. These changes might have been beneficial. It is doubtful that they would have pleased the late Charles Beard and his followers; it is even more doubtful that they would have facilitated the operation of unrestrained majority rule. Certainly that was not the intention of their proponents.

The Anti-Federalists were not latter-day democrats. Least of all were they majoritarians with respect to the national government. They were not confident that the people would always make wise and correct choices in either their constituent or electoral capacity, and many of them feared the oppression of one section in the community by a majority reflecting the interests of another. Above all, they consistently refused to accept legislative majorities as expressive either of justice or of the people's will. In short, they distrusted majority rule, at its source and through the only possible means of expression in governmental action over a large and populous nation, that is to say, through representation. The last thing in the world they wanted was a national democracy which would permit Congressional majorities to operate freely and without restraint. Proponents of this kind of majority rule have almost without exception been advocates of strong, positive action by the national government. The Anti-Federalists were not. Their philosophy was primarily one of limitations on power, and if they had had their way, the Constitution would have contained more checks and balances, not fewer. Indeed it seems safe to say that the Constitution could not have been ratified at all had it conformed to the standards of democracy which are implicit in the interpretation of Beard and his followers. A national government without separation of powers and checks and balances was not politically feasible. In this respect, then, I would suggest that his interpretation of the Constitution was unrealistic and unhistorical.

The Anti-Federalists may have followed democratic principles within the sphere of state government and possibly provided the impetus for the extension of power and privilege among the mass of the people, though it is significant that they did not advocate a broadening of the suffrage in 1787–1788 or the direct election of the Senate or the President. But they lacked both the faith and the vision to extend their principles nation-wide. It was the Federalists of 1787–1788 who created a national framework which would accommodate the later rise of democracy.

43

THE AMERICAN REVOLUTION:
REVISIONS IN NEED OF REVISING

EDMUND S. MORGAN

During the past fifty years three ideas have inspired research into the history of the eighteenth century in America and England. The earliest of these to appear, and the most fruitful of results, was the idea that American colonial history must be seen in the setting of the British Empire as a whole. We are all familiar today with the new insights and new discoveries that have grown out of this view: the great works of George Louis Beer and Charles McLean Andrews, the monumental synthesis of Professor Lawrence Gipson, which now approaches its culmination. This has been a great idea, and it has done more than any other to shape our understanding of the colonial past.

A second idea, which has affected in one way or another most of us who study colonial history, is that the social and economic divisions of a people will profoundly influence the course of their history. This idea received early application to American history in Carl Becker's study of New York politics on the eve of the Revolution and in Charles Beard's *An Economic Interpretation of the Constitution*. New York politics before the Revolution, Becker said, revolved around two questions, equally important, the question of home rule and that of who should rule at home.[1] Subsequent historians have found in Becker's aphorism a good description of the Revolutionary period as a whole. The conflict between different social groups now looms as large in our histories of the Revolution as the struggle against England. Like all seminal ideas, this one has sometimes been used as a substitute for research instead of a stimulus to it. Historians have been so convinced of the importance of social and economic divisions that they have uttered the wildest kind of nonsense, for example, about the social and economic basis of a religious movement like the Great Awakening of the 1740s. The view has nevertheless been productive of important new insights and new information.

The third idea, although it has had scarcely any effect as yet on the study of American history, has furnished the principal impetus to recent research in British history. It is a more complex idea, growing out of the discoveries of Sir Lewis Namier. The effect of these discoveries has been to attach a new importance to local as opposed to national forces. "It has been the greatest of Sir Lewis Namier's achievements," says Richard Pares, "to exhibit the personal and local nature of political issues and political power at this time."[2] Namier and his disciples, of

Mr. Morgan, professor of history at Yale University, delivered this paper on April 19, 1956, at a meeting of the Mississippi Valley Historical Association in Pittsburgh.

Ed. Note: This article was originally published in *William and Mary Quarterly*, 3d Ser., XIV (January 1957), 3–15.

[1] Carl Becker, *The History of Political Parties in the Province of New York, 1760–1776* (Madison, Wis., 1909), 22.

[2] Richard Pares, *King George III and the Politicians* (Oxford, 1953), 2.

whom Pares is the most notable, have destroyed the traditional picture of British politics in the age of the American Revolution. During this period, they tell us, there were no political parties in the modern sense, nor were there any political factions or associations with any principle or belief beyond that of serving selfish or local interests. The Rockingham Whigs, who made such a display of their opposition to the repressive measures against the colonies, were no different from the other squabbling factions except in their hypocritical pretense of standing for broader principles. And George III owed his control over Parliament not to bribery and corruption but simply to his constitutional position in the government and to his skill as a politician during a time when the House of Commons lacked effective leaders of its own.

Each of these three ideas, the imperial, the social or economic, and the Namierist, has had a somewhat similar effect on our understanding of the American Revolution. That effect has been to discredit, in different ways, the old Whig interpretation. The imperial historians have examined the running of the empire before the Revolution and pronounced it fair. The Navigation Acts, they have shown, were no cause for complaint. The Board of Trade did as good a job as could be expected. The Admiralty Courts were a useful means of maintaining fair play and fair trade on the high seas. Indeed, Professor Gipson tells us, the old colonial system "may not unfairly be compared to modern systems of state interference with the liberty of the subject in matters involving industry and trade, accepting the differences involved in the nature of the regulations respectively. In each case, individuals or groups within the state are forbidden to follow out lines of action that, while highly beneficial to those locally or personally concerned, are considered inimical to the larger national objectives."[3] In the light of such imperial benevolence and farsightedness, the unwillingness of the Americans to pay the trifling contribution demanded of them in the sixties and seventies becomes small and mean, and the resounding rhetoric of a Henry or an Otis or an Adams turns into the bombast of a demagogue.

The social and economic interpretation does nothing to redeem the fallen Revolutionary patriots but rather shows them up as hypocrites pursuing selfish interests while they mouth platitudes about democracy and freedom. Their objections to parliamentary taxation are reduced to mere tax evasion, with the arguments shifting as the character of the taxes shifted. Their insistence on freedom and equality is shown to be insincere, because in setting up their own governments they failed to establish universal suffrage or proportional representation. They were, it would appear, eager to keep one foot on the lower classes while they kicked the British with the other.

Namier and his followers have little to say about the American revolutionists but devote themselves to scolding the English Whigs. Though the Namierists generally achieve a sophisticated objectivity with regard to persons and parties, they sometimes seem fond of beating the Whigs in order—one suspects—to displease the Whig historians. For example, the unflattering portrait of Charles James Fox that emerges from Richard Pares's brilliant study must surely be read in part as a rebuke to Sir George Otto Trevelyan, or rather to those who have accepted

[3] Lawrence H. Gipson, *The British Empire before the American Revolution,* III (Caldwell, Idaho, 1936), 287.

Trevelyan's estimate of Fox. This deflation of Fox and Burke and the other Rockingham Whigs, while accomplished with scarcely a glance in the direction of the colonies, nevertheless deprives the American revolutionists of a group of allies whose high-minded sympathy had been relied upon by earlier historians to help demonstrate the justice of the American cause.

By the same token the righteousness of the Americans is somewhat diminished through the loss of the principal villain in the contest. George III is no longer the foe of liberty, seeking to subvert the British constitution, but an earnest and responsible monarch, doing his job to the best of his abilities. And those abilities, we are told, while not of the highest order, were not small either. George, in fact, becomes a sympathetic figure, and one can scarcely escape the feeling that the Americans were rather beastly to have made things so hard for him.

While the imperial, the economic, and the Namierist approaches have thus contributed in different ways to diminish the prestige of the American Revolution and its promoters, it is a curious fact that none of the ideas has produced any full-scale examination of the Revolution itself or of how it came about. The imperial historians have hitherto been occupied primarily in dissecting the workings of the empire as it existed before the Revolutionary troubles. Although their works have necessarily squinted at the Revolution in every sentence, the only direct confrontations have been brief and inconclusive.

The social and economic interpretation has been applied more extensively to different aspects of the Revolution, but surprisingly enough we still know very little about what the social and economic divisions actually were in most of the colonies and states at the time of the Revolution. Professor Schlesinger's analysis of the role of the merchant class[4] remains a fixed point of knowledge at the opening of the period, and Charles Beard's *Economic Interpretation of the Constitution* is a somewhat shakier foundation at the close of it, reinforced, however, by the work of Merrill Jensen.[5] Historians have bridged the gap between these two points with more assurance than information. There are, it is true, several illuminating studies of local divisions but not enough to warrant any firm conclusions about the role of economic and social forces in the Revolution as a whole. After thirty years we are only a little closer to the materials needed for such conclusions than J. Franklin Jameson was in 1926.

The Namierist approach, as already indicated, has been confined to events in England rather than America. Though the effect of such investigations has been to exonerate George III and discredit the English Whigs, the Revolution has not been a primary issue for Namier or Pares. One student of Professor Namier's, Eric Robson, made a preliminary excursion into the subject but confined his discussion primarily to military history.[6] And while Professor Charles Ritcheson has treated the place of the Revolution in British politics,[7] the implications of Namier's discoveries for developments on this side of the water remain unexplored.

---

[4] Arthur M. Schlesinger, *The Colonial Merchants and the American Revolution* (New York, 1918).

[5] Merrill Jensen, *The Articles of Confederation* (Madison, Wis., 1940); *The New Nation* (New York, 1950).

[6] Eric Robson, *The American Revolution in its Political and Military Aspects* (London, 1955).

[7] Charles Ritcheson, *British Politics and the American Revolution* (Norman, Okla., 1954).

Thus while the new ideas and new discoveries have altered our attitudes toward the American Revolution, they have done so for the most part indirectly, almost surreptitiously, without coming up against the Revolution itself. There is need for intensive and direct examination of all phases of the Revolution in the light of each of these ideas, and we may expect that in the next few years such examinations will be made. Professor Gipson has already begun. I should like to suggest, however, that we need not only to examine the Revolution in the light of the ideas but also to re-examine the ideas in the light of the Revolution; and in doing so we need also to examine them in relation to each other.

The Revolution is one of those brute facts which historians must account for, and it is a fact of central importance for ascertaining the meaning and limits of the three ideas we are discussing. I believe that each of the three needs revisions and will take them up in order.

While everyone will acknowledge the importance of the imperial idea and of the discoveries made under its influence, the net effect of that idea has been to emphasize the justice and beneficence of the British imperial system as it existed before the Revolution. May we not therefore pose a question to the imperial historians: if the empire was as fairly administered as you show it to have been, how could the Revolution have happened at all? In their preliminary skirmishes with this problem, imperial historians have frequently implied that the American revolutionists were moved, in part at least, by narrow or selfish views and stirred up by evil-minded agitators. But if historians are to sustain such a view in any full-scale consideration of the Revolution, they face a very difficult task: they must explain men like George Washington, John Adams, Thomas Jefferson, and Benjamin Franklin as agitators or as the dupes of agitators, or as narrow-minded men without the vision to see beyond provincial borders. After all due allowance is made for patriotic myopia, this still seems to me to be an impossible undertaking. Anyone who studies the Revolution can scarcely emerge without some degree of admiration for the breadth of vision that moved these men. In twenty-five years they created a new nation and endowed it with a government that still survives and now has the longest continuous history of any government in existence outside of England. The idea that they were narrow-minded simply will not wash. Nor is it possible to see them as the dupes of their intellectual inferiors. Samuel Adams, Patrick Henry, and James Otis may perhaps be cast as demagogues without seeming out of place, but not the giants of the period. If the British government could not run the empire without bringing on evils that appeared insufferable to men like Washington, Jefferson, John Adams, and Franklin, then the burden of proof would seem to be on those who maintain that it was fit to run an empire.

When the imperial historians are ready to attempt the proof, they must face a second task: they must explain away the character which the Namierist historians have given to the British statesmen of the period. The Namierists, as already indicated, have emphasized the parochial character of English politics in this period. They have cut the Whigs down to size, but they have cut down everyone else on the British political scene likewise. If Parliament was dominated by local interests, what becomes of imperial beneficence and farsightedness?

The whole effect of the Namierist discoveries, so far as the colonies are concerned, must be to show that British statesmen in the 1760s and 1770s, whether

47

in Parliament or in the Privy Council, were too dominated by local interests to be able to run an empire. There was no institution, no party, no organization through which imperial interests, as opposed to strictly British interests, could find adequate expression. In fact the Namierist view and the view of the imperial historians are directly at odds here: though neither group seems as yet to be aware of the conflict, they cannot both be wholly right, and the coming of the Revolution would seem to confirm the Namierist view and to cast doubt on the imperialist one. The achievements of the revolutionists and the failures of the British statesmen suggest in the strongest possible terms that it was the Americans who saw things in the large and the British who wore the blinders. If this is so, may it not be that the case for the beneficence and justice of the British Empire before the Revolution has been overstated?

In response to our argument ad hominem the imperialists may summon the aid of the economic interpretation to show that the Americans, however high-toned their arguments, were really moved by economic considerations of the basest kind. We may, however, call these considerations basic rather than base and offer our previous character witnesses against the economists too. There is no time to plead to every indictment here, but one may perhaps answer briefly the strongest yet offered, that of Charles Beard, and then suggest how the economic interpretation needs revision. Though Beard expressly disclaimed that his economic interpretation was the whole story, he gave not merely a one-sided view but a false one. All the evidence that Beard extracted from the records of the Constitutional Convention points toward the sordid conclusion that the delegates who held public securities also held undemocratic political views, motivated consciously or unconsciously by the desire to protect their investments. Beard consistently overlooked contradictory evidence. I will cite only two examples.

The first is his treatment of Roger Sherman, the delegate to the Constitutional Convention from Connecticut. Sherman, he notes, had risen from poverty to affluence and held nearly eight thousand dollars worth of public securities. Sherman's corresponding political philosophy he represents by the following statement: "Roger Sherman believed in reducing the popular influence in the new government to the minimum. When it was proposed that the members of the first branch of the national legislature should be elected, Sherman said that he was 'opposed to the election by the people, insisting that it ought to be by the state legislatures. The people, he said, immediately should have as little to do as may be about the government. They want information and are constantly liable to be misled.' "[8]

The quotation certainly supports Beard's view, but Beard failed to indicate what Sherman said at other times in the convention. On June 4, four days after the speech Beard quotes, Sherman was against giving the President a veto power, because he "was against enabling any one man to stop the will of the whole. No one man could be found so far above all the rest in wisdom." On June 21 he argued again for election of the House of Representatives by the state legislatures, but after election by the people had been decided upon, spoke for annual elections as against triennial, because "He thought the representatives ought to return home and mix with the people." On August 14 he was in favor of substantial pay

[8] Charles Beard, *An Economic Interpretation of the Constitution of the United States* (New York, 1913), 213–214.

for congressmen, because otherwise "men ever so fit could not serve unless they were at the same time rich."[9] Whatever explanation may be offered for these views, they suggest a much broader confidence in the people than might be inferred from the single remark by which Beard characterized the man.

It cannot be said that the statements which Beard neglected are concerned with an aspect of Sherman's views not relevant to the problem Beard was examining: they are certainly as relevant as the statement he did quote. His treatment of Pierce Butler, the delegate from South Carolina, is similar. Beard notes that Butler held public securities and that he argued for apportionment of representation according to wealth.[10] He neglects to mention that Butler, in spite of his security holdings, opposed full payment of the public debt, "lest it should compel payment as well to the Blood-suckers who had speculated on the distresses of others, as to those who had fought and bled for their country."[11] The statement is relevant, but directly opposed, to Beard's thesis.

It requires only a reading of the Convention debates to see that Beard's study needs revision.[12] But the trouble with the economic interpretation, as currently applied to the whole Revolutionary period, goes deeper. The trouble lies in the assumption that a conflict between property rights and human rights has been the persistent theme of American history from the beginning. It was undoubtedly the great theme of Beard's day, and Beard was on the side of human rights, where decent men belong in such a conflict. From the vantage point of twentieth-century Progressivism, he lined up the members of the Constitutional Convention, found their pockets stuffed with public securities, and concluded that they were on the wrong side.

It was a daring piece of work, and it fired the imagination of Beard's fellow progressives.[13] Vernon L. Parrington has recorded how it "struck home like a submarine torpedo—the discovery that the drift toward plutocracy was not a drift away from the spirit of the Constitution, but an inevitable unfolding from its premises." As a result of Beard's work, Parrington was able to see that "From the beginning . . . democracy and property had been at bitter odds."[14]

Parrington went on to construct his own image of American history in these terms, and he too had a powerful influence. Together he and Beard virtually captured the American past for Progressivism, a performance all the more remarkable when we consider that they did not enlist the revered founding fathers of the Constitution on their side.

It is time, however, that we had another look at the conflict between human

---

[9] *Records of the Federal Convention of 1787,* ed. Max Farrand (New Haven, 1911–1937), I, 99, 362; II, 291.

[10] Beard, *Economic Interpretation,* 81–82, 192.

[11] Farrand, *Records,* II, 392.

[12] Robert E. Brown's *Charles Beard and the Constitution* (Princeton, 1956) appeared too late to be of use in preparation of this paper, but the reader will find in it abundant additional evidence of deficiencies in Beard's use of the Convention records.

[13] See Douglass Adair, "The Tenth Federalist Revisited," *William and Mary Quarterly,* 3d Ser., VIII (1951), 48–67; Richard Hofstadter, "Beard and the Constitution: The History of an Idea," *American Quarterly,* II (1950), 195–213.

[14] Vernon L. Parrington, *Main Currents in American Thought* (New York, 1927–1930), III, 410.

rights and property rights; and the Revolutionary period is a good place to begin, for however strong the conflict may later have become, it was not a dominant one then. Anyone who studies the Revolution must notice at once the attachment of all articulate Americans to property. "Liberty and Property" was their cry, not "Liberty and Democracy." In the face of the modern dissociation of property from liberty, historians have often felt that this concern of the revolutionists for property was a rather shabby thing, and that the constitutional principles so much talked of, before 1776 as well as afterward, were invented to hide it under a more attractive cloak. But the Americans were actually quite shameless about their concern for property and made no effort to hide it, because it did not seem at all shabby to them. The colonial protests against taxation frankly and openly, indeed passionately, affirm the sanctity of property. And the passion is not the simple and unlovely passion of greed. For eighteenth-century Americans, property and liberty were one and inseparable, because property was the only foundation yet conceived for security of life and liberty: without security for his property, it was thought, no man could live or be free except at the mercy of another.

The revolutionists' coupling of property with life and liberty was not an attempt to lend respectability to property rights, nor was it an attempt to enlist the masses in a struggle for the special privileges of a small wealthy class. Property in eighteenth-century America was not associated with special privilege, as it came to be for later generations. Land was widely owned. A recent investigation has demonstrated that in Massachusetts, a key state in the Revolution, nearly every adult male could meet the property qualifications for the franchise.[15] We hear much from modern historians about the propertyless masses of the Revolutionary period, but it is altogether improbable that the mass of Americans were without property.

The Americans fought England because Parliament threatened the security of property. They established state constitutions with property qualifications for voting and officeholding in order to protect the security of property. And when the state governments seemed inadequate to the task, they set up the Federal government for the same purpose. The economic motive was present in all these actions, but it was present as the friend of universal liberty. Devotion to security of property was not the attitude of a privileged few but the fundamental principle of the many, inseparable from everything that went by the name of freedom and adhered to the more fervently precisely because it did affect most people so intimately.

What we have done in our social and economic interpretations of the Revolution is to project into eighteenth-century America a situation which existed in the nineteenth and early twentieth centuries, when property and the means of production became concentrated in the hands of a few, when liberty if it was to exist at all had to get along not only without the aid of property but in opposition to it. We seem now to be approaching a period when property, in another form, may again be widely distributed and may again become the friend rather than the enemy of liberty. Whether such is the case or not, as historians we should stop projecting into the eighteenth century the particular economic and

[15] Robert E. Brown, *Middle-Class Democracy and the Revolution in Massachusetts, 1691–1780* (Ithaca, N. Y., 1955).

social antagonisms that we have found in later generations. We may still believe that the American Revolution was in part a contest about who should rule at home, but we should beware of assuming that people took sides in that contest according to whether or not they owned property. And we should totally abandon the assumption that those who showed the greatest concern for property rights were not devoted to human rights.

The challenge of the Revolution to the Namier school of historians is less direct and less crucial, but it does pose one or two questions which these historians seem not to have confronted. The first is whether the new judgment of George III has not raised that monarch's reputation a little too high. Granted that George was neither the fool nor the knave he has hitherto been thought, granted that he was moved by a desire to maintain parliamentary supremacy rather than regal supremacy, it is nevertheless true that under his leadership England lost an important, if not the most important, part of her empire. The loss was not inevitable. All the objectives of the Americans before 1776 could have been attained within the empire, and would have cost the mother country little or nothing. George undoubtedly received a good deal of assistance from other politicians in losing the colonies, but the contention of the Namierists has been that the King still held a position of central responsibility in the British government in the 1760s and 1770s, a responsibility which they have shown that he shouldered and carried. If he was responsible then he must be held responsible. He must bear most of the praise or blame for the series of measures that alienated and lost the colonies, and it is hard to see how there can be much praise.

The other question that the Revolution poses for the Namierists may be more fundamental. Virtually no one in British politics, they argue, had any political principles that reached beyond local or factional interests. The argument, though convincingly presented, presumes a consistent hypocrisy or delusion on the part of the Whig opposition. It may be that the Whigs were hypocritical in their attack on George III and their support of the Americans. But if so why were they hypocritical in just the way they were? Why did they appeal to principles of government that later won acceptance? Can we be sure that it was only in order to attack their opponents? Can we be sure they were on the right side for the wrong reasons? I do not pretend to know the answers to these questions, but I am not quite comfortable about judgments of history in which people are condemned for being prematurely antimonarchical.

What I would suggest in conclusion is that the Whig interpretation of the American Revolution may not be as dead as some historians would have us believe, that George Bancroft may not have been so far from the mark as we have often assumed. Is it not time to ask again a few of the old questions that he was trying to answer? Let us grant that local interests were the keynote of British politics; we must still ask: how did the Americans, living on the edge of empire, develop the breadth of vision and the attachment to principle which they displayed in that remarkable period from 1763 to 1789? While English politics remained parochial and the empire was dissolving for lack of vision, how did the Americans generate the forces that carried them into a new nationality and a new human liberty?

The answer, I think, may lie in a comparatively neglected field of American scholarship. During the past fifty years our investigations of the colonial period have been directed primarily by the imperial idea and the social and economic one. We have seen the colonists as part of the empire or else we have seen them as the pawns of sweeping economic and social forces. What we have neglected is the very thing that the English have been pursuing in the study of their institutions. We have neglected, comparatively speaking at least, the study of local institutions, and it is in such a study that we may perhaps discover the answer to the fundamental question that moved Bancroft, the question of how a great nation with great principles of freedom was forged from thirteen quarrelsome colonies. What kind of institutions produced a Jefferson, a Madison, a Washington, a John Adams? Not imperial institutions certainly. The imperial machinery had no place for Americans except in performing local services. No American ever sat on the Board of Trade or the Privy Council. Few Americans ever came in contact with imperial officers. It was in local American institutions that these men gained their political experience.

Two generations ago Herbert Baxter Adams thought he had the clue to the question of where American liberty began, and he put a host of graduate students to work studying the local institutions of the colonies. As we all know, they did not find precisely what Adams was looking for, but they produced a prodigious number of studies, which are still the principal source of historical information about many colonial institutions. Some have been superseded by more recent scholarship, but we need more new studies of this kind, which will take advantage of what we have learned since Adams's time about the imperial setting and about social and economic forces.

We need to know how the individual's picture of society was formed. We need to study the social groupings in every colony: towns, plantations, counties, churches, schools, clubs, and other groups which occupied the social horizons of the individual colonist. We need to study political parties and factions in every colony. We need to study the way government worked at the local level. We need to study the county courts and the justices of the peace. We need to study the distribution of land and other forms of wealth from decade to decade and from place to place. We need to know so elementary a thing as the history of representation and the history of taxation in every colony. We have always known that the Revolution had something to do with the phrase, "no taxation without representation," and yet, after two generations of modern scholarship, how many scholars have studied the history of taxation in the colonies? Who really knows anything about the history of representation?

Without abandoning what we have gained from the imperial idea and from economic interpretations, we must dissect the local institutions which produced the American Revolution, the institutions from which were distilled the ideas that enabled men of that age to stand as the architects of modern liberty. The task has not been wholly neglected. A number of scholars have been quietly working at it. I will not attempt to name them here, but their discoveries are sufficient to show that this is the direction which scholarship in colonial history should now take and that the rewards will not be small.

Author's Postscript

What strikes me most forcefully in rereading this essay is how rapidly historical understanding of the Revolution has developed in the thirty-six years since its publication. The relatively simplistic views I complained of have given way to far more sophisticated interpretations. Studies of local institutions and of political and social divisions in each of the participating states have drawn a rich and complex picture of the way the Revolution affected different groups at different stages of the contest. What the colonists had to say about their motives and principles is no longer discounted as mere window dressing. The progression of their ideas is treated not as a story of shifts from one pretense to another but as a voyage of intellectual discovery. Charting its course has become a central preoccupation, with controversy centering not on whether the Revolutionaries meant what they said but rather on understanding precisely what they did mean.

The three revisions to which the title refers have indeed been revised. None of them has disappeared, nor do they deserve to disappear. The colonists must continue to be seen as part of an empire, not simply as prototypical Americans waiting for 1776. The divisions among them must not be dismissed as inconsequential, for they shaped the course of state and national politics throughout the Revolutionary period. Even the Namierist interpretation of British politics, though now discredited for its exclusive focus on structure, retains a relevance for any explanation of why Britain lost the colonies. But in each case I think it is fair to say that historians have refined the old views into something that conforms more closely to what the surviving sources tell us. Research in the period has been intense, and the level of discussion has risen steadily. It would please me to think that this essay has contributed in some way to the dynamics of that discussion, but the Revolution itself poses such a challenge to historians that they needed no stimulus from the likes of me. I am confident that revisions will continue and that they will continue to be themselves revised, refined, and refurbished.

RHETORIC AND REALITY IN
THE AMERICAN REVOLUTION

GORDON S. WOOD

If any catch phrase is to characterize the work being done on the American Revolution by this generation of historians, it will probably be "the American Revolution considered as an intellectual movement."[1] For we now seem to be fully involved in a phase of writing about the Revolution in which the thought of the Revolutionaries, rather than their social and economic interests, has become the major focus of research and analysis. This recent emphasis on ideas is not of course new, and indeed right from the beginning it has characterized almost all our attempts to understand the Revolution. The ideas of a period which Samuel Eliot Morison and Harold Laski once described as, next to the English revolutionary decades of the seventeenth century, the most fruitful era in the history of Western political thought could never be completely ignored in any phase of our history writing.[2]

It has not been simply the inherent importance of the Revolutionary ideas, those "great principles of freedom,"[3] that has continually attracted the attention of historians. It has been rather the unusual nature of the Revolution and the constant need to explain what on the face of it seems inexplicable that has compelled almost all interpreters of the Revolution, including the participants themselves, to stress its predominantly intellectual character and hence its uniqueness among Western revolutions. Within the context of Revolutionary historiography the one great effort to disparage the significance of ideas in the Revolution—an effort which dominated our history writing in the first half of the twentieth century— becomes something of an anomaly, a temporary aberration into a deterministic social and economic explanation from which we have been retreating for the past two decades. Since roughly the end of World War II we have witnessed a resumed and increasingly heightened insistence on the primary significance of conscious beliefs, and particularly of constitutional principles, in explaining what once again has become the unique character of the American Revolution. In the hands of idealist-minded historians the thought and principles of the Americans have consequently come to repossess that explanative force which the previous

Mr. Wood is a Fellow at the Institute of Early American History and Culture at Williamsburg, and a member of the Department of History, the College of William and Mary.

Ed. Note: This article was first published in *William and Mary Quarterly*, 3d Ser., XXIII (January 1966), 3–32.

[1] This is the title of a recent essay by Edmund S. Morgan in Arthur M. Schlesinger, Jr., and Morton White, eds., *Paths of American Thought* (Boston, 1963), 11–33.

[2] Samuel E. Morison, ed., "William Manning's *The Key of Libberty*," *William and Mary Quarterly*, 3d Ser., XIII (1956), 208.

[3] Edmund S. Morgan, "The American Revolution: Revisions in Need of Revising," *Wm. and Mary Qtly.*, 3d Ser., XIV (1957), 14.

generation of materialist-minded historians had tried to locate in the social structure.

Indeed, our renewed insistence on the importance of ideas in explaining the Revolution has now attained a level of fullness and sophistication never before achieved, with the consequence that the economic and social approach of the previous generation of behaviorist historians has never seemed more anomalous and irrelevant than it does at present. Yet paradoxically it may be that this preoccupation with the explanatory power of the Revolutionary ideas has become so intensive and so refined, assumed such a character, that the apparently discredited social and economic approach of an earlier generation has at the same time never seemed more attractive and relevant. In other words, we may be approaching a crucial juncture in our writing about the Revolution where idealism and behaviorism meet.

I

It was the Revolutionaries themselves who first described the peculiar character of what they had been involved in. The Revolution, as those who took stock at the end of three decades of revolutionary activity noted, was not "one of those events which strikes the public eye in the subversions of laws which have usually attended the revolutions of governments." Because it did not seem to have been a typical revolution, the sources of its force and its momentum appeared strangely unaccountable. "In other revolutions, the sword has been drawn by the arm of offended freedom, under an oppression that threatened the vital powers of society."[4] But this seemed hardly true of the American Revolution. There was none of the legendary tyranny that had so often driven desperate peoples into revolution. The Americans were not an oppressed people; they had no crushing imperial shackles to throw off. In fact, the Americans knew they were probably freer and less burdened with cumbersome feudal and monarchical restraints than any part of mankind in the eighteenth century. To its victims, the Tories, the Revolution was truly incomprehensible. Never in history, said Daniel Leonard, had there been so much rebellion with so "little real cause." It was, wrote Peter Oliver, "the most wanton and unnatural rebellion that ever existed."[5] The Americans' response was out of all proportion to the stimuli. The objective social reality scarcely seemed capable of explaining a revolution.

Yet no American doubted that there had been a revolution. How then was it to be justified and explained? If the American Revolution, lacking "those mad, tumultuous actions which disgraced many of the great revolutions of antiquity," was not a typical revolution, what kind of revolution was it? If the origin of the American Revolution lay not in the usual passions and interests of men, wherein did it lay? Those Americans who looked back at what they had been through could only marvel at the rationality and moderation, "supported by the energies

---

[4] [William Vans Murray], *Political Sketches, Inscribed to His Excellency John Adams* (London, 1787), 21, 48.

[5] [Daniel Leonard], *The Origin of the American Contest with Great-Britain . . . [by] Massachusettensis . . .* (New York, 1775), 40; Douglass Adair and John A. Schutz, eds., *Peter Oliver's Origin and Progress of the American Rebellion: A Tory View* (San Marino, 1963), 159.

of well weighed choice," involved in their separation from Britain, a revolution remarkably "without violence or convulsion."[6] It seemed to be peculiarly an affair of the mind. Even two such dissimilar sorts of Whigs as Thomas Paine and John Adams both came to see the Revolution they had done so much to bring about as especially involved with ideas, resulting from "a mental examination," a change in "the minds and hearts of the people."[7] The Americans were fortunate in being born at a time when the principles of government and freedom were better known than at any time in history. The Americans had learned "how to define the rights of nature,—how to search into, to distinguish, and to comprehend, the principles of physical, moral, religious, and civil liberty," how, in short, to discover and resist the forces of tyranny before they could be applied. Never before in history had a people achieved "a revolution by reasoning" alone.[8]

The Americans, "born the heirs of freedom,"[9] revolted not to create but to maintain their freedom. American society had developed differently from that of the Old World. From the time of the first settlements in the seventeenth century, wrote Samuel Williams in 1794, "every thing tended to produce, and to establish the spirit of freedom." While the speculative philosophers of Europe were laboriously searching their minds in an effort to decide the first principles of liberty, the Americans had come to experience vividly that liberty in their everyday lives. The American Revolution, said Williams, joined together these enlightened ideas with America's experience. The Revolution was thus essentially intellectual and declaratory: it "explained the business to the world, and served to confirm what nature and society had before produced." "All was the result of reason."[10] The Revolution had taken place not in a succession of eruptions that had crumbled the existing social structure, but in a succession of new thoughts and new ideas that had vindicated that social structure.

The same logic that drove the participants to view the Revolution as peculiarly intellectual also compelled Moses Coit Tyler, writing at the end of the nineteenth century, to describe the American Revolution as "pre-eminently a revolution caused by ideas, and pivoted on ideas." That ideas played a part in all revolutions Tyler readily admitted. But in most revolutions, like that of the French, ideas had been perceived and acted upon only when the social reality had caught up with them, only when the ideas had been given meaning and force by long-experienced "real evils." The American Revolution, said Tyler, had been different: it was directed "not against tyranny inflicted, but only against tyranny

---

[6] Simeon Baldwin, *An Oration Pronounced Before the Citizens of New-Haven, July 4th, 1788* . . . (New Haven, 1788), 10; [Murray], *Political Sketches,* 48; David Ramsay, *The History of the American Revolution* (Philadelphia, 1789), I, 350.

[7] Thomas Paine, *Letter to the Abbé Raynal* . . . (1782), in Philip S. Foner, ed., *The Complete Writings of Thomas Paine* (New York, 1945), II, 243; John Adams to H. Niles, Feb. 13, 1818, in Charles Francis Adams, ed., *The Works of John Adams* (Boston, 1850–1856), X, 282.

[8] William Pierce, *An Oration, Delivered at Christ Church, Savannah, on the 4th of July, 1788* . . . (Providence, [1788]), 6; Enos Hitchcock, *An Oration; Delivered July 4th, 1788* . . . (Providence, [1788]), 11.

[9] Petition to the King, Oct. 1774, in Worthington C. Ford, ed., *Journals of the Continental Congress, 1774–1789* (Washington, 1904–1937), I, 118.

[10] Samuel Williams, *The Natural and Civil History of Vermont* . . . (Walpole, New Hamp., 1794), vii, 372–373; Pierce, *Oration* . . . *4th July, 1788,* 8.

anticipated." The Americans revolted not out of actual suffering but out of reasoned principle. "Hence, more than with most other epochs of revolutionary strife, our epoch of revolutionary strife was a strife of ideas: a long warfare of political logic; a succession of annual campaigns in which the marshalling of arguments not only preceded the marshalling of armies, but often exceeded them in impression upon the final result."[11]

II

It is in this historiographical context developed by the end of the nineteenth century, this constant and at times extravagant emphasis on the idealism of the Revolution, that the true radical quality of the Progressive generation's interpretation of the Revolution becomes so vividly apparent. For the work of these Progressive historians was grounded in a social and economic explanation of the Revolutionary era that explicitly rejected the causal importance of ideas. These historians could scarcely have avoided the general intellectual climate of the first part of the twentieth century which regarded ideas as suspect. By absorbing the diffused thinking of Marx and Freud and the assumptions of behaviorist psychology, men had come to conceive of ideas as ideologies or rationalizations, as masks obscuring the underlying interests and drives that actually determined social behavior. For too long, it seemed, philosophers had reified thought, detaching ideas from the material conditions that produced them and investing them with an independent will that was somehow alone responsible for the determination of events.[12] As Charles Beard pointed out in his introduction to the 1935 edition of *An Economic Interpretation of the Constitution,* previous historians of the Constitution had assumed that ideas were "entities, particularities, or forces, apparently independent of all earthly considerations coming under the head of 'economic.'" It was Beard's aim, as it was the aim of many of his contemporaries, to bring into historical consideration "those realistic features of economic conflict, stress, and strain" which previous interpreters of the Revolution had largely ignored.[13] The product of this aim was a generation or more of historical writing about the Revolutionary period (of which Beard's was but the most famous expression) that sought to explain the Revolution and the formation of the Constitution in terms of socio-economic relationships and interests rather than in terms of ideas.[14]

---

[11] Moses Coit Tyler, *The Literary History of the American Revolution, 1763–1783* (New York, 1897), I, 8–9.

[12] For a bald description of the assumptions with which this generation of historians worked see Graham Wallas, *Human Nature in Politics,* 3d ed. (New York, 1921), 5, 45, 48–49, 83, 94, 96, 118, 122, 156.

[13] Charles A. Beard, *An Economic Interpretation of the Constitution* (New York, 1935), x, viii.

[14] While the Progressive historians were attempting to absorb and use the latest scientific techniques of the day nonbehaviorists in government departments and others with a traditional approach to political theory—men like Andrew C. McLaughlin, Edwin S. Corwin, William S. Carpenter, Charles M. McIlwain, and Benjamin F. Wright—were writing during this same period some of the best work that has ever been done on Revolutionary constitutional and political thought. However, because most of them were not, strictly speaking, historians, they never sought to explain the causes of the Revolution in terms of ideas.

Curiously, the consequence of this reversal of historical approaches was not the destruction of the old-fashioned conception of the nature of ideas. As Marx had said, he intended only to put Hegel's head in its rightful place; he had no desire to cut it off. Ideas as rationalization, as ideology, remained—still distinct entities set in opposition to interests, now however lacking any deep causal significance, becoming merely a covering superstructure for the underlying and determinative social reality. Ideas therefore could still be the subject of historical investigation, as long as one kept them in their proper place, interesting no doubt in their own right but not actually counting for much in the movement of events.

Even someone as interested in ideas as Carl Becker never seriously considered them to be in any way determinants of what happened. Ideas fascinated Becker, but it was as superstructure that he enjoyed examining them, their consistency, their logic, their clarity, the way men formed and played with them. In his *Declaration of Independence: A Study in the History of Political Ideas* the political theory of the Americans takes on an unreal and even fatuous quality. It was as if ideas were merely refined tools to be used by the colonists in the most adroit manner possible. The entire Declaration of Independence, said Becker, was calculated for effect, designed primarily "to convince a candid world that the colonies had a moral and legal right to separate from Great Britain." The severe indictment of the King did not spring from unfathomable passions but was contrived, conjured up, to justify a rebellion whose sources lay elsewhere. Men to Becker were never the victims of their thought, always the masters of it. Ideas were a kind of legal brief. "Thus step by step, from 1764 to 1776, the colonists modified their theory to suit their needs."[15] The assumptions behind Becker's 1909 behaviorist work on New York politics in the Revolution and his 1922 study of the political ideas in the Declaration of Independence were more alike than they at first might appear.

Bringing to their studies of the Revolution similar assumptions about the nature of ideas, some of Becker's contemporaries went on to expose starkly the implications of those assumptions. When the entire body of Revolutionary thinking was examined, these historians could not avoid being struck by its generally bombastic and overwrought quality. The ideas expressed seemed so inflated, such obvious exaggerations of reality, that they could scarcely be taken seriously. The Tories were all "wretched hirelings, and execrable parricides"; George III, the "tyrant of the earth," a "monster in human form"; the British soldiers, "a mercenary, licentious rabble of banditti," intending to "tear the bowels and vitals of their brave but peaceable fellow subjects, and *to wash the ground with a profusion of innocent blood.*"[16] Such extravagant language, it seemed, could be nothing but calculated deception, at best an obvious distortion of fact, designed to incite and mold a revolutionary fervor. "The stigmatizing of British policy as 'tyranny,' 'oppression' and 'slavery,'" wrote Arthur M. Schlesinger, the dean of the Progressive historians, "had little or no objective reality, at least prior to the

---

[15] Carl L. Becker, *The Declaration of Independence: A Study in the History of Political Ideas* (New York, 1922), 203, 207, 133.

[16] Quoted in Philip Davidson, *Propaganda and the American Revolution, 1763–1783* (Chapel Hill, 1941), 141, 373, 150.

Intolerable Acts, but ceaseless repetition of the charge kept emotions at fever pitch."[17]

Indeed, so grandiose, so overdrawn, it seemed, were the ideas that the historians were necessarily led to ask not whether such ideas were valid but why men should have expressed them. It was not the content of such ideas but the function that was really interesting. The Revolutionary rhetoric, the profusion of sermons, pamphlets, and articles in the patriotic cause, could best be examined as propaganda, that is, as a concerted and self-conscious effort by agitators to manipulate and shape public opinion. Because of the Progressive historians' view of the Revolution as the movement of class minorities bent on promoting particular social and economic interests, the conception of propaganda was crucial to their explanation of what seemed to be a revolutionary consensus. Through the use of ideas in provoking hatred and influencing opinion and creating at least "an appearance of unity," the influence of a minority of agitators was out of all proportion to their number. The Revolution thus became a display of extraordinary skillfulness in the manipulation of public opinion. In fact, wrote Schlesinger, "no disaffected element in history has ever risen more splendidly to the occasion."[18]

Ideas thus became, as it were, parcels of thought to be distributed and used where they would do the most good. This propaganda was not of course necessarily false, but it was always capable of manipulation. "Whether the suggestions are to be true or false, whether the activities are to be open or concealed," wrote Philip Davidson, "are matters for the propagandist to decide." Apparently ideas could be turned on or off at will, and men controlled their rhetoric in a way they could not control their interests. Whatever the importance of propaganda, its connection with social reality was tenuous. Since ideas were so self-consciously manageable, the Whigs were not actually expressing anything meaningful about themselves but were rather feigning and exaggerating for effect. What the Americans said could not be taken at face value but must be considered as a rhetorical disguise for some hidden interest. The expression of even the classic and well-defined natural rights philosophy became, in Davidson's view, but "the propagandist's rationalization of his desire to protect his vested interests."[19]

With this conception of ideas as weapons shrewdly used by designing propagandists, it was inevitable that the thought of the Revolutionaries should have been denigrated. The Revolutionaries became by implication hypocritical demagogues, "adroitly tailoring their arguments to changing conditions." Their political thinking appeared to possess neither consistency nor significance. "At best," said Schlesinger in an early summary of his interpretation, "an exposition of the political theories of the antiparliamentary party is an account of their retreat from one strategic position to another." So the Whigs moved, it was strongly suggested, easily if not frivolously from a defense of charter rights, to the rights of Englishmen, and finally to the rights of man, as each position was exposed and

[17] Arthur M. Schlesinger, *Prelude to Independence: The Newspaper War on Britain, 1764–1776* (New York, 1958), 34. For examples of the scientific work on which the propagandist studies drew, see note one in Sidney I. Pomerantz, "The Patriot Newspaper and the American Revolution," in Richard B. Morris, ed., *The Era of the American Revolution* (New York, 1939), 305.

[18] Davidson, *Propaganda*, 59; Schlesinger, *Prelude to Independence*, 20.

[19] Davidson, *Propaganda*, xiv, 46.

became untenable. In short, concluded Schlesinger, the Revolution could never be understood if it were regarded "as a great forensic controversy over abstract governmental rights."[20]

III

It is essentially on this point of intellectual consistency that Edmund S. Morgan has fastened for the past decade and a half in an attempt to bring down the entire interpretive framework of the socio-economic argument. If it could be shown that the thinking of the Revolutionaries was not inconsistent after all, that the Whigs did not actually skip from one constitutional notion to the next, then the imputation of Whig frivolity and hypocrisy would lose its force. This was a central intention of Morgan's study of the political thought surrounding the Stamp Act. As Morgan himself has noted and others have repeated, "In the last analysis the significance of the Stamp Act crisis lies in the emergence, not of leaders and methods and organizations, but of well-defined constitutional principles." As early as 1765 the Whigs "laid down the line on which Americans stood until they cut their connections with England. Consistently from 1765 to 1776 they denied the authority of Parliament to tax them externally or internally; consistently they affirmed their willingness to submit to whatever legislation Parliament should enact for the supervision of the empire as a whole."[21] This consistency thus becomes, as one scholar's survey of the current interpretation puts it, "an indication of American devotion to principle."[22]

It seemed clear once again after Morgan's study that the Americans were more sincerely attached to constitutional principles than the behaviorist historians had supposed, and that their ideas could not be viewed as simply manipulated propaganda. Consequently the cogency of the Progressive historians' interpretation was weakened if not unhinged. And as the evidence against viewing the Revolution as rooted in internal class-conflict continued to mount from various directions, it appeared more and more comprehensible to accept the old-fashioned notion that the Revolution was after all the consequence of "a great forensic controversy over abstract governmental rights." There were, it seemed, no deprived and depressed populace yearning for a participation in politics that had long been denied; no coherent merchant class victimizing a mass of insolvent debtors; no seething discontent with the British mercantile system; no privileged aristocracy, protected by law, anxiously and insecurely holding power against a clamoring democracy. There was, in short, no internal class upheaval in the Revolution.[23]

---

[20] Schlesinger, *Prelude to Independence,* 44; Arthur M. Schlesinger, *New Viewpoints in American History* (New York, 1923), 179.

[21] Edmund S. Morgan, "Colonial Ideas of Parliamentary Power, 1764-1766," *Wm. and Mary Qtly.,* 3d Ser., V (1948), 311, 341; Edmund S. and Helen M. Morgan, *The Stamp Act Crisis: Prologue to Revolution,* rev. ed. (New York, 1963), 369–370; Page Smith, "David Ramsay and the Causes of the American Revolution," *Wm. and Mary Qtly.,* 3d Ser., XVII (1960), 70–71.

[22] Jack P. Greene, "The Flight From Determinism: A Review of Recent Literature on the Coming of the American Revolution," *South Atlantic Quarterly,* LXI (1962), 257.

[23] This revisionist literature of the 1950s is well known. See the listings in Bernard Bailyn, "Political Experience and Enlightenment Ideas in Eighteenth-Century America," *American Historical Review,* LXVII (1961–1962), 341n; and in Greene, "Flight From Determinism," 235–259.

If the Revolution was not to become virtually incomprehensible, it must have been the result of what the American Whigs always contended it was—a dispute between Mother Country and colonies over constitutional liberties. By concentrating on the immediate events of the decade leading up to independence, the historians of the 1950s have necessarily fled from the economic and social determinism of the Progressive historians. And by emphasizing the consistency and devotion with which Americans held their constitutional beliefs they have once again focused on what seems to be the extraordinary intellectuality of the American Revolution and hence its uniqueness among Western revolutions. This interpretation, which, as Jack P. Greene notes, "may appropriately be styled neo-whig," has turned the Revolution into a rationally conservative movement, involving mainly a constitutional defense of existing political liberties against the abrupt and unexpected provocations of the British government after 1760. "The issue then, according to the neo-whigs, was no more and no less than separation from Britain and the preservation of American liberty." The Revolution has therefore become "more political, legalistic, and constitutional than social or economic." Indeed, some of the neo-Whig historians have implied not just that social and economic conditions were less important in bringing on the Revolution as we once thought, but rather that the social situation in the colonies had little or nothing to do with causing the Revolution. The Whig statements of principle iterated in numerous declarations appear to be the only causal residue after all the supposedly deeper social and economic causes have been washed away. As one scholar who has recently investigated and carefully dismissed the potential social and economic issues in pre-Revolutionary Virginia has concluded, "What remains as the fundamental issue in the coming of the Revolution, then, is nothing more than the contest over constitutional rights."[24]

In a different way Bernard Bailyn in a recent article has clarified and reinforced this revived idealistic interpretation of the Revolution. The accumulative influence of much of the latest historical writing on the character of eighteenth-century American society has led Bailyn to the same insight expressed by Samuel Williams in 1794. What made the Revolution truly revolutionary was not the wholesale disruption of social groups and political institutions, for compared to other revolutions such disruption was slight; rather it was the fundamental alteration in the Americans' structure of values, the way they looked at themselves and their institutions. Bailyn has seized on this basic intellectual shift as a means of explaining the apparent contradiction between the seriousness with which the Americans took their Revolutionary ideas and the absence of radical social and institutional change. The Revolution, argues Bailyn, was not so much the transformation as the realization of American society.

The Americans had been gradually and unwittingly preparing themselves for such a mental revolution since they first came to the New World in the seventeenth century. The substantive changes in American society had taken place in the course of the previous century, slowly, often imperceptibly, as a series of small piecemeal deviations from what was regarded by most Englishmen as the accepted orthodoxy in society, state, and religion. What the Revolution marked, so to

---

[24] Greene, "Flight From Determinism," 237, 257; Thad W. Tate, "The Coming of the Revolution in Virginia: Britain's Challenge to Virginia's Ruling Class, 1763–1776," *Wm. and Mary Qtly.*, 3d Ser., XIX (1962), 323–343, esp. 340.

speak, was the point when the Americans suddenly blinked and saw their society, its changes, its differences, in a new perspective. Their deviation from European standards, their lack of an established church and a titled aristocracy, their apparent rusticity and general equality, now became desirable, even necessary, elements in the maintenance of their society and politics. The comprehending and justifying, the endowing with high moral purpose, of these confusing and disturbing social and political divergences, Bailyn concludes, was the American Revolution.[25]

Bailyn's more recent investigation of the rich pamphlet literature of the decades before Independence has filled out and refined his idealist interpretation, confirming him in his "rather old-fashioned view that the American Revolution was above all else an ideological-constitutional struggle and not primarily a controversy between social groups undertaken to force changes in the organization of society." While Bailyn's book-length introduction to the first of a multivolumed edition of Revolutionary pamphlets makes no effort to stress the conservative character of the Revolution and indeed emphasizes (in contrast to the earlier article) its radicalism and the dynamic and transforming rather than the rationalizing and declarative quality of Whig thought, it nevertheless represents the culmination of the idealist approach to the history of the Revolution. For "above all else," argues Bailyn, it was the Americans' world-view, the peculiar bundle of notions and beliefs they put together during the imperial debate, "that in the end propelled them into Revolution." Through his study of the Whig pamphlets Bailyn became convinced "that the fear of a comprehensive conspiracy against liberty throughout the English-speaking world—a conspiracy believed to have been nourished in corruption, and of which, it was felt, oppression in America was only the most immediately visible part—lay at the heart of the Revolutionary movement." No one of the various acts and measures of the British government after 1763 could by itself have provoked the extreme and violent response of the American Whigs. But when linked together they formed in the minds of the Americans, imbued with a particular historical understanding of what constituted tyranny, an extensive and frightening program designed to enslave the New World. The Revolution becomes comprehensible only when the mental framework, the Whig world-view into which the Americans fitted the events of the 1760s and 1770s, is known. "It is the development of this view to the point of overwhelming persuasiveness to the majority of American leaders and the meaning this view gave to the events of the time, and not simply an accumulation of grievances," writes Bailyn, "that explains the origins of the American Revolution."[26]

It now seems evident from Bailyn's analysis that it was the Americans' peculiar conception of reality more than anything else that convinced them that tyranny was afoot and that they must fight if their liberty was to survive. By an empathic understanding of a wide range of American thinking Bailyn has been able to offer us a most persuasive argument for the importance of ideas in

---

[25] Bailyn, "Political Experience and Enlightenment Ideas," 339–351.

[26] Bernard Bailyn, ed., assisted by Jane N. Garrett, *Pamphlets of the American Revolution, 1750–1776* (Cambridge, Mass., 1965–), I, viii, 60, x, 20. The 200-page general introduction is entitled, "The Transforming Radicalism of the American Revolution."

bringing on the Revolution. Not since Tyler has the intellectual character of the Revolution received such emphasis and never before has it been set out so cogently and completely. It would seem that the idealist explanation of the Revolution has nowhere else to go.[27]

IV

Labeling the recent historical interpretations of the Revolution as "neo-whig" is indeed appropriate, for, as Page Smith has pointed out, "After a century and a half of progress in historical scholarship, in research techniques, in tools and methods, we have found our way to the interpretation held, substantially, by those historians who themselves participated in or lived through the era of, the Revolution." By describing the Revolution as a conservative, principled defense of American freedom against the provocations of the English government, the neo-Whig historians have come full circle to the position of the Revolutionaries themselves and to the interpretation of the first generation of historians.[28] Indeed, as a consequence of this historical atavism, praise for the contemporary or early historians has become increasingly common.

But to say "that the Whig interpretation of the American Revolution may not be as dead as some historians would have us believe" is perhaps less to commend the work of David Ramsay and George Bancroft than to indict the approach of recent historians.[29] However necessary and rewarding the neo-Whig histories have been, they present us with only a partial perspective on the Revolution. The neo-Whig interpretation is intrinsically polemical; however subtly presented, it aims to justify the Revolution. It therefore cannot accommodate a totally different, an opposing, perspective, a Tory view of the Revolution. It is for this reason that the recent publication of Peter Oliver's "Origin and Progress of the American Rebellion" is of major significance, for it offers us—"by attacking the hallowed traditions of the revolution, challenging the motives of the founding fathers, and depicting revolution as passion, plotting, and violence"—an explanation of what happened quite different from what we have been recently accustomed to.[30] Oliver's vivid portrait of the Revolutionaries with his accent on their vicious emotions and interests seriously disturbs the present Whiggish interpretation of the Revolution. It is not that Oliver's description of, say, John Adams as madly ambitious and consumingly resentful is any more correct than Adams's own description of himself as a virtuous and patriotic defender of liberty against tyranny. Both interpretations of Adams are in a sense right, but neither can comprehend the other because each is preoccupied with seemingly contradictory sets

63

---

[27] This is not to say, however, that work on the Revolutionary ideas is in any way finished. For examples of the re-examination of traditional problems in Revolutionary political theory see Richard Buel, Jr., "Democracy and the American Revolution: A Frame of Reference," *Wm. and Mary Qtly.*, 3d Ser., XXI (1964), 165–190; and Bailyn's resolution of James Otis's apparent inconsistency in *Revolutionary Pamphlets*, I, 100–103, 106–107, 121–123, 409–417, 546–552.

[28] Smith, "Ramsay and the American Revolution," 72.

[29] Morgan, "Revisions in Need of Revising," 13.

[30] Adair and Schutz, eds., *Peter Oliver's Origin*, ix. In the present neo-Whig context, Sidney S. Fisher, "The Legendary and Myth-Making Process in Histories of the American Revolution," in American Philosophical Society, *Proceedings*, LI (Philadelphia, 1912), 53–75, takes on a renewed relevance.

of motives. Indeed, it is really these two interpretations that have divided historians of the Revolution ever since.

Any intellectually satisfying explanation of the Revolution must encompass the Tory perspective as well as the Whig, for if we are compelled to take sides and choose between opposing motives—unconscious or avowed, passion or principle, greed or liberty—we will be endlessly caught up in the polemics of the participants themselves. We must, in other words, eventually dissolve the distinction between conscious and unconscious motives, between the Revolutionaries' stated intentions and their supposedly hidden needs and desires, a dissolution that involves somehow relating beliefs and ideas to the social world in which they operate. If we are to understand the causes of the Revolution we must therefore ultimately transcend this problem of motivation. But this we can never do as long as we attempt to explain the Revolution mainly in terms of the intentions of the participants. It is not that men's motives are unimportant; they indeed make events, including revolutions. But the purposes of men, especially in a revolution, are so numerous, so varied, and so contradictory that their complex interaction produces results that no one intended or could even foresee. It is this interaction and these results that recent historians are referring to when they speak so disparagingly of those "underlying determinants" and "impersonal and inexorable forces" bringing on the Revolution. Historical explanation which does not account for these "forces," which, in other words, relies simply on understanding the conscious intentions of the actors, will thus be limited. This preoccupation with men's purposes was what restricted the perspectives of the contemporaneous Whig and Tory interpretations; and it is still the weakness of the neo-Whig histories, and indeed of any interpretation which attempts to explain the events of the Revolution by discovering the calculations from which individuals supposed themselves to have acted.

No explanation of the American Revolution in terms of the intentions and designs of particular individuals could have been more crudely put than that offered by the Revolutionaries themselves. American Whigs, like men of the eighteenth century generally, were fascinated with what seemed to the age to be the newly appreciated problem of human motivation and causation in the affairs of the world. In the decade before independence the Americans sought endlessly to discover the supposed calculations and purposes of individuals or groups that lay behind the otherwise incomprehensible rush of events. More than anything else perhaps, it was this obsession with motives that led to the prevalence in the eighteenth century of beliefs in conspiracies to account for the confusing happenings in which men found themselves caught up. Bailyn has suggested that this common fear of conspiracy was "deeply rooted in the political awareness of eighteenth-century Britons, involved in the very structure of their political life"; it "reflected so clearly the realities of life in an age in which monarchical autocracy flourished, [and] in which the stability and freedom of England's 'mixed' constitution was a recent and remarkable achievement."[31] Yet it might also be argued that the tendency to see conspiracy behind what happened reflected as well the very enlightenment of the age. To attribute events to the designs and purposes of human agents seemed after all to be an enlightened advance over older beliefs in

[31] Bailyn, *Revolutionary Pamphlets,* I, 87, ix.

blind chance, providence, or God's interventions. It was rational and scientific, a product of both the popularization of politics and the secularization of knowledge. It was obvious to Americans that the series of events in the years after 1763, those "unheard of intolerable calamities, spring not of the dust, come not causeless." "Ought not the PEOPLE therefore," asked John Dickinson, "to watch? to observe facts? to search into causes? to investigate designs?"[32] And these causes and designs could be traced to individuals in high places, to ministers, to royal governors, and their lackeys. The belief in conspiracy grew naturally out of the enlightened need to find the human purposes behind the multitude of phenomena, to find the causes for what happened in the social world just as the natural scientist was discovering the causes for what happened in the physical world.[33] It was a necessary consequence of the search for connections and patterns in events. The various acts of the British government, the Americans knew, should not be "regarded according to the simple force of each, but as parts of a system of oppression."[34] The Whigs' intense search for the human purposes behind events was in fact an example of the beginnings of modern history.

In attempting to rebut those interpretations disparaging the colonists' cause, the present neo-Whig historians have been drawn into writing as partisans of the Revolutionaries. And they have thus found themselves entangled in the same kind of explanation used by the original antagonists, an explanation, despite obvious refinements, still involved with the discovery of motives and its corollary, the assessing of a personal sort of responsibility for what happened. While most of the neo-Whig historians have not gone so far as to see conspiracy in British actions (although some have come close),[35] they have tended to point up the blundering and stupidity of British officials in contrast to "the breadth of vision" that moved the Americans. If George III was in a position of central responsibility in the

[32] [Moses Mather], *America's Appeal to the Impartial World* . . . (Hartford, 1775), 59; [John Dickinson], *Letters from a Farmer in Pennsylvania to the Inhabitants of the British Colonies* (1768), in Paul L. Ford, ed., *The Life and Writings of John Dickinson* (Historical Society of Pennsylvania, *Memoirs*, XIV [Philadelphia, 1895]), II, 348. Dickinson hinged his entire argument on the ability of the Americans to decipher the "intention" of parliamentary legislation, whether for revenue or for commercial regulation. Ibid., 348, 364.

[33] See Herbert Davis, "The Augustan Conception of History," in J. A. Mazzeo, ed., *Reason and the Imagination: Studies in the History of Ideas, 1600–1800* (New York, 1962), 226–228; W. H. Greenleaf, *Order, Empiricism and Politics: Two Traditions of English Political Thought, 1500–1700* (New York, 1964), 166; R. N. Stromberg, "History in the Eighteenth Century," *Journal of the History of Ideas,* XII (1951), 300. It was against this "dominant characteristic of the historical thought of the age," this "tendency to explain events in terms of conscious action by individuals," that the brilliant group of Scottish social scientists writing at the end of the 18th century directed much of their work. Duncan Forbes, " 'Scientific' Whiggism: Adam Smith and John Millar," *Cambridge Journal,* VII (1954), 651, 653–654. While we have had recently several good studies of historical thinking in 17th-century England, virtually nothing has been done on the 18th century. See, however, J.G.A. Pocock, "Burke and the Ancient Constitution—A Problem in the History of Ideas," *The Historical Journal,* III (1960), 125–143; and Stow Persons, "The Cyclical Theory of History in Eighteenth Century America," *American Quarterly,* VI (1954), 147–163.

[34] [Dickinson], *Letters From a Farmer,* in Ford, ed., *Writings of Dickinson,* 388.

[35] Bailyn has noted that Oliver M. Dickerson, in chap. 7 of his *The Navigation Acts and the American Revolution* (Philadelphia, 1951), "adopts wholesale the contemporary Whig interpretation of the Revolution as the result of a conspiracy of 'King's Friends.'" Bailyn, *Revolutionary Pamphlets,* I, 724.

British government, as English historians have recently said, then, according to Edmund S. Morgan, "he must bear most of the praise or blame for the series of measures that alienated and lost the colonies, and it is hard to see how there can be much praise." By seeking "to define issues, fix responsibilities," and thereby to shift the "burden of proof" onto those who say the Americans were narrow and selfish and the empire was basically just and beneficent, the neo-Whigs have attempted to redress what they felt was an unfair neo-Tory bias of previous explanations of the Revolution;[36] they have not, however, challenged the terms of the argument. They are still obsessed with why men said they acted and with who was right and who was wrong. Viewing the history of the Revolution in this judicatory manner has therefore restricted the issues over which historians have disagreed to those of motivation and responsibility, the very issues with which the participants themselves were concerned.

The neo-Whig "conviction that the colonists' attachment to principle was genuine"[37] has undoubtedly been refreshing, and indeed necessary, given the Tory slant of earlier twentieth-century interpretations. It now seems clearer that the Progressive historians, with their naive and crude reflex conception of human behavior, had too long treated the ideas of the Revolution superficially if not superciliously. Psychologists and sociologists are now willing to grant a more determining role to beliefs, particularly in revolutionary situations. It is now accepted that men act not simply in response to some kind of objective reality but to the meaning they give to that reality. Since men's beliefs are as much a part of the given stimuli as the objective environment, the beliefs must be understood and taken seriously if men's behavior is to be fully explained. The American Revolutionary ideas were more than cooked up pieces of thought served by an aggressive and interested minority to a gullible and unsuspecting populace. The concept of propaganda permitted the Progressive historians to account for the presence of ideas but it prevented them from recognizing ideas as an important determinant of the Americans' behavior. The weight attributed to ideas and constitutional principles by the neo-Whig historians was thus an essential corrective to the propagandist studies.

Yet in its laudable effort to resurrect the importance of ideas in historical explanation much of the writing of the neo-Whigs has tended to return to the simple nineteenth-century intellectualist assumption that history is the consequence of a rational calculation of ends and means, that what happened was what was consciously desired and planned. By supposing "that individual actions and immediate issues are more important than underlying determinants in explaining particular events," by emphasizing conscious and articulated motives, the neo-Whig historians have selected and presented that evidence which is most directly and clearly expressive of the intentions of the Whigs, that is, the most well-defined, the most constitutional, the most reasonable of the Whig beliefs, those found in their public documents, their several declarations of grievances and causes. It is not surprising that for the neo-Whigs the history of the American Revolution should be more than anything else "the history of the Americans'

---

[36] Morgan, "Revisions in Need of Revising," 7, 13, 8; Greene, "Flight From Determinism," 237.

[37] Edmund S. Morgan, *The Birth of the Republic, 1763–89* (Chicago, 1956), 51.

search for principles."[38] Not only, then, did nothing in the Americans' economic and social structure really determine their behavior, but the colonists in fact acted from the most rational and calculated of motives: they fought, as they said they would, simply to defend their ancient liberties against British provocation.

By implying that certain declared rational purposes are by themselves an adequate explanation for the Americans' revolt, in other words that the Revolution was really nothing more than a contest over constitutional principles, the neo-Whig historians have not only threatened to deny what we have learned of human psychology in the twentieth century, but they have also in fact failed to exploit fully the terms of their own idealist approach by not taking into account all of what the Americans believed and said. Whatever the deficiencies and misunderstandings of the role of ideas in human behavior present in the propagandist studies of the 1930s, these studies did for the first time attempt to deal with the entirety and complexity of American Revolutionary thought—to explain not only all the well-reasoned notions of law and liberty that were so familiar but, more important, all the irrational and hysterical beliefs that had been so long neglected. Indeed, it was the patent absurdity and implausibility of much of what the Americans said that lent credence and persuasiveness to their mistrustful approach to the ideas. Once this exaggerated and fanatical rhetoric was uncovered by the Progressive historians, it should not have subsequently been ignored—no matter how much it may have impugned the reasonableness of the American response. No widely expressed ideas can be dismissed out of hand by the historian.

In his recent analysis of Revolutionary thinking Bernard Bailyn has avoided the neo-Whig tendency to distort the historical reconstruction of the American mind. By comprehending "the assumptions, beliefs, and ideas that lay behind the manifest events of the time," Bailyn has attempted to get inside the Whigs' mind, and to experience vicariously all of what they thought and felt, both their rational constitutional beliefs and their hysterical and emotional ideas as well. The inflammatory phrases, "slavery," "corruption," "conspiracy," that most historians had either ignored or readily dismissed as propaganda, took on a new significance for Bailyn. He came "to suspect that they meant something very real to both the writers and their readers: that there were real fears, real anxieties, a sense of real danger behind these phrases, and not merely the desire to influence by rhetoric and propaganda the inert minds of an otherwise passive populace."[39] No part of American thinking, Bailyn suggests—not the widespread belief in a ministerial conspiracy, not the hostile and vicious indictments of individuals, not the fear of corruption and the hope for regeneration, not any of the violent seemingly absurd distortions and falsifications of what we now believe to be true, in short, none of the frenzied rhetoric—can be safely ignored by the historian seeking to understand the causes of the Revolution.

Bailyn's study, however, represents something other than a more complete and uncorrupted version of the common idealist interpretations of the Revolution. By viewing from the "interior" the Revolutionary pamphlets, which were "to an unusual degree, *explanatory*," revealing "not merely positions taken

[38] Greene, "Flight From Determinism," 258; Morgan, *Birth of the Republic,* 3.
[39] Bailyn, *Revolutionary Pamphlets,* I, vii, ix.

but the reasons why positions were taken," Bailyn like any idealist historian has sought to discover the motives the participants themselves gave for their actions, to re-enact their thinking at crucial moments, and thereby to recapture some of the "unpredictable reality" of the Revolution.[40] But for Bailyn the very unpredictability of the reality he has disclosed has undermined the idealist obsession with explaining why, in the participants' own estimation, they acted as they did. Ideas emerge as more than explanatory devices, as more than indicators of motives. They become as well objects for analysis in and for themselves, historical events in their own right to be treated as other historical events are treated. Although Bailyn has examined the Revolutionary ideas subjectively from the inside, he has also analyzed them objectively from the outside. Thus, in addition to a contemporary Whig perspective, he presents us with a retrospective view of the ideas—their complexity, their development, and their consequences—that the actual participants did not have. In effect his essay represents what has been called "a Namierism of the history of ideas,"[41] a structural analysis of thought that suggests a conclusion about the movement of history not very different from Sir Lewis Namier's, where history becomes something "started in ridiculous beginnings, while small men did things both infinitely smaller and infinitely greater than they knew."[42]

In his *England in the Age of the American Revolution* Namier attacked the Whig tendency to overrate "the importance of the conscious will and purpose in individuals." Above all he urged us "to ascertain and recognize the deeper irrelevancies and incoherence of human actions, which are not so much directed by reason, as invested by it *ex post facto* with the appearances of logic and rationality," to discover the unpredictable reality, where men's motives and intentions were lost in the accumulation and momentum of interacting events. The whole force of Namier's approach tended to squeeze the intellectual content out of what men did. Ideas setting forth principles and purposes for action, said Namier, did not count for much in the movement of history.[43]

In his study of the Revolutionary ideas Bailyn has come to an opposite conclusion: ideas counted for a great deal, not only being responsible for the Revolution but also for transforming the character of American society. Yet in his hands ideas lose that static quality they have commonly had for the Whig historians, the simple statements of intention that so exasperated Namier. For Bailyn the ideas of the Revolutionaries take on an elusive and unmanageable quality, a dynamic self-intensifying character that transcended the intentions and desires of any of the historical participants. By emphasizing how the thought of the colonists was "strangely reshaped, turned in unfamiliar directions," by describing how the Americans "indeliberately, half-knowingly" groped toward "conclusions they could not themselves clearly perceive," by demonstrating how new beliefs and hence new actions were the responses not to desire but to the logic of

---

[40] Ibid., vii, viii, 17.

[41] J.G.A. Pocock, "Machiavelli, Harrington, and English Political Ideologies in the Eighteenth Century," *Wm. and Mary Qtly.*, 3d Ser., XXII (1965), 550.

[42] Sir Lewis Namier, *England in the Age of the American Revolution,* 2d ed. (London, 1961), 131.

[43] Ibid., 129.

developing situations, Bailyn has wrested the explanation of the Revolution out of the realm of motivation in which the neo-Whig historians had confined it.

With this kind of approach to ideas, the degree of consistency and devotion to principles become less important, and indeed the major issues of motivation and responsibility over which historians have disagreed become largely irrelevant. Action becomes not the product of rational and conscious calculation but of dimly perceived and rapidly changing thoughts and situations, "where the familiar meaning of ideas and words faded away into confusion, and leaders felt themselves peering into a haze, seeking to bring shifting conceptions somehow into focus." Men become more the victims than the manipulators of their ideas, as their thought unfolds in ways few anticipated, "rapid, irreversible, and irresistible," creating new problems, new considerations, new ideas, which have their own unforeseen implications. In this kind of atmosphere the Revolution, not at first desired by the Americans, takes on something of an inevitable character, moving through a process of escalation into levels few had intended or perceived. It no longer makes sense to assign motives or responsibility to particular individuals for the totality of what happened. Men were involved in a complicated web of phenomena, ideas, and situations, from which in retrospect escape seems impossible.[44]

By seeking to uncover the motives of the Americans expressed in the Revolutionary pamphlets, Bailyn has ended by demonstrating the autonomy of ideas as phenomena, where the ideas operate, as it were, over the heads of the participants, taking them in directions no one could have foreseen. His discussion of Revolutionary thought thus represents a move back to a deterministic approach to the Revolution, a determinism, however, which is different from that which the neo-Whig historians have so recently and self-consciously abandoned. Yet while the suggested determinism is thoroughly idealist—indeed never before has the force of ideas in bringing on the Revolution been so emphatically put—its implications are not. By helping to purge our writing about the Revolution of its concentration on constitutional principles and its stifling judicial-like preoccupation with motivation and responsibility, the study serves to open the way for new questions and new appraisals. In fact, it is out of the very completeness of his idealist interpretation, out of his exposition of the extraordinary nature—the very dynamism and emotionalism—of the Americans' thought that we have the evidence for an entirely different, a behaviorist, perspective on the causes of the American Revolution. Bailyn's book-length introduction to his edition of Revolutionary pamphlets is therefore not only a point of fulfillment for the idealist approach to the Revolution, it is also a point of departure for a new look at the social sources of the Revolution.

V

It seems clear that historians of eighteenth-century America and the Revolution cannot ignore the force of ideas in history to the extent that Namier

---

[44] Bailyn, *Revolutionary Pamphlets,* I, 90, x, 169, 140. See Hannah Arendt, *On Revolution* (New York, 1963), 173: "American experience had taught the men of the Revolution that action, though it may be started in isolation and decided upon by single individuals for very different motives, can be accomplished only by some joint effort in which the motivation of single individuals . . . no longer counts."

and his students have done in their investigations of eighteenth-century English politics. This is not to say, however, that the Namier approach to English politics has been crucially limiting and distorting. Rather it may suggest that the Namier denigration of ideas and principles is inapplicable for American politics because the American social situation in which ideas operated was very different from that of eighteenth-century England. It may be that ideas are less meaningful to a people in a socially stable situation. Only when ideas have become stereotyped reflexes do evasion and hypocrisy and the Namier mistrust of what men believe become significant. Only in a relatively settled society does ideology become a kind of habit, a bundle of widely shared and instinctive conventions, offering ready-made explanations for men who are not being compelled to ask any serious questions. Conversely, it is perhaps only in a relatively unsettled, disordered society, where the questions come faster than men's answers, that ideas become truly vital and creative.[45]

Paradoxically it may be the very vitality of the Americans' ideas, then, that suggests the need to examine the circumstances in which they flourished. Since ideas and beliefs are ways of perceiving and explaining the world, the nature of the ideas expressed is determined as much by the character of the world being confronted as by the internal development of inherited and borrowed conceptions. Out of the multitude of inherited and transmitted ideas available in the eighteenth century, Americans selected and emphasized those which seemed to make meaningful what was happening to them. In the colonists' use of classical literature, for example, "their detailed knowledge and engaged interest covered only one era and one small group of writers," Plutarch, Livy, Cicero, Sallust, and Tacitus—those who "had hated and feared the trends of their own time, and in their writing had contrasted the present with a better past, which they endowed with qualities absent from their own, corrupt era."[46] There was always, in Max Weber's term, some sort of elective affinity between the Americans' interests and their beliefs, and without that affinity their ideas would not have possessed the peculiar character and persuasiveness they did. Only the most revolutionary social needs and circumstances could have sustained such revolutionary ideas.[47]

When the ideas of the Americans are examined comprehensively, when all of the Whig rhetoric, irrational as well as rational, is taken into account, one cannot but be struck by the predominant characteristics of fear and frenzy, the exaggerations and the enthusiasm, the general sense of social corruption and disorder out of which would be born a new world of benevolence and harmony where Americans would become the "eminent examples of every divine and social

[45] See Sir Lewis Namier, *The Structure of Politics at the Accession of George III,* 2d ed. (London, 1961), 16; Sir Lewis Namier, "Human Nature in Politics," in *Personalities and Power: Selected Essays* (New York, 1965), 5–6.

[46] Bailyn, *Revolutionary Pamphlets,* I, 22. The French Revolutionaries were using the same group of classical writings to express their estrangement from the ancien régime and their hope for the new order. Harold T. Parker, *The Cult of Antiquity and the French Revolutionaries: A Study in the Development of the Revolutionary Spirit* (Chicago, 1937), 22–23.

[47] The relation of ideas to social structure is one of the most perplexing and intriguing in the social sciences. For an extensive bibliography on the subject see Norman Birnbaum, "The Sociological Study of Ideology (1940–60)," *Current Sociology,* IX (1960).

virtue."[48] As Bailyn and the propaganda studies have amply shown, there is simply too much fanatical and millennial thinking even by the best minds that must be explained before we can characterize the Americans' ideas as peculiarly rational and legalistic and thus view the Revolution as merely a conservative defense of constitutional liberties. To isolate refined and nicely reasoned arguments from the writings of John Adams and Jefferson is not only to disregard the more inflamed expressions of the rest of the Whigs but also to overlook the enthusiastic extravagance—the paranoiac obsession with a diabolical Crown conspiracy and the dream of a restored Saxon era—in the thinking of Adams and Jefferson themselves.

The ideas of the Americans seem, in fact, to form what can only be called a revolutionary syndrome. If we were to confine ourselves to examining the Revolutionary rhetoric alone, apart from what happened politically or socially, it would be virtually impossible to distinguish the American Revolution from any other revolution in modern Western history. In the kinds of ideas expressed the American Revolution is remarkably similar to the seventeenth-century Puritan Revolution and to the eighteenth-century French Revolution: the same general disgust with a chaotic and corrupt world, the same anxious and angry bombast, the same excited fears of conspiracies by depraved men, the same utopian hopes for the construction of a new and virtuous order.[49] It was not that this syndrome of ideas was simply transmitted from one generation or from one people to another. It was rather perhaps that similar, though hardly identical, social situations called forth within the limitations of inherited and available conceptions similar modes of expression. Although we need to know much more about the sociology of revolutions and collective movements, it does seem possible that particular patterns of thought, particular forms of expression, correspond to certain basic social experiences. There may be, in other words, typical modes of expression, typical kinds of beliefs and values, characterizing a revolutionary situation, at least within roughly similar Western societies. Indeed, the types of ideas manifested may be the best way of identifying a collective movement as a revolution. As one student of revolutions writes, "It is on the basis of a knowledge of men's beliefs that we can distinguish their behaviour from riot, rebellion or insanity."[50]

It is thus the very nature of the Americans' rhetoric—its obsession with corruption and disorder, its hostile and conspiratorial outlook, and its millennial vision of a regenerated society—that reveals as nothing else apparently can the American Revolution as a true revolution with its sources lying deep in the social structure. For this kind of frenzied rhetoric could spring only from the most

[48] Jacob Duché, *The American Vine, A Sermon, Preached . . . Before the Honourable Continental Congress, July 20th, 1775 . . .* (Philadelphia, 1775), 29.

[49] For recent discussions of French and Puritan revolutionary rhetoric see Peter Gay, "Rhetoric and Politics in the French Revolution," *Amer. Hist. Rev.,* LXVI (1960–1961), 664–676; Michael Walzer, "Puritanism as a Revolutionary Ideology," *History and Theory,* III (1963), 59–90. This entire issue of *History and Theory* is devoted to a symposium on the uses of theory in the study of history. In addition to the Walzer article, I have found the papers by Samuel H. Beer, "Causal Explanation and Imaginative Re-enactment," and Charles Tilly, "The Analysis of a Counter-Revolution," very stimulating and helpful.

[50] Bryan A. Wilson, "Millennialism in Comparative Perspective," *Comparative Studies in Society and History,* VI (1963–1964), 108. See also Neil J. Smelser, *Theory of Collective Behaviour* (London, 1962), 83, 120, 383.

severe sorts of social strain. The grandiose and feverish language of the Americans was indeed the natural, even the inevitable, expression of a people caught up in a revolutionary situation, deeply alienated from the existing sources of authority and vehemently involved in a basic reconstruction of their political and social order. The hysteria of the Americans' thinking was but a measure of the intensity of their revolutionary passions. Undoubtedly the growing American alienation from British authority contributed greatly to this revolutionary situation. Yet the very weakness of the British imperial system and the accumulating ferocity of American antagonism to it suggests that other sources of social strain were being fed into the revolutionary movement. It may be that the Progressive historians in their preoccupation with internal social problems were more right than we have recently been willing to grant. It would be repeating their mistake, however, to expect this internal social strain necessarily to take the form of coherent class conflict or overt social disruption. The sources of revolutionary social stress may have been much more subtle but no less severe.

Of all of the colonies in the mid-eighteenth century, Virginia seems the most settled, the most lacking in obvious social tensions. Therefore, as it has been recently argued, since conspicuous social issues were nonexistent, the only plausible remaining explanation for the Virginians' energetic and almost unanimous commitment to the Revolution must have been their devotion to constitutional principles.[51] Yet it may be that we have been looking for the wrong kind of social issues, for organized conflicts, for conscious divisions, within the society. It seems clear that Virginia's difficulties were not the consequence of any obvious sectional or class antagonism, Tidewater versus Piedmont, aristocratic planters versus yeomen farmers. There was apparently no discontent with the political system that went deep into the social structure. But there does seem to have been something of a social crisis within the ruling group itself, which intensely aggravated the Virginians' antagonism to the imperial system. Contrary to the impression of confidence and stability that the Virginia planters have historically acquired, they seemed to have been in very uneasy circumstances in the years before the Revolution. The signs of the eventual nineteenth-century decline of the Virginia gentry were, in other words, already felt if not readily apparent.

The planters' ability to command the acquiescence of the people seems extraordinary compared to the unstable politics of the other colonies. But in the years before independence there were signs of increasing anxiety among the gentry over their representative role. The ambiguities in the relationship between the Burgesses and their constituents erupted into open debate in the 1750s. And men began voicing more and more concern over the mounting costs of elections and growing corruption in the soliciting of votes, especially by "those who have neither natural nor acquired parts to recommend them."[52] By the late sixties and early seventies the newspapers were filled with warnings against electoral influence, bribery, and vote seeking. The freeholders were stridently urged to "strike at the Root of this growing Evil; be influenced by Merit alone," and avoid

---

[51] Tate, "Coming of the Revolution in Virginia," 324–343.

[52] Robert E. and B. Katherine Brown, *Virginia, 1705–1786: Democracy or Aristocracy?* (East Lansing, Mich., 1964), 236; Alexander White to Richard Henry Lee, 1758, quoted in J. R. Pole, "Representation and Authority in Virginia from the Revolution to Reform," *The Journal of Southern History,* XXIV (1958), 23.

electing "obscure and inferior persons."[53] It was as if ignoble ambition and demagoguery, one bitter pamphlet remarked, were a "Daemon lately come among us to disturb the peace and harmony, which had so long subsisted in this place."[54] In this context Robert Munford's famous play, *The Candidates,* written in 1770, does not so much confirm the planters' confidence as it betrays their uneasiness with electoral developments in the colony, "when coxcombs and jockies can impose themselves upon it for men of learning." Although disinterested virtue eventually wins out, Munford's satire reveals the kinds of threats the established planters faced from ambitious knaves and blockheads who were turning representatives into slaves of the people.[55]

By the eve of the Revolution the planters were voicing a growing sense of impending ruin, whose sources seemed in the minds of many to be linked more and more with the corrupting British connection and the Scottish factors, but for others frighteningly rooted in "our Pride, our Luxury, and Idleness."[56] The public and private writings of Virginians became obsessed with "corruption," "virtue," and "luxury." The increasing defections from the Church of England, even among ministers and vestrymen, and the remarkable growth of dissent in the years before the Revolution, "so much complained of in many parts of the colony," further suggests some sort of social stress. The strange religious conversions of Robert Carter may represent only the most dramatic example of what was taking place less frenziedly elsewhere among the gentry.[57] By the middle of the eighteenth century it was evident that many of the planters were living on the edge of bankruptcy, seriously overextended and spending beyond their means in an almost frantic effort to fulfill the aristocratic image they had created of themselves.[58] Perhaps the importance of the Robinson affair in the 1760s lies not

73

[53] Purdie and Dixon's *Virginia Gazette* (Williamsburg), Apr. 11, 1771; Rind's *Virginia Gazette,* Oct. 31, 1771. See Lester J. Cappon and Stella F. Duff, eds., *Virginia Gazette Index, 1736–1780* (Williamsburg, 1950), I, 351, for entries on the astounding increase in essays on corruption and cost of elections in the late 1760s and early 1770s.

[54] *The Defence of Injur'd Merit Unmasked; or, the Scurrilous Piece of Philander Dissected and Exposed to Public View. By a Friend to Merit, wherever found* (n. p., 1771), 10. Robert Carter chose to retire to private life in the early 1770s rather than adjust to the "new system of politicks" that had begun "to prevail generally." Quoted in Louis Morton, *Robert Carter of Nomini Hall: A Virginia Tobacco Planter of the Eighteenth Century* (Williamsburg, 1941), 52.

[55] Jay B. Hubbell and Douglass Adair, "Robert Munford's *The Candidates,*" *Wm. and Mary Qtly.,* 3d Ser., V (1948), 246, 238. The ambivalence in Munford's attitude toward the representative process is reflected in the different way historians have interpreted his play. Cf. ibid., 223–225, with Brown, *Virginia,* 236–237. Munford's fear of "men who aim at power without merit" was more fully expressed in his later play, *The Patriots,* written in 1775 or 1776. Courtlandt Canby, "Robert Munford's *The Patriots,*" *Wm. and Mary Qtly.,* 3d Ser., VI (1949), 437–503, quotation from 450.

[56] [John Randolph], *Considerations on the Present State of Virginia* ([Williamsburg], 1774), in Earl G. Swem, ed., *Virginia and the Revolution: Two Pamphlets, 1774* (New York, 1919), 16; Purdie and Dixon's *Virginia Gazette,* Nov. 25, 1773.

[57] Rind's *Virginia Gazette,* Sept. 8, 1774; Brown, *Virginia,* 252–254; Morton, *Robert Carter,* 231–250.

[58] See George Washington to George Mason, Apr. 5, 1769, in John C. Fitzpatrick, ed., *The Writings of George Washington* (Washington, 1931–1944), II, 502; Carl Bridenbaugh, *Myths and Realities: Societies of the Colonial South* (New York, 1963), 5, 10, 14, 16; Emory G. Evans, "Planter Indebtedness and the Coming of the Revolution in Virginia," *Wm. and Mary Qtly.,* 3d Ser., XIX (1962), 518–519.

in any constitutional changes that resulted but in the shattering effect the disclosures had on that virtuous image.[59] Some of the planters expressed openly their fears for the future, seeing the products of their lives being destroyed in the reckless gambling and drinking of their heirs, who, as Landon Carter put it, "play away and play it all away."[60]

The Revolution in Virginia, "produced by the wantonness of the Gentleman," as one planter suggested,[61] undoubtedly gained much of its force from this social crisis within the gentry. Certainly more was expected from the Revolution than simply a break from British imperialism, and it was not any crude avoidance of British debts.[62] The Revolutionary reforms, like the abolition of entail and primogeniture, may have signified something other than mere symbolic legal adjustments to an existing reality. In addition to being an attempt to make the older Tidewater plantations more economically competitive with lands farther west, the reforms may have represented a real effort to redirect what was believed to be a dangerous tendency in social and family development within the ruling gentry. The Virginians were not after all aristocrats who could afford having their entailed families' estates in the hands of weak or ineffectual eldest sons. Entail, as the preamble to the 1776 act abolishing it stated, had often done "injury to the morals of youth by rendering them independent of, and disobedient to, their parents."[63] There was too much likelihood, as the Nelson family sadly demonstrated, that a single wayward generation would virtually wipe out what had been so painstakingly built.[64] George Mason bespoke the anxieties of many Virginians when he warned the Philadelphia Convention in 1787 that "our own Children will in a short time be among the general mass."[65]

Precisely how the strains within Virginia society contributed to the creation of a revolutionary situation and in what way the planters expected independence and republicanism to alleviate their problems, of course, need to be fully explored. It seems clear, however, from the very nature of the ideas expressed that the sources of the Revolution in Virginia were much more subtle and complicated than a simple antagonism to the British government. Constitutional

74

---

[59] Rind's *Virginia Gazette,* Aug. 15, 1766. See Carl Bridenbaugh, "Violence and Virtue in Virginia, 1766: or The Importance of the Trivial," Massachusetts Historical Society, *Proceedings,* LXXVI (1964), 3–29.

[60] Quoted in Bridenbaugh, *Myths and Realities,* 27. See also Morton, *Robert Carter,* 223–225.

[61] John A. Washington to R. H. Lee, June 20, 1778, quoted in Pole, "Representation and Authority in Virginia," 28.

[62] Evans, "Planter Indebtedness," 526–527.

[63] Julian P. Boyd and others, eds., *The Papers of Thomas Jefferson* (Princeton, 1950–), I, 560. Most of our knowledge of entail and primogeniture in Virginia stems from an unpublished doctoral dissertation, Clarence R. Keim, "Influence of Primogeniture and Entail in the Development of Virginia" (University of Chicago, 1926). Keim's is a very careful and qualified study and conclusions from his evidence—other than the obvious fact that much land was held in fee simple—are by no means easy to make. See particularly pp. 56, 60–62, 110–114, 122, 195–196.

[64] Emory S. Evans, "The Rise and Decline of the Virginia Aristocracy in the Eighteenth Century: The Nelsons," in Darrett B. Rutman, ed., *The Old Dominion: Essays for Thomas Perkins Abernethy* (Charlottesville, 1964), 73–74.

[65] Max Farrand, ed., *The Records of the Federal Convention of 1787* (New Haven, 1911), I, 56; Bridenbaugh, *Myths and Realities,* 14, 16.

principles alone do not explain the Virginians' almost unanimous determination to revolt. And if the Revolution in the seemingly stable colony of Virginia possessed internal social roots, it is to be expected that the other colonies were experiencing their own forms of social strain that in a like manner sought mitigation through revolution and republicanism.

It is through the Whigs' ideas, then, that we may be led back to take up where the Progressive historians left off in their investigation of the internal social sources of the Revolution. By working through the ideas—by reading them imaginatively and relating them to the objective social world they both reflected and confronted—we may be able to eliminate the unrewarding distinction between conscious and unconscious motives, and eventually thereby to combine a Whig with a Tory, an idealist with a behaviorist, interpretation. For the ideas, the rhetoric, of the Americans was never obscuring but remarkably revealing of their deepest interests and passions. What they expressed may not have been for the most part factually true, but it was always psychologically true. In this sense their rhetoric was never detached from the social and political reality; and indeed it becomes the best entry into an understanding of that reality. Their repeated overstatements of reality, their incessant talk of "tyranny" when there seems to have been no real oppression, their obsession with "virtue," "luxury," and "corruption," their devotion to "liberty" and "equality"—all these notions were neither manipulated propaganda nor borrowed empty abstractions, but ideas with real personal and social significance for those who used them. Propaganda could never move men to revolution. No popular leader, as John Adams put it, has ever been able "to persuade a large people, for any length of time together, to think themselves wronged, injured, and oppressed, unless they really were, and saw and felt it to be so."[66] The ideas had relevance; the sense of oppression and injury, although often displaced onto the imperial system, was nonetheless real. It was indeed the meaningfulness of the connection between what the Americans said and what they felt that gave the ideas their propulsive force and their overwhelming persuasiveness.

It is precisely the remarkable revolutionary character of the Americans' ideas now being revealed by historians that best indicates that something profoundly unsettling was going on in the society, that raises the question, as it did for the Progressive historians, why the Americans should have expressed such thoughts. With their crude conception of propaganda the Progressive historians at least attempted to grapple with the problem. Since we cannot regard the ideas of the Revolutionaries as simply propaganda, the question still remains to be answered. "When 'ideas' in full cry drive past," wrote Arthur F. Bentley in his classic behavioral study, *The Process of Government,* "the thing to do with them is to accept them as an indication that something is happening; and then search carefully to find out what it really is they stand for, what the factors of the social life are that are expressing themselves through the ideas."[67] Precisely because they sought to understand both the Revolutionary ideas and American society, the behaviorist

---

[66] John Adams, "Novanglus," in Charles F. Adams, ed., *The Works of John Adams* (Boston, 1851), IV, 14.

[67] Arthur F. Bentley, *The Process of Government: A Study of Social Pressures* (Chicago, 1908), 152.

historians of the Progressive generation, for all of their crude conceptualizations, their obsession with "class" and hidden economic interests, and their treatment of ideas as propaganda, have still offered us an explanation of the Revolutionary era so powerful and so comprehensive that no purely intellectual interpretation will ever replace it.

Author's Postscript

If the tendency of subsequent scholarship is any indication, my 1966 article had very little influence on the historical profession. Much of the scholarship on the Revolution during the several decades following its publication ignored the "reality" of American society and instead concentrated very heavily on the "rhetoric" of the Revolution, which was by and large equated with something called "republicanism." I suppose my book *The Creation of the American Republic, 1776–1787*,[68] contributed its share to the so-called republican synthesis that emerged in the 1970s and 1980s to become something of a monster that has threatened to devour us all. My article, however, was supposed to tame the monster before it was unleashed.

When I wrote "Rhetoric and Reality," I had already essentially completed *Creation of the American Republic,* even though the book was published several years later. In that book I never intended to argue that the Revolution was fundamentally an ideological movement or that it could be explained solely in ideological terms. Indeed, I have never thought that one could explain anything fully by referring only to the beliefs of people. In writing the article I was well aware of the powerful implications of Bernard Bailyn's introduction to his *Pamphlets of the American Revolution,* which had just been published in 1965 and would become *The Ideological Origins of the American Revolution.*[69] As shatteringly important as I knew Bailyn's work to be, I thought it tried to explain the Revolution too much in terms of the professed beliefs of the participants. Thus I wrote "Rhetoric and Reality" as a corrective to the idealist tendency I saw in the neowhig historical literature of the 1950s and early 1960s that I believed had climaxed with Bailyn's stunning work. Without denying in any way the significance of ideas (after all, I had just completed a book on the political thought of the Revolution), I simply tried to urge historians not to get too carried away with exclusively intellectual explanations of the Revolution. I suggested that if we were ultimately to see the Revolution whole, from all sides, then we had to examine its social sources as well.

The problem with such a suggestion, aggravated by my wrongheaded title, was that it too easily reinforced the traditional assumptions of neoprogressive social history, which in the late 1960s and the 1970s, as Daniel T. Rodgers has recently reminded us, remained "reflexively dualistic: ideas versus behavior, rhetoric versus 'the concrete realities of life'; propaganda and mystification on the

---

[68] Chapel Hill, N. C., 1969.

[69] Bailyn, *Pamphlets of the American Revolution, 1750–1776* (Cambridge, Mass., 1965); Bailyn, *The Ideological Origins of the American Revolution* (Cambridge, Mass., 1967).

one hand, the real stuff on the other."[70] Despite my perverse title, I wrote the article as a protest against just such dualities, against such sharp separations of ideas from social circumstances. I wanted to acknowledge the importance of both ideas and underlying psychological and social determinants in shaping human behavior and yet avoid returning to the crude Beardian polarities of the past. In parts of *Creation of the American Republic* I tried to do just that, which is probably why so many historians could not decide what camp that book put me in.

Although cultural history of one sort or another has seized the day during the past generation (even the Marxists now write only cultural history), several historians have explicitly attempted to explore the linkages between culture and society that I suggested existed in the relatively stable colony of Virginia. Rhys Isaac in his *Transformation of Virginia*, T. H. Breen in his *Tobacco Culture*, Richard R. Beeman in his study of Lunenburg County, and Jack P. Greene in several articles have sought to relate social developments in Virginia to the ideology of the Revolution.[71] Although these works are very different, they are imaginative examples of what might be done. History that recognizes the importance of both culture and society, both consciousness and underlying social and material circumstances, is ultimately the kind of history we need to write.

77

---

[70] Rodgers, "Republicanism: The Career of a Concept," *Journal of American History*, LXXIX (1992), 25.

[71] Isaac, *The Transformation of Virginia, 1740–1790* (Chapel Hill, N. C., 1982). Breen, *Tobacco Culture: The Mentality of the Great Tidewater Planters on the Eve of Revolution* (Princeton, N. J., 1985). Beeman, *The Evolution of the Southern Backcountry: A Case Study of Lunenburg County, Virginia, 1746–1832* (Philadelphia, 1984). Greene, "Society, Ideology, and Politics: An Analysis of the Political Culture of Mid-Eighteenth-Century Virginia," in Richard M. Jellison, ed., *Society, Freedom, and Conscience: The Coming of the Revolution in Virginia, Massachusetts, and New York* (New York, 1976), 14–57; " 'Virtus et Libertas': Political Culture, Social Change, and the Origins of the American Revolution in Virginia, 1763–1766," in Jeffrey J. Crow and Larry E. Tise, eds., *The Southern Experience in the American Revolution* (Chapel Hill, N. C., 1978), 55–65; and "Character, Persona, and Authority: A Study of Alternative Styles of Political Leadership in Revolutionary Virginia," in W. Robert Higgins, ed., *The Revolutionary War in the South: Power, Conflict, and Leadership* (Durham, N. C., 1979), 3–42.

THE PURITAN ETHIC AND
THE AMERICAN REVOLUTION

EDMUND S. MORGAN

The American Revolution, we have been told, was radical and conservative, a movement for home rule and a contest for rule at home, the product of a rising nationality and the cause of that nationality, the work of designing demagogues and a triumph of statesmanship. John Adams said it took place in the minds and hearts of the people before 1776; Benjamin Rush thought it had scarcely begun in 1787. There were evidently many revolutions, many contests, divisions, and developments that deserve to be considered as part of the American Revolution. This paper deals in a preliminary, exploratory way with an aspect of the subject that has hitherto received little attention.[1] Without pretending to explain the whole exciting variety of the Revolution, I should like to suggest that the movement in all its phases, from the resistance against Parliamentary taxation in the 1760s to the establishment of a national government and national policies in the 1790s was affected, not to say guided, by a set of values inherited from the age of Puritanism.

These values or ideas, which I will call collectively the Puritan Ethic,[2] were not unconscious or subconscious, but were deliberately and openly expressed by men of the time. The men who expressed them were not Puritans, and few of the ideas included in the Puritan Ethic were actually new. Many of them had existed in other intellectual contexts before Puritanism was heard of, and many of them continue to exist today, as they did in the Revolutionary period, without the support of Puritanism. But Puritanism wove them together in a single rational pattern, and Puritans planted the pattern in America. It may be instructive, therefore, to identify the ideas as the Puritans defined and explained them before going on to the way in which they were applied in Revolutionary America after they had emerged from the Puritan mesh.

The values, ideas, and attitudes of the Puritan Ethic, as the term will be used here, clustered around the familiar idea of "calling." God, the Puritans believed, called every man to serve Him by serving society and himself in some useful,

Mr. Morgan is a member of the Department of History, Yale University.

Ed. Note: This article was originally published in *William and Mary Quarterly,* 3d Ser., XXIV (January 1967), 3–43.

[1] The author is engaged in a full-scale study of this theme. The present essay is interpretative, and citations have for the most part been limited to identifying the sources of quotations.

[2] I have chosen this term rather than the familiar "Protestant Ethic" of Max Weber, partly because I mean something slightly different and partly because Weber confined his phrase to attitudes prevailing while the religious impulse was paramount. The attitudes that survived the decline of religion he designated as the "spirit of capitalism." In this essay I have not attempted to distinguish earlier from later, though I am concerned with a period when the attitudes were no longer dictated primarily by religion.

productive occupation. Before entering on a trade or profession, a man must determine whether he had a calling to undertake it. If he had talents for it, if it was useful to society, if it was appropriate to his station in life, he could feel confident that God called him to it. God called no one to a life of prayer or to a life of ease or to any life that added nothing to the common good. It was a "foul disorder in any Commonwealth that there should be suffered rogues, beggars, vagabonds." The life of a monk or nun was no calling because prayer must be the daily exercise of every man, not a way for particular men to make a living. And perhaps most important, the life of the carefree aristocrat was no calling: "miserable and damnable is the estate of those that being enriched with great livings and revenues, do spend their days in eating and drinking, in sports and pastimes, not employing themselves in service for Church or Commonwealth."[3]

Once called to an occupation, a man's duty to the Maker Who called him demanded that he labor assiduously at it. He must shun both idleness, or neglect of his calling, and sloth, or slackness in it. Recreation was legitimate, because body and mind sometimes needed a release in order to return to work with renewed vigor. But recreation must not become an end in itself. One of the Puritans' objections to the stage was that professional players made recreation an occupation and thereby robbed the commonwealth of productive labor. The emphasis throughout was on productivity for the benefit of society.

In addition to working diligently at productive tasks, a man was supposed to be thrifty and frugal. It was good to produce but bad to consume any more than necessity required. A man was but the steward of the possessions he accumulated. If he indulged himself in luxurious living, he would have that much less with which to support church and society. If he needlessly consumed his substance, either from carelessness or from sensuality, he failed to honor the God who furnished him with it.

In this atmosphere the tolerance accorded to merchants was grudging. The merchant was suspect because he tended to encourage unnecessary consumption and because he did not actually produce anything; he simply moved things about. It was formally recognized that making exchanges could be a useful service, but it was a less essential one than that performed by the farmer, the shoemaker, or the weaver. Moreover, the merchant sometimes demeaned his calling by practicing it to the detriment rather than the benefit of society: he took advantage of his position to collect more than the value of his services, to charge what the market would bear. In short, he sometimes engaged in what a later generation would call speculation.

As the Puritan Ethic induced a suspicion of merchants, it also induced, for different reasons, a suspicion of prosperity. Superficial readers of Max Weber have often leapt to the conclusion that Puritans viewed economic success as a sign of salvation. In fact, Puritans were always uncomfortable in the presence of prosperity. Although they constantly sought it, although hard work combined with frugality could scarcely fail in the New World to bring it, the Puritans always felt more at ease when adversity made them tighten their belts. They knew that they must be thankful for prosperity, that like everything good in the world it came from God. But they also knew that God could use it as a temptation, that it could

---

[3] William Perkins, *Workes* (London, 1626–1631), I, 755–756.

lead to idleness, sloth, and extravagance. These were vices, not simply because they in turn led to poverty, but because God forbade them. Adversity, on the other hand, though a sign of God's temporary displeasure, and therefore a cause for worry, was also God's means of recalling a people to Him. When God showed anger man knew he must repent and do something about it. In times of drought, disease, and disaster a man could renew his faith by exercising frugality and industry, which were good not simply because they would lead to a restoration of prosperity, but because God demanded them.

The ambivalence of this attitude toward prosperity and adversity was characteristic of the Puritans: it was their lot to be forever improving the world, in full knowledge that every improvement would in the end prove illusory. While rejoicing at the superior purity of the churches they founded in New England, they had to tell themselves that they had often enjoyed more godliness while striving against heavy odds in England. The experience caused Nathaniel Ward, the "simple cobbler of Aggawam," to lament the declension that he was sure would overtake the Puritans in England after they gained the upper hand in the 1640s: "my heart hath mourned, and mine eyes wept in secret, to consider what will become of multitudes of my dear Country-men [in England], when they shall enjoy what they now covet."[4] Human flesh was too proud to stand success; it needed the discipline of adversity to keep it in line. And Puritans accordingly relished every difficulty and worried over every success.

This thirst for adversity found expression in a special kind of sermon, the Jeremiad, which was a lament for the loss of virtue and a warning of divine displeasure and desolation to come. The Jeremiad was a rhetorical substitute for adversity, designed to stiffen the virtue of the prosperous and successful by assuring them that they had failed. Nowhere was the Puritan Ethic more assiduously inculcated than in these laments, and it accordingly became a characteristic of the virtues which that ethic demanded that they were always seen to be expiring, if not already dead. Industry and frugality in their full vigor belonged always to an earlier generation, which the existing one must learn to emulate if it would avoid the wrath of God.

These ideas and attitudes were not peculiar to Puritans. The voluminous critiques of the Weber thesis have shown that similar attitudes prevailed widely among many groups and at many times. But the Puritans did have them, and so did their descendants in the time of the Revolution and indeed for long after it. It matters little by what name we call them or where they came from. "The Puritan Ethic" is used here simply as an appropriate shorthand phrase to designate them, and should not be taken to imply that the American Revolutionists were Puritans.

The Puritan Ethic as it existed among the Revolutionary generation had in fact lost for most men the endorsement of an omnipresent angry God. The element of divinity had not entirely departed, but it was a good deal diluted. The values and precepts derived from it, however, remained intact and were reinforced by a reading of history that attributed the rise and fall of empires to the acquisition and loss of the same virtues that God had demanded of the founders of New England. Rome, it was learned, had risen while its citizens worked at their

---

[4] Nathaniel Ward, *The Simple Cobbler of Aggawam in America* (London, 1647), 41.

callings and led lives of simplicity and frugality. Success as usual had resulted in extravagance and luxury. "The ancient, regular, and laborious life was relaxed and sunk in Idleness," and the torrent of vices thus let loose had overwhelmed the empire. In modern times the frugal Dutch had overthrown the extravagant Spanish.[5] The lesson of history carried the same imperatives that were intoned from the pulpit.

Whether they derived their ideas from history thus interpreted or from the Puritan tradition or elsewhere, Americans of the Revolutionary period in every colony and state paid tribute to the Puritan Ethic and repeated its injunctions. Although it was probably strongest among Presbyterians and Congregationalists like Benjamin Rush and Samuel Adams, it is evident enough among Anglicans like Henry Laurens and Richard Henry Lee and even among deists like Franklin and Jefferson. Jefferson's letters to his daughters sometimes sound as though they had been written by Cotton Mather: "It is your future happiness which interests me, and nothing can contribute more to it (moral rectitude always excepted) than the contracting a habit of industry and activity. Of all the cankers of human happiness, none corrodes it with so silent, yet so baneful a tooth, as indolence." "Determine never to be idle. No person will have occasion to complain of the want of time, who never loses any. It is wonderful how much may be done, if we are always doing."[6] And Jefferson of course followed his own injunction: a more methodically industrious man never lived.

The Puritan Ethic whether enjoined by God, by history, or by philosophy, called for diligence in a productive calling, beneficial both to society and to the individual. It encouraged frugality and frowned on extravagance. It viewed the merchant with suspicion and speculation with horror. It distrusted prosperity and gathered strength from adversity. It prevailed widely among Americans of different times and places, but those who urged it most vigorously always believed it to be on the point of expiring and in need of renewal.

The role of these ideas in the American Revolution—during the period, say, roughly from 1764 to 1789—was not explicitly causative. That is, the important events of the time can seldom be seen as the result of these ideas and never as the result solely of these ideas. Yet the major developments, the resistance to Great Britain, independence, the divisions among the successful Revolutionists, and the formulation of policies for the new nation, were all discussed and understood by men of the time in terms derived from the Puritan Ethic. And the way men understood and defined the issues before them frequently influenced their decisions.

I. The Origins of American Independence

In the first phase of the American Revolution, the period of agitation between the passage of the Sugar Act in 1764 and the outbreak of hostilities at Lexington in 1775, Americans were primarily concerned with finding ways to

[5] Purdie and Dixon's *Virginia Gazette* (Williamsburg), Sept. 5, 1771. Cf. *Pennsylvania Chronicle* (Philadelphia), Feb. 9–16, May 4–11, 1767; *Newport Mercury,* Mar. 7, 1774; and *Boston Evening Post,* Nov. 30, 1767.

[6] To Martha Jefferson, Mar. 28, May 5, 1787, in Julian Boyd et al., eds., *The Papers of Thomas Jefferson* (Princeton, 1950–), XI, 250, 349.

prevent British authority from infringing what they considered to be their rights. The principal point of contention was Parliament's attempt to tax them; and their efforts to prevent taxation, short of outright resistance, took two forms: economic pressure through boycotts and political pressure through the assertion of political and constitutional principles. Neither form of protest required the application of the Puritan Ethic, but both in the end were affected by it.

The boycott movements were a means of getting British merchants to bring their weight to bear on Parliament for the specific purpose of repealing tax laws. In each case the boycotts began with extralegal voluntary agreements among citizens not to consume British goods. In 1764–65, for instance, artisans agreed to wear only leather working clothes. Students forbore imported beer. Fire companies pledged themselves to eat no mutton in order to increase the supply of local wool. Backed by the nonconsumers, merchants of New York, Philadelphia, and Boston agreed to import no British goods until the repeal of the Stamp Act. The pressure had the desired effect: the Stamp Act was repealed and the Sugar Act revised. When the Townshend Acts and later the Coercive Acts were passed, new nonconsumption and nonimportation agreements were launched.[7]

From the outset these colonial boycott movements were more than a means of bringing pressure on Parliament. That is to say, they were not simply negative in intent. They were also a positive end in themselves, a way of reaffirming and rehabilitating the virtues of the Puritan Ethic. Parliamentary taxation offered Americans the prospect of poverty and adversity, and, as of old, adversity provided a spur to virtue. In 1764, when Richard Henry Lee got news of the Sugar Act, he wrote to a friend in London: "Possibly this step of the mother country, though intended to oppress and keep us low, in order to secure our dependence, may be subversive of this end. Poverty and oppression, among those whose minds are filled with ideas of British liberty, may introduce a virtuous industry, with a train of generous and manly sentiments."[8] And so it proved in the years that followed: as their Puritan forefathers had met providential disasters with a renewal of the virtue that would restore God's favor, the Revolutionary generation met taxation with a self-denial and industry that would hopefully restore their accustomed freedom and simultaneously enable them to identify with their virtuous ancestors.

The advocates of nonconsumption and nonimportation, in urging austerity on their countrymen, made very little of the effect that self-denial would have on the British government. Nonimportation and nonconsumption were preached as means of renewing ancestral virtues. Americans were reminded that they had been "of late years insensibly drawn into too great a degree of *luxury* and *dissipation*."[9] Parliamentary taxation was a blessing in disguise, because it produced the nonimportation and nonconsumption agreements. "Luxury," the people of the colonies were told, "has taken deep root among us, and to cure a people of luxury were an Herculean task indeed; what perhaps no power on earth but a British Parliament, in the very method they are taking with us, could possibly

---

[7] Arthur M. Schlesinger, *The Colonial Merchants and the American Revolution, 1763–1776* (New York, 1918), remains the best account of these movements.

[8] To [Unknown], May 31, 1764, in James C. Ballagh, ed., *The Letters of Richard Henry Lee* (New York, 1911), I, 7.

[9] *Boston Evening Post,* Nov. 16, 1767.

execute."[10] Parliamentary taxation, like an Indian attack in earlier years, was thus both a danger to be resisted and an act of providence to recall Americans from declension: "The Americans have plentifully enjoyed the delights and comforts, as well as the necessaries of life, and it is well known that an increase of wealth and affluence paves the way to an increase of luxury, immorality and profaneness, and here kind providence interposes; and as it were, obliges them to forsake the use of one of their delights, to preserve their liberty."[11] The principal object of this last homily was tea, which, upon being subjected to a Parliamentary duty, became luxurious and enervating. Physicians even discovered that it was bad for the health.[12]

In these appeals for self-denial, the Puritan Ethic acquired a value that had been only loosely associated with it hitherto: it became an essential condition of political liberty. An author who signed himself "Frugality" advised the readers of the *Newport Mercury* that "We may talk and boast of liberty; but after all, the industrious and frugal only will be free,"[13] free not merely because their self-denial would secure repeal of Parliamentary taxes, but because freedom was inseparable from virtue, and frugality and industry were the most conspicuous public virtues. The Americans were fortunate in having so direct and easy a way to preserve liberty, for importations, it now appeared, were mainly luxuries, "Baubles of Britain," "foreign trifles."[14] By barring their entrance, "by consuming *less* of what we are not really in want of, and by industriously cultivating and improving the natural advantages of our own country, we might save our *substance, even our lands,* from becoming the property of others, and we might effectually preserve our *virtue* and our *liberty,* to the latest posterity." Americans like Englishmen had long associated liberty with property. They now concluded that both rested on virtue: while liberty would expire without the support of property, property itself could not exist without industry and frugality. "Our enemies," they were assured, "very well know that dominion and property are closely connected; and that to impoverish us, is the surest way to enslave us. Therefore, if we mean still to be free, let us unanimously lay aside foreign superfluities, and encourage our own manufacture. SAVE YOUR MONEY AND YOU WILL SAVE YOUR COUNTRY!"[15]

There was one class of Americans who could take no comfort in this motto. The merchants, on whom nonimportation depended, stood to lose by the campaign for austerity, and it is not surprising that they showed less enthusiasm for it than the rest of the population. Their lukewarmness only served to heighten the suspicion with which their calling was still viewed. "Merchants have no country," Jefferson once remarked. "The mere spot they stand on does not constitute so strong an attachment as that from which they draw their gains."[16] And John

---

[10] *Va. Gazette* (Purdie and Dixon), June 1, 1769 (reprinted from *New York Chronicle*).

[11] *Newport Mercury,* Dec. 13, 1773.

[12] Ibid., Nov. 9, 1767, Nov. 29, 1773, Feb. 14, 28, 1774.

[13] Ibid., Feb. 28, 1774.

[14] *Boston Evening Post,* Nov. 9, 16, 1767; To Arthur Lee, Oct. 31, 1771, in H. A. Cushing, ed,, *The Writings of Samuel Adams* (New York, 1904–1908), II, 267.

[15] *Boston Evening Post,* Nov. 16, 1767; *Pennsylvania Journal* (Philadelphia), Dec. 10, 1767.

[16] To Horatio Spafford, Mar. 17, 1817, quoted in Boyd, ed., *Jefferson Papers,* XIV, 221.

Adams at the Continental Congress was warned by his wife's uncle that merchants "have no Object but their own particular Interest and they must be Contrould or they will ruin any State under Heaven."[17]

Such attitudes had been nourished by the merchants' behavior in the 1760's and 1770's. After repeal of the Stamp Act, Silas Downer, secretary of the Sons of Liberty in Providence, Rhode Island, wrote to the New York Sons of Liberty that "From many observations when the Stamp Act was new, I found that the Merchants in general would have quietly submitted, and many were zealous for it, always reciting the Difficulties their Trade would be cast into on Non Compliance, and never regarding the Interest of the whole Community."[18] When the Townshend Acts were passed, it was not the merchants but the Boston town meeting that took the lead in promoting nonimportation, and after the repeal of the Acts the merchants broke down and began importing while the duty on tea still remained. Samuel Adams had expected their defection to come much sooner for he recognized that the nonimportation agreements had "pressed hard upon their private Interest" while the majority of consumers could participate under the "happy Consideration that while they are most effectually serving their Country they are adding to their private fortunes."[19]

The merchants actually had more than a short-range interest at stake in their reluctance to undertake nonimportation. The movement, as we have seen, was not simply a means of securing repeal of the taxes to which merchants along with other colonists were opposed. The movement was in fact anticommercial, a repudiation of the merchant's calling. Merchants, it was said, encouraged men to go into debt. Merchants pandered to luxury. Since they made more on the sale of superfluous baubles than on necessities, they therefore pressed the sale of them to a weak and gullible public. What the advocates of nonimportation demanded was not merely an interruption of commerce but a permanent reduction, not to say elimination, of it. In its place they called for manufacturing, a palpably productive, useful calling.

The encouragement of manufacturing was an accompaniment to all the nonimportation, nonconsumption movements. New Yorkers organized a society specifically for that purpose, which offered bounties for the production of native textiles and other necessaries. The nonconsumption of mutton provided new supplies of wool, which housewives turned into thread in spinning matches (wheelwrights did a land-office business in spinning wheels). Stores began selling American cloth, and college students appeared at commencement in homespun. Tories ridiculed these efforts, and the total production was doubtless small, but it would be difficult to underestimate the importance of the attitude toward manufacturing that originated at this time. In a letter of Abigail Adams can be seen the way in which the Puritan Ethic was creating out of a Revolutionary protest movement the conception of a self-sufficient American economy. Abigail was writing to her husband, who was at the First Continental Congress, helping to

---

[17] Cotton Tufts to John Adams, Apr. 26, 1776, in L. H. Butterfield et al., eds., *Adams Family Correspondence* (Cambridge, Mass., 1963–), I, 395.

[18] Letter dated July 21, 1766, Peck Manuscripts, III, 3, Rhode Island Historical Society, Providence.

[19] To Stephen Sayre, Nov. 16, 1770, in Cushing, ed., *Writings of Samuel Adams,* II, 58.

frame the Continental Association for nonimportation, nonexportation, and nonconsumption:

> If we expect to inherit the blessings of our Fathers, we should return a little more to their primitive Simplicity of Manners, and not sink into inglorious ease. We have too many high sounding words, and too few actions that correspond with them. I have spent one Sabbeth in Town since you left me. I saw no difference in respect to ornaments, etc. etc. but in the Country you must look for that virtue, of which you find but small Glimerings in the Metropolis. Indeed they have not the advantages, nor the resolution to encourage their own Manufactories which people in the country have. To the Mercantile part, tis considerd as throwing away their own Bread; but they must retrench their expenses and be content with a small share of gain for they will find but few who will wear their Livery. As for me I will seek wool and flax and work willingly with my Hands, and indeed their is occasion for all our industry and economy.[20]

In 1774 manufacture retained its primitive meaning of something made by hand, and making things by hand seemed a fitting occupation for frugal country people who had always exhibited more of the Puritan Ethic than high-living city folk. Abigail's espousal of manufactures, with its defiant rejection of dependence on the merchants of the city, marks a step away from the traditional notion that America because of its empty lands and scarcity of people was unsuited to manufactures and must therefore obtain them from the Old World. Through the nonimportation movements the colonists discovered that manufacturing was a calling not beyond the capacities of a frugal, industrious people, however few in number, and that importation of British manufactures actually menaced frugality and industry. The result of the discovery was to make a connection with Britain seem neither wholly necessary nor wholly desirable, so that when the thought of independence at last came, it was greeted with less apprehension than it might otherwise have been.

Nonimportation had produced in effect a trial run in economic self-sufficiency. The trial was inconclusive as a demonstration of American economic capacity, but it carried immense significance intellectually, for it obliged the colonists to think about the possibility of an economy that would not be colonial. At the same time it confirmed them in the notion that liberty was the companion not only of property but of frugality and industry, two virtues that in turn fostered manufactures. The Puritan Ethic had shaped a protest movement into affirmations of value in which can be seen the glimmerings of a future national economic policy.

While engaged in their campaign of patriotic frugality, Americans were also articulating the political principles that they thought should govern free countries and that should bar Parliament from taxing them. The front line of defense against Parliament was the ancient maxim that a man could not be taxed except by his own consent given in person or by his representative. The colonists

---

[20] Oct. 16, 1774, in Butterfield, ed., *Adams Family Correspondence,* I, 173.

believed this to be an acknowledged principle of free government, indelibly stamped on the British Constitution, and they wrote hundreds of pages affirming it. In those pages the Puritan Ethic was revealed at the very root of the constitutional principle when taxation without representation was condemned as an assault on every man's calling. To tax a man without his consent, Samuel Adams said, was "against the plain and obvious rule of equity, whereby the industrious man is intitled to the fruits of his industry."[21] And the New York Assembly referred to the Puritan Ethic when it told Parliament that the effect of the sugar and stamp taxes would be to "dispirit the People, abate their Industry, discourage Trade, introduce Discord, Poverty, and Slavery."[22] In slavery, of course, there could be no liberty and no property and so no motive for frugality and industry. Uncontrolled Parliamentary taxation, like luxury and extravagance, was an attack not merely on property but on industry and frugality, for which liberty and property must be the expected rewards. With every protest that British taxation was reducing them to slavery, Americans reaffirmed their devotion to industry and frugality and their readiness to defy the British threat to them. Students of the American Revolution have often found it difficult to believe that the colonists were willing to fight about an abstract principle and have sometimes dismissed the constitutional arguments of the time as mere rhetoric. But the constitutional principle on which the colonists rested their case was not the product either of abstract political philosophy or of the needs of the moment. In the colonists' view, it was a means, hallowed by history, of protecting property and of maintaining those virtues, associated with property, without which no people could be free. Through the rhetoric, if it may be called that, of the Puritan Ethic, the colonists reached behind the constitutional principle to the enduring human needs that had brought the principle into being.

We may perhaps understand better the urgency both of the constitutional argument and of the drive toward independence that it ultimately generated, if we observe the growing suspicion among the colonists that the British government had betrayed its own constitution and the values which that constitution protected. In an earlier generation the colonists had vied with one another in praising the government of England. Englishmen, they believed, had suffered again and again from invasion and tyranny, had each time recovered control of their government, and in the course of centuries had developed unparalleled constitutional safeguards to keep rulers true to their callings. The calling of a ruler, as the colonists and their Puritan forebears saw it, was like any other calling: it must serve the common good; it must be useful, productive; and it must be assiduously pursued. After the Glorious Revolution of 1688, Englishmen had fashioned what seemed a nearly perfect instrument of government, a constitution that blended monarchy, aristocracy, and democracy in a mixture designed to avoid the defects and secure the benefits of each. But something had gone wrong. The human capacity for corruption had transformed the balanced government of King, Lords, and Commons into a single-minded body of rulers bent on their own enrichment and heedless of the public good.

---

[21] [*Boston Gazette,* Dec. 19, 1768], in Cushing, ed., *Writings of Samuel Adams,* I, 271.

[22] E. S. Morgan, ed., *Prologue to Revolution: Sources and Documents on the Stamp Act Crisis, 1764–1766* (Chapel Hill, 1959), 13.

A principal means of corruption had been the multiplication of officeholders who served no useful purpose but fattened on the labors of those who did the country's work. Even before the dispute over taxation began, few colonists who undertook trips to England failed to make unflattering comparisons between the simplicity, frugality, and industry that prevailed in the colonies and the extravagance, luxury, idleness, drunkenness, poverty, and crime that they saw in the mother country. To Americans bred on the values of the Puritan Ethic, England seemed to have fallen prey to her own opulence, and the government shared heavily in the corruption. In England, the most powerful country in the world, the visitors found the people laboring under a heavy load of taxes, levied by a government that swarmed with functionless placeholders and pensioners. The cost of government in the colonies, as Professor Gipson has shown, was vastly lower than in England, with the per capita burden of taxation only a fraction of that which Englishmen bore.[23] And whatever the costs of maintaining the empire may have contributed to the British burden, it was clear that the English taxpayers supported a large band of men who lived well from offices that existed only to pay their holders. Even an American like George Croghan, who journeyed to London to promote dubious speculative schemes of his own, felt uncomfortable in the presence of English corruption: "I am Nott Sorry I Came hear," he wrote, "as it will Larn Me to be Contented on a Litle farm in amerrica. . . . I am Sick of London and harttily Tierd of the pride and pompe."[24]

In the 1760s Americans were given the opportunity to gain the perspective of a Croghan without the need for a trip abroad. The Townshend Acts called for a reorganization of the customs service with a new set of higher officials, who would perforce be paid out of the duties they extracted from the colonists. In the establishment of this American Board of Customs Commissioners, Americans saw the extension of England's corrupt system of officeholding to America. As Professor Dickerson has shown, the Commissioners were indeed corrupt.[25] They engaged in extensive "customs racketeering" and they were involved in many of the episodes that heightened the tension between England and the colonies: it was on their request that troops were sent to Boston; the Boston Massacre took place before their headquarters; the *Gaspée* was operating under their orders. But it was not merely the official actions of the Commissioners that offended Americans. Their very existence seemed to pose a threat both to the Puritan Ethic and to the conscientious, frugal kind of government that went with it. Hitherto colonial governments had been relatively free of the evils that had overtaken England. But now the horde of placeholders was descending on America.

From the time the Commissioners arrived in Boston in November 1767, the newspapers were filled with complaints that "there can be no such thing as common good or common cause where mens estates are ravaged at pleasure to lavish on parasitical minions."[26] Samuel Adams remarked that the commissioners were

[23] L. H. Gipson, *The British Empire Before the American Revolution* . . . (New York, 1936–), X, 53–110; Gipson, *The Coming of the Revolution 1763–1775* (New York, 1954), 116–161.

[24] Quoted in T. P. Abernethy, *Western Lands and the American Revolution* (New York, 1937), 24.

[25] O. M. Dickerson, *The Navigation Acts and the American Revolution* (Philadelphia, 1951), 208–265.

[26] *Boston Evening Post*, Nov. 30, 1767.

"a useless and very expensive set of officers" and that they had power to appoint "as many officers under them as they please, for whose Support it is said they may sink the whole revenue."[27] American writers protested against the "legions of idle, lazy, and to say no worse, altogether useless customs house locusts, catterpillars, flies and lice."[28] They were "a parcel of dependant tools of arbitrary power, sent hither to enrich themselves and their Masters, on the Spoil of the honest and industrious of these colonies."[29] By 1774, when the debate between colonies and Parliament was moving into its final stages, town meetings could state it as an intolerable grievance "that so many unnecessary officers are supported by the earnings of honest industry, in a life of dissipation and ease; who, by being *properly* employed, might be useful members of society."[30]

The coming of the Customs Commissioners showed the colonists that the ocean barrier which had hitherto isolated them from the corruption of Britain was no longer adequate. Eventually, perhaps, Englishmen would again arise, turn out the scoundrels, and recall their government to its proper tasks. And Americans did not fail to support Englishmen like John Wilkes whom they thought to be working toward this end. But meanwhile they could not ignore the dangers on their own shores. There would henceforth be in their midst a growing enclave of men whose lives and values denied the Puritan Ethic; and there would be an increasing number of lucrative offices to tempt Americans to desert ancestral standards and join the ranks of the "parasitical minions." No American was sure that his countrymen would be able to resist the temptation. In 1766, after repeal of the Stamp Act, George Mason had advised the merchants of London that Americans were "not yet debauched by wealth, luxury, venality and corruption."[31] But who could say how long their virtue would withstand the closer subjection to British control that Whitehall seemed to be designing? Some Americans believed that the British were deliberately attempting to undermine the Puritan Ethic. In Boston Samuel Adams observed in 1771 that "the Conspirators against our Liberties are employing all their Influence to divide the people, . . . introducing Levity Luxury and Indolence and assuring them that if they are quiet the Ministry will alter their Measures."[32] And in 1772 Henry Marchant, a Rhode Island traveler in England wrote to his friend Ezra Stiles: "You will often hear the following Language—Damn those Fellows we shall never do any Thing with Them till we root out that cursed puritanick Spirit—How is this to be done?—keep Soldiers amongst Them, not so much to awe Them, as to debauch their Morals—Toss off to them all the Toies and Baubles that genius can invent to weaken their Minds, fill Them with Pride and Vanity, and beget in them all possible Extravagance in Dress and Living, that They may be kept poor and made wretched."[33]

---

[27] To Dennys De Berdt, May 14, 1768, in Cushing, ed., *Writings of Samuel Adams,* I, 216.

[28] *Newport Mercury,* June 21, 1773.

[29] Ibid., July 13, 1772.

[30] Resolves of Bristol, R. I., ibid., Mar. 21, 1774.

[31] Morgan, *Prologue to Revolution,* 160.

[32] To Arthur Lee, Oct. 31, 1771, in Cushing, ed., *Writings of Samuel Adams,* II, 266–267.

[33] Quoted in E. S. Morgan, *The Gentle Puritan: A Life of Ezra Stiles, 1727–1795* (New Haven, 1962), 265.

By the time the First Continental Congress came together in 1774, large numbers of leading Americans had come to identify Great Britain with vice and America with virtue, yet with the fearful recognition that virtue stands in perennial danger from the onslaughts of vice. Patrick Henry gave voice to the feeling when he denounced Galloway's plan for an intercolonial American legislature that would stand between the colonies and Parliament. "We shall liberate our Constituents," he warned, "from a corrupt House of Commons, but thro[w] them into the Arms of an American Legislature that may be bribed by that Nation which avows in the Face of the World, that Bribery is a Part of her System of Government."[34] A government that had succeeded in taxing seven million Englishmen (with the consent of their supposed representatives), to support an army of placeholders, would have no hesitation in using every means to corrupt the representatives of two and one half million Americans.

When the Second Congress met in 1775, Benjamin Franklin, fresh from London, could assure the members that their contrast of England and America was justified. Writing back to Joseph Priestley, he said it would "scarce be credited in Britain, that men can be as diligent with us from zeal for the public good, as with you for thousands per annum. Such is the difference between uncorrupted new states, and corrupted old ones."[35] Thomas Jefferson drew the contrast even more bluntly in an answer rejecting Lord North's Conciliatory Proposal of February 20, 1775, which had suggested that Parliament could make provisions for the government of the colonies. "The provisions we have made," said Jefferson, "are such as please our selves, and are agreeable to our own circumstances; they answer the substantial purposes of government and of justice, and other purposes than these should not be answered. We do not mean that our people shall be burthened with oppressive taxes to provide sinecures for the idle or the wicked."[36]

When Congress finally dissolved the political bands that had connected America with England, the act was rendered less painful by the colonial conviction that America and England were already separated as virtue is from vice. The British Constitution had foundered, and the British government had fallen into the hands of a luxurious and corrupt ruling class. There remained no way of preserving American virtue unless the connection with Britain was severed. The meaning of virtue in this context embraced somewhat more than the values of the Puritan Ethic, but those values were pre-eminent in it. In the eyes of many Americans the Revolution was a defense of industry and frugality, whether in rulers or people, from the assaults of British vice. The Puritan Ethic, in the colonists' political as in their economic thinking, prepared the way for independence.

89

[34] Sept. 28, 1774, in L. H. Butterfield et. al., eds., *Diary and Autobiography of John Adams* (Cambridge, Mass., 1961), II, 143.

[35] July 6, 1775, in E. C. Burnett, ed., *Letters of Members of The Continental Congress* (Washington, 1921–1936), I, 156.

[36] July 31, 1775, in Boyd, ed., *Jefferson Papers,* I, 232.

II. Who Should Rule at Home

Virtue, as everyone knew, was a fragile and probably fleeting possession. Even while defending it from the British, Americans worried about their own uneasy hold on it and eyed one another for signs of its departure. The war, of course, furnished the conditions of adversity in which virtue could be expected to flourish. On the day after Congress voted independence, John Adams wrote exultantly to Abigail of the difficulties ahead: "It may be the Will of Heaven that America shall suffer Calamities still more wasting and Distresses yet more dreadfull. If this is to be the Case, it will have this good Effect, at least: it will inspire Us with many Virtues, which We have not, and correct many Errors, Follies, and Vices, which threaten to disturb, dishonour, and destroy Us.—The Furnace of Affliction produces Refinement, in States as well as Individuals."[37] Thereafter, as afflictions came, Adams welcomed them in good Puritan fashion. But the war did not prove a sufficient spur to virtue, and by the fall of 1776 Adams was already observing that "There is too much Corruption, even in this infant Age of our Republic. Virtue is not in Fashion. Vice is not infamous."[38] Sitting with the Congress in Philadelphia, he privately yearned for General Howe to capture the town, because the ensuing hardship "would cure Americans of their vicious and luxurious and effeminate Appetites, Passions and Habits, a more dangerous Army to American Liberty than Mr. Howes."[39]

Within a year or two Americans would begin to look back on 1775 and 1776 as a golden age, when vice had given way to heroic self-denial, and luxury and corruption had not yet raised their heads. In revolutionary America as in Puritan New England the virtues of the Puritan Ethic must be quickened by laments for their loss.

Many of these eighteenth-century lamentations seem perfunctory—mere nostalgic ritual in which men purged their sins by confessing their inferiority to their fathers. But in the years after 1776 the laments were prompted by a genuine uneasiness among the Revolutionists about their own worthiness for the role they had undertaken. In the agitation against Britain they had repeatedly told themselves that liberty could not live without virtue. Having cast off the threat posed to both liberty and virtue by a corrupt monarchy, they recognized that the republican governments they had created must depend for their success on the virtue, not of a king or of a few aristocrats, but of an entire people. Unless the virtue of Americans proved equal to its tasks, liberty would quickly give way once again to tyranny and perhaps a worse tyranny than that of George III.

As Americans faced the problems of independence, the possibility of failure did not seem remote. By recalling the values that had inspired the resistance to British taxation they hoped to lend success to their venture in republican government. The Puritan Ethic thus continued to occupy their consciousness (and their letters, diaries, newspapers, and pamphlets) and to provide the framework within which alternatives were debated and sides taken.

---

[37] July 3, 1776, in Butterfield, ed., *Adams Family Correspondence,* II, 28.

[38] John to Abigail Adams, Sept. 22, 1776, ibid., II, 131.

[39] Same to same, Sept. 8, 1777, ibid., II, 338. Cf. pp. 169–170, 326.

Next to the task of defeating the British armies, perhaps the most urgent problem that confronted the new nation was to prove its nationality, for no one was certain that independent Americans would be able to get on with one another. Before the Revolution there had been many predictions, both European and American, that if independence were achieved it would be followed by bloody civil wars among the states, which would eventually fall prostrate before some foreign invader. The anticipated civil war did not take place for eighty-five years. Americans during those years were not without divisions, but they did manage to stay together. Their success in doing so, exemplified in the adoption of the Constitution of 1787, demonstrated that the divisions among them were less serious than they themselves had realized. Without attempting to examine the nature of the debates over the Constitution itself, I should like to show how the Puritan Ethic, while contributing to divisions among Americans, also furnished both sides with a common set of values that limited the extent and bitterness of divisions and thus helped to make a United States Constitution possible.

In the period after 1776 perhaps the most immediate threat to the American union was the possibility that the secession of the United States from Great Britain would be followed by a secession of the lower Mississippi and Ohio valleys from the United States. The gravity of the threat, which ended with the fiasco of the Burr Conspiracy, is difficult to assess, but few historians would deny that real friction between East and West existed.

The role of the Puritan Ethic in the situation was characteristic: each side tended to see the other as deficient in the same virtues. To westerners the eastern-dominated governments seemed to be in the grip of speculators and merchants determined to satisfy their own avarice by sacrificing the interests of the industrious farmers of the West. To easterners, or at least to some easterners, the West seemed to be filling up with shiftless adventurers, as lazy and lawless and unconcerned with the values of the Puritan Ethic as were the native Indians. Such men were unworthy of a share in government and must be restrained in their restless hunt for land and furs; they must be made to settle down and build civilized communities where industry and frugality would thrive.

The effects of these attitudes cannot be demonstrated at length here, but may be suggested by the views of a key figure, John Jay. As early as 1779, the French Ambassador, Conrad Alexandre Gérard, had found Jay one of the most reasonable members of Congress, that is, one of the members most ready to fall in with the Ambassador's instructions to discourage American expansion. Jay belonged to a group which suggested that Spain ought to close the Mississippi to American navigation in order to keep the settlers of the West "from living in a half-savage condition." Presumably the group reasoned that the settlers were mostly fur traders; if they were prevented from trading their furs through New Orleans, they might settle down to farming and thus achieve "an attachment to property and industry."[40] Whatever the line of reasoning, the attitude toward the West is clear, and

---

[40] John J. Meng, ed., *Despatches and Instructions of Conrad Alexandre Gérard . . .* (Baltimore, 1939), 531. Gérard reported of this group in February, 1779, "qu'ils desiroient fortement que Sa Majesté Catholique tint la clef du Mississippi de sorte que personne n'entrât du Mississippi dans l'Ocean ni de l'Ocean dans ce fleuve; mais qu'il falloit du Commerce aux peuplades dont il s'agit; que par là seulement on pourroit les empêcher de demeurer à demi Sauvages en les attachant à la propriété et à l'industrie."

Jay obliged the French Ambassador by volunteering the opinion that the United States was already too large.[41]

In 1786 Jay offered similar opinions to Jefferson, suggesting that settlement of the West should be more gradual, that Americans should be prevented from pitching their tents "through the Wilderness in a great Variety of Places, far distant from each other, and from those Advantages of Education, Civilization, Law, and Government which compact Settlements and Neighbourhood afford."[42] It is difficult to believe that Jay was unaffected by this attitude in the negotiations he was carrying on with the Spanish envoy Gardoqui over the right of the United States to navigate the Mississippi. When Jay presented Congress with a treaty in which the United States agreed to forgo navigation of the Mississippi in return for commercial concessions in Spain, it seemed, to westerners at least, that the United States Secretary for Foreign Affairs was willing to sacrifice their interests in favor of his merchant friends in the East.

Fortunately the conflict was not a lasting one. Jay was misinformed about the West, for the advance wave of fur traders and adventurers who pitched their tents far apart occupied only a brief moment in the history of any part of the West. The tens of thousands of men who entered Kentucky and Tennessee in the 1780s came to farm the rich lands, and they carried the values of the Puritan Ethic with them. As this fact became apparent, conflict subsided. Throughout American history, in fact, the West was perpetually turning into a new East, complete with industrious inhabitants, spurred by adversity, and pursuing their callings with an assiduity that the next generation would lament as lost.

Another sectional conflict was not so transitory. The South was not in the process of becoming northern or the North southern. And their differing interests were already discernible in the 1780s, at least to an astute observer like James Madison, as the primary source of friction among Americans. The difference arose, he believed, "principally from the effects of their having or not having slaves."[43]

The bearing of the Puritan Ethic on slavery, as on many other institutions, was complex and ambivalent. It heightened the conflict between those who did and those who did not have slaves. But it also, for a time at least, set limits to the conflict by offering a common ground on which both sides could agree in deploring the institution.

The Puritans themselves had not hesitated to enslave Indian captives or to sell and buy slaves. At the opening of the Revolution no state prohibited slavery. But the institution obviously violated the precepts of the Puritan Ethic: it deprived men of the fruits of their labor and thus removed a primary motive for industry and frugality. How it came into existence in the first place among a people devoted to the Puritan Ethic is a question not yet solved, but as soon as Americans began complaining of Parliament's assault on their liberty and property, it was difficult not to see the inconsistency of continuing to hold slaves. "I wish most

92

[41] Ibid., 433–434, 494.

[42] Dec. 14, 1786, in Boyd, ed., *Jefferson Papers*, X, 599.

[43] In Convention, June 30, 1787, in C. C. Tansill, ed., *Documents Illustrative of the Formation of the Union of the American States* (Washington, 1927), 310.

sincerely," Abigail Adams wrote to her husband in 1774, "there was not a Slave in the province. It allways appeard a most iniquitous Scheme to me—fight our-selfs for what we are daily robbing and plundering from those who have as good a right to freedom as we have."[44] Newspaper articles everywhere made the same point. As a result, slavery was gradually abolished in the northern states (where it was not important in the economy), and the self-righteousness with which New Englanders already regarded their southern neighbors was thereby heightened.

Although the South failed to abolish slavery, southerners like northerners recognized the threat it posed to the values that all Americans held. Partly as a result of that recognition, more slaves were freed by voluntary manumission in the South than by legal and constitutional abolition in the North. There were other reasons for hostility to slavery in both North and South, including fear of insurrection, humanitarianism, and apprehension of the wrath of God; but a pre-dominant reason, in the South at least, was the evil effect of slavery on the indus-try and frugality of both master and slave, but especially of the master.

A perhaps extreme example of this argument, divested of all considerations of justice and humanity, appeared in a Virginia newspaper in 1767. The author (who signed himself "Philanthropos"!) proposed to abolish slavery in Virginia by having the government lay a prohibitory duty on importation and then purchase one tenth of everyone's slaves every year. The purchase price would be recovered by selling the slaves in the West Indies. Philanthropos acknowledged that slaves were "used with more barbarity" in the West Indies than in Virginia but offered them the consolation "that this sacrifice of themselves will put a quicker period to a miserable life." To emancipate them and leave them in Virginia would be fatal, because they would probably "attempt to arrive at our possessions by force, rather than wait the tedious operation of labour, industry and time." But unless slavery was abolished in Virginia, the industry and frugality of the free population would expire. As it was, said Philanthropos, when a man got a slave or two, he sat back and stopped working. Promising young men failed to take up productive occupa-tions because they could get jobs as overseers. By selling off their slaves in the West Indies, Virginians would get the money to import white indentured servants and would encourage "our own common people, who would no longer be diverted from industry by the prospect of overseers places, to [enter] agriculture and the arts."[45]

Few opponents of slavery were so callous, but even the most humane stressed the effect of slavery on masters and the problems of instilling the values of indus-try in emancipated slaves. Thomas Jefferson hated slavery, but he hated idleness equally, and he would not have been willing to abolish slavery without making arrangements to preserve the useful activity it exacted from its victims. He had heard of one group of Virginia slaves who had been freed by their Quaker owners and kept as tenants on the land. The results had been unsatisfactory, because the ex-slaves had lacked the habits of industry and "chose to steal from their neigh-bors rather than work." Jefferson had plans to free his own slaves (after he freed himself from his creditors) by a gradual system which provided means for educat-ing the Negroes into habits of industry.[46] But Jefferson never put his scheme into

[44] Sept. 22, 1774, in Butterfield, ed., *Adams Family Correspondence,* I, 162.

[45] Reprinted in *Pa. Chronicle,* Aug. 31-Sept. 7, 1767. The Virginia paper in which it originally appeared has not been found.

[46] To Edward Bancroft, Jan. 26, 1788, in Boyd, ed., *Jefferson Papers,* XIV, 492.

practice. He and most other Southerners continued to hold slaves, and the result was as predicted: slavery steadily eroded the honor accorded work among southerners.

During the Revolutionary epoch, however, the erosion had not yet proceeded far enough to alienate North from South. Until well into the nineteenth century Southerners continued to deplore the effects of slavery on the industry and frugality at least of the whites. Until the North began to demand immediate abolition and the South began to defend slavery as a permanent blessing, leaders of the two sections could find a good deal of room for agreement in the shared values of the Puritan Ethic.

The fact that Americans of different sections could remain united came as something of a surprise. Even more surprising, so surprising that for a long time few could believe it, was the fact that party divisions in politics, instead of hindering, actually helped the cause of union. Parties or "factions" had been everywhere denounced in the eighteenth century. When men disagreed on political issues, each side was likely to accuse the other of being a party. Advocates of any measure preceded their arguments by disclaiming adherence to a party. And the last thing that the architects of the American national government wanted or anticipated was that it would fall into the hands of parties. But that of course is precisely what happened, and the result proved to be a blessing.

The unexpected success of the American party system has been the subject of continuous comment and congratulation among historians and political scientists ever since. Success, it seems clear, has depended in large part on the absence of any clear ideological difference between the major parties. It would be difficult, for example, for any but the most experienced historian, if presented with the Republican and Democratic platforms of the past hundred years, to distinguish one from the other. Our political disputes are peaceful, because both parties espouse similar principles and objectives and neither feels itself severely threatened by the other. And yet in any given issue or election neither side has difficulty in identifying friends and enemies. The members of any party recognize their own kind.

This situation has prevailed in American national politics from the outset. In the Continental Congress and in the first Congresses under the new Constitution, political divisions were unorganized. In the Continental Congress, partly because of rotation in office, groupings were transitory. But one finds the same absence of ideological difference and the same recognition by political partisans of their own kind. In the absence of party organization, one can see in these early divisions, even more clearly than in later ones, the forces that led some men to join one side and others another.[47]

---

[47] A work of major importance is Herbert James Henderson, "Party Politics in the Continental Congress, 1774–1783" (unpubl. Ph.D. diss., Columbia University, 1962). I arrived at the conclusions presented in the succeeding pages of this section, about the nature of the divisions in Congress in 1778 and 1779, by reading in the letters and papers of the members and then examining votes on specific issues. Dr. Henderson, who kindly allowed me to read his manuscript after my own investigation was completed, had independently studied the divisions in Congress during its first ten years, starting from an exhaustive statistical analysis of the voting. His study, which goes far beyond what I have attempted here, will greatly advance our understanding both of the American Revolution and of the origins of American political parties.

The first serious division in national politics after independence occurred in 1778 and 1779 over the conduct of the American envoy to France, Silas Deane; and the men who voted together in the divisions on that question often voted together on other seemingly unrelated questions. On each side, in other words, a kind of party was formed. If we examine the men on each side, together with their avowed principles and their application of those principles, if we examine the way a man regarded men on his own side and men on the other side, we will discover, I believe, that the Puritan Ethic, in this period at least, helped both to create political parties and to limit the differences between them.

The facts in the case of Silas Deane will probably never be fully known.[48] The question at issue was whether Deane had used public funds and public office for private gain, as was charged by another American agent abroad, Arthur Lee. When challenged by Congress, Deane was unable to produce vouchers to account for his expenditures, but he consistently maintained that the money had been spent on legitimate public business; and in the private papers that have survived he never admitted, even to himself, that he had done anything wrong. We know now a good deal more about him than the members of Congress did. We know, for example, that his close associate, Edward Bancroft, was a double agent. We know that Deane did engage in private speculation while in public office. But we still do not know that his transactions were any more dubious than those of, say, Robert Morris, who also mingled public and private funds and by so doing emerged as the financier of the Revolution. The members of Congress in 1778 and 1779, knowing even less than we do, were obliged to decide whether to honor Silas Deane's accounts. In a series of votes on questions relating to this issue the members had to make up their minds with very little to go on. Under the circumstances, it would not be surprising if they lined up according to the way in which Silas Deane struck them as a man. Those who found him to be their sort of person would take one side; those who distrusted that sort of person would take the other side.

What sort of person, then, was Silas Deane? He was, to begin with, an able man. He made a good impression at the First Continental Congress, and when Connecticut dropped him from its delegation, Congress sent him to France. In France he was indubitably successful in securing the supplies that made possible the success of the American armies at Saratoga. After Congress dismissed him and refused to honor his accounts, Deane became disillusioned with the patriot cause and in a series of letters to friends in Connecticut, unfortunately intercepted by the British, he argued that the war and the French alliance had corrupted his countrymen and that independence would consequently prove a curse instead of a blessing. In his native Connecticut he said, he had seen "thousands of industrious youth forced from the plough and other useful, homely occupations, and prematurely destroyed by the diseases, wants, and sufferings of a military life, whilst

95

---

[48] The complexity of the problems involved can be appreciated by anyone who reads the *Deane Papers,* published by the New-York Historical Society in its *Collections for 1886–1890.* Important aspects of the case are presented in Thomas P. Abernethy, "Commercial Activities of Silas Deane in France," *American Historical Review,* XXXIX (1933–1934), 477–485; Samuel F. Bemis, "British Secret Service and the French-American Alliance," ibid., XXIX (1923–24), 474–495; and Julian P. Boyd "Silas Deane: Death by a Kindly Teacher of Treason?" *William and Mary Quarterly,* 3d Ser., XVI (1959), 165–187, 319–342, 515–550.

the survivors, by exchanging their plain morals and honest industry for the habits of idleness and vice, appeared more likely to burthen than to benefit their country hereafter."[49] Silas Deane could avow his attachment to the values of the Puritan Ethic as ardently as any man.

But avowing the values was not quite the same as exemplifying them, and Deane as a person exhibited none of the moral austerity that ardent practitioners of the Puritan Ethic demanded. John Adams, always sensitive in these matters, was Deane's successor in the American mission to France. There he observed with distaste that Deane had taken extravagant lodgings in Paris in addition to his quarters with Benjamin Franklin at Passy.[50] Adams, though he always found Franklin's company trying, preferred to put up with it rather than cause the United States extra expense. Adams later recalled Deane as "a person of a plausible readiness and Volubility with his Tongue and his Pen, much addicted to Ostentation and Expence in Dress and Living but without any deliberate forecast or reflection or solidity of Judgment, or real Information."[51] Deane, on the other hand, found Adams absurdly spartan. "This man," he wrote, "who may have read much, appears to have retained nothing, except law knowledge and the fierce and haughty manners of the Lacedemonians and first Romans. These he has adopted as a perfect model to form a modern republican by."[52] If Adams could have read the criticism, he would have taken it as a tribute.

Adams, of course, was not a member of Congress when the Deane case was under debate, but Deane's characterization of Adams could easily have applied to the three men who led the fight against Deane: Samuel Adams of Massachusetts, Richard Henry Lee of Virginia, and Henry Laurens of South Carolina.

Samuel Adams thought of the Revolution as a holy war to save America from British corruption, and corruption to Adams meant luxury, extravagance, and avarice. During the nonimportation crusade he had worried about such weaknesses in the merchant battalion; and after independence merchants still failed to live up to the standards he expected of Americans. In 1778, detecting a spirit of avarice in Boston, he remarked, "but it rages only among the few, because perhaps, the few only are concerned at present in trade."[53] Even a little avarice was too much, however, for Adams, who had visions of Boston as the Sparta of America. Writing from Philadelphia to a Boston friend, he expressed concern about reports that the city had become exceedingly gay in appearance. "I would fain hope," he said, "this is confind to Strangers. Luxury and Extravagance are in my opinion totally destructive of those Virtues which are necessary for the Preservation of the Liberty and Happiness of the People. Is it true that the Review of the Boston Militia was closd with an expensive Entertainment? If it was, and the Example is followed by the Country, I hope I shall be excusd when I venture to pledge myself, that the Militia of that State will never be put on such a Footing as to become formidable to its Enemies."[54]

---

[49] To Jesse Root, May 20, 1781, in *Deane Papers,* IV, 350.

[50] Apr. 1778, in Butterfield, ed., *Diary and Autobiography of John Adams,* IV, 42.

[51] Nov.-Dec. 1775, ibid., III, 340.

[52] To John Jay, Nov. 1780, in *Deane Papers,* IV, 262.

[53] To Francis Lee [?] 1778, in Cushing, ed., *Writings of Samuel Adams,* IV, 19.

[54] To Samuel Savage, Oct. 6, 1778, ibid., IV, 67–68.

Richard Henry Lee, a brother of the man who first accused Deane, was a Virginia gentleman planter but not so strange an ally for Samuel Adams, as he might at first seem to be. The two had been in correspondence even before the First Continental Congress, and there they had sided together from the beginning. Although Lee was an Anglican and a slave-owner, he had spoken out against slavery (condemning it for its ill effect on industriousness) and by 1779 he was contemplating retirement to Massachusetts. "The hasty, unpersevering, aristocratic genius of the south," he confessed, "suits not my disposition, and is inconsistent with my ideas of what must constitute social happiness and security."[55] Lee never carried out his intention of retiring to Massachusetts and probably would not have been happy if he had, but he sometimes must have struck his contemporaries as a New Englander manqué. The French Ambassador Gérard not surprisingly mistook him for a Presbyterian, for he had, according to Gérard, "the severity of manners, and the gravity that is natural to Presbyterians."[56]

Lee had begun his attacks on political corruption in 1764 by sniffing out a scandal in the Virginia government: the Speaker of the House of Burgesses, John Robinson, who was also Treasurer, had been lending vast amounts in public funds to his political friends, and his friends included some of the best families in Virginia. The people involved were able to hush things up, but they did not forgive Lee for demanding an investigation.[57] The Deane affair, then, was not the first time he had caught men in high office with their fingers in the public till.

Henry Laurens, like Lee, was an Anglican, but the description of him by a fellow South Carolinian, David Ramsay, who knew him well, makes Laurens, too, sound like a Puritan: "In the performance of his religious duties Mr. Laurens was strict and exemplary. The emergency was great which kept him from church either forenoon or afternoon, and very great indeed which kept him from his regular monthly communion. With the bible he was intimately acquainted. Its doctrines he firmly believed, its precepts and history he admired, and was much in the habit of quoting and applying portions of it to present occurrences. He not only read the scriptures diligently to his family, but made all his children read them also. His family bible contained in his own hand-writing several of his remarks on passing providences." Ramsay also tells us that Laurens frowned on cardplaying and gambling. On some occasions in Charleston society when he could not avoid playing cards without being rude, he promptly paid if he lost, "but uniformly refused to receive what he won, esteeming it wrong to take any man's money without giving an equivalent."[58]

Laurens had himself been a merchant and a very methodical and assiduous one. After making a fortune, he transferred his activities from trade to planting. He seldom slept more than four hours a day, and he had a low opinion of gentlemen of leisure. Like Richard Henry Lee he had had a brush with corruption in

---

[55] Burnett, ed., *Letters of Members,* II, 155.

[56] "la sévérité des moeurs, et la gravité naturelle aux Presbytériens." Meng, ed., *Despatches of Gérard,* 569.

[57] Burton J. Hendrick, *The Lees of Virginia: Biography of a Family* (Boston, 1935), 101–105; David J. Mays, *Edmund Pendleton, 1721–1803: A Biography* (Cambridge, Mass., 1952), I, 174–208.

[58] David Ramsay, *The History of South Carolina from its first Settlement in 1670 to the Year 1808* (Charleston, 1809), II, 484, 485.

high places earlier in his career when the customs officers in Charleston seized a ship of his on a flimsy pretext. They had offered to release the ship in return for a bribe. Laurens had indignantly refused, and the officers, in collusion with a judge of the Admiralty Court, had succeeded in having the ship condemned and sold. Laurens had then written and published an account of the whole affair, including the attempt to shake him down.[59]

It was this episode that converted Laurens from staunch support of British authority to a deep suspicion of British corruption. But avarice among his own countrymen perturbed him even more. At the time when the Deane case came up, Laurens was serving as president of the Continental Congress. He had already denounced the "sacrilegious Robberies of public Money" by congressmen and military officers carrying on private trade in army supplies.[60] A little later he observed that many members of Congress, doubtless because they were themselves engaged in such practices, were ready to defend them, so that "he must be a pitiful rogue indeed, who, when detected, or suspected, meets not with powerful advocates among those, who in the present corrupt time, ought to exert all their powers in defence and support of these friend-plundered, much injured, and I was almost going to say, sinking States."[61]

Although Laurens was a merchant, he was so shocked by the activities of other merchants in and out of Congress that he wrote in despair in 1779: "Reduce us all to poverty and cut off or wisely restrict that bane of patriotism, Commerce, and we shall soon become Patriots, but how hard is it for a rich or covetous Man to enter heartily into the Kingdom of Patriotism?"[62] When Congress voted what Laurens considered too high salaries for the secretaries of its ministry abroad and elected Laurens's son to one of these positions, Laurens protested and informed his son that "men who are sincerely devoted to the service of their Country will not accept of Salaries which will tend to distress it."[63]

It is impossible to examine here the rank and file of Deane's opponents, but perhaps enough has been said to suggest what sort of person disliked Deane. It will come as no surprise that Deane's supporters were men more like himself. A principal supporter, of course, was Robert Morris, who had engaged deeply in trading enterprises with Deane but whose commercial empire extended throughout the country. At the outset of Deane's mission to France, Morris had directed him in both his private and his public investments and had advised him that "there never has been so fair an oppertunity of making a large Fortune."[64] At the time of the Deane affair, Morris was not a member of Congress, but he remained in Philadelphia, served in the Pennsylvania Assembly, and helped to marshal support for Deane. Deane's other defenders, like his opponents, were too numerous to bear examination in detail here, but they included men from the same states as his principal opponents.

---

[59] David D. Wallace, *The Life of Henry Laurens* . . . (New York, 1915); Dickerson, *Navigation Acts,* 224–231.

[60] Laurens to Rawlins Lowndes, May 17, 1778, in Burnett, ed., *Letters of Members,* III, 248.

[61] Laurens to John Houstoun, Aug. 27 [1778], ibid., III, 385.

[62] Laurens to William Livingston, Apr. 19 [1779], ibid., IV, 163.

[63] H. Laurens to John Laurens, Oct. 5, 1779, ibid., IV, 467.

[64] From Robert Morris, Aug. 11, 1776, in *Deane Papers,* I, 176.

In Massachusetts John Hancock was a Deane man, and it was Hancock who had provided the expensive entertainment for the militia which so disturbed Samuel Adams. Indeed Hancock, when inaugurated as Governor of Massachusetts in 1780, scandalized Adams by sponsoring a whole series of balls and parties. By introducing such "Scenes of Dissipation and Folly" Adams believed that Hancock endangered public virtue, and when virtue departed, liberty would accompany it. Adams accordingly considered Hancock a peril to the republic, as dangerous as the British.[65]

In Virginia Deane's supporters included most of the congressional delegates, apart from the Lees. Benjamin Harrison's position can be anticipated from John Adams's characterization of him at the Second Continental Congress as "an indolent, luxurious, heavy Gentleman," and as "another Sir John Falstaff, excepting in his Larcenies and Robberies, his Conversation disgusting to every Man of Delicacy or decorum, Obscaene, profane, impious, perpetually ridiculing the Bible, calling it the Worst Book in the World."[66] In Congress Harrison associated frequently with Hancock. He was also engaged in business with Robert Morris. When he got his son made Deputy Paymaster General of the Southern District, the son made a secret agreement with Morris to charge a premium of 2 per cent on any bills that either drew on the other in connection with public business.[67]

Carter Braxton, another supporter of Deane from Virginia was discovered in 1778 to have made a dubious deal with Morris and in 1779 was censured by Congress for sponsoring a privateer which captured a Portuguese vessel, an act that amounted to piracy, since the United States was not at war with Portugal and in fact was seeking Portuguese trade.[68] Braxton had been one of the many Virginians involved in the Robinson scandal.[69] The Lees tried to exclude such men from representing Virginia in Congress by securing passage in the Virginia legislature of a law requiring delegates to swear that they were not engaged and would not engage in trade.[70] But the delegates who took the oath evidently interpreted their business dealings as something other than trade.

From South Carolina Deane's advocate was William Henry Drayton, a man with whom Henry Laurens regularly disagreed. Their different characters were significantly revealed in an insignificant episode, when Drayton in 1779 urged Congress to authorize the celebration of Independence Day by an elaborate display of fireworks. In what Laurens called "a funny declamation," Drayton praised the Olympic games and other festivities by which nations celebrated their nativity. Laurens, outraged by the extravagance of celebrations in general, answered that "the Olympic Games of Greece and other fooleries brought on the desolation of Greece." When Drayton won approval for his motion and pointed out that the Olympic games "were calculated for improving bodily strength, to make men athletic and robust," Laurens was left to reflect in his diary, "Is drinking Madeira Wine from 5 to 9 o'clock, then sallying out to gaze at fire works, and

99

---

[65] Cushing, ed., *Writings of Samuel Adams*, IV, 208, 210, 227–230, 236–238, 241–242, 244–248; John C. Miller, *Sam Adams: Pioneer in Propaganda* (Boston, 1936), 359–369.

[66] Feb., Mar. 1776, in Butterfield, ed., *Diary and Autobiography of John Adams*, III, 367, 371.

[67] Abernethy, *Western Lands*, 159–160.

[68] Ibid., 215, 232.

[69] Mays, *Pendleton*, I, 180, 359.

[70] From Meriwether Smith, July 6, 1779, in Boyd, ed., *Jefferson Papers*, III, 28–29, 29n.

afterwards returning to Wine again, calculated to make men athletic and robust?"[71]

Two years earlier on the first anniversary of independence, Congress had also celebrated and there had also been a dissenter, William Williams of Connecticut, who wrote on July 5, 1777, to his friend Governor Trumbull: "Yesterday was in my opinion poorly spent in celebrating the anniversary of the Declaration of Independence . . . a great expenditure of Liquor, Powder etc. took up the Day, and of candles thro the City good part of the night."[72] By an interesting coincidence, William Williams was also an early opponent of Silas Deane. He had opposed Deane's election as a delegate to Congress; he had warned his friend Samuel Adams, as early as July 30, 1774, before the first Congress met, that Deane would be likely to place private interests above patriotism; and he had finally secured Deane's dismissal from the Connecticut delegation in 1775. Williams's own record in the Revolution, like Laurens's, was one of financial sacrifice.[73]

It would be impossible to prove conclusively that all the opponents of Silas Deane were frugal, industrious, and devoted to the common good or that all his advocates were addicted to trade, speculation, and profiteering. Men on both sides proclaimed their belief in the same values, but it seems likely that men like Adams, Lee, and Laurens recognized one another as kindred spirits and that men like Morris, Harrison, and Braxton did the same.[74] In the Continental Congress the turnover of delegates (required by the Articles of Confederation) prevented the formation of any durable parties, but in 1779 the groups that formed over the Deane issue tended to act together also in other divisions, such as the dispute over half pay for army officers and the dispute over war aims. In the latter dispute, for example, the French Ambassador found the friends of Deane far more amenable than the Adams-Lee-Laurens group, many of whom felt a sense of shame that the United States had been unable to fight its own battles without French financial and military assistance.[75]

The party divisions of 1778–79 seem to indicate that although most Americans made adherence to the Puritan Ethic an article of faith, some Americans were far more assiduous than others in exemplifying it. Since such men were confined to no particular section, and since men active in national politics could recognize their own kind from whatever section, political divisions in the early years of the republic actually brought Americans from all over the country into working harmony within a single group. And parties, instead of destroying the union, became a means of holding it together.

---

[71] Laurens, Notes, July 2, 1779, Burnett, ed., *Letters of Members,* IV, 293–294.

[72] Ibid., II, 401.

[73] Oscar Zeichner, *Connecticut's Years of Controversy, 1750–1776* (Chapel Hill, 1949), 322.

[74] Other active opponents of Deane included William Whipple of New Hampshire, James Lovell of Massachusetts, Roger Sherman of Connecticut, Nathaniel Scudder of New Jersey, and James Searle and William Shippen of Pennsylvania. Other advocates of Deane included Gouverneur Morris and John Jay of New York, Cyrus Griffin and Meriwether Smith of Virginia, William Carmichael of Maryland, and Henry Wynkoop of Pennsylvania.

[75] The solidity of the division is perhaps exaggerated in the extended reports on it by Gérard in Meng, ed., *Despatches of Gérard,* esp. 429–918, passim. On the half pay issue R. H. Lee parted from his anti-Deane allies.

Recent studies have shown that there was no continuity in the political divisions of the 1770s, 1780s, and 1790s, by demonstrating that the split between Federalists and Republicans in the 1790s cannot be traced to the preceding splits between reluctant and ardent revolutionaries of 1776 or between Federalists and Antifederalists of 1789. The continuity that a previous generation of historians had seen in the political history of these years has thus proved specious. It is tempting, however, to suggest that there may have been a form of continuity in American political history hitherto unnoticed, a continuity based on the attitudes we have been exploring. Although the divisions of 1778–79 did not endure, Americans of succeeding years continued to show differing degrees of attachment to the values of the Puritan Ethic. By the time when national political parties were organized in the 1790s, a good many other factors were involved in attracting men to one side or the other, far too many to permit discussion here. But the Puritan Ethic remained a constant ingredient, molding the style of American politics not only in the 1790s but long afterwards. Men on both sides, and seemingly the whole population, continued to proclaim their devotion to it by mourning its decline, and each side regularly accused the other of being deficient in it. It served as a weapon for political conflict but also as a tether which kept parties from straying too far apart. It deserves perhaps to be considered as one of the major reasons why American party battles have generally remained rhetorical and American national government has endured as a workable government.

III. An Economic Interpretation of the Constitution

As the Puritan Ethic helped to give shape to national politics, so too it helped to shape national policy, especially in the economic sphere. Before 1776 the economic policy of the American colonies had been made for them in London: they had been discouraged from manufacturing, barred from certain channels of trade, and encouraged to exploit the natural resources of the continent, especially its land. After 1776 the independent states were free to adopt, singly or collectively, any policy that suited them. At first the exigencies of the war against England directed every measure; but as the fighting subsided, Americans began to consider the economic alternatives open to them.

There appeared to be three possible kinds of activity: agriculture, manufacturing, and commerce. Of these, agriculture and commerce had hitherto dominated the American scene. Americans, in accepting the place assigned them under the British Navigation Acts, had seen the force of their own environment operating in the same direction as British policy: as long as the continent had an abundance of unoccupied land and a scarcity of labor, it seemed unlikely that its inhabitants could profitably engage in manufacturing. The nonimportation agreements had done much to dispel this opinion in America; and the war that followed, by interdicting trade in some regions and hindering it in others, had given a further spur to manufactures. By the time peace came numerous observers were able to point out fallacies in the supposition that manufacturing was not economically feasible in the United States. From England, Richard Price reminded Americans that their country contained such a variety of soils and climates that it was capable of "producing not only every *necessary,* but every *convenience* of life," and Americans were quick to agree.[76] They acknowledged that their population was small by comparison with Europe's and the numbers skilled in manufacturing even smaller. But they now discovered reasons why this deficiency was no insuperable handicap. People without regular employment, women and children for example, could be put to useful work in manufacturing. Moreover, if Americans turned to manufactures, many skilled artisans of the Old World, losing their New World customers, would move to America in order to regain them. Immigrants would come in large numbers anyhow, attracted by the blessings of republican liberty. And scarcity of labor could also be overcome by labor-saving machinery and by water and steam power.[77]

A few men like Thomas Jefferson continued to think manufacturing neither feasible nor desirable for Americans, but the economic vicissitudes of the postwar years subdued the voices of such men to a whisper. No one suggested that the country should abandon its major commitment to agriculture in favor of manufacturing, but it became a commonplace that too many Americans were engaged in commerce and that the moral, economic, and political welfare of the United States demanded a greater attention to manufacturing. The profiteering of merchants during the war had kept the old suspicions of that calling very much alive, so that long before the fighting stopped, people were worried about the effects of an unrestrained commerce on the independent United States. A Yale student reflected the mood in a declamation offered in July 1778. If the country indulged too freely in commerce, he warned, the result would be "Luxury with its train of the blackest vices, which will debase our manliness of sentiment, and spread a general dissolution of manners thro the Continent. This extensive Commerce is the most direct method to ruin our country, and we may affirm that we shall exist as an empire but a short space, unless it can be circumscribed within narrow limits."[78]

The prophecy seemed to be on the way to swift fulfillment within a year or two of the war's end. As soon as the peace treaty was signed, American merchants rushed to offer Americans the familiar British goods which they had done without for nearly a decade. The British gladly supplied the market, extending a liberal credit, and the result was a flood of British textiles and hardware in every state. As credit extended from merchant to tradesman to farmer and planter, Americans were caught up in an orgy of buying. But at the same time Britain barred American ships from her West Indies possessions, where American cattle, lumber, and foodstuffs had enjoyed a prime market. The British could now buy these articles in the United States at their own prices and carry them in their own ships, depriving the American merchant and farmer alike of accustomed profits. Hard

[76] Richard Price, *Observations on the Importance of the American Revolution* . . . (London, 1785), 75. Cf. *New Haven Gazette and Connecticut Magazine,* Nov. 16, 23, 1786; *American Mercury* (Hartford), Aug. 13, 1787.

[77] Hugh Williamson, *Letters from Sylvius to the Freemen Inhabitants of the United States* . . . (New York, 1787); Tench Coxe: *An Address to an Assembly of the Friends of American Manufactures* . . . (Philadelphia, 1787); *An Enquiry into the Principles on which a commercial system for the United States of America should be founded* . . . (Philadelphia, 1787); and *Observations on the Agriculture, Manufactures and Commerce of the United States* . . . (New York, 1789).

[78] Declamation, July 18, 1778, Yale University Archives, New Haven, Conn.

cash was rapidly drained off; debts grew to alarming proportions; and the buying boom turned to a sharp depression.[79]

Casting about for a remedy, some states turned to the old expedient of paper money. But to many Americans this was a cure worse than the disease and no real cure anyhow. The root of the trouble, they told themselves, was their own frivolity. Newspapers and pamphlets from one end of the continent to the other lamented the lost virtues that had inspired resistance to tyranny a few short years before. While Rome had enjoyed a republican simplicity for centuries, the United States seemed to have sunk into luxury and decay almost as soon as born. And who indulged this weakness, who coaxed Americans into this wild extravagance? It was the merchants. Shelves bulging with oversupplies of ribbons, laces, and yard goods, the merchants outdid themselves in appealing to every gullible woman and every foolish fop to buy. There was an oversupply, it seemed, not merely of ribbons and laces but of merchants, a breed of men, according to Hugh Williamson of North Carolina, "too lazy to plow, or labour at any other calling."[80] "What can we promise ourselves," asked another writer, "if we still pursue the same extensive trade? What, but total destruction to our manners, and the entire loss of our virtue?"[81]

The basic remedy must be frugality. The laments over luxury were a summons to Americans to tighten their belts, as they had done before in the face of adversity. And as they had also done in the earlier campaigns, they again linked frugality with nonimportation and with manufacturing for themselves, but this time with somewhat more confidence in the result. Manufacturing was now freed of the restrictions formerly imposed by the British; if once firmly established in the United States, it would help protect the very virtues that fostered it. An industrious, frugal people would manufacture for themselves, and in turn "Manufactures will promote industry, and industry contributes to health, virtue, riches and population."[82] Although the riches thus gained might constitute a danger to the virtues that begot them, they would not be as great a danger as riches arising from trade or speculation: "the evils resulting from opulence in a nation whose inhabitants are habituated to industry from their childhood, will never be so predominant as in those nations, whose riches are spontaneously produced, without labour or care."[83]

As manufactures were linked to virtue, so both were linked to the independent republican government for which Americans had been fighting. "America must adopt [a] new policy," David Ramsay insisted in 1785, "or she never will be independent in reality. We must import less and attend more to agriculture and manufactures."[84] It was now possible to see a new significance in England's old restraints on colonial manufacturing. Why had she prevented Americans from

---

[79] This picture of the economic history of the 1780s seems to have been universally accepted at the time. A typical statement is in Coxe, *Observations*, 59–64.

[80] Williamson, *Letters from Sylvius*, 30.

[81] *The American Museum*, I (Feb. 1787), 124.

[82] *Am. Mercury*, Aug. 13, 1787.

[83] *New Haven Gazette and Conn. Mag.*, Nov. 23, 1786.

[84] R. L. Brunhouse, ed., *David Ramsay, 1749–1815, Selections from his writings,* American Philosophical Society, *Transactions,* LV, Pt. 4 (1965), 87.

"working up those materials that God and nature have given us?" The answer was clear to a Maryland writer: because England knew "it was the only way to our real independence, and to render the habitable parts of our country truly valuable. What countries are the most flourishing and most powerful in the world? Manufacturing countries. It is not hills, mountains, woods, and rivers that constitute the true riches of a country. It is the number of industrious mechanic and manufacturing as well as agriculturing inhabitants. That a country composed of agricultivators and shepherds is not so valuable as one wherein a just proportion of the people attend to arts and manufactures, is known to every politician in Europe: And America will never feel her importance and dignity, until she alters her present system of trade, so ruinous to the interests, to the morals, and to the reputation of her citizens."[85]

Britain's extension of credit to American merchants, it now seemed, was only part of a perfidious plan to undermine through trade the independence she had acknowledged by treaty. Samuel Adams had once detected a British plan to destroy American liberty by introducing luxury and levity among the people. Having been thwarted in 1776, the British were now on the verge of success. As a South Carolina writer charged, they had let loose, "as from Pandora's box, a ruinous luxury, speculation, and extravagance, vitiated our taste, corrupted our manners, plunged the whole state into a private debt, never before equalled, and thro' the means of their trade, luxury, influence, and good things, brought the Republic into a dilemma, an example of which has not before happened in the world."[86] From France, where he was serving as ambassador, Thomas Jefferson could see that Britain by her liberal credits had put the whole United States in the same economic thralldom in which her merchants had held (and still held) the Virginia tobacco planters. From economic thralldom back to political thralldom was only a step. Unless the United States could break the grip, her experiment in independence was over.

Jefferson, while joining in the hymns to frugality (he thought extravagance a "more baneful evil than toryism was during the war"),[87] had a peculiar prejudice against manufacturing and hoped to break the British grip and achieve economic independence by gaining new commercial treaties with other countries.[88] But few of his countrymen shared his prejudice. In every state they told themselves to manufacture. Even if it cost more to make a coat or a pair of shoes or a plow or a gun in America, the price of foreign imports was independence. "No man," warned Hugh Williamson, drawing upon another precept of the Puritan Ethic, "is to say that a thing may be good for individuals which is not good for the public, or that our citizens may thrive by cheap bargains, while the nation is ruined by them." Considered in the light of the national interest, "every domestic

---

[85] *Am. Museum,* I (Feb. 1787), 124–125.

[86] [Anonymous], *A Few Salutary Hints, pointing out the Policy and Consequences of Admitting British Subjects to Engross our Trade and Become our Citizens* (Charleston printed, New York reprinted, 1786), 4.

[87] To John Page, May 4, 1786, in Boyd, ed., *Jefferson Papers,* IX, 445.

[88] These views are scattered throughout Jefferson's letters during his stay in France. See Boyd, ed., *Jefferson Papers,* VIII–XV. For a typical statement see letter to Thomas Pleasants, May 8, 1786, ibid., IX, 472–473.

manufacture is cheaper than a foreign one, for this plain reason, by the first nothing is lost to the country, by the other the whole value is lost—it is carried away never to return."[89]

Williamson, like many others, welcomed the economic depression as the kind of adversity that brings its own cure. Poverty might induce Americans of necessity to manufacture for themselves. Societies for the promotion of arts and manufactures sprang up everywhere, as they had in the 1760s and 1770s, and in Boston there was even a new nonimportation agreement.[90] But Americans as an independent nation were no longer confined to such informal and extralegal methods either in bringing pressure on the British or in encouraging their own manufactures. The states could now levy duties and prohibitions against foreign importations, and several did so. But the results served only to remind Americans of the importance of union. The old nonimportation agreements against the Townshend duties had foundered when the merchants of one colony gave way. In the 1780s the uncoordinated actions of individual states in penalizing foreign trade did not break the British grip on the American market, did not end the drainage of specie, and did not lead Britain to restore trading privileges in the West Indies, but they did become an unexpected source of bitterness and disunion. When states tried individually to regulate commerce, they often failed to discern the harmful repercussions of their measures in other states. As John Sullivan confessed, concerning the New Hampshire law, "it was a blow aimed at Britain but wounds us and our friends."[91]

The advocates of frugality and manufacturing did not conclude from such failures that trade needed no regulation or that it could not be regulated. "If we Americans do not choose to regulate it," one of them warned, "it will regulate us, till we have not a farthing left in our land. . . . unless we shortly regulate and correct the abuses of our trade by lopping off its useless branches, and establishing manufactures, we shall be corrected, perhaps even to our very destruction."[92] Even Thomas Jefferson, who had been impressed by Adam Smith's advocacy of free trade, thought that Smith's policy could not be adopted unilaterally.[93] As long as the other nations of the world continued to regulate trade, the United States could not survive without doing likewise. What the failure of individual state regulation showed was not that regulation was wrong but that it must be nationwide. As James Madison wrote to Jefferson in March 1786, "The States are every day giving proofs that separate regulations are more likely to set them by the ears, than to attain the common object."[94]

---

[89] Williamson, *Letters from Sylvius,* 13–14.

[90] *Am. Mercury,* Nov. 18, 1786.

[91] From John Sullivan, Mar. 4, 1786, in Boyd, ed., *Jefferson Papers,* IX, 314.

[92] *Am. Museum,* I (Mar. 1787), 213.

[93] To G. K. van Hogendorp, Oct. 13, 1785, in Boyd, ed., *Jefferson Papers,* VIII, 633. While Smith argued for free trade, he based his arguments on a new conception of the wealth of nations that stressed the achievement of maximum productivity. With this conception and with Smith's palpable hostility to merchants and their efforts to influence policy, the Americans could readily agree.

[94] Ibid., IX, 334.

Harmony in commercial regulations was needed not simply in order to promote American trade by united retaliation against British restrictions. Although merchants might look toward an increase in national authority with this end in view, farseeing observers had much larger goals: not merely to strike at British commerce in favor of American, but to strike at all commerce that threatened the nation's economic independence. The support that merchants gave the movement for a stronger central government has often blinded us to the larger aims of men like Madison and Hamilton who, as the latter put it, thought "continentally." What they wanted was to transform the still-colonial economy of the United States by directing the industry and productivity of its citizens toward a balanced self-sufficiency. The country, they knew, would remain predominantly agricultural for some years to come; and they also knew that it could support its own merchant class, as it had done under British rule. But merchants and farmers were not enough to give the nation true independence; and the merchants, if left to themselves, could easily bring ruin to the country. To attain true independence, the United States must achieve a balance in which manufacturing would find its place beside commerce and agriculture. When they demanded a national regulation of trade, continentally minded Americans had in mind as much the restraint as the encouragement of trade. They wanted not a southern economy or a New England economy, but an American economy, of the kind described some decades later by Henry Clay.

The possibility of such a harmonious economy did not seem visionary in 1789. Southerners already acknowledged that New Englanders would excel in manufacturing. The climate, the compact settlements, the absence of slavery all favored them. But it was pointed out that the New Englanders, as they turned their efforts to manufactures, would buy raw materials and foodstuffs from the South. Nationally minded southerners like Madison even spoke up for a national navigation act to confine American trade to American vessels, though they knew that in shipbuilding and commerce as in manufactures the New Englanders would surpass them.[95] Manufacturing, commerce, and agriculture were all necessary to an independent nation, and all three might need encouragement and protection, not only from foreign sources but from each other. Tench Coxe (who argued strongly for restraining commerce in favor of manufactures) expressed the larger concern for economic co-ordination when he warned that trade regulations must be phrased with great care, so as not to injure the various agricultural activities which occupied the bulk of the people throughout the country.[96] There was widespread agreement that economic co-ordination must be accomplished and that only a national, rather than a local, regulation of trade could do the job.[97] Not everyone who supported national regulation was moved by a large view of

---

[95] Jan. 22, 1786, Nov. 14, 1785, ibid., IX, 198, 203–204; Williamson, *Letters from Sylvius,* passim; *A few Salutary Hints,* passim; St. George Tucker, *Reflections on the Policy and Necessity of Encouraging the Commerce of the Citizens of the United States of America* . . . (Richmond, 1785), passim.

[96] Coxe, *An Enquiry into the Principles,* passim.

[97] Examples will be found in *A Few Salutary Hints,* 16; Tucker, *Reflections,* 16; William Barton, *The True Interest of the United States, and Particularly of Pennsylvania, Considered* . . . (Philadelphia, 1786).

the national interest. Doubtless many merchants were looking merely for better trading opportunities, farmers for higher prices, would-be manufacturers for protection. But because national regulation could offer something to everyone, and because the appeal of the ancient virtues could also be harnessed to it, men who did see its larger implications for national independence were able to enlist powerful support behind it.

There were, of course, many forces working simultaneously toward the establishment of an effective national government in the 1780s, and perhaps economic forces were not the most important. It has been shown that Charles Beard's interpretation of the economic forces leading to the Constitution was without adequate foundation, and economic interpretations thus far advanced in place of Beard's have been only more complex versions of his. But another economic interpretation of the Constitution may be suggested: Americans from the time of their first nonimportation agreements against England had been groping toward a national economic policy that would bestow freedom from domination by outsiders. Long before the country had a national government capable of executing it, the outlines of that policy were visible, and the national government of 1789 was created, in part at least, in order to carry it out. Only an independent national economy could guarantee the political independence that Americans had declared in 1776, and only an independent national economy could preserve the virtue, the industry, frugality, and simplicity that Americans had sought to protect from the luxury and corruption of Great Britain. By 1787 it had become clear that none of these objectives could be attained without a national government empowered to control trade—and through trade all other parts of the national economy.

It is altogether fitting that the United States, which first acted as a government when the Continental Congress undertook the nonimportation, nonexportation, nonconsumption Association of 1774, gained a permanent effective government when Americans again felt an urgent need to control trade. There was in each case an immediate objective, to bring pressure on the British, and in each case a larger objective, to build American economic and moral strength. As the Philadelphia Convention was drafting its great document, Tench Coxe expressed a hope which many members of that body cherished equally with the members of the First Continental Congress, that the encouragement of manufacturing would "lead us once more into the paths of virtue by restoring frugality and industry, those potent antidotes to the vices of mankind and will give us real independence by rescuing us from the tyranny of foreign fashions, and the destructive torrent of luxury."[98] Patriotism and the Puritan Ethic marched hand in hand from 1764 to 1789.

The vicissitudes of the new national government in carrying out a national economic policy form another story, and one full of ironies. Alexander Hamilton, the brilliant executor of the policy, had scarcely a grain of the Puritan Ethic in him and did not hesitate to enroll the merchant class in his schemes. Hamilton, for purely economic and patriotic reasons, favored direct encouragement of

---

[98] Coxe, *An Address to Friends of Manufactures,* 29–30. Coxe was not a member of the Convention. He was addressing, in Philadelphia, a group "convened for the purpose of establishing a Society for the Encouragement of Manufactures and the Useful Arts."

manufactures by the national government; but the merchants whom he had gathered behind him helped to defeat him. Thomas Jefferson, devoted to the values of the Puritan Ethic but prejudiced against manufactures, fought against governmental support of them, yet in the end adopted the measures that turned the country decisively toward manufacturing.

The Puritan Ethic did not die with the eighteenth century. Throughout our history it has been there, though it has continued to be in the process of expiring. One student of the Jacksonian period has concluded that politics in the 1830s and 1840s was dominated by an appeal for restoration of the frugality and simplicity which men of that generation thought had prevailed in the preceding one. The most popular analysis of American society after the second World War was a lament for the loss of inner-directedness (read simplicity, industry, frugality) which had been replaced by other-directedness (read luxury, extravagance). The Puritan Ethic has always been known by its epitaphs. Perhaps it is not quite dead yet.

Author's Postscript

This essay was intended as a preliminary summary of a volume never written. In reading colonial newspapers of the Revolutionary period I had been surprised to find that arguments for nonimportation agreements had focused not on the pressure they would bring on Parliament to repeal colonial taxes but rather on the incentives they would offer Americans to work hard and be more frugal. At some point I decided to do a full-scale study of attitudes toward work in America and how they affected the course of our history from the beginnings to the present. Since the idea came to me from the time of the Revolution, I would begin by reading everything I could find from that time, trying to pick up in the middle the threads that would run through the study.

After spending several years in the voluminous correspondence and publications of the Revolutionists, I knew it was time to identify and define the main themes that were emerging. This article was the result, published as I turned back to the sixteenth century to see what attitudes toward work the English brought with them to America and how they applied them when they arrived. I never got beyond the first colony in what was originally supposed to be the opening volume of a series, *American Slavery, American Freedom: The Ordeal of Colonial Virginia*. The prospect of continuing on the same scale was too daunting. Perhaps someone more capable than I will one day write the major study I contemplated.

JACK TAR IN THE STREETS: MERCHANT SEAMEN IN THE POLITICS OF REVOLUTIONARY AMERICA

JESSE LEMISCH

Here comes Jack Tar, his bowed legs bracing him as if the very Broadway beneath his feet might begin to pitch and roll.[1] In his dress he is, in the words of a superior, "very nasty and negligent," his black stockings ragged, his long, baggy trousers tarred to make them waterproof.[2] Bred in "that very shambles of language," the merchant marine, he is foul-mouthed, his talk alien and suspect.[3] He is Jolly Jack, a bull in a china shop, always, in his words, "for a Short Life and a Merry one," and, in the concurring words of his superiors, "concerned only for the present . . . incapable of thinking of, or inattentive to, future welfare," "like froward Childeren not knowing how to judge for themselves."[4]

Mr. Lemisch is a visiting member of the Department of History, Northwestern University. An earlier version of this article was read at a meeting of the Organization of American Historians, Cincinnati, Ohio, April 1966. A grant and a fellowship from the American Council of Learned Societies aided the research.

Ed. Note: This article was originally published in *William and Mary Quarterly*, 3d Ser., XXV (July 1968), 371–407.

[1] His walk was sometimes described as a "waddle," *New-York Gazette; or the Weekly Post-Boy*, Sept. 3, 1759. Seamen were often called Jack Tar in England and in the colonies, for example, ibid., Oct. 15, 1770. The term was used more or less interchangeably along with "seaman," "sailor," and "mariner," with the latter frequently connoting "master" (as in Panel of Jurors [n.d.], New York Supreme Court, Pleadings P-2689, Office of County Clerk, Hall of Records, New York City, where seven of ten "mariners" are identifiable as captains by comparison with such sources as *The Burghers of New Amsterdam and the Freemen of New York, 1675–1866* [New-York Historical Society, *Collections*, XVIII (New York, 1886)], passim; *N.-Y. Gaz.; Weekly Post-Boy*, passim; and the especially valuable list of privateer captains in Stuyvesant Fish, *The New York Privateers, 1756–1763* [New York, 1945], 83–90). In this article Jack Tar is a merchant seaman, a "sailor" is in the Royal Navy, and a "mariner" is the captain of a merchant vessel. If a source calls a man a "mariner" or a "sailor" I have had to have evidence that he was in fact a merchant seaman before I would count him as one. For a useful discussion of terms see I. M. V., "Note," *Mariner's Mirror*, VII (1921), 351.

[2] [George Balfour], "Memorandum," *Mariners Mirror*, VIII (1922), 248. For the seaman's dress see *Abstracts of Wills on File in the Surrogate's Office, City of New York* (N.-Y. Hist. Soc., Coll., XXV–XLI [New York, 1893–1909]), VI, III; descriptions of dress scattered throughout Admiralty Group, Class 98, Piece 11–14, Public Record Office. Hereafter cited as Adm. 98/11–14; *N.-Y. Gaz.; Weekly Post-Boy*, Dec. 10, 1759, Oct. 14, Dec. 16, 1762, Nov. 3, 1763, Mar. 6, June 26, 1766, Oct. 1, 1767, Jan. 29, 1770, July 6, 1772; Samuel Eliot Morison, *John Paul Jones* (Boston, 1959), 72. A pair of useful illustrations appears in *Mariner's Mirror*, IX (1923), 128.

[3] J. R. Hutchinson, *The Press-Gang, Afloat and Ashore* (New York, 1913), 29. See *The Acts and Resolves . . . of the Province of Massachusetts Bay . . .* (Boston, 1869–1922), III, 318–319, for an act of Feb. 10, 1747, prescribing the stocks and whipping for seamen guilty of "profane cursing or swearing." For a landsman's version of some seamen's dialogue, see *N.-Y. Gaz.; Weekly Post-Boy*, Dec. 10, 1767.

[4] Robert E. Peabody, "The Naval Career of Captain John Manley of Marblehead," Essex

Clothes don't make the man, nor does language; surely we can do better than these stereotypes. Few have tried. Maritime history, as it has been written, has had as little to do with the common seaman as business history has had to do with the laborer. In that *mischianza* of mystique and elitism, "seaman" has meant Sir Francis Drake, not Jack Tar; the focus has been on trade, exploration, the great navigators, but rarely on the men who sailed the ships.[5] Thus we know very little about Jack. Samuel Eliot Morison is one of the few who have tried to portray the common seaman. In an influential anecdote in *The Maritime History of Massachusetts* Morison has described a "frequent occurrence" in early New England. A farmer's boy, called by the smell or the sight of the sea, suddenly runs off; three years later he returns as a man, marries the hired girl, and lives "happily ever after." This experience, Morison tells us, was "typical of the Massachusetts merchant marine," where the "old salt" was almost non-existent and where there never was "a native deep-sea proletariat." The ships were sailed by wave after wave of "adventure-seeking boys," drawn by high wages and wanderlust. If they recovered, they took their earnings, married, and bought a farm; if not, these "young, ambitious seamen culled from the most active element of a pushing race" stayed on and rose to become masters in a merchant marine distinguished from its class-ridden European counterparts by easy mobility.[6]

There is much to support Morison's tableau. Even if the mystique of the sea has been no more than mystique, still it has existed and exerted a powerful force. Washington, Franklin, and thousands of others did suffer attacks of "sea fever."[7] Seamen were, as Morison says, young men, averaging in one sample slightly over twenty-four, with many like John Paul Jones who went to sea at thirteen and even some who went at eight.[8] Many of them "hove in hard at the Hause-hole"[9]

Institute, *Historical Collections,* XLV (1909), 25; Ralph D. Paine, *The Ships and Sailors of Old Salem* (New York, 1909), 23; John Cremer, *Ramblin' Jack . . . ,* ed. R. Reynell Bellamy (London, 1936), 38–39; Congressman Edward Livingston, Apr. 10, 1798, United States, Congress, *Debates and Proceedings in the Congress of the United States . . .* (Washington, D.C., 1834–1856), 5th Cong., 2d sess., 1388. Hereafter cited as *Annals of Congress;* Colvill to Admiralty, Nov. 12, 1765, Adm. 1/482.

[5] The bibliography is endless: a typical recent instance is Edmund O. Sawyer, *America's Sea Saga* (New York, 1962), foreword, 185, "a tale of unending courage" by a retired lieutenant colonel who now lives in Hollywood where he "plays an active role in the relentless crusade against the Communist conspiracy." Although there is much of use in *American Neptune,* the magazine's definition of maritime history has been too genteel, dwelling too often on such matters as ship design and construction, yachting, reminiscences, and model-building. On the other hand, even the W.P.A. Writer's Program neglected the seamen in *Boston Looks Seaward* (Boston, 1941) and in *A Maritime History of New York* (Garden City, N. Y., 1941).

[6] Samuel Eliot Morison, *The Maritime History of Massachusetts* (Boston, 1921), 105–107, 111; see also Morison, *John Paul Jones,* 22–23.

[7] Mason L. Weems, *The Life of Washington,* ed. Marcus Cunliffe (Cambridge, Mass., 1962), xxxv, 27; Douglas S. Freeman, *George Washington* (New York, 1948–1957), I, 190–199; Jesse Lemisch, ed., *Benjamin Franklin: The Autobiography and Other Writings* (New York, 1961), 23; Elmo Paul Hohman, *Seamen Ashore* (New Haven, 1952), 217, calls this kind of motivation "positive"; see ibid., for "negative" motives.

[8] Morison, *John Paul Jones,* 11; sixty-one American seamen of ascertainable age listed in *Muster Rolls of New York Provincial Troops: 1755–1764* (N.-Y. Hist. Soc., *Coll.,* XXIV [New York, 1892]), passim, average 24.3 years; Cremer, *Ramblin' Jack,* ed. Bellamy, 38.

[9] The phrase appears in Cremer, *Ramblin' Jack,* ed. Bellamy, 31–32, and in Morison, *Maritime History,* 107.

and became masters of their own vessels; later, while their sons and grandsons added to their wealth, they retired, perhaps to their farms, and wrote proud histories of their successes.[10] Some, like Nicholas Biddle, found the navy a better outlet for their ambitions than the merchant service.[11] Others, following Morison's pattern, quit the sea early and turned to farming.[12] For many there was mobility between generations and between trades.[13] Seamen and landsmen might be distinct classes in Europe, but in America, men such as Albert Gallatin who knew both the Old World and the New found no "material distinction."[14] So Jack Tar seems to have been simply the landsman gone to sea, indistinguishable from his fellows ashore, and, together with them, on his way to prosperity.

If the seaman was a clean young farm-boy on the make—and likely to succeed—why was Josiah Franklin so apprehensive lest young Benjamin "break loose and go to sea"? Why did Josiah fight his son's "strong inclination to go to sea" by frantically trying to make of him a joiner, a brick-layer, a turner, a brazier, a tallow-chandler, a cutler, a printer—anything, so long as it would keep him on land?[15] Why did Washington's uncle suggest that young George would better become a planter or even an apprentice to a tinker, while explicitly urging that he not become a seaman?[16]

"All masters of vessels are warned not to harbor, conceal, or employ him, as they will answer for it, as the law directs."[17] To a fleeing apprentice, dissatisfied with the "bondage" of work ashore,[18] to a runaway slave, the sea might appear

[10] See for example, Mary Barney, ed., *A Biographical Memoir of the Late Commodore Joshua Barney* (Boston, 1832); Thomas Dring, *Recollections of the Jersey Prison-Ship*, ed. Albert G. Greene (Providence, 1829); Ebenezer Fox, *The Adventures of Ebenezer Fox in the Revolutionary War* (Boston, 1847?); Christopher Hawkins, *The Adventures of Christopher Hawkins* (New York, 1864); Paine, *Ships and Sailors of Salem*, 100, 117–119; James A. Henretta, "Economic Development and Social Structure in Colonial Boston," *William and Mary Quarterly*, 3d Ser., XXII (1965), 76.

[11] Joseph Galloway to Benjamin Franklin, Apr. 23, 1771, Franklin Papers, III, 50, American Philosophical Society, Philadelphia.

[12] "In America . . . all sorts of people turn farmers—where no mechanic or artizan—sailor—soldier—servant, etc. but what, if they get money, take land, and turn farmers." Harry J. Carman, ed., *American Husbandry* (New York, 1939), 124.

[13] The sons of captains might find themselves apprenticed to gentlemen or to butchers or barbers as well as to other mariners. See, for example, *Burghers of New Amsterdam*, 577–578, 617, 620; *Indentures of Apprentices*, 1718–1727 (N.-Y. Hist. Soc., *Coll.*, XLII [New York, 1910]), 122–123, 140, 142–143, 150, 155, 166, 169, 181, 188, 189, 193, 195.

[14] Albert Gallatin, Apr. 10, 1798, *Annals of Congress*, 5th Cong., 2d sess., 1392; J. Hector St. John de Crèvecoeur, *Letters from an American Farmer* (New York, 1957), 122, has similar observations about American "sea-faring men," but he seems to be describing only whalers.

[15] Lemisch, ed., *Franklin*, 23, 25–26. History apparently repeated itself in the next generation. Franklin's son William "left my house unknown to us all, and got on board a privateer, from whence I fetched him." Benjamin Franklin to Jane Mecom [June ? 1748], Leonard W. Labaree et al., eds., *The Papers of Benjamin Franklin* (New Haven, 1959–), III, 303.

[16] Freeman, *Washington*, I, 198–199. For some other instances of opposition by families of young men who expressed the intention of going to sea, see Barney, ed., *Memoir*, 3–4, and Fox, *Adventures*, 29, 36, 40.

[17] This is a composite of advertisements appearing in almost every colonial newspaper. See, for example, *N.-Y. Gaz.; Weekly Post-Boy*, May 17, 24, 1764, June 27, 1765.

[18] The term is used by Fox, *Adventures*, 18, describing his situation in 1775. In an interesting passage ibid., 17–19, he sees in the movement for independence a cause of a general "spirit of

the only real shelter. Men with no experience at sea tried to pass for seamen and before long discovered that they had indeed become seamen. Others were seamen, apprenticed in one vessel and fled to another. Still others, deserted soldiers, bail-jumpers, thieves, and murderers, had gotten into trouble with the law.[19] And others went to sea entirely unwillingly, originally impressed—perhaps from jail—into the navy, or tricked into the merchant service by crimps.[20] These were the floaters who drifted and slipped their moorings, the suicides, the men whose wives—if they had wives—ran off with other men; the beneficiaries in their wills—when they left wills—were innkeepers.[21] Hitherto, argued a proponent of a United States navy in 1782, the merchant marine had been "the resource of necessity, accident or indulgence."[22]

The merchant marine was a place full of forces beyond the seaman's control: death and disease, storms, and fluctuations in employment. Indeed, the lack of "old salts" in Morison's merchant marine might reflect a sombre irony: was the average seaman young because mobility rapidly brought him to another trade or because seamen died young?[23] A man in jail, said Dr. Johnson, was at least safe

---

insubordination" among American youth at the time. For another runaway, see Bushnell, *Adventures of Hawkins,* 10, 60–61.

[19] See *N.-Y. Gaz.; Weekly Post-Boy,* Sept. 3, Dec. 20, 1759, Oct. 14, Dec. 26, 1762, July 21, Oct. 6, Nov. 3, 1763, Mar. 29, May 10, 24, July 19, Sept. 6, 20, 1764, Apr. 4, 18, June 27, 1765, June 29, July 6, 1772; *New-York Journal: or the General Advertiser,* May 13, 1773. For a Negro seaman see log of *Hunter,* Sept. 8, 1758, Adm. 51/465. Some Negro seamen were free and some received their freedom as a reward for service in warships. Benjamin Quarles, *The Negro in the American Revolution* (Chapel Hill, 1961), 84; Robert McColley, *Slavery and Jeffersonian Virginia* (Urbana, 1964), 89. But Negroes also served at sea and in related maritime trades as part of their bondage and were sometimes advertised as "brought up from his Infancy to the sea." William Waller Hening, *The Statutes at Large . . . of Virginia* (Richmond, 1809–1823), XI, 404; *N.-Y. Gaz.; Weekly Post-Boy,* Mar. 26, 1761, July 7, Aug. 18, Nov. 17, 1763; Samuel Hallett in *American Loyalists: Transcripts of the Commission of Enquiry into the Losses and Services of the American Loyalists . . . 1783–1790,* XIX, 207, New York Public Library; George William Edwards, *New York as an Eighteenth-Century Municipality, 1731–1776* (New York, 1917), 178.

[20] For crimps, see Hutchinson, *Press-Gang,* 48–49. Hohman, *Seamen Ashore,* 273–274, dates the development of crimping in America between 1830 and 1845, but there were crimps in Norfolk in 1767. See Captain Jeremiah Morgan to Governor Francis Fauquier, Sept. 11, 1767, Adm. 1/2116, Library of Congress transcript.

[21] *N.-Y. Gaz.; Weekly Post-Boy,* Sept. 30, 1773; *The King* v. *Jane the Wife of Thomas Dun,* Indictment for Bigamy, filed Oct. 26, 1763, N. Y. Supreme Court, Pleadings K-41. Although no statistical conclusions are possible, to a surprising extent the beneficiaries in a sample of seamen's wills are not wives but rather brothers and sisters, friends and innkeepers, *Abstracts of Wills,* VI, 111, 226; VII, 12, 38, 148, 397; VIII, 98; XI, 194.

[22] *Independent Chronicle* (Boston), Sept. 5, 1782.

[23] For some reflections on mortality in the merchant marine see Ralph Davis, *The Rise of the English Shipping Industry in the Seventeenth and Eighteenth Centuries* (London, 1962), 156. As late as the 1840s Massachusetts seamen, with an average age at death of 42.47 years, died younger than farmers, clergymen, lawyers, physicians, blacksmiths, carpenters, merchants, and laborers. Only painters, fishermen, manufacturers, mechanics, and printers are listed as having shorter lives in Lemuel Shattuck et al., *Report of the Sanitary Commission of Massachusetts, 1850* (Cambridge, Mass., 1948), 87. For employment see *N. Y. Journal or Gen. Adv.,* Oct. 5, 1775; Thomas Paine, *The Complete Writings,* ed. Philip S. Foner (New York, 1945), I, 33; in addition, a kind of unemployment is built into the profession; a seaman ashore is generally unemployed. See Hohman, *Seamen Ashore,* 209.

from drowning, and he had more room, better food, and better company. The Quaker John Woolman was one of the few sensitive enough to see that if the "poor bewildered sailors" drank and cursed, the fault lay not so much in themselves as in the harsh environment and the greed of employers. Nor was the road up through the hawse-hole so easy as Morison asserts. That the few succeeded tells us nothing of the many; only the successful left autobiographies.[24] Perhaps the sons of merchants and ship-masters made it, along with the captain's brother-in-law [25] and those who attended schools of navigation,[26] but what of the "poor lads bound apprentice" who troubled Woolman, those whose wages went to their masters? What of the seamen in Morison's own Boston who died too poor to pay taxes and who were a part of what James Henretta has called "the bottom" of Boston society?[27] What of those who went bankrupt with such frequency in Rhode Island?[28] Why, at the other end of the colonies, did Washington's uncle warn that it would be "very difficult" to become master of a Virginia vessel and not worth trying?[29]

The presence of such men, fugitives and floaters, powerless in a tough environment, makes wanderlust appear an ironic parody of the motives which made at least some men go to sea. Catch the seaman when he is not pandering to your romanticism, said former seaman Frederick Law Olmsted a century later, and he will tell you that he hates the sight of blue water, he hates his ship, his officers, and his messmates—and he despises himself. Melville's Ishmael went to sea when he felt grim, hostile, and suicidal: "It is a way I have of driving off the spleen." No matter what we make of Ishmael, we cannot possibly make him into one of Morison's "adventure-seeking boys." Others, perhaps, but not Ishmael. The feelings of eighteenth-century Americans toward seafaring and seamen, and what evidence we have of the reasons men had for going to sea indicate that there were many like Ishmael in the colonial period, too, who left the land in flight and fear, outcasts, men with little hope of success ashore. These were the dissenters from the American mood. Their goals differed from

[24] Quoted in Davis, *Rise of English Shipping*, 154; John Woolman, *The Journal of John Woolman and A Plea for the Poor* (New York, 1961), 206, 192–193, 196. For comments on elitism in the writings of Morison and of other historians of early America, see Jesse Lemisch, "The American Revolution Seen from the Bottom Up," in Barton J. Bernstein, ed., *Towards a New Past: Dissenting Essays in American History* (New York, 1968), 3–45.

[25] Barney, ed., *Memoir*, 10. For the relative prospects of the sons of merchants and masters as opposed to others in the English merchant marine, see Davis, *Rise of English Shipping*, 117.

[26] For such schools see Boston Registry Department, *Records Relating to the Early History of Boston* (Boston, 1876–1909), XIII, 2, 204; Carl Bridenbaugh, *Cities in Revolt* (New York, 1955), 377.

[27] Woolman, *Journal*, 195; *Bethune* v. *Warner*, May 27, 1724, Admiralty Court, Boston, Minute Book II (1718–1726), 177, Office of Clerk, Supreme Judicial Court, Suffolk County, Mass.; Boston Reg. Dept., *Records of Boston*, XIV, 88–89, 94–95; Henretta, "Economic Development," 85; see also Jackson T. Main, *The Social Structure of Revolutionary America* (Princeton, 1965), 74.

[28] Only three occupational groups exceeded "mariners" in the number of insolvency petitions filed with the Rhode Island legislature from 1756 to 1828. See Peter J. Coleman, "The Insolvent Debtor in Rhode Island, 1745–1828," *Wm. and Mary Qtly.*, 3d Ser., XXII (1965), 422n. Mr. Coleman has stated in conversation with the author that the "mariners" appear to be predominantly common seamen.

[29] Freeman, *Washington*, I, 199.

their fellows ashore; these were the rebels, the men who stayed on to become old salts.[30]

Admiralty law treated seamen in a special way, as "wards." Carl Ubbelohde says that seamen favored the colonial Vice Admiralty Courts as "particular tribunals in case of trouble," and Charles M. Andrews and Richard B. Morris agreed that these courts were "guardians of the rights of the seamen." The benefits of being classified as a "ward" are dubious, but, regardless of the quality of treatment which admiralty law accorded to seamen, it certainly does not follow that, all in all, the colonial seaman was well treated by the law. Indeed, if we broaden our scope to include colonial law generally, we find an extraordinarily harsh collection of laws, all justifying Olmsted's later claim that American seamen "are more wretched, and are governed more by threats of force than any other civilized laborers of the world."[31] There are laws providing for the whipping of disobedient seamen and in one case for their punishment as "seditious"; laws prohibiting seamen in port from leaving their vessels after sundown and from traveling on land without certificates of discharge from their last job; laws empowering "every free white person" to catch runaway seamen.[32] We find other laws, less harsh, some seeming to protect the seaman: laws against extending credit to seamen and against arresting them for debt, and against entertaining them in taverns for more than one hour per day; laws against selling them liquor and prohibiting them from playing with cards or dice; laws waiving imprisonment for seamen convicted of cursing; laws requiring masters to give discharge certificates to their seamen and laws prohibiting hiring without such certificates.[33] Finally, there are

[30] Frederick Law Olmsted, *A Journey in the Back Country* . . . (New York, 1860), 287. Morison, *Maritime History,* offers no evidence for the assertion that his anecdote of the adventurous farm-boy is "typical" and that Massachusetts "has never had a native deep-sea proletariat." In the absence of such evidence and in the light of the evidence offered above for the existence of a very different type there is no basis for a claim that either group was "typical." My contention about the nature of the merchant marine is limited and negative. The presence of runaway slaves, thieves, murderers, fugitives, and floaters, *in addition* to Morison's adventure-seekers prevents any statement about typicality until we can offer quantitative evidence. Meanwhile all that we can say is that both types existed and that it is misleading to view the colonial merchant marine as a homogenous entity.

[31] Carl Ubbelohde, *The Vice-Admiralty Courts and the American Revolution* (Chapel Hill, 1960), 20, 159–160; Charles M. Andrews, introduction to Dorothy S. Towle, ed., *The Records of the Vice Admiralty Court of Rhode Island, 1716–1752* (Washington, 1936), 60; Richard B. Morris, *Government and Labor in Early America* (New York, 1946), 232, 256; Olmsted, *Journey,* 287. Ubbelohde, Morris, and Andrews do not contend that the seaman was well treated by the law in an overall sense. Ubbelohde and Morris show that the seaman was better treated in Vice Admiralty Courts than in courts of common law; but when the focus moves to colonial legislation the hostility of the law emerges as the central fact for the seaman.

[32] Hening, *Statutes of Virginia,* IV, 107–108; VI, 26; E. B. O'Callaghan, ed., *Laws and Ordinances of New Netherland, 1638–1674* (Albany, 1868), 11–12. This law also prevented landsmen from going aboard vessels without authorization from the director of the West India Company. On June 13, 1647, two seamen convicted of tearing down a copy of this law attached to their vessel's mainmast were sentenced to be chained to a wheelbarrow and employed at hard labor on bread and water for three months. I.N.P. Stokes, *The Iconography of Manhattan Island, 1498–1909* (New York, 1915–1928), IV, 87. Thomas Cooper, ed., *The Statutes at Large of South Carolina* (Columbia, 1836–1841), III, 736.

[33] See the laws cited in Morris, *Government and Labor,* 230, n. 2; *Minutes of the Common Council of the City of New York, 1675–1776* (New York, 1905), I, 223, 372; *Acts and Resolves,* I, 142, 560; III, 318–319; IV, 73; James T. Mitchell and Henry Flanders, eds., *Statutes at Large of Pennsylvania from 1682 to 1801* (Harrisburg, 1896–1908), II, 239–240; Albert S. Batchellor and Henry H.

laws which clearly do help the seaman: laws requiring masters to provide "good and sufficient diet and accommodation" and providing for redress if the master refused; laws providing punishment for masters who "immoderately beat, wound, or maim" their seamen; laws providing that seamen's contracts be written.[34]

These harsh or at best paternalistic laws[35] add up to a structure whose purpose is to assure a ready supply of cheap, docile labor.[36] Obedience, both at sea and ashore, is the keystone.[37] Charles Beard at his most rigidly mechanistic would doubtless have found the Constitution merely mild stuff alongside this blatantly one-sided class legislation. Today's historians of the classless society would do well to examine the preambles of these laws, written in a more candid age, by legislatures for which, even by Robert Brown's evidence, most seamen could not vote.[38] Again and again these laws aim to inhibit acts of seamen which may do "prejudice to masters and owners of vessells" or constitute a "manifest detriment of . . . trade."[39] The seamen's interests are sacrificed to the merchants', and even the laws which seem friendly to the seaman benefit the master. Laws against giving credit, arresting, and suing aim to keep the seaman available rather than involved in a lawsuit or imprisoned; the certificates and written contracts seek to

---

Metcalf, *Laws of New Hampshire* (Manchester, 1904–1922), I, 691; J. Hammond Trumbull and C. J. Hoadly, eds., *The Public Records of the Colony of Connecticut (1636–1776)* (Hartford, 1850–1890), III, 54; *Charters and General Laws of the Colony and Province of Massachusetts* (Boston, 1814), 185; Cooper, ed., *Statutes of South Carolina*, III, 735, 736; Hening, *Statutes of Virginia*, IV, 108–110; VI, 25, 28.

[34] Hening, *Statutes of Virginia*, IV, 109–110, VI, 27. *Colonial Laws of New York from the Year 1664 to the Revolution* . . . (Albany, 1894–1896), IV, 484–485; Morris, *Government and Labor*, 230, n. 5 and 7.

[35] Eugene T. Jackman, "Efforts Made Before 1825 to Ameliorate the Lot of the American Seaman: With Emphasis on his Moral Regeneration," *American Neptune*, XXIV (1964), 109, describes legislation for seamen after the Revolution as "paternalistic." As late as 1897 the Supreme Court declared that "seamen are treated by Congress, as well as by the Parliament of Great Britain, as deficient in that full and intelligent responsibility for their acts which is accredited to ordinary adults." Hobman, *Seamen Ashore*, 214.

[36] Morris, *Government and Labor*, 230, agrees with this statement in a somewhat more limited form.

[37] See Deposition of Commander Arthur Tough [1742], Gertrude MacKinney, ed., *Pennsylvania Archives*, 8th Ser. (Harrisburg, 1931–1935), IV, 2993.

[38] Robert E. Brown, *Middle-Class Democracy and the Revolution in Massachusetts, 1691–1780* (Ithaca, 1955), 27–30, acknowledges that the "city proletariat" constituted "the largest disfranchised group" and strongly implies that itinerant seamen could not vote. Even so, Brown has stated the case too optimistically. By including propertied captains under the ambiguous label "mariner," he has disguised the fact, legible in his own evidence, that the "mariners" who could vote were captains and the common seamen could not. See John Cory, "Statistical Method and the Brown Thesis on Colonial Democracy, With a Rebuttal by Robert E. Brown," *Wm. and Mary Qtly.*, 3d Ser., XX (1963), 257. For Brown's acknowledgment of the error see ibid., 272. Arthur M. Schlesinger, *The Colonial Merchants and the American Revolution, 1763–1776* (New York, 1918), 28, includes seamen in a list of those who were "for the most part, unenfranchised." For an assertion that "sailors" could vote based on evidence that *masters* could compare Jacob R. Marcus, *Early American Jewry* (Philadelphia, 1953), II, 231, and B. R. Carroll, ed., *Historical Collections of South Carolina* (New York, 1836), II, 441.

[39] Trumbull and Hoadly, *Public Records of Connecticut*, III, 54; Cooper, ed., *Statutes of South Carolina*, II, 54; III, 735; for other legislation containing similar phrases see Batchellor and Metcalf, *Laws of New Hampshire*, I, 691; *Minutes of the Common Council of New York*, I, 223; *Colonial Laws of New York*, IV, 483; Hening, *Statutes of Virginia*, IV, 107.

115

prevent desertion and to protect the master against what would today be called a "strike";[40] the laws protecting seamen against immoderate punishment and requiring adequate food and accommodation are implicitly weak in that they require that dependents make open complaint against their superiors.[41] Sometimes this limitation is made explicit, as in a South Carolina law of 1751 whose stated purpose is "TO DISCOURAGE FRIVOLOUS AND VEXATIOUS ACTIONS AT LAW BEING BROUGHT BY SEAMEN AGAINST MASTERS AND COMMANDERS."[42]

Thus if we think of Jack Tar as jolly, childlike, irresponsible, and in many ways surprisingly like the Negro stereotype, it is because he was treated so much like a child, a servant, and a slave. What the employer saw as the necessities of an authoritarian profession were written into law and culture: the society that wanted Jack dependent made him that way and then concluded that that was the way he really was.[43]

II

Constantly plagued by short complements, the Royal Navy attempted to solve its manning problems in America, as in England, by impressment.[44] Neil Stout has recently attributed these shortages to "death, illness, crime, and desertion" which were in turn caused largely by rum and by the deliberate

---

[40] For instance, *Colonial Laws of New York,* IV, 484 (later disallowed), required a written contract in order to end such practices as this: "very often when Ships and vessels come to be cleared out . . . the Seamen refuse to proceed with them, without coming to new agreements for increasing their wages and many of them will Leave their Ships and Vessels and not proceed on their voyages which puts the owners of such ships and vessels to Great Trouble and Charges." The act also mentions subterfuges of seamen but fails to acknowledge the possibility that masters might also use subterfuge. For a "mutiny" which clearly expressed a labor grievance see below, 406.

[41] See the procedure provided in Hening, *Statutes of Virginia,* IV, 109–110. See also Morris, *Government and Labor,* 268.

[42] Cooper, ed., *Statutes of South Carolina,* III, 735.

[43] For examples of the similarity between life at sea and life on the plantation compare Morris, *Government and Labor,* 230, 247, 256, 262, 274, and McColley, *Slavery and Jeffersonian Virginia,* 103. For Frederick Olmsted's comments on the similarity, based on his own experience at sea in 1843–1844, see *The Cotton Kingdom,* ed. Arthur M. Schlesinger (New York, 1953), 453. For the image of the seaman in literature see Harold F. Watson, *The Sailor in English Fiction and Drama, 1550–1880* (New York, 1931), 159–160, and passim.

[44] For shortages which led to impressment see, for example, Capt. Thos. Miles to Admiralty, Jan. 31, 1705/6, Adm. 1/2093; Lord Cornbury to Lords of Trade, Oct. 3, 1706, E. B. O'Callaghan, ed., *Documents Relative to the Colonial History of the State of New York* (Albany, 1853–1887), IV, 1183–1185; Captain A. Forrest to Lt. Gov. Spencer Phips, Oct. 26, 1745, Adm. 1/1782. For a detailed record of such shortages see items headed "The State and Condition of His Majesty's Ships and Sloops" appearing frequently, scattered throughout Admirals' Dispatches, Adm. 1/480–486. For impressment in the colonies see Neil R. Stout, "Manning the Royal Navy in North America, 1763–1775," *American Neptune,* XXIII (1963), 174–185, and Neil R. Stout, "The Royal Navy in American Waters, 1760–1775" (unpubl. Ph.D. diss., University of Wisconsin, 1962), 359–395; R. Pares, "The Manning of the Navy in the West Indies, 1702–63," Royal Historical Society, *Transactions,* 4th Ser., XX (1937), 31–60; Dora Mae Clark, "The Impressment of Seamen in the American Colonies," in *Essays in Colonial History Presented to Charles McLean Andrews by his Students* (New Haven, 1931), 198–224; Jesse Lemisch, "Jack Tar vs. John Bull: The Role of New York's Seamen in precipitating the Revolution" (unpubl. Ph.D. diss., Yale University, 1962), 12–51. Two useful accounts primarily dealing with impressment in England may be found in Hutchinson, *Press-Gang,* passim, and Daniel A. Baugh, *British Naval Administration in the Age of Walpole* (Princeton, 1965), 147–240.

enticements of American merchants.[45] Rum and inveiglement certainly took a high toll, but to focus on these two causes of shortages is unfairly to shift the blame for impressment onto its victims. The navy itself caused shortages. Impressment, said Thomas Hutchinson, caused desertion, rather than the other way around.[46] Jack Tar had good reasons for avoiding the navy. It would, a young Virginian was warned, "cut him and staple him and use him like a Negro, or rather, like a dog"; James Otis grieved at the loss of the "flower" of Massachusetts's youth "by ten thousands" to a service which treated them little better than "hewers of wood and drawers of water." Discipline was harsh and sometimes irrational, and punishments were cruel.[47] Water poured into sailors' beds, they went mad, and died of fevers and scurvy.[48] Sickness, Benjamin Franklin noted, was more common in the navy than in the merchant service and more frequently fatal.[49] In a fruitless attempt to prevent desertion, wages were withheld and men shunted about from ship to ship without being paid.[50] But the accumulation of even three or four years' back wages could not keep a man from running.[51] And why should it have? Privateering paid better in wartime, and wages were higher in the merchant service; even laborers ashore were better

[45] Stout, "Manning the Royal Navy," 176–177, suggests the possibility of other causes when he notes that desertion was high "whatever the causes," but he mentions no cause other than rum and inveiglement. The Admiralty made the seamen's "natural Levity" another possible reason for desertion. Admiralty to Gov. Thomas on Impressments, 1743, *Pennsylvania Archives*, 1st Ser. (Philadelphia, 1852–1856), I, 639; see also Massachusetts Historical Society, *Journals of the House of Representatives of Massachusetts* (Boston, 1919–), XX, 84, 98; Colvill to Admiralty, Aug. 8, 1765, Adm. 1/482; Pares, "Manning the Navy," 31, 33–34.

[46] Hutchinson to Richard Jackson, June 16, 1768, G. G. Wolkins, "The Seizure of John Hancock's Sloop 'Liberty,'" Massachusetts Historical Society, *Proceedings,* LV (Boston, 1923), 283.

[47] Freeman, *Washington,* I, 199; James Otis, *The Rights of the British Colonies Asserted and Proved* (Boston, 1764) in Bernard Bailyn, ed., *Pamphlets of the American Revolution, 1750–1776* (Cambridge, Mass., 1965), I, 464. Flogging was universal and men received as many as 600 and 700 lashes. Colvill to Admiralty, Nov. 12, 1765, Adm. 1/482. For obscenity the tongue was scraped with hoop-iron. There were punishments for smiling in the presence of an officer. One captain put his sailors' heads in bags for trivial offenses. Hutchinson, *Press-Gang,* 31–36. And, of course, the captain might go mad, as did Captain Robert Bond of *Gibraltar*. Admiral Gambier to Admiralty, Oct. 10, 1771, Adm. 1/483, log of *Gibraltar,* Feb. 10, 14, 1771, Adm. 51/394.

[48] Log of *Arethusa,* Dec. 28, 1771, Adm. 51/59; Petition of Jeremiah Raven, [fall 1756], Letters as to Admission of Pensioners to Greenwich Hospital, 1756–1770, Adm. 65/81, an excellent source for the discovery of the effects of service in the navy on health. See also the items headed "Weekly Account of Sick and Wounded Seamen" in Admirals' Dispatches, for example, Admiral Gambier to Admiralty, May 6, June 10, July 20, 27, 1771, Adm. 1/483; Nov. 9, 1771, Aug. 29, 1772, Adm. 1/484.

[49] Remarks on Judge Foster's Argument in Favor of . . . Impressing Seamen, Jared Sparks, ed., *The Works of Benjamin Franklin,* II (Boston, 1844), 333. Sparks gives this no date; John Bigelow, ed., *The Complete Works of Benjamin Franklin* (New York, 1887–1888), IV, 70, dates it 1767; Helen C. Boatfield of the Papers of Benjamin Franklin, Yale University, dates it post-1776.

[50] Pares, "Manning the Navy," 31–38; Roland G. Usher, Jr., "Royal Navy Impressment during the American Revolution," *Mississippi Valley Historical Review,* XXXVII (1950–1951), 686. At the time of the Mutiny at the Nore the crew of one ship had not been paid in 15 years, Hutchinson, *Press-Gang,* 44.

[51] Mr. William Polhampton to Lords of Trade, Mar. 6, 1711, O'Callaghan, ed., *Docs. Rel. Col. Hist. N. Y.,* V, 194. A seaman who deserted his ship would leave an "R"—for "run"—written against his name in the ship's book. See Hutchinson, *Press-Gang,* 151, for a song which urges seamen to flee the press-gang and "leave 'em an R in pawn!"

paid.[52] Thus Stout's claim that the navy was "forced" to press is only as accurate as the claim that the South was forced to enslave Negroes. Those whose sympathies lie with the thousands of victims of this barbaric practice—rather than with naval administrators—will see that the navy pressed because to be in the navy was in some sense to be a slave, and for this we must blame the slave owners rather than the slaves.[53]

Impressment angered and frightened the seamen, but it pervaded and disrupted all society, giving other classes and groups cause to share a common grievance with the press-gang's more direct victims: just about everyone had a relative at sea.[54] Whole cities were crippled. A night-time operation in New York in 1757 took in eight hundred men, the equivalent of more than one-quarter of the city's adult male population.[55] Impressment and the attendant shortage of men may have been a critical factor in the stagnancy of "the once cherished now depressed, once flourishing now sinking Town of Boston."[56] H. M. S. Shirley's log lists at least ninety-two men pressed off Boston in five months of 1745–1746; Gramont received seventy-three pressed men in New York in three days in 1758; Arethusa took thirty-one in two days off Virginia in 1771.[57] Binges such as these left the communities where they occurred seriously harmed. Preachers' congregations

---

[52] Peter Warren to Admiralty, Sept. 8, 1744, Adm. 1/2654; Mr. William Polhampton to Lords of Trade, Mar. 6, 1711, O'Callaghan, ed., Docs. Rel. Col. Hist. N. Y., V, 194; Admiralty to Thomas, 1743, Pa. Arch., 1st Ser., I, 638–639; Morris, Government and Labor, 247–248. The navy's most imaginative response to the problem was sporadic and abortive attempts to limit the wages given to merchant seamen, but the inviting differential remained. When the navy offered bounties for enlistment, this merely served to induce additional desertions by men who could pick up a month's pay simply by signing up. Pares, "Manning the Navy," 33–34; Hutchinson, Press-Gang, 22, 48–49; Remarks on Judge Foster's Argument, Sparks, ed., Works of Franklin, II, 333; N.-Y. Gaz.; Weekly Post-Boy, Mar. 31, Apr. 21, 1755, Mar. 11, 1771.

[53] Stout, "Manning the Royal Navy," 182. England abolished the press-gang in 1833, Hutchinson, Press-Gang, 311. Parliament abolished slavery in the British colonies in the same year.

[54] At least in Pennsylvania and New Jersey, according to the Independent Chronicle (Boston), Sept. 5, 1782.

[55] Three thousand men participated in this massive operation. Three or four hundred of those seized were released. Lord Loudoun to Pitt, May 30, 1757, Gertrude S. Kimball, ed., Correspondence of William Pitt (New York, 1906), I, 69; Paul L. Ford, ed., The Journals of Hugh Gaine, Printer (New York, 1902), II, 8–9; May 20, 1757, The Montresor Journals (N.-Y. Hist. Soc., Coll., XIV [New York, 1882]), 150–151; Benjamin Cutter, History of the Cutter Family of New England (Boston, 1871), 67; Evarts B. Greene and Virginia D. Harrington, American Population before the Federal Census of 1790 (New York, 1932), 101, 1756 census.

[56] Boston is so described in a petition of the town meeting to the House of Representatives, Mar. 11, 1745/6, Mass. Hist. Soc., Mass. House Journals, XXII, 204. This petition is but one of many attributing the depletion of Boston's population in part to impressment. For a table indicating a downward trend in Boston's population after 1743 see Stuart Bruchey, ed., The Colonial Merchant: Sources and Readings (New York, 1966), 11. I am indebted to Joel Shufro, a graduate student at the University of Chicago, for the suggestion of a connection between impressment and the decline of Boston.

[57] Log of Shirley, Dec. 25, 1745-May 17, 1746, Adm. 51/4341; log of Gramont, Apr. 25–27, 1758, Adm. 51/413; log of Arethusa, Mar. 19–20, 1771, Adm. 51/59. Shirley's haul was not mentioned in the Boston Evening Post or in the records of any American governmental body. Here is but one instance in which the serious grievance of 92 Americans has previously gone unnoticed. Such grievances are nonetheless real and play a causal role despite their invisibility to historians. On the other hand, overdependence on British sources is apt to be extremely

took flight, and merchants complained loudly about the "many Thousands of Pounds of Damage."[58] "Kiss my arse, you dog," shouted the captain as he made off with their men, leaving vessels with their fires still burning, unmanned, finally to be wrecked.[59] They took legislators and slaves, fishermen and servants.[60] Seamen took to the woods or fled town altogether, dreading the appearance of a man-of-war's boat—in the words of one—as a flock of sheep dreaded a wolf's appearance.[61] If they offered to work at all, they demanded inflated wages and refused to sail to ports where there was danger of impressment.[62] "New York and Boston," Benjamin Franklin commented during the French and Indian War, "have so often found the Inconvenience of . . . Station Ships that they are very indifferent about having them: The Pressing of their Men and thereby disappointing Voyages, often hurting their Trade more than the Enemy hurts it." Even a ferryboat operator complained as people shunned the city during a press; food and fuel grew short and their prices rose.[63]

From the very beginning the history of impressment in America is a tale of venality, deceit, and vindictiveness. Captains kept deserters and dead men on ships' books, pocketing their provision allowances. In 1706 a captain pressed men and literally sold them to short-handed vessels; his midshipman learned the

misleading. Either because of sloppiness or because of the clouded legality of impressment, official records seem more often to ignore the practice or to distort it than to complement information from American sources. Admiral Charles Hardy neglected to mention the massive press in New York in 1757 in his correspondence with the Admiralty. See May-June 1757, Adm. 1/481. The absence of impressment in *Triton's Prize*'s log in 1706, Adm. 51/1014, is contradicted in Lord Cornbury to Lords of Trade, Oct. 3, 1706, O'Callaghan, ed., *Docs. Rel. Col. Hist. N. Y.*, IV, 1183–1185. Sometimes logs show what seems to be purposeful distortion: *Diana*, whose log, Apr. 15, 1758, Adm. 51/4162, reveals only that she "saluted with 9 Guns" *Prince of Orange* privateer, in fact pressed her hands, *Montresor Journal*, 152. In another instance St. John "received on board a Boat Load of Ballast," log, July 16, 1764, Adm. 51/3961, which seems in fact to have consisted of hogs, sheep, and poultry stolen from the people of Martha's Vineyard, *Newport Mercury*, July 23, 1764. See below n. 69.

[58] *Boston Evening Post*, Sept. 3, 1739, July 6, 1741.

[59] Deposition of Nathaniel Holmes, July 18, 1702, Deposition of John Gullison, July 17, 1702, Lt. Gov. Thomas Povey to Lords Commissioners for Trade and Plantations, July 20, 1702, Colonial Office Group, Class 5, Piece 862, Public Record Office. Hereafter cited as C. O. 5/862; *Boston Evening Post*, Dec. 14, 1747; *N.-Y. Gaz.; Weekly Post-Boy*, Jan. 14, 1771.

[60] Peter Woodbery and John Tomson to Governor William Phips, July 1, 2, 1692, C. O. 5/751; James and Drinker to [?], Oct. 29, 1756, James and Drinker Letterbook 1, Historical Society of Pennsylvania, Philadelphia; *Boston Evening Post*, Dec. 9, 1745; Mass. Hist. Soc., *Mass. House Journals*, II, 300–301, XXXIII, Pt. ii, 433; *N.-Y. Gaz.; Weekly Post-Boy*, July 12, 1764.

[61] Mass. Hist. Soc., *Mass. House Journals*, XXXV, 267; William Shirley to Gideon Wanton, June 6, 1745, Charles H. Lincoln, ed., *Correspondence of William Shirley* (New York, 1912), I, 227; Mr. Colden to Lords of Trade, Aug. 30, 1760, O'Callaghan, ed., *Docs. Rel. Col. Hist. N. Y.*, VII, 446; Andrew Sherburne, *Memoirs of Andrew Sherburne* (Utica, 1828), 68.

[62] Mass. Hist. Soc., *Mass. House Journals*, XXXV, 267; James and Drinker to Nehemiah Champion, July 13, 1757, James and Drinker Letterbook, I, 145.

[63] Franklin to Joseph Galloway, Apr. 7, 1759, Labaree et al., eds., *Papers of Benjamin Franklin*, VIII, 315-316; Morris, *Government and Labor*, 274; Mr. Colden to Lords of Trade, Aug. 30, 1760, O'Callaghan, ed., *Docs. Rel. Col. Hist. N. Y.*, VII, 446; Mass. Hist. Soc., *Mass. House Journals*, XVIII, 202; XX, 84; Boston Reg. Dept., *Records of Boston*, XVII, 125. See also Gerard G. Beekman to William Beekman, July 3, 1764, Philip L. White, ed., *The Beekman Mercantile Papers*, 1746–1799 (New York, 1956), I, 469.

business so well that after his dismissal he became a veritable entrepreneur of impressment, setting up shop in a private sloop. Another commander waited until New York's governor was away to break a no-press agreement and when the governor returned he seriously considered firing on the Queen's ship.[64] In Boston in 1702 the lieutenant-governor did fire, responding to merchants' complaints. "Fire and be damn'd," shouted the impressing captain as the shots whistled through his sails. The merchants had complained that the press was illegal under 1697 instructions which required captains and commanders to apply to colonial governors for permission to press.[65] These instructions, a response to complaints of "irregular proceedings of the captains of some of our ships of war in the impressing of seamen," had clearly not put an end to irregularities.[66] In 1708 a Parliament fearful of the disruptive effect of impressment on trade forbade the practice in America. In the sixty-seven years until the repeal in 1775 of this "Act for the Encouragement of the Trade to America" there was great disagreement as to its meaning and indeed as to its very existence. Did the Sixth of Anne, as the act was called, merely prohibit the navy from impressing and leave governors free to do so? At least one governor, feeling "pinioned" under the law, continued impressing while calling it "borrowing."[67] Was the act simply a wartime measure, which expired with the return of peace in 1713?[68] Regardless of the dispute, impressment continued, routine in its regularity, but often spectacular in its effects.[69]

[64] William Polhampton to the Lords of Trade, Mar. 6, 1711, Lord Cornbury to Lords of Trade, Oct. 3, Dec. 14, 1706, O'Callaghan, ed., *Docs. Rel. Col. Hist. N. Y.,* V, 194; IV, 1183–1184, 1190–1191. The captain later publicly declared that he hated the whole province and would not help a New York vessel in distress at sea if he met one, Lord Cornbury to Lords of Trade, July 1, 1708, ibid., V, 60. It seems increasingly to have become common practice to press after a public declaration that there would be no press, for example, *Boston Evening Post,* Dec. 9, 23, 1745; log of *Shirley,* Dec. 25, 1745-May 17, 1746, Adm. 51/4341.

[65] Lieutenant Governor Thomas Povey to Lords Commissioners for Trade and Plantations, July 20, 1702, Memorial of Thomas Povey, [July, 1702], Deposition of Nathaniel Holmes, July 18, 1702, Deposition of John Arnold and John Roberts, July 18, 1702, C. O. 5/862.

[66] For instructions to royal governors giving them sole power to press in their province see Leonard W. Labaree, ed., *Royal Instructions to British Colonial Governors, 1670–1776* (New York, 1935), I, 442–443; Instructions for the Earl of Bellomont, Aug. 31, 1697, Copy of . . . Lovelace's Instructions, n.d., O'Callaghan, ed., *Docs. Rel. Col. Hist. N. Y.,* IV, 287; V, 101. See also Clark, "Impressment of Seamen," in *Essays to Andrews,* 202–205.

[67] *Calendar of Council Minutes, 1668–1783* (New York State Library, *Bulletin* 58 [Mar. 1902]), 229, 230; Stokes, *Iconography of Manhattan,* IV, 465, 973; V, 99–101; Chief Justice . . . Opinion, June 30, 1709, Report of the Councill, July 3, 1709, Governor Hunter to Secretary St. John, Sept. 12, 1711, O'Callaghan, ed., *Docs. Rel. Col. Hist. N. Y.,* V, 100, 102, 254–255.

[68] In 1716 the attorney-general declared, "I am of Opinion, that the whole American Act was intended . . . only for the War," *Massachusetts Gazette* (Boston), June 17, 1768. Governor Shirley of Massachusetts agreed in 1747, despite the fact that, along with other colonial governors, he was still instructed to enforce the Sixth of Anne and had indeed sworn to do so, The Lords Justices to William Shirley, Sept. 10, 1741, Lincoln, ed., *Correspondence of Shirley,* I, 74–76; Stout, *Royal Navy,* 391. Twenty-two years later Governor Hutchinson feared that John Adams might publicize the act. The Admiralty continued to instruct American commanders to obey the act after Queen Anne's War, for example, see Admiralty to Captain Balcher, Mar. 9, 1714, Adm. 2/48, but ceased so to instruct them in 1723, Clark, "Impressment of Seamen," in *Essays to Andrews,* 211. Of course, the act's repeal in 1775 indicated that it had been on the books, if no place else, all that time.

[69] Stout's claim in *Royal Navy,* 366, that the navy began pressing again only in 1723 illustrates

Boston was especially hard-hit by impressment in the 1740s, with frequent incidents throughout the decade and major explosions in 1745 and 1747. Again and again the town meeting and the House of Representatives protested, drumming away at the same themes: impressment was harmful to maritime commerce and to the economic life of the city in general and illegal if not properly authorized.[70] In all this the seaman himself becomes all but invisible. The attitude towards him in the protests is at best neutral and often sharply antagonistic. In 1747 the House of Representatives condemned the violent response of hundreds of seamen to a large-scale press as "a tumultuous riotous assembling of armed Seamen, Servants, Negroes, and others . . . tending to the Destruction of all Government and Order." While acknowledging that the people had reason to protest, the House chose to level *its* protest against "the most audacious Insult" to the governor, Council, and House. And the town meeting, that stronghold of democracy, offered its support to those who took "orderly" steps while expressing its "Abhorence of such illegal Criminal Proceedings" as those undertaken by the seamen "and other persons of mean and Vile Condition."[71]

Protests such as these reflect at the same time both unity and division in colonial society. All kinds of Americans—both merchants and seamen—opposed impressment, but the town meeting and the House spoke for the merchant, not the seaman. They opposed impressment not for its effect on the seaman but for its effect on commerce. Thus their protests express antagonism to British policy at the same time that they express class division. These two themes continue and develop in American opposition to impressment in the three decades between the Knowles Riots of 1747 and the Declaration of Independence.

During the French and Indian War the navy competed with privateers for seamen.[72] Boston again protested against impressment, and then considered authorizing the governor to press, "provided said Men be impressed from inward-bound Vessels from Foreign Parts only, and that none of them be Inhabitants of this Province."[73] In 1760 New York's mayor had a naval captain arrested on the complaint of two shipmasters who claimed that he had welched on a deal to exchange two men he had pressed for two others they were willing to furnish.[74] With the return of peace in 1763 admirals and Americans alike had reason to

121

again the dangers of over-reliance on British sources in such controversial matters. That the Admiralty continued to instruct commanders not to press does not mean that they did not in fact press. *Shark* pressed in Boston in 1720, Mass. Hist. Soc., *Mass. House Journals,* II, 300–301; interestingly, her log for Oct.-Nov. 1720, Adm. 51/892, contains no mention of the fact.

[70] See, for example, Mass. Hist. Soc., *Mass. House Journals,* XVIII, 202; XX, 98–99; XXII, 76–77, 204–205.

[71] Ibid., XXIV, 212; Boston Reg. Dept., *Records of Boston,* XIV, 127. Bridenbaugh, *Cities in Revolt,* 117, sees the law of 1751 for suppressing riots as in part a response to the Knowles Riots; he calls the law "brutal" even for its own day and a "triumph for the reactionaries."

[72] See, for example, Lord Loudoun to Pitt, Mar. 10, May 30, 1757, Kimball, ed., *Correspondence of Pitt,* I, 19, 69; Lieutenant-Governor De Lancey to Secretary Pitt, Mar. 17, 1758, O'Callaghan, ed., *Docs. Rel. Col. Hist. N. Y.,* VII, 343.

[73] Mass. Hist. Soc., *Mass. House Journals,* XXXIII, Pt. ii, 434; XXXIV, Pt. i, 134; Boston Reg. Dept., *Records of Boston,* XIX, 96–97; log of *Hunter,* Aug. 31, 1758, Adm. 51/465. The Council voted such authorization, but the House did not concur.

[74] Capt. George Ant. Tonyn to Admiralty, Mar. 1, 1760, Depositions of Peter Vail and Singleton Church, Jan. 15, 16, 1760, Adm. 1/2588.

suppose that there would be no more impressment.[75] But the Admiralty's plans for a large new American fleet required otherwise, and impressment began again in the spring of 1764 in New York, where a seven-week hot press was brought to a partial stop by the arrest of one of the two offending captains.[76] In the spring and summer a hunt for men between Maine and Virginia by four naval vessels brought violent responses, including the killing of a marine at New York; another fort, at Newport, fired on another naval vessel.[77]

Along with the divisions there was a certain amount of unity. Seamen who fled after violently resisting impressment could not be found—probably because others sheltered them—and juries would not indict them. Captains were prevented from impressing by the threat of prosecution.[78] And in 1769 lawyer John Adams used the threat of displaying the statute book containing the Sixth of Anne to frighten a special court of Admiralty into declaring the killing of an impressing lieutenant justifiable homicide in necessary self-defense.[79]

There were two kinds of impressment incidents: those in which there was immediate self-defense against impressment, usually at sea, and those in which crowds ashore, consisting in large part of seamen, demonstrated generalized opposition to impressment. This is what the first kind of incident sounded like: a volley of musketry and the air full of langrage, grapeshot, round shot, hammered shot, double-headed shot, even rocks. "Come into the boat and be damned, you Sorry Son of a Whore or else Ile breake your head, and hold your tongue." Small arms, swords and cutlasses, blunderbusses, clubs and pistols, axes, harpoons, fishgigs, twelve-pounders, six-pounders, half-pounders. "You are a parsill of Raskills." Fired five shots to bring to a snow from North Carolina, pressed four. "You have no right to impress me . . . If you step over that line . . . by the eternal God of Heaven, you are a dead man." "Aye, my lad, I have seen many a brave fellow before now."[80]

[75] Admiral Colvill, Journal, Mar. 19, 1764, Adm. 50/4; Colvill to Admiralty, May 19, 1764, Adm. 1/482; *N.-Y. Gaz.; Weekly Post-Boy,* July 18, 1765.

[76] Stout, *Royal Navy,* 72–73, citing Admiralty to Egremont, Jan. 5, 1763, State Papers Group, Class 42, Piece 43, Public Record Office. Hereafter cited as S.P. 42/43; Captain Jno. Brown to Admiralty, May 16, 1764, Adm. 1/1494; log of *Coventry,* Mar. 31, 1764, Adm. 51/213, indicates impressment on that date; compare Stout, *Royal Navy,* 379, 393n.

[77] Admiral Colvill, Journal, June 4, 1764, Adm. 50/4; Colvill to Admiralty, June 18, 1764, Adm. 1/482. On the violence at New York see log of *Jamaica,* June 8, 1764, Adm. 51/3874; *N.-Y. Gaz.; Weekly Post-Boy,* July 12, 1764; Report of the Grand Jury, Aug. 2, 1764, New York Supreme Court Minute Book (July 31, 1764-Oct. 28, 1764), 7. On the violence at Newport see log of *St. John,* July 10, 1764, Adm. 51/3961; Captain Smith to Colvill, July 12, 1764, in Colvill to Admiralty, Aug. 24, 1764, Adm. 1/482; John Temple to Treasury, Sept. 9, 1765, Treasury Group, Class 1, Piece 442, Library of Congress transcript.

[78] *The King* v. *Osborn Greatrakes* and *The King* v. *Josiah Moore,* Oct. 24, 28, 30, Nov. 11–17, 1760, New York Supreme Court Minute Book (1756–1761), 1–6, 200, 209, 215; Henry B. Dawson, *The Sons of Liberty in New York* (New York, 1859), 53; *N.-Y. Gaz.; Weekly Post-Boy,* July 12, 1764; Report of Grand Jury, Aug. 2, 1764, New York Supreme Court Minute Book (July 31, 1764-Oct. 28, 1767), 7; Colvill to Admiralty, Aug. 5, 1766, Adm. 1/482.

[79] Charles Francis Adams, ed., *The Works of John Adams* (Boston, 1850–1856), II, 225n-226n, and "The Inadmissable Principles of the King of England's Proclamation of October 16, 1807, Considered" [1809], IX, 317–318; Thomas Hutchinson, *The History of the Colony and Province of Massachusetts-Bay,* ed. Lawrence S. Mayo (Cambridge, Mass., 1936), III, 167n; log of *Rose,* Apr. 22, 1769, Adm. 51/804; Admiral Hood to Admiralty, May 5, 1769, Adm. 1/483.

[80] *The King* v. *Ship Sampson,* Examination of Hugh Mode, Pilot, taken Aug. 19, 1760, N. Y.

Here is hostility and bloodshed, a tradition of antagonism. From the beginning, impressment's most direct victims—the seamen—were its most active opponents. Bernard Bailyn's contention that "not a single murder resulted from the activities of the Revolutionary mobs in America" does not hold up if extended to cover resistance to impressment; there were murders on both sides. Perhaps the great bulk of incidents of this sort must remain forever invisible to the historian, for they often took place out of sight of friendly observers, and the only witness, the navy, kept records which are demonstrably biased and faulty, omitting the taking of thousands of men.[81] But even the visible records provide a great deal of information. This much we know without doubt: seamen did not go peacefully. Their violence was purposeful, and sometimes they were articulate. "I know who you are," said one, as reported by John Adams and supported by Thomas Hutchinson. "You are the lieutenant of a man-of-war, come with a press-gang to deprive me of my liberty. You have no right to impress me. I have retreated from you as far as I can. I can go no farther. I and my companions are determined to stand upon our defence. Stand off."[82] (It was difficult for Englishmen to fail to see impressment in such terms—even a sailor *doing* the pressing could feel shame over "fighting with honest sailors, to deprive them of their liberty.")[83]

Ashore, seamen and others demonstrated their opposition to impressment with the only weapon which the unrepresentative politics of the day offered

---

Supreme Court, Pleadings K-304; *N.-Y. Gaz.; Weekly Post-Boy*, May 1, 1758, Aug. 7, 1760; Captain J. Hale to Admiralty, Aug. 28, 1760, Adm. 1/1895; William McCleverty to Admiralty, July 31, 1760, Adm. 1/2172; Howard Thomas, *Marine Willett* (Prospect, N. Y. 1954) 3-4. Deposition of John Gullison, July 17, 1702, Deposition of Woodward Fay, July 17, 1702, C. O. 5/862; log of *Magdelen*, Apr. 6, 1771, Adm. 51/3984, describing the loss during a press "by Accident" of a sword and musquet—apparently a common accident; see also log of *Arethusa*, Apr. 18, 1772, Adm. 51/59; Weyman's *New-York Gazette*, Aug. 25, 1760; Admiral Hood to Admiralty, May 5, 1769, Adm. 1/483; paraphrase of log of *Shirley*, Jan. 17, 1746, Adm. 51/4341; "Inadmissable Principles" [1809], Adams, ed., *Works of Adams*, IX. 318.

[81] Bailyn, ed., *Pamphlets*, I, 581. Six Englishmen of varying ranks were killed while pressing in the 1760s. In addition to the incidents just discussed in which a lieutenant of marines was murdered on June 8, 1764, while pressing at New York and in which John Adams's clients-to-be, accused of murdering a lieutenant off Cape Ann Apr. 22, 1769, got off with justifiable homicide in self-defense, four sailors were shot to death at New York, Aug. 18, 1760. Cadwallader Colden to Lords of Trade, Aug. 30, 1760, O'Callaghan, ed., *Docs. Rel. Col. Hist. N. Y.*, VII, 446; *The King* v. *Osborn Greatrakes* and *the King* v. *Josiah Moore*, Oct. 24, 28, 30, Nov. 11 17, 1760, New York Supreme Court Minute Book (1756–1761), 1–16, 200, 209, 215; *The King* v. *Ship Sampson*, Examination of Hugh Mode, Pilot, taken Aug. 19, 1760, N. Y. Supreme Court, Pleadings K-304; Capt. J. Hale to Admiralty, Aug. 28, 1760, Adm. 1/1895; Weyman's *N.-Y. Gaz.*, Aug. 25, 1760; Dawson, *Sons of Liberty*, 51–54. Governor Cadwallader Colden called the last incident murder, but the jury refused to indict. For some instances of Americans killed while resisting impressment see deposition of William Thwing, Nathaniel Vaill, and Thomas Hals, July 15, 1702, C. O. 5/862; Governor Hunter to Secretary St. John, Sept. 12, 1711, O'Callaghan, ed., *Docs. Rel. Col. Hist. N. Y.*, V, 254–255 (conviction of murder); Bridenbaugh, *Cities in Revolt*, 114–115; *N.-Y. Gaz.; Weekly Post-Boy*, Aug. 7, 1760. There is every reason to suppose that this list is partial. See above n. 57.

[82] "Inadmissable Principles" [1809], Adams, ed., *Works of Adams*, IX, 318, quotes Michael Corbet, commenting that Corbet displayed "the cool intrepidity of a Nelson, reasoned, remonstrated, and laid down the law with the precision of a Mansfield." Hutchinson, *History of Massachusetts-Bay*, ed. Mayo, III, 167n, notes that Corbet and his companions "swore they would die before they would be taken, and that they preferred death to slavery."

[83] "Inadmissable Principles" [1809], Adams, ed., *Works of Adams*, IX, 317–318.

them—riot. In Boston several thousand people responded to a nighttime impressment sweep of the harbor and docks with three days of rioting beginning in the early hours of November 17, 1747. Thomas Hutchinson reported that "the lower class were beyond measure enraged." Negroes, servants, and hundreds of seamen seized a naval lieutenant, assaulted a sheriff and put his deputy in the stocks, surrounded the governor's house, and stormed the Town House where the General Court was sitting. The rioters demanded the seizure of the impressing officers, the release of the men they had pressed, and execution of a death sentence which had been levied against a member of an earlier press-gang who had been convicted of murder. When the governor fled to Castle William—some called it "abdication"—Commodore Knowles threatened to put down what he called "arrant rebellion" by bombarding the town. The governor, who, for his part, thought the rioting a secret plot of the upper class, was happily surprised when the town meeting expressed its "Abhorence" of the seamen's riot.[84]

After the French and Indian War press riots increased in frequency. Armed mobs of whites and Negroes repeatedly manhandled captains, officers, and crews, threatened their lives, and held them hostage for the men they pressed. Mobs fired at pressing vessels and tried to board them; they threatened to burn one, and they regularly dragged ships' boats to the center of town for ceremonial bonfires. In Newport in June 1765, five hundred seamen, boys, and Negroes rioted after five weeks of impressment. "Sensible" Newporters opposed impressment but nonetheless condemned this "Rabble." In Norfolk in 1767 Captain Jeremiah Morgan retreated, sword in hand, before a mob of armed whites and Negroes. "Good God," he wrote to the governor, "was your Honour and I to prosecute all the Rioters that attacked us belonging to Norfolk there would not be twenty left unhang'd belonging to the Toun."[85] According to Thomas Hutchinson, the *Liberty* Riot in Boston in 1768 may have been as much against impressment as against the seizure of Hancock's sloop: *Romney* had pressed before June 10, and on that day three officers were forced by an angry crowd "arm'd with Stones" to release a man newly pressed from the Boston packet.[86] *Romney* pressed another

---

[84] Hutchinson, *History of Massachusetts-Bay,* ed. Mayo, II, 330–331, 333; Mass. Hist. Soc., *Mass. House Journals,* XXIV, 212; Bridenbaugh, *Cities in Revolt,* 115–117; Boston Reg. Dept., *Records of Boston,* XIV, 127; William Shirley to Lords of Trade, Dec. 1, 1747, Lincoln, ed., *Correspondence of Shirley,* I, 412–419, is the best single account. Shirley says that only the officers responded to his call for the militia.

[85] *Newport Mercury,* June 10, 1765; Captain Jeremiah Morgan to Governor Francis Fauquier, Sept. 11, 1767, Adm. 1/2116; log of *St. John,* July 10, 1764, Adm. 51/3961; Remarks of Thomas Hill in Colvill to Admiralty, July 26, 1764, Colvill to Admiralty, Jan. 12, Sept. 21, 1765, Adm. 1/482; log of *Maidstone,* June 5, 1765, Adm. 51/3897; Captain Smith to Colvill, July 12, 1764 (extract) in Colvill to Admiralty, Aug. 24, 1764, Adm. 1/482; *N.-Y. Gaz.; Weekly Post-Boy,* July 12, 1764; Thomas Laugharne to Admiral Colvill, Aug. 11, 1764 (extract) in Colvill to Admiralty, Aug. 24, 1764, Adm. 1/482; Stout's contention, "Manning the Royal Navy," 185, that "there is no recorded case of impressment on shore during the 1760s and 1770s, although the Navy did capture some deserters on land" is inaccurate. See Captain Jeremiah Morgan to Governor Francis Fauquier, Sept. 11, 1767, Adm. 1/2116, and *Pennsylvania Chronicle and Universal Advertiser* (Philadelphia), Oct. 26, 1767.

[86] For impressment by *Romney,* see log, June 10, 1768, Adm. 51/793; Mayo, ed., *Hist.,* III, 139. Oliver M. Dickerson, *The Navigation Acts and the American Revolution* (Philadelphia, 1951), 238, sees the riot as growing out of the seizure and has the support of most sources. Massachusetts Council to Governor Gage, Oct. 27, 1768, Bowdoin-Temple Papers, I, 120, Massachusetts Historical Society, Boston; Admiral Hood to Admiralty, July 11, 1768, Adm. 1/483;

man, and on June 14, after warding off "many wild and violent proposals," the town meeting petitioned the governor against both the seizure and impressment; the instructions to their representatives (written by John Adams) quoted the Sixth of Anne at length. On June 18 two councillors pleaded with the governor to procure the release of a man pressed by *Romney* "as the peace of the Town seems in a great measure to depend upon it."[87]

There were other impressment riots at New York in July of 1764 and July of 1765;[88] at Newport in July of 1764;[89] at Casco Bay, Maine, in December 1764.[90] Incidents continued during the decade following, and impressment flowered on the very eve of the Revolution. Early in 1775 the practice began to be used in a frankly vindictive and political way—because a town had inconvenienced an admiral, or because a town supported the Continental Congress.[91] Impresses were ordered and took place from Maine to Virginia.[92] In September a bundle of press warrants arrived from the Admiralty, along with word of the repeal of the Sixth

---

Hutchinson, *History of Massachusetts-Bay,* III, 136. On the other hand Thomas Hutchinson also spoke of impressment as adding "more fewel to the great stock among us before." Mass. Hist. Soc., *Proceedings, 1921–1922* (Boston, 1923), 283. Clark, "Impressment of Seamen," in *Essays to Andrews,* 219, describes the rioting as a response to impressment alone by a mob "which seemed to be always ready to resent any infringement of American liberties." Dickerson, *Navigation Acts,* 219–220, attributes the burning of a boat belonging to the customs collector to the mob's failure to locate *Romney's* press boat. In 1922 G. G. Wolkins, "Seizure of Liberty," 250, speculated that "impressment of seamen, rather than the seizure of John Hancock's goods, was perhaps the genesis of what happened." L. Kinvin Wroth and Hiller B. Zobel, eds., *Legal Papers of John Adams* (Cambridge, Mass., 1965), II, 179n, summarize: "Boston's position was that the employment of the *Romney,* already despised for the impressment activities of her captain, brought on the riot of 10 June." The riot seems to have been caused by a combination of factors among which impressment has been given too little attention.

[87] Boston Reg. Dept., *Records of Boston,* XX, 296; [Thomas Hutchinson], State of the Disorders, Confusion and Misgovernment, which have lately prevailed . . . in . . . Massachusetts, June 21, 1770, C. O. 5/759, Pt. 4; Report of Resolves Relating to Riot of June 10, June 14, 1768, James Bowdoin and Royall Tyler to Jno. Corner, June 18, 1768, Bowdoin-Temple Papers, I, 102, 104; *Mass. Gaz.* (Boston), Nov. 10, 1768. For Adams's authorship, see L. H. Butterfield et al., eds., *Diary and Autobiography of John Adams* (New York, 1964), III, 291; Adams, ed., *Works of Adams,* III, 501.

[88] *N.-Y. Gaz.; Weekly Post-Boy,* July 12, 1764, July 18, 1765; Thos. Lagharne to Admiral Colvill, Aug. 11, 1764 (extract) in Colvill to Admiralty, July 26, Aug. 24, 1764, Adm. 1/482; *Weyman's N. Y. Gaz.,* July 18, 1765.

[89] Captain Smith to Colvill, July 12, 1764 (extract) in Colvill to Admiralty, Aug. 24, 1764, Adm. 1/482; Remarks of Thomas Hill in Colvill to Admiralty, July 26, 1764, Adm. 1/482; log of *Squirrel,* July 10, 1764, Adm. 51/929; log of *St. John,* July 10, 1764, Adm. 51/3961; *Newport Mercury,* July 16, 1764.

[90] Colvill to Admiralty, Jan. 12, 1765, Adm. 1/482; log of *Gaspée,* Dec. 8, 10, 12, 1764, Adm. 51/3856.

[91] Graves to Admiralty, Feb. 20, 1775, Adm. 1/485; *N. Y. Journal or Gen. Adv.,* Feb. 23, 1775; Margaret Wheeler Willard, ed., *Letters on the American Revolution, 1774–1776* (Boston, 1925), 65–66.

[92] Graves to Admiralty, Apr. 11, 1775, Mowat to Graves, May 4, 1775, in Graves to Admiralty, May 13, 1775, Barkley to Graves, June 5, 1775, in Graves to Admiralty, June 22, 1775, Montagu to Graves, June 17, 1775, in Graves to Admiralty, July 17, 1775, Adm. 1/485; log of *Scarborough,* May 14, 1775, Adm. 51/867; log of *Fowey,* July 16, 23, 1775, Adm. 51/375. Despite the troubles at Marblehead in February, *Lively* was still pressing there in May, Graves to Admiralty, May 13, 1775, Adm. 1/485.

of Anne. What had been dubious was now legal. Up and down the coast, officers rejoiced and went to work.[93]

Long before 1765 Americans had developed beliefs about impressment, and they had expressed those beliefs in words and deeds. Impressment was bad for trade and it was illegal. As such, it was, in the words of the Massachusetts House in 1720, "a great Breach on the Rights of His Majesties Subjects." In 1747 it was a violation of "the common Liberty of the Subject," and in 1754 "inconsistent with Civil Liberty, and the Natural Rights of Mankind."[94] Some felt in 1757 that it was even "abhorrent to the English Constitution."[95] In fact, the claim that impressment was unconstitutional was wrong. (Even *Magna Charta* was no protection. *Nullus liber homo capiatur* did not apply to seamen.)[96] Instead impressment indicated to Benjamin Franklin "that the constitution is yet imperfect, since in so general a case it doth not secure liberty, but destroys it." "If impressing seamen is of right by common law in Britain," he also remarked, "slavery is then of right by common law there; there being no slavery worse than that sailors are subjected to."[97]

For Franklin, impressment was a symptom of injustice built into the British Constitution. In *Common Sense* Tom Paine saw in impressment a reason for rejecting monarchy. In the Declaration of Independence Thomas Jefferson included impressment among the "Oppressions" of George III; later he likened the practice to the capture of Africans for slavery. Both "reduced [the victim] to . . . bondage by force, in flagrant violation of his own consent, and of his natural right in his own person."[98]

Despite all this, and all that went before, we have thought little of impressment as an element in explaining the conduct of the common man in the American Revolution.[99] Contemporaries knew better. John Adams felt that a

[93] Admiralty to Graves, June 24, Sept. 29, 1775, Adm. 2/549, 550; Graves to Admiralty, Sept. 12, 1775, List of . . . Press Warrants, Jan. 27, 1776, in Graves to Admiralty, Jan. 1776, Adm. 1/486; Shuldham to Arbuthnot, June 5, 1776, in Shuldham to Admiralty, July 24, 1776, Adm. 1/484.

[94] Mass. Hist. Soc., *Mass. House Journals,* II, 300–301; Freeman, *Washington,* I, 199; *N.-Y. Gaz.; Weekly Post-Boy,* Aug. 12, 1754.

[95] Mass. Hist. Soc., *Mass. House Journals,* XXXIII, Pt. ii, 434.

[96] Hutchinson, *Press-Gang,* 5–7.

[97] Sparks, ed., *Works of Franklin,* II, 338, 334. For opposition to impressment on the part of the Genevan democrat, Jean Louis De Lolme, and by the British radical John Wilkes, see Robert R. Palmer, *The Age of the Democratic Revolution* (Princeton, 1959), 148. *N.-Y. Gaz.; Weekly Post-Boy,* Dec. 31, 1770; *Annual Register . . . for 1771* (London, 1772), 67, 68, 70–71; R. W. Postgate, *That Devil Wilkes* (New York, 1929), 182; Percy Fitzgerald, *The Life and Times of John Wilkes* (London, 1888), II, 120.

[98] Paine, *Writings,* ed. Foner, I, 11. For later attacks on impressment by Paine see ibid., I, 449, II, 476. The complaint in the Declaration of Independence alludes to impressment after the outbreak of fighting: "He has constrained our fellow Citizens taken Captive on the high Seas to bear Arms against their Country, to become the executioners of their friends and Brethren, or to fall themselves by their Hands." Carl L. Becker, *The Declaration of Independence* (New York, 1958), 190, 156, 166. Thomas Jefferson to Dr. Thomas Cooper, Sept. 10, 1814, Andrew A. Lipscomb and Albert Ellery Bergh, eds., *The Writings of Thomas Jefferson,* XIV (Washington, 1907), 183.

[99] James Fulton Zimmerman, *Impressment of American Seamen* (New York, 1925), esp. 11–17, treats the practice as almost nonexistent before the Revolution, giving the pre-revolutionary

tactical mistake by Thomas Hutchinson on the question of impressment in 1769 would have "accelerated the revolution. . . . It would have spread a wider flame than Otis's ever did, or could have done."[100] Ten years later American seamen were being impressed by *American* officers. The United States Navy had no better solution for "public Necessities" than had the Royal Navy. Joseph Reed, President of Pennsylvania, complained to Congress of "Oppressions" and in so doing offered testimony to the role of *British* impressment in bringing on revolution. "We cannot help observing how similar this Conduct is to that of the British Officers during our Subjection to Great Brittain and are persuaded it will have the same unhappy effects viz., an estrangement of the Affections of the People from the Authority under which they act which by an easy Progression will proceed to open Opposition to the immediate Actors and Bloodshed."[101] Impressment had played a role in the estrangement of the American people from the British government. It had produced "Odium" against the navy, and even six-year-olds had not been too young to have learned to detest it.[102] The anger of thousands of victims did not vanish. Almost four decades after the Declaration of Independence an orator could still arouse his audience by tapping a folk-memory of impressment by the same "haughty, cruel, and gasconading nation" which was once again trying to enslave free Americans.[103]

III

The seamen's conduct in the 1760s and 1770s makes more sense in the light of previous and continued impressment. What may have seemed irrational violence can now be seen as purposeful and radical. The pattern of rioting as political expression, established as a response to impressment was now adapted and broadened as a response to the Stamp Act. In New York General Gage described the "insurrection" of October 31, 1765, and following as "composed of great numbers of Sailors." The seamen, he said, were "the only People who may be properly Stiled Mob," and estimates indicate that between a fifth and a fourth of New York's rioters were seamen. The disturbances began among the seamen—

127

phenomenon only the briefest consideration, and concluding, on the basis of speculative evidence, that impressment was rare in the colonies. The author does not understand the Sixth of Anne and thinks it was repealed in 1769. Clark, "Impressment of Seamen," in *Essays to Andrews*, 202; Paine, *Ships and Sailors of Salem*, 65; George Athan Billias, *General John Glover and Marblehead Mariners* (New York, 1960), 31; Bridenbaugh, *Cities in Revolt*, 114–117, 308–310; Bernhard Knollenberg, *Origin of the American Revolution: 1759–1766* (New York, 1961), 12, 179–181, all see impressment as contributing in some way to the revolutionary spirit.

[100] Adams, ed., *Works of Adams*, II, 226n. Neil Stout, "Manning the Royal Navy," 182–184, suggests that impressment did not become a "great issue" of the American Revolution because American "radicals" did not *make* an issue of it and especially because of the failure of John Adams's attempt to make a "*cause célèbre*" in 1769. Stout's approach sides with the navy and minimizes the *reality* of impressment as a grievance. Its implication is that the seaman had in fact no genuine grievance and that he acted in response to manipulation.

[101] Pres. Reed to Pres. of Congress, 1779, Oct. 21, 1779, *Pa. Archives*, 1st Ser., VII, 762. Reed renewed his complaint of these "Opressions" in the following year, Reed to Pennsylvania Delegates in Congress, 1780, ibid., 1st Ser., VIII, 643.

[102] Colvill to Admiralty, Aug. 8, 1765, Adm. 1/482; Sherburne, *Memoirs*, 68.

[103] William M. Willett, *A Narrative of the Military Actions of Colonel Marinus Willett, Taken Chiefly from his own Manuscript* (New York, 1831), 149–151. On the level of leadership impressment

especially former privateersmen—on October 31. On November 1 they had marched, led primarily by their former captains; later they rioted, led by no one but themselves. Why? Because they had been duped by merchants, or, if not by merchants, then certainly by lawyers. So British officials believed—aroused by these men who meant to use them, the seamen themselves had nothing more than plunder on their minds. In fact, at that point in New York's rioting when the leaders lost control, the seamen, who were then in the center of town, in an area rich for plunder, chose instead to march in an orderly and disciplined way clear across town to do violence to the home and possessions of an English major whose provocative conduct had made him the obvious political enemy. Thus the "rioting" was actually very discriminating.[104]

Seamen and non-seamen alike joined to oppose the Stamp Act for many reasons,[105] but the seamen had two special grievances: impressment and the effect of England's new attitude toward colonial trade. To those discharged by the navy at the end of the war and others thrown out of work by the death of privateering were added perhaps twenty thousand more seamen and fishermen who were thought to be the direct victims of the post-1763 trade regulations.[106] This

---

was not a major cause of the American Revolution. But the extent to which the articulate voice a grievance is rarely an adequate measure of the suffering of the inarticulate. Since it is unrealistic to suppose that the victims of impressment forgot their anger, the question becomes not, why was impressment irrelevant to the American Revolution—for it had to be relevant, in this sense—but, rather, why were the articulate not *more* articulate about the seamen's anger? In part, perhaps, because much impressment took place offshore and was invisible to all but the seamen directly involved. But the leaders had always perceived even visible impressment more as an interference with commerce than as a form of slavery. As the Revolution approached, impressment as human slavery interested them even less than Negro slavery did; the gap between Jack Tar and the men who made laws for him continued. The failure of the elite to see impressment more clearly as a political issue means only that they failed, as we have, to listen to the seamen.

[104] General Gage to Secretary Conway, Nov. 4, Dec. 21, 1765, Clarence Edwin Carter, ed., *The Correspondence of General Thomas Gage . . . 1763–1775* (New Haven, 1931), I, 70–71, 79; *N.-Y. Gaz.; Weekly Post-Boy,* Nov. 7, 1765, estimates that there were four to five hundred seamen in the mob; Nov. 1, 7, 1765, *Montresor Journal,* 336, 339, estimates the total mob at "about 2000" and is the only source describing the participation of a professional group other than seamen, estimating 300 carpenters; R. R. Livingston to General Monckton, Nov. 8, 1765, Chalmers Manuscripts, IV, New York Public Library, for a note signed "Sons of Neptune"; Lieutenant-Governor Colden to Secretary Conway, Nov. 5, 9, 1765, O'Callaghan, ed., *Docs. Rel. Col. Hist. N. Y.,* VII, 771–774; *New York Mercury,* Nov. 4, 1765. For additional information on the leadership of privateer captains, especially Isaac Sears, see William Gordon, *History of the Rise, Progress, and Establishment of the United States of America* (London, 1788), I, 185-186. The navy continued to press during the crisis. See log of *Guarland,* Apr. 22, 1766, Adm. 51/386; Apr. 22, 1766, *Montresor Journal,* 361. Impressment also limited the navy's activities against the rioting. "As most of our men are imprest," wrote a captain in answer to a governor's request for men to put down a mob, "there is a great risque of their deserting." Marines were needed as sentries to keep the men from deserting. Archibald Kennedy to Cadwallader Colden, Nov. 1, 1765, *The Letters and Papers of Cadwallader Colden* (N.-Y. Hist. Soc., *Coll.,* L-LVI [New York, 1918–1923]), VII, 85–86.

[105] For a fuller account of the seamen's opposition to the Stamp Act see Lemisch, "Jack Tar vs. John Bull," 76–128.

[106] *N.-Y. Gaz.; Weekly Post-Boy,* May 19, 1763; "Essay on the trade of the Northern Colonies," ibid., Feb. 9, 1764. Even admirals were worried about the prospects of postwar unemployment, Colvill to Admiralty, Nov. 9, 1762, Adm. I/482. During the French and Indian War 18,000 American seamen had served in the Royal Navy, *Annual Register . . . for 1778* (London, 1779), 201, and a large additional number had been privateersmen. Fifteen to twenty thousand had

problem came to the fore in the weeks following November 1, 1765, when the Stamp Act went into effect. The strategy of opposition chosen by the colonial leadership was to cease all activities which required the use of stamps. Thus maritime trade came to a halt in the cities.[107] Some said that this was a cowardly strategy. If the Americans opposed the Stamp Act, let them go on with business as usual, refusing outright to use the stamps.[108] The leaders' strategy was especially harmful to the seamen, and the latter took the more radical position—otherwise the ships would not sail. And this time the seamen's radicalism triumphed over both colonial leadership and British officials. Within little more than a month the act had been largely nullified. Customs officers were allowing ships to sail without stamps, offering as the reason the fear that the seamen, "who are the people that are most dangerous on these occasions, as their whole dependance for a subsistence is upon Trade," would certainly "commit some terrible Mischief." Philadelphia's customs officers feared that the seamen would soon "compel" them to let ships pass without stamps. Customs officers at New York yielded when they heard that the seamen were about to have a meeting.[109]

Customs officers had worse luck on other days. Seamen battled them throughout the 1760s and 1770s. In October 1769 a Philadelphia customs officer

---

sailed in 224 privateers out of New York alone, 5670 of them in 1759, Fish, *New York Privateers*, 4, 54–82; Bridenbaugh, *Cities in Revolt*, 62. A New York merchants' petition of Apr. 20, 1764, expressed the fear that seamen thrown out of work by the Sugar Act might drift into foreign merchant fleets, *Journal of the Votes and Proceedings of the General Assembly of the Colony of New York* (New York, 1764–1766), II, 742–743. On the eve of the Revolution maritime commerce employed approximately 30,000–35,000 American seamen, Carman, ed., *American Husbandry*, 495–496; John Adams to the President of Congress, June 16, 1780, Francis Wharton, ed., *The Revolutionary Diplomatic Correspondence of the United States* (Washington, 1889), III, 789. I am presently assembling data which will allow more detailed statements on various demographic matters involving seamen, such as their numbers, comparisons with other occupations, their origins and permanence. For some further quantitative information on seamen in various colonial ports, see in addition to the sources cited immediately above, Evarts B. Greene and Richard B. Morris, *A Guide to the Principal Sources for Early American History (1600–1800) in the City of New York,* 2d ed., rev. (New York, 1953), 265; E. B. O'Callaghnn, ed., *The Documentary History of the State of New York,* I (Albany, 1849), 493; Governor Clinton's Report on the Province of New York, May 23, 1749, Report of Governor Tryon on the Province of New York, June 11, 1774, O'Callaghan, ed., *Docs. Rel. Col. Hist. N. Y.,* VI, 511, VIII, 446; Main, *Social Structure,* 38–39; Benjamin W. Labaree, *Patriots and Partisans* (Cambridge, Mass., 1962), 5; John R. Bartlett, ed., *Records of the Colony of Rhode Island and Providence Plantations . . .* (Providence, 1856–1865), VI, 379.

[107] See, for example, James and Drinker to William Starkey, Oct. 30, 1765, James and Drinker Letterbook; *N.-Y. Gaz.; Weekly Post-Boy,* Dec. 19, 1765.

[108] See, for example, *N.-Y. Gaz.; Weekly Post-Boy,* Nov. 28, Dec. 5, 1765. For a fuller account of this dispute, see Jesse Lemisch, "New York's Petitions and Resolves of December 1765: Liberals vs. Radicals," New-York Historical Society, *Quarterly,* XLIX (1965), 313–326.

[109] Edmund S. and Helen M. Morgan, *The Stamp Act Crisis* (Chapel Hill, 1953), 162. For a fuller account of the nullification of the Stamp Act, see ibid., 159–179. The seamen's strategy may have been more effective in bringing about repeal than was the strategy of the leaders. Commenting on Parliament's secret debates, Lawrence Henry Gipson, "The Great Debate in the Committee of the Whole House of Commons on the Stamp Act, 1766, as Reported by Nathaniel Ryder," *Pennsylvania Magazine of History and Biography,* LXXXVI (1962), 10–41, notes that merchant pressure was only the "ostensible cause" of repeal and that many members were influenced by the violent resistance in America. I am indebted to E. S. Morgan for calling Ryder's notes to my attention.

was attacked by a mob of seamen who also tarred, feathered, and nearly drowned a man who had furnished him with information about illegally imported goods. A year later a New Jersey customs officer who approached an incoming vessel in Delaware Bay had *his* boat boarded by armed seamen who threatened to murder him and came close to doing so. When the officer's son came to Philadelphia, he was similarly treated by a mob of seamen; there were one thousand seamen in Philadelphia at the time, and according to the customs collector there, they were "always ready" to do such "mischief."[110] This old antagonism had been further politicized in 1768 when, under the American Board of Customs Commissioners, searchers began to break into sea chests and confiscate those items not covered by cockets, thus breaking an old custom of the sea which allowed seamen to import small items for their own profit. Oliver M. Dickerson has described this new "Invasion of Seamen's Rights" as a part of "customs racketeering" and a cause of animosity between seamen and customs officers.[111]

Many of these animosities flared in the Boston Massacre. What John Adams described as "a motley rabble of saucy boys, negroes and molattoes, Irish teagues and out landish jack tarrs," including twenty or thirty of the latter, armed with clubs and sticks, did battle with the soldiers. Their leader was Crispus Attucks, a mulatto seaman; he was shot to death in front of the Custom House.[112] One of the seamen's reasons for being there has been too little explored. The Massacre grew out of a fight between workers and off-duty soldiers at a ropewalk two days before.[113] That fight, in turn, grew out of the long-standing practice in the British army of allowing off-duty soldiers to take civilian employment. They did so, in Boston and elsewhere, often at wages which undercut those offered to

[110] John Swift to Commissioners of Customs, Oct. 13, 1769, Customs Commissioners to Collector and Comptroller at Philadelphia, Oct. 23, 1769, John Hatton, A State of the Case, Nov. 8, 1770, John Hatton to John Swift, Nov. 9, 1770, Customs Commissioners at Boston to Collector and Comptroller at Philadelphia, Jan. 1771, John Swift to Customs Commissioners, Feb. 11, 1772, John Swift to Customs Commissioners, Nov. 15, 1770, Collector and Comptroller at Philadelphia to Customs Commissioners, Dec. 20, 1770, Philadelphia Custom House Papers, X, 1205, 1209, 1286, 1288; XI; XII; X, 1291–1292; XI, Hist. Soc. Pa. Swift made the customary contention that the seamen rioted because their captains told them to. For a qualification of this contention see Arthur L. Jensen, *The Maritime Commerce of Colonial Philadelphia* (Madison, 1963), 152. For a mob which attacked a collector of customs and others at the time of the Stamp Act and which may have been led by a seaman, see Morgan and Morgan, *Stamp Act Crisis,* 191–194; log of *Cygnet,* Aug. 29, 30, 1765, Adm. 51/223; Captain Leslie to Admiral Colvill, Aug. 30, 31, 1765, Adm. 1/482.

[111] Dickerson, *Navigation Acts,* 218–219. On seamen's right to import, see Morris, *Government and Labor,* 238–239.

[112] On the participation of seamen in the Boston Massacre see testimony of Robert Goddard, Oct. 25, 1770; Ebenezer Bridgham, Nov. 27, 1770; James Bailey, Nov. 28, Dec. 4, 1770; James Thompson, Nov. 30, 1770; all in Wroth and Zobel, eds., *Legal Papers of Adams,* III, 57–58, 103–106, 114–115, 115n–120n, 188, 189n, 268–269; also Frederick Kidder, *History of the Boston Massacre, March 5, 1770* (Albany, 1870), 288. For Adams's description, see Wroth and Zobel, eds., *Legal Papers of Adams,* III, 266. For Attucks see testimony of James Bailey, Nov. 28, 1770, of Patrick Keeton, Nov. 30, 1770, ibid., III, 114–115, 115n–120n, 191–192, 262, 268–269; Kidder, *Boston Massacre,* 29n–30n, 287; Hutchinson, *History of Massachusetts-Bay,* ed. Mayo, III, 196; *Boston Herald,* Nov. 19, 1890 [sic.]; John Hope Franklin, *From Slavery to Freedom* (New York, 1956), 127.

[113] Lt. Col. W. Dalrymple to Hillsborough, Mar. 13, 1770, C. O. 5/759, Pt. 3, Library of Congress photostat; Capt. Thos. Rich to Admiralty, Mar. 11, 1770, Adm. 1/2388; Morris, *Government and Labor,* 190–192.

Americans—including unemployed seamen who sought work ashore—by as much as 50 per cent.[114] In hard times this led to intense competition for work, and the Boston Massacre was in part a product of this competition. Less well known is the Battle of Golden Hill, which arose from similar causes and took place in New York six weeks before. In January 1770 a gang of seamen went from house to house and from dock to dock, using clubs to drive away the soldiers employed there and threatening anyone who might rehire them.[115] In the days of rioting which followed and which came to be called the Battle of Golden Hill, the only fatality was a seaman, although many other seamen were wounded in the attempt to take vengeance for the killing.[116] The antipathy between soldiers and seamen was so great, said John Adams, "that they fight as naturally when they meet, as the elephant and Rhinoceros."[117]

IV

To wealthy Loyalist Judge Peter Oliver of Massachusetts, the common people were only "Rabble"—like the "Mobility of all Countries, perfect Machines, wound up by any Hand who might first take the Winch." The people were "duped," "deceived," and "deluded" by cynical leaders who could "turn the Minds of the great Vulgar." Had they been less ignorant, Americans would have spurned their leaders, and there would have been no Revolution.[118] I have tested this generalization and found it unacceptable, at least in its application to colonial seamen. Obviously the seamen did not cause the American Revolution. But neither were they simply irrational fellows who moved only when others manipulated them. I have attempted to show that the seaman had a mind of his own and genuine reasons to act, and that he did act—purposefully. The final test of this purposefulness must be the Revolution itself. Here we find situations in which the seamen are separated from those who might manipulate them and thrown into great physical danger; if they were manipulated or duped into rebellion, on their own we might expect them to show little understanding of or enthusiasm for the war.

To a surprising extent American seamen remained Americans during the Revolution. Beaumarchais heard from an American in 1775 that seamen, fishermen, and harbor workers had become an "army of furious men, whose actions are all animated by a spirit of vengeance and hatred" against the English, who had

---

[114] *The Times,* Broadsides, 1770–21, New-York Historical Society, New York City; Morris, *Government and Labor,* 190n.

[115] *N.-Y. Gaz.; Weekly Post-Boy,* Feb. 5, 1770, reports on the gang of seamen which went from dock to dock turning out soldiers. *The Times,* N.-Y. Hist. Soc. Broadsides, 1770–21 describes what could only be the same group and adds the threat of vengeance.

[116] *N.-Y. Gaz.; Weekly Post-Boy,* Jan. 22, Feb. 5, 1770; Dawson, *Sons of Liberty,* 117n; William J. Davis, "The Old Bridewell," in Henry B. Dawson, *Reminiscences of the Park and its Vicinity* (New York, 1855), 61. Thomas Hutchinson noted the death of the seaman and believed that the Battle of Golden Hill "encouraged" Boston, thus leading to the Boston Massacre, Hutchinson, *History of Massachusetts-Bay,* ed. Mayo, III, 194.

[117] Wroth and Zobel, eds., *Legal Papers of Adams,* III, 262. See also John Shy, *Toward Lexington* (Princeton, 1965), 309.

[118] Douglass Adair and John A. Schutz, eds., *Peter Oliver's Origin and Progress of the American Rebellion: A Tory View* (San Marino, Calif., 1961), 65, 94–95, 48, 158, 39, 162, 165.

destroyed their livelihood "and the liberty of their country."[119] The recent study of loyalist claimants by Wallace Brown confirms Oliver Dickerson's earlier contention that "the volumes dealing with loyalists and their claims discloses an amazing absence of names" of seamen. From a total of 2786 loyalist claimants whose occupations are known Brown found only 39, 1.4 per cent, who were seamen (or pilots). (It is possible to exclude fishermen and masters but not pilots from his figures.) In contrast, farmers numbered 49.1 per cent, artisans 9.8 per cent, merchants and shopkeepers 18.6 per cent, professionals 9.1 per cent, and officeholders 10.1 per cent. Although as Brown states, the poor may be underrepresented among the claimants, "the large number of claims by poor people, and even Negroes, suggests that this is not necessarily true."[120]

An especially revealing way of examining the seamen's loyalties under pressure is to follow them into British prisons.[121] Thousands of them were imprisoned in such places as the ship *Jersey,* anchored in New York harbor, and Mill and Forton prisons in England. Conditions were abominable. Administration was corrupt, and in America disease was rife and thousands died.[122] If physical discomfort was less in the English prisons than in *Jersey,* the totality of misery may have been as great, with prisoners more distant from the war and worse informed about the progress of the American cause. Lost in a no-man's land between British refusal to consider them prisoners of war and Washington's unwillingness in America to trade trained soldiers for captured seamen, these men had limited opportunities for exchange. Trapped in this very desperate situation, the men were offered a choice: they could defect and join the Royal Navy. To a striking extent the

[119] Louis de Loménie, *Beaumarchais and His Times,* trans. Henry S. Edwards (London, 1856), III, 110. See also Paine, *Writings,* ed. Foner, I, 33.

[120] Dickerson, *Navigation Acts,* 219, offers no explanation of the extent or method of his search. Wallace Brown, *The King's Friends* (Providence, 1965), 263, 287–344. Although Brown states that those listed on pages 261–263 "make up 100 per cent of the claimants," he has excluded those whose occupations are unknown without noting the exclusion. He has also made some minor errors in his calculations, ibid., 261–263, 295, 300, 313. The figures given in the text are my own computations based on corrected totals. I would like to thank Mr. Brown for his assistance in clearing up some of these errors. My own examination of New York materials in Loyalist Transcripts, I–VIII, XLI–XLVIII, and Lorenzo Sabine, *Biographical Sketches of Loyalists of the American Revolution with an Historical Essay* (Boston, 1864), turned up very few loyalist seamen, some of whom were obviously captains. See for example, Alpheus Avery and Richard Jenkins, Loyalist Transcripts, XVIII, 11–15, XLIII, 495–504. Brown, *King's Friends,* 307–308, also finds five out of a total of nine New York loyalist "seamen" are masters.

[121] See Morison, *John Paul Jones,* 165–166. "The unpleasant subject of the treatment of American naval prisoners during the war afforded fuel for American Anglophobes for a century or more, and there is no point in stirring it up again." For a plea that the horrors of the prisons not be forgotten see *New Hampshire Gazette* (Portsmouth), Feb. 9, 1779. The following brief account of the prisons in England and America summarizes my full-length study, "Jack Tar in the Darbies: American Seamen in British Prisons during the Revolution," to be completed shortly.

[122] On the prison ships the standard work at present is James Lenox Banks, *David Sproat and Naval Prisoners in the War of the Revolution with Mention of William Lenox, of Charlestown* (New York, 1909). This contains many useful documents, but the commentary is a one-sided whitewash written by a descendant who was not above ignoring evidence that Sproat elicited favorable accounts of conditions in *Jersey* through threats and bribery. Compare ibid., 12–14, 81–84, with Danske Dandridge, *American Prisoners of the Revolution* (Charlottesville, 1911), 419–423.

prisoners remained patriots,[123] and very self-consciously so. "Like brave men, they resisted, and swore that they would never lift a hand to do any thing on board of King George's ships."[124] The many who stayed understood the political significance of their choice as well as the few who went. "What business had he to sell his Country, and go to the worst of Enemies?"[125] Instead of defecting they engaged in an active resistance movement. Although inexperienced in self-government and segregated from their captains, on their own these men experienced no great difficulties in organizing themselves into disciplined groups. "Notwithstanding they were located within the absolute dominions of his Britanic majesty," commented one, the men "adventured to form themselves into a republic, framed a constitution and enacted wholesome laws, with suitable penalties."[126] Organized, they resisted, celebrating the Fourth of July under British bayonets, burning their prisons, and escaping. Under these intolerable conditions, seamen from all over the colonies discovered that they shared a common conception of the cause for which they fought.[127]

At the Constitutional Convention Benjamin Franklin spoke for the seamen:

It is of great consequence that we shd. not depress the virtue and public spirit of our common people; of which they displayed a great deal during the war, and which contributed principally to the favorable issue of it. He related the honorable refusal of the American seamen who were carried in great numbers into the British prisons during the war, to redeem themselves from misery or to seek their fortunes, by entering on board of the Ships of the Enemies to their Country; contrasting their patriotism with a contemporary instance in which the British seamen made prisoners by the Americans, readily entered on the ships of the latter on being promised a share of the prizes that might be made out of their own Country.[128]

[123] For instance, computations based on a list of prisoners in Mill Prison from May 27, 1777, to Jan. 21, 1782, from the *Boston Gaz.,* June 24, July 1, 8, 1782, indicate that 7.7% of 1013 men entered the king's service. This figure may be slightly distorted by the presence of a small number of non-Americans, but there is almost precise confirmation in Adm. 98/11–14 which lists only 190 out of a total of 2579 Americans, 7.4%, entered from all English prisons. This figure is slightly inflated. See Adm. 98/13, 108. See also John Howard, *The State of the Prisons in England and Wales,* 3d ed. (Warrington, Eng., 1784), 185, 187, 188, 192, 194. I am indebted to John K. Alexander, a graduate student at the University of Chicago, for these figures and for valuable assistance in connection with the prisons.

[124] Charles Herbert, *A Relic of the Revolution* (Boston, 1847), 157. See also entry for Aug. 19, 1778, in Marion S. Coan, "A Revolutionary Prison Diary: the Journal of Dr. Jonathan Haskins," *New England Quarterly,* XVII (1944), 430. Clearly there is plagiarism here, as there is in many other, but by no means all, entries in the two journals. For a contention that Haskins is the plagiarist, see John K. Alexander, "Jonathan Haskins' Mill Prison 'Diary': Can It Be Accepted at Face Value?" ibid., XL (1967), 561–564.

[125] William Russell, "Journal," Dec. 31, 1781, Paine, *Ships and Sailors of Salem,* 155.

[126] Sherburne, *Memoirs,* 81. For a prisoners' committee in Forton Prison see Jan. 27, 1779, Adm. 98/11, 442–444; for a trial in Mill Prison for "the crime of profanely damning of the Honrbl. Continental Congress," see Mar. 4, 1778, in Coan, "Revolutionary Prison Diary," 305. For self-government in *Jersey,* see Dring, *Recollections,* ed. Greene, 84–86.

[127] For example, Dring, *Recollections,* ed. Greene, 97–116; Herbert, *Relic of the Revolution,* 142; Russell, July 4, 1781, Paine, *Ships and Sailors of Salem,* 142. For a celebration of the British defeat at Yorktown, see Benjamin Golden to Benjamin Franklin, Dec. 2, 1781, Franklin Papers, XXIII, 94.

[128] Max Farrand, ed., *The Records of the Federal Convention of 1787,* rev. ed. (New Haven, 1937), II, 204–205.

Franklin spoke *against limiting* the franchise, not *for broadening* it: he praised the seamen, but with a hint of condescension, suggesting that it would be prudent to grant them a few privileges. A decade later a French traveller noticed that "except the laborer in ports, and the common sailor, everyone calls himself, and is called by others, a *gentleman*."[129] Government was still gentleman's government: more people were defined as gentlemen, but Jack Tar was not yet among them.

V

Bernard Bailyn has recently added needed illumination to our understanding of pre-Revolutionary crowd action. Bailyn has disagreed with Peter Oliver and with modern historians who have concurred in describing pre-Revolutionary rioters as mindless, passive, and manipulated: "far from being empty vessels," rioters in the decade before the outbreak of fighting were "politically effective" and "shared actively the attitudes and fears" of their leaders; theirs was a "'fully-fledged political movement'"[130] Thus it would seem that Bailyn has freed himself from the influencial grasp of Gustave Le Bon.[131] But Bailyn stopped short of total rejection. Only in 1765, he says, was the colonial crowd "transformed" into a political phenomenon. Before then it was "conservative"—like crowds in seventeenth- and eighteenth-century England, aiming neither at social revolution nor at social reform, but only at immediate revenge. Impressment riots and other "demonstrations by transient sailors and dock workers," Bailyn says, expressed no "deep-lying social distress" but only a "diffuse and indeliberate antiauthoritarianism"; they were "ideologically inert."[132]

[129] Duke de la Rochefoucauld Liancourt, *Travels through the United States of North America . . . ,* trans. H. Neuman (London, 1799), II, 672, quoted in Staughton Lynd and Alfred Young, "After Carl Becker: The Mechanics and New York City Politics, 1774–1801," *Labor History,* V (1964), 220.

[130] Bailyn, ed., *Pamphlets,* 581–583, 740, n. 10; Bailyn quotes the last phrase from George Rudé, "The London 'Mob' of the Eighteenth Century," *Historical Journal,* II (1959), 17. Bailyn is here contending that the post-1765 crowd was more highly developed than its English counterpart which was, according to Rudé, not yet "a fully-fledged political movement." See also Gordon S. Wood, "A Note on Mobs in the American Revolution," *Wm. and Mary Qtly.,* 3d Ser., XXIII (1966), 635–642.

[131] See Gustave Le Bon, *The Crowd* (New York, 1960). For a critique of interpretations of the American Revolution which seem to echo Le Bon, see Lemisch, "American Revolution," in Bernstein, ed., *Towards a New Past,* passim. Two useful discussions which place Le Bon and those he has influenced in the context of the history of social psychology (and of history) are George Rudé, *The Crowd in History* (New York, 1964), 3–15, and Roger W. Brown, "Mass Phenomena," in Gardner Lindzey, ed., *Handbook of Social Psychology* (Cambridge, Mass., 1954), II, 833–873. Both Rudé and Brown describe Le Bon's bias as "aristocratic." Also relevant are some of the studies in Duane P. Schultz, ed., *Panic Behavior* (New York, 1964), especially Alexander Mintz, "Non-Adaptive Group Behavior," 84–107.

[132] Bailyn, ed., *Pamphlets,* 581–583, citing Max Beloff, *Public Order and Popular Disturbances, 1660–1714* (London, 1938), 33, 153, 155, calls Beloff "the historian of popular disturbances in pre-industrial England," thus bypassing at least one other candidate for the title, George Rudé, whom he describes as "an English historian of eighteenth-century crowd phenomena." Rudé has shown in *The Crowd in History* and elsewhere that the crowd was purposeful, disciplined, and discriminating, that "in the eighteenth century the typical and ever recurring form of social protest was the riot." Rudé finds in Beloff echoes of Burke and Taine. Thus, the European foundation for Bailyn's interpretation of the pre-1765 American crowd is somewhat one-sided. Compare with Bailyn R. S. Longley's extremely manipulative "Mob Activities in

Other historians have seen the colonial seamen—and the rest of the lower class—as mindless and manipulated, both before and after 1765.[133] The seeming implication behind this is that the seamen who demonstrated in colonial streets did so as much out of simple vindictiveness or undisciplined violence as out of love of liberty. Certainly such motivation would blend well with the traditional picture of the seaman as rough and ready. For along with the stereotype of Jolly Jack—and in part belying that stereotype—is bold and reckless Jack, the exotic and violent.[134] Jack *was* violent; the conditions of his existence were violent. Was his violence non-political? Sometimes. The mob of seventy to eighty yelling, club-swinging, out-of-town seamen who tried to break up a Philadelphia election in 1742 had no interest in the election; they had been bought off with money and liquor.[135]

Other violence is not so clear-cut. Edward Thompson has seen the fighting out of significant social conflict in eighteenth-century England "in terms of Tyburn, the hulks and the Bridewells on the one hand; and crime, riot, and mob action on the other."[136] Crime and violence among eighteenth-century American seamen needs reexamination from such a perspective. Does "mutiny" adequately describe the act of the crew which seized *Black Prince*, re-named it *Liberty*, and chose their course and a new captain by voting? What shall we call the conduct of 150 seamen who demanded higher wages by marching along the streets of Philadelphia with clubs, unrigging vessels, and forcing workmen ashore? If "mutiny" is often the captain's name for what we have come to call a "strike," perhaps we might also detect some significance broader than mere criminality in the seamen's frequent assaults on captains and thefts from them.[137] Is it not in some sense a political act for a seaman to tear off the mast a copy of a law which says that disobedient seamen will be punished as "seditious"?

135

Revolutionary Massachusetts," *New Eng. Qtly.*, VI (1933), 108: "Up to 1765, the Massachusetts mob was not political. Even after this date, its political organization was gradual, but it began with the Stamp Act."

[133] For a further discussion see Lemisch, "American Revolution," in Bernstein, ed., *Towards a New Past*, passim. Bailyn, ed., *Pamphlets*, 581, is not entirely clear on the situation *after* 1765. He denies that "Revolutionary mobs" in America were in fact "revolutionary" and questions their "meliorist aspirations."

[134] For rough and ready Jack see Watson, *Sailor in English Fiction*, 45, 159–160; Hohman, *Seamen Ashore*, 217.

[135] *Pa. Archives*, 8th Ser., IV, 2971, 2987, 2995–2998, 3009; "Extracts from the Gazette, 1742," Labaree et al., eds., *Papers of Benjamin Franklin*, II, 363–364. Yet even these men can be shown to have had some ideas; their shouts, which included attacks on "Broad-brims," "Dutch dogs," and "You damned Quakers . . . Enemies to King GEORGE," are similar to those of the European "Church and King" rioters. See Rudé, *Crowd in History*, 135–148; E. J. Hobsbawm, *Primitive Rebels* (New York, 1965), 110, 118, 120–123.

[136] E. P. Thompson, *The Making of the English Working Class* (New York, 1964), 60.

[137] Deposition of Thomas Austin, Dec. 10, 1769, in Hutchinson to Hillsborough, Dec. 20, 1769, C. O. 5/759, Pt. 2, Library of Congress Transcript; *Pennsylvania Packet* (Philadelphia), Jan. 16, 1779; *Colonial Records of Pennsylvania 1683–1790* (Harrisburg, 1852–1853), XI, 664–665; J. Thomas Scharf and Thompson Westcott, *History of Philadelphia, 1609–1884* (Philadelphia, 1884), I, 403. For some crimes of seamen against masters see *The King* v. *John Forster*, Indictment for Petty Larceny, filed Oct. 23, 1772, N. Y. Supreme Court, Pleadings K-495; Deposition of Cap. Elder and Examination of John Forster, sworn Oct. 20, 1772, N. Y. Supreme Court, Pleadings K-457; *N.-Y. Gaz.; Weekly Post-Boy*, Feb. 2, 1764.

Impressment meant the loss of freedom, both personal and economic, and, sometimes, the loss of life itself. The seaman who defended himself against impressment felt that he was fighting to defend his "liberty," and he justified his resistance on grounds of "right."[138] It is in the concern for liberty and right that the seaman rises from vindictiveness to a somewhat more complex awareness that certain values larger than himself exist and that he is the victim not only of cruelty and hardship but also, in the light of those values, of injustice. The riots ashore, whether they be against impressment, the Stamp Act, or competition for work express that same sense of injustice. And here, thousands of men took positive and effective steps to demonstrate their opposition to both acts and policies.

Two of England's most exciting historians have immensely broadened our knowledge of past and present by examining phenomena strikingly like the conduct and thought of the seamen in America. These historians have described such manifestations as "sub-political" or "pre-political," and one of them has urged that such movements be "seriously considered not simply as an unconnected series of individual curiosities, as footnotes to history, but as a phenomenon of general importance and considerable weight in modern history."[139] When Jack Tar went to sea in the American Revolution, he fought, as he had for many years before, quite literally, to protect his life, liberty, and property. It might be extravagant to call the seamen's conduct and the sense of injustice which underlay it in any fully developed sense ideological or political; on the other hand, it makes little sense to describe their ideological content as zero. There are many worlds and much of human history in that vast area between ideology and inertness.

Author's Postscript

"There are no sources," said Edmund Morgan when I proposed, late in the 'fifties, to do a dissertation at Yale on the politics of merchant seamen in Revolutionary New York. Later, Morgan good-naturedly liked to tell the story on himself: "That's the last time I'll ever say that to a graduate student."

As an undergraduate student of Morgan's in 1955, I had read widely in colonial history. As I read more in graduate study, seamen seemed to be everywhere, but with the exception of Richard B. Morris's landmark *Government and Labor in Early America* (New York, 1946), they were dismissed as Jolly Jack—mindless, manipulated, without politics, just drunk and blowing off steam. This characterization of their rioting as irrational offended my sense that it is the historian's task to explain.

Morgan's answer to me as a graduate student incited me further. I had a passion to document those for whom sources were said to be nonexistent. I might just as well have thrived professionally by projecting ancient Roman life from images on coins. As a child, I loved the TV panel of anthropologists and archaeologists who guessed (sometimes erroneously) the provenance of unlabeled artifacts, often connecting visual conventions to time and place: "Pointed ears . . . Peru . . . around 5,000 B.C." Such intriguing evidentiary puzzles and the kind of thinking that solves them have always delighted me.

---

[138] See above, p. 123.

[139] Thompson, *Making of the English Working Class,* 55, 59, 78; Hobsbawm, *Primitive Rebels,* 2, 7, 10.

"Jack Tar" was cooking as a dissertation from 1958 to 1962. I wrote about riots and movements before the 'sixties became The Sixties. In those dark ages, academic thought contained much bigotry haughtily presented as political neutrality: contempt for the lower classes, racism, antiradicalism, fancy reactionary theories, and a worship of strong men. By the time "Jack Tar in the Streets" was published in 1968, I had experienced riot and Movement. This put me in a better position to understand past protest than were those who sided with authority. Edward Thompson, Eric Hobsbawm, and George Rudé provided solid theoretical underpinnings. But I got little help in looking at history in new ways from colonial historians. My University of Chicago colleague Daniel Boorstin enjoyed what he called my "sea stories" but could not abide my introduction of the notion of class. Firing me, William McNeill said, "Your convictions interfered with your scholarship." Great Institutions began to shun me (including, for many years, the Institute of Early American History and Culture).

My article reflected mostly new work done after the dissertation stage. Some of this involved opening up new sources such as first-person reminiscences by Revolutionary veterans. Like other historians of my generation, I used old sources in new ways: Admiralty records for the realities of impressment; little bits and pieces from court records, statutes, legislative records, loyalist claims, newspapers. I had also learned to imagine the kinds of situations that might produce abundant documentation, such as riot—a window into Jack's politics—the Revolutionary prisons—a laboratory for the study of his loyalties. In particular, I quested after Jack's words, denying his "inarticulateness." I assumed reasoning capacity among rioters and a concern for liberty and right. I assumed that impressment was barbaric and that colonial elites' relative silence about it reflected, not the absence of grievance, but their failure to listen to seamen.

Today, social history prospers. But writing about ordinary people is not necessarily "history from the bottom up." Much is missing in the new social history.

Where is human agency, often lost among the Great Forces? Where is consciousness, in a history whose quest for quantifiable sources still too often projects consciousness from social structure? Where are the moral passion and identification that are needed to understand people's consciousness and concerns for justice and right? Social history has become too academicized and deactivated.

When they tell you there are no sources for history "from the bottom up," be skeptical. Look at old sources in new ways. Have the patience to assemble the bits of data. Imagine the kind of sources you would need and then seek them. They are there. Only imagine. Of course, it might help were another such time as The Sixties to come, to clear our heads and help us to see the world plainly.

137

POPULAR UPRISINGS AND CIVIL AUTHORITY IN EIGHTEENTH-CENTURY AMERICA

PAULINE MAIER

It is only natural that the riots and civil turbulence of the past decade and a half have awakened a new interest in the history of American mobs. It should be emphasized, however, that scholarly attention to the subject has roots independent of contemporary events and founded in long-developing historiographical trends. George Rudé's studies of pre-industrial crowds in France and England, E. J. Hobsbawm's discussion of "archaic" social movements, and recent works linking eighteenth-century American thought with English revolutionary tradition have all, in different ways, inspired a new concern among historians with colonial uprisings.[1] This discovery of the early American mob promises to have a significant effect upon historical interpretation. Particularly affected are the Revolutionary struggle and the early decades of the new nation, when events often turned upon well-known popular insurrections.

Eighteenth-century uprisings were in some important ways different than those of today—different in themselves, but even more in the political context within which they occurred. As a result they carried different connotations for the American Revolutionaries than they do today. Not all eighteenth-century mobs simply defied the law: some used extralegal means to implement official demands or to enforce laws not otherwise enforceable, others in effect extended the law in urgent situations beyond its technical limits. Since leading eighteenth-century Americans had known many occasions on which mobs took on the defense of the public welfare, which was, after all, the stated purpose of government, they were

Mrs. Maier is a member of the Department of History, University of Massachusetts.

Ed. Note: This article was originally published in *William and Mary Quarterly,* 3d Ser., XXVII (January 1970), 3–35.

[1] See the following by George Rudé: *The Crowd in the French Revolution* (Oxford, 1959); "The London 'Mob' of the Eighteenth Century," *The Historical Journal,* II (1959), 1–18; *Wilkes and Liberty: A Social Study of 1763 to 1774* (Oxford, 1962); *The Crowd in History: A Study of Popular Disturbances in France and England, 1730–1848* (New York, 1964). See also E. J. Hobsbawm, *Primitive Rebels: Studies in Archaic Forms of Social Movement in the 19th and 20th Centuries* (New York, 1959), esp. "The City Mob," 108–125. For recent discussions of the colonial mob see: Bernard Bailyn, *Pamphlets of the American Revolution* (Cambridge, Mass., 1965), I, 581–584; Jesse Lemisch, "Jack Tar in the Streets: Merchant Seamen in the Politics of Revolutionary America," *William and Mary Quarterly,* 3d Ser., XXV (1968), 371–407; Gordon S. Wood, "A Note on Mobs in the American Revolution," *Wm. and Mary Qtly.,* 3d Ser., XXIII (1966), 635–642, and more recently Wood's *Creation of the American Republic, 1776–1787* (Chapel Hill, 1969), passim, but esp. 319–328. Wood offers an excellent analysis of the place of mobs and extralegal assemblies in the development of American constitutionalism. Hugh D. Graham and Ted R. Gurr, *Violence in America: Historical and Comparative Perspectives* (New York, 1969) primarily discusses uprisings of the 19th and 20th centuries, but see the chapters by Richard M. Brown, "Historical Patterns of Violence in America," 45–84, and "The American Vigilante Tradition," 154–226.

less likely to deny popular upheavals all legitimacy than are modern leaders. While not advocating popular uprisings, they could still grant such incidents an established and necessary role in free societies, one that made them an integral and even respected element of the political order. These attitudes, and the tradition of colonial insurrections on which they drew, not only shaped political events of the Revolutionary era, but also lay behind many laws and civil procedures that were framed during the 1780s and 1790s, some of which still have a place in the American legal system.

I

Not all colonial uprisings were identical in character or significance. Some involved no more than disorderly vandalism or traditional brawls such as those that annually marked Pope's Day on November 5, particularly in New England. Occasional insurrections defied established laws and authorities in the name of isolated private interests alone—a set of Hartford County, Connecticut, landowners arose in 1722, for example, after a court decision imperiled their particular land titles. Still others—which are of interest here—took on a broader purpose, and defended the interests of their community in general where established authorities failed to act.[2] This common characteristic linked otherwise diverse rural uprisings in New Jersey and the Carolinas. The insurrectionists' punishment of outlaws, their interposition to secure land titles or prevent abuses at the hands of legal officials followed a frustration with established institutions and a belief that justice and even security had to be imposed by the people directly.[3] The earlier Virginia tobacco insurrection also illustrates this common pattern well: Virginians began tearing up young tobacco plants in 1682 only after Governor Thomas Culpeper forced the quick adjournment of their assembly, which had been called to curtail tobacco planting during an economic crisis. The insurrections in Massachusetts a little over a century later represent a variation on this theme. The insurgents in Worcester, Berkshire, Hampshire, Middlesex, and Bristol counties— often linked together as members of "Shays's Rebellion"—forced the closing of civil courts, which threatened to send a major portion of the local population to debtors' prison, only until a new legislature could remedy their pressing needs.[4]

[2] Carl Bridenbaugh, *Cities in the Wilderness: The First Century of Urban Life in America, 1625–1742* (New York, 1964), 70–71, 223–224, 382–384; and Carl Bridenbaugh, *Cities in Revolt: Urban Life in America, 1743–1776* (New York, 1964), 113–118; Charles J. Hoadly, ed., *The Public Records of the Colony of Connecticut* . . . (Hartford, 1872), VI, 332–333, 341–348.

[3] See particularly Richard M. Brown, *The South Carolina Regulators* (Cambridge, Mass., 1963). There is no published study of the New Jersey land riots, which lasted over a decade and were due above all to the protracted inability of the royal government to settle land disputes stemming from conflicting proprietary grants made in the late 17th century. See, however, "A State of Facts concerning the Riots and Insurrections in New Jersey, and the Remedies Attempted to Restore the Peace of the Province," William A. Whitehead et al., eds., *Archives of the State of New Jersey* (Newark, 1883), VII, 207–226. On other rural insurrections see Irving Mark, *Agrarian Conflicts in Colonial New York, 1711–1775* (New York, 1940), Chap. IV, V; Staughton Lynd, "The Tenant Rising at Livingston Manor," *New-York Historical Society Quarterly*, XLVIII (1964), 163–177; Matt Bushnell Jones, *Vermont in the Making, 1750–1777* (Cambridge, Mass., 1939), Chap. XII, XIII; John R. Dunbar, ed., *The Paxton Papers* (The Hague, 1957), esp. 3–51.

[4] Richard L. Morton, *Colonial Virginia* (Chapel Hill, 1960), I, 303–304; Jonathan Smith, "The

This role of the mob as extralegal arm of the community's interest emerged, too, in repeated uprisings that occurred within the more densely settled coastal areas. The history of Boston, where by the mid-eighteenth century "public order . . . prevailed to a greater degree than anywhere else in England or America," is full of such incidents. During the food shortage of 1710, after the governor rejected a petition from the Boston selectmen calling for a temporary embargo on the exportation of foodstuffs one heavily laden ship found its rudder cut away, and fifty men sought to haul another outward bound vessel back to shore. Under similar circumstances Boston mobs again intervened to keep foodstuffs in the colony in 1713 and 1729. When there was some doubt a few years later whether or not the selectmen had the authority to seize a barn lying in the path of a proposed street, a group of townsmen, their faces blackened, levelled the structure and the road went through. Houses of ill fame were attacked by Boston mobs in 1734, 1737, and 1771; and in the late 1760s the *New-York Gazette* claimed that mobs in Providence and Newport had taken on responsibility for "disciplining" unfaithful husbands. Meanwhile in New London, Connecticut, another mob prevented a radical religious sect, the Rogerenes, from disturbing normal Sunday services, "a practice they . . . [had] followed more or less for many years past; and which all the laws made in that government, and executed in the most judicious manner could not put a stop to."[5]

Threats of epidemic inspired particularly dramatic instances of this community oriented role of the mob. One revealing episode occurred in Massachusetts in 1773–1774. A smallpox hospital had been built on Essex Island near Marblehead "much against the will of the multitude" according to John Adams. "The patients were careless, some of them wantonly so; and others were suspected of designing to spread the smallpox in the town, which was full of people who had not passed through the distemper." In January 1774 patients from the hospital who tried to enter the town from unauthorized landing places were forcefully prevented from doing so; a hospital boat was burned; and four men suspected of stealing infected clothes from the hospital were tarred and feathered, then carted from Marblehead to Salem in a long cortege. The Marblehead town meeting finally won the proprietors' agreement to shut down the hospital; but after some twenty-two new cases of smallpox broke out in the town within a few days "apprehension became general," and some "Ruffians" in disguise hastened the hospital's demise by burning the nearly evacuated building. A military watch of forty men were needed for several nights to keep the peace in Marblehead.[6]

Depression of 1785 and Daniel Shays' Rebellion," *Wm. and Mary Qtly.*, 3d Ser., V (1948), 86–87, 91.

[5] Bridenbaugh, *Cities in Revolt,* 114; Bridenbaugh, *Cities in the Wilderness,* 196, 383, 388–389; Edmund S. and Helen M. Morgan, *The Stamp Act Crisis,* rev. ed. (New York, 1963), 159; Anne Rowe Cunningham, ed., *Letters and Diary of John Rowe, Boston Merchant, 1759–1762, 1764–1779* (Boston, 1903), 218. On the marriage riots, see *New-York Gazette* (New York City), July 11, 1765—and note, that when the reporter speaks of persons "concern'd in such unlawful Enterprises" he clearly is referring to the husbands, not their "Disciplinarians." On the Rogerenes, see item in *Connecticut Gazette* (New Haven), Apr. 5, 1766, reprinted in Lawrence H. Gipson, *Jared Ingersoll* (New Haven, 1920), 195, n. 1.

[6] John Adams, "Novanglus," in Charles F. Adams, ed., *The Works of John Adams* (Boston,

A similar episode occurred in Norfolk, Virginia, when a group of wealthy residents decided to have their families inoculated for smallpox. Fears arose that the lesser disease brought on by the inoculations would spread and necessitate a general inoculation, which would cost "more money than is circulating in Norfolk" and ruin trade and commerce such that "the whole colony would feel the effects." Local magistrates said they could not interfere because "the law was silent in the matter." Public and private meetings then sought to negotiate the issue. Despite a hard-won agreement, however, the pro-inoculation faction persisted in its original plan. Then finally a mob drove the newly inoculated women and children on a five-mile forced march in darkness and rain to the common Pest House, a three-year old institution designed to isolate seamen and others, particularly Negroes, infected with smallpox.[7]

These local incidents indicate a willingness among many Americans to act outside the bounds of law, but they cannot be described as anti-authoritarian in any general sense. Sometimes in fact—as in the Boston bawdy house riot of 1734, or the Norfolk smallpox incident—local magistrates openly countenanced or participated in the mob's activities. Far from opposing established institutions, many supporters of Shays's Rebellion honored their leaders "by no less decisive marks of popular favor than elections to local offices of trust and authority."[8] It was above all the existence of such elections that forced local magistrates to reflect community feelings and so prevented their becoming the targets of insurrections. Certainly in New England, where the town meeting ruled, and to some extent in New York, where aldermen and councilmen were annually elected, this was true; yet even in Philadelphia, with its lethargic closed corporation, or Charleston, which lacked municipal institutions, authority was normally exerted by residents who had an immediate sense of local sentiment. Provincial governments were also for the most part kept alert to local feelings by their elected assemblies. Sometimes, of course, uprisings turned against domestic American institutions—as in Pennsylvania in 1764, when the "Paxton Boys" complained that the colony's Quaker assembly had failed to provide adequately for their defense against the Indians. But uprisings over local issues proved *extra-institutional* in character more often than they were anti-institutional; they served the community where no law existed, or intervened beyond what magistrates thought they could do officially to cope with a local problem.

The case was different when imperial authority was involved. There legal authority emanated from a capital an ocean away, where the colonists had no

---

1850–1856), IV, 76–77; Salem news of Jan. 25 and Feb. 1, 1774, in *Providence Gazette* (Rhode Island), Feb. 5, and Feb. 12, 1774.

[7] Letter from "Friend to the Borough and county of Norfolk," in Purdie and Dixon's *Virginia Gazette Postscript* (Williamsburg), Sept. 8, 1768, which gives the fullest account. This letter answered an earlier letter from Norfolk, Aug. 6, 1768, available in Rind's *Va. Gaz. Supplement* (Wmsbg.), Aug. 25, 1768. See also letter of Cornelius Calvert in Purdie and Dixon's *Va. Gaz.* (Wmsbg.), Jan. 9, 1772. Divisions over the inoculation seemed to follow more general political lines. See Patrick Henderson, "Smallpox and Patriotism, The Norfolk Riots, 1768–1769," *Virginia Magazine of History and Biography,* LXXIII (1965), 413–424.

[8] James Madison to Thomas Jefferson, Mar. 19, 1787, in Julian P. Boyd, ed., *The Papers of Thomas Jefferson* (Princeton, 1950–), XI, 223.

integral voice in the formation of policy, where governmental decisions were based largely upon the reports of "king's men" and sought above all to promote the king's interests. When London's legal authority and local interest conflicted, efforts to implement the edicts of royal officials were often answered by uprisings, and it was not unusual in these cases for local magistrates to participate or openly sympathize with the insurgents. The colonial response to the White Pine Acts of 1722 and 1729 is one example. Enforcement of the acts was difficult in general because "the various elements of colonial society . . . seemed inclined to violate the pine laws—legislatures, lumbermen, and merchants were against them, and even the royal governors were divided." At Exeter, New Hampshire, in 1734 about thirty men prevented royal officials from putting the king's broad arrow on some seized boards; efforts to enforce the acts in Connecticut during the 1750s ended after a deputy of the surveyor-general was thrown in a pond and nearly drowned; five years later logs seized in Massachusetts and New Hampshire were either "rescued" or destroyed.[9] Two other imperial issues that provoked local American uprisings long before 1765 and continued to do so during the Revolutionary period were impressment and customs enforcement.

As early as 1743 the colonists' violent opposition to impressment was said to indicate a "Contempt of Government." Some captains had been mobbed, the Admiralty complained, "others emprisoned, and afterwards held to exorbitant Bail, and are now under Prosecutions carried on by Combination, and by joint Subscription towards the expense." Colonial governors, despite their offers, furnished captains with little real aid either to procure seamen or "even to protect them from the Rage and Insults of the People." Two days of severe rioting answered Commodore Charles Knowles's efforts to sweep Boston harbor for able-bodied men in November 1747. Again in 1764 when Rear Admiral Lord Alexander Colville sent out orders to "procure" men in principal harbors between Casco Bay and Cape Henlopen, mobs met the ships at every turn. When the *St. John* sent out a boat to seize a recently impressed deserter from a Newport wharf, a mob protected him, captured the boat's officer, and hurled stones at the crew; later fifty Newporters joined the colony's gunner at Fort George in opening fire on the king's ship itself. Under threat to her master the *Chaleur* was forced to release four fishermen seized off Long Island, and when that ship's captain went ashore at New York a mob seized his boat and burned it in the Fields. In the spring of 1765 after the *Maidstone* capped a six-month siege of Newport harbor by seizing "all the Men" out of a brigantine from Africa, a mob of about five hundred men similarly seized a ship's officer and burned one of her boats on the Common. Impressment also met mass resistance at Norfolk in 1767 and was a major cause of the famous *Liberty* riot at Boston in 1768.[10]

---

[9] Bernhard Knollenberg, *Origin of the American Revolution: 1759–1766* (New York, 1965), 126, 129. See also Robert G. Albion, *Forests and Sea Power* (Cambridge, Mass., 1926), 262–263, 265. Joseph J. Malone, *Pine Trees and Politics* (Seattle, 1964), includes less detail on the forceful resistance to the acts.

[10] Admiralty to Gov. George Thomas, Sept. 26, 1743, in Samuel Hazard et al., eds., *Pennsylvania Archives* (Philadelphia, 1852–1949), I, 639. For accounts of the Knowles riot, see Gov. William Shirley to Josiah Willard, Nov. 19, 1747, Shirley's Proclamation of Nov. 21, 1747, and his letter to the Board of Trade, Dec. 1, 1747, in Charles H. Lincoln, ed., *The Correspondence of William Shirley . . . 1731–1760* (New York, 1912), I, 406–419; see also Thomas Hutchinson, *History of the Province of Massachusetts-Bay,* ed. Lawrence S. Mayo

Like the impressment uprisings, which in most instances sought to protect or rescue men from the "press," customs incidents were aimed at impeding the customs service in enforcing British laws. Tactics varied, and although incidents occurred long before 1764—in 1719, for example, Caleb Heathcote reported a "riotous and tumultuous" rescue of seized claret by Newporters—their frequency, like those of the impressment "riots," apparently increased after the Sugar Act was passed and customs enforcement efforts were tightened. The 1764 rescue of the *Rhoda* in Rhode Island preceded a theft in Dighton, Massachusetts, of the cargo from a newly seized vessel, the *Polly,* by a mob of some forty men with blackened faces. In 1766 again a mob stoned a customs official's home in Falmouth (Portland), Maine, while "Persons unknown and disguised" stole sugar and rum that had been impounded that morning. The intimidation of customs officials and of the particularly despised customs informers also enjoyed a long history. In 1701 the South Carolina attorney general publicly attacked an informer "and struck him several times, crying out, this is the Informer, this is he that will ruin the country." Similar assaults occurred decades later, in New Haven in 1766 and 1769, and New London in 1769, and were then often distinguished by their brutality. In 1771 a Providence tidesman, Jesse Saville, was seized, stripped, bound hand and foot, tarred and feathered, had dirt thrown in his face, then was beaten and "almost strangled." Even more thorough assaults upon two other Rhode Island tidesmen followed in July 1770 and upon Collector Charles Dudley in April 1771. Finally, customs vessels came under attack: the *St. John* was shelled at Newport in 1764 where the customs ship *Liberty* was sunk in 1769—both episodes that served as prelude to the destruction of the *Gaspée* outside Providence in 1772.[11]

(Cambridge, Mass., 1936), II, 330–333; and *Reports of the Record Commissioners of Boston* (Boston, 1885), XIV, 127–130. David Lovejoy, *Rhode Island Politics and the American Revolution, 1760–1776* (Providence, 1958), 36–39, and on the *Maidstone* in particular see "O. G." in *Newport Mercury* (Rhode Island), June 10, 1765. Bridenbaugh, *Cities in Revolt,* 309–311; documents on the *St. John* episode in *Records of the Colony of Rhode Island and Providence Plantations* (Providence, 1856–1865), VI, 427–430. George G. Wolkins, "The Seizure of John Hancock's Sloop 'Liberty,'" Massachusetts Historical Society, *Proceedings* (1921–1923), LV, 239–284. See also Lemisch, "Jack Tar," *Wm. and Mary Qtly.,* 3d Ser., XXV (1968), 391–393; and Neil R. Stout, "Manning the Royal Navy in North America, 1763–1775," *American Neptune,* XXIII (1963), 179–181.

[11] Heathcote letter from Newport, Sept. 7, 1719, *Records of the Colony of Rhode Island,* IV, 259–260; Lovejoy, *Rhode Island Politics,* 35–39. There is an excellent summary of the *Polly* incident in Morgan, *Stamp Act Crisis,* 59, 64–67; and see also *Providence Gaz.* (R. I.), Apr. 27, 1765. On the Falmouth incident see the letter from the collector and comptroller of Falmouth, Aug. 19, 1766, Treasury Group I, Class 453, Piece 182, Public Records Office. Hereafter cited as T. 1/453, 182. See also the account in Appendix I of Josiah Quincy, Jr., *Reports of the Cases Argued and Adjudged in the Superior Court of Judicature of the Province of Massachusetts Bay, between 1761 and 1772* (Boston, 1865), 446–447. W. Noel Sainsbury et al., eds., *Calendar of State Papers, Colonial Series, America and the West Indies* (London, 1910), *1701,* no. 1042, xi, a. A summary of one of the New Haven informer attacks is in Willard M. Wallace, *Traitorous Hero: The Life and Fortunes of Benedict Arnold* (New York, 1954), 20–23. Arnold's statement on the affair which he led is in Malcolm Decker, *Benedict Arnold, Son of the Havens* (Tarrytown, N. Y., 1932), 27–29. Gipson, in *Jared Ingersoll,* 277–278, relates the later incidents. For the New London informer attacks, see documents of July 1769 in T. 1/471. On the Saville affair see Saville to collector and comptroller of customs in Newport, May 18, 1769, T. 1/471, and *New York Journal* (New York City), July 6, 1769. On later Rhode Island incidents see Dudley and John Nicoll to governor of Rhode Island, Aug. 1, 1770, T. 1/471. Dudley to commissioners of customs at Boston,

Such incidents were not confined to New England. Philadelphia witnessed some of the most savage attacks, and even the surveyor of Sassafras and Bohemia in Maryland—an office long a sinecure, since no ships entered or cleared in Sassafras or Bohemia—met with violence when he tried to execute his office in March 1775. After seizing two wagons of goods being carried overland from Maryland toward Duck Creek, Pennsylvania, the officer was overpowered by a "licentious mob" that kept shouting "Liberty and Duck Creek forever" as it went through the hours-long rituals of tarring and feathering him and threatening his life. And at Norfolk, Virginia, in the spring 1766 an accused customs informer was tarred and feathered, pelted with stones and rotten eggs, and finally thrown in the sea where he nearly drowned. Even Georgia saw customs violence before independence, and one of the rare deaths resulting from a colonial riot occurred there in 1775.[12]

White Pine, impressment, and customs uprisings have attracted historians' attention because they opposed British authority and so seemed to presage the Revolution. In fact, however, they had much in common with many exclusively local uprisings. In each of the incidents violence was directed not so much against the "rich and powerful"[13] as against men who—as it was said after the Norfolk smallpox incident—"in every part of their conduct . . . acted very inconsistently as good neighbors or citizens." The effort remained one of safeguarding not the interests of isolated groups alone, but the community's safety and welfare. The White Pine Acts need not have provoked this opposition had they applied only to trees of potential use to the Navy, and had they been framed and executed with concern for colonial rights. But instead the acts reserved to the Crown all white pine trees including those "utterly unfit for masts, yards, or bowsprits," and prevented colonists from using them for building materials or lumber exportation even in regions where white pine constituted the principal forest growth. As a

Newport, Apr. 11, 1771, T. 1/482. On the destruction of the *Liberty* see documents in T. 1/471, esp. comptroller and collector to the governor, July 21, 1769.

[12] On Philadelphia violence see William Sheppard to commissioners of customs, Apr. 21, 1769, T. 1/471; Deputy Collector at Philadelphia John Swift to commissioners of customs at Boston, Oct. 13, 1769, ibid.; and on a particularly brutal attack on the son of customsman John Hatton, see Deputy Collector John Swift to Boston customs commissioners, Nov. 15, 1770, and related documents in T. 1/476. See also Alfred S. Martin, "The King's Customs: Philadelphia, 1763–1774," *Wm. and Mary Qtly.*, 3d Ser., V (1948), 201–216. Documents on the Maryland episode are in T. 1/513, including the following: Richard Reeve to Grey Cooper, Apr. 19, 1775; extracts from a Council meeting, Mar. 16, 1775; deposition of Robert Stratford Byrne, surveyor of His Majesty's Customs at Sassafras and Bohemia, and Byrne to customs commissioners, Mar. 17, 1775. On the Virginia incident see William Smith to Jeremiah Morgan, Apr. 3, 1766, Colonial Office Group, Class 5, Piece 1331, 80, Public Record Office. Hereafter cited as C. O. 5/1331, 80. W. W. Abbot, *The Royal Governors of Georgia, 1754–1775* (Chapel Hill, 1959), 174-175. These customs riots remained generally separate from the more central intercolonial opposition to Britain that emerged in 1765. Isolated individuals like John Brown of Providence and Maximilian Calvert of Norfolk were involved in both the organized intercolonial Sons of Liberty and in leading mobs against customs functionaries or informers. These roles, however, for the most part were unconnected, that is, there was no radical program of customs obstruction per se. Outbreaks were above all local responses to random provocations and, at least before the Townshend duties, usually devoid of explicit ideological justifications.

[13] Hobsbawm, *Primitive Rebels,* 111. For a different effort to see class division as relevant in 18th century uprisings, see Lemisch, "Jack Tar," *Wm. and Mary Qtly.*, 3d Ser., XXV (1968), 387.

result the acts "operated so much against the convenience and even necessities of the inhabitants," Surveyor John Wentworth explained, that "it became almost a general interest of the country" to frustrate the acts' execution. Impressment offered a more immediate effect, since the "press" could quickly cripple whole towns. Merchants and masters were affected as immediately as seamen: the targeted port, as Massachusetts' Governor William Shirley explained in 1747, was drained of mariners by both impressment itself and the flight of navigation to safer provinces, driving the wages for any remaining seamen upward. When the press was of long duration, moreover, or when it took place during a normally busy season, it could mean serious shortages of food or firewood for winter, and a general attrition of the commercial life that sustained all strata of society in trading towns. Commerce seemed even more directly attacked by British trade regulations, particularly by the proliferation of customs procedures in the mid-1760s that seemed to be in no American's interest, and by the Sugar Act with its virtual prohibition of the trade with the foreign West Indies that sustained the economies of colonies like Rhode Island. As a result even when only a limited contingent of sailors participated in a customs incident officials could suspect—as did the deputy collector at Philadelphia in 1770—that the mass of citizens "in their Hearts" approved of it.[14]

Because the various uprisings discussed here grew out of concerns essential to wide sections of the community, the "rioters" were not necessarily confined to the seamen, servants, Negroes, and boys generally described as the staple components of the colonial mob. The uprising of Exeter, New Hampshire, townsmen against the king's surveyor of the woods in 1754 was organized by a member of the prominent Gillman family who was a mill owner and a militia officer. Members of the upper classes participated in Norfolk's smallpox uprising, and Cornelius Calvert, who was later attacked in a related incident, protested that leading members of the community, doctors and magistrates, had posted securities for the good behavior of the "Villains" convicted of mobbing him. Captain Jeremiah Morgan complained about the virtually universal participation of Norfolkers in an impressment incident of 1767, and "all the principal Gentlemen in Town" were supposedly present when a customs informer was tarred and feathered there in 1766. Merchant Benedict Arnold admitted leading a New Haven mob against an informer in 1766; New London merchants Joseph Packwood and Nathaniel Shaw commanded the mob that first accosted Captain William Reid the night the *Liberty* was destroyed at Newport in 1769, just as John Brown, a leading Providence merchant, led that against the *Gaspée*. Charles Dudley reported in April 1771 that the men who beat him in Newport "did not come from the . . . lowest class of Men," but were "stiled Merchants and the Masters of their Vessels"; and again in 1775 Robert Stratford Byrne said many of his Maryland and Pennsylvania attackers were "from Appearance . . . Men of

145

---

[14] "Friends to the borough and county of Norfolk," Purdie and Dixon's *Va. Gaz. Postscript.* (Wmsbg.), Sept. 8, 1768. Wentworth quoted in Knollenberg, *Origin of American Revolution,* 124–125. Lemisch, "Jack Tar," *Wm. and Mary Qtly.,* 3d Ser., XXV (1968), 383–385. Shirley to Duke of Newcastle, Dec. 31, 1747, in Lincoln, ed., *Shirley Correspondence,* I, 420–423. Dora Mae Clark, "The Impressment of Seamen in the American Colonies," *Essays in Colonial History Presented to Charles McLean Andrews* (New Haven, 1931), 199–200; John Swift to Boston customs commissioners, Nov. 15, 1770, T. 1/476.

Property." It is interesting, too, that during Shays's Rebellion—so often considered a class uprising—"men who were of good property and owed not a shilling" were said to be "involved in the train of desperado's to suppress the courts."[15]

Opposition to impressment and customs enforcement in itself was not, moreover, the only cause of the so-called impressment or customs "riots." The complete narratives of these incidents indicate again not only that the crowd acted to support local interests, but that it sometimes enforced the will of local magistrates by extralegal means. Although British officials blamed the *St. John* incident upon that ship's customs and impressment activities, colonists insisted that the confrontation began when some sailors stole a few pigs and chickens from a local miller and the ship's crew refused to surrender the thieves to Newport officials. Two members of the Rhode Island council then ordered the gunner of Fort George to detain the schooner until the accused seamen were delivered to the sheriff, and "many People went over the Fort to assist the Gunner in the Discharge of his Duty." Only after this uprising did the ship's officers surrender the accused men.[16] Similarly, the 1747 Knowles impressment riot in Boston and the 1765 *Maidstone* impressment riot in Newport broke out after governors' request for the release of impressed seamen had gone unanswered, and only after the outbreaks of violence were the governors' requests honored. The crowd that first assembled on the night the *Liberty* was destroyed in Newport also began by demanding the allegedly drunken sailors who that afternoon had abused and shot at a colonial captain, Joseph Packwood, so they could be bound over to local magistrates for prosecution.[17]

146

[15] Malone, *Pine Trees,* 112. "Friends to the borough and county of Norfolk," Purdie and Dixon's *Va. Gaz. Postscrpt.* (Wmsbg.), Sept. 8, 1768; Calvert letter, ibid., Jan. 9, 1772. Capt. Jeremiah Morgan, quoted in Lemisch, "Jack Tar," *Wm. and Mary Qtly.,* 3d Ser., XXV (1968), 391; and William Smith to Morgan, Apr. 3, 1766, C. O. 5/1331, 80. Decker, *Benedict Arnold,* 27–20; deposition of Capt. William Reid on the *Liberty* affair, July 21, 1769, T. 1/471; Ephraim Bowen's narrative on the *Gaspée* affair, *Records of the Colony of Rhode Island,* VII, 68–73; Charles Dudley to Boston customs commissioners, Apr. 11, 1771, T. 1/482, and deposition by Byrne, T. 1/513. Edward Carrington to Jefferson, June 9, 1787, Boyd, ed., *Jefferson Papers,* XI, 408; and see also Smith, "Depression of 1785," *Wm. and Mary Qtly.,* 3d Ser., V (1948), 88—of the 21 men indicted for treason in Worcester during the court's April term 1787, 15 were "gentlemen" and only 6 "yeomen."

[16] Gov. Samuel Ward's report to the Treasury lords, Oct. 23, 1765, Ward Manuscripts, Box 1, fol. 58, Rhode Island Historical Society, Providence. See also deposition of Daniel Vaughn of Newport—Vaughn was the gunner at Fort George—July 8, 1764, Chalmers Papers, Rhode Island, fol. 41, New York Public Library, New York City. For British official accounts of the affair, see Lieut. Hill's version in James Munro, ed., *Acts of the Privy Council of England, Colonial Series* (London, 1912), VI, 374–376, and the report of John Robinson and John Nicoll to the customs commissioners, Aug. 30, 1765, Privy Council Group, Class I, Piece 51, Bundle 1 (53a), Public Record Office. Hill, whose report was drawn up soon after the incident, does not contradict Ward's narrative, but seems oblivious of any warrant-granting process on shore; Robinson and Nicoll—whose report was drawn up over a year later, and in the midst of the Stamp Act turmoil—claimed that a recent customs seizure had precipitated the attack upon the *St. John.*

[17] On the Knowles and *Maidstone* incidents see above, n. 10. On the *Liberty* affair see documents in T. 1/471, esp. the deposition of Capt. William Reid, July 21, 1769, and that of John Carr, the second mate, who indicates that the mob soon forgot its scheme of delivering the crew members to the magistrates.

In circumstances such as these, the "mob" often appeared only after the legal channels of redress had proven inadequate. The main thrust of the colonists' resistance to the White Pine Acts had always been made in their courts and legislatures. Violence broke out only in local situations where no alternative was available. Even the burning of the *Gaspée* in June 1772 was a last resort. Three months before the incident a group of prominent Providence citizens complained about the ship's wanton severity with all vessels along the coast and the colony's governor pressed their case with the fleet's admiral. The admiral, however, supported the *Gaspée's* commander, Lieutenant William Dudingston; and thereafter, the *Providence Gazette* reported, Dudingston became "more haughty, insolent and intolerable, . . . personally ill treating every master and merchant of the vessels he boarded, stealing sheep, hogs, poultry, etc. from farmers round the bay, and cutting down their fruit and other trees for firewood." Redress from London was possible but time-consuming, and in the meantime Rhode Island was approaching what its governor called "the deepest calamity" as supplies of food and fuel were curtailed and prices, especially in Newport, rose steeply. It was significant that merchant John Brown finally led the Providence "mob" that seized the moment in June when the *Gaspée* ran aground near Warwick, for it was he who had spearheaded the effort in March 1772 to win redress through the normal channels of government.[18]

II

There was little that was distinctively American about the colonial insurrections. The uprisings over grain exportations during times of dearth, the attacks on brothels, press gangs, royal forest officials, and customsmen, all had their counterparts in seventeenth- and eighteenth-century England. Even the Americans' hatred of the customs establishment mirrored the Englishman's traditional loathing of excise men. Like the customsmen in the colonies, they seemed to descend into localities armed with extraordinary prerogative powers. Often, too, English excisemen were "thugs and brutes who beat up their victims without compunction or stole or wrecked their property" and against whose extravagances little redress was possible through the law.[19] Charges of an identical character were made in the colonies against customsmen and naval officials as well, particularly after 1763 when officers of the Royal Navy were commissioned as deputy members of the customs service,[20] and a history of such accusations lay

---

[18] Malone, *Pine Trees,* 8–9, and passim. *Records of the Colony of Rhode Island,* VII, 60, 62–63, 174–175, including the deposition of Dep. Gov. Darius Sessions, June 12, 1772, and Adm. Montagu to Gov. Wanton, Apr. 8, 1772. Also, Wanton to Hillsborough, June 16, 1772, and Ephraim Bowen's narrative, ibid., 63–73, 90–92. *Providence Gaz.* (R. I.), Jan. 9, 1773.

[19] Max Beloff, *Public Order and Popular Disturbances, 1660–1714* (London, 1938), passim; Albion, *Forests and Sea Power,* 263; J. H. Plumb, *England in the Eighteenth Century* (Baltimore, 1961 [orig. publ., Oxford, 1950]), 66.

[20] See, for example, "A Pumkin" in the *New London Gazette* (Connecticut), May 14, 18, 1773; "O. G." in *Newport Merc.* (R. I.), June 10, 1765; *New London Gaz.* (Conn.), Sept. 22, 1769; complaints of Marylander David Bevan, reprinted in Rind's *Va. Gaz.* (Wmsbg.), July 27, 1769, and *New London Gaz.* (Conn.), July 21, 1769. Stout, "Manning the Royal Navy," *American Neptune,* XXIII (1963), 174. For a similar accusation against a surveyor-general of the king's woods, see Albion, *Forests and Sea Power,* 262.

behind many of the best-known waterfront insurrections. The Americans' complaints took on particular significance only because in the colonies those officials embodied the authority of a "foreign" power. Their arrogance and arbitrariness helped effect "an estrangement of the Affections of the People from the Authority under which they act," and eventually added an emotional element of anger against the Crown to a revolutionary conflict otherwise carried on in the language of law and right.[21]

The focused character of colonial uprisings also resembled those in England and even France where, Rudé has pointed out, crowds were remarkably single-minded and discriminating.[22] Targets were characteristically related to grievances: the Knowles rioters sought only the release of the impressed men; they set free a captured officer when assured he had nothing to do with the press, and refrained from burning a boat near Province House for fear the fire would spread. The Norfolk rioters, driven by fear of smallpox, forcefully isolated the inoculated persons where they would be least dangerous. Even the customs rioters vented their brutality on customs officers and informers alone, and the Shaysite "mobs" dispersed after closing the courts which promised most immediately to effect their ruin. So domesticated and controlled was the Boston mob that it refused to riot on Saturday and Sunday nights, which were considered holy by New Englanders.[23]

When colonists compared their mobs with those in the Mother Country they were struck only with the greater degree of restraint among Americans. "These People bear no Resemblance to an English Mob," John Jay wrote of the Shaysites in December 1786, "they are more temperate, cool and regular in their Conduct—they have hitherto abstained from Plunder, nor have they that I know of committed any outrages but such as the accomplishment of their Purpose made necessary." Similar comparisons were often repeated during the Revolutionary conflict, and were at least partially grounded in fact. When Londoners set out to "pull down" houses of ill fame in 1688, for example, the affair spread, prisons were opened, and disorder ended only when troops were called out. But when eighteenth-century Bostonians set out on the same task, there is no record that their destruction extended beyond the bordellos themselves. Even the violence of the customs riots—which contrast in that regard from other American incidents—can sometimes be explained by the presence of volatile foreign seamen. The attack on the son of customsman John Hatton, who was nearly killed in a Philadelphia riot, occurred, for example, when the city was crowded by over a

---

[21] Joseph Reed to the president of Congress, Oct. 21, 1779, in Hazard et al., eds., *Pennsylvania Archives*, VII, 762. Five years earlier Reed had tried to impress upon Lord Dartmouth the importance of constraining Crown agents in the colonies if any reconciliation were to be made between Britain and the colonies. See his letter to Earl of Dartmouth, Apr. 4, 1774, in William B. Reed, *Life and Correspondence of Joseph Reed* (Philadelphia, 1847), I, 56–57. For a similar plea, again from a man close to the American Revolutionary leadership, see Stephen Sayre to Lord Dartmouth, Dec. 13, 1766, Dartmouth Papers, D 1778/2/258, William Salt Library, Stafford, England.

[22] Rudé, *Crowd in History*, 60, 253–254. The restraint exercised by 18th century mobs has often been commented upon. See, for example, Wood, "A Note on Mobs," *Wm. and Mary Qtly.*, 3d Ser., XXIII (1966), 636–637.

[23] Joseph Harrison's testimony in Wolkins, "Seizure of Hancock's Sloop '*Liberty*,' " Mass. Hist. Soc., *Proceedings*, LV, 254.

thousand seamen. His attackers were apparently Irish crew members of a vessel he and his father had tried to seize off Cape May, and they were "set on," the Philadelphia collector speculated, by an Irish merchant in Philadelphia to whom the vessel was consigned. One of the most lethal riots in the history of colonial America, in which rioters killed five people, occurred in a small town near Norfolk, Virginia, and was significantly perpetrated entirely by British seamen who resisted the local inhabitants' efforts to reinstitute peace.[24] During and immediately after the Revolutionary War some incidents occurred in which deaths are recorded; but contemporaries felt these were historical aberrations, caused by the "brutalizing" effect of the war itself. "Our citizens, from a habit of putting . . . [the British] to death, have reconciled their minds to the killing of each other," South Carolina Judge Aedanus Burke explained.[25]

To a large extent the pervasive restraint and virtual absence of bloodshed in American incidents can best be understood in terms of social and military circumstance. There was no large amorphous city in America comparable to London, where England's worst incidents occurred. More important, the casualties even in eighteenth-century British riots were rarely the work of rioters. No deaths were inflicted by the Wilkes, Anti-Irish, or "No Popery" mobs, and only single fatalities resulted from other upheavals such as the Porteous riots of 1736. "It was authority rather than the crowd that was conspicuous for its violence to life and limb": all 285 casualties of the Gordon riots, for example, were rioters.[26] Since a regular army was less at the ready for use against colonial mobs, casualty figures for American uprisings were naturally much reduced.

To some extent the general tendency toward a discriminating purposefulness was shared by mobs throughout western Europe, but within the British Empire the focused character of popular uprisings and also their persistence can be explained in part by the character of law enforcement procedures. There were no professional police forces in the eighteenth century. Instead the power of government depended traditionally upon institutions like the "hue and cry," by which the community in general rose to apprehend felons. In its original medieval form the "hue and cry" was a form of summary justice that resembled modern lynch law. More commonly by the eighteenth century magistrates turned to the *posse commitatus,* literally the "power of the country," and in practice all able-bodied men a sheriff might call upon to assist him. Where greater and more organized

149

[24] Jay to Jefferson, Dec. 14, 1786, Boyd, ed., *Jefferson Papers*, X, 597. Beloff, *Public Order*, 30. John Swift to Boston customs commissioners, Nov. 15, 1770, Gov. William Franklin's Proclamation, Nov. 17, 1770, and John Hutton to Boston custom commissioners, Nov. 20, 1770, T. 1/476. The last mentioned riot occurred in November 1762. A cartel ship from Havana had stopped for repairs in October. On Nov. 21 a rumor spread that the Spaniards were murdering the inhabitants, which drew seamen from His Majesty's ship, *Arundel,* also in the harbor, into town, where the seamen drove the Spaniards into a house, set fire to it, and apparently intended to blow it up. A dignitary of the Spanish colonial service, who had been a passenger on the cartel ship, was beaten and some money and valuables were stolen from him. Local men tried to quell the riot without success. It was eventually put down by militiamen from Norfolk. See "A Narrative of a Riot in Virginia in November 1762," T. 1/476.

[25] Burke and others to the same effect, quoted in Jerome J. Nadelhaft, "The Revolutionary Era in South Carolina, 1775–1788" (unpubl. Ph.D. diss., University of Wisconsin, 1965), 151–152. See also account of the "Fort Wilson" riot of October 1779 in J. Thomas Scharf and Thompson Westcott, *History of Philadelphia, 1609–1884* (Philadelphia, 1884), I, 401–403.

[26] Rudé, *Crowd in History,* 255–257.

support was needed, magistrates could call out the militia.[27] Both the *posse* and the militia drew upon local men, including many of the same persons who made up the mob. This was particularly clear where these traditional mechanisms failed to function effectively. At Boston in September 1766 when customsmen contemplated breaking into the house of merchant Daniel Malcom to search for contraband goods, Sheriff Stephen Greenleaf threatened to call for support from members of the very crowd suspected of an intent to riot; and when someone suggested during the Stamp Act riots that the militia be raised Greenleaf was told it had already risen. This situation meant that mobs could naturally assume the manner of a lawful institution, acting by habit with relative restraint and responsibility. On the other hand, the militia institutionalized the practice of forcible popular coercion and so made the formation of extralegal mobs more natural that J. R. Western has called the militia "a relic of the bad old days," and hailed its passing as "a step towards . . . bringing civilization and humanity into our [English] political life."[28]

These law enforcement mechanisms left magistrates virtually helpless whenever a large segment of the population was immediately involved in the disorder, or when the community had a strong sympathy for the rioters. The Boston militia's failure to act in the Stamp Act riots, which was repeated in nearly all the North American colonies, recapitulated a similar refusal during the Knowles riot of 1747.[29] If the mob's sympathizers were confined to a single locality, the governor could try to call out the militias of surrounding areas, as Massachusetts Governor William Shirley began to do in 1747, and as, to some extent, Governor Francis Bernard attempted after the rescue of the *Polly* in 1765.[30] In the case of sudden uprisings, however, these peace-keeping mechanisms were at best partially effective since they required time to assemble strength, which often made the effort wholly pointless. When the disorder continued and the militia either failed to appear or proved insufficient, there was, of course, the army, which was used periodically in the eighteenth century against rioters in England and Scotland. Even in America peacetime garrisons tended to be placed where they might serve to maintain law and order. But since all Englishmen shared a fear of standing

[27] On the "hue and cry" see Frederick Pollock and Frederic W. Maitland, *The History of English Law before the Time of Edward I* (Cambridge, Eng., 1968 [orig. publ., Cambridge, Eng., 1895]), II, 578–580, and William Blackstone, *Commentaries on the Laws of England* (Philadelphia, 1771), IV, 290–291. John Shy, *Toward Lexington: The Role of the British Army in the Coming of the American Revolution* (Princeton, 1965), 40. The English militia underwent a period of decay after 1670 but was revived in 1757. See J. R. Western, *The English Militia in the Eighteenth Century* (London, 1965).

[28] Greenleaf's deposition, T. 1/446; *Providence Gaz.* (R. I.), Aug. 24, 1765. Western, *English Militia,* 74.

[29] Gov. William Shirley explained the militia's failure to appear during the opening stages of the Knowles riot by citing the militiamen's opposition to impressment and consequent sympathy for the rioters. See his letter to the Lords of Trade, Dec. 1, 1747, in Lincoln, ed., *Shirley Correspondence,* I, 417–418. The English militia was also unreliable. It worked well against invasions and unpopular rebellions, but was less likely to support the government when official orders "clashed with the desires of the citizens" or when ordered to protect unpopular minorities. Sir Robert Walpole believed "that if called on to suppress smuggling, protect the turnpikes, or enforce the gin act, the militia would take the wrong side." Western, *English Militia,* 72–73.

[30] Shirley to Josiah Willard, Nov. 19, 1747, Lincoln, ed., *Shirley Correspondence,* I, 407; Bernard's orders in *Providence Gaz.* (R. I.), Apr. 27, 1765.

armies the deployment of troops had always to be a sensitive and carefully limited recourse. Military and civil spheres of authority were rigidly separated, as was clear to Lord Jeffery Amherst, who refused to use soldiers against antimilitary rioters during the Seven Years' War because that function was "entirely foreign to their command and belongs of right to none but the civil power." In fact troops could be used against British subjects, as in the suppression of civil disorder, only upon the request of local magistrates. This institutional inhibition carried, if anything, more weight in the colonies. There royal governors had quickly lost their right to declare martial law without the consent of the provincial councils that were, again, usually filled with local men.[31]

For all practical purposes, then, when a large political unit such as an entire town or colony condoned an act of mass force, problems were raised "almost insoluble without rending the whole fabric of English law." Nor was the situation confined to the colonies. After describing England's institutions for keeping the peace under the later Stuarts, Max Beloff suggested that no technique for maintaining order was found until nineteenth-century reformers took on the task of reshaping urban government. Certainly by the 1770s no acceptable solution had been found—neither by any colonists, nor "anyone in London, Paris, or Rome, either," as Carl Bridenbaugh has put it. To even farsighted contemporaries like John Adams the weakness of authority was a fact of the social order that necessarily conditioned the way rulers could act. "It is vain to expect or hope to carry on government against the universal bent and genius of the people," he wrote, "we may whimper and whine as much as we will, but nature made it impossible when she made man."[32]

The mechanisms of enforcing public order were rendered even more fragile since the difference between legal and illegal applications of mass force was distinct in theory, but sometimes indistinguishable in practice. The English common law prohibited riot, defined as an uprising of three or more persons who performed what Blackstone called an "unlawful act of violence" for a private purpose. If the act was never carried out or attempted the offense became unlawful assembly; if some effort was made toward its execution, rout; and if the purpose of the uprising was public rather than private—tearing down whore houses, for example, or destroying all enclosures rather than just those personally affecting the insurgents—the offense became treason since it constituted a usurpation of the king's function, a "levying war against the King." The precise legal offense lay not so much in the purpose of the uprising as in its use of force and violence "wherein the Law does not allow the Use of such Force." Such unlawful assumptions of force were carefully distinguished by commentators upon the common law from other occasions on which the law authorized a use of force. It was, for example, legal for force to be used by a sheriff, constable, "or perhaps even . . . a private Person" who assembled "a competent Number of People, in Order with Force to suppress Rebels, or Enemies, or Rioters"; for a justice of the peace to raise the *posse* when opposed in detaining lands, or for Crown officers to raise "a

151

---

[31] Shy, *Toward Lexington,* 39–40, 44, 47, 74. Amherst, quoted in J. C. Long, *Lord Jeffery Amherst* (New York, 1933), 124.

[32] Shy, *Toward Lexington,* 44; Beloff, *Public Order,* 157–158; Bridenbaugh, *Cities in Revolt,* 297; C. F. Adams, ed., *Works of Adams,* IV, 74–75, V, 209.

Power as may effectually enable them to over-power any . . . Resistance" in the execution of the King's writs.[33]

In certain situations these distinctions offered at best a very uncertain guide as to who did or did not exert force lawfully. Should a *posse* employ more force than was necessary to overcome overt resistance, for example, its members acted illegally and were indictable for riot. And where established officials supported both sides in a confrontation, or where the legality of an act that officials were attempting to enforce was itself disputed, the decision as to who were or were not rioters seemed to depend upon the observer's point of view. Impressment is a good example. The colonists claimed that impressment was unlawful in North America under an act of 1708, while British authorities and some—but not all—spokesmen for the government held that the law had lapsed in 1713. The question was settled only in 1775, when Parliament finally repealed the "Sixth of Anne." Moreover, supposing impressment could indeed be carried on, were press warrants from provincial authorities still necessary? Royal instructions of 1697 had given royal governors the "sole power of impressing seamen in any of our plantations in America or in sight of them." Admittedly that clause was dropped in 1708, and a subsequent parliamentary act of 1746, which required the full consent of the governor and council before impressment could be carried on within their province, applied only to the West Indies. Nonetheless it seems that in 1764 the Lords of the Admiralty thought the requirement held throughout North America.[34] With the legality of impressment efforts so uncertain, especially when opposed by local authorities, it was possible to see the press gangs as "rioters" for trying en masse to perpetrate an unlawful act of violence. In that case the local townsmen who opposed them might be considered lawful defenders of the public welfare, acting much as they would in a *posse*. In 1770 John Adams cited opposition to press gangs who acted without warrants as an example of the lawful use of force; and when the sloop of war *Hornet* swept into Norfolk, Virginia, in September 1767 with a "bloody riotous plan . . . to impress seamen, without consulting the Mayor, or any other magistrate," the offense was charged to the pressmen. Roused by the watchman, who called out *"a riot by man of war's men,"* the inhabitants rose to back the magistrates, and not only secured the release of the impressed men but also imprisoned ten members of the press gang. The ship's captain, on the other hand, condemned the townsmen as "Rioters." Ambiguity was present, too, in Newport's *St. John* clash, which involved both impressment and criminal action on the part of royal seamen and culminated with Newporters firing on the king's ship. The Privy Council in England promptly classified the incident as a riot, but the Rhode Island governor's report boldly maintained that "the people meant nothing but to assist [the magistrates] in apprehending the Offenders" on the vessel, and even suggested that "their Conduct be honored with his Majesty's royal Approbation."[35]

---

[33] The definition of the common law of riot most commonly cited—for example, by John Adams in the Massacre trials—was from William Hawkins, *A Treatise of the Pleas of the Crown* (London, 1716), I, 155–159. See also, Blackstone, *Commentaries,* IV, 146–147, and Edward Coke, *The Third Part of the Institutes of the Laws of England* (London, 1797), 176.

[34] Clark, "Impressment of Seamen," *Essays in Honor of Andrews,* 198–224; Stout, "Manning the Royal Navy," *American Neptune,* XXIII (1963), 178–179; and Leonard W. Labaree, ed., *Royal Instructions to British Colonial Governors, 1670–1776* (New York, 1935), I, 442–443.

[35] L. Kinvin Wroth and Hiller B. Zobel, eds., *Legal Papers of John Adams* (Cambridge, Mass.,

The enforcement of the White Pine Acts was similarly open to legal dispute. The acts seemed to violate both the Massachusetts and Connecticut charters; the meaning of provisions exempting trees growing within townships (act of 1722) and those which were "the property of private persons" (act of 1729) was contested, and royal officials tended to work on the basis of interpretations of the laws that Bernhard Knollenberg has called farfetched and, in one case, "utterly untenable." The Exeter, New Hampshire, "riot" of 1734, for example, answered an attempt of the surveyor to seize boards on the argument that the authorization to seize logs from allegedly illegally felled white pine trees in the act of 1722 included an authorization to seize processed lumber. As a result, Knollenberg concluded, although the surveyors' reports "give the impression that the New Englanders were an utterly lawless lot, . . . in many if not most cases they were standing for what they believed, with reason, were their legal and equitable rights in trees growing on their own lands."[36]

Occasions open to such conflicting interpretations were rare. Most often even those who sympathized with the mob's motives condemned its use of force as illegal and unjustifiable. That ambiguous cases did arise, however, indicates that legitimacy and illegitimacy, *posses* and rioters, represented but poles of the same spectrum. And where a mob took upon itself the defense of the community, it benefited from a certain popular legitimacy even when the strict legality of its action was in doubt, particularly among a people taught that the legitimacy of law itself depended upon its defense of the public welfare.

Whatever quasi-legal status mobs were accorded by local communities was reinforced, moreover, by formal political thought. "Riots and rebellions" were often calmly accepted as a constant and even necessary element of free government. This acceptance depended, however, upon certain essential assumptions about popular uprisings. With words that could be drawn almost verbatim from John Locke or any other English author of similar convictions, colonial writers posited a continuing moderation and purposefulness on the part of the mob. "Tho' innocent Persons may sometimes suffer in popular Tumults," observed a 1768 writer in the *New York Journal*, "yet the general Resentment of the People is principally directed according to Justice, and the greatest Delinquent feels it most." Moreover, upheavals constituted only occasional interruptions in well-governed societies. "Good Laws and good Rulers will always be obey'd and respected"; "the Experience of all Ages proves, that Mankind are much more likely to submit to bad Laws and wicked Rulers, than to resist good ones." "Mobs and Tumults," it was often said, "never happen but thro' Oppression and a scandalous Abuse of Power."[37]

1965), III, 253. Account of the Norfolk incident by George Abyvon, Sept. 5, 1767, in Purdie and Dixon's *Va. Gaz.* (Wmsbg.), Oct. 1, 1767. Capt. Morgan quoted in Lemisch, "Jack Tar," *Wm. and Mary Qtly.*, 3d Ser., XXV (1968), 391. Munro, ed., *Acts of the Privy Council, Colonial Series*, VI, 374; Gov. Samuel Ward to Treasury lords, Oct. 23, 1765, Ward MSS, Box 1, fol. 58.

[36] Knollenberg, *Origin of the Revolution*, 122–130; Albion, *Forests and Sea Power*, 255–258.

[37] *N. Y. Jour.* (N.Y.C.), Aug. 18, 1768 (the writer was allegedly drawing together arguments that had recently appeared in the British press); and *N. Y. Jour. Supplement* (N.Y.C.), Jan. 4, 1770. Note also that Jefferson accepted Shays's rebellion as a sign of health in American institutions only after he had been assured by men like Jay that the insurgents had acted purposely and

In the hands of Locke such remarks constituted relatively inert statements of fact. Colonial writers, however, often turned these pronouncements on their heads such that observed instances of popular disorder became prima facie indictments of authority. In 1747, for example, New Jersey land rioters argued that "from their Numbers, Violences, and unlawful Actions" it was to be "inferred that . . . they are wronged and oppressed, or else they would never *rebell agt. the Laws.*" Always, a New York writer said in 1770, when "the People of any Government" become "turbulent and uneasy," it was above all "a certain Sign of Maladministration." Even when disorders were not directly levelled against government they provided "strong proofs that something is much amiss in the state" as William Samuel Johnson put it; that—in Samuel Adams's words—the "wheels of good government" were "somewhat clogged." Americans who used this argument against Britain in the 1760's continued to depend upon it two decades later when they reacted to Shays's Rebellion by seeking out the public "Disease" in their own independent governments that was indicated by the "Spirit of Licentiousness" in Massachusetts.[38]

Popular turbulence seemed to follow so naturally from inadequacies of government that uprisings were often described with similes from the physical world. In 1770 John Adams said that there were "Church-quakes and state-quakes in the moral and political world, as well as earthquakes, storms and tempests in the physical." Two years earlier a writer in the *New York Journal* likened popular tumults to "Thunder Gusts" which "commonly do more Good than Harm." Thomas Jefferson continued the imagery in the 1780s, particularly with his famous statement that he liked "a little rebellion now and then" for it was "like a storm in the atmosphere." It was, moreover, because of the "imperfection of all things in this world," including government, that Adams found it "vain to seek a government in all points free from a possibility of civil wars, tumults and seditions." That was "a blessing denied to this life and preserved to complete the felicity of the next."[39]

If popular uprisings occurred "in all governments at all times," they were nonetheless most able to break out in free governments. Tyrants imposed order and submission upon their subjects by force, thus dividing society, as Jefferson said, into wolves and sheep. Only under free governments were the people "nervous," spirited, jealous of their rights, ready to react against unjust provocations; and this being the case, popular disorders could be interpreted as "Symptoms of a

---

moderately, and after he had concluded that the uprising represented no continuous threat to established government. "An insurrection in one of the 13. states in the course of 11. years that they have subsisted amounts to one in any particular state in 143 years, say a century and a half," he calculated. "This would not be near as many as has happened in every other government that has ever existed," and clearly posed no threat to the constitutional order as a whole. To David Hartley, July 2, 1787, Boyd, ed., *Jefferson Papers,* XI, 526.

[38] John Locke, *The Second Treatise of Government,* paragraphs 223–225. "A State of Facts Concerning the Riots . . . in New Jersey," *New Jersey Archives,* VII, 217. *N. Y. Jour., Supp.* (N.Y.C.), Jan. 4, 1770. Johnson to Wm. Pitkin, Apr. 29, 1768, Massachusetts Historical Society, *Collections,* 5th Ser., IX (1885), 275. Adams as "Determinus" in *Boston Gazette,* Aug. 8, 1768; and Harry A. Cushing, ed., *The Writings of Samuel Adams* (New York, 1904–1908), I, 237. Jay to Jefferson, Oct. 27, 1786, Boyd, ed., *Jefferson Papers,* X, 488.

[39] Wroth and Zobel, eds., *Adams Legal Papers,* III, 249–250; *N. Y. Jour. Supp.* (N.Y.C.), Aug. 18, 1768; Jefferson to Abigail Adams, Feb. 22, 1787, Boyd, ed., *Jefferson Papers,* XI, 174. C. F. Adams, ed., *Works of Adams,* IV, 77, 80 (quoting Algernon Sydney).

strong and healthy Constitution" even while they indicated some lesser short-coming in administration. It would be futile, Josiah Quincy, Jr., said in 1770, to expect "that pacific, timid, obsequious, and servile temper, so predominant in more despotic governments" from those who lived under free British institutions. From "our happy constitution," he claimed, there resulted as "very natural Effects" an "impatience of injuries, and a strong resentment of insults."[40]

This popular impatience constituted an essential force in the maintenance of free institutions. "What country can preserve it's [sic] liberties if their rulers are not warned from time to time that their people preserve the spirit of resistance?" Jefferson asked in 1787. Occasional insurrections were thus "an evil . . . productive of good": even those founded on popular error tended to hold rulers "to the true principles of their institution" and generally provided "a medecine necessary for the sound health of government." This meant that an aroused people had a role not only in extreme situations, where revolution was requisite, but in the normal course of free government. For that reason members of the House of Lords could seriously argue—as A.J.P. Taylor has pointed out—that "rioting is an essential part of our constitution"; and for that reason, too, even Massachusetts's conservative Lieutenant Governor Thomas Hutchinson could remark in 1768 that "mobs a sort of them at least are constitutional."[41]

III

It was, finally, the interaction of this constitutional role of the mob with the written law that makes the story of eighteenth-century popular uprisings complexity itself.[42] If mobs were appreciated because they provided a check on power, it was always understood that, insofar as upheavals threatened "running to

---

[40] Jefferson to Edward Carrington, Jan. 16, 1787, Boyd, ed., *Jefferson Papers*, XI, 49, and Rev. James Madison to Jefferson, Mar. 28, 1787, ibid., 252. Wroth and Zobel, eds., *Adams Legal Papers*, III, 250. Quincy's address to the jury in the soldiers' trial after the Boston Massacre in Josiah Quincy, *Memoir of the Life of Josiah Quincy, Junior, of Massachusetts Bay, 1744–1775*, ed. Eliza Susan Quincy, 3d ed. (Boston, 1875), 46. See also Massachusetts Assembly's similar statement in its address to Gov. Hutchinson, Apr. 24, 1770, Hutchinson, *History of Massachusetts-Bay*, ed. Mayo, III, 365–366. This 18th century devotion to political "jealousy" resembles the doctrine of "vigilance" that was defended by 19th century vigilante groups. See Graham and Gurr, *Violence in America*, 179–183.

[41] Jefferson to William Stephen Smith, Nov. 13, 1787, Boyd, ed., *Jefferson Papers*, XII, 356, Jefferson to Carrington, Jan. 16, 1787, ibid., XI, 49, Jefferson to James Madison, Jan. 30, 1787, ibid., 92–93. Taylor's remarks in "History of Violence," *The Listener*, CXXIX (1968), 701. ("Members of the House of Lords . . . said . . . if the people really don't like something, then they work our carriages and tear off our wigs and throw stones through the windows of our town-houses. And this is an essential thing to have if you are going to have a free country.") Hutchinson to [John or Robert] Grant, July 27, 1768, Massachusetts Archives, XXVI, 317, State House, Boston. See also the related story about John Selden, the famous 17th century lawyer, told to the House of Commons in Jan. 1775 by Lord Camden and recorded by Josiah Quincy, Jr., in the "Journal of Josiah Quincy, Jun., During his Voyage and Residence in England from September 28th, 1774, to March 3d, 1775," Massachusetts Historical Society, *Proceedings*, L (1916–1917), 462–463. Selden was asked what lawbook contained the laws for resisting tyranny. He replied he did not know, "but I'll tell [you] what is most certain, that it has always been the custom of England—and the Custom of England is the *Law of the Land*."

[42] On the developing distinction Americans drew between what was legal and constitutional, see Wood, *Creation of the American Republic*, 261–268.

such excesses, as will overturn the whole system of government," "strong dis-couragements" had to be provided against them. For eighteenth-century Americans, like the English writers they admired, liberty demanded the rule of law. In extreme situations where the rulers had clearly chosen arbitrary power over the limits of law, men like John Adams could prefer the risk of anarchy to continued submission because "anarchy can never last long, and tyranny may be perpetual," but only when "there was any hope that the fair order of liberty and a free constitution would arise out of it." This desire to maintain the orderly rule of law led legislatures in England and the colonies to pass antiriot statutes and to make strong efforts—in the words of a 1753 Massachusetts law—to discounte-nance "a mobbish temper and spirit in . . . the inhabitants" that would oppose "all government and order."[43]

The problem of limiting mass violence was dealt with most intensely over a sustained period by the American Revolutionary leadership, which has perhaps suffered most from historians' earlier inattention to the history of colonial upris-ings. So long as it could be maintained—as it was only fifteen years ago—that political mobs were "rare or unknown in America" before the 1760s, the Revolutionaries were implicitly credited with their creation. American patriots, Charles McLean Andrews wrote, were often "lawless men who were nothing more than agitators and demagogues" and who attracted a following from the riffraff of colonial society. It now seems clear that the mob drew on all elements of the population. More important, the Revolutionary leaders had no need to create mob support. Instead they were forced to work with a "permanent entity," a traditional crowd that exerted itself before, after, and even during the Revolutionary struggle over issues unrelated to the conflict with Britain, and that, as Hobsbawm has noted, characteristically aided the Revolutionary cause in the opening phases of conflict but was hard to discipline thereafter.[44]

In focusing popular exuberance the American leaders could work with long-established tendencies in the mob toward purposefulness and responsibility. In doing so they could, moreover, draw heavily upon the guidelines for direct action that had been defined by English radical writers since the seventeenth century. Extralegal action was justified only when all established avenues to redress had failed. It could not answer casual errors or private failings on the part of the mag-

[43] *N. Y. Jour. Supp.* (N.Y.C.), Jan. 4, 1770; Wroth and Zobel, eds., *Adams Legal Papers,* III, 250, and C. F. Adams, ed., *Works of Adams,* VI, 151. Adams's views were altered in 1815, ibid., X, 181. It is noteworthy that the Boston town meeting condemned the Knowles rioters not simply for their method of opposing impressment but because they insulted the governor and the legislature, and the Massachusetts Assembly acted against the uprising only after Gov. Shirley had left Boston and events seemed to be "tending to the destruction of all government and order." Hutchinson, *History of Massachusetts-Bay,* ed. Mayo, II, 332–333. *Acts and Resolves of the Province of Massachusetts Bay,* III, 647. (Chap. 18 of the Province laws, 1752–1753, "An Act for Further Preventing all Riotous, Tumultuous and Disorderly Assemblies or Companies or Persons. . . .") This act, which was inspired particularly by Pope's Day violence, was renewed after the Boston Massacre in 1770 even though the legislature refused to renew its main Riot Act of 1751. Ibid., IV, 87.

[44] Arthur M. Schlesinger, "Political Mobs and the American Revolution, 1765–1776," *Proceedings of the American Philosophical Society,* XCIX (1955), 246; Charles M. Andrews, *The Colonial Background of the American Revolution,* rev. ed. (New Haven, 1939), 176; Charles M. Andrews, "The Boston Merchants and the Non-Importation Movement," Colonial Society of Massachusetts, *Transactions,* XIX (1916–1917), 241; Hobsbawm, *Primitive Rebels,* 111, 123–124.

istrates, but had to await fundamental public abuses so egregious that the "whole people" turned against their rulers. Even then, it was held, opposition had to be measured so that no more force was exerted than was necessary for the public good. Following these principles colonial leaders sought by careful organization to avoid the excesses that first greeted the Stamp Act. Hutchinson's query after a crowd in Connecticut had forced the resignation of stampman Jared Ingersoll— whether "such a public regular assembly can be called a mob"—could with equal appropriateness have been repeated during the tea resistance, or in 1774 when Massachusetts *mandamus* councillors were forced to resign.[45]

From the first appearance of an organized resistance movement in 1765, moreover, efforts were made to support the legal magistrates such that, as John Adams said in 1774, government would have "as much vigor then as ever" except where its authority was specifically under dispute. This concern for the maintenance of order and the general framework of law explains why the American Revolution was largely free from the "universal tumults and all the irregularities and violence of mobbish factions [that] naturally arise when legal authority ceases." It explains, too, why old revolutionaries like Samuel Adams or Christopher Gadsden disapproved of those popular conventions and committees that persisted after regular independent state governments were established in the 1770s. "Decency and Respect [are] due to Constitutional Authority," Samuel Adams said in 1784, "and those Men, who under any Pretence or by any Means whatever, would lessen the Weight of Government lawfully exercised must be Enemies to our happy Revolution and the Common Liberty."[46]

In normal circumstances the "strong discouragements" to dangerous disorder were provided by established legislatures. The measures enacted by them to deal with insurrections were shaped by the eighteenth-century understanding of civil uprisings. Since turbulence indicated above all some shortcoming in government, it was never to be met by increasing the authorities' power of suppression. The "weakness of authority" that was a function of its dependence upon popular support appeared to contemporary Americans as a continuing virtue of British institutions, as one reason why rulers could not simply dictate to their subjects and why Britain had for so long been hailed as one of the freest nations in Europe. It was "far less dangerous to the Freedom of a State" to allow "the laws to be trampled upon, by the licence among the rabble . . . than to dispence with their force by an act of power." Insurrections were to be answered by reform, by attacking the "Disease"—to use John Jay's term of 1786—that lay behind them rather than by suppressing its "Symptoms." And ultimately, as William Samuel Johnson observed in 1768, "the only effectual way to prevent them is to govern with wisdom, justice, and moderation."[47]

---

[45] Hutchinson to Thomas Pownall, [Sept. or Oct. 1765], Mass. Archives, XXVI, 157. Pauline Maier, "From Resistance to Revolution: American Radicals and the Development of Intercolonial Opposition to Britain, 1765–1776" (unpubl. Ph.D. diss., Harvard University, 1968), I, 37–45, 72–215.

[46] C. F. Adams, ed., *Works of Adams*, IV, 51; Rev. Samuel Langdon's election sermon to third Massachusetts Provincial Congress, May 31, 1775, quoted in Richard Frothingham, *Life and Times of Joseph Warren* (Boston, 1865), 499; Samuel Adams to Noah Webster, Apr. 30, 1784, Cushing, ed., *Writings of Samuel Adams*, IV, 305–306. On Gadsden see Richard Walsh, *Charleston's Sons of Liberty* (Columbia, 1959), 87.

[47] *N. Y. Jour. Supp.* (N.Y.C.), Jan. 4, 1770; Jay to Jefferson, Oct. 27, 1786, Boyd, ed., *Jefferson*

In immediate crises, however, legislatures in both England and America resorted to special legislation that supplemented the common law prohibition of riot. The English Riot Act of 1714 was passed when disorder threatened to disrupt the accession of George I; a Connecticut act of 1722 followed a rash of incidents over land title in Hartford County; the Massachusetts act of 1751 answered "several tumultuous assemblies" over the currency issue and another of 1786 was enacted at the time of Shays's Rebellion. The New Jersey legislature passed an act in 1747 during that colony's protracted land riots; Pennsylvania's Riot Act of 1764 was inspired by the Paxton Boys; North Carolina's of 1771 by the Regulators; New York's of 1774 by the "land wars" in Charlotte and Albany County.[48] Always the acts specified that the magistrates were to depend upon the *posse* in enforcing their provisions, and in North Carolina on the militia as well. They differed over the number of people who had to remain "unlawfully, riotously, and tumultuously assembled together, to the Disturbance of the Publick Peace" for one hour after the reading of a prescribed riot proclamation before becoming judicable under the act. Some colonies specified lesser punishments than the death penalty provided for in the English act, but the American statutes were not in general more "liberal" than the British. Two of them so violated elementary judicial rights that they were subsequently condemned—North Carolina's by Britain, and New York's act of 1774 by a later, Revolutionary state legislature.[49]

In one important respect, however, the English Riot Act was reformed. Each colonial riot law, except that of Connecticut, was enacted for only one to three years, whereas the British law was perpetual. By this provision colonial legislators avoided the shortcoming which, it was said, was "more likely to introduce *arbitrary Power* than even an *Army* itself," because a perpetual riot act meant that "in all future time" by "reading a Proclamation" the Crown had the power "of hanging up their Subjects wholesale, or of picking out Those, to whom they have the greatest Dislike." If the death penalty was removed, the danger was less. When, therefore, riot acts without limit of time were finally enacted—as Connecticut had done in 1722, Massachusetts in 1786, New Jersey in 1797—the punishments were considerably milder, providing, for example, for imprisonment not exceeding six months in Connecticut, one year in Massachusetts, and three years in New Jersey.[50]

Papers, X, 488; Johnson to William Pitkin, July 23, 1768, Massachusetts Historical Society, *Collections,* 5th Ser., IX, 294–295.

[48] *The Statutes at Large* [of Great Britain] (London, 1786), V, 4–6; Hoadly, ed., *Public Records of Connecticut,* VI, 346–348 for the law, and see also 332–333, 341–348; *Acts and Resolves of Massachusetts Bay,* III, 544–546, for the Riot Act of 1751, and see also Hutchinson, *History of Massachusetts-Bay,* ed. Mayo, III, 6–7; and *Acts and Laws of the Commonwealth of Massachusetts* (Boston, 1893), 87–88, for Act of 1786; "A State of Facts Concerning the Riots . . . in New Jersey," *N. J. Archives,* VII, 211–212, 221–222; *The Statutes at Large of Pennsylvania . . .* (n. p., 1899), VI, 325–328; William A. Saunders, ed., *The Colonial Records of North Carolina* (Raleigh, 1890), VIII, 481–486; *Laws of the Colony of New York in the Years 1774 and 1775* (Albany, 1888), 38–43.

[49] See additional instruction to Gov. Josiah Martin, Saunders, ed., *Colonial Records of North Carolina,* VIII, 515–516; and *Laws of the State of New York* (Albany, 1886), I, 20.

[50] *The Craftsman* (London, 1731), VI, 263–264. Connecticut and Massachusetts laws cited in

Riot legislation, it is true, was not the only recourse against insurgents, who throughout the eighteenth century could also be prosecuted for treason. The colonial and state riot acts suggest, nonetheless, that American legislators recognized the participants in civil insurrections as guilty of a crime peculiarly complicated because it had social benefits as well as damages. To some degree, it appears, they shared the idea expressed well by Jefferson in 1787: that "honest republican governors" should be "so mild in their punishments of rebellions, as not to discourage them too much."[51] Even in countering riots the legislators seemed as intent upon preventing any perversion of the forces of law and order by established authorities as with chastising the insurgents. Reform of the English Riot Act thus paralleled the abolition of constitutent treasons—a traditional recourse against enemies of the Crown—in American state treason acts of the Revolutionary period and finally in Article III of the Federal Constitution.[52] From the same preoccupation, too, sprang the limitations placed upon the regular army provided for in the Constitution in part to assure the continuation of republican government guaranteed to the states by Article IV, Section iv. Just as the riot acts were for so long limited in duration, appropriations for the army were never to extend beyond two years (Article I, Section viii, 12); and the army could be used within a state against domestic violence only after application by the legislature or governor, if the legislature could not be convened (Article IV, Section iv).

A continuing desire to control authority through popular action also underlay the declaration in the Second Amendment that "a well regulated Militia being necessary to the security of a free State," citizens were assured the "right . . . to keep and bear Arms." The militia was meant above all "to prevent the establishment of a standing army, the bane of liberty"; and the right to bear arms—taken in part from the English Bill of Rights of 1689—was considered a standing threat to would-be tyrants. It embodied "a public allowance, under due restrictions, of the *natural right of resistance and self preservation,* when the sanctions of society and laws are found *insufficient* to restrain the *violence of oppression.*" And on the basis of their eighteenth-century experience, Americans could consider that right to be "perfectly harmless. . . . If the government be equitable; if it be reasonable in its exactions; if proper attention be paid to the education of children in knowledge, and religion," Timothy Dwight declared, "few men will be disposed to use arms, unless for their amusement, and for the defence of themselves and their country."[53]

The need felt to continue the eighteenth-century militia as a counterweight to government along with the efforts to outlaw rioting and to provide for the use of a standing army against domestic insurrections under carefully defined circum-

---

n. 45; and *Laws of the State of New Jersey* (Trenton, 1821), 279–281.

[51] Jefferson to Madison, Jan. 30, 1787, Boyd, ed., *Jefferson Papers,* XI, 93.

[52] See Bradley Chapin, "Colonial and Revolutionary Origins of the American Law of Treason," *Wm. and Mary Qtly.,* 3d Ser., XVII (1960), 3–21.

[53] Elbridge Gerry in Congressional debates, quoted in Irving Brant, *The Bill of Rights, Its Origin and Meaning* (Indianapolis, 1965), 486; Samuel Adams, quoting Blackstone, as "E. A." in *Boston Gaz.,* Feb. 27, 1769, and Cushing, ed., *Writings of Samuel Adams,* I, 317. Timothy Dwight, quoted in Daniel J. Boorstin, *The Americans: The Colonial Experience* (New York, 1958), 353.

stances together illustrate the complex attitude toward peacekeeping that pre-vailed among the nation's founders. The rule of law had to be maintained, yet complete order was neither expected nor even desired when it could be pur-chased, it seemed, only at the cost of forcefully suppressing the spirit of a free people. The constant possibility of insurrection—as institutionalized in the mili-tia—was to remain an element of the United States Constitution, just as it had played an essential role in Great Britain's.

This readiness to accept some degree of tumultuousness depended to a large degree upon the lawmakers' own experience with insurrections in the eighteenth century, when "disorder" was seldom anarchic and "rioters" often acted to defend law and justice rather than to oppose them. In the years after indepen-dence this toleration declined, in part because mass action took on new dimen-sions. Nineteenth-century mobs often resembled in outward form those of the previous century, but a new violence was added. Moreover, the literal assumption of popular rule in the years after Lexington taught many thoughtful Revolutionary partisans what was for them an unexpected lesson—that the peo-ple were "as capable of despotism as any prince," that "public liberty was no guarantee after all of private liberty."[54] With home rule secured, attention focused more exclusively upon minority rights, which mob action had always to some extent imperiled. And the danger that uprisings carried for individual freedom became ever more egregious as mobs shed their former restraint and burned Catholic convents, attacked nativist speakers, lynched Mormons, or destroyed the presses and threatened the lives of abolitionists.

Ultimately, however, changing attitudes toward popular uprisings turned upon fundamental transformations in the political perspective of Americans after 1776. Throughout the eighteenth century political institutions had been viewed as in a constant evolution: the colonies' relationship with Britain and with each other, even the balance of power within the governments of various colonies, remained unsettled. Under such circumstances the imputations of governmental shortcoming that uprisings carried could easily be accepted and absorbed. But after Independence, when the form and conduct of the Americans' governments were under their exclusive control, and when those governments represented, moreover, an experiment in republicanism on which depended their own happi-ness and "that of generations unborn," Americans became less ready to endure domestic turbulence or accept its disturbing implications. Some continued to argue that "distrust and dissatisfaction" on the part of the multitude were "always the consequence of tyranny or corruption." Others, however, began to see domestic turbulence not as indictments but as insults to government that were likely to discredit American republicanism in the eyes of European observers. "Mobs are a reproach to Free Governments," where all grievances could be legal-ly redressed through the courts or the ballot box, it was argued in 1783. They originated there "not in Oppression, but in Licentiousness," an "ungovernable spirit" among the people. Under republican governments even that distrust of power colonists had found so necessary for liberty, and which uprisings seemed to manifest, could appear outmoded. "There is some consistency in being jealous of power in the hands of those who assume it by birth . . . and over whom we have

---

[54] Wood, *Creation of the American Republic*, 410.

no controul . . . as was the case with the Crown of England over America," another writer suggested. "But to be jealous of those whom we chuse, the instant we have chosen them" was absurd: perhaps in the transition from monarchy to republic Americans had "bastardized" their ideas by placing jealousy where confidence was more appropriate.[55] In short, the assumptions behind the Americans' earlier toleration of the mob were corroded in republican America. Old and new attitudes coexisted in the 1780s and even later. But the appropriateness of popular uprisings in the United States became increasingly in doubt after the Federal Constitution came to be seen as the final product of long-term institutional experimentation, "a momentous contribution to the history of politics" that rendered even that most glorious exertion of popular force, revolution itself, an obsolete resort for Americans.[56]

Yet this change must not be viewed exclusively as a product of America's distinctive Revolutionary achievement. J. H. Plumb has pointed out, that a century earlier, when England passed beyond her revolutionary era and progressed toward political "stability," radical ideology with its talk of resistance and revolution was gradually left behind. A commitment to peace and permanence emerged from decades of fundamental change. In America as in England this stability demanded that operative sovereignty, including the right finally to decide what was and was not in the community's interest, and which laws were and were not constitutional, be entrusted to established governmental institutions. The result was to minimize the role of the people at large, who had been the ultimate arbiters of those questions in English and American Revolutionary thought. Even law enforcement was to become the task primarily of professional agencies. As a result in time all popular upheavals alike became menacing efforts to "pluck up law and justice by the roots," and riot itself gradually became defined as a purposeless act of anarchy, "a blind and misguided outburst of popular fury," of "undirected violence with no articulated goals."[57]

161

Author's Postscript

I backed into the rich material that provided the basis for "Popular Uprisings and Civil Authority." During the spring of 1962, in desperate need of a paper topic for a graduate seminar in early American history—a subject about which I knew almost nothing—I remembered an odd fact I'd picked up from a book on eighteenth-century England: there were Americans in the Supporters of the Bill of Rights, a group formed in London to back the radical John Wilkes. With the

---

[55] Judge Aedanus Burke's Charge to the Grand Jury at Charleston, June 9, 1783, in *South-Carolina Gazette and General Advertiser* (Charleston), June 10, 1783; "A Patriot," ibid., July 15, 1783; and "Another Patriot," ibid., July 29, 1783; and on the relevance of jealousy of power, see a letter to Virginia in ibid., Aug. 9, 1783. "Democratic Gentle-Touch," *Gazette of the State of South Carolina* (Charleston), May 13, 1784.

[56] Wood, *Creation of the American Republic,* 612–614.

[57] J. H. Plumb, *The Origins of Political Stability, England 1675–1725* (Boston, 1967), xv, 187; John Adams on the leaders of Shays's Rebellion in a letter to Benjamin Hitchborn, Jan. 27, 1787, in C. F. Adams, ed., *Works of Adams,* IX, 551; modern definitions of riot in "Riot Control and the Use of Federal Troops," *Harvard Law Review,* LXXXI (1968), 643.

encouragement of the instructor, a young Harvard professor named Bernard Bailyn, I set out to see what I could learn about those colonial Wilkites. The fruits of that effort include an article published in the *William and Mary Quarterly* in 1963 and, five years later, a dissertation that eventually saw print as *From Resistance to Revolution* (New York, 1972).

I wasn't far into my research when I began to suspect that the relationship between American popular leaders and their followers was at odds with established wisdom on the subject. According to historians of the "progressive" tradition—whose interpretation of the Revolution was still being dismantled, point by point, in the 1960s—"radicals" had introduced popular violence into America during the Stamp Act crisis. My sources suggested, however, that radicals of the 1760s in both England and America were far more concerned with restraining their followers than with raising mobs or inciting violence. The more I studied the "crowd"—an unsatisfactory word then considered more politically correct than the good old eighteenth-century term "mob"—the more convinced I became that it was more firmly rooted in the Anglo-American past than progressive historians had recognized. My dissertation included a chapter on popular uprisings in an opening unit on traditions that shaped American resistance to Britain between 1765 and 1776. When I revised that chapter as an article, I expanded its contents, bringing in uprisings from the 1780s and 1790s and suggesting how attitudes and practices shifted with the establishment of republican government. By then, in retrospect, I had moved far beyond my 1967 ignorance of early America. My old ambition to become a historian of modern America was also long gone—I was hooked on the eighteenth century.

The continued interest in the article depends, I think, in part on how carefully its claims were limited. It made no pretense to cover all colonial uprisings but focused on one important, recurrent type within a defined period of time. In that way the article established a historical model against which studies of other uprisings have been compared. Clearly, the eighteenth-century phenomenon I studied was different from the "civil disobedience" or "violent protest" that flourished in a more modern sociopolitical context. On the other hand, even the most destructive modern riots share traits with their eighteenth-century ancestors. My Massachusetts Institute of Technology colleague Robert M. Fogelson tells the story of a looter in the 1965 Watts riot who, while walking down the street with a television in his arms, stopped to wait for the street light to change. It probably never crossed the man's mind that he had some resemblance to colonial Bostonians who wouldn't riot on the Sabbath.

EVANGELICAL REVOLT:
THE NATURE OF THE BAPTISTS' CHALLENGE
TO THE TRADITIONAL ORDER IN VIRGINIA,
1765 TO 1775

RHYS ISAAC

An intense struggle for allegiance had developed in the Virginia countryside during the decade before the Revolution. Two eye-witness accounts may open to us the nature of the conflict. First, a scene vividly remembered and described by the Reverend James Ireland etches in sharp profile the postures of the forces in contest. As a young man Ireland, who was a propertyless schoolmaster of genteel origin, had cut a considerable figure in Frederick County society. His success had arisen largely from his prowess at dancing and his gay facility as a satiric wit. Then, like many other young men at this time (ca. 1768), he came deeply "under conviction of sin" and withdrew from the convivialities of gentry society. When an older friend and patron of Ireland heard that his young protégé could not be expected at a forthcoming assembly, this gentleman, a leader in county society, sensed the challenge to his way of life that was implicit in Ireland's withdrawal. He swore instantly that "there could not be a dance in the settlement without [Ireland] being there, and if they would leave it to him, he would convert [him], and that to the dance, on Monday; and they would see [Ireland] lead the ball that day." Frederick County, for all its geographical spread, was a close community. Young James learned that his patron would call, and dreaded the coming test of strength:

163

> When I viewed him riding up, I never beheld such a display of pride arising from his deportment, attitude and jesture; he rode a lofty elegant horse, . . . his countenance appeared to me as bold and daring as satan himself, and with a commanding authority [he] called upon me, if I were there to come out, which I accordingly did, with a fearful and timorous heart. But O! how quickly can God level pride. . . . For no sooner did he behold my disconsolate looks, emaciated countenance and solemn aspect, than he . . . was riveted to the beast he rode on. . . . As soon as he could articulate a little his eyes fixed upon me, and his first address was this; "In the name of the Lord, what is the matter with you?"[1]

Mr. Isaac is a member of the Department of History, La Trobe University, Australia. He would like to thank all those who helped this study with encouragement and critical advice, particularly Stephen G. Kurtz, Thad W. Tate, Allan Martin, John Salmond, Inga Clendinnen, and Greg and Donna Dening. A deep debt of gratitude is owed to the Virginia Baptist Historical Society and the Virginia State Library for their cooperation in making available microfilm of the Baptist church books.

Ed. Note: This article was originally published in *William and Mary Quarterly*, 3d Ser., XXXI (July 1974), 345–368.

[1] James Ireland, *The Life of the Reverend James Ireland* . . . (Winchester, Va., 1819), 83, 84–85.

The evident overdramatization in this account is its most revealing feature for it is eloquent concerning the tormented convert's heightened awareness of the contrast between the social world he was leaving and the one he was entering.

The struggle for allegiance between these social worlds had begun with the Great Awakening in the 1740s, but entered into its most fierce and bitter phase with the incursions of the "New Light" Separate Baptists into the older parts of Virginia in the years after 1765.[2] The social conflict was not over the distribution of political power or of economic wealth, but over the ways of men and the ways of God. By the figures in the encounter described we may begin to know the sides drawn: on the one hand, a mounted gentleman of the world with "commanding authority" responding to challenge; on the other, a guilt-humbled, God-possessed youth with "disconsolate looks . . . and solemn aspect."

A second scene—this time in the Tidewater—reveals through actions some characteristic responses of the forces arrayed. From a diary entry of 1771 we have a description of the disruption of a Baptist meeting by some gentlemen and their followers, intent on upholding the cause of the established Church:

> Brother Waller informed us . . . [that] about two weeks ago on the Sabbath Day down in Caroline County he introduced the worship of God by singing. . . . The Parson of the Parish [who had ridden up with his clerk, the sheriff, and some others] would keep running the end of his horsewhip in [Waller's] mouth, laying his whip across the hymn book, etc. When done singing [Waller] proceeded to prayer. In it he was violently jerked off the stage; they caught him by the back part of his neck, beat his head against the ground, sometimes up, sometimes down, they carried him through a gate that stood some considerable distance, where a gentleman [the sheriff] gave him . . . twenty lashes with his horsewhip. . . . Then Bro. Waller was released, went back singing praise to God, mounted the stage and preached with a great deal of liberty.[3]

Violence of this kind had become a recurrent feature of social-religious life in Tidewater and Piedmont. We must ask: What kind of conflict was this? What was it that aroused such antagonism? What manner of man, what manner of movement, was it that found liberty in endurance under the lash?

[2] For a valuable account of the triumph of evangelicalism in Virginia, 1740 to 1790, see Wesley M. Gewehr, *The Great Awakening in Virginia, 1740–1790* (Durham, N. C., 1930). The rate at which the Separate Baptists were spreading may be seen by the following summary: 1769—7 churches, 3 north of the James River; May 1771—14 churches (1,335 members); May–Oct. 1774—54 churches (4,004 members), 24 north of the James River. Ibid., 117. In the manuscript notes of Morgan Edwards references to at least 31 disruptions of meetings, by riot and/or arrest, occurring before 1772 can be identified; 13 of these appear to have been plebeian affairs, 8 gentry-led, and 10 unspecified. Morgan Edwards, Materials toward a History of the Baptists in the Province of Virginia, 1772 passim, MS, Furman University Library, Greenville, S. C. (microfilm kindly supplied by the Historical Commission, Southern Baptist Convention, Nashville, Tenn.).

[3] John Williams's Journal, May 10, 1771, in Lewis Peyton Little, *Imprisoned Preachers and Religious Liberty in Virginia* (Lynchburg, Va., 1938), 230–231. A similar account by Morgan Edwards indicates that the men were mounted and mentions who the principals were. Materials, 75–76.

The continuation of the account gives fuller understanding of the meaning of this "liberty" and of the true character of this encounter. Asked "if his nature did not interfere in the time of violent persecution, when whipped, etc.," Waller "answered that the Lord stood by him . . . and poured his love into his soul without measure, and the brethren and sisters about him singing praises . . . so that he could scarcely feel the stripes . . . rejoicing . . . that he was worthy to suffer for his dear Lord and Master."[4]

Again we see contrasted postures: on the one hand, a forceful, indeed brutal, response to the implicit challenge of religious dissidence; on the other, an acceptance of suffering sustained by shared emotions that gave release—"liberty." Both sides were, of course, engaged in combat, yet their modes of conducting themselves were diametrically opposite. If we are to understand the struggle that had developed, we must look as deeply as possible into the divergent styles of life, at the conflicting visions of what life should be like, that are reflected in this episode.

Opposites are intimately linked not only by the societal context in which they occur but also by the very antagonism that orients them to each other. The strength of the fascination that existed in this case is evident from the recurrent accounts of men drawn to Baptist meetings to make violent opposition, who, at the time or later, came "under conviction" and experienced conversion.[5] The study of a polarity such as we find in the Virginia pre-Revolutionary religious scene should illuminate not only the conflict but also some of the fundamental structures of the society in which it occurred. A profile of the style of the gentry, and of those for whom they were a pattern, must be attempted. Their values, and the system by which these values were maintained, must be sketched. A somewhat fuller contrasting picture of the less familiar Virginia Baptist culture must then be offered, so that its character as a radical social movement is indicated.

The gentry style, of which we have seen glimpses in the confrontation with Baptists, is best understood in relation to the concept of honor—the proving of prowess.[6] A formality of manners barely concealed adversary relationships; the essence of social exchange was overt self-assertion.

Display and bearing were important aspects of this system. We can best get a sense of the self-images that underlay it from the symbolic importance of horses. The figure of the gentleman who came to call Ireland back to society was etched on his memory as mounted on a "lofty . . . elegant horse." It was noted repeatedly in the eighteenth century that Virginians would "go five miles to catch a horse, to ride only one mile upon afterwards."[7] This apparent absurdity had its logic in the necessity of being mounted when making an entrance on the social scene. The role of the steed as a valuable part of proud self-presentation is suggested by

---

[4] Williams, Journal, in Little, *Imprisoned Preachers,* 231.

[5] For examples see Edwards, Materials, 34, 54, 55, 73.

[6] For the sake of clarity a single "gentry style" is here characterized. Attention is focused on the forms that appear to have been most pervasive, perhaps because most adapted to the circumstances of common life. It is not, however, intended to obscure the fact that there were divergent and more refined gentry ways of life. The development within the genteel elite of styles formed in negation of the predominant mores will be the subject of a full separate analysis. I am indebted to Jack P. Greene for advice on this point.

[7] J.F.D. Smyth, quoted in Jane Carson, *Colonial Virginians at Play* (Williamsburg, Va., 1965), 103–104. See also the comments of Hugh Jones and Edward Kimber, ibid., 103.

the intimate identification of the gentry with their horses that was constantly manifested through their conversation. Philip Fithian, the New Jersey tutor, sometimes felt that he heard nothing but "Loud disputes concerning the Excellence of each others Colts . . . their Fathers, Mothers (for so they call the Dams) Brothers, Sisters, Uncles, Aunts, Nephews, Nieces, and Cousins to the fourth Degree!"[8]

Where did the essential display and self-assertion take place? There were few towns in Virginia; the outstanding characteristic of settlement was its diffuseness. Population was rather thinly scattered in very small groupings throughout a forested, river-dissected landscape. If there is to be larger community in such circumstances, there must be centers of action and communication. Insofar as cohesion is important in such an agrarian society, considerable significance must attach to the occasions when, coming together for certain purposes, the community realizes itself. The principal public centers in traditional Virginia were the parish churches and the county courthouses, with lesser foci established in a scatter of inns or "ordinaries." The principal general gatherings apart from these centers were for gala events such as horse race meetings and cockfights. Although lacking a specifically community character, the great estate house was also undoubtedly a very significant locus of action. By the operation of mimetic process and by the reinforcement of expectations concerning conduct and relationships, such centers and occasions were integral parts of the system of social control.[9]

The most frequently held public gatherings at generally distributed centers were those for Sunday worship in the Anglican churches and chapels. An ideal identification of parish and community had been expressed in the law making persistent absence from church punishable. The continuance of this ideal is indicated by the fact that prosecutions under the law occurred right up to the time of the Revolution.[10]

Philip Fithian has left us a number of vivid sketches of the typical Sunday scene at a parish church, sketches that illuminate the social nature and function of this institution. It was an important center of communication, especially among the elite, for it was "a general custom on Sundays here, with Gentlemen to invite one another home to dine, after Church; and to consult about, determine their common business, either before or after Service," when they would engage in discussing "the price of Tobacco, Grain etc. and settling either the lineage, Age,

---

[8] Hunter Dickinson Farish, ed., *Journal & Letters of Philip Vickers Fithian 1773–1774: A Plantation Tutor of the Old Dominion* (Williamsburg, Va., 1957), 177–178.

[9] I am unable to find a serviceable alternative for this much abused term. The concept has tended to be directed toward the operations of rules and sanctions, the restraint of the pursuit of self-interest, and the correction of deviant motivation. See *International Encyclopedia of the Social Sciences*, XIV (New York, 1968), 381–396. A different emphasis is adopted in this article, drawing attention to more fundamental aspects, namely, those processes by which cultural criteria of "proper" motivation and "true" self-interest are established and reinforced in a particular society. Closely related are the mechanisms whereby individuals' perceptions and valuations of their own and others' identities are shaped and maintained. My conceptualization derives from the ideas of "reality-maintenance" (almost of continuous socialization) which are fully developed in Peter L. Berger and Thomas Luckmann, *The Social Construction of Reality: A Treatise in the Sociology of Knowledge* (Garden City, N. Y., 1966), 72–73, 84, 166–175, and passim.

[10] Little, *Imprisoned Preachers*, 265–266, 291.

or qualities of favourite Horses." The occasion also served to demonstrate to the community, by visual representation, the rank structure of society. Fithian's further description evokes a dramatic image of haughty squires trampling past seated hoi polloi to their pews in the front. He noted that it was "not the Custom for Gentlemen to go into Church til Service is beginning, when they enter in a Body, in the same manner as they come out."[11]

Similarly, vestry records show that fifty miles to the south of Fithian's Westmoreland County the front pews of a King and Queen County church were allocated to the gentry, but the pressure for place and precedence was such that only the greatest dignitaries (like the Corbins) could be accommodated together with their families; lesser gentlemen represented the honor of their houses in single places while their wives were seated farther back.[12]

The size and composition of the ordinary congregations in the midst of which these representations of social style and status took place is as yet uncertain, but Fithian's description of a high festival is very suggestive on two counts: "This being Easter-Sunday, all the Parish seem'd to meet together High, Low, black, White all come out."[13] We learn both that such general attendance was unusual, and that at least once a year full expression of ritual community was achieved. The whole society was then led to see itself in order.

The county courthouse was a most important center of social action. Monthly court days were attended by great numbers, for these were also the times for markets and fairs. The facts of social dominance were there visibly represented by the bearing of the "gentlemen justices" and the respect they commanded. On court days economic exchange was openly merged with social exchange (both plentifully sealed by the taking of liquor) and also expressed in conventional forms of aggression—in banter, swearing, and fighting.[14]

The ruling gentry, who set the tone in this society, lived scattered across broad counties in the midst of concentrations of slaves that often amounted to black villages. Clearly the great houses that they erected in these settings were important statements: they expressed a style, they asserted a claim to dominance. The lavish entertainments, often lasting days, which were held in these houses performed equally important social functions in maintaining this claim, and in establishing communication and control within the elite itself. Here the convivial contests that were so essential to traditional Virginia social culture would issue in their most elaborate and stylish performances.[15]

[11] Farish, ed., *Journal of Fithian*, 29, 167.

[12] C. G. Chamberlayne, ed., *The Vestry Book of Stratton Major Parish, King and Queen County, Virginia, 1729–1783* (Richmond, Va., 1931), 167.

[13] Farish, ed., *Journal of Fithian*, 89. See also 137.

[14] Charles S. Sydnor, *American Revolutionaries in the Making: Political Practices in Washington's Virginia* (New York, 1965 [orig. publ. Chapel Hill, N. C., 1952]), 74–85. This is the incomparable authority for the nature and function of county court days, and for the rank, etc., of the justices. Chap. 4 makes clear the importance of liquor in social intercourse. That the custom of gentlemen establishing their "liberality" by "treating" their inferiors was not confined to the time of elections is suggested by Col. Wager's report "that he usually treated the members of his militia company with punch after the exercises were over." Ibid., 58.

[15] Farish, ed., *Journal of Fithian*, passim; Carson, *Colonial Virginians at Play*, passim.

The importance of sporting occasions such as horse racing meets and cock-fights for the maintenance of the values of self-assertion, in challenge and response, is strongly suggested by the comments of the marquis de Chastellux concerning cockfighting. His observations, dating from 1782, were that "when the principal promoters of this diversion [who were certainly gentry] propose to [match] their champions, they take great care to announce it to the public; and although there are neither posts, nor regular conveyances, this important news spreads with such facility, that the planters for thirty or forty miles round, attend, some with cocks, but all with money for betting, which is sometimes very considerable."[16] An intensely shared interest of this kind, crossing but not leveling social distinctions, has powerful effects in transmitting style and reinforcing the leadership of the elite that controls proceedings and excels in the display.

Discussion so far has focused on the gentry, for *there* was established in dominant form the way of life the Baptists appeared to challenge. Yet this way was diffused throughout the society. All the forms of communication and exchange noted already had their popular acceptances with variations appropriate to the context, as can be seen in the recollections of the young Devereux Jarratt. The son of a middling farmer-artisan, Jarratt grew up totally intimidated by the proximity of gentlemen, yet his marked preference for engagement "in keeping and exercising race-horses for the turf . . . in taking care of and preparing game-cocks for a match and main" served to bind him nonetheless into the gentry social world, and would, had he persisted, have brought him into contact—gratifying contact—with gentlemen. The remembered images of his upbringing among the small farmers of Tidewater New Kent County are strongly evocative of the cultural continuum between his humble social world and that of the gentry. In addition to the absorbing contest pastimes mentioned, there were the card play, the gathering at farmhouses for drinking (cider not wine), violin playing, and dancing.[17]

The importance of pastime as a channel of communication, and even as a bond, between the ranks of a society such as this can hardly be too much stressed. People were drawn together by occasions such as horse races, cockfights, and dancing as by no other, because here men would become "known" to each other—"known" in the ways which the culture defined as "real." Skill and daring in that violent duel, the "quarter race"; coolness in the "deep play" of the betting that necessarily went with racing, cockfighting, and cards—these were means whereby Virginia males could prove themselves.[18] Conviviality was an essential part of the social exchange, but through its soft coating pressed a harder structure of contest, or "emulation" as the contemporary phrase had it. Even in dancing this was so. Observers noted not only the passion for dancing—"*Virginians* are of genuine Blood—They will dance or die!"—but also the marked preference for

168

[16] Quoted in Carson, *Colonial Virginians at Play,* 160 and passim. For evidence of genteel patronage of the sport see ibid., 156–157.

[17] Devereux Jarratt, *The Life of the Reverend Devereux Jarratt* . . . (Baltimore, 1806), 14, 19, 20, 23, 31, 42–44. It is interesting to note that although religious observance played a minimal part in Jarratt's early life, the Bible was the book from which he (and other small farmers' sons presumably) learned to read. A base was thereby prepared for evangelical culture. Ibid., 20–21.

[18] Carson, *Colonial Virginians at Play,* passim. For an intensely illuminating discussion of the social significance of "deep play" in gambling see Clifford Geertz, "Deep Play: Notes on the Balinese Cockfight," *Daedalus,* CI (Winter, 1972), 1–37.

the jig—in effect solo performances by partners of each sex, which were closely watched and were evidently competitive.[19] In such activities, in social contexts high or low, enhanced eligibility for marriage was established by young persons who emerged as virtuosos of the dominant style. Situations where so much could happen presented powerful images of the "good life" to traditional Virginians, especially young ones. It was probably true, as alleged, that religious piety was generally considered appropriate only for the aged.[20]

When one turns to the social world of the Baptists, the picture that emerges is so striking a negative of the one that has just been sketched that it must be considered to have been structured to an important extent by processes of reaction to the dominant culture.

Contemporaries were struck by the contrast between the challenging gaiety of traditional Virginia formal exchange and the solemn fellowship of the Baptists, who addressed each other as "Brother" and "Sister" and were perceived as "the most melancholy people in the world"—people who "cannot meet a man upon the road, but they must ram a text of Scripture down his throat."[21] The finery of a gentleman who might ride forth in a gold-laced hat, sporting a gleaming Masonic medal, must be contrasted with the strict dress of the Separate Baptist, his hair "cut off" and such "superfluous forms and Modes of Dressing . . . as cock't hatts" explicitly renounced.[22]

Their appearance was austere, to be sure, but we shall not understand the deep appeal of the evangelical movement, or the nature and full extent of its challenging contrast to the style and vision of the gentry-oriented social world, unless we look into the rich offerings beneath this somber exterior. The converts were proffered some escape from the harsh realities of disease, debt, overindulgence and deprivation, violence and sudden death, which were the common lot of small farmers. They could seek refuge in a close, supportive, orderly community, "a congregation of faithful persons, called out of the world by divine grace, who mutually agree to live together, and execute gospel discipline among them."[23] Entrance into this community was attained by the relation of a personal experience of profound importance to the candidates, who would certainly be heard with respect, however humble their station. There was a community resonance

169

---

[19] Farish, ed., *Journal of Fithian*, 177; Carson, *Colonial Virginians at Play*, 21–35.

[20] Jarratt wrote of "*Church people*, that, generally speaking, none went to the *table* [for communion] except a few of the more aged," *Life*, 102; and Ireland, "I . . . determined to pursue the pleasures . . . until I arrived to such an advance in years, that my nature would . . . enjoy no further relish. . . . A merciful God . . . would accept of a few days or weeks of my sincere repenting," *Life*, 59. Likewise it may be noted that religiosity only enters markedly into the old-man phase of Landon Carter's diary. Jack P. Greene, ed., *The Diary of Colonel Landon Carter of Sabine Hall, 1752–1778*, 2 vols. (Charlottesville, Va., 1965), passim.

[21] David Thomas, *The Virginian Baptist . . .* (Baltimore, 1774), 59; Robert B. Semple, *A History of the Rise and Progress of the Baptists in Virginia*, ed. G. W. Beale (Richmond, Va., 1894), 30.

[22] Farish, ed., *Journal of Fithian*, 69; Upper King and Queen Baptist Church, King and Queen County, Records, 1774–1816, Sept. 16, 1780. (Microfilm of this and subsequently cited Baptist church books kindly provided by the Virginia Baptist Historical Society, Richmond.)

[23] John Leland, *The Virginia Chronicle* (Fredericksburg, Va., 1790), 27. See also Thomas, *The Virginian Baptist*, 24–25.

for deep feelings, since, despite their sober face to the outside world, the Baptists encouraged in their religious practice a sharing of emotion to an extent far beyond that which would elicit crushing ridicule in gentry-oriented society.[24] Personal testimonies of the experiences of simple folk have not come down to us from that time, but the central importance of the ritual of admission and its role in renewing the common experience of ecstatic conversion is powerfully evoked by such recurrent phrases in the church books as "and a dore was opened to experience." This search for deep fellow-feeling must be set in contrast to the formal distance and rivalry in the social exchanges of the traditional system.[25]

The warm supportive relationship that fellowship in faith and experience could engender appears to have played an important part in the spread of the movement. For example, about the year 1760 Peter Cornwell of Fauquier County sought out in the backcountry one Hays of pious repute, and settled him on his own land for the sake of godly companionship. "Interviews between these two families were frequent . . . their conversation religious . . . in so much that it began to be talked of abroad as a very strange thing. Many came to see them, to whom they related what God did for their souls . . . to the spreading of serious-ness through the whole neighbourhood."[26]

A concomitant of fellowship in deep emotions was comparative equality. Democracy is an ideal, and there are no indications that the pre-Revolutionary Baptists espoused it as such, yet there can be no doubt that these men, calling each other brothers, who believed that the only authority in their church was the meeting of those in fellowship together, conducted their affairs on a footing of equality in sharp contrast to the explicit preoccupation with rank and precedence that characterized the world from which they had been called. Important Baptist church elections generally required unanimity and might be held up by the doubts of a few. The number of preachers who were raised from obscurity to play an epic role in the Virginia of their day is a clear indication of the opportunities for fulfillment that the movement opened up to men who would have found no other avenue for public achievement. There is no reason to doubt the contempo-rary reputation of the early Virginia Baptist movement as one of the poor and unlearned. Only isolated converts were made among the gentry, but many among the slaves.[27]

170

---

[24] The Baptists, it was sneered, were "always sighing, groaning, weeping." To which Thomas replied, "It is true lively Christians are apt to weep much, but that is often with joy instead of sorrow." *The Virginian Baptist,* 59.

[25] Chestnut Grove Baptist Church, or Albemarle-Buck Mountain Baptist Church, Records, 1773–1779, 1792–1811, passim. Ireland tells how, when he had given the company of travel-ers to the Sandy Creek Association of 1769 an account of "what the Lord had done for my soul. . . . They were very much affected . . . so much so that one of the ministers embraced me in his arms." *Life,* 141.

[26] Edwards, Materials, 25–26.

[27] Thomas, *The Virginian Baptist,* 54. See also Semple, *History of the Baptists in Virginia,* 29, 270, and Leland, *Virginia Chronicle,* 23. I have not as yet been able to attempt wealth-status correla-tions for ministers, elders, deacons, and ordinary members of the churches. It must be noted that the role which the small group of gentry converts played (as one might expect from the history of other radical movements) assumed an importance out of all proportion to their numbers. See Morattico Baptist Church, Lancaster County, Records (1764), 1778–1814, passim, and Chesterfield Baptist Church, Lancaster County, Records, 1773–1788, for the role of the "rich" Eleazer Clay.

The tight cohesive brotherhood of the Baptists must be understood as an explicit rejection of the formalism of traditional community organization. The antithesis is apparent in the contrast between Fithian's account of a parish congregation that dispersed without any act of worship when a storm prevented the attendence of both parson and clerk, and the report of the Baptist David Thomas that "when no minister . . . is expected, our people meet notwithstanding; and spend . . . time in praying, singing, reading, and in religious conversation."[28]

The popular style and appeal of the Baptist Church found its most powerful and visible expression in the richness of its rituals, again a total contrast to the "prayrs read over in haste" of the colonial Church of England, where even congregational singing appears to have been a rarity.[29] The most prominent and moving rite practiced by the sect was adult baptism, in which the candidates were publicly sealed into fellowship. A scrap of Daniel Fristoe's journal for June 15–16, 1771, survives as a unique contemporary description by a participant:

> (Being sunday) about 2000 people came together; after preaching [I] heard others that proposed to be baptized. . . . Then went to the water where I preached and baptized 29 persons. . . . When I had finished we went to a field and making a circle in the center, there laid hands on the persons baptized. The multitude stood round weeping, but when we sang *Come we that love the lord* and they were so affected that they lifted up their hands and faces towards heaven and discovered such chearful countenances in the midst of flowing tears as I had never seen before.[30]

The warm emotional appeal at a popular level can even now be felt in that account, but it must be noted that the scene was also a vivid enactment of a community within and apart from *the* community. We must try to see that closed circle for the laying on of hands through the eyes of those who had been raised in Tidewater or Piedmont Virginia with the expectation that they would always have a monistic parish community encompassing all the inhabitants within its measured liturgical celebrations. The antagonism and violence that the Baptists aroused then also become intelligible.

The celebration of the Lord's Supper frequently followed baptism, in which circumstances it was a further open enactment of closed community. We have some idea of the importance attached to this public display from David Thomas's justification:

> should we forbid even the worst of men, from viewing the solemn representation of his [the LORD JESUS CHRIST's] dying agonies? May not the sight of this mournful tragedy, have a tendency to alarm stupid creatures . . . when GOD himself is held forth . . . trembling, failing, bleeding, yea, expiring under the intollerable pressure of that wrath due to [sin]. . . . And therefore, this ordinance

171

---

[28] Farish, ed., *Journal of Fithian,* 157; Thomas, *The Virginian Baptist,* 34.

[29] Farish, ed., *Journal of Fithian,* 167, 195.

[30] Morgan Edwards, Notes, in Little, *Imprisoned Preachers,* 243. See also Leland, *Virginia Chronicle,* 36: "At times appointed for baptism the people generally go singing to the water in grand procession: I have heard many souls declare they first were convicted or first found pardon going to, at, or coming from the water."

should not be put under a bushel, but on a candlestick, that all may enjoy the illumination.[31]

We may see the potency attributed to the ordinances starkly through the eyes of the abashed young John Taylor who, hanging back from baptism, heard the professions of seven candidates surreptitiously, judged them not saved, and then watched them go "into the water, and from thence, as I thought, seal their own damnation at the Lord's table. I left the meeting with awful horror of mind."[32]

More intimate, yet evidently important for the close community, were the rites of fellowship. The forms are elusive, but an abundance of ritual is suggested by the simple entry of Morgan Edwards concerning Falls Creek: "In this church are admitted, Evangelists, Ruling Elders, deaconesses, laying on of hands, feasts of charity, anointing the sick, kiss of charity, washing feet, right hand of fellowship, and devoting children." Far from being mere formal observances, these and other rites, such as the ordaining of "apostles" to "pervade" the churches, were keenly experimented with to determine their efficacy.[33]

Aspects of preaching also ought to be understood as ritual rather than as formal instruction. It was common for persons to come under conviction or to obtain ecstatic release "under preaching," and this established a special relationship between the neophyte and his or her "father in the gospel." Nowhere was the ritual character of the preaching more apparent than in the great meetings of the Virginia Separate Baptist Association. The messengers would preach to the people along the way to the meeting place and back; thousands would gather for the Sunday specially set aside for worship and preaching. There the close independent congregational communities found themselves merged in a great and swelling collective.[34] The varieties of physical manifestations such as crying out and falling down, which were frequently brought on by the ritualized emotionalism of such preaching, are too well known to require description.

Virginia Baptist sermons from the 1770s have not survived, perhaps another indication that their purely verbal content was not considered of the first importance. Ireland's account of his early ministry (he was ordained in 1769) reveals the ritual recurrence of the dominant themes expected to lead into repentance those who were not hardened: "I began first to preach . . . our awful apostasy by the fall; the necessity of repentance unto life, and of faith in the Lord Jesus Christ . . . our helpless incapacity to extricate ourselves therefrom I stated and urged."[35]

172

---

[31] Thomas, *The Virginian Baptist,* 35–36; Albemarle Baptist Church Book, June 18, 1774.

[32] John Taylor, *A History of Ten Baptist Churches* . . . (Frankfort, Ky., 1823), 296.

[33] Edwards, Materials, 56; Albemarle Baptist Church Book, Aug. 1776; Semple, *History of the Baptists in Virginia,* 81.

[34] Ireland, *Life,* 191; Taylor, *History of Ten Baptist Churches,* 7, 16; Semple, *History of the Baptists in Virginia,* 63; Garnett Ryland, *The Baptists of Virginia, 1699–1926* (Richmond, Va., 1955), 53–54.

[35] Ireland, *Life,* 185. Laboring day and night, "preaching three times a day very often, as well as once at night," he must have kept himself in an *exalté,* near trance-like condition. His instruction to those who came to him impressed with "their helpless condition" is also illuminating. "I would immediately direct them where their help was to be had, and that it was their duty to be as much engaged . . . as if they thought they could be saved by their own works, but not to rest upon such engagedness." Ibid., 186.

As "seriousness" spread, with fear of hell-fire and concern for salvation, it was small wonder that a gentleman of Loudoun County should find to his alarm "that the *Anabaptists* . . . growing very numerous . . . seem to be increasing in afluence [influence?]; and . . . quite destroying pleasure in the Country; for they encourage ardent Pray'r; strong and constant faith, and an intire Banishment of *Gaming, Dancing,* and Sabbath-Day Diversions."[36] That the Baptists were drawing away increasing numbers from the dominant to the insurgent culture was radical enough, but the implications of solemnity, austerity, and stern sobriety were more radical still, for they called into question the validity—indeed the propriety—of the occasions and modes of display and association so important in maintaining the bonds of Virginia's geographically diffuse society. Against the system in which proud men were joined in rivalry and convivial excess was set a reproachful model of an order in which God-humbled men would seek a deep sharing of emotion while repudiating indulgence of the flesh. Yet the Baptist movement, although it must be understood as a revolt against the traditional system, was not primarily negative. Behind it can be discerned an impulse toward a tighter, more effective system of values and of exemplary conduct to be established and maintained within the ranks of the common folk.

In this aspect evangelicalism must be seen as a popular response to mounting social disorder. It would be difficult—perhaps even impossible—to establish an objective scale for measuring disorder in Virginia. What can be established is that during the 1760s and 1770s disorder was perceived by many as increasing. This has been argued for the gentry by Jack P. Greene and Gordon S. Wood, and need not be elaborated here. What does need to be reemphasized is that the gentry's growing perception of disorder was focused on those forms of activity which the Baptists denounced and which provided the main arenas for the challenge and response essential to the traditional "good life." It was coming to be felt that horse racing, cockfighting, and card play, with their concomitants of gambling and drinking, rather than serving to maintain the gentry's prowess, were destructive of it and of social order generally. Display might now be negatively perceived as "luxury."[37]

Given the absence of the restraints imposed by tight village community in traditional Virginia, disorder was probably an even more acute problem in the lower than in the upper echelons of society—more acute because it was compounded by the harshness and brutality of everyday life, and most acute in proportion to the social proximity of the lowest stratum, the enslaved. The last named sector of society, lacking sanctioned marriage and legitimated familial authority, was certainly disorderly by English Protestant standards, and must therefore have had a disturbing effect on the consciousness of the whole community.[38]

173

[36] Farish, ed., *Journal of Fithian,* 72.

[37] Greene, ed., *Landon Carter Diary,* I, 14, 17–19, 21, 25, 33, 39, 44, 47, 52–53; Gordon S. Wood, "Rhetoric and Reality in the American Revolution," *William and Mary Quarterly,* 3d Ser., XXIII 1966), 27–31; Jack P. Greene, "Search for Identity: An Interpretation of the Meaning of Selected Patterns of Social Response in Eighteenth-Century America," *Journal of Social History,* III (1969–1970), 196–205.

[38] Gerald W. Mullin, *Flight and Rebellion: Slave Resistance in Eighteenth-Century Virginia* (New

As the conversion experience was at the heart of the popular evangelical movement, so a sense of a great burden of guilt was at the heart of the conversion experience. An explanation in terms of social process must be sought for the sudden widespread intensification and vocal expression of such feelings, especially when this is found in areas of the Virginia Piedmont and Tidewater where no cultural tradition existed as preconditioning for the communal confession, remorse, and expiation that characterized the spread of the Baptist movement. The hypothesis here advanced is that the social process was one in which popular perceptions of disorder in society—and hence by individuals in themselves—came to be expressed in the metaphor of "sin." It is clear that the movement was largely spread by revolt from within, not by "agitators" from without. Commonly the first visit of itinerant preachers to a neighborhood was made by invitation of a group of penitents already formed and actively meeting together. Thus the "spread of seriousness" and alarm at the sinful disorder of the traditional world tended to precede the creation of an emotional mass movement "under preaching."[39] A further indication of the importance of order-disorder preoccupations for the spread of the new vision with its contrasted life style was the insistence on "works." Conversion could ultimately be validated among church members only by a radical reform of conduct. The Baptist church books reveal the close concern for the disciplinary supervision of such changes.[40]

Drunkenness was a persistent problem in Virginia society. There were frequent cases in the Baptist records where censure, ritual excommunication, and moving penitence were unable to effect a lasting cure. Quarreling, slandering, and disputes over property were other endemic disorders that the churches sought patiently and endlessly to control within their own communities.[41] With its base in slavery, this was a society in which contest readily turned into disorderly violence. Accounts of the occasion, manner, and frequency of wrestling furnish a horrifying testimony to the effects of combining a code of honor with the coarseness of life in the lower echelons of society. Hearing that "by appointment is to be fought this Day . . . two fist Battles between four young Fellows," Fithian noted the common causes of such conflicts, listing numbers of trivial affronts such as that one "has in a merry hour call'd [another] a *Lubber,* . . . or a *Buckskin,* or a *Scotchman,* . . . or offered him a dram without wiping the mouth of the Bottle." He noted also the savagery of the fighting, including "Kicking, Scratching, Biting,

174

York, 1972), passim. This article owes an incalculable debt to Mullin's powerful and creative analysis of the dominant Virginia culture.

[39] Edwards, *Materials,* 25, 69, 89, 90; Semple, *History of the Baptists in Virginia,* 19–20, 25, 26, 32, 33, 227, 431.

[40] I have closely read the following Baptist church records for the period up to 1790: Broad Run Baptist Church, Fauquier County, Records, 1762–1837; Chesterfield Baptist Church, Recs.; Chestnut Grove/Albemarle Church, Recs.; Hartwood-Potomac Baptist Church Book, Stafford County, 1771–1859; Mill Creek Baptist Church, Berkeley County, Records (1757), 1805–1928; Mill Swamp Baptist Church, Isle of Wight County, Records (1774), 1777–1790; Morattico Baptist Church, Recs.; Smith's Creek Baptist Church, Shenandoah and Rockingham counties, Records, 1779–1809 (1805); Upper King and Queen Baptist Church, Recs.

[41] Upper King and Queen Baptist Church, Recs., Jan. 20, 1781; Morattico Baptist Church, Recs., May 30, 1781, et seq.; Mill Swamp Baptist Church, Recs., Sept. 17, 1779; Broad Run Baptist Church, Recs., July 27, 1778.

. . . Throtling, Gouging [the eyes], Dismembring [the private parts]. . . . This spectacle . . . generally is attended with a crowd of People!" Such practices prevailed throughout the province.[42] An episode in the life of one of the great Baptist preachers, John, formerly "swearing Jack," Waller, illustrates both prevailing violence and something of the relationship between classes. Waller and some gentry companions were riding on the road when a drunken butcher addressed them in a manner they considered insolent. One of the gentlemen had a horse trained to rear and "paw what was before him," which he then had it do to frighten the butcher. The man was struck by the hooves and died soon after. Tried for manslaughter, the company of gentlemen was acquitted on a doubt as to whether the injury had indeed caused the butcher's death.[43] The episode may have helped prepare Waller for conversion into a radically opposed social world.

Nowhere does the radicalism of the evangelical reaction to the dominant values of self-assertion, challenge, and response of the gentry-oriented society reveal itself so clearly as in the treatment of physical aggression. In the Baptist community a man might come forward by way of confession with an accusation against himself for "Geting angry Tho in Just Defence of himself in Despute." The meeting of another church was informed that its clerk, Rawley Hazard, had been approached on his own land and addressed in "Very scurrilous language" and then assaulted, and that he then "did defend himself against this sd Violence, that both the Assailant and Defendent was much hurt." The members voted that the minister "do Admonish Brother Rawley . . . in the presents of the Church . . . saying that his defence was Irregular."[44]

A further mark of their radicalism, and without doubt the most significant aspect of the quest for a system of social control centered in the people, was the inclusion of slaves as "brothers" and "sisters" in their close community. When the Baptists sealed the slaves unto eternal life, leading them in white robes into the water and then back to receive the bread and wine, they were also laying upon them responsibility for godly conduct, demanding an internalization of strict Protestant Christian values and norms. They were seeking to create an orderly moral community where hitherto there had seemed to be none.

The slaves were members and therefore subject to church discipline. The incidence of excommunication of slaves, especially for the sin of adultery, points to the desire of the Baptists to introduce their own standards of conduct, including stable marital relationships, among slaves.[45] A revealing indication of the perception of the problem in this area is found in the recurrent phrase that was sometimes given as the sole reason for excommunication: "walking disorderly." Discipline was also clearly directed toward inculcating a sense of duty in the slaves, who could be excommunicated for "disobedience and Aggrevation to [a] master."[46]

---

[42] Farish, ed., *Journal of Fithian,* 183; Carson, *Colonial Virginians at Play,* 164–168.

[43] Edwards, Materials, 72.

[44] Chestnut Grove/Albemarle Baptist Church, Recs., Dec. 1776; Morattico Baptist Church, Recs., Feb. 17, 1783.

[45] Mill Swamp Baptist Church, Recs., Mar. 13, 1773.

[46] Morattico Baptist Church, Recs., Oct. 8, 1780. The role of the slaves in the 18th-century Baptist movement remains obscure. They always carried with them their slave identity, being

The recurrent use of the words "order," "orderly," "disorderly" in the Baptist records reveals a preoccupation that lends further support to the hypothesis that concern for the establishment of a securer system of social control was a powerful impulse for the movement. "Is it orderly?" is the usual introduction to the queries concerning right conduct that were frequently brought forward for resolution at monthly meetings.[47]

With alarm at perceived disorder must also be associated the deep concern for Sabbath-day observance that is so strongly manifested in autobiographies, apologetics, and church books. It appears that the Virginia method of keeping the Sabbath "with sport, merriment, and dissipation" readily served to symbolize the disorder perceived in society. It was his observation of this that gave Ireland his first recorded shock. Conversely, cosmic order was affirmed and held up as a model for society in the setting aside on the Lord's Day of worldly pursuits, while men expressed their reverence for their Maker and Redeemer.[48]

When the Baptist movement is understood as a rejection of the style of life for which the gentry set the pattern and as a search for more powerful popular models of proper conduct, it can be seen why the ground on which the battle was mainly fought was not the estate or the great house, but the neighborhood, the farmstead, and the slave quarter. This was a contemporary perception, for it was generally charged that the Baptists were "continual fomenters of discord" who "not only divided good neighbours, but slaves and their masters; children and their parents . . . wives and their husbands." The only reported complaint against the first preachers to be imprisoned was of "their running into private houses and making dissensions."[49] The struggle for allegiance in the homesteads between a style of life modeled on that of the leisured gentry and that embodied in evangelicalism was intense. In humbler, more straitened circumstances a popular culture based on the code of honor and almost hedonist values was necessarily less securely established than among the more affluent gentry. Hence the anxious aggressiveness of popular anti-New Light feeling and action.[50]

---

designated "Gresham's Bob" or the like, or even "the property of." Yet it is reported that the slaves of William Byrd's great estates in Mecklenburg County were among the first proselytes to the Separate Baptists in Virginia. "Many of these poor slaves became bright and shining Christians. The breaking up of Byrd's quarters scattered these blacks into various parts. It did not rob them of their religion. It is said that through their labors in the different neighborhoods . . . many persons were brought to the knowledge of the truth, and some of them persons of distinction." Semple, *History of the Baptists in Virginia*, 291–292. The valuable researches of W. Harrison Daniel show that hearing of experience, baptism, and disciplining of whites and blacks took place in common. Black preachers were not uncommon and swayed mixed congregations. "In the 1780's one predominantly white congregation in Gloucester County chose William Lemon, a Negro, as its pastor." Segregation of the congregation does not begin to appear in the records until 1811. Daniel, "Virginia Baptists and the Negro in the Early Republic," *Virginia Magazine of History and Biography*, LXXX (1972), 62, 60–69.

[47] Mill Swamp Baptist Church, Recs., Mar. 13, June 9, 1778; Hartwood-Potomac Baptist Church, Recs., 1776, 9–10.

[48] Ireland, *Life*, 44; Thomas, *The Virginian Baptist*, 34–35.

[49] Thomas, *The Virginian Baptist*, 57: John Blair to the King's Attorney in Spotsylvania County, July 16, 1768, in Little, *Imprisoned Preachers*, 100–101.

[50] Jarratt, *Life*, 23, 31, 38; Farish, ed., *Journal of Fithian*, 73; Semple, *History of the Baptists in Virginia*, passim.

The Baptists did not make a bid for control of the political system—still less did they seek a leveling or redistribution of worldly wealth. It was clearly a mark of the strength of gentry hegemony and of the rigidities of a social hierarchy with slavery at its base that the evangelical revolt should have been so closely restricted in scope. Yet the Baptists' salvationism and sabbatarianism effectively redefined morality and human relationships; their church leaders and organization established new and more popular foci of authority, and sought to impose a radically different and more inclusive model for the maintenance of order in society. Within the context of the traditional monistic, face-to-face, deferential society such a regrouping necessarily constituted a powerful challenge.

The beginnings of a cultural disjunction between gentry and sections of the lower orders, where hitherto there had been a continuum, posed a serious threat to the traditional leaders of the community; their response was characteristic. The popular emotional style, the encouragement given to men of little learning to "exercise their gifts" in preaching, and the preponderance of humble folk in the movement gave to the proud gentry their readiest defense—contempt and ridicule. The stereotype of the Baptists as "an ignorant . . . set . . . of . . . the contemptible class of the people," a "poor and illiterate sect" which "none of the rich or learned ever join," became generally established. References in the *Virginia Gazette* to "ignorant enthusiasts" were common, and there could appear in its columns without challenge a heartless satire detailing "A Receipt to make an Anabaptist Preacher": "Take the Herbes of Hypocrisy and Ambition, . . . of the Seed of Dissention and Discord one Ounce, . . . one Pint of the Spirit of Self-Conceitedness."[51]

An encounter with some gentlemen at an inn in Goochland County is recorded by Morgan Edwards, a college-educated Pennsylvania Baptist minister. He noted the moderation of the gentry in this area, yet their arrogant scorn for dissenters in general, and for Baptists in particular, is unmistakable from the dialogue reported. Since Edwards had just come from Georgia, they began with ribald jests about "mr Whitefield's children . . . by the squaw" and continued as follows:

Esq[uire] U: Pray are you not a clergyman? . . .
Capt. L: Of the church of England I presume?
N[orthern] M[inister]: No, Sir; I am a clergyman of a better church than that; for she is a persecutor.
Omnes: Ha! Ha! Ha! . . .
Esq. U: Then you are one of the fleabitten clergy?
N. M.: Are there fleas in this bed, Sir?
Esq. U: I ask, if you are a clergyman of the itchy true blue kirk of Scotland? . . .
Capt. L. (whispers): He is ashamed to own her for fear you should scratch him 'Squire.'. . .
[When they have discovered that this educated man, who shows such address in fencing with words, is a Baptist minister, they discuss the subject bibulously among themselves.]

---

[51] Little, *Imprisoned Preachers,* 36; Thomas, *The Virginian Baptist,* 54. See also Semple, *History of the Baptists in Virginia,* 29; Leland, *Virginia Chronicle,* 23; *Virginia Gazette* (Purdie and Dixon), Oct. 31, 1771.

Esq. U: He is no baptist . . . I take him to be one of the Georgia law[ye]rs.
Mr. G: For my part I believe him to be a baptist minister. There are some clever fellows among them. . . .
Major W: I confess they have often confounded me with their arguments and texts of Scripture; and if any other people but the baptists professed their religion I would make it my religion before tomorrow.[52]

The class of folk who filled the Baptist churches were a great obstacle to gentry participation. Behind the ridicule and contempt, of course, lay incomprehension, and behind that, fear of this menacing, unintelligible movement. The only firsthand account we have of a meeting broken up by the arrest of the preachers tells how they "were carried before the magistrate," who had them taken "one by one into a room and examined our pockets and wallets for firearms." He accused them of "carrying on a mutiny against the authority of the land." This sort of dark suspicion impelled David Thomas, in his printed defense of the Baptists, to reiterate several times that "We concern not ourselves with the government . . . we form no intrigues . . . nor make any attempts to alter the constitution of the kingdom to which as men we belong."[53]

Fear breeds fantasy. So it was that alarmed observers put a very crude interpretation on the emotional and even physical intimacy of this intrusive new society. Its members were associated with German Anabaptists, and a "historical" account of the erotic indulgences of that sect was published on the front page of the *Virginia Gazette*.[54]

Driven by uneasiness, although toughened by their instinctive contempt, some members of the establishment made direct moves to assert proper social authority and to outface the upstarts. Denunciations from parish pulpits were frequent. Debates were not uncommon, being sought on both sides. Ireland recalled vividly an encounter that reveals the pride and presumption of the gentlemen who came forward in defense of the Church of England. Captain M'Clanagan's place was thronged with people, some of whom had come forty miles to hear John Pickett, a Baptist preacher of Fauquier County. The rector of a neighboring parish attended with some leading parishioners "who were as much prejudiced . . . as he was." "The parson had a chair brought for himself, which he placed three or four yards in front of Mr. Pickett . . . taking out his pen, ink and paper, to take down notes of what he conceived to be false doctrine." When Pickett had finished, "the Parson called him a schismatick, a broacher of false doctrines . . . [who] held up damnable errors that day." Pickett answered adequately (it appeared to Ireland), but "when contradicted it would in

---

[52] Edwards, Materials, 86–88.

[53] John Waller to an unknown fellow Baptist, Aug. 12, 1771, in Little, *Imprisoned Preachers*, 276; Thomas, *The Virginian Baptist*, 33, 36.

[54] *Va. Gaz.* (Purdie and Dixon), Oct. 4, 1770. Thomas states that there is no evil which "has not been reported of us." *The Virginian Baptist*, 6. There is in a letter of James Madison a reference to the "Religion . . . of some enthusiasts, . . . of such a nature as to fan the amorous fire." Madison to William Bradford, Apr. 1, 1774, in William T. Hutchinson and William M. E. Rachal, eds., *The Papers of James Madison*, I (Chicago, 1962), 112. See also Richard J. Hooker, ed., *The Carolina Backcountry on the Eve of the Revolution* (Chapel Hill, N. C., 1953), 98, 100–104, 113–117, for more unrestrained fantasies concerning the emergent Southern Baptists.

a measure confuse him." So Ireland, who had been raised a gentleman, took it on himself to sustain the Baptist cause. The parson immediately "wheeled about on his chair . . . and let out a broadside of his eloquence, with an expectation, no doubt, that he would confound me with the first fire." However, Ireland "gently laid hold of a chair, and placed . . . it close by him, determined to argue." The contest was long, and "both gentlemen and ladies," who had evidently seated themselves near the parson, "would repeatedly help him to scripture, in order to support his arguments." When the debate ended (as the narrator recalled) in the refutation of the clergyman, Ireland "addressed one of the gentlemen who had been so officious in helping his teacher; he was a magistrate . . . 'Sir, as the dispute between the Parson and myself is ended, if you are disposed to argue the subject over again, I am willing to enter upon it with you.' He stretched out his arm straight before him, at that instant, and declared that I should not come nigher than that length." Ireland "concluded what the consequence would be, therefore made a peaceable retreat."[55] Such scenes of action are the stuff of social structure, as of social conflict, and require no further comment.

Great popular movements are not quelled, however, by outfacing, nor are they stemmed by the ridicule, scorn, or scurrility of incomprehension. Moreover, they draw into themselves members of all sections of society. Although the social worlds most open to proselytizing by the Baptists were the neighborhoods and the slave quarters, there were converts from the great houses too. Some of the defectors, such as Samuel Harris, played a leading role in the movement.[56] The squirearchy was disturbed by the realization that the contemptible sect was reaching among themselves. The exchanges between Morgan Edwards and the gentlemen in the Goochland inn were confused by the breakdown of the stereotype of ignorance and poverty. Edwards's cultured facility reminded the squires that "there are some clever fellows among [the Baptists]. I heard one Jery Walker support a petition of theirs at the assembly in such a manner as surprised us all, and [made] our witts draw in their horns."[57] The pride and assurance of the gentry could be engaged by awareness that their own members might withdraw from their ranks and choose the other way. The vigorous response of Ireland's patron to the challenge implicit in his defection provides a striking example.

The intensity of the conflict for allegiance among the people and, increasingly, among the gentry, makes intelligible the growing frequency of violent clashes of the kind illustrated at the beginning of this article. The violence was, however, one-sided and self-defeating. The episode of April 1771 in which the parson brutally interfered with the devotions of the preacher, who was then horsewhipped by the sheriff, must have produced a shock of revulsion in many quarters. Those who engaged in such actions were not typical of either the Anglican clergy or the country gentlemen. The extreme responses of some, however, show the anxieties to which all were subject, and the excesses in question could only heighten the tension.

[55] Ireland, *Life*, 129–134.

[56] Although Samuel Harris, renouncing the world, gave up his newly built country seat to be a meetinghouse for his church, the role of patron died hard. He would kill cattle for love feasts that were held there. Edwards, Materials, 57.

[57] Ibid., 88. The scene was concluded by the genteel Baptist being offered and accepting hospitality. He finally left the neighborhood with an assurance from his host "that he would never talk any more against the Baptists." Ibid., 89.

Disquiet was further exacerbated by the fact that the law governing dissent, under which the repressive county benches were intent on acting, was of doubtful validity, and became the subject of public controversy in the fall of 1771.[58] This controversy, combined with the appalling scenes of disorder and the growing numbers of Separate Baptists, led the House of Burgesses to attempt action in its spring 1772 session. The Separates had shown renewed tendencies to intransigence as recently as May 1771, when a move was strongly supported to deny fellowship to all ministers who submitted to the secular authority by applying for permission to preach. The fact that eight months later the House of Burgesses received a petition for easier licensing conditions was a sign that a compromise was at last being sought. Nevertheless, prejudices were so strong that the bill that the Burgesses approved was considerably more restrictive than the English act that had hitherto been deemed law in the colony.[59]

The crisis of self-confidence which the evangelical challenges and the failure of forceful responses were inducing in the Virginia gentry was subtly revealed in March 1772 by the unprecedented decision of the House, ordinarily assertive of its authority, not to send the engrossed bill to the Council, but to have it printed and referred to the public for discussion. Nearly two years later, in January 1774, the young James Madison, exultant about the progress of the American cause in the aftermath of the Boston Tea Party, despaired of Virginia on account of religious intolerance. He wrote that he had "nothing to brag of as to the State and Liberty" of his "Country," where "Poverty and Luxury prevail among all sorts" and "that diabolical Hell conceived principle of persecution rages." In April of the same year he still had little hope that a bill would pass to ease the situation of dissenters. In the previous session "such incredible and extravagant stories" had been "told in the House of the monstrous effects of the Enthusiasm prevalent among the Sectaries and so greedily swallowed by their Enemies that . . . they lost footing by it." Burgesses "who pretend too much contempt to examine into their principles . . . and are too much devoted to the ecclesiastical establishment to hear of the Toleration of Dissentients" were likely to prevail once again.[60] Madison's foreboding was correct inasmuch as the old regime in Virginia never accomplished a legal resolution of the toleration problem.

The Revolution ultimately enshrined religious pluralism as a fundamental principle in Virginia. It rendered illegitimate the assumptions concerning the nature of community religious corporateness that underlay aggressive defense against the Baptists. It legitimated new forms of conflict, so that by the end of the century the popular evangelists were able to counterattack and symbolize social revolution in many localities by having the Episcopal Church's lands and even communion plate sold at auction. But to seek the conclusion to this study in such political-constitutional developments would be a deflection, for it has focused on a brief period of intense, yet deadlocked conflict in order to search out the social-cultural configurations of the forces that confronted each other. The diametrical

---

[58] *Va. Gaz.* (Purdie and Dixon), Aug. 15, 22, 1771; *Va. Gaz.* (Rind), Aug. 8, 1771.

[59] *Va. Gaz.* (Rind), Mar. 26, 1772. Especially severe were provisions designed to curb activities among the slaves.

[60] Madison to Bradford, Jan. 24, Apr. 1, 1774, in Hutchinson and Rachal, eds., *Madison Papers,* I, 106, 112.

opposition of the swelling Baptist movement to traditional mores shows it to have been indeed a radical social revolt, indicative of real strains within society.

Challenging questions remain. Can some of the appeal of the Revolution's republican ideology be understood in terms of its capacity to command the allegiance of both self-humbled evangelicals and honor-upholding gentry? What different meanings did the republican ideology assume within the mutually opposed systems of values and belief? And, looking forward to the post-Revolutionary period, what was the configuration—what the balance between antagonistic cultural elements—when confrontation within a monistic framework had given way to accommodation in a more pluralist republican society? These questions are closely related to the subject that this study has endeavored to illuminate—the forms and sources of popular culture in Virginia, and the relationship of popular culture to that of the gentry elite.

Author's Postscript

"Evangelical Revolt" was prepared as an intended part of a larger study of the American Revolution in Virginia. It was an element in a program of what I came to call "dramaturgic ethnography," according to which I would review the actions of all sorts of Virginians on the "stages" great and small where they "performed." I would interpret what they communicated to themselves and to each other by the style and content of their actions, much as a theater critic might interpret action on an actual stage. By reviewing new forms of action I would trace the varieties of involvement in the transformation of their worlds by which ordinary people made the Revolution—or, rather, revolutions, since I saw, and still see, a religious revolution parallel to and as important as the political one. In my book, *The Transformation of Virginia, 1740–1790*,[61] I sought to trace those popular paths from the world as it had been at mid-eighteenth century to the world as it had come to be by the century's end.

There have not been great controversies among early Americanists over my ethnographic interpretation of the American Revolution in Virginia. The main challenge to rethinking it has come rather from a critical-theory position within the larger field of American studies. In 1990, Jean-Christophe Agnew published a retrospect on my work, seeing in it a key instance of the way Clifford Geertz is beguiling historians from their traditional responsibilities. Agnew's proposition, baldly summed up, is that a Geertzian meaning-oriented approach cannot explain what happened because it is unable to deal with the operations in history of terrifying power—power such as was manifested in the institution of slavery so fundamental to Revolutionary Virginia society.[62]

There is no contest with Agnew's position insofar as he argues that accounts of the Revolution and of emergent United States society are seriously deficient if they do not dwell on the operations of terrifying power in its gendered, racial, and class forms. I will continue to assert, however, in defense of the ethnographic approach, that effective power is always sustained by systems that communicate meanings. In this conviction I am reinforced by the presentations of a great

[61] Chapel Hill, N. C., 1982.

[62] See Agnew, "History and Anthropology: Scenes from a Marriage," *Yale Journal of Criticism*, III (1990), 29–50.

historian-anthropologist, whose work tracks repeatedly across the domain of early American history.[63]

Those who exercise power continuously must always construct theaters for their acts of power. We shall understand neither the positive transformations nor the tragic limitations of the American Revolution—nor yet the glories and the torments of the nation it brought into being—unless we attend closely to all those "theaters" of often cruel power, domestic, local, regional, and national.

[63] See Greg Dening, *Mr. Bligh's Bad Language: Passion, Power, and Theater on the Bounty* (New York, 1992), and Rhys Isaac, "On Explanation, Text, and Terrifying Power in Ethnographic History," *Yale J. Crit.*, VI (1993), 217–236.

THE PLANTER'S WIFE: THE EXPERIENCE OF WHITE WOMEN IN SEVENTEENTH-CENTURY MARYLAND

LOIS GREEN CARR AND LORENA S. WALSH

Four facts were basic to all human experience in seventeenth-century Maryland. First, for most of the period the great majority of inhabitants had been born in what we now call Britain. Population increase in Maryland did not result primarily from births in the colony before the late 1680s and did not produce a predominantly native population of adults before the first decade of the eighteenth century. Second, immigrant men could not expect to live beyond age forty-three, and 70 percent would die before age fifty. Women may have had even shorter lives. Third, perhaps 85 percent of the immigrants, and practically all the unmarried immigrant women, arrived as indentured servants and consequently married late. Family groups were never predominant in the immigration to Maryland and were a significant part for only a brief time at midcentury. Fourth, many more men than women immigrated during the whole period.[1] These facts—immigrant predominance, early death, late marriage, and sexual imbalance—created circumstances of social and demographic disruption that deeply affected family and community life.

We need to assess the effects of this disruption on the experience of women in seventeenth-century Maryland. Were women degraded by the hazards of servitude in a society in which everyone had left community and kin behind and in which women were in short supply? Were traditional restraints on social conduct weakened? If so, were women more exploited or more independent and powerful than women who remained in England? Did any differences from English experience which we can observe in the experience of Maryland women survive the transformation from an immigrant to a predominantly native-born society with its own kinship networks and community traditions? The tentative argument put forward here is that the answer to all these questions is Yes. There were degrading aspects of servitude, although these probably did not characterize the lot of most women; there were fewer restraints on social conduct, especially in

183

Ms. Carr is the historian and Ms. Walsh a research associate at the St. Mary's City Commission. The authors wish to thank Russell R. Menard for sharing his data and insights into family history in the Chesapeake.

Ed. Note: This article was originally published in *William and Mary Quarterly,* 3d Ser., XXXIV (October 1977), 542–571.

[1] Russell R. Menard, "Economy and Society in Early Colonial Maryland" (Ph.D. diss., University of Iowa, 1975), 153–212, and "Immigrants and Their Increase: The Process of Population Growth in Early Colonial Maryland," in Aubrey C. Land, Lois Green Carr, and Edward C. Papenfuse, eds., *Law, Society, and Politics in Early Maryland* (Baltimore, 1977), 88–110, hereafter cited as Menard, "Immigrants and Their Increase"; Lorena S Walsh and Russell R. Menard, "Death in the Chesapeake: Two Life Tables for Men in Early Colonial Maryland," *Maryland Historical Magazine,* LXIX (1974), 211–227. In a sample of 806 headrights Menard found only two unmarried women who paid their own passage ("Economy and Society," 187).

courtship, than in England; women were less protected but also more powerful than those who remained at home; and at least some of these changes survived the appearance in Maryland of New World creole communities. However, these issues are far from settled, and we shall offer some suggestions as to how they might be further pursued.

Maryland was settled in 1634, but in 1650 there were probably no more than six hundred persons and fewer than two hundred adult women in the province. After that time population growth was steady; in 1704 a census listed 30,437 white persons, of whom 7,163 were adult women.[2] Thus in discussing the experience of white women in seventeenth-century Maryland we are dealing basically with the second half of the century.

Marylanders of that period did not leave letters and diaries to record their New World experience or their relationships to one another. Nevertheless, they left trails in the public records that give us clues. Immigrant lists kept in England and documents of the Maryland courts offer quantifiable evidence about the kinds of people who came and some of the problems they faced in making a new life. Especially valuable are the probate court records. Estate inventories reveal the kinds of activities carried on in the house and on the farm, and wills, which are usually the only personal statements that remain for any man or woman, show something of personal attitudes. This essay relies on the most useful of the immigrant lists and all surviving Maryland court records, but concentrates especially on the surviving records of the lower Western Shore, an early settled area highly suitable for tobacco. Most of this region comprised four counties: St. Mary's, Calvert, Charles, and Prince George's (formed in 1696 from Calvert and Charles). Inventories from all four counties, wills from St. Mary's and Charles, and court proceedings from Charles and Prince George's provide the major data.[3]

Because immigrants predominated, who they were determined much about the character of Maryland society. The best information so far available comes from lists of indentured servants who left the ports of London, Bristol, and Liverpool. These lists vary in quality but at the very least they distinguish immigrants by sex and general destination. A place of residence in England is usually given, although it may not represent the emigrant's place of origin; and age and occupation are often noted. These lists reveal several characteristics of immigrants to the Chesapeake and, by inference, to Maryland.[4]

[2] Menard, "Immigrants and Their Increase," Fig. I; William Hand Browne et al., eds., *Archives of Maryland* (Baltimore 1883–), XXV, 256, hereafter cited as *Maryland Archives*.

[3] Court proceedings for St. Mary's and Calvert counties have not survived.

[4] The lists of immigrants are found in John Camden Hotten, ed., *The Original Persons of Quality; Emigrants; Religious Exiles; Political Rebels; . . . and Others Who Went from Great Britain to the American Plantations, 1600–1700* (London, 1874); William Dodgson Bowman, ed., *Bristol and America: A Record of the First Settlers in the Colonies of North America, 1654–1685* (Baltimore, 1967 [orig. publ. London, 1929]); C.D.P. Nicholson, comp., *Some Early Emigrants to America* (Baltimore, 1965); Michael Ghirelli, ed., *A List of Emigrants to America, 1682–1692* (Baltimore, 1968); and Elizabeth French, ed., *List of Emigrants to America from Liverpool, 1697–1707* (Baltimore, 1962 [orig. publ. Boston, 1913]). Folger Shakespeare Library, MS, V. B. 16 (Washington, D. C.), consists of 66 additional indentures that were originally part of the London records. For studies of these lists see Mildred Campbell, "Social Origins of Some Early Americans," in James Morton Smith, ed., *Seventeenth-Century America: Essays in Colonial History* (Chapel Hill, N. C., 1959), 63–89; David W. Galenson, "'Middling People' or 'Common Sort'?: The Social Origins of Some Early Americans Reexamined," *William and Mary Quarterly*

Servants who arrived under indenture included yeomen, husbandmen, farm laborers, artisans, and small tradesmen, as well as many untrained to any special skill. They were young: over half of the men on the London lists of 1683–1684 were aged eighteen to twenty-two. They were seldom under seventeen or over twenty-eight. The women were a little older; the great majority were between eighteen and twenty-five, and half were aged twenty to twenty-two. Most servants contracted for four or five years service, although those under fifteen were to serve at least seven years.[5] These youthful immigrants represented a wide range of English society. All were seeking opportunities they had not found at home.

However, many immigrants—perhaps about half[6]—did not leave England with indentures but paid for their passage by serving according to the custom of the country. Less is known about their social characteristics, but some inferences are possible. From 1661, customary service was set by Maryland laws that required four-year (later five-year) terms for men and women who were twenty-two years or over at arrival and longer terms for those who were younger. A requirement of these laws enables us to determine something about age at arrival of servants who came without indentures. A planter who wished to obtain more than four or five years of service had to take his servant before the county court to have his or her age judged and a written record made. Servants aged over twenty-one were not often registered, there being no incentive for a master to pay court fees for those who would serve the minimum term. Nevertheless, a comparison of the ages of servants under twenty-two recorded in Charles County, 1658–1689, with those under twenty-two on the London list is revealing. Of Charles County male servants (N = 363), 77.1 percent were aged seventeen or under, whereas on the London list (N = 196), 77.6 percent were eighteen or over. Women registered in Charles County court were somewhat older than the men, but among those under twenty-two (N = 107), 5.5 percent were aged twenty-one, whereas on the London list (N = 69), 46.4 percent had reached this age. Evidently, some immigrants who served by custom were younger than those who came indentured, and this age difference probably characterized the two groups as a whole. Servants who were not only very young but had arrived without the protection of a written contract were possibly of lower social origins than were servants who came under indenture. The absence of skills among Charles County servants who served by custom supports this supposition.[7]

(forthcoming). See also Menard, "Immigrants and Their Increase," Table 4.1, and "Economy and Society," Table VIII-6; and Lorena S. Walsh, "Servitude and Opportunity in Charles County," in Land, Carr, and Papenfuse, eds., Law, Society, and Politics in Early Maryland, 112–114, hereafter cited as Walsh, "Servitude and Opportunity."

[5] Campbell, "Social Origins of Some Early Americans," in Smith, ed., Seventeenth-Century America, 74–77; Galenson, "'Middling People' or 'Common Sort'?" WMQ (forthcoming). When the ages recorded in the London list (Nicholson, comp., Some Early Emigrants) and on the Folger Library indentures for servants bound for Maryland and Virginia are combined, 84.5% of the men (N = 354) are found to have been aged 17 to 30, and 54.9% were 18 through 22. Of the women (N = 119), 81.4% were 18 through 25; 10% were older, 8.3% younger, and half (51.2%) immigrated between ages 20 and 22. Russell Menard has generously lent us his abstracts of the London list.

[6] This assumption is defended in Walsh, "Servitude and Opportunity," 129.

[7] Ibid., 112–114, describes the legislation and the Charles County data base. There is some reason to believe that by 1700, young servants had contracts more often than earlier. Figures from

Whatever their status, one fact about immigrant women is certain: many fewer came than men. Immigrant lists, headright lists, and itemizations of servants in inventories show severe imbalance. On a London immigrant list of 1634–1635 men outnumbered women six to one. From the 1650s at least until the 1680s most sources show a ratio of three to one. From then on, all sources show some, but not great, improvement. Among immigrants from Liverpool over the years 1697–1707 the ratio was just under two and one half to one.[8]

Why did not more women come? Presumably, fewer wished to leave family and community to venture into a wilderness. But perhaps more important, women were not as desirable as men to merchants and planters who were making fortunes raising and marketing tobacco, a crop that requires large amounts of labor. The gradual improvement in the sex ratio among servants toward the end of the century may have been the result of a change in recruiting the needed labor. In the late 1660s the supply of young men willing to emigrate stopped increasing sufficiently to meet the labor demands of a growing Chesapeake population. Merchants who recruited servants for planters turned to other sources, and among these sources were women. They did not crowd the ships arriving in the Chesapeake, but their numbers did increase.[9]

To ask the question another way, why did women come? Doubtless, most came to get a husband, an objective virtually certain of success in a land where women were so far outnumbered. The promotional literature, furthermore, painted bright pictures of the life that awaited men and women once out of their time; and various studies suggest that for a while, at least, the promoters were not being entirely fanciful. Until the 1660s, and to a less degree the 1680s, the expanding economy of Maryland and Virginia offered opportunities well beyond those available in England to men without capital and to the women who became their wives.[10]

Nevertheless, the hazards were also great, and the greatest was untimely death. Newcomers promptly became ill, probably with malaria, and many died. What proportion survived is unclear; so far no one has devised a way of measuring it. Recurrent malaria made the woman who survived seasoning less able to withstand other diseases, especially dysentery and influenza. She was especially

186

---

the London list include the Folger Library indentures.

[8] Menard, "Immigrants and Their Increase," Table I.

[9] Menard, "Economy and Society," 336–356; Lois Green Carr and Russell R. Menard, "Servants and Freedmen in Early Colonial Maryland," in Thad W. Tate and David A. Ammerman, eds., *Essays on the Chesapeake in the Seventeenth Century* (Chapel Hill, N. C., forthcoming); E. A. Wrigley, "Family Limitation in Pre-Industrial England," *Economic History Review,* 2d Ser., XIX (1966), 82–109; Michael Drake, "An Elementary Exercise in Parish Register Demography," ibid., XIV (1962), 427–445; J. D. Chambers, *Population, Economy, and Society in Pre-Industrial England* (London, 1972).

[10] John Hammond, *Leah and Rachel, or, the Two Fruitful Sisters Virginia and Mary-land . . . ,* and George Alsop, *A Character of the Province of Mary-land . . . ,* in Clayton Colman Hall, ed., *Narratives of Early Maryland, 1633–1684,* Original Narratives of Early American History (New York, 1910), 281–308, 340–387; Russell R. Menard, P.M.G. Harris, and Lois Green Carr, "Opportunity and Inequality: The Distribution of Wealth on the Lower Western Shore of Maryland, 1638–1705," *Md. Hist. Mag.,* LXIX (1974), 169–184; Russell R. Menard, "From Servant to Freeholder: Status Mobility and Property Accumulation in Seventeenth-Century Maryland," *WMQ,* 3d Ser., XXX (1973), 37–64; Carr and Menard, "Servants and Freedmen," in Tate and Ammerman, eds., *Essays on the Chesapeake;* Walsh, "Servitude and Opportunity," 111–133.

vulnerable when pregnant. Expectation of life for everyone was low in the Chesapeake, but especially so for women.[11] A woman who had immigrated to Maryland took an extra risk, though perhaps a risk not greater than she might have suffered by moving from her village to London instead.[12]

The majority of women who survived seasoning paid their transportation costs by working for a four- or five-year term of service. The kind of work depended on the status of the family they served. A female servant of a small planter—who through about the 1670s might have had a servant[13]—probably worked at the hoe. Such a man could not afford to buy labor that would not help with the cash crop. In wealthy families women probably were household servants, although some are occasionally listed in inventories of well-to-do planters as living on the quarters—that is, on plantations other than the dwelling plantation. Such women saved men the jobs of preparing food and washing linen but doubtless also worked in the fields.[14] In middling households experience must have varied. Where the number of people to feed and wash for was large, female servants would have had little time to tend the crops.

Tracts that promoted immigration to the Chesapeake region asserted that female servants did not labor in the fields, except "nasty" wenches not fit for other tasks. This implies that most immigrant women expected, or at least hoped, to avoid heavy field work, which English women—at least those above the cottager's status—did not do.[15] What proportion of female servants in Maryland found themselves demeaned by this unaccustomed labor is impossible to say, but this must have been the fate of some. A study of the distribution of female servants among wealth groups in Maryland might shed some light on this question. Nevertheless, we still would not know whether those purchased by the poor or sent to work on a quarter were women whose previous experience suited them for field labor.

An additional risk for the woman who came as a servant was the possibility of bearing a bastard. At least 20 percent of the female servants who came to Charles County between 1658 and 1705 were presented to the county court for this cause.[16] A servant woman could not marry unless someone was willing to pay her master for the term she had left to serve.[17] If a man made her pregnant, she could not marry him unless he could buy her time. Once a woman became free, however, marriage was clearly the usual solution. Only a handful of free women

187

---

[11] Walsh and Menard, "Death in the Chesapeake," *Md. Hist. Mag.,* LXIX (1974), 211–227; Darrett B. and Anita H. Rutman, "Of Agues and Fevers: Malaria in the Early Chesapeake," *WMQ,* 3d Ser., XXXIII (1976), 31–60.

[12] E. A. Wrigley, *Population and History* (New York, 1969), 96–100.

[13] Menard, "Economy and Society," Table VII-5.

[14] Lorena S. Walsh, "Charles County, Maryland, 1658–1705: A Study in Chesapeake Political and Social Structure" (Ph.D. diss., Michigan State University, 1977), chap. 4.

[15] Hammond, *Leah and Rachel,* and Alsop, *Character of the Province,* in Hall, ed., *Narratives of Maryland,* 281–308, 340–387; Mildred Campbell, *The English Yeoman Under Elizabeth and the Early Stuarts,* Yale Historical Publications (New Haven, Conn., 1942), 255–261; Alan Everitt, "Farm Labourers," in Joan Thirsk, ed., *The Agrarian History of England and Wales, 1540–1640* (Cambridge, 1967), 432.

[16] Lorena S. Walsh and Russell R. Menard are preparing an article on the history of illegitimacy in Charles and Somerset counties, 1658–1776.

[17] Abbot Emerson Smith, *Colonists in Bondage: White Servitude and Convict Labor in America,*

were presented in Charles County for bastardy between 1658 and 1705. Since few free women remained either single or widowed for long, not many were subject to the risk. The hazard of bearing a bastard was a hazard of being a servant.[18]

This high rate of illegitimate pregnancies among servants raises lurid questions. Did men import women for sexual exploitation? Does John Barth's Whore of Dorset have a basis outside his fertile imagination?[19] In our opinion, the answers are clearly No. Servants were economic investments on the part of planters who needed labor. A female servant in a household where there were unmarried men must have both provided and faced temptation, for the pressures were great in a society in which men outnumbered women by three to one. Nevertheless, the servant woman was in the household to work—to help feed and clothe the family and make tobacco. She was not primarily a concubine.

This point could be established more firmly if we knew more about the fathers of the bastards. Often the culprits were fellow servants or men recently freed but too poor to purchase the woman's remaining time. Sometimes the master was clearly at fault. But often the father is not identified. Some masters surely did exploit their female servants sexually. Nevertheless, masters were infrequently accused of fathering their servants' bastards, and those found guilty were punished as severely as were other men. Community mores did not sanction their misconduct.[20]

A female servant paid dearly for the fault of unmarried pregnancy. She was heavily fined, and if no one would pay her fine she was whipped. Furthermore, she served an extra twelve to twenty-four months to repay her master for the "trouble of his house" and labor lost, and the fathers often did not share in this payment of damages. On top of all, she might lose the child after weaning unless by then she had become free, for the courts bound out bastard children at very early ages.[21]

English life probably did not offer a comparable hazard to young unmarried female servants. No figures are available to show rates of illegitimacy among those who were subject to the risk,[22] but the female servant was less restricted in England than in the Chesapeake. She did not owe anyone for passage across the Atlantic; hence it was easier for her to marry, supposing she happened to become

---

1607–1776 (Chapel Hill, N. C., 1947), 271–273. Marriage was in effect a breach of contract.

[18] Lois Green Carr, "County Government in Maryland, 1689–1709" (Ph.D. diss., Harvard University, 1968), text, 267–269, 363. The courts pursued bastardy offenses regardless of the social status of the culprits in order to ensure that the children would not become public charges. Free single women were not being overlooked.

[19] John Barth, *The Sot-Weed Factor* (New York, 1960), 429.

[20] This impression is based on Walsh's close reading of Charles County records, Carr's close reading of Prince George's County records, and less detailed examination by both of all other 17th-century Maryland court records.

[21] Walsh, "Charles County, Maryland," chap. 4; Carr, "County Government in Maryland," chap. 4, n. 269. Carr summarizes the evidence from Charles, Prince George's, Baltimore, Talbot, and Somerset counties, 1689–1709, for comparing punishment of fathers and mothers of bastards. Leniency toward fathers varied from county to county and time to time. The length of time served for restitution also varied over place and time, increasing as the century progressed. See Charles County Court and Land Records, MS, L #1, ff. 276–277, Hall of Records, Annapolis, Md. Unless otherwise indicated, all manuscripts cited are at the Hall of Records.

[22] Peter Laslett and Karla Osterveen have calculated illegitimacy ratios—the percentage of

pregnant while in service. Perhaps, furthermore, her temptations were fewer. She was not 3,000 miles from home and friends, and she lived in a society in which there was no shortage of women. Bastards were born in England in the seventeenth century, but surely not to as many as one-fifth of the female servants.

Some women escaped all or part of their servitude because prospective husbands purchased the remainder of their time. At least one promotional pamphlet published in the 1660s described such purchases as likely, but how often they actually occurred is difficult to determine.[23] Suggestive is a 20 percent difference between the sex ratios found in a Maryland headright sample, 1658–1681, and among servants listed in lower Western Shore inventories for 1658–1679.[24] Some of the discrepancy must reflect the fact that male servants were younger than female servants and therefore served longer terms; hence they had a greater chance of appearing in an inventory. But part of the discrepancy doubtless follows from the purchase of women for wives. Before 1660, when sex ratios were even more unbalanced and the expanding economy enabled men to establish themselves more quickly, even more women may have married before their terms were finished.[25]

Were women sold for wives against their wills? No record says so, but nothing restricted a man from selling his servant to whomever he wished. Perhaps some women were forced into such marriages or accepted them as the least evil. But the man who could afford to purchase a wife—especially a new arrival—was usually already an established landowner.[26] Probably most servant women saw an opportunity in such a marriage. In addition, the shortage of labor gave women some bargaining power. Many masters must have been ready to refuse to sell a woman who was unwilling to marry a would-be purchaser.

If a woman's time was not purchased by a prospective husband, she was virtually certain to find a husband once she was free. Those famous spinsters,

---

bastard births among all births registered—in 24 English parishes, 1581–1810. The highest ratio over the period 1630–1710 was 2.4. Laslett and Osterveen, "Long Term Trends in Bastardy in England: A Study of the Illegitimacy Figures in the Parish Registers and in the Reports of the Registrar General, 1561–1960," *Population Studies,* XXVII (1973), 267. In Somerset County, Maryland, 1666–1694, the illegitimacy ratio ranged from 6.3 to 11.8. Russell R. Menard, "The Demography of Somerset County, Maryland: A Preliminary Report" (paper presented to the Stony Brook Conference on Social History, State University of New York at Stony Brook, June 1975), Table XVI. The absence of figures for the number of women in these places of childbearing age but with no living husband prevents construction of illegitimacy rates.

[23] Alsop, *Character of the Province,* in Hall, ed., *Narratives of Maryland,* 358.

[24] Maryland Headright Sample, 1658–1681 (N = 625); 257.1 men per 100 women; Maryland Inventories, 1658–1679 (N = 584): 320.1 men per 100 women. Menard, "Immigrants and Their Increase," Table I.

[25] A comparison of a Virginia Headright Sample, 1648–1666 (N = 4272) with inventories from York and Lower Norfolk counties, 1637–1675 (N = 168) shows less, rather than more, imbalance in inventories as compared to headrights. This indicates fewer purchases of wives than we have suggested for the period after 1660. However, the inventory sample is small.

[26] Only 8% of tenant farmers who left inventories in four Maryland counties of the lower Western Shore owned labor, 1658–1705. St. Mary's City Commission Inventory Project, "Social Stratification in Maryland, 1658–1705" (National Science Foundation Grant GS-32272), hereafter cited as "Social Stratification." This is an analysis of 1,735 inventories recorded from 1658 to 1705 in St. Mary's, Calvert, Charles, and Prince George's counties, which together constitute most of the lower Western Shore of Maryland.

Margaret and Mary Brent, were probably almost unique in seventeenth-century Maryland. In the four counties of the lower Western Shore only two of the women who left a probate inventory before the eighteenth century are known to have died single.[27] Comely or homely, strong or weak, any young woman was too valuable to be overlooked, and most could find a man with prospects.

The woman who immigrated to Maryland, survived seasoning and service, and gained her freedom became a planter's wife. She had considerable liberty in making her choice. There were men aplenty, and no fathers or brothers were hovering to monitor her behavior or disapprove her preference. This is the modern way of looking at her situation, of course. Perhaps she missed the protection of a father, a guardian, or kinfolk, and the participation in her decision of a community to which she felt ties. There is some evidence that the absence of kin and the pressures of the sex ratio created conditions of sexual freedom in courtship that were not customary in England. A register of marriages and births for seventeenth-century Somerset County shows that about one-third of the immigrant women whose marriages are recorded were pregnant at the time of the ceremony—nearly twice the rate in English parishes.[28] There is no indication of community objection to this freedom so long as marriage took place. No presentments for bridal pregnancy were made in any of the Maryland courts.[29]

The planter's wife was likely to be in her mid-twenties at marriage. An estimate of minimum age at marriage for servant women can be made from lists of indentured servants who left London over the years 1683–1684 and from age judgments in Maryland county court records. If we assume that the 112 female indentured servants going to Maryland and Virginia whose ages are given in the London lists served full four-year terms, then only 1.8 percent married before age twenty, but 68 percent after age twenty-four.[30] Similarly, if the 141 women whose ages were judged in Charles County between 1666 and 1705 served out their terms according to the custom of the country, none married before age twenty-two, and half were twenty-five or over.[31] When adjustments are made for the ages at which wives may have been purchased, the figures drop, but even so the majority of women waited until at least age twenty-four to marry.[32] Actual

[27] Sixty women left inventories. The status of five is unknown. The two who died single died in 1698. Menard, "Immigrants and Their Increase," Table 1.

[28] Menard, "Demography of Somerset County," Table XVII; Daniel Scott Smith and Michael S. Hindus, "Premarital Pregnancy in America, 1640–1971: An Overview," *Journal of Interdisciplinary History,* V (1975), 541. It was also two to three times the rate found in New England in the late 17th century.

[29] In Maryland any proceedings against pregnant brides could have been brought only in the civil courts. No vestries were established until 1693, and their jurisdiction was confined to the admonishment of men and women suspected of fornication unproved by the conception of a child. Churchwardens were to inform the county court of bastardies. Carr, "County Government in Maryland," text, 148–149, 221–223.

[30] The data are from Nicholson, comp., *Some Early Emigrants.*

[31] Charles County Court and Land Records, MSS, C #1 through B #2.

[32] Available ages at arrival are as follows:

Age	under	12	13	14	15	16	17	18	19	20	21	22	23	24	25	26	27	28	29	30
Indentured (1682–1687)				1	1	6	2	9	9	8	29	19	6	5	6	2	3	1	2	3
Unindentured (1666–1705)		8	5	12	4	7	18	16	13	34	9	11	2	1	1					

age at marriage in Maryland can be found for few seventeenth-century female immigrants, but observations for Charles and Somerset counties place the mean age at about twenty-five.[33]

Because of the age at which an immigrant woman married, the number of children she would bear her husband was small. She had lost up to ten years of her childbearing life[34]—the possibility of perhaps four or five children, given the usual rhythm of childbearing.[35] At the same time, high mortality would reduce both the number of children she would bear over the rest of her life and the number who would live. One partner to a marriage was likely to die within seven years, and the chances were only one in three that a marriage would last ten years.[36] In these circumstances, most women would not bear more than three or four children—not counting those stillborn—to any one husband, plus a posthumous child were she the survivor. The best estimates suggest that nearly a quarter, perhaps more, of the children born alive died during their first year and that 40 to 55 percent would not live to see age twenty.[37] Consequently, one of her children would probably die in infancy, and another one or two would fail to reach adulthood. Wills left in St. Mary's County during the seventeenth century show the results. In 105 families over the years 1660 to 1680 only twelve parents left more than three children behind them, including those conceived but not yet born. The average number was 2.3, nearly always minors, some of whom might die before reaching adulthood.[38]

Terms of service for women without indentures from 1666 on were 5 years if they were aged 22 at arrival; 6 years if 18–21; 7 years if 15–17; and until 22 if under 15. From 1661 to 1665 these terms were shorter by a year and women under 15 served until age 21. If we assume that (1) indentured women served 4 years; (2) they constituted half the servant women; (3) women under age 12 were not purchased as wives; (4) 20% of women aged 12 or older were purchased; and (5) purchases were spread evenly over the possible years of service, then from 1666, 73.9% were 23 or older at marriage, and 66.0% were 24 or older; 70.8% were 23 or older from 1661 to 1665, and 55.5% were 24 or older. Mean ages at eligibility for marriage, as calculated by dividing person-years by the number of women, were 24.37 from 1666 on and 23.42 from 1661 to 1665. All assumptions except (3) and (5) are discussed above. The third is made on the basis that native girls married as young as age 12.

[33] Walsh, "Charles County, Maryland," chap. 2; Menard, "Demography of Somerset County," Tables XI, XII.

[34] The impact of later marriages is best demonstrated with age-specific marital fertility statistics. Susan E. Norton reports that women in colonial Ipswich, Massachusetts, bore an average of 7.5 children if they married between ages 15 and 19; 7.1 if they married between 20 and 24; and 4.5 if they married after 24. Norton, "Population Growth in Colonial America: A Study of Ipswich, Massachusetts," *Pop. Studies*, XXV (1971), 444. Cf. Wrigley, "Family Limitation in Pre-Industrial England," *Econ. Hist. Rev.*, 2d Ser., XIX (1966), 82–109.

[35] In Charles County the mean interval between first and second and subsequent births was 30.8, and the median was 27.3 months. Walsh, "Charles County, Maryland," chap. 2. Menard has found that in Somerset County, Maryland, the median birth intervals for immigrant women between child 1 and child 2, child 2 and child 3, child 3 and child 4, and child 4 and child 5 were 26, 26, 30, 27 months, respectively ("Demography of Somerset County," Table XX).

[36] Walsh, "Charles County, Maryland," chap. 2.

[37] Walsh and Menard, "Death in the Chesapeake," *Md. Hist. Mag., LXIX (1974), 222.*

[38] Menard, using all Maryland wills, found a considerably lower number of children per family in a similar period: 1.83 in wills probated 1660–1665; 2.20 in wills probated 1680–1684 ("Economy and Society," 198). Family reconstitution not surprisingly produces slightly higher figures, since daughters are often underrecorded in wills but are recorded as frequently as sons in

For the immigrant woman, then, one of the major facts of life was that although she might bear a child about every two years, nearly half would not reach maturity. The social implications of this fact are far-reaching. Because she married late in her childbearing years and because so many of her children would die young, the number who would reach marriageable age might not replace, or might only barely replace, her and her husband or husbands as child-producing members of the society. Consequently, so long as immigrants were heavily predominant in the adult female population, Maryland could not grow much by natural increase.[39] It remained a land of newcomers.

This fact was fundamental to the character of seventeenth-century Maryland society, although its implications have yet to be fully explored. Settlers came from all parts of England and hence from differing traditions—in types of agriculture, forms of landholding and estate management, kinds of building construction, customary contributions to community needs, and family arrangements, including the role of women. The necessities of life in the Chesapeake required all immigrants to make adaptations. But until the native-born became predominant, a securely established Maryland tradition would not guide or restrict the newcomers.

If the immigrant woman had remained in England, she would probably have married at about the same age or perhaps a little later.[40] But the social consequences of marriage at these ages in most parts of England were probably different. More children may have lived to maturity and even where mortality was as high newcomers are not likely to have been the main source of population growth.[41] The locally born would still dominate the community, its social organization, and its traditions. However, where there were exceptions, as perhaps in London, late age at marriage, combined with high mortality and heavy immigration, may have had consequences in some ways similar to those we have found in Maryland.

A hazard of marriage for seventeenth-century women everywhere was death in childbirth, but this hazard may have been greater than usual in the Chesapeake. Whereas in most societies women tend to outlive men, in this malaria-ridden area it is probable that men outlived women. Hazards of childbirth provide the likely reason that Chesapeake women died so young. Once a woman in the

---

birth registers. In 17th-century Charles County the mean size of all reconstituted families was 2.75. For marriages contracted in the years 1658–1669 (N = 118), 1670–1679 (N = 79), and 1680–1689 (N = 95), family size was 3.15, 2.58, and 2.86, respectively. In Somerset County, family size for immigrant marriages formed between 1665 and 1695 (N = 41) was 3.9. Walsh, "Charles County, Maryland," chap. 2; Menard, "Demography of Somerset County," Table XXI.

[39] For fuller exposition of the process see Menard, "Immigrants and Their Increase."

[40] P. E. Razell, "Population Change in Eighteenth-Century England. A Reinterpretation," *Econ. Hist. Rev.*, 2d Ser., XVIII (1965), 315, cites mean age at marriage as 23.76 years for 7,242 women in Yorkshire, 1662–1714, and 24.6 years for 280 women of Wiltshire, Berkshire, Hampshire, and Dorset, 1615–1621. Peter Laslett, *The World We Have Lost: England before the Industrial Age,* 2d ed. (London, 1971), 86, shows a mean age of 23.58 for 1,007 women in the Diocese of Canterbury, 1619–1690. Wrigley, "Family Limitation in Pre-Industrial England," *Econ. Hist. Rev.,* 2d Ser., XIX (1966), 87, shows mean ages at marriage for 259 women in Colyton, Devon, ranging from 26.15 to 30.0 years, 1600–1699.

[41] For a brief discussion of Chesapeake and English mortality see Walsh and Menard, "Death in the Chesapeake," *Md. Hist. Mag.,* LXIX (1974), 224–225.

Chesapeake reached forty-five, she tended to outlive men who reached the same age. Darrett and Anita Rutman have found malaria a probable cause of an exceptionally high death rate among pregnant women, who are, it appears, peculiarly vulnerable to that disease.[42]

This argument, however, suggests that immigrant women may have lived longer than their native-born daughters, although among men the opposite was true. Life tables created for men in Maryland show that those native-born who survived to age twenty could expect a life span three to ten years longer than that of immigrants, depending upon the region where they lived. The reason for the improvement was doubtless immunities to local diseases developed in childhood.[43] A native woman developed these immunities, but, as we shall see, she also married earlier than immigrant women usually could and hence had more children.[44] Thus she was more exposed to the hazards of childbirth and may have died a little sooner. Unfortunately, the life tables for immigrant women that would settle this question have so far proved impossible to construct.

However long they lived, immigrant women in Maryland tended to outlive their husbands—in Charles County, for example, by a ratio of two to one. This was possible, despite the fact that women were younger than men at death, because women were also younger than men at marriage. Some women were widowed with no living children, but most were left responsible for two or three. These were often tiny, and nearly always not yet sixteen.[45]

This fact had drastic consequences, given the physical circumstances of life. People lived at a distance from one another, not even in villages, much less towns. The widow had left her kin 3,000 miles across an ocean, and her husband's family was also there. She would have to feed her children and make her own tobacco crop. Though neighbors might help, heavy labor would be required of her if she had no servants, until—what admittedly was usually not difficult—she acquired a new husband.

In this situation dying husbands were understandably anxious about the welfare of their families. Their wills reflected their feelings and tell something of how they regarded their wives. In St. Mary's and Charles counties during the seventeenth century, little more than one-quarter of the men left their widows with

[193]

[42] George W. Barclay, *Techniques of Population Analysis* (New York, 1958), 136n; Darrett B. and Anita H. Rutman "'Now-Wives and Sons-in-Law': Parental Death in a Seventeenth-Century Virginia County," in Tate and Ammerman, eds., *Essays on the Chesapeake;* Rutman and Rutman, "Of Agues and Fevers," *WMQ,* 3d Ser., XXXIII (1976), 31–60. Cf. Peter H. Wood, *Black Majority: Negroes in Colonial South Carolina from 1670 through the Stono Rebellion* (New York, 1974), chap. 3.

[43] Walsh and Menard, "Death in the Chesapeake," *Md. Hist. Mag.,* LXIX (1974), 211–227; Menard, "Demography of Somerset County."

[44] In Charles County immigrant women who ended childbearing years or died before 1705 bore a mean of 3.5 children (N = 59); the mean for natives was 5.1 (N = 42). Mean completed family size in Somerset County for marriages contracted between 1665 and 1695 was higher, but the immigrant-native differential remains. Immigrant women (N = 17) bore 6.1 children, while native women (N = 16) bore 9.4. Walsh, "Charles County, Maryland," chap. 2; Menard, "Demography of Somerset County," Table XXI.

[45] Among 1,735 decedents who left inventories on Maryland's lower Western Shore, 1658–1705, 72% died without children or with children not yet of age. Only 16% could be proved to have a child of age. "Social Stratification."

no more than the dower the law required—one-third of his land for her life, plus outright ownership of one-third of his personal property. (See Table 1.) If there were no children, a man almost always left his widow his whole estate. Otherwise there were a variety of arrangements. (See Table 2.)

During the 1660s, when testators begin to appear in quantity, nearly a fifth of the men who had children left all to their wives, trusting them to see that the children received fair portions. Thus in 1663 John Shircliffe willed his whole estate to his wife "towards the maintenance of herself and my children into whose tender care I do Commend them Desireing to see them brought up in the fear of God and the Catholick Religion and Chargeing them to be Dutiful and obedient to her."[46] As the century progressed, husbands tended instead to give the wife all or a major part of the estate for her life, and to designate how it should be distributed after her death. Either way, the husband put great trust in his widow, considering that he knew she was bound to remarry. Only a handful of men left estates to their wives only for their term of widowhood or until the children came of age. When a man did not leave his wife a life estate, he often gave her land outright or more than her dower third of his movable property. Such bequests were at the expense of his children and showed his concern that his widow should have a maintenance which young children could not supply.

A husband usually made his wife his executor and thus responsible for paying his debts and preserving the estate. Only 11 percent deprived their wives of such powers.[47] In many instances, however, men also appointed overseers to assist their wives and to see that their children were not abused or their property embezzled. Danger lay in the fact that a second husband acquired control of all his wife's property, including her life estate in the property of his predecessor. Over half of the husbands who died in the 1650s and 1660s appointed overseers to ensure that their wills were followed. Some trusted to the overseers' "Care and good Conscience for the good of my widow and fatherless children." Others more explicitly made overseers responsible for seeing that "my said child . . . and the other [expected child] (when pleases God to send it) may have their right Proportion of my Said Estate and that the said Children may be bred up Chiefly in the fear of God."[48] A few men—but remarkably few—authorized overseers to remove children from households of stepfathers who abused them or wasted their property.[49] On the whole, the absence of such provisions for the protection of the children points to the husband's overriding concern for the welfare of his widow and to his confidence in her management, regardless of the certainty of her remarriage. Evidently, in the politics of family life women enjoyed great respect.[50]

---

[46] Wills, I, 172.

[47] From 1640 to 1710, 17% of the married men named no executor. In such cases, the probate court automatically gave executorship to the wife unless she requested someone else to act.

[48] Wills, I, 96, 69.

[49] Ibid., 193–194, 167, V, 82. The practice of appointing overseers ceased around the end of the century. From 1690 to 1710, only 13% of testators who made their wives executors appointed overseers.

[50] We divided wills according to whether decedents were immigrant, native born, or of unknown origins, and found no differences in patterns of bequests, choice of executors, or tendency to appoint overseers. No change occurred in 17th-century Maryland in these respects as a native-born population began to appear.

TABLE 1

Bequests of Husbands to Wives,
St. Mary's and Charles Counties, Maryland, 1640 to 1710

		Dower or Less	
	N	N	%
1640s	6	2	54
1650s	24	7	29
1660s	65	18	28
1670s	86	21	24
1680s	64	17	27
1690s	83	23	28
1700s	74	25	34
Totals	402	113	28

Source: Wills I–XIV, Hall of Records, Annapolis, Md.

195

TABLE 2

Bequests of Husbands to Wives with Children,
St. Mary's and Charles Counties, Maryland, 1640 to 1710

	N	N	%	N	%	N	%	N	%	N	%	N	%
1640s	3	1	33	33								2	67
1650s	16	1	6	2	13	1	6	1	6	4	25	7	44
1660s	45	8	1	8	18	2	4	3	7	9	20	15	33
1670s	61	4	7	21	34	2	3	3	5	13	21	18	30
1680s	52	5	10	19	37	2	4	2	4	11	21	13	25
1690s	69	1	1	31	45	7	10	2	3	10	14	18	26
1700s	62			20	32	6	40	2	3	14	23	20	32
Totals	308	20	6	101	33	20	6	13	4	61	20	93	30

Source: Wills I–XIV.

We have implied that this respect was a product of the experience of immigrants in the Chesapeake. Might it have been instead a reflection of English culture? Little work is yet in print that allows comparison of the provisions for Maryland widows with those made for the widows of English farmers. Possibly, Maryland husbands were making traditional wills which could have been written in the communities they left behind. However, Margaret Spufford's recent study of three Cambridgeshire villages in the late sixteenth century and early seventeenth century suggests a different pattern. In one of these villages, Chippenham, women usually did receive a life interest in the property, but in the other two they did not. If the children were all minors, the widow controlled the property until the oldest son came of age, and then only if she did not remarry. In the majority of cases adult sons were given control of the property with instructions for the support of their mothers. Spufford suggests that the pattern found in Chippenham must have been very exceptional. On the basis of village censuses in six other counties, dating from 1624 to 1724, which show only 3 percent of widowed people heading households that included a married child, she argues that if widows commonly controlled the farm, a higher proportion should have headed such households. However, she also argues that widows with an interest in land would not long remain unmarried.[51] If so, the low percentage may be deceptive. More direct work with wills needs to be done before we can be sure that Maryland husbands and fathers gave their widows greater control of property and family than did their English counterparts.

Maryland men trusted their widows, but this is not to say that many did not express great anxiety about the future of their children. They asked both wives and overseers to see that the children received "some learning." Robert Sly made his wife sole guardian of his children but admonished her "to take due Care that they be brought up in the true fear of God and instructed in such Literature as may tend to their improvement." Widowers, whose children would be left without any parent, were often the most explicit in prescribing their upbringing. Robert Cole, a middling planter, directed that his children "have such Education in Learning as [to] write and read and Cast accompt I mean my three Sonnes my two daughters to learn to read and sew with their needle and all of them to be keept from Idleness but not to be keept as Comon Servants." John Lawson required his executors to see that his two daughters be reared together, receive learning and sewing instruction, and be "brought up to huswifery."[52] Often present was the fear that orphaned children would be treated as servants and trained only to work in the fields.[53] With stepfathers in mind, many fathers provided that their sons should be independent before the usual age of majority, which for girls was sixteen but for men twenty-one. Sometimes fathers willed that their sons should inherit when they were as young as sixteen, though more often eighteen. The sons could then escape an incompatible stepfather, who could no longer exploit their labor or property. If a son was already close to age sixteen, the father might bind him to his mother until he reached majority or his mother died, whichever came first. If she lived, she could watch out for his welfare, and his

[51] Margaret Spufford, *Contrasting Communities: English Villagers in the Sixteenth and Seventeenth Centuries* (Cambridge, 1974), 85–90, 111–118, 161–164.

[52] Wills, I, 422, 182, 321.

[53] For example, ibid., 172, 182.

labor could contribute to her support. If she died, he and his property would be free from a stepfather's control.[54]

What happened to widows and children if a man died without leaving a will? There was great need for some community institution that could protect children left fatherless or parentless in a society where they usually had no other kin. By the 1660s the probate court and county orphans' courts were supplying this need.[55] If a man left a widow, the probate court—in Maryland a central government agency—usually appointed her or her new husband administrator of the estate with power to pay its creditors under court supervision. Probate procedures provided a large measure of protection. These required an inventory of the movable property and careful accounting of all disbursements, whether or not a man had left a will. William Hollis of Baltimore County, for example, had three stepfathers in seven years, and only the care of the judge of probate prevented the third stepfather from paying the debts of the second with goods that had belonged to William's father. As the judge remarked, William had "an uncareful mother."[56]

Once the property of an intestate had been fully accounted and creditors paid, the county courts appointed a guardian who took charge of the property and gave bond to the children with sureties that he or she would not waste it. If the mother were living, she could be the guardian, or if she had remarried, her new husband would act. Through most of the century bond was waived in these circumstances, but from the 1690s security was required of all guardians, even of mothers. Thereafter the courts might actually take away an orphan's property from a widow or stepfather if she or he could not find sureties—that is, neighbors who judged the parent responsible and hence were willing to risk their own property as security. Children without any parents were assigned new families, who at all times found surety if there were property to manage. If the orphans inherited land, English common law allowed them to choose guardians for themselves at age fourteen—another escape hatch for children in conflict with stepparents. Orphans who had no property, or whose property was insufficient to provide an income that could maintain them, were expected to work for their guardians in return for their maintenance. Every year the county courts were expected to check on the welfare of orphans of intestate parents and remove them or their property from guardians who abused them or misused their estates. From 1681, Maryland law required that a special jury be impaneled once a year to report neighborhood knowledge of mistreatment of orphans and hear complaints.

This form of community surveillance of widows and orphans proved quite effective. In 1696 the assembly declared that orphans of intestates were often better cared for than orphans of testators. From that time forward, orphans' courts were charged with supervision of all orphans and were soon given powers to remove any guardians who were shown false to their trusts, regardless of the arrangements laid down in a will. The assumption was that the deceased parent's main concern was the welfare of the child, and that the orphans' court, as "father

---

[54] Lorena S. Walsh, "'Till Death Do Us Part': Marriage and Family in Charles County, Maryland, 1658–1705," in Tate and Ammerman, eds., *Essays on the Chesapeake.*

[55] The following discussion of the orphans' court is based on Lois Green Carr, "The Development of the Maryland Orphans' Court, 1654–1715," in Land, Carr, and Papenfuse, eds., *Law, Society, and Politics in Early Maryland,* 41–61.

[56] Baltimore County Court Proceedings, D, ff. 385–386.

to us poor orphans," should implement the parent's intent. In actual fact, the courts never removed children—as opposed to their property—from a household in which the mother was living, except to apprentice them at the mother's request. These powers were mainly exercised over guardians of orphans both of whose parents were dead. The community as well as the husband believed the mother most capable of nurturing his children.

Remarriage was the usual and often the immediate solution for a woman who had lost her husband.[57] The shortage of women made any woman eligible to marry again, and the difficulties of raising a family while running a plantation must have made remarriage necessary for widows who had no son old enough to make tobacco. One indication of the high incidence of remarriage is the fact that there were only sixty women, almost all of them widows, among the 1,735 people who left probate inventories in four southern Maryland counties over the second half of the century.[58] Most other women must have died while married and therefore legally without property to put through probate.

One result of remarriage was the development of complex family structures. Men found themselves responsible for stepchildren as well as their own offspring, and children acquired half-sisters and half-brothers. Sometimes a woman married a second husband who himself had been previously married, and both brought children of former spouses to the new marriage. They then produced children of their own. The possibilities for conflict over the upbringing of children are evident, and crowded living conditions, found even in the households of the wealthy, must have added to family tensions. Luckily, the children of the family very often had the same mother. In Charles County, at least, widows took new husbands three times more often than widowers took new wives.[59] The role of the mother in managing the relationships of half-brothers and half-sisters or stepfathers and stepchildren must have been critical to family harmony.

Early death in this immigrant population thus had broad effects on Maryland society in the seventeenth century. It produced what we might call a pattern of serial polyandry, which enabled more men to marry and to father families than the sex ratios otherwise would have permitted. It produced thousands of orphaned children who had no kin to maintain them or preserve their property, and thus gave rise to an institution almost unknown in England, the orphans' court, which was charged with their protection. And early death, by creating families in which the mother was the unifying element, may have increased her authority within the household.

When the immigrant woman married her first husband, there was usually no property settlement involved, since she was unlikely to have any dowry. But her remarriage was another matter. At the very least, she owned or had a life interest in a third of her former husband's estate. She needed also to think of her children's interests. If she remarried, she would lose control of the property. Consequently, property settlements occasionally appear in the seventeenth-century court records between widows and their future husbands. Sometimes she and her intended signed an agreement whereby he relinquished his rights to the use of her

[57] In 17th-century Charles County two-thirds of surviving partners remarried within a year of their spouse's death. Walsh, "Charles County, Maryland," chap. 2.

[58] See n. 26.

[59] Walsh, "'Till Death Do Us Part,'" in Tate and Ammerman, eds., *Essays on the Chesapeake*.

children's portions. Sometimes he deeded to her property which she could dispose of at her pleasure.[60] Whether any of these agreements or gifts would have survived a test in court is unknown. We have not yet found any challenged. Generally speaking, the formal marriage settlements of English law, which bypassed the legal difficulties of the married woman's inability to make a contract with her husband, were not adopted by immigrants, most of whom probably came from levels of English society that did not use these legal formalities.

The wife's dower rights in her husband's estate were a recognition of her role in contributing to his prosperity, whether by the property she had brought to the marriage or by the labor she performed in his household. A woman newly freed from servitude would not bring property, but the benefits of her labor would be great. A man not yet prosperous enough to own a servant might need his wife's help in the fields as well as in the house, especially if he were paying rent or still paying for land. Moreover, food preparation was so time-consuming that even if she worked only at household duties, she saved him time he needed for making tobacco and corn. The corn, for example, had to be pounded in the mortar or ground in a handmill before it could be used to make bread, for there were very few water mills in seventeenth-century Maryland. The wife probably raised vegetables in a kitchen garden; she also milked the cows and made butter and cheese, which might produce a salable surplus. She washed the clothes, and made them if she had the skill. When there were servants to do field work, the wife undoubtedly spent her time entirely in such household tasks. A contract of 1681 expressed such a division of labor. Nicholas Maniere agreed to live on a plantation with his wife and child and a servant. Nicholas and the servant were to work the land; his wife was to "Dresse the Victualls milk the Cowes wash for the servants and Doe allthings necessary for a woman to doe upon the s[ai]d plantation."[61]

We have suggested that wives did field work; the suggestion is supported by occasional direct references in the court records. Mary Castleton, for example, told the judge of probate that "her husband late Deceased in his Life time had Little to sustaine himselfe and Children but what was produced out of ye ground by ye hard Labour of her the said Mary."[62] Household inventories provide indirect evidence. Before about 1680 those of poor men and even middling planters on Maryland's lower Western Shore—the bottom two-thirds of the married decedents[63]—show few signs of household industry, such as appear in equivalent English estates.[64] Sheep and woolcards, flax and hackles, and spinning wheels all

---

[60] Ibid.

[61] *Maryland Archives*, LXX, 87. See also ibid., XLI, 210, 474, 598, for examples of allusions to washing clothes and dairying activities. Water mills were so scarce that in 1669 the Maryland assembly passed an act permitting land to be condemned for the use of anyone willing to build and operate a water mill. Ibid., II, 211–214. In the whole colony only four condemnations were carried out over the next 10 years. Ibid., LI, 25, 57, 86, 381. Probate inventories show that most households had a mortar and pestle or a handmill.

[62] Testamentary Proceedings, X, 184–185. Cf. Charles County Court and Land Records, MS, I #1, ff. 9–10, 259.

[63] Among married decedents before 1680 (N = 308), the bottom two-thirds (N = 212) were those worth less than £150. Among all decedents worth less than £150 (N = 451), only 12 (about 3%) had sheep or yarn-making equipment, "Social Stratification."

[64] See Everitt, "Farm Labourers," in Thirsk, ed., *Agrarian History of England and Wales*, 422–426, and W. G. Hoskins, *Essays in Leicestershire History* (Liverpool, 1950), 134.

were a rarity, and such things as candle molds were nonexistent. Women in these households must have been busy at other work. In households with bound labor the wife doubtless was fully occupied preparing food and washing clothes for family and hands. But the wife in a household too poor to afford bound labor—the bottom fifth of the married decedent group—might well tend tobacco when she could.[65] Eventually, the profits of her labor might enable the family to buy a servant, making greater profits possible. From such beginnings many families climbed the economic ladder in seventeenth-century Maryland.[66]

The proportion of servantless households must have been larger than is suggested by the inventories of the dead, since young men were less likely to die than old men and had had less time to accumulate property. Well over a fifth of the households of married men on the lower Western Shore may have had no bound labor. Not every wife in such households would necessarily work at the hoe—saved from it by upbringing, ill-health, or the presence of small children who needed her care—but many women performed such work. A lease of 1691, for example, specified that the lessee could farm the amount of land which "he his wife and children can tend."[67]

Stagnation of the tobacco economy, beginning about 1680, produced changes that had some effect on women's economic role.[68] As shown by inventories of the lower Western Shore, home industry increased, especially at the upper ranges of the economic spectrum. In these households women were spinning yarn and knitting it into clothing.[69] The increase in such activity was far less in the households of the bottom fifth, where changes of a different kind may have increased the pressures to grow tobacco. Fewer men at this level could now purchase land, and a portion of their crop went for rent.[70] At this level, more wives than before may have been helping to produce tobacco when they could. And by this time they were often helping as a matter of survival, not as a means of improving the family position.

---

[65] Among married decedents, the bottom fifth were approximately those worth less than £30. Before 1680 these were 17% of the married decedents. By the end of the period, from 1700 to 1705, they were 22%. Before 1680, 92% had no bound labor. From 1700 to 1705, 95% had none. Less than 1% of all estates in this wealth group had sheep or yarn-making equipment before 1681. "Social Stratification."

[66] On opportunity to rise from the bottom to the middle see Menard, "From Servant to Freeholder," *WMQ,* 3d Ser., XXX (1973), 37–64; Walsh, "Servitude and Opportunity," 111–133, and Menard, Harris, and Carr, "Opportunity and Inequality," *Md. Hist. Mag.,* LXIX (1974), 169–184.

[67] Charles County Court and Land Records, MS, R #1, f. 193.

[68] For 17th-century economic development see Menard, Harris, and Carr, "Opportunity and Inequality," *Md. Hist. Mag.,* LXIX (1974), 169–184.

[69] Among estates worth £150 or more, signs of diversification in this form appeared in 22% before 1681 and in 67% after 1680. Over the years 1700–1705, the figure was 62%. Only 6% of estates worth less than £40 had such signs of diversification after 1680 or over the period 1700–1705. Knitting rather than weaving is assumed because looms were very rare. These figures are for all estates. "Social Stratification."

[70] After the mid-1670s information about landholdings of decedents becomes decreasingly available, making firm estimates of the increase in tenancy difficult. However, for householders in life cycle 2 (married or widowed decedents who died without children of age) the following table is suggestive. Householding decedents in life cycle 2 worth less than £40 (N = 255) were 21% of all decedents in this category (N = 1,218).

So far we have considered primarily the experience of immigrant women. What of their daughters? How were their lives affected by the demographic stresses of Chesapeake society?

One of the most important points in which the experience of daughters differed from that of their mothers was the age at which they married. In this woman-short world, the mothers had married as soon as they were eligible, but they had not usually become eligible until they were mature women in their middle twenties. Their daughters were much younger at marriage. A vital register kept in Somerset County shows that some girls married at age twelve and that the mean age at marriage for those born before 1670 was sixteen and a half years.

Were some of these girls actually child brides? It seems unlikely that girls were married before they had become capable of bearing children. Culturally, such a practice would fly in the face of English, indeed Western European, precedent, nobility excepted. Nevertheless, the number of girls who married before age sixteen, the legal age of inheritance for girls, is astonishing. Their English counterparts ordinarily did not marry until their mid- to late twenties or early thirties. In other parts of the Chesapeake, historians have found somewhat higher ages at marriage than appear in Somerset, but everywhere in seventeenth-century Maryland and Virginia most native-born women married before they reached age twenty-one.[71] Were such early marriages a result of the absence of fathers? Evidently not. In Somerset County, the fathers of very young brides—those under sixteen—were usually living.[72] Evidently, guardians were unlikely to allow such marriages, and this fact suggests that they were not entirely approved. But the shortage of women imposed strong pressures to marry as early as possible.

Not only did native girls marry early, but many of them were pregnant before the ceremony. Bridal pregnancy among native-born women was not as common as among immigrants. Nevertheless, in seventeenth-century Somerset County 20 percent of native brides bore children within eight and one half

	£0–19				£20 39			
	Deced- ents	Land Unkn.	With Land	With Land	Deced- ents	Land Unkn.	With Land	With Land
	N	N	N	%	N	N	N	%
To 1675	10	0	7	70	34	2	29	91
1675 on	98	22	40	53	113	16	64	66

In computing percentages, unknowns have been distributed according to knowns.

A man who died with a child of age was almost always a landowner, but these were a small proportion of all decedents (see n. 45).

Several studies provide indisputable evidence of an increase in tenancy on the lower Western Shore over the period 1660–1706. These compare heads of households with lists of landowners compiled from rent rolls made in 1659 and 1704–1706. Tenancy in St. Mary's and Charles counties in 1660 was about 10%. In St. Mary's, Charles, and Prince George's counties, 1704–1706, 30–35% of householders were tenants. Russell R. Menard, "Population Growth and Land Distribution in St. Mary's County, 1634–1710" (ms. report, St. Mary's City Commission, 1971, copy on file at the Hall of Records); Menard, "Economy and Society," 423; Carr, "County Government in Maryland," text, 605.

[71] Menard, "Immigrants and Their Increase," Table III; n. 40 above.

[72] Menard, "Demography of Somerset County," Table XIII.

months of marriage. This was a somewhat higher percentage than has been reported from seventeenth-century English parishes.[73]

These facts suggest considerable freedom for girls in selecting a husband. Almost any girl must have had more than one suitor, and evidently many had freedom to spend time with a suitor in a fashion that allowed her to become pregnant. We might suppose that such pregnancies were not incurred until after the couple had become betrothed, and that they were consequently an allowable part of courtship, were it not that girls whose fathers were living were usually not the culprits. In Somerset, at least, only 10 percent of the brides with fathers living were pregnant, in contrast to 30 percent of those who were orphans.[74] Since there was only about one year's difference between the mean ages at which orphan and non-orphan girls married, parental supervision rather than age seems to have been the main factor in the differing bridal pregnancy rates.[75]

Native girls married young and bore children young; hence they had more children than immigrant women. This fact ultimately changed the composition of the Maryland population. Native-born females began to have enough children to enable couples to replace themselves. These children, furthermore, were divided about evenly between males and females. By the mid-1680s, in all probability, the population thus began to grow through reproductive increase, and sexual imbalance began to decline. In 1704 the native-born preponderated in the Maryland assembly for the first time and by then were becoming predominant in the adult population as a whole.[76]

This appearance of a native population was bringing alterations in family life, especially for widows and orphaned minors. They were acquiring kin. St. Mary's and Charles counties wills demonstrate the change.[77] (See Table 3.) Before 1680, when nearly all those who died and left families had been immigrants, three-

---

[73] Ibid., Table XVII; P.E.H. Hair, "Bridal Pregnancy in Rural England in Earlier Centuries," *Pop. Studies,* XX (1966), 237; Chambers, *Population, Economy, and Society in England,* 75; Smith and Hindus, "Premarital Pregnancy in America," *Jour. Interdisciplinary Hist.,* V (1975), 537–570.

[74] Menard, "Demography of Somerset County," Table XVIII.

[75] Adolescent subfecundity might also partly explain lower bridal pregnancy rates among very young brides.

[76] Menard develops this argument in detail in "Immigrants and Their Increase." For the assembly see David W. Jordan, "Political Stability and the Emergence of a Native Elite in Maryland, 1660–1715," in Tate and Ammerman, eds., *Essays on the Chesapeake.* In Charles County, Maryland, by 1705 at least half of all resident landowners were native born. Walsh, "Charles County, Maryland," chaps. 1, 7.

[77] The proportion of wills mentioning non-nuclear kin can, of course, prove only a proxy of the actual existence of these kin in Maryland. The reliability of such a measure may vary greatly from area to area and over time, depending on the character of the population and on local inheritance customs. To test the reliability of the will data, we compared them with data from reconstituted families in 17th-century Charles County. These reconstitution data draw on a much broader variety of sources and include many men who did not leave wills. Because of insufficient information for female lines, we could trace only the male lines. The procedure compared the names of all married men against a file of all known county residents, asking how many kin in the male line might have been present in the county at the time of the married man's death. The proportions for immigrants were in most cases not markedly different from those found in wills. For native men, however, wills were somewhat less reliable indicators of the presence of such kin; when non-nuclear kin mentioned by testate natives were compared with kin found by reconstitution, 29% of the native testators had non-nuclear kin present in the county who were not mentioned in their wills.

quarters of the men and women who left widows and/or minor children made no mention in their wills of any other kin in Maryland. In the first decade of the eighteenth century, among native-born testators, nearly three-fifths mention other kin, and if we add information from sources other than wills—other probate records, land records, vital registers, and so on—at least 70 percent are found to have had such local connections. This development of local family ties must have been one of the most important events of early Maryland history.[78]

Historians have only recently begun to explore the consequences of the shift from an immigrant to a predominantly native population.[79] We would like to suggest some changes in the position of women that may have resulted from this transition. It is already known that as sexual imbalance disappeared, age at first marriage rose, but it remained lower than it had been for immigrants over the second half of the seventeenth century. At the same time, life expectancy improved, at least for men. The results were longer marriages and more children who reached maturity.[80] In St. Mary's County after 1700, dying men far more often than earlier left children of age to maintain their widows, and widows may have felt less inclination and had less opportunity to remarry.[81]

We may speculate on the social consequences of such changes. More fathers were still alive when their daughters married, and hence would have been able to exercise control over the selection of their sons-in-law. What in the seventeenth

[78] Not surprisingly, wills of immigrants show no increase in family ties, but these wills mention adult children far more often than earlier. Before 1680, only 11% of immigrant testators in St. Mary's and Charles counties mention adult children in their wills; from 1700 to 1710, 37% left adult children to help the family. Two facts help account for this change. First, survivors of early immigration were dying in old age. Second, proportionately fewer young immigrants with families were dying, not because life expectancy had improved, but because there were proportionately fewer of them than earlier. A long stagnation in the tobacco economy that began about 1680 had diminished opportunities for freed servants to form households and families. Hence, among immigrants the proportion of young fathers at risk to die was smaller than in earlier years.

In the larger population of men who left inventories, 18.2% had adult children before 1681, but in the years 1700–1709, 50% had adult children. "Social Stratification."

[79] Examples of some recent studies are Carole Shammas, "English-Born and Creole Elites in Turn-of-the-Century Virginia," in Tate and Ammerman, eds., *Essays on the Chesapeake;* Jordan, "Political Stability and the Emergence of a Native Elite in Maryland," ibid.; Lois Green Carr, "The Foundations of Social Order: Local Government in Colonial Maryland," in Bruce C. Daniels, ed., *Town and Country: Essays on the Structure of Local Government in the American Colonies* (Middletown, Conn., forthcoming); Menard, "Economy and Society," 396–440.

[80] Allan Kulikoff has found that in Prince George's County the white adult sex ratio dropped significantly before the age of marriage rose. Women born in the 1720s were the first to marry at a mean age above 20, while those born in the 1740s and marrying in the 1760s, after the sex ratio neared equality, married at a mean age of 22. Marriages lasted longer because the rise in the mean age at which men married—from 23 to 27 between 1700 and 1740—was more than offset by gains in life expectancy. Kulikoff, "Tobacco and Slaves: Population, Economy, and Society in Eighteenth-Century Prince George's County, Maryland" (Ph.D. diss. Brandeis University, 1976), chap. 3; Menard, "Immigrants and Their Increase."

[81] Inventories and related biographical data have been analyzed by the St. Mary's City Commission under a grant from the National Endowment for the Humanities, "The Making of a Plantation Society in Maryland" (R 010585–74–267). From 1700 through 1776 the percentage of men known to have had children, and who had an adult child at death, ranged from a low of 32.8% in the years 1736–1738 to a high of 61.3% in the years 1707–1709. The figure was over 50% for 13 out of 23 year-groups of three to four years each. For the high in 1707–1709 see comments in n. 78.

TABLE 3

Resident Kin of Testate Men and Women Who Left Minor Children,
St. Mary's and Charles Counties, Maryland, 1640 to 1710

	Families	*No Kin*	*Only Wife*	*Grown Child*	*Other Kin*
	N	*% Families*	*% Families*	*% Families*	*% Families*
			A		
1640–1669	95	23	43	11	23
1670–1679	76	17	50	7	26
1700–1710	71	6	35^a	25	34^b
			B		
1700–1710					
Immigrant	41	10	37	37	17
Native	30		33^c	10	57^d

[a] If information found in other records is included, the percentage is 30.
[b] If information found in other records is included, the percentage is 39.
[c] If information found in other records is included, the percentage is 20.
[d] If information found in other records is included, the percentage is 70.

For a discussion of wills as a reliable source for discovery of kin see n. 78. Only 8 testators were natives of Maryland before 1680s; hence no effort has been made to distinguish them from immigrants.

Source: Wills I-XIV.

century may have been a period of comparative independence for women, both immigrant and native, may have given way to a return to more traditional European social controls over the creation of new families. If so, we might see the results in a decline in bridal pregnancy and perhaps a decline in bastardy.[82]

[82] On the other hand, these rates may show little change. The restraining effect of increased parental control may have been offset by a trend toward increased sexual activity that appears to have become general throughout Western Europe and the United States by the mid-19th century. Smith and Hindus, "Premarital Pregnancy in America," *Jour. Interdisciplinary Hist.*, V (1975), 537–570; Edward Shorter, "Female Emancipation, Birth Control, and Fertility in European History," *American Historical Review*, LXXVIII (1973), 605–640.

We may also find the wife losing ground in the household polity, although her economic importance probably remained unimpaired. Indeed, she must have been far more likely than a seventeenth-century immigrant woman to bring property to her marriage. But several changes may have caused women to play a smaller role than before in household decision-making.[83] Women became proportionately more numerous and may have lost bargaining power.[84] Furthermore, as marriages lasted longer, the proportion of households full of stepchildren and half-brothers and half-sisters united primarily by the mother must have diminished. Finally, when husbands died, more widows would have had children old enough to maintain them and any minor brothers and sisters. There would be less need for women to play a controlling role as well as less incentive for their husbands to grant it. The provincial marriage of the eighteenth century may have more closely resembled that of England than did the immigrant marriage of the seventeenth century.

If this change occurred, we should find symptoms to measure. There should be fewer gifts from husbands to wives of property put at the wife's disposal. Husbands should less frequently make bequests to wives that provided them with property beyond their dower. A wife might even be restricted to less than her dower, although the law allowed her to choose her dower instead of a bequest.[85] At the same time, children should be commanded to maintain their mothers.

St Mary's County wills show some of the symptoms (see Table 4). Bequests of dower or less grew by nearly two-fifths, from 30 to 41 percent. On the other hand, widowhood restrictions did not increase, nor did fathers often exhort children to help their mothers or give them living space. Still, as demographic conditions became more normal and traditional family networks appeared, St. Mary's County widows began to lose ground to their children. This phenomenon deserves further study.

It is time to issue a warning. Whether or not Maryland women in a creole society lost ground, the argument hinges on an interpretation of English behavior that also requires testing. Either position supposes that women in seventeenth-century Maryland obtained power in the household which wives of English farmers did not enjoy. Much of the evidence for Maryland is drawn from the disposition of property in wills. If English wills show a similar pattern, similar inferences might be drawn about English women. We have already discussed evidence from English wills that supports the view that women in Maryland were favored; but the position of seventeenth-century English women—especially those not of gentle status—has been little explored.[86] A finding of little difference

[83] Page Smith has suggested that such a decline in the wife's household authority had occurred in the American family by—at the latest—the beginning of the 19th century (*Daughters of the Promised Land: Women in American History* [Boston, 1970], chaps. 3, 4).

[84] There is little doubt that extreme scarcity in the early years of Chesapeake history enhanced the worth of women in the eyes of men. However, as Smith has observed, "the functioning of the law of supply and demand could not in itself have guaranteed status for colonial women. Without a ideological basis, their privileges could not have been initially established or subsequently maintained" (ibid., 38–39). In a culture where women were seriously undervalued, a shortage of women would not necessarily improve their status.

[85] Acts 1699, chap. 41, *Maryland Archives*, XXII, 542.

[86] Essays by Cicely Howell and Barbara Todd, printed or made available to the authors since this

between bequests to women in England and in Maryland would greatly weaken the argument that demographic stress created peculiar conditions especially favorable to Maryland women.

If the demography of Maryland produced the effects here described, such effects should also be evident elsewhere in the Chesapeake. The four characteristics of the seventeenth-century Maryland population—immigrant predominance, early death, late marriage, and sexual imbalance—are to be found everywhere in the region, at least at first. The timing of the disappearance of these peculiarities may have varied from place to place, depending on date of settlement or rapidity of development, but the effect of their existence upon the experience of women should be clear. Should research in other areas of the Chesapeake fail to find women enjoying the status they achieved on the lower Western Shore of Maryland, then our arguments would have to be revised.[87]

Work is also needed that will enable historians to compare conditions in Maryland with those in other colonies. Richard S. Dunn's study of the British West Indies also shows demographic disruption.[88] When the status of wives is studied, it should prove similar to that of Maryland women. In contrast were demographic conditions in New England, where immigrants came in family groups, major immigration had ceased by the mid-seventeenth century, sex ratios balanced early, and mortality was low.[89] Under these conditions, demographic disruption must have been both less severe and less prolonged. If New England women achieved status similar to that suggested for women in the Chesapeake, that fact will have to be explained. The dynamics might prove to have been different;[90] or a dynamic we have not identified, common to both areas, might turn

article was written, point out that customary as opposed to freehold tenures in England usually gave the widow the use of the land for life, but that remarriage often cost the widow this right. The degree to which this was true requires investigation. Howell, "Peasant Inheritance in the Midlands, 1280–1700," in Jack Goody, Joan Thirsk, and E. P. Thompson, eds., *Family and Inheritance: Rural Society in Western Europe, 1200–1800* (Cambridge, 1976), 112–155; Todd, "'In Her Free Widowhood': Succession to Property and Remarriage in Rural England, 1540–1800" (paper delivered to the Third Berkshire Conference of Women Historians, June 1976).

[87] James W. Deen, Jr., "Patterns of Testation: Four Tidewater Counties in Colonial Virginia," *American Journal of Legal History,* XVI (1972), 154–176, finds a life interest in property for the wife the predominant pattern before 1720. However, he includes an interest for widowhood in life interest and does not distinguish a dower interest from more than dower.

[88] Richard S. Dunn, *Sugar and Slaves: The Rise of the Planter Class in the English West Indies, 1624–1713* (Chapel Hill, N. C., 1972), 326–334. Dunn finds sex ratios surprisingly balanced, but he also finds very high mortality, short marriages, and many orphans.

[89] For a short discussion of this comparison see Menard, "Immigrants and Their Increase."

[90] James K. Somerville has used Salem, Massachusetts, wills from 1660 to 1770 to examine women's status and importance within the home ("The Salem [Mass.] Woman in the Home, 1660–1770," *Eighteenth-Century Life,* I [1974], 11–14). See also Alexander Keyssar, "Widowhood in Eighteenth-Century Massachusetts: A Problem in the History of the Family," *Perspectives in American History,* VIII (1974), 83–119, which discusses provisions for 22 widows in 18th-century Woburn, Massachusetts. Both men find provisions for houseroom and care of the widow's property enjoined upon children proportionately far more often than we have found in St. Mary's County, Maryland, where we found only five instances over 136 years. However, part of this difference may be a function of the differences in age at widowhood in the two regions. Neither Somerville nor Keyssar gives the percentage of widows who received a life interest in property, but their discussions imply a much higher proportion than we have found of women whose interest ended at remarriage or the majority of the oldest son.

TABLE 4

Bequests of Husbands to Wives with Children,
St. Mary's County, Maryland, 1710–1777

	All Estate			All or Dwelling Plantation for Life		All or Dwelling Plantation for Widowhood[a]		More than Dower in Other Form		Dower or Less or Unknown[b]	
Date	N	N	%	N	%	N	%	N	%	N	%
1710–1719	39	1	3	12	32	2	5	10	26	14	37
1720–1729	65	4	6	23	35	0	0	15	23	23	35
1730–1739	58	2	3	17	29	5	9	9	16	25	43
1740–1749	73	1	1	20	27	6	8	10	14	36	49
1750–1759	78	2	3	26	33	11	14	8	10	31	39
1760–1769	92	2	2	35	38	10	11	5	5	40	43
1770–1777	66	1	3	17	26	10	15	12	18	26	39
Totals	471	13	3	150	32	44	9	69	15	195	41

[a]Includes instances of all or dwelling plantation for minority of child (N = 11).
[b]Includes instances of provisions for maintenance or houseroom (N = 5).
Source: Wills XIII–XLI.
Ed. Note: This table is a revision of the table printed in the original published article.

out to have been the primary engine of change. And, if women in England shared the status—which we doubt—conditions in the New World may have had secondary importance. The Maryland data establish persuasive grounds for a hypothesis, but the evidence is not all in.

Authors' Postscript

"The Planter's Wife," which began life in 1975 as the Bernard Steiner Lecture at the Maryland Historical Society, was born of collaborative research at the Maryland Hall of Records as part of a museum enterprise. The St. Mary's City Commission (now the Historic St. Mary's City Commission) had established a research program in history and archaeology—a program still in place—to explore the site of Maryland's seventeenth-century capital and make it come alive for visitors. Our colleagues in this research, Russell R. Menard and P.M.G. Harris, were as much creators of this essay as were we. In addition, a bevy of scholars also working at the Hall of Records shared data and methods and provided daily conversation that tested and improved everyone's perceptions as we learned together. The broad range of topics and discussion enriched not only this essay but the work of all of us.

The part of our essay that perhaps has attracted the most attention focuses on inheritance and the decisions husbands and fathers made in distributing family property. We must warn readers that there are difficulties in standardizing the provisions of wills that we did not foresee when we first wrote. After publication of "The Planter's Wife," we discovered that hidden discrepancies in interpreting wills had led to errors in Table 4 and required a modification of our findings for the eighteenth century. These changes have been incorporated into later reprintings of the essay, including this one.

The essay offers a hypothesis intended to encourage further exploration— that in the early modern New World setting, at least among the British, the demographic structure of society had basic effects on the family polity—effects that can be seen in the decisions of testators in distributing power over property and the upbringing of children. We have refined our thinking on this subject considerably. Carr has found within the Chesapeake region far more variation in testation practices than we had expected. Trevor Burnard's work in Jamaica, published in this journal, presents a case in which demographic stress did not produce results entirely parallel to ours.[91] There are complexities being discovered that will surely enhance understanding of the connections between demographic and social developments.

We both still work for museums, although Lorena Walsh has exchanged St. Mary's City for Colonial Williamsburg. In retrospect, we think that our museum experience has broadened our outlook and interests as scholars. In trying to recreate past experiences, we have approached people's lives in as holistic a way as we could devise; and in writing of the experience of women, we have thought of our work as part of a human history, not as a history of women.

---

[91] Lois Green Carr, "Inheritance in the Colonial Chesapeake," in Ronald Hoffman and Peter J. Albert, eds., *Women in the Age of the American Revolution* (Charlottesville, Va., 1989), 155–208; Trevor Burnard, "Inheritance and Independence: Women's Status in Early Colonial Jamaica," *WMQ*, 3d Ser., XLVIII (1990), 93–114.

FAMILIES AND FARMS:
MENTALITÉ IN PRE-INDUSTRIAL AMERICA

JAMES A. HENRETTA

The history of the agricultural population of pre-industrial America remains to be written. As a result of quantitative investigations of wealth distribution and social mobility; of rates of birth, marriage, and death; and of patterns of inheritance, officeholding, and church membership, there is an ever-growing mass of data that delineates the *structures* of social existence in the small rural communities that constituted the core of American agricultural society in the North before 1830. But what of the *consciousness* of the inhabitants, the mental or emotional or ideological aspects of their lives? And what of the relationship between the two? Can a careful statistical analysis of people's lives—a precise description of their patterns of social action—substantiate at least limited statements as to their motivations, values, and goals?

A number of historians have attempted to establish a connection between the subsistence activities of the agricultural population and its institutional, ideological, and cultural existence. Consider, for example, the entrepreneurial interpretation implicit in James T. Lemon's highly regarded quantitative analysis of the eighteenth-century agricultural society of Southeastern Pennsylvania:

> A basic stress in these essays is on the "liberal" middle-class orientation of many of the settlers. . . . "Liberal" I use in the classic sense, meaning placing individual freedom and material gain over that of public interest. Put another way, the people planned for themselves much more than they did for their communities. . . . This is not to say that the settlers were "economic men," single-minded maximizing materialists. Few could be, or even wanted to be. Nevertheless, they defended their liberal propensities in a tenacious manner. . . . Undoubtedly their view was fostered by a sense that the environment was "open." As individualists, they were ready in spirit to conquer the limitless continent, to subdue the land.[1]

Mr. Henretta is a member of the Department of History at the University of California, Los Angeles. Earlier versions of this paper were presented at the University of Rochester, the Charles Warren Center at Harvard, and the Shelby Cullom Davis Center at Princeton. Mr. Henretta wishes to express special gratitude for the written criticisms and suggestions offered by Patricia Wilson, Jonathan Wiener, Fred Matthews, Jeffrey Nelson, Richard Dunn, Gary Nash, Peter Kolchin, Daniel Scott Smith, and Sam Bass Warner, and for the oral commentaries of Lawrence Stone, R. Jackson Wilson, and Bernard Bailyn.

Ed. Note: This article was originally published in *William and Mary Quarterly*, 3d Ser., XXXV (January 1978), 3–32.

[1] *The Best Poor Man's Country: A Geographical Study of Early Southeastern Pennsylvania* (Baltimore, 1972), xv.

However overburdened with reservations and qualifications, the general thrust of this depiction of values and aspirations is clear enough. Lemon's settlers were individualists, enterprising men and women intent upon the pursuit of material advantage at the expense of communal and non-economic goals.

Can the "consciousness" with which Lemon has endowed these early Pennsylvanians be verified by historical evidence? The question is important, for many of the statistical data presented by Lemon do not support this description of the inhabitants' "orientation," " spirit," or "propensities." Take the pattern of residence. It is true that the predominance of isolated farmsteads—rather than nucleated villages—suggests that these men and women were planning "for themselves much more than . . . for their communities." But what of the presence of clusters of ethnic and religious groups? Such voluntary concentrations of like-minded settlers indicate the importance of *communal* values, of people who preferred to share a religious or ethnic identity. Here the author's evidence contradicts his conclusion. "Most of the people who came during this period," Lemon writes of the years between 1700 and 1730, "settled together in areas and communities defined by nationality or denomination. . . . Language and creed thus exerted considerable influence on the whereabouts of people. Yet groups were mixed in several areas, for example on the Lancaster Plain."[2]

This exception only confirms the rule. Nearly every historian who has studied ethnic settlement patterns in the colonial period has stressed the existence of communal concentrations. In the Middle Colonies, for example, patterns of spatial segregation appeared among the Dutch in Newark, New Jersey, and to some extent among Quakers and Seventh Day Baptists in the same area. Most of the German immigrants who arrived in Lancaster, Pennsylvania, in 1744 settled on the lots laid out by Dr. Adam Simon Kuhn, the leading German resident, rather than on land offered by the English proprietor, Alexander Hamilton. These linguistic and religious ties extended beyond settlement patterns to encompass economic relationships. Every one of the one hundred names inscribed in the account book of Henry King—shoemaker, butcher, and currier of Second River, New Jersey, in 1775—was of Dutch origin; and the main business connections of the merchants of Lancaster, whether they were Jewish or Quaker or German, were with their co-religionists in Philadelphia.[3]

Is an individualist spirit fully compatible with these communal settlement patterns and this religiously determined economic activity? It is possible, of course, that these ethnic or linguistic preferences facilitated the pursuit of individual economic gain, and that the patronage of the shop of a fellow church member brought preferred treatment and lower prices. But the weight of the evidence indicates that these decisions were not made for narrowly economic or strictly utilitarian reasons: the felt need to maintain a linguistic or religious identity was as important a consideration as the fertility of the soil or the price of the land in determining where a family would settle. The "calculus of advantage" for these

---

[2] Ibid., 221.

[3] Dennis P. Ryan, "Six Towns: Continuity and Change in Revolutionary New Jersey, 1770–1792" (Ph.D. diss., New York University, 1974), 57–71; Jerome H. Wood, Jr., "Conestoga Crossroads: The Rise of Lancaster, Pennsylvania, 1730–1789" (Ph.D. diss., Brown University, 1969), 53, 114–115, 129–131.

men and women was not mere pecuniary gain, but encompassed a much wider range of social and cultural goals.[4]

These ethnic, linguistic, or religious ties did not reflect a coherent ideological system, a planned *communitarian* culture similar to the highly organized Moravian settlement at Bethlehem, Pennsylvania.[5] These bonds among families, neighbors, and fellow church members were informal; nonetheless, they circumscribed the range of individual action among the inhabitants of Pennsylvania and laid the foundations for a rich and diverse cultural existence. These community-oriented patterns of social interaction emerge clearly from Lemon's quantitative data, yet they do not figure prominently in his conclusion. He has not explained the complexity of the settlers' existence but has forced their lives into the mold of a timeless, placeless concept of "liberal individualism."

A similar discrepancy between data and interpretation appears in Lemon's analysis of the economic goals and achievements of the inhabitants of eighteenth-century Pennsylvania. What becomes of the open environment and the conquering spirit when "tenant farming was much more frequent than we might expect[.] . . . [I]n 1760 and 1782 about 30 per cent of Lancaster's and Chester's married taxpayers were landless" and an additional 15 percent of the total number of taxpayers in Chester County were single freemen—mostly young men without landed property. With nearly 45 percent of the members of the adult white male population without land of their own, the gap between evidence and conclusion is so obvious that it must be confronted; and what better way than by evoking the spirit of Frederick Jackson Turner? "As long as the frontier was open," Lemon writes, "many people were able to move, and as a result frustrations were dampened and the liberal values of the original inhabitants of the colony were upheld."[6]

This is an appealing interpretation, especially since it admits the necessary connection between the structure of opportunity offered by a given environment and the consciousness of the inhabitants, but it is not completely satisfactory. It assumes that the migrants came with "liberal" values, with an expectation that most adult males would own a freehold estate and that anything less than this would generate anger and frustration. Neither the basic proposition nor its corollary is acceptable, for both fail to convey the settlers' conception of social reality, their understanding of the structural components of age and wealth.

To be "young" in this agricultural society (as in most) was either to be landless or without sufficient land to support a family. As Philip J. Greven, Daniel Scott Smith, and Robert A. Gross have shown, male parents normally retained

---

[4] Nor, in E. A. Wrigley's definition, was their society modern—one in which "the unit is the individual or, at the widest, the nuclear family" and "the utilities to be maximized are concentrated in a narrower band and are pursued with a new urgency" ("The Process of Modernization and the Industrial Revolution in England," *Journal of Interdisciplinary History*, III [1972], 233, 229).

[5] Gillian Lindt Gollin, *Moravians in Two Worlds: A Study of Changing Communities* (New York, 1967).

[6] Lemon, *Best Poor Man's Country*, 94, 97; James T. Lemon and Gary B. Nash, "The Distribution of Wealth in Eighteenth-Century America: A Century of Change in Chester County, Pennsylvania, 1693–1802," *Journal of Social History*, II (1968), Table I. Since indentured and hired servants are not included in the categories of married freeholder or single freeman, the proportion of landless males may be greater than 45%.

legal control of a sizable portion of the family estate until death, in order to ensure their financial well-being in old age, and the economic security of their widows was carefully protected by dower rights.[7] Nor were these cultural restraints on the transmission of improved property the only, or even the main, obstacle to the economic prospects of the next generation. For the high rate of natural increase constantly threatened to overwhelm the accumulated capital resources of many of these northern farm families. There was never sufficient cleared and improved property, or livestock, or farm equipment, or adequate housing to permit most young men and women to own a farm. In five small agricultural towns in New Jersey in the 1770s, for example, one-half of all white males aged eighteen to twenty-five were without land, while another 29 percent of this age group owned fifty acres or less. And in Concord, Massachusetts, the percentage of landless males (many of whom were young) remained at 30 percent from 1750 to 1800. This correlation between age and wealth persisted throughout the life-cycle; all of the males in the lowest quintile of the taxable population in East Guilford, Connecticut, in 1740 were below the age of forty, while every person in the highest quintile was that age or above.[8]

The accumulation of financial resources by aging men brought them higher status and political power. In Concord, between 1745 and 1774, the median age of selectmen at the time of their first election to office was forty-five, a pattern that obtained in Dedham and Watertown as well.[9] Indeed, the correlation among age, wealth, status, and power in these agricultural communities indicates the profound importance of age as a basic principle of social differentiation. And so it appeared to the Reverend William Bentley of Salem on a visit to Andover in 1793; the country people, he noted, assembled to dance "in classes due to their ages, not with any regard to their condition, as in the Seaport Towns."[10] In such

[7] Philip J. Greven, Jr., "Family Structure in Seventeenth-Century Andover, Massachusetts," *William and Mary Quarterly,* 3d Ser., XXIII (1966), 234–256, and *Four Generations: Population, Land, and Family in Colonial Andover, Massachusetts* (Ithaca, N. Y., 1970); Daniel Scott Smith, "Parental Power and Marriage Patterns: An Analysis of Historical Trends in Massachusetts," *Journal of Marriage and the Family,* XXXV (1973), 419–428; Robert A. Gross, *The Minutemen and Their World* (New York, 1976), 210, n. 22. These authors interpret this use of economic power as an attempt by parents to control the marriage age and the subsequent family life of their children. This may have been the *effect* of delayed transmission; the prime *cause,* however, was probably the parents' concern with financial security during their old age. The exercise of parental authority (with the resulting generational conflict) was not an end in itself but simply the by-product of the prudent fiscal management of productive property. Some of the difficulties in interpreting these data are explored by Maris Vinovskis, "American Historical Demography Review Essay," *Historical Methods Newsletter,* IV (Sept. 1971), 141–148.

[8] Ryan, "Six Towns," 273 (Table 61); Robert A. Gross, "The Problem of Agricultural Crisis in Eighteenth-Century New England: Concord, Massachusetts, as a Test Case" (unpubl. paper, 1975), 7; John J. Waters, "A Yankee Village's Last Hundred Years: Guilford, Connecticut, in the Eighteenth Century" (unpubl. paper, 1975), Table I. The Wisconsin tax lists for 1860 indicate that a man one year older than another had, on the average, 7.8% more wealth than his younger counterpart. Lee Soltow, *Patterns of Wealthholding in Wisconsin Since 1850* (Madison, Wis., 1971), 8. Soltow finds a "pattern of wealth increase from age 20 to 50 or 55, with a tapering after this age" in rural areas; and that age and nativity account for roughly 60% of the inequality in the distribution of wealth (ibid., 46, 42).

[9] Gross, *Minutemen,* 196; Kenneth A. Lockridge and Alan Kreider, "The Evolution of Massachusetts Town Government, 1640 to 1740," *WMQ,* 3d Ser., XXIII (1966), 566.

[10] *The Diary of William Bentley, D. D. . . . ,* II (Salem, Mass., 1907), 17.

an age-stratified society economic "success" was not usual (and not expected) until the age of thirty-five, forty, or even forty-five. Propertied status was the product of one or two decades of work as a laborer or tenant, or of the long-delayed inheritance of the parental farm. The ownership of a freehold estate was the *goal* of young male farmers and their wives; it was not—even in the best of circumstances—a universal condition among adult males at any one point in time. Age stratification thus constituted an important aspect of what Michael Zuckerman has neatly conceptualized as the "social context" of political activity in these small and ethnically homogeneous agricultural settlements.[11] The economic dependence and powerlessness of young adults was a fact of life, the proper definition of social reality.

If cultural norms legitimated an age-stratified society in the minds of most northern farmers, then the character of social and economic life accustomed them to systematic inequalities in the distribution of wealth. Consider the evidence. In southeastern Pennsylvania in 1760 and again in 1782, the top 40 percent of the taxable population owned 70 percent of the assessed wealth, while the top 10 percent controlled 33 percent. On the 1784 tax list of Newtown, Long Island, the proportions were nearly identical, with the top 40 percent owning 73 percent of the wealth, and the richest 10 percent holding 37 percent. In both places, inequality increased steadily from the end of the seventeenth century even as the rate of natural population growth declined—a clear indication of advancing social differentiation (and not simply age stratification). And in Newtown, at least, the bulk of the poor population in 1784 was composed not of "younger sons or older men" but of workers in the prime of their productive lives.[12]

The westward migration of this excess farm population was of crucial importance, although not for the precise reasons suggested by Turner and Lemon. Young men and women without a landed inheritance moved to newly settled communities not as yeomen but as aspirants to that status; they hoped to make the difficult climb up the agricultural "ladder" from laborer to tenant to freeholder. This geographical movement, in turn, helped to maintain social stability in long-settled agricultural towns. One-third of all adult males in Goshen, Connecticut, in 1750 were without land; but two decades later a majority of these men had left the town and 70 percent of those who remained had obtained property through marriage, inheritance, or the savings from their labor. A new landless group of unmarried sons, wage laborers, and tenant farmers had appeared in Goshen by 1771, again encompassing one-third of the adult males. A similar process of out-migration and property accumulation would characterize many of

---

[11] "The Social Context of Democracy in Massachusetts," *WMQ*, 3d Ser., XXV (1968), 523–544. Zuckerman's analysis is not sufficiently critical of Robert E. Brown's work, even as it provides a better conceptual framework for evaluating the importance of a widespread suffrage. Age stratification is ignored, as are economic inequality and the increasing appearance of religious conflict. For a more detailed analysis of Zuckerman's work (and that of Greven, John Demos, and Kenneth Lockridge) see James A. Henretta, "The Morphology of New England Society in the Colonial Period," *Jour. Interdisciplinary Hist.*, II (1971), 379–398.

[12] Lemon, *Best Poor Man's Country*, 11 (Table 1); Jessica Kross Ehrlich, "A Town Study in Colonial New York: Newtown, Queens County (1642–1790)" (Ph.D. diss., University of Michigan, 1974), 178, 164 (Table 13). The data for Concord indicate that in 1770–1771 the top 20% of the population owned 48% of the land and 56% of the town's wealth but paid only 42.7% of the total tax (Gross, *Minutemen*, 212, 220, 231).

the lives of this landless group, but throughout the northern region there was a steady increase in the number of permanent tenant farmers as the century progressed.[13]

The renewed expropriation of aboriginal lands during the early nineteenth century brought a partial reversal of this trend. Massive westward migration enabled a rapidly growing Euro-American population to *preserve* an agricultural society composed primarily of yeoman freeholding families in many eastern areas, and to *extend* these age- and wealth-stratified communities into western regions.[14] This movement did not, however, produce less stratified communities in the Northwest states, nor did it assure the universal ownership of land. Within a few decades of settlement the wealth structure of the frontier states was nearly indistinguishable from that in the agricultural areas of the more densely settled east. In Trempealeau County, Wisconsin, in 1870 the poorest 10 percent of the propertied population owned less than 1 percent of all assessed wealth, while the most affluent 10 percent controlled 39 percent. This distribution was almost precisely the same as that in those regions of Vermont from which many of the inhabitants of this farming county had recently migrated.[15] "On no frontier," Neil McNall concludes from an intensive study of the settlement of the rich Genesee Valley in upstate New York between 1790 and 1860, "was there an easy avenue to land ownership for the farmer of limited means."[16]

Evidence from a variety of geographic locations indicates, therefore, that Lemon has presented an overly optimistic description of the agricultural economy of early America and has falsely ascribed a "liberal" consciousness to the inhabitants of eighteenth-century Pennsylvania. His analysis is not unique. A number of historians of colonial New England have offered similar interpretations of an entrepreneurial mentality among the majority of the agricultural population. Sometimes the ascription is implicit and perhaps inadvertent, as in the case of Philip Greven's path-breaking analysis of Andover, which focuses attention on

214

---

[13] Jackson Turner Main, *The Social Structure of Revolutionary America* (Princeton, N. J., 1965), 176. For a carefully documented analysis of the agricultural ladder see Clarence H. Danhof, *Change in Agriculture: The Northern United States, 1820–1870* (Cambridge, Mass., 1969), 78–115.

[14] The alternative was a class-stratified society, composed of a few owners of large properties and a mass of wage laborers—an agricultural proletariat. See, for example, J. Harvey Smith, "Work Routine and Social Structure in a French Village: Cruzy in the Nineteenth Century," *Jour. Interdisciplinary Hist.*, V (1975), 362.

[15] Merle Curti et al., *The Making of an American Community: A Case Study of Democracy in a Frontier County* (Stanford, Calif., 1959), chap. 4. Inequality in the Old Northwest was less acute than in Frederick and Berkeley counties in the Shenandoah Valley of Virginia in 1788, where the top 10% of the landowners held nearly 50% of the land, or in the "cotton South," where the top decile controlled between 50% and 55% of the total wealth in 1850 and 1860. See Robert D. Mitchell, "Agricultural Change and the American Revolution: A Virginia Case Study," *Agricultural History*, XLVII (Apr. 1973), 131, and Gavin Wright, "'Economic Democracy' and the Concentration of Agricultural Wealth in the Cotton South, 1850–1860," *Agricultural Hist.*, XLIV (1970), 63–85.

[16] Neil Adams McNall, *An Agricultural History of the Genesee Valley, 1790–1860* (Philadelphia, 1952), 240–241. For the rapid and extensive emergence of farm tenancy in Illinois and Iowa see Paul W. Gates, "Frontier Estate Builders and Farm Laborers," in Richard Hofstadter and Seymour Martin Lipset, eds., *Turner and the Sociology of the Frontier* (New York, 1968), 105, 115–116.

the single economic variable of land transmission. Was the preservation of a landed inheritance the concern of *most* Andover families or only that of the very select group of substantially endowed first settlers and their descendants whom Greven has studied? The pattern of family life, geographic mobility, and economic values may have been very different among later arrivals to Andover—those who had less land to pass on to the next generation—yet this group constituted a majority of the town's population by the eighteenth century. Or what of the pervasive entrepreneurial outlook among Connecticut farmers which is posited by Richard L. Bushman in his stimulating examination of the transition *From Puritan To Yankee?*[17] Bushman's interpretation of the Great Awakening is predicated upon the emergence of an accumulation-oriented pattern of behavior, and yet little—if any—evidence is presented to demonstrate its existence among the mass of the population.

Indeed, the only work which attempts explicitly to demonstrate the predominance of entrepreneurial values among the farming population of New England is the small but influential study by Charles S. Grant, *Democracy in the Connecticut Frontier Town of Kent.* According to Grant, the one-hundred-odd male settlers who arrived in Kent during the late 1730s and the 1740s were "remarkably uniform . . . prosperous enough to buy proprietary shares and to accumulate large amounts of land." They were "versatile and ambitious," and the economic opportunity available in Kent—"fertile (but stony) farming land, . . . deposits of iron ore, and abundant water power for . . . mills"—induced in these settlers "not placid contentment, but an almost frenzied determination to try a hand at everything."[18] Thus "virtually every family settled on a farm which . . . usually produced a salable surplus"; "virtually every family had some member involved as operator or part owner of an ironworks"; and "virtually every early settler was an avid land speculator." By the time of the American Revolution this activity had produced "a population raised on an economic tradition of land speculation and individualistic venturing" which refused to make "economic sacrifices" for the sake of Independence.[19] While Grant indicates that there may have been "humble subsistence farmers" and "obscure yeomen" in the town, he "is impressed not so much with the contented subsistence way of life as with the drive for profits." Indeed, he devotes a chapter to "The Drive For Profits," and concludes it by stressing the acquisitiveness of the economic elite, the "aggressive opportunists" whose ethical standards were "part and parcel of the spirit of Kent." "One sees in certain of the Kent settlers not so much the contended yeoman, certainly not the 'slave' toiling for his master, but perhaps the embryo John D. Rockefeller."[20]

Even when stated in more historically realistic language, Grant's argument is not sustained by his evidence. He begins by distorting much of the allegedly opportunistic and profit-seeking economic activity in Kent by calling it "nonagri-

---

[17] Subtitled: *Character and the Social Order in Connecticut, 1690–1765* (Cambridge, Mass., 1967). The possible bias in Greven's work is suggested in Vinovskis, "American Historical Demography Review Essay," *Historical Methods Newsletter,* IV (Sept. 1971), 142–145.

[18] (New York, 1961), 99, 29, 169–170.

[19] Ibid., 170, 42, 53, 171.

[20] Ibid., 78, 29, 54, 53.

cultural." In actuality, most of the nonfarm enterprises were sawmills, gristmills, fulling mills, and tanneries. These were profit-seeking businesses, but they were also social necessities in a rural community; all were intimately connected to agricultural production. With the exception of the iron industry (the development of which lends some support to Grant's thesis), these enterprises produced primarily for a local market and were so crucial to the welfare of the inhabitants that they were supported by communal action. Following the long New England tradition of material inducements to skilled artisans, the proprietors of the town voted an extra lot in the first division to Ebenezer Barnum "on condition he build a sawmill by the last of December next and also a gristmill in two years."[21] Thus the mere existence of most of these "non-agricultural" enterprises will not substantiate Grant's interpretation. They were traditional, not new, enterprises, practical necessities rather than dramatic innovations, and the product of communal legislation as much as of an adventurous individualism.

A second distortion appears when Grant argues that "the most significant aspect of this enterprise . . . would seem to be the magnitude of profit-seeking activity." "Altogether," he indicates, "209 men were investors in nonagricultural enterprise at Kent between 1739 and 1800."[22] But what is the significance of this number? Neither in his monograph nor in his dissertation does Grant indicate the aggregate number of adult males who lived in Kent during this sixty-year period; yet this total is crucial, for it represents the number of *potential* investors. The statistical material that is available suggests that at least one thousand (and probably one thousand five hundred) adult males worked and resided in Kent during this period; thus the 209 resident "profit-seekers" constituted only 15–20 percent of the potential investing population.[23] What Grant has depicted as the activity and the ethos of most of the inhabitants of Kent becomes, at most, the enterprise and outlook of a well-to-do upper class.

In an attempt to demonstrate the pervasiveness of this entrepreneurial outlook in Kent, Grant adduces another type of evidence. His position—based more on assumption than on argument—is that the sale of "surplus" agricultural products on the market constitutes prima facie evidence of a profit-oriented attitude. Considered abstractly, this is a weak line of reasoning, if only because of the word "surplus" itself. This term, as it was widely used in America until the middle of the nineteenth century, clearly indicated that market sales were a secondary rather than a primary consideration: the "surplus" was what was left over after the yearly subsistence requirements of the farm household had been met.[24]

Even if this faulty reasoning is ignored, the factual evidence will not sustain Grant's argument that a majority of these farmsteads produced a surplus which

---

[21] This vote (as well as the fact that there was a common field system in Kent in the early 1740s) is mentioned in Grant's "A History of Kent, 1738–1796: Democracy on Connecticut's Frontier" (Ph.D. diss., Columbia University, 1957), 43, 57–58, although not in the published version.

[22] Grant, *Democracy in Kent,* 44.

[23] Grant notes that 474 adult males lived in Kent between 1738 and 1760 and that 525 adult males lived in or moved through Kent in the four years 1774–1777. Since some of these 999 men were undoubtedly "double-counted," the total number was somewhat less; but because this calculation pertains only to 26 years out of a total of 62, the total number of resident adult males during this period must have been at least 1,000.

[24] Danhof, *Change in Agriculture,* 17–18.

could be sold or exchanged. Grant himself states that 40 of the 103 farms in Kent in 1796 could provide only enough foodstuffs for the sustenance of their occupants. And this estimate is undoubtedly too low, since his computations assume a grain harvest of twenty-five bushels per acre for both corn and wheat. Such yields might be attained on the best land (and then only for the first harvests), but reliable data from areas as far apart as Massachusetts, Pennsylvania, Virginia, and North Carolina indicate average yields of fifteen bushels per acre for corn and eight to twelve bushels for wheat.[25] If these yields are assumed, the proportion of Kent farmsteads that produced even a small salable surplus drops from two-thirds to one-third; only the most productive farms—15–20 percent of the total—could have produced enough to engage in extensive market transactions.

Why was this case? Was the soil too poor? The climate too forbidding? Or were the aspirations of the settlers too limited? What was the economic and cultural consciousness of the mass of the agricultural population? These questions raise fundamental issues pertaining to the nature of social reality and the sources of human motivation; and their resolution must begin with an investigation of the epistemological premises of the entrepreneurial school of agricultural historians. Once again, Charles Grant offers an ideal entrée, this time as he explicitly acknowledges the source of his interpretation: "Hofstadter suggests," Grant explains in a footnote, "that where the yeoman practiced only subsistence farming, he did so out of necessity (lack of transportation and markets) and not because he was enamored of this way of life. The yeoman farmer wanted profits."[26] At issue here is not the validity of the argument but the assumptions on which it is based. Following Hofstadter, Grant effects a radical disjunction between the constraints imposed by the material and social environment and the yeoman's consciousness. The "drive for profits" simply exists, even given the "lack of transportation and markets." The subsistence way of life does not seem to affect or alter the sensibility of the farmer; consciousness is divorced from condition.

Contemporary observers who spoke to this issue assumed a rather different relationship between environmental opportunities and human goals. "We know," wrote one migrant to the Genesee Valley in 1810, "that people who live far from markets and cannot sell their produce, naturally become indolent and vicious." "There can be no industry without motive," another migrant warned the readers of *The Plough Boy* in 1820, "and it appears to me [that without markets] there is

---

[25] Grant, *Democracy in Kent,* 34, n. 3. The computations appear only in the dissertation, pp. 67–68, 78–79, where heavy reliance is placed on the yields reported in *American Husbandry.* This anonymous work, published in 1775, is criticized for its inflated estimates of farm yields in Harry Roy Merrens, *Colonial North Carolina in the Eighteenth Century: A Study in Historical Geography* (Chapel Hill, N. C., 1964), chap. 6, n. 11. Merrens also provides more reliable estimates (pp. 110ff.), as does Lemon, "Household Consumption in Eighteenth-Century America and Its Relationship to Production and Trade: The Situation Among Farmers in Southeastern Pennsylvania," *Agricultural Hist.,* XLI (1967), 59–70, and *Best Poor Man's Country,* 152–153 (Table 27). In Concord, average grain yields—corn and wheat combined—increased from 12.2 to 15 bushels per acre between 1771 and 1801 (Gross, *Minutemen,* 231), while Mitchell reports wheat yields of 10 bushels per acre in the newly settled Shenandoah Valley ("Agricultural Change," *Agricultural Hist.,* XLVII [1973], 129).

[26] Grant, *Democracy in Kent,* 191. The reference is to Richard Hofstadter, "The Myth of the Happy Yeoman," *American Heritage,* VII (Apr. 1956), 43–53.

great danger that our people will soon limit their exertions to the raising of food for their families."[27] A somewhat similar point had been made in the mid-eighteenth century by William Byrd II when he came upon a fertile allotment that "would be a valuable tract of land in any country but North Carolina, where, for want of navigation and commerce, the best estate affords little more than a coarse subsistence." All were agreed that "convenience and a ready market is the life of a settler—not cheap lands."[28]

Such astute contemporary perceptions constituted the empirical foundations for the argument propounded in 1916 by Percy Bidwell, the leading modern historian of early American agriculture. Why should the farmer specialize, "why should he exert himself to produce a surplus," Bidwell asked in his classic analysis of the rural economy of New England, when there was no market in which to sell it, when "the only return he could expect would be a sort of psychological income?"[29] Bidwell's logic is still compelling, for it is based on epistemological principles that command assent. It recognized, if only implicitly, that there was a considerable diversity of motivation and of economic values among the farm population. In this respect, it echoed the observation of another contemporary. "Farming may be so conducted as to be made profitable, or merely to afford a living[,] or to run out the farm," a Massachusetts writer noted in 1849. "Taking the land as it averages in the state, this depends more on the farmer than on the soil." At the same time, Bidwell insisted that everyone was affected by the structural possibilities and limitations of the society, whatever their cultural propensities or economic aspirations. There was a direct relationship between the material environment, on the one hand, and the consciousness and activity of the population on the other. This understanding informs Bidwell's account and renders it far superior to that of the entrepreneurial school of agricultural historians. "Potatoes are very much used and increased attempts are making to raise them for market," Bidwell quotes the Reverend Samuel Goodrich of Ridgefield, Connecticut (c. 1800), "but the distance from the market is so great that it is not expected the practice will be general."[30] Acquisitive hopes had yielded to geographic realities.

A convincing interpretation of northern agriculture must begin, therefore, not with an ascribed consciousness but rather with an understanding of the dimensions of economic existence. These varied significantly from one region to another, primarily as a result of differential access to an urban or an international market. Yet in every area similar cultural constraints circumscribed the extent of involvement in the market economy. Indeed, the tension between the demands of the market and the expectations stemming from traditional social relationships was a fact of crucial significance in the lives of this pre-industrial population.

Given the absence of an external market, there was no alternative to subsistence or semi-subsistence production.[31] Following the settlement of an inland

---

[27] Quoted in McNall, *Agricultural History of the Genesee Valley,* 104.

[28] Louis B. Wright, ed., *The Prose Works of William Byrd of Westover: Narratives of a Colonial Virginian* (Cambridge, Mass., 1966), 184; McNall, *Agricultural History of the Genesee Valley,* 96.

[29] Percy W. Bidwell, "Rural Economy in New England at the Beginning of the Nineteenth Century," Connecticut Academy of Arts and Sciences, *Transactions,* XX (1916), 330.

[30] Ibid., 317n; The Massachusetts quotation is from Danhof, *Change in Agriculture,* 134.

[31] By these terms I mean limited participation in a commercial market economy. As the preceding quotations suggest, most farm families had enough land, equipment, and labor to raise as

region, for example, there would be a flurry of barter transactions, as established settlers exchanged surplus foodstuffs, seeds, and livestock for the scarce currency and manufactured items brought by newly arrived migrants. Subsequently, the diversification of the local economy created a small demand for farm produce among artisans and traders. Yet neither of these consuming groups was large. Migrants quickly planted their own crops, and most rural artisans cultivated extensive gardens and kept a few head of livestock. The economy had stabilized at a low level of specialization.

This system of local exchange, moreover, did not constitute a market economy in the full sense of the term. Many of these transactions were direct ones—between producers of different types of goods and services—without the involvement of a merchant, broker, or other middlemen. Farm men and women exchanged wheat for tools, meat for furniture, or vegetables for cloth, because their families had a specific personal use for the bartered product. They would attempt to drive a hard bargain or to make a good deal in their negotiations with the blacksmith, cabinetmaker, or seamstress—to insist, for example, on a carefully crafted, high-quality product. Yet their goal was not profit but the acquisition of a needed item for use. "Robt Griffins wife got 10 cocks of hay from me which she is to pay in butter," Matthew Patten of Bedford, New Hampshire, noted in his diary in the 1770s; "I asked her 2£ for a cock." Even when an artisan or merchant would "sell" goods to a farmer and record the obligation in monetary terms, it was assumed that the debt would continue (usually without interest) until it was balanced in a subsequent barter transaction of "Country Produce at Market price."[32]

A market existed, therefore, and it regulated the overall terms of trade among farmers, artisans, and merchants. But this price system was not sovereign; it was often subordinated, in the conduct of daily existence, to barter transactions based on exchange value—what an item was worth to a specific individual. Some goods could not be purchased at any price because they were spoken for by friends, neighbors, or kinfolk. "I went to joseph Farmers and [to] Alexanders to buy some corn," Patten noted in 1770, "but Farmers was all promised and Alexander wood [would] not take 2 pistereens a bushel and I got none."[33] The maximizing of profit was less important to these producers than the meeting of household needs and the maintaining of established social relationships within the community. And it was this "subsistence farm society" which Jackson T. Main correctly specifies as "the most common type throughout New England and perhaps in the entire

---

much food as they could consume. Thus their living standards (in terms of calories and protein) could rise even if they did not engage in extensive market transactions. The pressure of population on resources inhibited such advances, but there were no near-famines or subsistence crises in the northern colonies, as there were, for instance, in France in the 1690s.

[32] Max George Schumacher, *The Northern Farmer and His Markets during the Late Colonial Period*, Dissertations in American Economic History (New York, 1975), 88, 83. For further detail see *The Diary of Matthew Patten of Bedford, N. H. from Seventeen Fifty-Four to Seventeen Eighty-Eight* (Concord, 1903).

[33] Schumacher, *Northern Farmer*, 20. My argument in these two paragraphs is based on Michael Merrill's "Self-Sufficiency and Exchange in the Rural Economy of the United States," *Radical History Review*, VII (1977).

North" until the end of the eighteenth century.[34] As Bidwell argued, "the revolution in agriculture, as well as the breaking down of the self-sufficient village life, awaited the growth of a [large, urban] non-agricultural population."[35]

A commercially oriented agriculture began to develop after 1750, in response to lucrative urban and European markets for American grain. Yet the size of these new trading networks should not be overestimated. The meat exports of the entire state of Connecticut between 1768 and 1773 would have been absorbed by an additional urban population of twenty-two thousand—a city the size of New York; and the shipments of grain from Connecticut ports were even smaller. Exports of wheat and flour from the Middle Colonies during these years were far more substantial, with the annual average equivalent to 2.1 million bushels of wheat. Still, the amount of wheat consumed by the residents of these colonies was nearly twice as large (3.8 million bushels per year). And wheat was normally cultivated on only one-third of the acreage devoted to the production of grain, most of which was corn that was consumed by livestock. The "surplus" wheat exported to foreign markets thus remained a relatively small part of total production (15–20 percent), even for commercially minded family farmers.[36] As late as 1820, "the portion of farm products not consumed within the northern rural community" and sold on all outside markets, both foreign and domestic, amounted to only 25 percent of the total.[37]

Given the existence of a growing European market—a demand for wheat that brought a price rise of 100 percent during the second half of the eighteenth century—the slow and limited commercialization of northern agriculture is significant. Far more dramatic changes were occurring in the South, on slave plantations rather than on family farms. During the years from 1768 to 1773 wheat and flour exports from Virginia and Maryland amounted to 25 percent of the total from the "bread-basket" colonies of New York and Pennsylvania. This "striking expansion of the wheat belt" to the southern colonies after 1750 clearly indicated, as Max Schumacher has argued, "that production on the individual [northern] farms was not elastic enough to cope with the rising wheat market."[38]

---

[34] Main, *Social Structure*, 18. Another important characteristic of many of these communities was an extensive debt structure. Grant notes a "vast tangle of debts" in Kent, with each adult male having an average of 20 creditors in the 1770s. There was no concentration of debts in the hands of a moneylending class; most of the obligations were small, often ran for years, and frequently cancelled each other out. When Elizur Price died in 1777, he had 20 creditors but was himself owed money by 17 men. In more commercial settlements there was a distinct financial elite. When Elisha Hurlbut, a merchant of Windham, Conn., died in 1771, he was owed a total of £590 by no fewer than 77 debtors, and during the preceding 12 years had initiated 212 debt actions (13% of the total) in Windham County Court. See William F. Willingham, "Windham, Connecticut: Profile of a Revolutionary Community, 1775–1818" (Ph.D. diss., Northwestern University, 1972), 77–91, 240–261. The debt structure in Newtown, N. Y., remained extensive as late as 1790, while that in Lancaster, Pa., conformed to the Windham pattern. Ehrlich, "Town Study in Colonial New York," 151–154; Wood, "Conestoga Crossroads," 167–168.

[35] Bidwell, "Rural Economy," Conn. Academy of Arts and Sci., *Trans.*, XX (1916), 353.

[36] Schumacher, *Northern Farmer*, 33, 42 and 42n for the macro-estimates; Lemon, *Best Poor Man's Country*, Tables 27 and 28, and 180–181 indicates that 8 of 26 cultivated acres on a typical farm of 125 acres would be planted in wheat and that 50 bushels of grain (out of a total of 295) would be available for sale or exchange.

[37] Danhof, *Change in Agriculture*, 11, 2.

[38] Schumacher, *Northern Farmer*, 142. See also 110, 154, 167.

The high cost of inland transport was one factor that inhibited the expansion of northern wheat production. A bushel of wheat could be shipped 164 miles on the Hudson River from Albany to New York City in 1769 for fourpence, or 5 percent of its wholesale value, but the proportion rose to 18 percent for a journey of the same distance on the shallow and more difficult waters of the upper Delaware River in Pennsylvania. And the cost of land transportation was much higher. Even in 1816, when the price of grain was high in Philadelphia, the cost of transporting wheat from 50 miles outside the city amounted to one-fourth of the selling price.[39]

Technological restraints and cultural preferences placed even greater limitations on the expansion of wheat production on the family farms of the north. Thomas Jefferson isolated the crucial variable when he noted, in 1793, that planters "allow that every laborer will manage ten acres of wheat, except at harvest." The inefficiency of the sickle, which limited the amount a worker could reap to one-half or three-quarters of an acre per day, placed a severe constraint upon the cultivation of wheat. Large-scale production—with annual yields of 1,000 bushels from 100 acres—was attempted only by those northern producers who were prepared to bid for scarce wage labor during the short harvest season or who controlled a captive labor supply of indentured servants or black slaves. In Somerset County, New Jersey, one farmer relied on the assistance of six blacks to harvest his 80 acres of wheat, while a Trenton proprietor had three blacks to reap 20 acres.[40] Such entrepreneurial farmers were exceptions. They entered the market not only to buy necessities and to sell their surplus but also to buy labor—slaves, servants, wage workers—in order to make a profit. Their farms were "capitalistic" enterprises in the full sense of the term: privately owned productive properties which were operated for profit through a series of market-oriented contractual relationships.

Even in the most market-oriented areas of the Middle Colonies, many farmers participated in the commercial capitalist economy in a much more limited way and with rather different goals. Lacking slaves or indentured servants and unwilling to bid for wage labor, they planted only 8 to 10 acres of wheat each year, a crop that could conveniently be harvested by the farmer, one or two growing sons, and (in some cases) his wife. Of the normal yield of 80 to 100 bushels, 60 would be consumed by the family or saved for seed; the surplus of 20 to 40 bushels would be sold on the Philadelphia market, bringing a cash income in the early 1770s of £5 to £10 sterling. The ordinary male farmer, Lemon concludes, was content to produce "enough for his family and . . . to sell a surplus in the market to buy what he deemed necessities."[41] There was little innovative,

[39] Ibid., 57–59; George Rogers Taylor, *The Transportation Revolution, 1815–1860* (*Economic History of the United States,* IV [New York, 1951]), 133.

[40] Jefferson to President Washington, June 28, 1793, in Andrew A. Lipscomb and Albert E. Bergh, eds., *The Writings of Thomas Jefferson,* IX (Washington, D. C., 1903), 142.

[41] Lemon, *Best Poor Man's Country,* 180; see also Tables 27 and 28 and 179–183. Was there a "motivationally subsistent agricultural class" in the North similar to that found among the poor white population in the South? "A common practice of [southern white cotton] farmers in plantation areas," Julius Rubin has argued, "was to raise the minimal amount of cash crop needed to buy a narrow and rigid range of necessities: tobacco, lead, powder and sugar." For these men, mere participation in the international economy was neither an indication of nor

risk-taking behavior; there was no determined pursuit of profit. Indeed, the account books of these farm families indicate that they invariably chose the security of diversified production rather than hire labor to produce more wheat or to specialize in milk production. Economic gain was important to these men and women, yet it was not their dominant value. It was subordinate to (or encompassed by) two other goals: the yearly subsistence and the long-run financial security of the family unit.

Thus, the predominance of subsistence or semi-subsistence productive units among the yeoman farming families of the northern colonies was not only the result of geographic or economic factors—the ready access to a reliable, expanding market. These men and women were enmeshed also in a web of social relationships and cultural expectations that inhibited the free play of market forces. Much of the output of their farms was consumed by the residents, most of whom were biologically or legally related and who were not paid wages for their labor. A secondary group of consumers consisted of the inhabitants of the local area, members of a community often based on ties of kinship, language, religion, or ethnicity. An impersonal price system figured prominently in these transactions, but goods were often bartered for their exchange value or for what was considered a "just price." Finally, a small (but growing) proportion of the total production of these farms was "sold" on an external market through a series of formal commercial transactions.

If freehold ownership and participation in these urban and international markets meant that northern agriculture did not have many of the characteristics of a closed peasant or a pre-capitalist economy,[42] they do not imply that this system of

---

conducive to the development of an entrepreneurial mentality. See Julius Rubin, "Urban Growth and Regional Development," in David T. Gilchrist, ed., *The Growth of the Seaport Cities, 1790–1825: Proceedings of a Conference Sponsored by the Eleutherian Mills-Hagley Foundation March 17–19, 1966* (Charlottesville, Va., 1967), 15. Two other works that begin to examine the values, behavior, and life style of the poor white agricultural population of the South are Rhys Isaac, "Evangelical Revolt: The Nature of the Baptists' Challenge to the Traditional Order . . . ," *WMQ*, 3d Ser., XXXI (1974), 345–368, and Aubrey C. Land, "Economic Base and Social Structure: The Northern Chesapeake in the Eighteenth Century," *Journal of Economic History*, XXV (1965), 639–654.

[42] There are a number of other reasons for not describing this as a "peasant society," as Kenneth A. Lockridge has done in *A New England Town, The First Hundred Years: Dedham, Massachusetts, 1636–1736* (New York, 1970). Dedham was simply not analogous to the subjugated aboriginal settlements which Eric Wolf depicted as "closed corporate peasant communities" ("Closed Corporate Peasant Communities in Mesoamerica and Central Java," *Southwestern Journal of Anthropology*, X [1957], 1–18). A more realistic comparison is with the peasant societies of early modern Western Europe; and the differences are sufficiently great as to render use of the term unwise in the American context. There were few landlords and no nobility in the northern colonies; the settlement pattern was diffuse rather than nucleated by the 18th century; the central government was weak; the role of the church was limited and the established Congregational churches of New England were non-hierarchical in structure; and the system of property relationships was contractual and malleable. Finally, these American farming communities constituted the central core of the society; they were not "part-societies" and "part-cultures" (in the definition of peasant society advanced by Robert Redfield), dependent upon and exploited by a metropolitan elite.

If a historical analogy is required, then the "post-reform" peasant societies of 19th-century Western Europe are the most appropriate, not those of the ancien régime. See, for example, Walter Goldschmidt and Evelyn Jacobson Kunkel, "The Structure of the Peasant Family," *American Anthropologist*, N. S., LXXIII (1971), 1058–1076. Then, too, the pattern of *family*

production and exchange was modern or that its members were motivated primarily by liberal, entrepreneurial, individualist, or capitalist values. Nor is it sufficient to describe these farming communities as "transitional" between the ideal-types of traditional and modern or pre-capitalist and capitalist. To adopt such an idealist approach is to substitute typology for analysis, to suggest a teleological model of historical development, and to ignore the specific features of this social and economic system. Rather, one must point to its central features: the community was distinguished by age- and wealth-stratification and (usually) by ethnic or religious homogeneity, while on the family level there was freehold property ownership, a household mode of production, limited economic possibilities and aspirations, and a safety-first subsistence agriculture within a commercial capitalist market structure. And then one must seek an understanding of the "coping strategies" used by individuals, groups, and governments to reconcile the competing demands, the inherent tensions, and the immanent contradictions posed by this particular configuration of historical institutions and cultural values.

It would be premature, at this point, to attempt a complete analysis of the *mentalité* of the pre-industrial yeoman population. Yet a preliminary examination may suggest both a conceptual framework for future research and the character of certain widely accepted values, goals, and behavioral norms. An important, and perhaps controversial, premise should be made explicit at the beginning. It is assumed that the behavior of the farm population constitutes a crucial (although not a foolproof) indicator of its values and aspirations. This epistemological assumption has an interpretive implication, for it focuses attention on those activities that dominated the daily lives of the population in the case of this particular society, on the productive tasks that provided food, clothing, and shelter.

This process of production and capital formation derived much of its emotive and intellectual meaning from the cultural matrix—from the institutional character of the society. Work was arranged along familial lines rather than controlled communally or through a wage system. This apparently simple organizational fact was a crucial determinant of the historical consciousness of this farming population. For even as the family gave symbolic meaning and emotional significance to subsistence activities, its own essence was shaped by the character of the productive system. There was a complex relationship between the agricultural labor and property system of early America and its rural culture; and it is that matrix of productive activities, organizational structures, and social values which the following analysis attempts (in a very preliminary fashion) to reconstruct.[43]

---

behavior and values may be similar among small freeholding farmers, whether they live in a yeoman or in a peasant *society:* compare, for example, Greven's Andover families with those analyzed in Lutz K. Berkner, "The Stem Family and the Development Cycle of the Peasant Household: An Eighteenth-Century Austrian Example," *American Historical Review,* LXXVII (1972), 398–418.

[43] The exciting work of E. P. Thompson on the agricultural society of 18th-century England, "The Moral Economy of the English Crowd in the Eighteenth Century," *Past and Present,* L (Feb. 1971), 76–136, and "Patrician Society, Plebian Culture," *Jour. Soc. Hist.,* VII (1974), 382–405, focuses on conflicts engendered by consumption shortages and by asymmetrical authority relationships. It assumes, but does not investigate in detail, class- or wealth-related production differences. A similar concentration on authority, especially in its religious aspects, characterizes the excellent work of Rhys Isaac (see n. 41 above). Ultimately, it will be necessary to specify the relationships among productive activity, religious inclination, and the system of authority.

Because the primary economic unit—the family—was also the main social institution, production activities had an immense impact on the entire character of agrarian life. Family relationships could not be divorced from economic considerations; indeed, the basic question of power and authority within the family hinged primarily on legal control over the land and—indirectly—over the labor needed to work it. The parents (principally the husband) enjoyed legal possession of the property—either as freeholders, tenants, or sharecroppers—but they were dependent on their children for economic support in their old age. Their aim, as Greven has pointed out, was to control the terms and the timing of the transfer of economic resources to the succeeding generation.[44]

The intimate relationship between agricultural production and parental values, between economic history and family history, is best approached through a series of case studies. The first of these small family dramas began in 1739 with the arrival in Kent, Connecticut, of Joseph Fuller. At one time or another Fuller was an investor in an iron works, a "typical speculative proprietor," and a "rich squatter" who tried to deceive the Connecticut authorities into granting him (and his partner Joshua Lassell) 4,820 acres of provincial land. Fuller's energy, ambition, and activities mark him as an entrepreneur, even a "capitalist." Yet his behavior must be seen in the widest possible context, and the motivation assessed accordingly. When this restless man arrived in Kent at the age of forty (with his second wife), he was the father of seven sons, aged two to sixteen; thirteen years later, when his final petition for a land grant was rejected, he had nine sons, aged eleven to twenty-nine years, and five daughters. With fourteen children to provide with land, dowries, or currency, Fuller *had* to embark on an active career if he wished to keep his children (and himself and his wife in their old age) from a life of landless poverty.

In the event, fecundity overwhelmed the Fullers' financial ingenuity. None of the children of Joseph Fuller ever attained a rating on the tax list equal to the highest recorded for their father, and a similar pattern prevailed among the sons of the third generation. The total resources of the Fuller "clan" (for such it had become) grew constantly over time—with nine second- and twelve third-generation males appearing on the tax lists of Kent—but their per capita wealth declined steadily.[45] The gains of one generation, the slow accumulation of capital resources through savings and invested labor, had been dispersed among many heirs.

Such divisions of limited resources inevitably roused resentment and engendered bitter battles within farm families. Ultimately, the delicate reciprocal economic relationship between parents and children might break down completely. Insufficiency of land meant that most children would have to be exiled—apprenticed to wealthier members of the community or sent out on their own as landless laborers—and that parents would have to endure a harsh old age, sharing their small plot with the remaining heir. High fertility and low mortality threatened each generation of children with the loss of class status; the unencumbered inheritance of a freehold estate was the exception, not the rule.

Even in these circumstances—as a second example will suggest—the ideal for

[44] Greven, "Family Structure," *WMQ*, 3d Ser., XXIII (1966), 234–256, and *Four Generations*.

[45] Grant, *Democracy in Kent*, 101, "Diminishing Property: Three Generations of Fullers," Table 13. See also 17, 47–50, 67, 71.

many dispossessed children remained property ownership and eventual control of the transfer process with regard to their own offspring. "My parents were poor," an "Honest Farmer" wrote to the *Pennsylvania Packet* in 1786,

> and they put me at twelve years of age to a farmer, with whom I lived till I was twenty one. . . . I married me a wife—and a very working young woman she was—and we took a farm of forty acres on rent. . . . In ten years I was able to buy me a farm of sixty acres on which I became my own tenant. I then, in a manner, grew rich and soon added another sixty acres, with which I am content. My estate increased beyond all account. I bought several lots of out-land for my children, which amounted to seven when I was forty-five years old.
>
> About this time I married my oldest daughter to a clever lad, to whom I gave one hundred acres of my out-land.[46]

Was this "success story" typical? Did the "Honest Farmer" minimize the difficulties of his own ascent and exaggerate the prospects of his seven children, each of whom would have to be provided with land, livestock, or equipment? It is clear, at any rate, that this Pennsylvanian enjoyed a crucial advantage over Joseph Fuller; he could accumulate capital through the regular sale of his surplus production on the market, and offer economic assistance to his children. His grandchildren, moreover, would grow up in the more fully developed commercial economy of the early nineteenth century. Ten years of work as a farm laborer—and an intense commitment to save—would now yield a capital stock of five hundred dollars. With this sum invested in equipment, livestock, and supplies, it would then be feasible to rent a farm, "with the prospect of accumulating money at a rate perhaps double that possible by wage work."[47] To begin with less than five hundred dollars was to increase dependence on the landlord—to accept a half-and-half division of the produce rather than a two-thirds share. In either case, there was a high financial and psychological price to be paid. For many years these young adults would be "dependent," would work as wage laborers without security, as sharecroppers without land, or as mortgagors without full independence; their labor would enrich freeholders, landlords, and bankers even as it moved them closer to real economic freedom.

This process is readily apparent in a third case study, an archetypical example of the slow but successful accumulation of productive agricultural property in the mid-nineteenth century. In 1843 a young farmer in Massachusetts bought an old farm of 85 acres for $4,337; "in order to pay for it, I mortgaged it for $4,100, paying only $237, all that I had, after buying my stock." Nine years later it was clear that some progress had been made, for he had "paid up about $600 on the mortgage, and laid out nearly $2,000 in permanent improvements on my buildings and farm." This hard-working farmer was "a little nearer the harbor than I was when I commenced the voyage," but he was still $3,500 in debt and had interest payments of $250 to make each year.[48] These obligations might be met in

[46] Quoted in Stevenson W. Fletcher, *Pennsylvania Agriculture and Country Life, 1640–1840* (Harrisburg, 1950), 315.

[47] Danhof, *Change in Agriculture,* 91 and 78–115.

[48] Ibid., 112; quotations are from Amasa Walker, ed., *Transactions of the Agricultural Societies in the State of Massachusetts, for 1852 . . .* (Boston, 1853), 93–94.

225

ten or fifteen years, but by then new debts would have to be incurred in order to provide working capital for his children. This farmer would die a property owner, but at least some of his offspring would face a similarly time-consuming and difficult climb up the agricultural ladder.

Two features of the long-term process of capital formation through agricultural production revealed by these case studies stand out as particularly important, one static and the other dynamic. The recurrent factor was the continual pressure of population on the existing capital stock; the rate of natural increase constantly threatened to outstrip the creation of new productive resources: cleared land, machinery, housing, and livestock. This danger is demonstrable in the case of the Fuller clan, and its specter lurks in the prose of the "Honest Farmer" and his younger accumulation-oriented counterpart in Massachusetts. Economic prosperity was the result of unremitting labor by each generation. Only as farm parents began consciously to limit their fertility were they able to pass on sizable estates to their children—and this occurred primarily after 1830.[49]

What changed—from the seventeenth to the early nineteenth century—was the increased rate of capital formation stemming from the expansion of the market economy; the growing importance of "unearned" profits because of the rise in the value of land and of other scarce commodities; and the extent to which middlemen dominated the processes of agricultural production and of westward migration. These three developments were interrelated. All were aspects of an increasingly important system of commercial agriculture that generated antagonistic social relationships and incipient class divisions. These alterations brought greater prosperity to those farmers whose geographic locations and cultural values were conducive to market activity. The new structural possibilities undoubtedly induced other producers (who might otherwise have been content with their subsistence existence) to raise their output, perhaps even to alter their mode of production by hiring labor or purchasing farm machinery. Certainly, the boom in land values enabled those settlers with substantial estates to reap windfall profits. They had not always purchased their land with speculative resale in mind, but they benefited nonetheless from social and economic forces beyond their control: the surge in population and in agricultural prices both in the American colonies and in Western Europe. Finally, there were individuals and groups who sought to manage the new system of production and exchange. By the mid-eighteenth century, merchants and land speculators had appeared as crucial factors in the westward movement of population, and within another fifty years bankers and mortgage companies were also extracting a share of agricultural production. At some times and places the monetary liens imposed by middlemen and substantial landowners were justified; they represented fair returns for services rendered. More often, the farm population—especially those of its members who were young or landless—paid a disproportionate price for access to the productive system because bankers, speculators, and merchants were able to use their political and economic power to set the terms of exchange in order to gain a greater share

---

[49] Robert Wells, "Family Size and Fertility Control in Eighteenth-Century America: A Study of Quaker Families," *Population Studies*, XXV (1971), 73–82, traces the beginning of this process, while the sequel is explored by Richard A. Easterlin, "Population Change and Farm Settlement in the Northern United States," *Jour. of Econ. Hist.*, XXXVI (1976), 45–75.

of the growing wealth of the society than was warranted by their entrepreneurial contribution.[50]

Even as this process of economic specialization and structural change was taking place, the family persisted as the basic unit of agricultural production, capital formation, and property transmission. This is a point of some importance, for it suggests that alterations in the macro-structure of a society or an economic system do not inevitably or immediately induce significant changes in its micro-units. Social or cultural change is not always systemic in nature, and it proceeds in fits and starts. Old cultural forms persist (and sometimes flourish) within new economic structures; there are "lags" as changes in one sphere of life are gradually reconciled with established values and patterns of behavior.

And so it was in the case of the pre-industrial yeoman family. Changes in societal structure did not alter the basic character of the farm family (although the proportion of such families in the population steadily decreased). As the case studies suggest, the agricultural family remained an extended lineal one; each generation lived in a separate household, but the character of production and inheritance linked these conjugal units through a myriad of legal, moral, and customary bonds. Rights and responsibilities stretched across generations. The financial welfare of both parents and children was rooted in the land and in the equipment and labor needed to farm it. Parents therefore influenced their children's choice of marriage partners. Their welfare, or that of their other children, might otherwise be compromised by the premature division of assets which an early marriage entailed.[51] The line was more important than the individual; the patrimony was to be conserved for lineal purposes.

227

The historical significance of these lineal values was immense. The emphasis on the line or upon the welfare of the entire family, for example, inhibited the emergence of individualism. When the members of this agricultural society traced the contours of their cultural landscape, they began with the assumption—as John Demos has amply demonstrated—that the basic unit was a family, "a little commonwealth," not a man (and still less a woman) "for himself," in their disparaging phrase.[52] This stress on family identity also shaped the character—and often confined the scope—of entrepreneurial activity and capitalist enterprise. Lemon's analysis indicates that most male farmers in Pennsylvania preferred family labor (including the assistance of nearby relatives) to that provided by indentured servants, slaves, or wage laborers. Religious membership was also circumscribed by cultural values, especially in the Congregational churches of New England. As Edmund Morgan argued thirty years ago (in an hypothesis recently supported

---

[50] On this controversial topic see McNall, *Genesee Valley*, 14, 48, 63–64, 240–241, and chap. 4. A favorable view of the tenancy system is offered by Sung Bok Kim, "A New Look at the Great Landlords of Eighteenth-Century New York," *WMQ*, 3d Ser., XXVII (1970), 581–614. Kim succeeds only in demonstrating that their own financial interests often prompted landlords to offer reasonable terms to their tenants; he does not demonstrate the inherent superiority of the tenancy system or that it was not more exploitative than, for instance, the grants of the New England governments during the 17th century or of the U. S. government under the Homestead Acts.

[51] See the discussion in n. 7 above.

[52] John Demos, *A Little Commonwealth: Family Life in Plymouth Colony* (New York, 1970), 77–78.

with quantitative evidence by Gerald Moran), Puritanism quickly became a "tribal" cult, with family lineage the prime determinant of elect status.[53]

Nevertheless, lineal values were not always dominant. And they were often affected by the emergent market economy; indeed, the commercial family–capitalism of the early modern period and the small father-son businesses of the nineteenth century represented striking adaptations of the lineal ideal.[54] Equally significant alterations took place in rural areas, in response to the pressure of population on agricultural resources. In the seventeenth century many settlers had attempted to identify the family with a specific piece of land, to ensure its continued existence by rooting it firmly in space. Thus, in 1673, Ebenezer Perry of Barnstable, Massachusetts, entailed his land to his son Ebenezer and to the latter's "eldest son surviving and so on to the male heirs of his body lawfully begotten forever."[55] Other early inhabitants of Massachusetts preferred to bequeath the family homestead to the youngest son—ultimogeniture—both because this would allow elder siblings to leave the farm at an early age and because the youngest son often came to maturity just as the parents were ready to retire. In either case, the transmission of property was designed to link one generation with the next, and both with "family land."

When the pressure on family resources made it impossible to provide all surviving sons with a portion of the original family estate, the settlers devised alternative strategies of heirship. Some parents uprooted the family and moved to a newly settled area where it would be possible to maintain traditional lineal ties between generations. "The Squire's House stands on the Bank of [the] Susquehannah," Philip Fithian reported from the frontier region of northeastern Pennsylvania in 1775. "He tells me . . . he will be able to settle all his Sons and his fair Daughter *Betsy* on the Fat of the Earth."[56] Other farmers remained in the old community and sought desperately to settle their children on nearby lands. The premature death of one son brought the Reverend Samuel Chandler of Andover, Massachusetts, to remember that he had "been much distressed for land, for his children," and to regret that "he took so much care . . . [for] one is taken away and needs none."[57] From nearby Concord, Benjamin Barrett petitioned the General Court for a grant of land in New Hampshire, since he and many other residents were "without land for their posterity"; yet when this request was

---

[53] Edmund S. Morgan, *The Puritan Family: Religion and Domestic Relations in Seventeenth-Century New England* (Boston, 1944), chap. 6; Gerald Francis Moran, "The Puritan Saint: Religious Experience, Church Membership, and Piety in Connecticut, 1736–1776" (Ph.D. diss., Rutgers Univ., 1974). Moran has analyzed the membership of a number of Congregational churches in Connecticut between the time of their founding (1630s and 1640s) and 1800. He finds that 60 to 70% of all members during that period were either the original founders or their descendants.

[54] See, for example, Bernard Bailyn, "Communications and Trade: The Atlantic in the Seventeenth Century," *Jour. Econ. Hist.*, XIII (1953), 378–387, esp. 380–382.

[55] Quoted in John J. Waters, "The Traditional World of the New England Peasants: A View from Seventeenth-Century Barnstable," *New England Historical and Genealogical Register*, CXXX (1976), 4.

[56] July 26, 1775, Robert Greenhalgh Abion and Leonidas Dodson, eds., *Philip Vickers Fithian: Journal, 1775–1776, Written on the Virginia-Pennsylvania Frontier* . . . (Princeton, N. J., 1934), 71; Jack Goody, "Strategies of Heirship," *Comparative Studies in Society and History*, XV (1973), 3–20.

[57] Samuel Chandler, diary entry for Dec. 23, 1745, quoted in Greven, *Four Generations*, 254.

granted, none of the petitioners migrated to the new settlement. When Barrett died in 1728, the income from these western lands helped to settle two sons on his Concord estate and two younger sons on farms in nearby Worcester County.[58]

This imaginative use of western land rights to subsidize the local settlement of offspring may have been fairly widespread. Of the forty-one men who were the original purchasers of proprietary shares in Kent, Connecticut, twenty-five did not become inhabitants of the town but sold their rights to residents, relatives, and neighbors. Still, the limited availability of arable land in the older communities of New England and the Middle Colonies ruled out this option for most parents. The best they could do was to finance the migration of some children while keeping intact the original farmstead. Both in Newtown, Long Island, and in German areas of Pennsylvania in the eighteenth century, fathers commonly willed the family farm to the eldest son, requiring him to pay a certain sum of money to his younger brothers and his sisters. In other cases, the farm was "sold" to one son or son-in-law, with the "profits" of the transaction being divided among the other children—daughters usually receiving one-half the amount bestowed on the sons.[59]

These attempts by individual farmers to preserve a viable family estate reflected a set of values that was widespread in the community and which eventually received a formal legal sanction. When the appraisers of intestate property in Concord, Massachusetts, reported that a property could not be divided "without Spoiling the Whole," the probate court granted the farm intact to one heir (usually the eldest son), requiring him to compensate his brothers and sisters for their shares in the estate.[60] Such rulings confirmed the societal norm: even as New England parents wrote wills that divided their lands, they encouraged or directed their children to reconstitute viable economic units, with regard to both size and access. As Mark Hasket of Rochester, Massachusetts, wrote in his will: "my sons shall not any of them debar or hinder one another from having a way over each others Land when and where there may be ocation for it."[61]

There were other respects in which the central position of the lineal family (rather than the conjugal unit or the individual) was reflected in the legal system. On the death of her husband, a wife normally received the "right" to one-third of the real property of the estate. Yet this control was strictly limited: it usually lapsed upon remarriage and, even more significant, did not include the privilege of sale. The widow's "third" had to be preserved intact, so that upon her death the property could revert to the heirs of the estate. More important than the

229

---

[58] Gross, *Minutemen*, 80.

[59] Ehrlich, "Town Study in Colonial New York," 123–127; John C. Gagliardo, "Germans and Agriculture in Colonial Pennsylvania," *Pennsylvania Magazine of History and Biography*, LXXXIII (1959), 192–198; Greven, *Four Generations*, 234–245. Ryan records a typical intergenerational arrangement: "Samuel Day, having seven sons, could only provide an estate for three sons, leaving them to pay sons David, Robert, Abraham and Jared £100 apiece" ("Six Towns," 85).

[60] Gross, "Problem of Agricultural Crisis in Eighteenth-Century New England," 8. Of the landed estates settled in probate in Concord between 1738 and 1775, 60% were not divided; only 25% were divided among three or more heirs.

[61] Quoted in Waters, "Traditional World of New England Peasants," *NEHGR*, CXXX (1976), 7; Danhof, *Change in Agriculture*, 80.

economic freedom of the widow—her rights as an individual—was the protection of the estate and the line of succession. These deeply held values were preserved even in the more diverse, money-oriented economy of eastern Massachusetts in the eighteenth century; the law was changed to permit widows to sell family property, but the court carefully regulated such transactions to ensure that the capital of the estate would be used for the support of the child-heirs.[62] Property was "communal" within the family, with the limits of alienation strictly limited by custom or by law. Even as the link to the land was broken the intimate tie between the estate and the lineal family was reaffirmed.

These traditional notions of family identity were subjected to considerable strain by the mid-nineteenth century. The psychological dimensions of the economic changes that diminished the importance of the family farm as the basic productive unit are revealed, in an oblique fashion, in the naming patterns practiced by parents in Hingham, Massachusetts. During the colonial period, most parents in this agricultural settlement did not perceive their children as "unique *per se*." If a child died, his or her existence was perpetuated indirectly, for the same forename was normally given to the next infant of the same sex, especially when the dead child carried the same name as one of the parents. This necronymic pattern, with its obvious emphasis on the line rather than the individual, persisted in Hingham until the 1840s. So also did the tendency of parents to name their first children after themselves—to entail the parental name, as it were, and thus to stress the continuity between generations.[63] As economic change altered the structure and character of Hingham society, these lineal conceptions of identity gradually yielded to more individualistic ones. After 1800 first sons were given the same forenames as their fathers but a distinctive middle name. This was a subtle and complex compromise, for these middle names were often family names as well (the mother's surname, for example)—yet another manifestation of the persistence of traditional forms in a time of transition.

It is significant that this shift toward a distinctive personal identity—toward individualism—has been traced in Hingham, Massachusetts, one of the oldest English settlements in America, and not on the frontier. A similar development may have resulted from (or accompanied) the westward movement, but it is equally likely—Frederick Jackson Turner to the contrary—that lineal family values were *more* important than individualism in the new farming communities of the old Northwest. For farm families usually trained and encouraged their children "to succeed *them*, rather than to 'succeed' by rising in the social system."[64]

[62] Alexander Keyssar, "Widowhood in Eighteenth-Century Massachusetts: A Problem in the History of the Family," *Perspectives in American History*, VIII (1974), 100–111.

[63] Daniel Scott Smith, "Child-Naming Patterns and Family Structure Change: Hingham, Massachusetts, 1640–1880" (unpub. paper, 1975), 10. Over 60% of first sons and over 70% of first daughters bore the same forename as their parents in 17th-century Hingham families, and the proportions remained high until the first children of the 1861–1880 marriage cohorts, when "the respective fractions are two-fifths and one-sixth."

[64] The quotation refers to the socialization process in a "tradition-directed" culture, as described by David Riesman, *The Lonely Crowd: A Study of the Changing American Character* (New Haven, Conn., 1950), 40, 17–18. See also Joseph F. Kett, "Adolescence and Youth in Nineteenth-Century America," *Jour. Interdisciplinary Hist.*, II (1971), 283–299. As Nancy Cott and R. Jackson Wilson have pointed out to me, the agricultural journals of the 1830s are filled with articles and letters expressing parental concern over the urban migration of farm youth; such sentiments suggest the persistence of lineal, farming-oriented values.

The young adults of thriving farm communities were not forced to confront the difficult problems of occupational choice and psychological identity as were those from depressed and overcrowded rural environments or growing cities. The dimensions of existence had expanded in the East, even as the eighteenth-century patterns of farm life, community stratification, and family identity were being recreated, in a modified form, in the new settlements of the West.

In some of these older and crowded communities in New England and the Middle States, lineal family values remained important well into the nineteenth century because they were consistent, at least temporarily, with rural industrialization and an emergent market economy. Fathers and mature sons continued to farm the (now depleted or subdivided) land while mothers, daughters, and younger sons turned their talents and energies to the production of textiles, shoes, and other items. The period between 1775 and 1815 was "the heyday of domestic manufactures" in America.[65]

The family factory assumed major economic importance as a result of the commercial dislocations produced by the War for Independence; household production of linen and woolen cloth was increased to compensate for the lack of English imports. Subsequently, this enlarged productive capacity was systematically organized by American entrepreneurs. In some cases, merchants sought out new markets for household manufactures and then capitalized part of the productive process itself, providing necessary materials and credit through the "putting out" system. Tens of thousands of "Negro shoes" were sold to southern slaveholders by Quaker merchants from Lynn, Massachusetts; and this productive network extended far back into the New England countryside. An even more important product of the rural family factory was wearing apparel. In New York State the production of textiles increased steadily until 1825, when the per capita output of household looms amounted to 8.95 yards.[66]

This extraordinary household output was made possible not only by the existence of a regional or national market—the product of a mature merchant-directed commercial capitalism—but also by the peculiar evolution of the factory system. By the late eighteenth century certain operations which were difficult in the home—such as fulling, carding, dyeing, and spinning in the case of textile production—had been assumed, with constantly increasing efficiency, by small mills. This process of specialization was as yet incomplete; eventually the weaving of cloth (as well as the preparation of the yarn) would be removed from the home and placed in the factory. For the moment—indeed for more than a generation—this final stage in the "evolution of the simple household industry into the . . . factory system" was held in abeyance by technological constraints, and the family factory reigned supreme.[67] Rural industrialization expanded the productive capacity of the society and systematically integrated female labor into the market economy; but it did so without removing the family from the center of economic life.

---

[65] Lewis C. Gray, *History of Agriculture in the Southern United States to 1860*, I (Washington, 1933), 455; Rolla Milton Tryon, *Household Manufactures in the United States, 1640–1860* (New York, 1966 [orig. publ. Chicago, 1917]), esp. 243–276.

[66] Paul G. Faler, "Workingmen, Mechanics and Social Change: Lynn, Massachusetts, 1800–1860" (Ph.D. diss., University of Wisconsin, 1971), 41–43; Taylor, *Transportation Revolution*, 212–213; Tryon, *Household Manufactures*, 190, 276–279, 370–371, and Tables 12, 16, 18.

[67] Tryon, *Household Manufactures*, 243–259, 272–276; Danhof, *Change in Agriculture*, 20–21.

One result was to perpetuate, for another generation, the delicate and reciprocally beneficial economic relationship between eastern farm parents and their offspring. The intergenerational exchange of youthful labor for an eventual inheritance had been threatened in the mid-eighteenth century by land scarcity, which diminished the financial security of aging parents and their ability or willingness to assist their children. Some young adults implicitly rebuked their parents by migrating; others stayed and exercised a gentle form of coercion. Nineteen percent of all first births registered in Concord, Massachusetts, in the 1740s were premaritally conceived, and the proportion rose to 40 percent in Concord, Hingham, and many other northern communities by the end of the century. "If they were again in the same circumstances," one observer noted, these young men and women "would do the same again, because otherwise they could not obtain their parents' consent to marry."[68] Once the legal and financial concessions were extracted from reluctant parents, marriage quickly followed. Both parents and children shunned illegitimacy; both accepted the cultural norm of stable family existence.

Whatever their economic weakness and vulnerability to youthful persuasion, parents retained significant power over their offspring. Affective bonds remained strong, and they were augmented by the power of the state. Young men who wished to work outside the household unit before they attained their legal majority were obliged to buy their economic freedom, undertaking in written contracts to pay their parents a certain sum in return for the privilege. Similarly, the first New England mill girls turned at least a portion of their earnings over to their parents; they were working outside the home but not for themselves as unattached individuals.[69] The lineal family remained predominant, in large part because there were few other institutions in early nineteenth-century America that could assume its social and economic functions—few schools, insurance companies, banks, or industries to provide training and capital for the new generation, and comfort and security for the old. Only a major structural change in the society itself—the widespread appearance of non-familial social, economic, and political organizations—would undermine the institutions of lineage; until this occurred there were simply no "alternatives to the family as a source of provision for a number of crucially important needs."[70]

The lineal family—not the conjugal unit and certainly not the unattached individual—thus stood at the center of economic and social existence in northern agricultural society in pre-industrial America. The interlocking relationship between the biological life cycle and the system of agricultural (and domestic) production continued to tie the generations together even as the wider economic structure was undergoing a massive transformation and as the proportion of farming families in the population was steadily declining. Most men, women and

[68] Quoted in Daniel Scott Smith and Michael S. Hindus, "Premarital Pregnancy in America, 1640–1971: An Overview and Interpretation," *Jour. Interdisciplinary Hist.,* V (Spring 1975), 557; Gross, *Minutemen,* 217, 235.

[69] Joseph F. Kett, "Growing Up in Rural New England, 1800–1840," in Tamara K. Hareven, ed., *Anonymous Americans: Explorations in Nineteenth-Century Social History* (Englewood Cliffs, N. J., 1971), 1–16; Joan W. Scott and Louise A. Tilly, "Women's Work and the Family in Nineteenth-Century Europe," *Comparative Studies in Soc. and Hist.,* XV (Jan. 1975), 36–64.

[70] Michael Anderson, *Family Structure in Nineteenth-Century Lancashire* (Cambridge, 1971), 96.

children in this yeoman society continued to view the world through the prism of family values. This cultural outlook—this inbred pattern of behavior—set certain limits on personal autonomy, entrepreneurial activity, religious membership, and even political imagery.[71] Lineal family values did not constitute, by any means, the entire world view—the *mentalité*—of the agricultural population, but they did define a central tendency of that consciousness, an abiding core of symbolic and emotive meaning; and, most important of all, they constituted a significant and reliable guide to behavior amid the uncertainties of the world.

Author's Postscript

How did I come to conclude in "Families and Farms" that most rural folk were not agrarian entrepreneurs? In *The Evolution of American Society,* published six years previously, I had posited the existence in eighteenth-century America of a "new entrepreneurial personality" that "knew no geographic or social limits." Drawing on Charles Grant's work, I had depicted the farmers of Kent, Connecticut, as men with "materialistic values" and as exemplars "of the capitalistic ethos and behavior patterns which had become pervasive in the rural as well as the urban sector of the northern economy."[72] What changed my mind?

In a word: the classroom. As I taught the new social history to undergraduates and graduates, I became convinced that the widespread presence of an entrepreneurial personality was very unlikely given the character of many aspects of family and community life. That perception prompted me to reexamine the evidence on which Grant's interpretation (and similar accounts by James Lemon and others) was based.[73] It was the weakness of that evidence that ultimately caused me to advance a counter-interpretation of the *mentalité* of northern farm families.

But that was not the end of matter. Having rejected the sovereignty of the market and the predominance of acquisitive values in colonial America, how could I explain the emergence of a capitalist economy and society by the early nineteenth century? The answer to that question took shape in several articles written during the 1980s and collected in *The Origins of American Capitalism.*[74] I have no illusions that the restatement and elaboration of my interpretation outlined there will silence my critics but I hope it will advance the debate. In any event, I have had my say and, because I am now pursuing other scholarly interests, happily leave the discussion to others.[75]

---

[71] An extended discussion of the importance of family imagery in 18th-century politics, political theory, and the War for Independence is Edwin G. Burrows and Michael Wallace, "The American Revolution: The Ideology and Psychology of National Liberation," *Perspectives in Am. Hist.,* VI (1972), 167–306.

[72] Henretta, *The Evolution of American Society, 1700–1815* (Lexington, Mass., 1973), 103.

[73] Lemon, *Best Poor Man's Country,* Bushman, *From Puritan to Yankee,* Richard Hofstadter, "The Myth of the Happy Yeoman," *American Heritage,* VII (April 1956), 43–53.

[74] Henretta, *Origins of American Capitalism: Collected Essays* (Boston, 1991).

[75] For a balanced treatment (and attempted resolution) of the debate see Allan Kulikoff, *The Agrarian Origins of American Capitalism* (Charlottesville, Va., 1992), chaps. 1, 2.

George Robert Twelves Hewes (1742–1840): A Boston Shoemaker and the Memory of the American Revolution

ALFRED F. YOUNG

Late in 1762 or early in 1763, George Robert Twelves Hewes, a Boston shoe-maker in the last year or so of his apprenticeship, repaired a shoe for John Hancock and delivered it to him at his uncle Thomas Hancock's store in Dock Square. Hancock was pleased and invited the young man to "come and see him on New Year's day, and bid him a happy New-Year," according to the custom of the day, a ritual of noblesse oblige on the part of the gentry. We know of the episode through Benjamin Bussey Thatcher, who interviewed Hewes and wrote it up for his *Memoir* of Hewes in 1835. On New Year's Day, as Thatcher tells the story, after some urging by his master,

> George washed his face, and put his best jacket on, and proceeded straight-away to the Hancock House (as it is still called). His heart was in his mouth, but assuming a cheerful courage, he knocked at the front door, and took his hat off. The servant came:
>
> "Is 'Squire Hancock at home, Sir?" enquired Hewes, making a bow.
>
> He was introduced directly to the *kitchen,* and requested to seat himself, while report should be made above stairs. The man came down directly, with a new varnish of civility suddenly spread over his face. He ushered him into the 'Squire's sitting-room, and left him to make his obeisance. Hancock remembered him, and addressed him kindly. George was anxious to get through, and he commenced a desperate speech—"as pretty a one," he says, "as he any way knew how,"—intended to announce the purpose of his visit, and to accomplish it, in the same breath.

This essay would not have been possible without the help of a large number of scholars, librarians, and descendants and friends of the Hewes family. I acknowledge each of these at the relevant point. I wish to express my special appreciation to three scholars who read and commented on the essay in several drafts: Jesse Lemisch, Gary Nash, and Lawrence W. Towner. Michael Kammen and James Henretta also offered valuable reactions to an early draft. My debt to Jesse Lemisch is large; he helped me to work out problems too numerous to mention and provided a pioneering example of a biography of an ordinary person in "The American Revolution and the American Dream: A Life of Andrew Sherburne, a Pensioner of the Navy of the Revolution" (Columbia University Seminar on Early American History and Culture, 1975) to be published in his *The American Revolution and the American Dream.* I have also profited from the criticism of colleagues at the Conference on the "New" Labor History and the New England Working Class, Smith College, 1979; the Graduate Colloquium, Northern Illinois University; and the Newberry Library Seminar in Early American History. Research for the paper was completed on a Newberry Library-National Endowment for the Humanities Fellowship.

Ed. Note: This article was originally published in *William and Mary Quarterly,* 3d Ser., XXXVIII (October 1981), 561–623.

"Very well, my lad," said the 'Squire—now take a chair, my lad."

He sat down, scared all the while (as he now confesses) "almost to death," while Hancock put his hand into his breeches-pocket and pulled out a crown-piece, which he placed softly in his hand, thanking him at the same time for his punctual attendance, and his compliments. He then invited his young friend to drink his health—called for wine—poured it out for him—and ticked glasses with him,—a feat in which Hewes, though he had never seen it performed before, having acquitted himself with a creditable dexterity, hastened to make his bow again, and secure his retreat, though not till the 'Squire had extorted a sort of half promise from him to come the next New-Year's—which, for a rarity, he never discharged.[1]

The episode is a demonstration of what the eighteenth century called deference.

Another episode catches the point at which Hewes had arrived a decade and a half later. In 1778 or 1779, after one stint in the war on board a privateer and another in the militia, he was ready to ship out again, from Boston. As Thatcher tells the story: "Here he enlisted, or engaged to enlist, on board the Hancock, a twenty-gun ship, but not liking the manners of the Lieutenant very well, who ordered him one day in the streets to take his hat off to him—which he refused to do for any man,—he went aboard the 'Defence,' Captain Smedley, of Fairfield Connecticut."[2] This, with a vengeance, is the casting off of deference.

What had happened in the intervening years? What had turned the young shoemaker tongue-tied in the face of his betters into the defiant person who would not take his hat off for any man? And why should stories like this have stayed in his memory sixty and seventy years later?

George Robert Twelves Hewes was born in Boston in 1742 and died in Richfield Springs, New York, in 1840. He participated in several of the principal political events of the American Revolution in Boston, among them the Massacre and the Tea Party, and during the war he served as a privateersman and militiaman. A shoemaker all his life, and intermittently or concurrently a fisherman, sailor, and farmer, he remained a poor man. He never made it, not before the war in Boston, not at sea, not after the war in Wrentham and Attleborough, Massachusetts, not in Otsego County, New York. He was a nobody who briefly became a somebody in the Revolution and, for a moment near the end of his life, a hero.

Hewes might have been unknown to posterity save for his longevity and a shift in the historical mood that rekindled the "spirit of '76." To Americans of the 1830s the Boston Tea Party had become a leading symbol of the Revolution, and Hewes lived long enough to be thought of as one of the last surviving participants, perhaps the very last. In 1833, when James Hawkes "discovered" him in the "obscurity" of upstate New York, Hewes was ninety-one but thought he was ninety-eight, a claim Hawkes accepted when he published the first memoir of

235

[1] A Bostonian [Benjamin Bussey Thatcher], *Traits of the Tea Party; Being a Memoir of George R. T. Hewes, One of the Last of Its Survivors; With a History of That Transaction; Reminiscences of the Massacre, and the Siege, and Other Stories of Old Times* (New York: Harper & Brothers, 1835), 52–55, hereafter cited as Thatcher, *Memoir of Hewes*.

[2] Ibid., 226–227.

Hewes that year.[3] Thus in 1835 when Hewes was invited to Boston, people thought that this survivor of one of the greatest moments of the Revolution was approaching his one hundredth birthday and on "the verge of eternity," as a Fourth of July orator put it.[4] He became a celebrity, the guest of honor on Independence Day, the subject of a second biography by Thatcher and of an oil portrait by Joseph Cole, which hangs today in Boston's Old State House.

To Thatcher, Hewes was one of the "humble classes" that made the success of the Revolution possible. How typical he was we can only suggest at this point in our limited knowledge of the "humble classes." Probably he was as representative a member of the "lower trades" of the cities and as much a rank-and-file participant in the political events and the war as historians have found. The two biographies, which come close to being oral histories (and give us clues to track down Hewes in other ways), provide an unusually rich cumulative record, over a very long period of time, of his thoughts, attitudes, and values. Consequently, we can answer, with varying degrees of satisfaction, a number of questions about one man of the "humble classes." About the "lower trades": why did a boy enter a craft with such bleak prospects as shoemaking? what was the life of an apprentice? what did it mean to be a shoemaker and a poor man in Boston? About the Revolution: what moved such a rank-and-file person to action? what action did he take? may we speak of his "ideology"? does the evidence of his loss of deference permit us to speak of change in his consciousness? About the war: how did a poor man, an older man, a man with a family exercise his patriotism? what choices did he make? About the results of the Revolution: how did the war affect him? to what extent did he achieve his life goals? why did he go west? what did it mean to be an aged veteran of the Revolution? What, in sum, after more than half a century had passed, was the meaning of the Revolution to someone still in the "humble classes"?

236

I

A wide variety of sources can be used to check Hewes's recollections, fill in what is missing in the biographies, and supply context. But to get at Hewes, the historian has essentially a major double task: separating him from his biographers and sifting the memories of a man in his nineties to recover actions and feelings from sixty to eighty years before. The problem is familiar to scholars who have used the rich body of W.P.A. narratives of former slaves taken down by interviewers in the 1930s and who have had to ask: who recorded these recollections, under what circumstances, and with what degree of skill? how does memory function in the aged? what is remembered best and least? how do subsequent emotions and values color or overlie the memory of events in the distant past?[5]

[3] A Citizen of New York [James Hawkes], *A Retrospect of the Boston Tea-Party, with a Memoir of George R. T. Hewes, a Survivor of the Little Band of Patriots Who Drowned the Tea in Boston Harbour in 1773* (New York: S. Bliss, printer, 1834), hereafter cited as Hawkes, *Retrospect.*

[4] *Evening Mercantile Journal* (Boston), July 6, 1835.

[5] C. Vann Woodward, "History from Slave Sources," *American Historical Review,* LXXIX (1974), 470–481. For the related problems in slave memoirs see John W. Blassingame, *The Slave Community: Plantation Life in the Antebellum South,* rev. ed. (New York, 1979), 369–378.

237

George Robert Twelves Hewes, "The Centenarian," by Joseph G. Cole, Boston, 1835. Courtesy, The Bostonian Society, Old State House, Boston.

The two biographies of Hewes were part of "a spate" of narratives of the Revolution by ordinary soldiers and sailors that appeared in print, especially from the 1820s on.[6] Together with the autobiographies, diaries, and journals, unpublished at the time, we know of at least 500 such first-person accounts of men who saw military service.[7] Much of this remembering was stimulated by the pension laws of 1818 and especially of 1832 that required veterans to submit, in lieu of written records, "a very full account" of their military service. These laws produced no less than 80,000 personal narratives—Hewes's among them—which are finally coming under the scrutiny of historians.[8]

Hawkes and Thatcher had different strengths and weaknesses. We know hardly anything about James Hawkes; he took the pseudonym "A New Yorker" and published in New York City. He may have been a journalist.[9] He discovered Hewes by an "accidental concurrence of events" and interviewed him in his familiar surroundings in Richfield Springs over several days in 1833 around the Fourth of July. Hawkes's virtue was that he tried to take down Hewes in the first person, although more often than not he lapsed into the third person or interrupted Hewes's narrative with long digressions, padding the story. He did not know enough about either the Revolution or Boston to question Hewes or follow up his leads, and he had a tendency to use Hewes as an exemplar of the virtues of Benjamin Franklin and selfless patriotism. But in his ignorance he allowed Hewes to structure his own story and convey his own feelings. Thus the book at times has an "as told to" flavor, and when Hawkes allows Hewes to speak, we can agree that "his language is remarkable for its grammatical simplicity and correctness."[10]

Benjamin Bussey Thatcher, on the other hand, intruded, as the language of his account of the visit to John Hancock suggests. He could not resist embellish-

---

[6] Michael Kammen, *A Season of Youth: The American Revolution and the Historical Imagination* (New York, 1978), 26; Richard M. Dorson, ed., *America Rebels: Narratives of the Patriots,* 2d ed. rev. (New York, 1966), 17. Dorson, defining "narrative" somewhat loosely, counted over 200 entries in the Library of Congress catalog; in his appendix he lists 37, 11 of which appeared between 1822 and 1833.

[7] J. Todd White and Charles H. Lesser, eds., *Fighters for Independence: A Guide to Sources of Biographical Information on Soldiers and Sailors of the American Revolution* (Chicago, 1977), lists under "Diaries, Journals and Autobiographies" 538 entries, both published and in manuscript. Walter Wallace, "'Oh, Liberty! Oh, Virtue! Oh, My Country!' An Exploration of the Minds of New England Soldiers During the American Revolution" (M. A. thesis, Northern Illinois University, 1974), is based on 164 published diaries. Also relevant is Jesse Lemisch, "The American Revolution Bicentennial and the Papers of Great White Men," American Historical Association, *Newsletter,* IX (Nov., 1971), 7–21, as well as "The Papers of Great White Men," *Maryland Historian,* VI (1975), 43–50, and "The Papers of a Few Great Black Men and a Few Great White Women," ibid., 60–66.

[8] John C. Dann, ed., *The Revolution Remembered: Eyewitness Accounts of the War for Independence* (Chicago, 1980), introduction. For other scholars who have made use of the pension applications see the works cited in sec. VI below. John Shy and Dann are directing a project, "Data Bank for American Revolutionary Generation," William L. Clements Library, University of Michigan, Ann Arbor, Mich., based on samples from the 1818 and 1832 pension applications.

[9] Cataloguers attribute the book to James Hawkes on the basis of the copyright entry on the overleaf of the title page. I am indebted to Walter Wallace for searching for Hawkes in the New York Public Library, unfortunately without success.

[10] The body of Hawkes's book with the memoir runs 115 pages, about 27,000 words; a lengthy preface and an appendix bring it to 206 pages.

ing Hewes's stories or inventing dialogue. He brought to Hewes the same compassion for the lowly and sense of the uses of history that he brought to other historical subjects. A Boston gentleman, reformer, abolitionist, Bowdoin graduate, and lawyer, at the age of twenty-six he had written a short biography of Phillis Wheatley, Boston's black poet of the eighteenth century, a memoir of a Liberian missionary, and four volumes on American Indians, two of them collections of biographies.[11] Thatcher talked to Hewes on the latter's "triumphal" return to Boston in 1835, walked him around town, primed his memory. He lifted almost everything in Hawkes (without attribution) but also extracted a good many new anecdotes, especially about Hewes's youth, and expanded others about the Revolution. Occasionally he was skeptical; he read old newspapers and talked to other survivors to check the background. Thatcher thus added to the record, although in a form and tone that often seem more his own than Hewes's. And while his interests as a reformer led him to inquire, for example, about schools and slavery in Hewes's Boston, they also led him to dissociate Hewes from the "mob," probably with some distortion. Thus Thatcher's portrayal, while fuller than Hawkes's, is also more flawed.[12]

Hewes's remembering, once distinguished from the overlay of these biographies, also had strengths and weaknesses. He was, to begin with, in remarkable physical condition. In 1833 Hawkes found his "physical and intellectual" powers "of no ordinary character." "I have generally enjoyed sound health," Hewes said. He showed few signs of his advanced age. His hair was light brown, salted with gray, and he had most of it. He was not bent down by his years but was "so perfectly erect" and moved "with so much agility and firmness . . . that he might be taken for a man in all the vigour of youth." He regularly walked two or three miles each day, and for his sessions with Hawkes he walked five miles back and forth to Hawkes's lodgings. He was of such an "active disposition" that Hawkes found he would hardly stay put long enough to be interviewed. When Hewes became excited, his "dark blue eyes," which Hawkes called "an index to an intelligent and vigorous mind," would "sparkle with a glow of lustre."[13] Thatcher was impressed with "a strength and clearness in his faculties" often not present in men twenty years younger. "Both his mental and bodily faculties are wonderfully hale. He converses with almost the promptness of middle life." His mind did not wander. He answered questions directly, and "he can seldom be detected in any redundancy or deficiency of expression." He was not garrulous.[14]

Both men were amazed at Hewes's memory. Thatcher found it "so extraordinary" that at times it "absolutely astonished" him.[15] Hewes recounted details from many stages of his life: from his childhood, youth, and young adulthood, from the years leading up to the Revolution, from seven years of war. While he

239

---

[11] *Dictionary of American Biography,* s.v. "Thatcher, Benjamin Bussey." See also Nehemiah Cleaveland, *History of Bowdoin College. With Biographical Sketches of its Graduates . . . ,* ed. Alpheus Spring Packard (Boston, 1882), 356–358.

[12] Thatcher's book has 242 pages, about 49,000 words, plus a short appendix.

[13] Hawkes, *Retrospect,* 13–16, 85–93.

[14] Thatcher, *Memoir of Hewes,* iv, 250–253.

[15] Ibid., 250, and examples at 52, 89, 95, 112.

told next to nothing about the next half-century of his life, his memory of recent events was clear. He graphically recalled a trip to Boston in 1821. He remembered names, a remarkable array of them that Thatcher checked.[16] He remembered how things looked; he even seemed to recall how things tasted. Most important, he remembered his own emotions, evoking them once again. He seems to have kept no diary or journal, and by his own claim, which Hawkes accepted, he had not read any accounts of the Tea Party or by implication any other events of the Revolution.[17]

His mind worked in ways that are familiar to students of the processes of memory.[18] Thus he remembered more for Thatcher in Boston in 1835 than for Hawkes in Richfield Springs in 1833. This is not surprising; he was warmed up and was responding to cues as he returned to familiar scenes and Thatcher asked him pointed questions. Having told many episodes of his life before—to his children and grandchildren, and to children and adults in Richfield Springs—he thus had rehearsed them and they came out as adventure stories.

His memory also displayed common weaknesses. He had trouble with his age, which may not have been unusual at a time when birthdays were not much celebrated and birth certificates not issued.[19] He had trouble with sequences of events and with the intervals of time between events. He was somewhat confused, for example, about his military tours of duty, something common in other veterans' narratives.[20] He also got political events in Boston somewhat out of order, telescoping what for him had become one emotionally. Or he told his good stories first, following up with the less interesting ones. All this is harmless enough. He remembered, understandably, experiences that were pleasant, and while he did well with painful experiences that had been seared into him—like childhood punishments and the Boston Massacre—he "forgot" other experiences that were humiliating. There are also many silences in his life story, and where these cannot be attributed to his biographers' lack of interest (as in his humdrum life from 1783 to 1833), because his memory is so good we are tempted to see significance in these silences.

All in all, we are the beneficiaries in Hewes of a phenomenon psychologists recognize in "the final stage of memory" as "life review," characterized by "sudden emergence of memories and a desire to remember, and a special candour which goes with a feeling that active life is over, achievement is completed." A British historian who has taken oral history from the aged notes that "in this final

---

[16] For example, Hewes gave Hawkes, who had no way of prompting or correcting him, the more or less correct names and occupations of the five victims of the Boston Massacre, five leading loyalist officials, and half-a-dozen relatives he visited in 1821. A typical error was "Leonard Pitt" for Lendell Pitts as his "Captain" at the Tea Party.

[17] Hawkes, *Retrospect,* 28.

[18] See Ian M. L. Hunter, *Memory* (London, 1957), esp. chap. 6.

[19] According to John R. Sellers, "many [veterans who applied for pensions under the 1818 act] did not know how old they were" ("The Origins and Careers of New England Soldiers, Non-Commissioned Officers, and Privates in the Massachusetts Continental Line" [unpubl. paper, American Historical Association, 1972], 4–5, cited with the author's permission). Sellers was able to compute the ages of 396 men in a sample of 546.

[20] Dann, ed., *Revolution Remembered,* xx. For examples in which narratives faulty in some respects still checked out as essentially credible, see ibid., 204–211, 240–250, 268–274.

stage there is a major compensation for the longer interval and the selectivity of the memory process, in an increased willingness to remember, and commonly too a diminished concern for fitting the story to the social norms of the audience. Thus bias from both repression and distortion becomes a less inhibiting difficulty, for both teller and historian."[21]

On balance, Hewes's memory was strong, yet what he remembered, as well as the meaning he attached to it, inevitably was shaped by his values, attitudes, and temperament. There was an overlay from Hewes as well as his biographers. First, he had a stake, both monetary and psychic, in his contribution to the Revolution. He had applied for a pension in October 1832; by the summer of 1833, when he talked to Hawkes, it had been granted. He had also become a personage of sorts in his own locale, at least on the Fourth of July. And when he talked with Thatcher he was bathed in Boston's recognition. Thus though he did not have to prove himself (as did thousands of other veterans waiting for action on their applications), he had spent many years trying to do just that. Moreover, he had to live up to his reputation and had the possibility of enhancing it.

Secondly, he may have imposed an overlay of his current religious values on the younger man. He had generally been "of a cheerful mind," he told Hawkes, and Thatcher spoke of the "cheerfulness and evenness of his temper."[22] There is evidence for such traits earlier in his life. In his old age, however, he became a practicing Methodist—composed in the assurance of his own salvation, confident of his record of good deeds, and forgiving to his enemies. As a consequence he may well have blotted out some contrary feelings he had once held. One suspects he had been a much more angry and aggressive younger man than he or his biographers convey.

Finally, in the 1830s he lived in a society that no longer bestowed the deference once reserved for old age and had never granted much respect to poor old shoemakers.[23] In the Revolution for a time it had been different; the shoemaker won recognition as a citizen; his betters sought his support and seemingly deferred to him. This contributed to a tendency, as he remembered the Revolution, not so much to exaggerate what he had done—he was consistently modest in his claims for himself—as to place himself closer to some of the great men of the time than is susceptible to proof. For a moment he was on a level with his betters. So he thought at the time, and so it grew in his memory as it disappeared in his life. And in this memory of an awakening to citizenship and recognition from his betters we shall argue—a memory with both substance and shadow—lay the meaning of the Revolution to George Hewes.

---

[21] Paul Thompson, *The Voice of the Past: Oral History* (Oxford, 1978), 113 and chap. 4. For a remarkable example of this in a black sharecropper interviewed in his 85th year see Theodore Rosengarten, *All God's Dangers: The Life of Nate Shaw* (New York, 1974). See also John Neuenschwander, "Remembrance of Things Past: Oral Historians and Long-Term Memory," *Oral History Review,* VI (1978), 45–53.

[22] Hawkes, *Retrospect,* 93; Thatcher, *Memoir of Hewes,* 251.

[23] See David Hackett Fischer, *Growing Old in America,* expanded ed. (New York, 1978), esp. chap. 2.

II

In 1756, when Hewes was fourteen, he was apprenticed to a shoemaker. Why did a boy become a shoemaker in mid-eighteenth-century Boston? The town's shoemakers were generally poor and their prospects were worsening. From 1756 to 1775, eight out of thirteen shoemakers who died and left wills at probate did not even own their own homes.[24] In 1790, shoemakers ranked thirty-eighth among forty-four occupations in mean tax assessments.[25]

It was not a trade in which boys were eager to be apprentices. Few sons continued in their father's footsteps, as they did, for example, in prosperous trades like silversmithing or shipbuilding.[26] Leatherworkers, after mariners, headed the list of artisans who got their apprentices from the orphans, illegitimate children, and boys put out to apprenticeship by Boston's Overseers of the Poor.[27] In England, shoemaking was a trade with proud traditions, symbolized by St. Crispin's Day, a shoemakers' holiday, a trade with a reputation for producing poets, philosophers, and politicians, celebrated by Elizabethan playwrights as "the gentle craft."[28] But there were few signs of a flourishing shoemaker culture in Boston before the Revolution. In children's lore shoemakers were proverbially poor, like the cobbler in a Boston chapbook who "labored hard and took a great deal of pains for a small livelihood."[29] Shoemakers, moreover, were low in status. John Adams spoke of shoemaking as "too mean and dimi[nu]tive an Occupation" to hold a client of his who wanted to "rise in the World."[30]

[24] Based on a computer print-out of all wills at probate entered at Suffolk County Court, kindly loaned to me by Gary B. Nash. For analysis of the context see his "Urban Wealth and Poverty in Pre-Revolutionary America," *Journal of Interdisciplinary History,* VI (1976), 545–584, and *The Urban Crucible: Social Change, Political Consciousness, and the Origins of the American Revolution* (Cambridge, Mass., and London, 1979), chap. 7. Before 1735, eight shoemakers on the probate list ended up in the top 10% of wealthholders (albeit most at the bottom of that bracket), but from 1736 to 1775 only one did.

[25] Allan Kulikoff, "The Progress of Inequality in Revolutionary Boston," *William and Mary Quarterly,* 3d Ser., XXVIII (1971), 375–412; James A. Henretta, "Economic Development and Social Structure in Colonial Boston," ibid., XXII (1965), 75–92. The 1771 tax assessment does not list occupations; the 1780 assessment, which does, is incomplete; the 1790 list is the first point at which occupations can be measured for wealth.

[26] In Nash's list of 61 shoemakers, 1685–1775, 7 names are repeated, appearing twice; after 1752, no name is repeated (see above, n. 24). For examples of trades passed down within families see Esther Forbes, *Paul Revere & the World He Lived In* (Boston, 1942). For a family engaged in shipbuilding over six generations see Bernard Farber, *Guardians of Virtue: Salem Families in 1800* (New York, 1972), 104–108.

[27] Lawrence W. Towner, "The Indentures of Boston's Poor Apprentices: 1734–1805," Colonial Society of Massachusetts, *Transactions,* XLIII (1966), 417–468. The maritime, shipbuilding, and leather trades each accounted for about 8% of the boys; about 40% went into husbandry. From 1751 to 1776, 26 boys were put out to cordwainers, 6 in Boston, 20 in country towns.

[28] Eric Hobsbawm and Joan Scott, "Political Shoemakers," *Past and Present,* No. 89 (1980), 86–114, which the authors kindly allowed me to see in MS. See also Peter Burke, *Popular Culture in Early Modern Europe* (London, 1978), 38–39.

[29] *The Most Delightful History of the King and the Cobler . . .* ([Boston, 1774]), reprinted from an English chapbook; and also printed in *Crispin Anecdotes; Comprising Interesting Notices of Shoemakers . . .* (Sheffield, Eng., 1827).

[30] John Adams, June 17, 1760, in L. H. Butterfield et al., eds., *Diary and Autobiography of John Adams,* I (Cambridge, Mass., 1961), 135.

Where one ended up in life depended very much on where one started out. George was born under the sign of the Bulls Head and Horns on Water Street near the docks in the South End. His father—also named George—was a tallow chandler and erstwhile tanner. Hewes drew the connections between his class origins and his life chances as he began his narrative for Hawkes:

> My father, said he, was born in Wrentham in the state of Massachusetts, about twenty-eight miles from Boston. My grandfather having made no provision for his support, and being unable to give him an education, apprenticed him at Boston to learn a mechanical trade. . . .

> In my childhood, my advantages for education were very limited, much more so than children enjoy at the present time in my native state. My whole education which my opportunities permitted me to acquire, consisted only of a moderate knowledge of reading and writing; my father's circumstances being confined to such humble means as he was enabled to acquire by his mechanical employment, I was kept running of errands, and exposed of course to all the mischiefs to which children are liable in populous cities.[31]

Hewes's family on his father's side was "no better off than what is called in New England *moderate,* and probably not as good."[32] The American progenitor of the line seems to have come from Wales and was in Salisbury, near Newburyport, in 1677, doing what we do not know. Solomon Hewes, George Robert's grandfather, was born in Portsmouth, New Hampshire, in 1674, became a joiner, and moved with collateral members of his family to Wrentham, originally part of Dedham, near Rhode Island. There he became a landholder; most of his brothers were farmers; two became doctors, one of whom prospered in nearby Providence. His son—our George's father—was born in 1701,[33] On the side of his mother, Abigail Seaver, Hewes's family was a shade different. They had lived for four generations in Roxbury, a small farming town immediately south of Boston across the neck. Abigail's ancestors seem to have been farmers, but one was a minister.[34] Her father, Shubael, was a country cordwainer who owned a house, barn, and two acres. She was born in 1711 and married in 1728.[35]

George Robert Twelves Hewes, born August 25, 1742, was the sixth of nine children, the fourth of seven sons. Five of the nine survived childhood—his three older brothers, Samuel, Shubael, and Solomon, and a younger brother, Daniel. He was named George after his father, Robert after a paternal uncle, and the unlikely Twelves, he thought, for his mother's great uncle, "whose Christian

---

[31] Hawkes, *Retrospect,* 17–18.

[32] Thatcher, *Memoir of Hewes,* 11.

[33] For a very full genealogy and family history of the several branches of the Hewes family see Eben Putnam, comp., *Lieutenant Joshua Hewes: A New England Pioneer and Some of his Descendants . . .* (New York, 1913).

[34] William B. Trask, "The Seaver Family," *New-England Historical and Genealogical Register,* XXVI (1872), 303–323.

[35] Will of Shubael Seaver, Suffolk Co. Probate Court, LII, 20–21, a copy of which was provided by Gary Nash.

name was Twelve, for whom she appeared to have great admiration. Why he was called by that singular name I never knew." More likely, his mother was honoring her own mother, also Abigail, whose maiden name was Twelves.[36]

The family heritage to George, it might be argued, was more genetic than economic. He inherited a chance to live long: the men in the Seaver line were all long-lived. And he inherited his size. He was unusually short—five feet, one inch. "I have never acquired the ordinary weight or size of other men," Hewes told Hawkes, who wrote that "his whole person is of a slight and slender texture." In old age he was known as "the little old man."[37] Anatomy is not destiny, but Hewes's short size and long name helped shape his personality. It was a big name for a small boy to carry. He was the butt of endless teasing jibes—George Robert what?—that Thatcher turned into anecdotes the humor of which may have masked the pain Hewes may have felt.[38]

"Moderate" as it was, Hewes had a sense of family. Wrentham, town of his grandfather and uncles, was a place he would be sent as a boy, a place of refuge in the war, and after the war his home. He would receive an inheritance three times in his life, each one a reminder of the importance or potential importance of relatives. And he was quite aware of any relative of status, like Dr. Joseph Warren, a distant kinsman on his mother's side.[39]

His father's life in Boston had been an endless, futile struggle to succeed as a tanner. Capital was the problem. In 1729 he bought a one-third ownership in a tannery for £600 in bills of credit. Two years later, he sold half of his third to his brother Robert, who became a working partner. The two brothers turned to a rich merchant, Nathaniel Cunningham, who put up £3500 in return for half the profits. The investment was huge: pits, a yard, workshops, hides, bark, two horses, four slaves, journeymen. For a time the tannery flourished. Then there was a disastrous falling out with Cunningham: furious fights, a raid on the yards, debtors' jail twice for George, suits and countersuits that dragged on in the courts for years. The Hewes brothers saw themselves as "very laborious" artisans who "managed their trade with good skill," only to be ruined by a wealthy, arrogant merchant. To Cunningham, they were incompetent and defaulters. Several years before George Robert was born, his father had fallen back to "butchering, tallow chandlering, hog killing, soap boiling &c."[40]

The family was not impoverished. George had a memory as a little boy of boarding a ship with his mother to buy a small slave girl "at the rate of two dollars a pound."[41] And there was enough money to pay the fees for his early schooling. But beginning in 1748, when he was six, there was a series of family tragedies. In 1748 an infant brother, Joseph, died, followed later in the year by his sister

---

[36] Trask, "Seaver Family," *NEHGR,* XXVI (1872), 306; Putnam, comp., *Joshua Hewes,* 318.

[37] Hawkes, *Retrospect,* 18, 86.

[38] Thatcher, *Memoir of Hewes,* 26–33. Hewes did not volunteer these anecdotes to Hawkes.

[39] Ibid., 129, 132. Warren was his grandmother's sister's son.

[40] Petitions by Nathaniel Cunningham and George and Robert Hewes, 1740–1743, MS, Massachusetts Archives, Manufactures, LIX, 316–319, 321–324, 334–337, 342–345, State House, Boston. I am indebted to Ruth Kennedy for running down Hewes and his family in a variety of legal and other sources in Boston, and to Gary Nash for his help in interpreting the sources.

[41] Thatcher, *Memoir of Hewes,* 38.

Abigail, age thirteen, and brother Ebenezer, age two. In 1749 his father died suddenly of a stroke, leaving the family nothing it would seem, his estate tangled in
debt and litigation.[42] George's mother would have joined the more than one
thousand widows in Boston, most of whom were on poor relief.[43] Sometime
before 1755 she died. In 1756 Grandfather Seaver died, leaving less than £15 to
be divided among George and his four surviving brothers. Thus in 1756, at the
age of fourteen, when boys were customarily put out to apprenticeship, George
was an orphan, the ward of his uncle Robert, as was his brother Daniel, age
twelve, each with a legacy of £2 17s. 4d. Uncle Robert, though warmly recol-
lected by Hewes, could not do much to help him: a gluemaker, he was struggling
to set up his own manufactory.[44] Nor could George's three older brothers, whom
he also remembered fondly. In 1756 they were all in the "lower" trades. Samuel,
age twenty-six, and Solomon, twenty-two, were fishermen; Shubael, twenty-
four, was a butcher.

The reason why George was put to shoemaking becomes clearer: no one in
the family had the indenture fee to enable him to enter one of the more lucrative
"higher" trades. Josiah Franklin, also a tallow chandler, could not make his son
Benjamin a cutler because he lacked the fee.[45] But in shoemaking the prospects
were so poor that some masters would pay to get an apprentice. In addition,
George was too small to enter trades that demanded brawn; he could hardly have
become a ropewalk worker, a housewright, or a shipwright. Ebenezer McIntosh,
the Boston shoemaker who led the annual Pope's Day festivities and the Stamp
Act demonstrations, was a small man.[46] The trade was a sort of dumping ground
for poor boys who could not handle heavy work. Boston's Overseers of the Poor
acted on this assumption in 1770;[47] So did recruiting officers for the American

245

---

[42] Letter of Administration, Estate of George Hewes, Suffolk Co. Probate Court, 1766, Docket
No. 13906.

[43] Alexander Keyssar, "Widowhood in Eighteenth-Century Massachusetts: A Problem in the
History of the Family," *Perspectives in American History,* VIII (1974), 98, 116–119. A census of
1742 showed 1,200 widows, "one thousand whereof are in low circumstances," in a population
of 16,382 (Nash, *Urban Crucible,* 172).

[44] Petition of Robert Hewes, Nov. 1752, MS, Mass. Archs., Manufactures, LIX, 372–374. He is
not to be confused with Robert Hewes (1751–1830) of Boston, a highly successful glassmaker
(*DAB,* s.v. "Hewes, Robert"), or the father of this man, also Robert, who migrated from
England c. 1751. See petitions of Robert Hewes to the General Court, May 25 and June 8,
1757 (in a different hand from that of Uncle Robert), Mass. Archs., Manufactures, LIX,
434–435.

[45] Benjamin Franklin, *The Autobiography of Benjamin Franklin,* ed. Leonard W. Labaree et al.
(New Haven, Conn., 1964), 57.

[46] George P. Anderson, "Ebenezer McIntosh: Stamp Act Rioter and Patriot," Col. Soc. Mass.,
Trans., XXVI (1927), 15–64 (hereafter cited as Anderson, "Ebenezer McIntosh"), and "A Note
on Ebenezer McIntosh," ibid., 348–361.

[47] The Overseers of the Poor first put out Thomas Banks, age eight, to a farmer, William
Williams. In 1770 Williams informed the Overseer that Thomas "is now seventeen years . . .
old and about as big as an ordinary Country boy of thirteen . . . and scarcely able to perform the
service of one of our boys of that age," and so he placed him with a cordwainer. Williams to
Royal Tyler, Jan. 23, 1770, in Towner, "Boston's Poor Apprentices," Col. Soc. Mass., *Trans.,*
LXIII (1966), 430–431.

navy forty years later.[48] The same was true in Europe.[49] Getting into a good trade required "connections"; the family connections were in the leather trades, through Uncle Robert, the gluemaker, or brother Shubael, the butcher. Finally, there was a family tradition. Grandfather Shubael had been a cordwainer, and on his death in 1756 there might even have been a prospect of acquiring his tools and lasts. In any case, the capital that would be needed to set up a shop of one's own was relatively small. And so the boy became a shoemaker—because he had very little choice.

III

Josiah Franklin had known how important it was to place a boy in a trade that was to his liking. Otherwise there was the threat that Benjamin made explicit: he would run away to sea. Hawkes saw the same thrust in Hewes's life: shoemaking "was never an occupation of his choice," he "being inclined to more active pursuits."[50] George was the wrong boy to put in a sedentary trade that was not to his liking. He was what Bostonians called "saucy"; he was always in Dutch. The memories of his childhood and youth that Thatcher elicited were almost all of defying authority—his mother, his teachers at dame school, his schoolmaster, his aunt, his shoemaker master, a farmer, a doctor.

Hewes spoke of his mother only as a figure who inflicted punishment for disobedience. The earliest incident he remembered could have happened only to a poor family living near the waterfront. When George was about six, Abigail Hewes sent him off to the nearby shipyards with a basket to gather chips for the fire. At the water's edge George put the basket aside, straddled some floating planks to watch the fish, fell in, and sank to the bottom. He was saved only when some ship carpenters saw the basket without the boy, "found him motionless on the bottom, hooked him out with a boat hook, and rolled him on a tar barrel until signs of life were discovered." His mother nursed him back to health. Then she flogged him.[51]

The lesson did not take, nor did others in school. First there was a dame school with Miss Tinkum, wife of the town crier. He ran away. She put him in a dark closet. He dug his way out. The next day she put him in again. This time he discovered a jar of quince marmalade and devoured it. A new dame school with "mother McLeod" followed. Then school with "our famous Master Holyoke,"

---

[48] James Biddle to David Conner, Aug. 9, 1813, Fourth Auditor Accounts Numerical Series, #1141, Record Group 217, National Archives, kindly brought to my attention by Christopher McKee.

[49] Hobsbawm and Scott write that "there is a good deal of evidence that small, weak or physically handicapped boys were habitually put to this trade" ("Political Shoemakers," *Past and Present*, No. 89 [1980], 96–97).

[50] Hawkes, *Retrospect*, 23–24; Franklin, *Autobiography*, ed. Labaree et al., 57. For a boy whose threats forced his parents to allow him to go to sea see Lemisch, "Life of Andrew Sherburne," sec. III.

[51] Thatcher, *Memoir of Hewes*, 17–18. For a boy in the laboring classes who fell into a cistern of rain water and was rescued from drowning see Isaiah Thomas, *Three Autobiographical Fragments . . .* (Worcester, Mass., 1962), 7.

which Hewes remembered as "little more than a series of escapes made or attempted from the reign of the birch."[52]

Abigail Hewes must have been desperate to control George. She sent him back after one truancy with a note requesting Holyoke to give him a good whipping. Uncle Robert took pity and sent a substitute note. Abigail threatened, "If you run away again I shall go to school with you myself."[53] When George was about ten, she took the final step: she sent him to Wrentham to live with one of his paternal uncles. Here, George recalled, "he spent several years of his boyhood . . . in the monotonous routine of his Uncle's farm." The only incident he recounted was of defying his aunt. His five-year-old cousin hit him in the face with a stick "without any provocation." George cursed the boy out, for which his aunt whipped him, and when she refused to do the same with her son, George undertook to "chastise" him himself. "I caught my cousin at the barn" and applied the rod. The aunt locked him up but his uncle let him go, responsive to his plea for "equal justice."[54]

Thus when George entered his apprenticeship, if he was not quite the young whig his biographers made him out to be, he was not a youth who would suffer arbitrary authority easily. His master, Downing, had an irascible side and was willing to use a cowhide. Hewes lived in Downing's attic with a fellow apprentice, John Gilbert. All the incidents Hewes recalled from this period had two motifs: petty defiance and a quest for food. There was an escapade on a Saturday night when the two apprentices made off for Gilbert's house and bought a loaf of bread, a pound of butter, and some coffee. They returned after curfew to encounter an enraged Downing, whom they foiled by setting pans and tubs for him to trip over when he came to the door. There was an excursion to Roxbury on Training Day, the traditional apprentices' holiday in Boston, with fellow apprentices and his younger brother. Caught stealing apples, they were taken before the farmer, who was also justice of the peace and who laughed uproariously at Hewes's name and let him go. There was an incident with a doctor who inoculated Hewes and a fellow worker for smallpox and warned them to abstain from food. Sick, fearful of death, Hewes and his friend consumed a dish of venison in melted butter and a mug of flip—and lived to tell the tale.[55]

These memories of youthful defiance and youthful hunger lingered on for seventy years: a loaf of bread and a pound of butter, a parcel of apples, a dish of venison. This shoemaker's apprentice could hardly have been well fed or treated with affection.

The proof is that Hewes tried to end his apprenticeship by the only way he saw possible: escape to the military. "After finding that my depressed condition would probably render it impracticable for me to acquire that education requisite for civil employments," he told Hawkes, "I had resolved to engage in the military service of my country, should an opportunity present." Late in the 1750s, possibly

247

---

[52] Thatcher, *Memoir of Hewes,* 18–26.

[53] Ibid., 25.

[54] Hawkes, *Retrospect,* 21–22.

[55] Thatcher, *Memoir of Hewes,* 29–47. Thatcher presented this story as occurring shortly after Hewes became 21, which might make it 1764, the year of a massive smallpox inoculation campaign in Boston.

in 1760, as the fourth and last of England's great colonial wars with France ground on and his majesty's army recruiters beat their drums through Boston's streets, Hewes and Gilbert tried to enlist. Gilbert was accepted, but Hewes was not. Recruiting captains were under orders to "enlist no Roman-Catholic, nor any under five feet two inches high without their shoes." "I could not pass muster," Hewes told Hawkes, "because I was not tall enough."[56] As Thatcher embroiders Hawkes's story, Hewes then "went to the shoe shop of several of his acquaintances and heightened his heels by several taps [;] then stuffing his stocking with paper and rags," he returned. The examining captain saw through the trick and rejected him again. Frustrated, humiliated, vowing he would never return to Downing, he took an even more desperate step: he went down to the wharf and tried to enlist on a British ship of war. "His brothers, however, soon heard of it and interfered," and, in Thatcher's words, "he was compelled to abandon that plan." Bostonians like Solomon and Samuel Hewes, who made their living on the waterfront, did not need long memories to remember the city's massive resistance to the impressment sweeps of 1747 and to know that the British navy would be, not escape, but another prison.[57]

About this time, shoemaker Downing failed after fire swept his shop (possibly the great fire of 1760).[58] This would have freed Hewes of his indenture, but he was not qualified to be a shoemaker until he had completed apprenticeship. As Hewes told it, he therefore apprenticed himself "for the remainder of his minority," that is, until he turned twenty-one, to Harry Rhoades, who paid him $40. In 1835 he could tell Thatcher how much time he then had left to serve, down to the month and day. Of the rest of his "time" he had no bad memories.[59]

248 Apprenticeship had a lighter side. Hewes's anecdotes give tantalizing glimpses into an embryonic apprentice culture in Boston to which other sources attest— glimpses of pranks played on masters, of revelry after curfew, of Training Day, when the militia displayed its maneuvers and there was drink, food, and "frolicking" on the Common. One may speculate that George also took part in the annual Pope's Day festival, November 5, when apprentices, servants, artisans in the lower trades, and young people of all classes took over the town, parading effigies of Pope, Devil, and Pretender, exacting tribute from the better sort, and engaging in a battle royal between North End and South End Pope's Day "companies."[60]

---

[56] Hawkes, *Retrospect*, 23–25. See also *By His Excellency William Shirley, Esq.* . . . (Boston, Apr. 17, 1755), with the eligibility requirement, and *By His Excellency Thomas Pownall* . . . (Boston, Apr. 10, 1758, and Mar. 14, 1760), broadsides, Lib. Cong.

[57] Thatcher, *Memoir of Hewes*, 47–49. For the anti-impressment riots of 1747 see Jesse Lemisch, "Jack Tar in the Streets: Merchant Seamen in the Politics of Revolutionary America," *WMQ*, 3d Ser., XXV (1968), 371–407, and John Lax and William Pencak, "The Knowles Riot and the Crisis of the 1740's in Massachusetts," *Perspectives Am. Hist.*, X (1976), 163–214.

[58] This may have been the great fire of 1760. I find no record of a Downing in the claims filed by 365 sufferers in "Records Relating to the Early History of Boston," *Report of the Record Commissioners of the City of Boston* (Boston, 1876–1909), XXIX, hereafter cited as *Record Commissioners' Reports,* but the published records are incomplete.

[59] Thatcher spelled his name Rhoades (*Memoir of Hewes*, 49–50). Henry Roads is listed as a cordwainer assigned an apprentice Oct. 30, 1752, in Towner, "Boston's Poor Apprentices," Col. Soc. Mass., *Trans.*, XLIII (1966), Table, [441]. If the apprenticeship ran the customary seven years, Rhoades (or Roads) would have needed another one in 1760, which would fit Hewes's story.

[60] Alfred Young, "Pope's Day, Tar and Feathers, and Cornet Joyce, Jun: From Ritual to

Hewes's stories of his youth, strained as they are through Thatcher's condescension, hint at his winning a place for himself as the small schoolboy who got
the better of his elders, the apprentice who defied his master, perhaps even a
leader among his peers. There are also hints of the adult personality. Hewes was
punished often, but if childhood punishment inured some to pain, it made Hewes
reluctant to inflict pain on others. He developed a generous streak that led him to
reach out to others in trouble. When Downing, a broken man, was on the verge
of leaving for Nova Scotia to start anew, Hewes went down to his ship and gave
him half of the $40 fee Rhoades had paid him. Downing broke into tears. The
story smacks of the Good Samaritan, of the Methodist of the 1830s counting his
good deeds; and yet the memory was so vivid, wrote Thatcher, that "his features
light up even now with a gleam of rejoicing pride." Hewes spoke later of the
"tender sympathies of my nature."[61] He did not want to be, but he was a fit candidate for the "gentle craft" he was about to enter.

IV

In Boston from 1763, when he entered his majority, until 1775, when he
went off to war, Hewes never made a go of it as a shoemaker. He remembered
these years more fondly than he had lived them. As Hawkes took down his story,
shifting from the third to the first person:

> Hewes said he cheerfully submitted to the course of life to which his
> destinies directed.
>
> He built him a shop and pursued the private avocation of his trade for a
> considerable length of time, until on the application of his brother he was
> induced to go with him on two fishing voyages to the banks of New
> Foundland, which occupied his time for two years.
>
> After the conclusion of the French war . . . he continued at Boston,
> except the two years absence with his brother.
>
> During that period, said Hewes, when I was at the age of twenty-six, I
> married the daughter of Benjamin Sumner, of Boston. At the time of our
> intermarriage, the age of my wife was seventeen. We lived together very
> happily seventy years. She died at the age of eighty-seven.
>
> At the time when the British troops were first stationed at Boston, we
> had several children, the exact number I do not recollect. By our industry
> and mutual efforts we were improving our condition.[62]

Thatcher added a few bits to this narrative, some illuminating. The "little
shop was at the head of Griffin's Wharf," later the site of the Tea Party. Benjamin
Sumner, "if we mistake not," was a "sexton of one of the principal churches in

249

Rebellion in Boston" (unpubl. MS, Anglo-American Labor Historians' Conference, 1973). See
also Thomas, *Three Autobiographical Fragments,* 22–25, for one apprentice's near-fatal participation.

[61] Thatcher, *Memoir of Hewes,* 50–52. For another anecdote about a gift of food during the siege
of Boston see ibid., 204.

[62] Hawkes, *Retrospect,* 26–27.

town." His wife was a "washer-woman" near the Mill Pond, assisted by her five daughters. Hewes courted one of the girls when he "used to go to the house regularly every Saturday night to pay Sally for the week's washing." The father was stern, the swain persistent, and after a couple of years George and Sally were married. "The business was good, and growing better," Thatcher wrote, "especially as it became more and more fashionable to encourage our own manufactures."[63]

The reality was more harsh. What kind of shoemaker was Hewes? He had his own shop—this much is clear, but the rest is surmise. There were at that time in Boston about sixty to seventy shoemakers, most of whom seem to have catered to the local market.[64] If Hewes was typical, he would have made shoes to order, "bespoke" work; this would have made him a cordwainer. And he would have repaired shoes; this would have made him a cobbler. Who were his customers? No business records survive. A shoemaker probably drew his customers from his immediate neighborhood. Located as he was near the waterfront and the ropewalks, Hewes might well have had customers of the "meaner" sort. In a ward inhabited by the "middling" sort he may also have drawn on them. When the British troops occupied Boston, he did some work for them. Nothing suggests that he catered to the "carriage trade."[65]

Was his business "improving" or "growing better"? Probably it was never very good and grew worse. From his own words we know that he took off two years on fishing voyages with his brothers. He did not mention that during this period he lived for a short time in Roxbury.[66] His prospects were thus not good enough to keep him in Boston. His marriage is another clue to his low fortune. Sally (or Sarah) Sumner's father was a sexton so poor that his wife and daughters had to take in washing. The couple was married by the Reverend Samuel Stillman of the First Baptist Church, which suggests that this was the church that Benjamin Sumner served.[67] Though Stillman was respected, First Baptist was not

---

[63] Thatcher, *Memoir of Hewes,* 58–64.

[64] My estimate. There were 78 shoemakers in Boston in 1790, when there were 2,995 people on the assessment rolls in a population of 18,000 (Kulikoff, "Progress of Inequality," *WMQ,* 3d Ser., XXVIII [1971], 412). I count 26 shoemakers in 1780, when there were 2,225 on the assessment rolls in a population of less than 15,000 and at a time when poorer men were apt to be at war (Boston Assessing Dept., *Assessors' "Talking Books" of the Town of Boston 1780* [Boston, 1912]). If the population of Boston was 20% smaller in 1774 than in 1790, with a proportional loss of shoemakers, it would have included 63 shoemakers. For comparisons of occupational breakdowns see Jacob Price, "Economic Function and the Growth of American Port Towns in the Eighteenth Century," *Perspectives Am. Hist.,* VIII (1974), 176, 181.

[65] See Thatcher, *Memoir of Hewes,* 39–40, 85, for evidence that he made and repaired shoes. Griffin's Wharf was in the area of the tenth and eleventh wards where in 1771 the mean tax assessment was £193 and £254, twice as high as the mean in the crowded North End wards but considerably below the mean of £695 in the center of town (see Kulikoff, "Progress of Inequality," *WMQ,* 3d Ser., XXVIII [1971], 395, map).

[66] Putnam, comp., *Joshua Hewes,* 335.

[67] "Boston Town Records," in *Record Commissioners' Reports,* III, 65; "Boston Marriages, 1752–1809," ibid., XXX, 65; and Samuel Stillman, "Record of Marriages from the Year 1761" indicate marriage by Stillman. The records of the First Baptist Church, including the Minutes, List of Adult Baptisms and Pew Proprietors Record Book, do not show the names of either the Sumners or the Heweses as members or of Sumner (or anyone else) as sexton (MS, Andover Newton Theological Seminary, Andover, Mass.). Researched by Elaine Weber Pascu.

"one of the principal churches in town," as Thatcher guessed, but one of the poorest and smallest, with a congregation heavy with laboring people, sailors, and blacks.[68] Marriage, one of the few potential sources of capital for an aspiring tradesman, as Benjamin Franklin made clear in his autobiography, did not lift Hewes up.

Other sources fill in what Hewes forgot. He married in January 1768. In September 1770 he landed in debtors' prison. In 1767 he had contracted a debt of £6 8s. 3d. to Thomas Courtney, a merchant tailor, for "making a sappled coat & breeches of fine cloth." The shoemaker bought this extravagant outfit when he was courting. What other way was there to persuade Sally's parents that he had good prospects? Over the three years since, he had neither earned enough to pay the debt nor accumulated £9 property that might be confiscated to satisfy it. "For want of Goods or Estate of the within named George Robt Twelve Hewes, I have taken his bodey & committed him to his majesty's goal [sic] in Boston," wrote Constable Thomas Rice on the back of the writ. There may have been a touch of political vindictiveness in the action: Courtney was a rich tory later banished by the state.[69] Who got Hewes out of jail? Perhaps his uncle Robert, perhaps a brother.

Once out of jail, Hewes stayed poor. The Boston tax records of 1771, the only ones that have survived for these years, show him living as a lodger in the house of Christopher Ranks, a watchmaker, in the old North End. He was not taxed for any property.[70] In 1773 he and his family, which now included three children, were apparently living with his uncle Robert in the South End; at some time during these years before the war they also lived with a brother.[71] After almost a decade on his own, Hewes could not afford his own place. In January 1774 he inadvertently summed up his condition and reputation in the course of a violent street encounter. Damned as "a rascal" and "a vagabond" who had no right to "speak to a gentleman in the street," Hewes retorted that he was neither "and though a poor man, in as good credit in town" as his well-to-do antagonist.[72]

251

---

[68] The First Baptist Church had "not 70 members" before 1769 and about 80 more during the next three years (Isaac Backus, *History of New England, with Particular Reference to the . . . Baptists,* III [Boston, 1796], 125–126). See also Nathan Eusebius Wood, *The History of the First Baptist Church of Boston* (1665–1899) (Philadelphia, 1899), 266–267. After the great fire of 1760 the church gave £143 to charity compared, for example, to £1862 from Old South and £418 from Old North. See Franklin Bowditch Dexter, ed., *Extracts from the Itineraries and Other Miscellanies of Ezra Stiles . . .* (New Haven, Conn., 1916), 120.

[69] Writ of Attachment on George Robert Twelves Hewes, including Hewes's note of indebtedness to Courtney, Sept. 3, 1770, Suffolk Co. Court, Case #89862. Ruth Kennedy discovered this document. For Courtney see E. Alfred Jones, *The Loyalists of Massachusetts: Their Memorials, Petitions and Claims* (London, 1930), 103.

[70] Bettye Hobbs Pruitt, ed., *The Massachusetts Tax Valuation List of 1771* (Boston, 1978), 14–15. Hewes is listed only for one "Polls Rateable." Christopher Ranks is listed as the owner. Stephanie G. Wolf brought this publication to my attention. Ranks is listed in the Thwing File, Massachusetts Historical Society, as a shopkeeper in 1750, a clockmaker in 1751, and a watchmaker in 1788.

[71] Thatcher, *Memoir of Hewes,* 84, 204.

[72] *Massachusetts Gazette and Boston Weekly News-Letter,* Jan. 27, 1774, discussed below, sec. V.

The economic odds were against a Boston shoemaker thriving these years. Even the movement "to encourage our manufactures" may have worked against him, contrary to Thatcher. The patriot boycott would have raised his hopes; the Boston town meeting of 1767 put men's and women's shoes on the list of items Bostonians were encouraged to buy from American craftsmen.[73] But if this meant shoes made in Lynn—the manufacturing town ten miles to the north that produced 80,000 shoes in 1767 alone—it might well have put Hewes at a competitive disadvantage, certainly for the ladies' shoes for which Lynn already had a reputation. And if Hewes was caught up in the system whereby Lynn masters were already "putting out" shoes in Boston, he would have made even less.[74] Whatever the reason, the early 1770s were hard times for shoemakers; Ebenezer McIntosh also landed in debtors' jail in 1770.[75]

As a struggling shoemaker, what would have been Hewes's aspirations? He does not tell us in so many words, but "the course of his life," Hawkes was convinced, was marked "by habits of industry, integrity, temperance and economy"; in other words, he practiced the virtues set down by "another soap boiler and tallow chandler's son" (Thatcher's phrase for Benjamin Franklin). "From childhood," Hewes told Hawkes, "he has been accoustomed to rise very early and expose himself to the morning air; that his father compelled him to do this from his infancy." ("Early to bed, Early to rise, makes a man healthy, wealthy and wise.") "I was often . . . admonished," said Hewes, "of the importance of faithfulness in executing the commands of my parents, or others who had a right to my services." Thatcher also reported that "he makes it a rule to rise from the table with an appetite, and another to partake of but a single dish at a meal." ("A Fat kitchen makes a lean will, as Poor Richard says.")[76]

Poor Richard spoke to and for artisans at every level—masters, journeymen, and apprentices—whose goal was "independence" or "a competency" in their trade. What he advocated, we need remind ourselves, "was not unlimited acquisition but rather prosperity, which was the mid-point between the ruin of extravagance and the want of poverty. The living he envisaged was a decent middling wealth, which could only be attained through unremitting labor and

[73] See *At a meeting of the Freeholders . . . the 28th of October, 1767* (Boston, 1767), broadside, Mass. Hist. Soc.

[74] Blanche Evans Hazard, *The Organizations of the Boot and Shoe Industry in Massachusetts before 1875* (Cambridge, Mass., 1921), 128, chap. 6, and appendices on 256–264. Lynn shoes were being sold in Boston at public auctions by the hundred pair, dozen pair, or single pair. Moreover, there were several hundred petty retailers, predominantly women, who would have been driven to the wall by the boycott and eager to sell such items. See Thatcher, *Memoir of Hewes,* 139–140, for a reprint of a newspaper notice, Feb. 14, 1770, from Isaac Vibert implying a putting-out system.

[75] *Peter Oliver's Origin & Progress of the American Rebellion: A Tory View,* ed. Douglass Adair and John A. Schutz (San Marino, Calif., 1961), 54–55. Similarly in 1771, one in six Philadelphia shoemakers was on poor relief (see Billy G. Smith, "Material Lives of Laboring Philadelphians, 1750 to 1800," *WMQ*, 3d Ser., XXXVIII [1981], 163–202).

[76] Hawkes, *Retrospect,* 20, 89, 92; Thatcher, *Memoir of Hewes,* 251–252; Richard Saunders, *Poor Richard Improved: Being an Almanac and Ephemeris . . . for the Year of Our Lord 1758 . . .* (Philadelphia, 1758), also appearing as *Father Abraham's Speech . . .* (Boston, n.d. [1758, 1760]), a compilation of aphorisms from the previous 26 almanacs. See Leonard W. Labaree et al., eds., *The Papers of Benjamin Franklin,* VII (New Haven, Conn., 1963), 326–355.

self-control."[77] Hewes's likely goal, then, was to keep his shop so that his shop would keep him.

But he could no more live by Poor Richard's precepts than could Franklin. "Industry" must have come hard. He was in an occupation "never of his choice." How could he "stick to his last" when he was "inclined towards more active pursuits"? "Avoid, above all else, debt," counselled Poor Richard, warning that "fond pride of dress is sure a very curse; E'er Fancy you consult, consult your purse." But Hewes surrendered to pride and as a consequence to the warden of the debtors' jail. "Economy"—that is, saving—produced no surplus. And so he would succumb, when war presented the opportunity, to the gamble for sudden wealth. He was as much the object as the exemplar of Poor Richard's advice, as indeed was Franklin himself.

If Hewes's memories softened such realities, in other ways his silences spoke. He said nothing about being part of any of Boston's traditional institutions— church, town meeting, or private associations. He was baptized in Old South, a Congregational church, and married by the minister of the First Baptist Church; there is no evidence that he took part in either.[78] In his old age a convert to Methodism, a churchgoer, and Bible reader, he reminisced to neither biographer about the religion of youth.

Nor does he seem to have taken part in town government. He was not a taxpayer in 1771. He probably did not own enough property to qualify as a voter for either provincial offices ($£40$ sterling) or town offices ($£20$ sterling).[79] Recollecting the political events of the Revolution, he did not speak of attending town meetings until they became what patriots called meetings of "the whole body of the people," without regard to property. The town had to fill some two hundred minor positions; it was customary to stick artisans with the menial jobs. Hewes's father was hogreeve and measurer of boards. Harry Rhoades held town offices. McIntosh was made a sealer of leather, Hewes was appointed to nothing.[80]

He does not seem to have belonged to any associations. McIntosh was in a

---

[77] J. E. Crowley, *This Sheba, Self: The Conceptualization of Economic Life in Eighteenth-Century America*, The Johns Hopkins University Studies in Historical and Political Science, XCII (Baltimore, 1974), 84. See especially James A. Henretta, "The Study of Social Mobility: Ideological Assumptions and Conceptual Bias," *Labor History*, XVIII (1977), 165–178.

[78] Hewes is listed in the baptismal records of Old South as having been christened on Sept. 26, 1742 (O. S.). See Thatcher, *Memoir of Hewes*, 255. There is no other trace of Hewes in Old South records, searched by Elaine W. Pascu. I am indebted to Charles W. Akers for help in identifying and locating Boston church records.

[79] Chilton Williamson, *American Suffrage: From Property to Democracy, 1760–1860* (Princeton, N. J., 1960), 13, 16. See *Notification to Voters, William Cooper, Town Clerk, May 1, 1768*, publicizing the property requirement, and Notification, Mar. 17, 1768, warning that "a strict scrutiny will be made as to the qualification of voters" (broadsides, Lib. Cong.). The average total vote in annual elections at official town meetings from 1763 to 1774 was 555; the high was 1,089 in 1763 (see Alan and Catherine Day, "Another Look at the Boston Caucus," *Journal of American Studies*, V [1971], 27–28).

[80] For the father see Putnam, comp., *Joshua Hewes*, 321, and for McIntosh see Anderson, "Ebenezer McIntosh," 26–28. I find no record of Hewes in "Records Relating to the Early History of Boston," in *Record Commissioners' Reports*, XIV-XX. For the wealth of leaders of the town meeting see Edward M. Cook, Jr., *The Fathers of the Towns: Leadership and Community Structure in Eighteenth-Century New England*, The Johns Hopkins University Studies in Historical and Political Science, XCIV (Baltimore, 1976), chaps. 2, 3.

fire company. So was Hewes's brother Shubael. Hewes was not. Shubael and a handful of prosperous artisans became Masons. Hewes did not.[81] It was not that he was a loner. There was simply not much for a poor artisan to belong to.[82] There was no shoemakers' society or general society of mechanics. Shoemakers had a long tradition of taking ad hoc collective action, as did other Boston craftsmen, and Hewes may have participated in such occasional informal activities of the trade.[83] Very likely he drilled in the militia with other artisans on Training Day (size would not have barred him). He seems to have known many artisans and recalled their names in describing events. So it is not hard to imagine him at a South End tavern enjoying a mug of flip with Adam Colson, leatherworker, or Patrick Carr, breechesmaker. Nor is it difficult to imagine him in the streets on November 5, in the South End Pope's Day company captained by McIntosh. After all what else was there in respectable Boston for him to belong to? All this is conjecture, but it is clear that, though he lived in Boston proper, he was not part of proper Boston—not until the events of the Revolution.

V

Between 1768 and 1775, the shoemaker became a citizen—an active participant in the events that led to the Revolution, an angry, assertive man who won recognition as a patriot. What explains the transformation? We have enough evidence to take stock of Hewes's role in three major events of the decade: the Massacre (1770), the Tea Party (1773), and the tarring and feathering of John Malcolm (1774).

Thatcher began the story of Hewes in the Revolution at the Stamp Act but based his account on other sources and even then claimed no more than that Hewes was a bystander at the famous effigy-hanging at the Liberty Tree, August 14, 1765, that launched Boston's protest. "The town's-people left their work—and Hewes, his hammer among the rest—to swell the multitude." The only episode for which Thatcher seems to have drawn on Hewes's personal recollection was the celebration of the repeal of the act in May 1766, at which Hewes remembered drinking from the pipe of madeira that John Hancock set out on the Common. "Such a day has not been seen in Boston before or since," wrote Thatcher.[84]

It is possible that Thatcher's bias against mobs led him to draw a curtain over Hewes's role. It is reasonable to suppose that if Hewes was a member of the South End Pope's Day company, he followed McIntosh who was a major leader

---

[81] For Shubael see Putnam, comp., *Joshua Hewes,* 332, and for McIntosh see Anderson, "Ebenezer McIntosh," 25.

[82] For the low level of associations see Richard D. Brown, "Emergence of Voluntary Associations in Massachusetts, 1760–1830," *Journal of Voluntary Action Research,* II (1973), 64–73.

[83] Mary Roys Baker, "Anglo-Massachusetts Trade Union Roots, 1130–1790," *Labor Hist.,* XIV (1973), 335, 362, 365–367, 371, 381–33, 388, 394.

[84] Thatcher, *Memoir of Hewes,* 68, 72. For crowd events in Boston the most reliable guide is Dirk Hoerder, *Crowd Action in Revolutionary Massachusetts, 1765–1780* (New York, 1977). Hoerder has generously shared with me his detailed knowledge. I also draw on my forthcoming book on the laboring classes in Boston in the Revolutionary era.

of the crowd actions of August 14 and 26, the massive processions of the united North and South End companies on November 1 and 5, and the forced resignation of stampmaster Andrew Oliver in December. But it is not likely; in fact, he may well have been off on fishing voyages in 1765. Perhaps the proof is negative: when Hewes told Hawkes the story of his role in the Revolution, he began not at the Stamp Act but at the Massacre, five years later. On the night of the Massacre, March 5, Hewes was in the thick of the action. What he tells us about what brought him to King Street, what brought others there, and what he did during and after this tumultuous event gives us the perspective of a man in the street.

The presence of British troops in Boston beginning in the summer of 1768— four thousand soldiers in a town of fewer than sixteen thousand inhabitants— touched Hewes personally. Anecdotes about soldiers flowed from him. He had seen them march off the transports at the Long Wharf; he had seen them every day occupying civilian buildings on Griffin's Wharf near his shop. He knew how irritating it was to be challenged by British sentries after curfew (his solution was to offer a swig of rum from the bottle he carried).

More important, he was personally cheated by a soldier. Sergeant Mark Burk ordered shoes allegedly for Captain Thomas Preston, picked them up, but never paid for them. Hewes complained to Preston, who made good and suggested he bring a complaint. A military hearing ensued, at which Hewes testified. The soldier, to Hewes's horror, was sentenced to three hundred fifty lashes. He "remarked to the court that if he had thought the fellow was to be punished so severely for such an offense, bad as he was, he would have said nothing about it." And he saw others victimized by soldiers. He witnessed an incident in which a soldier sneaked up behind a woman, felled her with his fist, and "stripped her of her bonnet, cardinal muff and tippet." He followed the man to his barracks, identified him (Hewes remembered him as Private Kilroy, who would appear later at the Massacre), and got him to give up the stolen goods, but decided this time not to press charges.[85] Hewes was also keenly aware of grievances felt by the laboring men and youths who formed the bulk of the crowd—and the principal victims—at the Massacre.[86] From Hawkes and Thatcher three causes can be pieced together.

First in time, and vividly recalled by Hewes, was the murder of eleven-year-old Christopher Seider on February 23, ten days before the Massacre. Seider was one of a large crowd of schoolboys and apprentices picketing the shop of Theophilus Lilly, a merchant violating the anti-import resolutions. Ebenezer Richardson, a paid customs informer, shot into the throng and killed Seider. Richardson would have been tarred and feathered, or worse, had not whig leaders intervened to hustle him off to jail. At Seider's funeral, only a week before the

---

[85] Thatcher, *Memoir of Hewes,* 84–87. Bostonians were "shocked by the frequency and severity of corporal punishment in the army" (John Shy, *Toward Lexington: The Role of the British Army in the Coming of the American Revolution* [Princeton, N. J., 1965], 308).

[86] Hawkes, *Retrospect,* 31–32. My statement on the composition of the crowd is based on my analysis of participants, witnesses, and victims identified in the trial record, depositions, etc., and is supported by Hoerder, *Crowd Action,* 223–234, and James Barton Hunt, "The Crowd and the American Revolution: A Study of Urban Political Violence in Boston and Philadelphia, 1763–1776" (Ph.D. diss., University of Washington, 1973), 471–479.

Massacre, five hundred boys marched two by two behind the coffin, followed by two thousand or more adults, "the largest [funeral] perhaps ever known in America," Thomas Hutchinson thought.[87]

Second, Hewes emphasized the bitter fight two days before the Massacre between soldiers and workers at Gray's ropewalk down the block from Hewes's shop. Off-duty soldiers were allowed to moonlight, taking work from civilians. On Friday, March 3, when one of them asked for work at Gray's, a battle ensued between a few score soldiers and ropewalk workers joined by others in the maritime trades. The soldiers were beaten and sought revenge. Consequently, in Thatcher's words, "quite a number of soldiers, in a word, were determined to have a row on the night of the 5th."[88]

Third, the precipitating events on the night of the Massacre, by Hewes's account, were an attempt by a barber's apprentice to collect an overdue bill from a British officer, the sentry's abuse of the boy, and the subsequent harassment of the sentry by a small band of boys that led to the calling of the guard commanded by Captain Preston. Thatcher found this hard to swallow—"a dun from a greasy barber's boy is rather an extraordinary explanation of the origin, or one of the occasions, of the massacre of the 5th of March"—but at the trial the lawyers did not. They battled over defining "boys" and over the age, size, and degree of aggressiveness of the numerous apprentices on the scene.[89]

Hewes viewed the civilians as essentially defensive. On the evening of the Massacre he appeared early on the scene at King Street, attracted by the clamor over the apprentice. "I was soon on the ground among them," he said, as if it were only natural that he should turn out in defense of fellow townsmen against what was assumed to be the danger of aggressive action by soldiers. He was not part of a conspiracy; neither was he there out of curiosity. He was unarmed, carrying neither club nor stave as some others did. He saw snow, ice, and "missiles" thrown at the soldiers. When the main guard rushed out in support of the sentry, Private Kilroy dealt Hewes a blow on his shoulder with his gun. Preston ordered the townspeople to disperse. Hewes believed they had a legal basis to refuse: "they were in the king's highway, and had as good a right to be there" as Preston.[90]

[87] Hawkes, *Retrospect,* 43; Thatcher, *Memoir of Hewes,* 88–95. Hewes told about the event after he recounted the Massacre. He correctly remembered Seider, reported as "Snider" by Thomas Hutchinson and other contemporaries. His recollection is borne out in essentials by Hoerder, *Crowd Action,* 216–223. See Hutchinson to Thomas Hood, Feb. 23, 1770; to Gen. Gage, Feb. 25, 1770; and to Lord Hillsborough, Feb. 28, 1770, Hutchinson Transcripts, Houghton Library, Harvard University, Cambridge, Mass.

[88] Hawkes, *Retrospect,* 31–32; Thatcher, *Memoir of Hewes,* 96–99. For verification by another contemporary see "Recollections of a Bostonian," from the *Boston Centinel,* 1821–1822, reprinted in Hezekiah Niles, *Principles and Acts of the Revolution in America . . .* (Baltimore, 1822), 430–431. For the fray at the ropewalk, accepted as a precipitating cause by contemporaries on both sides, see Richard B. Morris, *Government and Labor in Early America* (New York, 1946), 190–192.

[89] Hawkes, *Retrospect,* 30–31; Thatcher, *Memoir of Hewes,* 118–119. For the trial see L. Kinvin Wroth and Hiller B. Zobel, eds., *Legal Papers of John Adams* (Cambridge, Mass. 1965), III, 50, 52, 56, 93–94, 108.

[90] Hawkes, *Retrospect,* 29. For the event itself see Hiller B. Zobel, *The Boston Massacre* (New York, 1970), in conjunction with Jesse Lemisch, "Radical Plot in Boston (1770): A Study in the

The five men killed were all workingmen. Hewes claimed to know four: Samuel Gray, a ropewalk worker; Samuel Maverick, age seventeen, an apprentice to an ivory turner; Patrick Carr, an apprentice to a leather breeches worker; and James Caldwell, second mate on a ship—all but Christopher Attucks. Caldwell, "who was shot in the back was standing by the side of Hewes, and the latter caught him in his arms as he fell," helped carry him to Dr. Thomas Young in Prison Lane, then ran to Caldwell's ship captain on Cold Lane.[91]

More than horror was burned into Hewes's memory. He remembered the political confrontation that followed the slaughter, when thousands of angry townspeople faced hundreds of British troops massed with ready rifles. "The people," Hewes recounted, "then immediately chose a committee to report to the governor the result of Captain Preston's conduct, and to demand of him satisfaction."[92] Actually the "people" did not choose a committee "immediately." In the dark hours after the Massacre a self-appointed group of patriot leaders met with officials and forced Hutchinson to commit Preston and the soldiers to jail. Hewes was remembering the town meeting the next day, so huge that it had to adjourn from Fanueil Hall, the traditional meeting place that held only twelve hundred, to Old South Church, which had room for five to six thousand. This meeting approved a committee to wait on the officials and then adjourned, but met again the same day, received and voted down an offer to remove one regiment, then accepted another to remove two. This was one of the meetings at which property bars were let down.[93]

What Hewes did not recount, but what he had promptly put down in a deposition the next day, was how militant he was after the Massacre. At 1:00 A.M., like many other enraged Bostonians, he went home to arm himself. On his way back to the Town House with a cane he had a defiant exchange with Sergeant Chambers of the 29th Regiment and eight or nine soldiers, "all with very large clubs or cutlasses." A soldier, Dobson, "ask'd him how he far'd; he told him very badly to see his townsmen shot in such a manner, and asked him if he did not think it was a dreadful thing." Dobson swore "it was a fine thing" and "you shall see more of it." Chambers "seized and forced" the cane from Hewes, "saying I had no right to carry it. I told him I had as good a right to carry a cane as they had to carry clubs."[94]

The Massacre had stirred Hewes to political action. He was one of ninety-nine Bostonians who gave depositions for the prosecution that were published by the town in a pamphlet. Undoubtedly, he marched in the great funeral procession for the victims that brought the city to a standstill. He attended the tempestuous trial of Ebenezer Richardson, Seider's slayer, which was linked politically with the Massacre. ("He remembers to this moment, even the precise words of the

---

Use of Evidence," *Harvard Law Review*, LXXXIV (1970), 485–504, and Pauline Maier, "Revolutionary Violence and the Relevance of History," *JIH*, II (1971), 119–135.

[91] Hawkes, *Retrospect*, 29–32; Thatcher, *Memoir of Hewes*, 110–112.

[92] Hawkes, *Retrospect*, 30.

[93] Zobel, *Boston Massacre*, 206–209; Hoerder, *Crowd Action*, 232.

[94] Deposition No. 75, in *A Short Narrative of the Horrid Massacre in Boston . . . To Which is Added an Appendix . . .* (Boston, 1770), 61. Thatcher reprinted this in *Memoir of Hewes*, 116–118. Hewes's deposition testified to the soldiers' threats to kill more civilians and to someone entering the Custom House at the time of the Massacre, both themes emphasized by whig leaders.

Judge's sentence," wrote Thatcher.)[95] He seems to have attended the trial of the soldiers or Preston or both.

It was in this context that he remembered something for which there is no corroborating evidence, namely, testifying at Preston's trial on a crucial point. He told Hawkes:

> When Preston, their captain, was tried, I was called as one of the witnesses, on the part of the government, and testified, that I believed it was the same man, Captain Preston, that ordered his soldiers to make ready, who also ordered them to fire. Mr. John Adams, former president of the United States, was advocate for the prisoners, and denied the fact, that Captain Preston gave orders to his men to fire; and on his cross examination of me asked whether my position was such, that I could see the captain's lips in motion when the order to fire was given; to which I answered, that I could not.[96]

Perhaps so: Hewes's account is particular and precise, and there are many lacunae in the record of the trial (we have no verbatim transcript) that modern editors have assiduously assembled. Perhaps not: Hewes may have "remembered" his brother Shubael on the stand at the trial of the soldiers (although Shubael was a defense witness) or his uncle Robert testifying at Richardson's trial. Or he may have given pre-trial testimony but was not called to the stand.[97]

In one sense, it does not matter. What he was remembering was that he had become involved. He turned out because of a sense of kinship with "his townsmen" in danger; he stood his ground in defense of his "rights"; he was among the "people" who delegated a committee to act on their behalf; he took part in the legal process by giving a deposition, by attending the trials, and, as he remembered it, by testifying. In sum, he had become a citizen, a political man.

Four years later, at the Tea Party on the night of December 16, 1773, the citizen "volunteered" and became the kind of leader for whom most historians have never found a place. The Tea Party, unlike the Massacre, was organized by the radical whig leaders of Boston. They mapped the strategy, organized the public meetings, appointed the companies to guard the tea ships at Griffin's Wharf

---

[95] Thatcher, *Memoir of Hewes,* 95. Thatcher did not give the words. I suspect that what Hewes remembered was the verdict brought in by the jury after a dramatic trial repeatedly interrupted by what Peter Oliver called "a vast concourse of rabble." The verdict was "Guilty of Murder," at which "the Court Room resounded with Expressions of Pleasure" (*Oliver's Origin & Progress,* ed. Adair and Schutz, 86). The judges delayed the sentence until the crown granted a pardon. The case aroused a furor. See Wroth and Zobel, eds., *Legal Papers of Adams,* II, 396–430, and Zobel, *Boston Massacre,* chap. 15, and 423–426. For the way in which the killing of Seider and the killings of the Boston Massacre were linked politically see *A Monumental Inscription in the Fifth of March Together with a few lines on the Enlargement of Ebenezer Richardson Convicted of Murder* [1772], broadside, Mass. Hist. Soc.

[96] Hawkes, *Retrospect,* 32. Thatcher does not even mention this claim of Hewes, possibly because he was skeptical.

[97] Wroth and Zobel, eds. *Legal Papers of Adams,* III, has no record of Hewes at the trial, but see L. H. Butterfield's "Descriptive List of Sources and Documents": "This operation has been a good deal like that of an archeological team reconstructing a temple from a tumbled mass of architectural members, some missing, many mutilated, and most of them strewn over a wide area" (ibid., 34). For Shubael Hewes see ibid., 176–177, 224–275, and for Robert Hewes ibid., II, 405, 418.

(among them Daniel Hewes, George's brother), and planned the official boarding parties. As in 1770, they converted the town meetings into meetings of "the whole body of the people," one of which Hutchinson found "consisted principally of the Lower ranks of the People & even Journeymen Tradesmen were brought in to increase the number & the Rabble were not excluded yet there were divers Gentlemen of Good Fortunes among them."[98]

The boarding parties showed this same combination of "ranks." Hawkes wrote:

> On my inquiring of Hewes if he knew who first proposed the project of destroying the tea, to prevent its being landed, he replied that he did not; neither did he know who or what number were to volunteer their services for that purpose. But from the significant allusion of some persons in whom I had confidence, together with the knowledge I had of the spirit of those times, I had no doubt but that a sufficient number of associates would accompany me in that enterprise.[99]

The recollection of Joshua Wyeth, a journeyman blacksmith, verified Hewes's story in explicit detail: "It was proposed that young men, not much known in town and not liable to be easily recognized should lead in the business." Wyeth believed that "most of the persons selected for the occasion were apprentices and journeymen, as was the case with myself, living with tory masters." Wyeth "had but a few hours warning of what was intended to be done."[100] Those in the officially designated parties, about thirty men better known, appeared in well-prepared Indian disguises. As nobodies, the volunteers—anywhere from fifty to one hundred men—could get away with hastily improvised disguises. Hewes said he got himself up as an Indian and daubed his "face and hands with coal dust in the shop of blacksmith." In the streets "I fell in with many who were dressed, equipped and painted as I was, and who fell in with me and marched in order to the place of our destination."

At Griffin's Wharf the volunteers were orderly, self-disciplined, and ready to accept leadership.

> When we arrived at the wharf, there were three of our number who assumed an authority to direct our operations, to which we readily submitted. They divided us into three parties, for the purpose of boarding the three ships which contained the tea at the same time. The name of him who commanded the division to which I was assigned was Leonard Pitt [Lendell Pitts].

[98] Hutchinson to Lord Dartmouth, Dec. 3, 1773, Hutchinson Transcripts. For Daniel Hewes see Francis S. Drake, *Tea Leaves: Being a Collection of Letters and Documents Relating to the Shipment of Tea* . . . (Boston, 1884), xlvi.

[99] Hawkes, *Retrospect*, 36–37. Hewes's account is verified in its essentials by Hoerder, *Crowd Action*, 257–264, and is not inconsistent with the less detailed account in Benjamin Woods Labaree, *The Boston Tea Party* (New York, 1964), chap. 7. For analysis of the participants see Hoerder, *Crowd Action*, 263–264, and Hunt, "The Crowd and the American Revolution," 481, 485.

[100] Joshua Wyeth, "Revolutionary Reminiscence," *North American*, I (1827), 195, brought to my attention by Richard Twomey.

The names of the other commanders I never knew. We were immediately ordered by the respective commanders to board all the ships at the same time, which we promptly obeyed.

But for Hewes there was something new: he was singled out of the rank and file and made an officer in the field.

The commander of the division to which I belonged, as soon as we were on board the ship, appointed me boatswain, and ordered me to go to the captain and demand of him the keys to the hatches and a dozen candles. I made the demand accordingly, and the captain promptly replied, and delivered the articles; but requested me at the same time to do no damage to the ship or rigging. We then were ordered by our commander to open the hatches, and take out all the chests of tea and throw them overboard, and we immediately proceeded to execute his orders; first cutting and splitting the chests with our tomahawks, so as thoroughly to expose them to the effects of the water. In about three hours from the time we went on board, we had thus broken and thrown overboard every tea chest to be found in the ship; while those in the other ships were disposing of the tea in the same way, at the same time. We were surrounded by British armed ships, but no attempt was made to resist us. We then quietly retired to our several places of residence, without having any conversation with each other, or taking any measures to discover who were our associates.[101]

This was Hewes's story, via Hawkes. Thatcher, who knew a good deal more about the Tea Party from other sources, accepted it in its essentials as an accurate account. He also reported a new anecdote which he treated with skepticism, namely, that Hewes worked alongside John Hancock throwing tea overboard. And he added that Hewes, "whose whistling talent was a matter of public notoriety, acted as a boatswain," that is, as the officer whose duty it was to summon men with a whistle. That Hewes was a leader is confirmed by the reminiscence of Thompson Maxwell, a teamster from a neighboring town who was making a delivery to Hancock the day of the event. Hancock asked him to go to Griffin's Wharf. "I went accordingly, joined the band under one Captain Hewes; we mounted the ships and made tea in a trice; this done I took my team and went home as any honest man should."[102] "Captain" Hewes—it was not impossible.

As the Tea Party ended, Hewes was stirred to further action on his own initiative, just as he had been in the hours after the Massacre. While the crews were throwing the tea overboard, a few other men tried to smuggle off some of the tea scattered on the decks. "One Captain O'Connor whom I well knew," said Hewes, "came on board for that purpose, and when he supposed he was not noticed, filled his pockets, and also the lining of his coat. But I had detected him, and gave information to the captain of what he was doing. We were ordered to take him into custody, and just as he was stepping from the vessel, I seized him by

---

[101] Hawkes, *Retrospect,* 38–39.

[102] Thatcher, *Memoir of Hewes,* 180–181, 261. Maxwell's reminiscence is in *NEHGR,* XXII (1868), 58.

the skirt of his coat, and in attempting to pull him back, I tore it off." They scuffled. O'Connor recognized him and "threatened to 'complain to the Governor.' 'You had better make your will first,' quoth Hewes, doubling his fist expressively," and O'Connor escaped, running the gauntlet of the crowd on the wharf. "The next day we nailed the skirt of his coat, which I had pulled off, to the whipping post in Charlestown, the place of his residence, with a label upon it," to shame O'Connor by "popular indignation."[103]

A month later, at the third event for which we have full evidence, Hewes won public recognition for an act of courage that almost cost his life and precipitated the most publicized tarring and feathering of the Revolution. The incident that set it off would have been trivial at any other time. On Tuesday, January 25, 1774, at about two in the afternoon, the shoemaker was making his way back to his shop after his dinner. According to the very full account in the *Massachusetts Gazette,*

> Mr. George-Robert-Twelves Hewes was coming along Fore-Street, near Captain Ridgway's, and found the redoubted John Malcolm, standing over a small boy, who was pushing a little sled before him, cursing, damning, threatening and shaking a very large cane with a very heavy ferril on it over his head. The boy at that time was perfectly quiet, notwithstanding which Malcolm continued his threats of striking him, which Mr. Hewes conceiving if he struck him with that weapon he must have killed him out-right, came up to him, and said to him, Mr. Malcolm I hope you are not going to strike this boy with that stick.[104]

Malcolm had already acquired an odious reputation with patriots of the lower sort. A Bostonian, he had been a sea captain, an army officer, and recently an employee of the customs service. He was so strong a supporter of royal authority that he had traveled to North Carolina to fight the Regulators and boasted of having a horse shot out from under him. He had a fiery temper. As a customs informer he was known to have turned in a vessel to punish sailors for petty smuggling, a custom of the sea. In November 1773, near Portsmouth, New Hampshire, a crowd of thirty sailors had "genteely tarr'd and feather'd" him, as the *Boston Gazette* put it: they did the job over his clothes. Back in Boston he made "frequent complaints" to Hutchinson of "being hooted at in the streets" for this by "tradesmen"; and the lieutenant governor cautioned him, "being a passionate man," not to reply in kind.[105]

The exchange between Malcolm and Hewes resonated with class as well as political differences:

---

[103] Hawkes, *Retrospect,* 40–41; Thatcher, *Memoir of Hewes,* 182–183.

[104] *Mass. Gaz. and Boston Wkly News-Letter,* Jan. 27, Feb. 3, 1774. Hewes told this story to Hawkes essentially as reported in this paper but with only some of the dialogue. He may have kept the clipping. Thatcher added dialogue based on the account in the paper but also extracted additional details from Hewes not in either the *Gazette* or Hawkes.

[105] Frank W. C. Hersey, "Tar and Feathers: The Adventures of Captain John Malcolm," Col. Soc. Mass., *Trans.,* XXXIV (1941), 429–473, which also reprints the documents. The full letter, Hutchinson to Lord Dartmouth, Jan. 28, 1774, is in K. G. Davis, ed., *Documents of the American Revolution, 1770–1783,* VIII (Shannon, Ireland, 1972), 25–27.

261

Malcolm returned, you are an impertinent rascal, it is none of your business. Mr. Hewes then asked him, what had the child done to him. Malcolm damned him and asked him if he was going to take his part? Mr. Hewes answered no further than this, that he thought it was a shame for him to strike the child with such a club as that, if he intended to strike him. Malcolm on that damned Mr. Hewes, called him a vagabond, and said he would let him know he should not speak to a gentleman in the street. Mr. Hewes returned to that, he was neither a rascal nor vagabond, and though a poor man was in as good credit in town as he was. Malcolm called him a liar, and said he was not, nor ever would be. Mr. Hewes retorted, be that as it will, I never was tarred nor feathered any how. On this Malcolm struck him, and wounded him deeply on the forehead, so that Mr. Hewes for some time lost his senses. Capt. Godfrey, then present, interposed, and after some altercation, Malcolm went home.[106]

Hewes was rushed to Joseph Warren, the patriot doctor, his distant relative. Malcolm's cane had almost penetrated his skull. Thatcher found "the indentation as plainly perceptible as it was sixty years ago." So did Hawkes. Warren dressed the wound, and Hewes was able to make his way to a magistrate to swear out a warrant for Malcolm's arrest "which he carried to a constable named Justice Hale."[107] Malcolm, meanwhile, had retreated to his house, where he responded in white heat to taunts about the half-way tarring and feathering in Portsmouth with "damn you let me see the man that dare do it better."

In the evening a crowd took Malcolm from his house and dragged him on a sled into King Street "amidst the huzzas of thousands." At this point "several gentlemen endeavoured to divert the populace from their intention." The ensuing dialogue laid bare the clash of conceptions of justice between the sailors and laboring people heading the action and Sons of Liberty leaders. The "gentlemen" argued that Malcolm was "open to the laws of the land which would undoubtedly award a reasonable satisfaction to the parties he had abused," that is, the child and Hewes. The answer was political. Malcolm "had been an old impudent and mischievious [sic] offender—he had joined in the murders at North Carolina—he had seized vessels on account of sailors having a bottle or two of gin on board—he had in other words behaved in the most capricious, insulting and daringly abusive manner." He could not be trusted to justice. "When they were told the law would have its course with him, they asked what course had the law taken with Preston or his soldiers, with Capt. Wilson or Richardson? And for their parts they had seen so much partiality to the soldiers and customhouse officers by the present Judges, that while things remained as they were, they would, on all such occasions, take satisfaction their own way, and let them take it off."[108] The references were to Captain Preston who had been tried and found innocent of the Massacre, the soldiers who had been let off with token punishment, Captain John

---

[106] *Mass. Gaz. and Boston Wkly News-Letter,* Jan. 27, 1774.

[107] Thatcher, *Memoir of Hewes,* 132; Hawkes, *Retrospect,* 33–35.

[108] *Mass. Gaz. and Boston Wkly News-Letter,* Jan. 27, 1774. For other comments from the crowd see *Boston-Gazette, and Country Journal,* Jan. 31, 1774.

Wilson, who had been indicted for inciting slaves to murder their masters but never tried,[109] and Ebenezer Richardson, who had been tried and found guilty of killing Seider, sentenced, and then pardoned by the crown.

The crowd won and proceeded to a ritualized tarring and feathering, the purpose of which was to punish Malcolm, force a recantation, and ostracize him.

> With these and such like arguments, together with a gentle crouding of persons not of their way of thinking out of the ring they proceeded to elevate Mr. Malcolm from his sled into a cart, and stripping him to buff and breeches, gave him a modern jacket [a coat of tar and feathers] and hied him away to liberty-tree, where they proposed to him to renounce his present commission, and swear that he would never hold another inconsistent with the liberties of his country; but this he obstinately refusing, they then carted him to the gallows, passed a rope round his neck, and threw the other end over the beam as if they intended to hang him: But this manoeuvre he set at defiance. They then basted him for some time with a rope's end, and threatened to cut his ears off, and on this he complied, and they then brought him home.[110]

Hewes had precipitated an electrifying event. It was part of the upsurge of spontaneous action in the wake of the Tea Party that prompted the whig leaders to promote a "Committee for Tarring and Feathering" as an instrument of crowd control. The "Committee" made its appearance in broadsides signed by "Captain Joyce, Jun.," a sobriquet meant to invoke the bold cornet who had captured King Charles in 1647.[111] The event was reported in the English newspapers, popularized in three or four satirical prints, and dramatized still further when Malcolm went to England, where he campaigned for a pension and ran for Parliament (without success) against John Wilkes, the leading champion of America. The event confirmed the British ministry in its punitive effort to bring rebellious Boston to heel.[112]

What was lost to the public was that Hewes was at odds with the crowd. He wanted justice from the courts, not a mob; after all, he had sworn out a warrant against Malcolm. And he could not bear to see cruel punishment inflicted on a man, any more than on a boy. As he told the story to Thatcher, when he returned and saw Malcolm being carted away in tar and feathers, "his instant impulse was to push after the procession as fast as he could, with a blanket to put over his shoulders. He overtook them [the crowd] at his brother's [Shubael's]

---

[109] Hawkes, *Retrospect*, 44; Zobel, *Boston Massacre*, 102.

[110] *Mass. Gaz. and Boston Wkly News-Letter*, Jan. 27, 1774.

[111] See Albert Matthews, "Joyce, Jun," Col. Soc. Mass., *Pubs.*, VIII (1903), 89–104, and Young, "Pope's Day, Tar and Feathers," sec. VI.

[112] For the newspaper accounts and prints see R.T.H. Halsey, *The Boston Port Bill as Pictured by a Contemporary London Cartoonist* (New York, 1904), 82–94, 121n, 132–133; Mary Dorothy George, comp., *Catalogue of Political and Personal Satires . . . in the British Museum*, V (London, 1935), no. 5232, 168–169; and Donald Creswell, comp., *The American Revolution in Drawings and Prints; A Checklist of 1765–1790 Graphics in the Library of Congress* (Washington, D. C., 1975), nos. 668–670. For the impact on the king and his ministers see Peter Orlando Hutchinson, comp., *The Diary and Letters of His Excellency Thomas Hutchinson . . .*, I (London, 1883), 164.

house and made an effort to relieve him; but the ruffians who now had the charge of him about the cart, pushed him aside, and warned him to keep off." This may have been the Good Samaritan of 1835, but the story rings true. While "the very excitement which the affront must have wrought upon him began to rekindle," Hewes conveyed no hatred for Malcolm.[113]

The denouement of the affair was an incident several weeks later. "Malcolm recovered from his wounds and went about as usual. 'How do you do, Mr. Malcolm?' said Hewes, very civilly, the next time he met him. 'Your humble servant, Mr. George Robert Twelves Hewes,' quoth he,—touching his hat genteely as he passed by. 'Thank ye,' thought Hewes, 'and I am glad you have learned *better manners at last.*'"[114] Hewes's mood was one of triumph. Malcolm had been taught a lesson. The issue was respect for Hewes, a patriot, a poor man, an honest citizen, a decent man standing up for a child against an unspeakably arrogant "gentleman" who was an enemy of his country.

Hewes's role in these three events fits few of the categories that historians have applied to the participation of ordinary men in the Revolution. He was not a member of any organized committee, caucus, or club. He did not attend the expensive public dinners of the Sons of Liberty. He was capable of acting on his own volition without being summoned by any leaders (as in the Massacre). He could volunteer and assume leadership (as in the Tea Party). He was at home on the streets in crowds but he could also reject a crowd (as in the tarring and feathering of Malcolm). He was at home in the other places where ordinary Bostonians turned out to express their convictions: at funeral processions, at meetings of the "whole body of the people," in courtrooms at public trials. He recoiled from violence to persons if not to property. The man who could remember the whippings of his own boyhood did not want to be the source of pain to others, whether Sergeant Burk, who tried to cheat him over a pair of shoes, or John Malcolm, who almost killed him. It is in keeping with his character that he should have come to the aid of a little boy facing a beating.

Nevertheless, Hewes was more of a militant than he conveyed or his biographers recognized in 1833 and 1835. He was capable of acting on his own initiative in the wake of collective action at both the Massacre and the Tea Party. He had "public notoriety," Thatcher tells us for his "whistling talent"; whistling was the customary way of assembling a crowd.[115] According to Malcolm, Hewes was among the "tradesmen" who had "several times before affronted him" by "hooting" at him in the streets.[116] And the patriots whose names stayed with him included Dr. Thomas Young and William Molineaux, the two Sons of Liberty who replaced Ebenezer McIntosh as "mob" leaders.[117]

What moved Hewes to action? It was not the written word; indeed there is no sign he was much of a reader until old age, and then it was the Bible he read. "My whole education," he told Hawkes, "consisted of only a moderate

<hr />

[113] Thatcher, *Memoir of Hewes,* 132.

[114] Ibid., 133.

[115] Ibid., 181, 263; *Oliver's Origin & Progress,* ed. Adair and Schutz, 74–75.

[116] Hutchinson to Lord Dartmouth, Jan. 28, 1774, in Davis, ed., *Documents of the Revolution,* 25–27.

[117] Hawkes, *Retrospect,* 42–44.

knowledge of reading and writing."[118] He seems to have read one of the most sensational pamphlets of 1773, which he prized enough to hold onto for more than fifty years, but he was certainly not like Harbottle Dorr, the Boston shop-keeper who pored over every issue of every Boston newspaper, annotating Britain's crimes for posterity.[119]

Hewes was moved to act by personal experiences that he shared with large numbers of other plebeian Bostonians. He seems to have been politicized, not by the Stamp Act, but by the coming of the troops after 1768, and then by things that happened to him, that he saw, or that happened to people he knew. Once aroused, he took action with others of his own rank and condition—the laboring classes who formed the bulk of the actors at the Massacre, the Tea Party, and the Malcolm affair—and with other members of his family: his uncle Robert, "known for a staunch Liberty Boy," and his brother Daniel, a guard at the tea ship. Shubael, alone among his brothers, became a tory.[120] These shared experiences were interpreted and focused more likely by the spoken than the written word and as much by his peers at taverns and crowd actions as by leaders in huge public meetings.

As he became active politically he may have had a growing awareness of his worth as a shoemaker. McIntosh was clearly the man of the year in 1765; indeed, whigs were no less fearful than loyalists that "the Captain General of the Liberty Tree" might become the Masaniello of Boston.[121] After a shoemaker made the boot to hang in the Liberty Tree as an effigy of Lord Bute, "Jack Cobler" served notice that "whenever the Public Good requires my services, I shall be ready to distinguish myself." In 1772 "Crispin" began an anti-loyalist diatribe by saying, "I am a shoemaker, a citizen, a free man and a freeholder." The editor added a post-script justifying "Crispin's performance" and explaining that "it should be known what common people, even *coblers* think and feel under the present administration."[122] In city after city, "cobblers" were singled out for derision by conservatives for leaving their lasts to engage in the body politic.[123] Hewes could not have been unaware of all this; he was part of it.

---

[118] Ibid., 18–19.

[119] Ibid., 87. Hewes made an allusion to having brought with him what could only have been *Copy of Letters Sent to Great Britain, by His Excellency Thomas Hutchinson, the Hon. Andrew Oliver, and Several Other Persons* . . . (Boston, 1773). See Bernard Bailyn, *The Ordeal of Thomas Hutchinson* (Cambridge, Mass., 1974), 222–224. For Dorr see Bailyn, "The Index and Commentaries of Harbottle Dorr," Mass. Hist. Soc., *Proceedings,* LXXXV (1973), 21–35, and Barbara Wilhelm, *The American Revolution as a Leadership Crisis: The View of a Hardware Store Owner,* West Georgia College Studies in the Social Sciences, XV (Carrollton, Ga., 1976), 43–54.

[120] Robert Hewes attended the 1769 dinner commemorating the Stamp Act action of 1765 (see "An Alphabetical List of the Sons of Liberty who Dined at Liberty Tree, Dorchester, August 14, 1769," MS, Mass. Hist. Soc.). "Parson Thatcher" called Robert "a great Liberty Man" in 1775 (see Thatcher, *Memoir of Hewes,* 217). Daniel Hewes was a guard at the tea ships, Nov. 30, 1773 (see Drake, *Tea Leaves,* xlvi). For Shubael Hewes, who testified for the defense at the Massacre trial, see Putnam, comp., *Joshua Hewes,* 331.

[121] See Alfred Young, "The Rapid Rise and Decline of Ebenezer McIntosh" (MS, Shelby Cullum Davis Center, Princeton Univ., Jan. 1976).

[122] "Jack Cobler," *Massachusetts Gazette* (Boston), Feb. 20, 1776; "Crispin," *Massachusetts Spy* (Boston), Jan. 16, 1772.

[123] For derogatory references in New York, Baltimore, and Savannah see Philip S. Foner, *Labor*

He may also have responded to the rising demand among artisans for support of American manufacturers, whether or not it brought him immediate benefit. He most certainly subscribed to the secularized Puritan ethic—self-denial, industry, frugality—that made artisans take to the nonimportation agreement with its crusade against foreign luxury and its vision of American manufactures. And he could easily have identified with the appeal of the Massachusetts Provincial Congress of 1774 that equated the political need "to encourage agriculture, manufacturers and economy so as to render this state as independent of every other state as the nature of our country will admit" with the "happiness of particular families" in being "independent."[124]

But what ideas did Hewes articulate? He spoke of what he did but very little of what he thought. In the brief statement he offered Hawkes about why he went off to war in 1776, he expressed a commitment to general principles as they had been brought home to him by his experiences. "I was continually reflecting upon the unwarrantable sufferings inflicted on the citizens of Boston by the usurpation and tyranny of Great Britain, and my mind was excited with an unextinguishable desire to aid in chastising them." When Hawkes expressed a doubt "as to the correctness of his conduct in absenting himself from his family," Hewes "emphatically reiterated" the same phrases, adding to a "desire to aid in chastising them" the phrase "and securing our independence."[125] This was clearly not an afterthought; it probably reflected the way many others moved toward the goal of Independence, not as a matter of original intent, but as a step made necessary when all other resorts failed. Ideology thus did not set George Hewes apart from Samuel Adams or John Hancock. The difference lies in what the Revolution did to him as a person. His experiences transformed him, giving him a sense of citizenship and personal worth. Adams and Hancock began with both; Hewes had to arrive there, and in arriving he cast off the constraints of deference.

The two incidents with which we introduced Hewes's life measure the distance he had come: from the young man tongue-tied in the presence of John Hancock to the man who would not take his hat off to the officer of the ship named *Hancock*. Did he cast off his deference to Hancock? Hewes's affirmation of his worth as a human being was a form of class consciousness. Implicit in the idea, "I am as good as any man regardless of rank or wealth," was the idea that any poor man might be as good as any rich man. This did not mean that all rich men were bad. On the contrary, in Boston, more than any other major colonial seaport, a majority of the merchants were part of the patriot coalition; "divers Gentelmen of Good Fortunes," as Hutchinson put it, were with the "Rabble." This blunted class consciousness. Boston's mechanics, unlike New York's or Philadelphia's, did not develop mechanic committees or a mechanic

---

and the American Revolution (Westport, Conn., 1976), 120, 197, 151, and for Charleston see Richard Walsh, *Charleston's Sons of Liberty: A Study of the Artisans, 1763–1789* (Columbia, S. C., 1959), 70.

[124] Edmund S. Morgan, "The Puritan Ethic and the American Revolution," *WMQ*, 3d Ser., XXIV (1967), 3–43, esp. sec. II; "Declaration of the Massachusetts Provincial Congress, Dec. 8, 1774," in Merrill Jensen, ed., *English Historical Documents: American Colonial Documents to 1776* (New York, 1955), 823–825. Thatcher dwelled on the patriot promotion of American manufactures without, however, attributing such ideas to Hewes (*Memoir of Hewes*, 58–60).

[125] Hawkes, *Retrospect*, 62, 64.

consciousness before the Revolution. Yet in Boston the rich were forced to defer to the people in order to obtain or retain their support. Indeed, the entire public career of Hancock from 1765 on—distributing largesse, buying uniforms for Pope's Day marchers, building ships to employ artisans—can be understood as an exercise of this kind of deference, proving his civic virtue and patriotism.[126]

This gives meaning to Hewes's tale of working beside Hancock at the Tea Party—"a curious reminiscence," Thatcher called it, "but we believe it a mistake."

> Mr. Hewes, however, positively affirms, as of his own observation, that *Samuel Adams and John Hancock were both actively engaged in the process of destruction.* Of the latter he speaks more particularly, being entirely confident that he was himself at one time engaged with him in the demolition of the same chest of tea. He recognized him not only by his *ruffles* making their appearance in the heat of the work, from under the disguise which pretty thoroughly covered him,—and by his figure, and gait;—but by his features, which neither his paint nor his loosened club of hair behind wholly concealed from a close view;—and by his voice also, for he exchanged with him an Indian *grunt,* and the expression *"me know you,"* which was a good deal used on that occasion for a countersign.[127]

Thatcher was justifiably skeptical; it is very unlikely that Hancock was there. Participants swore themselves to secrecy; their identity was one of the best-kept secrets of the Revolution. In fact, in 1835 Thatcher published in an appendix the first list of those "more or less actively engaged" in the Tea Party as furnished by "an aged Bostonian," clearly not Hewes.[128] Hancock was not named. More important, it was not part of the patriot plan for the well-known leaders to be present. When the all-day meeting that sanctioned the action adjourned, the leaders, including Hancock, stayed behind conspicuously in Old South.[129] Still, there can be little question that Hewes was convinced at the time that Hancock was on the ship: some gentlemen were indeed present; it was reasonable to assume that Hancock, who had been so conspicuous on the tea issue, was there; Hewes knew what Hancock looked like; he was too insistent about details for his testimony to be dismissed as made up. And the way he recorded it in his mind at the time was the way he stored it in his memory.

Hewes in effect had brought Hancock down to his own level. The poor shoemaker had not toppled the wealthy merchant; he was no "leveller." But the rich and powerful—the men in "ruffles"—had become, in his revealing word, his "associates." John Hancock and George Hewes breaking open the same chest at the Tea Party remained for Hewes a symbol of a moment of equality. To the

267

[126] Charles W. Akers, "John Hancock: Notes for a Reassessment" (unpubl. paper, Univ. of Michigan-Flint Conference, Oct. 1976), which the author kindly allowed me to read.

[127] Thatcher, *Memoir of Hewes,* 192–193.

[128] Ibid., 261–262.

[129] L.F.S. Upton, "Proceedings of Ye Body Respecting the Tea," *WMQ,* 3d Ser., XXII (1965), 298. The standard sources are dubious. See Edward L. Pierce, "Recollections as a Source of History," Mass. Hist. Soc., *Procs.,* 2d Ser., X (1896), 473–490, and Labaree, *Boston Tea Party,* 144, and chap. 7.

shoemaker, one suspects, this above all was what the Revolutionary events of Boston meant, as did the war that followed.

VI

Hewes's decisions from 1775 to 1783—his choice of services and the timing and sequence of his military activities—suggest a pattern of patriotism mingled with a hope to strike it rich and a pressing need to provide for his family.

After the outbreak of hostilities at Lexington and Concord in April 1775, Boston became a garrison town; patriot civilians streamed out—perhaps ten thousand of them—Tory refugees moved in, and the number of British troops grew to 13,500 by July. Hewes sent his wife and children to Wrentham—his father's native town—where they would be safe with relatives. His brother Daniel did the same; Solomon went elsewhere; Shubael alone stayed with the British, as butcher-general to General Gage. George himself remained—"imprisoned," as he remembered it—prevented like other able-bodied men from leaving the city. He made a living as a fisherman; the British allowed him to pass in and out of the harbor in exchange for the pick of the day's catch. He was in Boston nine weeks, was harassed by soldiers on the street, witnessed the Battle of Bunker Hill from a neck of land far out in the bay (he "saw [Joseph Warren] fall"), and saw the corpses of British soldiers "chucked" into an open pit at one end of the Common. One morning he bade good-bye to Shubael, hid his shoemaker's tools under the deck of a small boat borrowed from a tory, and, after a narrow scrape with British guards, made good an escape with two friends to nearby Lynn. The Committee of Safety took him to Cambridge, where General Washington plied him with questions about conditions in Boston—an interview we shall return to. Then he made his way south to Wrentham.[130]

Hewes's record of service thereafter can be reconstructed with reasonable accuracy by matching what he claimed in his pension application in 1832 and told his biographers against information from official records and other contemporary sources.[131] After some months, very likely in the fall of 1776, he enlisted on a pri-

---

[130] Hawkes, *Retrospect,* 59–62; Thatcher, *Memoir of Hewes,* 198–220. For verification of the context see Richard Frothingham, *History of the Siege of Boston* . . . (Boston, 1849), and Justin Winsor, ed., *The Memorial History of Boston, Including Suffolk County Massachusetts* . . . , III (Boston, 1881), chap. 2. The Hewes family was not listed among the 5,000 or more Boston families who received charity from the Friends, although over a score of shoemakers were (see Henry J. Cadbury, "Quaker Relief during the Siege of Boston," Col. Soc. Mass., *Trans.,* XXXIV [1943], 39–179).

[131] Hewes claimed five separate stints, two as a privateersman and three in the militia, in his Pension Application and Statement of Service, Military Service Records, MS, No. 14748, Nat'l Archs., hereafter cited as Pension Application. The two privateering expeditions can be verified from corroborative evidence (see below, nn. 144, 145). Of his three claims for militia service, two are verified in Massachusetts Secretary of the Commonwealth, *Massachusetts Soldiers and Sailors in the Revolutionary War* (Boston, 1896–1908), VII, 792–793, s.v. "Hewes, George" and "Hewes, George R. T.," hereafter cited as *Mass. Soldiers.* This compilation attests to one of the three months he claimed for 1777 (Sept. 25–Oct. 30) and more than the three months he claimed for 1781 (July 23–Nov. 8). Using unnamed "official records" that could only have been the as-yet-unpublished MS records in the Mass. Archs., Putnam found evidence for four separate enlistments, one more than Hewes claimed, two of which (1777 and 1781) are printed in *Mass. Soldiers,* VII, and two of which (Aug. 17–Sept. 9, 1778, and July 28–Oct. 21, 1780) are

vateer at Providence on a voyage north that lasted about three months. He returned to Wrentham and a year later, in the fall of 1777, served in the militia from one to three months. In late August 1778 he served again, most likely for one month. In February 1779 he made a second privateering voyage, this time out of Boston, an eventful seven-and-a-half-month trip to the South and the West Indies. In 1780 he very likely was in the militia again from late July to late October, and in 1781 he definitely was in the militia at the same time of year. That was his final tour of duty: in the closing years of the war, to avoid the Massachusetts draft, he hired a substitute. All these enlistments were out of Attleborough, the town immediately south of Wrentham.[132] All were as a private; he did not rise in the ranks.

Several things stand out in this record. Hewes did not go at once, not until he provided for his family. He remembered that he did not make his first enlistment until "about two years after the battle of Bunker Hill," although actually it was closer to a year or fifteen months.[133] He served often, twice at sea, at least four and possibly five times in the militia, but not at all in the Continental army, which would have meant longer periods away from home. For almost all of these stints he volunteered; once he was drafted; once he sent a substitute; he drew these distinctions carefully.[134]

This record, put alongside what we know about other Massachusetts men in the war, places Hewes a good cut above the average. He served at least nine

---

not (see Putnam, comp., *Joshua Hewes,* 335–336). Putnam's 1778 finding verifies Hewes's pension claim for three months in 1778 for dates he did not specify (but which places him at the Battle of Newport Island at the right period). Hewes did not claim the 1780 stint Putnam found. There is corroboration for his pension claims in the Attleborough records (see below, n. 132). There is thus good evidence for his two privateering claims, direct verification for two of his militia claims, and evidence for two more he did not claim.

[132] George Hewes's name is not on the militia musters for Attleborough reprinted in John Daggett, *Sketch of the History of Attleborough from its Settlement to the Present Time* (Boston, 1894 [orig. publ. Dedham, Mass., 1834]), 134–145. In his petition of 1832 Hewes indicated several times that he returned to his family at Wrentham but enlisted at Attleborough. The explanation may be that "these lists comprise all the *town* enlistments, not individual enlistments of certain citizens elsewhere in which the town would have no monetary interest" (Daggett, *Sketch of Attleborough,* 143n). The Attleborough evidence, however, corroborates Hewes's claims: (1) The town's units were in the three campaigns Hewes claimed in 1777, 1778, and 1781. (2) Caleb Richardson, the officer Hewes listed twice as his captain, served in the Attleborough militia. He is listed as captain for six tours of duty, the dates of two of which (1778 and 1780) coincide with Hewes's claims (*Mass. Soldiers,* XIII, 230). (3) Luke Drury is listed as Lt. Col. Commandant for the service at West Point that Hewes claimed under "Col. Drury" in 1781 (ibid., IV, 987).

[133] In his Pension Application Hewes said he went on board the privateer *Diamond* "about two years after the battle of Bunker Hill," adding, "sometime in the month of April." This would have made it in 1777. But the two vessels whose names he remembered as prizes were taken in Oct. and Dec. 1776. If it was a three months' voyage, as Hewes remembered, this would have meant the *Diamond* sailed about Sept. 1776. See below, n. 144.

[134] The clerk wrote that Hewes "enlisted as a volunteer on board of a privateer"; he "volunteered into a company of militia"; "he again volunteered into a company of militia"; but finally, "he enlisted . . . into a company of militia" (Pension Application). Hewes also told Hawkes that in "a hot press for men to go and recapture Penobscot" from the British "I volunteered to go with a Mr. Saltonstall, who was to be the commander of the expedition, which for some cause, however, failed" (*Retrospect,* 72). This was the naval expedition of July-Aug. 1779, led by Capt. Dudley Saltonstall, which ended in disaster.

months in the militia and ten-and-a-half months at sea—about twenty months in all. In Concord, most men "were credited with under a half a year's time";[135] in Peterborough, New Hampshire, only a third did "extensive service" of over a year.[136] Hewes served less than the thirty-three months of the average man in the Continental army.[137] He was not one of the men whom John Shy has called the "hard core" of Revolutionary fighters, like the shoemaker "Long Bill" Scott of Peterborough. But neither was he one of the sunshine patriots Robert Gross found in Concord who came out for no more than a few militia stints early in the war. He served over the length of the fighting. Like others who put in this much time, he was poor; even in Concord after 1778, soldiers in the militia as well as the army "were men with little or nothing to lose."[138] Hewes was in his mid-thirties; he and Sarah had four children by 1776, six by 1781. He spent most of the years of war at home providing for them, doing what, he did not say, but possibly making shoes for the army like other country cordwainers.[139] His patriotism was thus tempered by the need for survival.

Going to war was a wrenching experience. When Hewes told his wife he intended to "take a privateering cruise," she "was greatly afflicted at the prospect of our separation, and my absence from a numerous family of children, who needed a father's parental care." Taught from boyhood to repress his emotions ("I cannot cry," Thatcher reported him saying when punishment loomed), Hewes cut the pain of parting by a ruse.

> On the day which I had appointed to take my departure, I came into the room where my wife was, and inquired if all was ready? She pointed in silence to my knapsack. I observed, that I would put it on and walk with it a few rods, to see if it was rightly fitted to carry with ease. I went out, to return no more until the end of my cruise. The manly fortitude which becomes the soldier, could not overcome the tender sympathies of my nature. I had not courage to encounter the trial of taking a formal leave. When I had arrived at a solitary place on my way, I sat down for a few moments, and sought to allay the keenness of my grief by giving vent to a profusion of tears.[140]

Why was privateering Hewes's first choice? Privateering, as Jesse Lemisch has put it, was legalized piracy with a share of the booty for each pirate.[141] Under a state or Continental letter of marque, a privately owned ship was authorized to take enemy vessels as prizes. The government received a share, as did the owners

---

[135] Robert A. Gross, *The Minutemen and Their World* (New York, 1976), 149.

[136] John Shy, *A People Numerous and Armed: Reflections on the Military Struggle for American Independence* (New York, 1976), 171.

[137] John Resch to author, May 29, 1980, based on research cited in n. 166 below.

[138] Gross, *Minutemen,* 151.

[139] For example, see the petition of Sylvanus Wood of Woburn, Mass., in Dann, ed., *Revolution Remembered,* 8.

[140] Hawkes, *Retrospect,* 62–63.

[141] The phrase and analysis are from Lemisch, "Jack Tar Goes A'Privateering" (unpubl. MS). I am indebted to Christopher McKee for sharing his unrivaled knowledge of naval sources.

and crew, prorated by rank. During the seven years of war, the United States commissioned 2,000 privateers, 626 in Massachusetts alone, which itself issued 1,524 commissions. In 1776, when Hewes made his decision, Abigail Adams spoke of "the rage for privateering" in Boston, and James Warren told Samuel Adams that "a whole country" was "privateering mad."[142]

War for Hewes meant opportunity: a chance to escape from a humdrum occupation never to his liking; to be at thirty-five what had been denied at sixteen—a fighting man; above all, a chance to accumulate the capital that could mean a house, a new shop, apprentices and journeymen, perhaps a start in something altogether new. He was following a path trod by tens of thousands of poor New Englanders ever since the wars against the French in the 1740s and 1750s.[143] As an economic flyer, however, privateering ultimately proved disastrous for Hewes.

His first voyage went well. He sailed on the *Diamond* out of Providence, attracted possibly by an advertisement that promised fortune and adventure. They captured three vessels, the last of which Hewes brought back to Providence as a member of the prize crew. He said nothing about his share; by inference he got enough to whet his appetite but not enough to boast about. He also nearly drowned off Newfoundland when a line he and two shipmates were standing on broke.[144]

His second voyage was shattering. He went on the Connecticut ship of war *Defence,* commanded by Captain Samuel Smedley and sailing from Boston with the *Oliver Cromwell*. The *Defence* and the *Cromwell* captured two richly laden vessels and later, after a layover in Charleston, South Carolina, two British privateers; on the way home, the *Defence* stopped a ship and relieved the tory passengers of their money. The prize money from the two privateers alone was $80,000.[145] But Hewes got nothing. His share was supposed to be $250, "but some pretext was

---

[142] Gardner Weld Allen, *Massachusetts Privateers of the Revolution* (Mass. Hist. Soc., *Collections,* LXXVII [Boston, 1927]), 716–717; James Warren to Samuel Adams, Aug. 15, 1776, in Henry Steele Commager and Richard B. Morris, eds., *The Spirit of 'Seventy-Six: The Story of the American Revolution as Told by Participants,* II (New York, 1958), 965; Abigail Adams to John Adams, Sept. 29, 1776, in L. H. Butterfield et al. eds., *Adams Family Correspondence,* II (Cambridge, Mass., 1963), 135.

[143] Nash, *Urban Crucible,* chaps. 3, 7.

[144] Hawkes, *Retrospect,* 64–67; Thatcher, *Memoir of Hewes,* 220–226. William P. Sheffield verifies Hewes's recollections of the vessel, commander (Thomas Stacey), owner (John Brown), and the names of the captured prizes: the *Live Oak,* listed as taken in Dec. 1776, and the *Mary and Joseph,* listed as taken Oct. 1776 (but by the *Montgomery* under Stacey) (*Privateersmen of Newport* [Newport, R. I., 1883], 64).

[145] Hawkes, *Retrospect,* 67–72; Thatcher, *Memoir of Hewes,* 227–257. Hewes's recollections of the details of this voyage are verified in Louis F. Middlebrook, *History of Maritime Connecticut during the American Revolution* (Salem, Mass., 1925), I, 44, 51–52, 65, II, 285–286, 303–304, 306–310, 313–316. Hewes is not on the crew list, I conclude, because Capt. Smedley, who did not give him his wages, eliminated his name (ibid., I, 70–73). For other vivid details of the encounters of the *Defence* verifying Hewes, see the diary of a sailor on the accompanying ship *Cromwell* in Samuel W. Boardman [ed.], *Log-Book of Timothy Boardman. Kept on Board the Privateer Oliver Cromwell . . .* (Albany, N. Y., 1885), entries Apr. 7–30, 1778. For additional verification see the petition of Abel Woodworth, also on the *Cromwell,* in Dann, ed., *Revolution Remembered,* 319–320. See also Gardner W. Allen, *A Naval History of the American Revolution,* I (New York, 1913), 321–323.

always offered for withholding my share from me; so that I have never received one cent of it." When he asked for his wages, Captain Smedley "told me he was about fitting out an expedition to the West Indies, and could not, without great inconvenience, spare the money then; but said he would call on his way to Providence . . . and would pay me; but I never saw him afterwards. Neither have I, at any time since, received a farthing, either of my share of prize money or wages."[146]

There was an adventurous side to privateering. His stories stress the thrill of the chase, the intrepid maneuvering of his ship in battle, the excitement of a boarding party. They also deal with the prosaic. He remembered manning the pumps on the leaking *Defence* "for eight days and eight nights to keep us from sinking." He remembered before battle that "we sat up all night . . . we made bandages, scraped lint, so that we might be prepared to dress wounds as we expected to have a hard time of it."[147] The man of tender sympathies did not become a bloodthirsty buccaneer.

Most important of all was the memory that at sea he had participated in making decisions and that the captains had shown deference to their crews. On his first voyage, the initial agreement was for a cruise of seven weeks. "When that term had expired," said Hewes, "and we had seen no enemy during the time, we were discouraged, and threatened to mutiny, unless he would return." Captain Stacey asked for one more week, after which he promised to sail home if they saw nothing, "to which we assented." On the second voyage, when the *Defence* sighted enemy ships and Captain Smedley "asked us if we were willing to give chase to them, we assented, we were all ready to go and risk our lives with him." In Charleston, their tour of duty legally over, Smedley proposed a five-day extension when the British privateers were sighted. "Our Captain put it to a vote, and it was found we were unanimously agreed to make the cruise."[148] One hesitates to call this process democratic: even the captain of a pirate ship could not function without the support of his crew. What Hewes remembered was that the captains deferred to him and his mates, not the other way around.

This is the motif of his encounter with George Washington in 1775. When Hewes and his fellow escapees from Boston were taken to Washington's headquarters at Craigie House in Cambridge, the Reverend Peter Thatcher recognized him as the nephew of the "staunch Liberty Man" Robert Hewes. Washington invited Hewes into his parlor—"with him, alone. There he told him his story, every word of it, from beginning to end, and answered all his questions besides." Washington, in Hewes's words, "didn't *laugh,* to be sure, but *looked amazing good-natured* you may depend." Washington then treated him and his companions to punch and invited them and Thatcher to a meal. All this is entirely possible. Washington was considering an invasion of Boston; he would have welcomed intelligence from a street-wise man just out of the town, and as a Virginia planter he knew the importance of the gesture of hospitality. Hewes also claimed that "Madam Washington waited upon them at table all dinner-time,"

272

---

[146] Hawkes, *Retrospect,* 71–72. Ira Dye has very kindly checked for Hewes in the computerized naval records of the Continental Congress, 1774–1789, Nat'l Archs., but without success.

[147] Hawkes, *Retrospect,* 68.

[148] Ibid., 65, 68.

but this is improbable, and Thatcher the biographer erred in stating that she was "known to have been with her husband at the date of the adventure."[149]

In military duty on land there was no recognition of this sort from his betters, though he was in the militia, by reputation the most democratic branch of service. Even his adventures were humdrum. The "general destination" of his units, he told Hawkes, was "to guard the coasts." He saw action at the Battle of Newport Island in August 1778 under General John Sullivan. He remembered "an engagement" at Cobblehill, "in which we beat them with a considerable slaughter of their men." He remembered rowing through the darkness in silence in an attack on a British fort that had to be aborted when one of the rowers talked. He remembered the grim retreat from Newport Island, crossing the waters at Howland's Ferry. On duty at West Point in 1781 he went out on forays against the "cowboys," lawless bands pillaging Westchester County. In all this activity he claimed no moment of glory; there was a lot of marching; a lot of sentry duty; much drudgery.[150] If he mended shoes for soldiers, as did other shoemakers in the ranks, he did not speak of it. And military service did not kindle in him an ambition to rise, as it did in a number of other shoemakers who became officers.[151]

After all this service it hurt to be subjected to an inequitable draft. As Hewes explained to Hawkes with considerable accuracy, Massachusetts required all men of military age to serve "or to form themselves into classes of nine men, and each class to hire an able bodied man, on such terms as they could, and pay him for his services, while they were to receive their pay of the state." Attleborough instituted such a procedure early in 1781. Why did Hewes refuse to go? He was frank with Hawkes: the "extreme exigencies" of his family and the "pressure of his circumstances" forced him to "withdraw his services from the army." The decision was painful, and it was costly. Hewes's substitute "demanded . . . specie while we received nothing of the government but paper money, of very little value, and continually depreciating."[152]

Thatcher was right: his service was "poorly rewarded." Hewes was one of "the mass of people, at large; such as had little property to fight for, or to lose, on

273

---

[149] Thatcher, *Memoir of Hewes,* 216–220. Hewes did not tell this story to Hawkes, who reported Hewes as saying, "I went on shore at a safe place, and repaired straitway to my family at Wrentham" (*Retrospect,* 61). Thatcher elicited the story as he did several others about famous people. For the Washingtons at Cambridge see Douglas Southall Freeman, *George Washington: A Biography,* III (New York, 1951), 405, 477, 580–581. Hewes spoke of being in Boston nine weeks, which means his escape would have been late Aug. or early Sept., about the time Washington was considering an attack on Boston. Martha Washington did not arrive until Dec. 11, 1775. Thatcher reported one other encounter with a famous man during the war, an episode at the Newport Island action, Aug. 1778, in which Hewes claimed he rescued James Otis, who was "roaming about the lines in one of his unhappy spells of derangement" (*Memoir of Hewes,* 238). I have not been able to prove or disprove this incident.

[150] Hawkes, *Retrospect,* 73–74; Thatcher, *Memoir of Hewes,* 237–240.

[151] For shoemakers as officers see Don Higginbotham, *The American War of Independence: Military Attitudes, Policies, and Practice, 1763–1789* (New York, 1971), 400, and Shy, *People Numerous and Armed,* 163–179. For shoemaker officers mending shoes see the Baroness von Riedesel's comments cited in Forbes, *Paul Revere,* 336.

[152] Hawkes, *Retrospect,* 74–75; Daggett, *Sketch of Attleborough,* 128; Jonathan Smith, "How Massachusetts Raised Her Troops in the Revolution," *Mass. Hist. Soc., Procs.,* LV (1921), 345–370.

one hand, and could reasonably expect to gain still less, either in the way of emolument or distinction on the other."[153] Instead, the inequities of civilian life were repeated on an even crasser scale. The rich could easily afford a substitute; the men who had already fought paid through the nose for one. The ship's officers got their share of the prize; the poor sailor got neither prize money nor wages.

But the war meant more than this to Hewes. It left a memory of rights asserted (by a threat of mutiny) and rights respected by captains who put decisions to a vote of the crew, and of the crew giving assent. It was a memory, above all, of respect from his betters: from General Washington at Cambridge, from captains Stacey and Smedley at sea, and from John Hancock in Boston. For a moment, it had been a world that marched to the tune of the old English nursery rhyme supposedly played at Cornwallis's surrender, "The World Turned Upside Down." Then "in a trice" Hewes's world came right side up—but little, if any, better than before.

VII

For thirty-three years, from 1783 to about 1815, George Hewes almost eludes us. We know that at the end of the war he did not return to Boston but stayed in Wrentham; that he produced a large family; that after the War of 1812 he moved to Otsego County, New York. But we hardly know what he did these years. His biographers were uninterested. Hawkes said he was in "laborious pursuits either in some agricultural or mechanical employment." Later lore had it that he returned to the sea and "for many years" was "a mate on merchant vessels in the West Indies trade," lore that has been impossible to verify.[154] Legal documents refer to him in 1796–1797 as a "yeoman" and in 1810 as a "cordwainer."[155] These clues are not inconsistent. Wrentham in those years was a small inland farming town of about 2,000 people, no more than a good day's walk to the port of Providence.[156] If Hewes was a cordwainer, he would have had to be a farmer

274

---

[153] Thatcher, *Memoir of Hewes,* 242–243. How much Hewes made can only be guessed: in privateering, very little on his first voyage, nothing on his second. For militia duty in 1777 Attleborough paid £3 a month plus a £2 bounty; in 1778, £2 8s. a month and £5 a month bonus (Daggett, *Sketch of Attleborough,* 124, 126). Thus if Hewes served nine months, he might have earned £27 in pay and perhaps the same as a bounty. As a resident of Wrentham he might have been attracted to Attleborough by extra pay for nonresidents. Had he wanted to make money from land service he could have enlisted in the Continental army; in 1778 Attleborough was offering £30 a month plus a bounty of £30 for army enlistments.

[154] Hawkes, *Retrospect,* 74–75; James G. Wilson, "The Last Survivor of the Boston Tea Party," *American Historical Register,* N. S., I (1897), 5, hereafter cited as Wilson, "Last Survivor." See Ira Dye, "Early American Merchant Seafarers," American Philosophical Society, *Proceedings,* CXX (1976), 331–360. After 1796 the federal government issued protection certificates to merchant seamen who requested them. Dye has generously checked for Hewes in abstracts of the surviving certificates, but without success. Providence, however, was not checked.

[155] See a will of Joseph Hewes [1796] summarized in Putnam, comp., *Joshua Hewes,* 327–338, and in Bristol County Northern District Registry of Deeds Record Book, two conveyances dated Mar. 18, 1797, in Book 76, p. 126, and Sept. 10, 1810, in Book 91, p. 453, copies of which were kindly provided by Alfred Florence, Assistant Register of Deeds, Bristol County, Taunton, Mass.

[156] Jordan D. Fiore, *Wrentham, 1673–1973: A History* (Wrentham, Mass., 1973), 136–140.

too, as were most country shoemakers. If he went to sea, he would have had to fall back on landlubber pursuits, especially in his later years. There were few "old salts" in their fifties or sixties.

All we may say with certainty is that he came out of the war poor and stayed poor. By 1783, he had turned forty, and had very little to show for it. That he did not go back to Boston, that he did not visit there more than a few times until 1821, tells us how small a stake he had in his native city. In this he was like at least a thousand other Bostonians—for the most part "the poorest and least successful"—who migrated elsewhere.[157] "The shop which I had built in Boston, I lost," he told Hawkes. British troops "appropriated it for the purpose of a wash and lumber house, and eventually pulled it down and burnt it up."[158] He owned no real estate. After seven years of war he could hardly count on customers waiting at his door. There was really nothing to go back to. Uncle Robert had died. His brothers were still there: Solomon was a fisherman and Daniel a mason, but Shubael could list himself as gentleman. Hewes bore his loyalist brother no ill will; he named a son Shubael in 1781. But his own low estate, compared to his brother's success, must have rankled.

There is no evidence that he acquired land in Wrentham. The census names him; the records of real estate bought and sold do not.[159] The town's tax records of the 1790s list him only as a "poll rateable," owning neither real nor personal taxable property. In 1796, at the age of fifty-four, he was assessed thirty-three cents for his Massachusetts poll tax, seven cents for his county tax, fifty cents for his town tax.[160] He may possibly have been joint owner of property listed in someone else's name; more likely he rented or lived on a relative's land.[161] His uncle Joseph, a Providence physician who died in 1796, willed George and Sarah

275

[157] Kulikoff, "Progress of Inequality," *WMQ*, 3d Ser., XXVIII (1971), 402. "By 1790, 45 per cent of the taxpayers in town in 1780 had disappeared from tax lists." Of 2,225 individuals on the assessors' books in 1780, 1,000 were missing in 1790. The rate of persistence was only 42% for those paying no rent, and 52% for those paying from £1 to £20, but 66% for those paying from £100 to £199, and 74% for those paying over £200 (ibid., 401–402).

[158] Hawkes, *Retrospect*, 72.

[159] U. S. Bureau of the Census, *Heads of Families at the First Census of the United States Taken in the Year 1790: Massachusetts* (Washington, D. C., 1908), Wrentham, 210, lists a George Hewes; Laraine Welch, comp., *Massachusetts 1800 Census* (Bountiful, Utah, 1973), Norfolk County, 174, lists George R. L. Hewes; Ronald Jackson et al., *Massachusetts 1810 Census Index* (Bountiful, Utah, 1976), does not list Hewes. Anne Lehane Howard, a title examiner, of Quincy, Mass., finds no record of Hewes buying or selling real estate in Suffolk or Norfolk counties in the Suffolk Co. Registry of Deeds, 1695–1899.

[160] The Wrentham tax records, incomplete and in disarray, were examined at the Assessor's Office, Wrentham, with the cooperation of Lois McKennson, Assessor, by Gregory Kaster and Patricia Reeve. Hewes is listed only as a poll rateable for 1791, 1792, 1794, 1796, and 1797; he does not appear in the other available tax lists for 1780, 1798, 1799, and 1817. Daniel Scott Smith helped interpret these data. Kaster did not find Hewes in "Massachusetts Direct Tax of 1798," MS, New England Historical and Genealogical Society, Boston. This was a dwelling tax.

[161] One tax list, for 1793, lists Solomon Hewes for £1 4s. under commonwealth real estate assessment and £5 4s. 5d. town tax. He is listed immediately above George R. T. Hewes. This possibly is Solomon his eldest son (1771–1834), who entered his majority in 1792 and would marry in Wrentham in 1794. However, Anne Lehane Howard finds no record of a Solomon Hewes buying or selling property in the Suffolk Co. Registry of Deeds after the death of grandfather Solomon Hewes (1674?–1756).

one thirty-sixth share of the estate—$580.25. The windfall helped keep him going. In 1810 he finally became a property holder in Attleborough: a co-owner, with eighteen others, of "a burying yard."[162]

That Hewes stayed poor is also suggested by what little we know about his children. Sarah Hewes gave birth to fifteen, it would seem, of whom we have the names of eleven, three girls and eight boys, possibly all who survived birth. Six were born by 1781, the rest by 1796 at the latest. The naming pattern suggests the strength of family attachments: Sally for her mother; Mary and Elizabeth for aunts, Hewes's father's sisters; Solomon, Daniel, and Shubael after his brothers (and Solomon also for his grandfather, Shubael also for Sally's relative). One son was named Eleven, and the last-born, George Robert Twelves Fifteen.[163] What can we make of this? A mischievous sense of humor? His own long name, the subject of teasing in his youth, after all had been a way of getting attention. Perhaps the only inheritance a poor shoemaker-farmer-seaman could guarantee— especially to his eleventh and fifteenth children—was a name that would be a badge of distinction as his had been.

Hewes could do little for this brood. Solomon, the first-born, became a shoemaker—undoubtedly trained by his father. Robert became a blacksmith. For the other sons we know no occupations. Of the daughters, two of the three married late—Elizabeth at twenty-two but Sarah (also Sally) in her mid-thirties and Mary at thirty-two—understandable when a father could not provide a suitor with dowry, position, or a sought-after craft skill.[164]

For a while the Heweses lived in Attleborough, but the only trace they left is the share of the "burying yard."[165] Attleborough was not much different from Wrentham; a farming town closer to Providence, it also had a few of the mills that dotted southern New England these years. For opportunity the family would have to move much farther away. And so they did, like tens of thousands of families who left New England in the 1790s and early 1800s, and like a large number of New England veterans.[166] Robert, Sally who married William Morrison, and

[162] See Bristol County Conveyance, n. 155 above.

[163] Putnam, comp., *Joshua Hewes,* 334–335, 353–357, lists nine children, leaving space between Robert and Eleven for three unnamed children, and between Eleven and Fifteen for three more. A relative sent in the names of two "missing" children as Asa and Walter (ibid., Addendum, 601–602). Fifteen was identified as the fifteenth child in a newspaper account (*Providence Journal* reprinted in *Columbian Centinel* [Boston], July 1, 1835). For the significance of child-naming practices see Daniel Scott Smith, "Child-Naming Patterns and Family Structure Change: Hingham, Massachusetts, 1640–1880" (Newberry Papers in Family and Community History, No. 76–5, Jan. 1977), and Herbert G. Gutman, *The Black Family in Slavery and Freedom, 1750–1925* (New York, 1976), chap. 5.

[164] *Vital Records of Wrentham, Massachusetts to the Year 1850,* III (Boston, 1910), 321, lists Sarah Hewes, born about 1769, marrying William Morason (sic), Nov. 27, 1806. *Vital Records of Attleboro, Massachusetts . . . to 1849* (Salem, Mass., 1934), 456, lists Eliza (sic) Hewes, born 1773, marrying Preserved Whipple, "both of Attleboro," Mar. 19, 1795, and Mary Hewes "of Wrentham," born 1777, marrying Abel Jillison of Attleborough, Jan. 21, 1809.

[165] The clerk put down that Hewes "resided in Wrentham and Attlebury [sic] since the Revolution" (Pension Application, Oct. 16, 1832). The only evidence for Hewes's residence at Attleborough is Elizabeth's marriage record of 1795 (see above, n. 164). The conveyance of the "burying yard," Mar. 10, 1810 (see above, n. 155), lists Hewes as a "cordwainer of *Wrentham*." I have not conducted a search of the tax records of Attleborough.

[166] For the migration from Attleborough see Daggett, *Sketch of Attleborough,* 664–665. John Resch found in a sample of applicants under the 1818 pension law that "a third of the total no

Elizabeth who married Preserved Whipple moved to Otsego County, New York. George Fifteen went first to Connecticut, then to Richfield Springs, finally to Michigan. Solomon also moved to Otsego County for a while, then went down east to Union, Maine, where he acquired twenty-eight acres. Eleven went to Kentucky.[167]

What had become these years of George Hewes, the citizen? We have only one thing to go on. According to family tradition, during the War of 1812 he tried to enlist in the navy as a boatswain but was turned down; tried to ship out on the frigate *Constitution;* then tried to join Commodore Perry's fleet on Lake Erie. There is even a story that he walked to Braintree to enlist ex-President John Adams's support.[168] Two sons we know saw service, Eleven in the Kentucky militia, under General Henry Clay, and George Fifteen in Connecticut. Such patriotism in Wrentham, where there was "no rush of men" to arms, would have been extraordinary.[169] It meant that the War of 1812 was a second War of Independence to Hewes; and to have sons who responded meant that the father had passed on well the heritage of the Revolution.

At the end of the war, perhaps before, George and Sarah Hewes went west to Richfield Springs. George was seventy-four, Sarah sixty-five. His family was dispersed, but three or four children were already in Otsego County or accompanied him there. Did he mean to spend his declining years in retirement with his family? He was still vigorous. One suspects he went in search of the "living," the "independence," that had eluded the artisan and the recognition that had eluded the citizen. He had gone from city to sea to small town; now he would try again in a place where at the least he would be with sons and daughters. And so he left Wrentham about 1815, as he had left Boston in 1775, probably with not much more than the tools of his trade. Only this time he had an old soldier's uniform as well.

277

VIII

In New York, Hewes did not find independence either for himself or through his children. For the last decade of his life he did not even have the haven of family. He did find recognition.

Richfield Springs, sixty-five miles west of Albany and eighteen north of Cooperstown, was no longer frontier country after 1815. Otsego County had been opened up in the 1790s by Judge William Cooper, the novelist's father,

---

longer lived in the regions where their units originated and another 20 per cent appeared to have moved to a different state within the same region" ("Poverty, the Elderly and Federal Welfare: The 1818 Revolutionary War Pension Act" [unpubl. paper, Organization of American Historians, 1980], 9). For another veteran who went west see Lemisch, "Life of Andrew Sherburne," sec. XII.

[167] Putnam, comp, *Joshua Hewes,* 353–357.

[168] Ibid., 339; Wilson, "Last Survivor," 5. Wilson heard the story of the walk out in Otsego County. There S. Crippin, the clerk who endorsed Hewes's pension application at Richfield Springs in 1832, wrote on it: "He was a soldier in the Late War as well as in the Revolution." Hewes himself made no such claim to Hawkes or Thatcher. Hewes's name does not appear on any of the checking lists in the Adams Papers, Mass. Hist. Soc., for either John or John Quincy Adams, kindly checked for me by Malcolm Freiberg.

[169] Fiore, *Wrentham,* 100. The War of 1812 pension applications of Eleven and George Fifteen are reported in Putnam, comp, *Joshua Hewes,* 357–358.

who boasted of settling 50,000 families. The pioneers were already moving away to find more fertile land on better terms in western New York or the Old Northwest. Richfield Springs was located in a beautiful area of rolling hills and low mountain peaks, of streams and lakes. In the 1820s, after mineral waters were discovered, it became a resort town. But its prosperity was uneven. It did not get a post office until 1829.[170]

What did Hewes do these years? We have more to go on for the last twenty-five years of his life than for the three decades before: Hawkes's account is supplemented by some fascinating reminiscences by Hewes's contemporaries collected in 1896 by the historian James Grant Wilson. According to "an old jesting rhyme attributed to James Fenimore Cooper who knew honest Hewes,"

> Old Father Hewes, he makes good shoes,
> And sews them well together
> It has no heels but those he steals
> And begs his upper leather.[171]

Hewes, then, was once again a shoemaker.

He and Sally lived in "a small house which his son Robert had built for him" on Robert's land.[172] Sarah Morrison was nine miles away in German Flats and Elizabeth Whipple was also in the area, each with a large and growing family. Fifteen lived nearby for a time, a property holder; so did Solomon. As before, their father had no house or land of his own.[173]

He can hardly have prospered. The clue is that when Daniel, his last surviving brother, died in 1821, Hewes travelled with Robert to Boston for five days in a one-horse wagon to secure their legacy. For the third time in his life a will loomed—Grampa Shubael left £2 17s. 6d. in 1756, and Uncle Joseph, $580.25 in 1796—a windfall so important when there were no other prospects of accumulation. George's brother Solomon had died in 1816, Shubael in 1813. Daniel left an estate that came to $2,900 after expenses; he willed a third to Hewes and his children. Hewes considered his share "a considerable sum," but it could not have stretched very far. "For some years," Hawkes wrote in

---

[170] Duane Hamilton Hurd, *History of Otsego County, New York* (Philadelphia, 1878), 298–306, passim, W. T. Bailey, *Richfield Springs and Vicinity* . . . (New York, 1874), passim. I am indebted to Ethylyn Morse Hawkins, local historian, for sharing her knowledge with me, and the following friends of the Hewes family for answering inquiries: Vern Steele of Las Vegas, Nev., and Harry B. Carson of Golden, Colo.

[171] Wilson, "Last Survivor," 5.

[172] Hawkes, *Retrospect,* 94. "New York State Census for 1820: Otsego County," the handwritten takers' book, 163, lists George R. T. Hewes as living with his wife, and Robert Hewes below him with his family, and, 160, George R. T. F. Hewes, that is, Fifteen. The 1830 census lists only Robert Hewes but with one free white male "of ninety and under one hundred" living with him, confirming Hawkes.

[173] For running Hewes down assiduously in the property records, vital records, and newspapers of Otsego County I am especially indebted to Marion Brophy, Special Collections Librarian, New York State Historical Association, Cooperstown, as well as to Wendell Tripp, Chief of Library Services, and Wayne Wright, Edith R. Empey, and Susan Filupeit of the library staff. Marion Brophy found no record of Hewes's owning property but found Fifteen owning land in Richfield Springs, corroborating Hawkes.

1833, Robert had "contributed what was necessary" to support his father and mother.[174]

Sarah died in 1828, aged 87 years and 9 months, the tombstone said. Actually she was 77. It is difficult to bring Sarah out from her husband's shadow. He spoke of her with affection: "we lived together very happily," he told Hawkes; he expected to see her in heaven. He had hardly married her for money; he had courted her for two years. He was grief-stricken when he left her in wartime. He called her Sally, not Sarah, certainly not Mrs. Hewes. What was her role? A washerwoman before she was married, she labored a lifetime as a housewife, without servants. She bore, it seems, fifteen children and raised eleven of them. She was illiterate; unlike her husband, she signed her name with a mark. A daughter of a sexton, she may well have been religious. Certainly, she was apolitical; had she been a "Daughter of Liberty," Thatcher, who dwelt on the subject, would have caught it. When George got home from the Tea Party and told her his story, "'Well George,' said she, at the end of it, *did you bring me home a lot of it?*'" "We shouldn't wonder," Thatcher added, "if Mrs. Hewes was more of a tea-drinker than a Whig." Or, we might add, more of a woman struggling to make ends meet on a shoemaker's income.[175]

After she died, it was all downhill. George moved from one child to another, each so poor they could not long provide for him. At first, he lived with Robert, who soon after, "having met with some misfortune, was obliged to sell his house" and move farther west. For a while he was "a sojourner among friends." Then he moved in with his daughter and son-in-law, the Morrisons, but stayed only a year. "Morrison and his wife had several children," wrote Hawkes, "and were, as they are now very poor . . . Morrison not being able by his manuel [sic] services to provide for his family but a mere subsistence." Hewes had a "severe sickness." Next he took up "a short residence with a son who resides near Richfield Springs," very likely George, Jr. Soon after, he "fell down a stairway on some iron ware," severely lacerating both legs. He healed with remarkable speed for a man his age, but a son with eight children to feed could not provide "for his comfortable support." Finally, a "worthy gentleman" in the neighborhood took the old man in, and it was there that Hawkes found him in 1833, "pressed down by the iron hand of poverty" and "supported by the charity of his friends." His children had failed and, in the classic style of poor pioneers, were moving on to greener fields. They and his grandchildren would scatter, most to the Midwest, some to California, some still in mechanic trades in Boston.[176]

In the fall of 1832 Hewes applied successfully for a veteran's pension. He may have applied earlier, for Hawkes spoke of a "long and expensive process" begun about fifteen or twenty years before. If true, Hewes must have been

279

---

[174] Hawkes, *Retrospect*, 77–78, 94; Will of Daniel Hewes, recorded July 16, 1821, Suffolk Co. Probate Court, and Aug. 5, 1822, Record Book 120, 129, for the final sum, $2,904.79, located by Ruth Kennedy.

[175] Tombstone, Lakeview Cemetery, Richfield Springs. For Sarah's signature as a mark see the 1797 conveyances above, n. 155. For the Tea Party see Thatcher, *Memoir of Hewes,* 186, and for Hewes on her age see Hawkes, *Retrospect,* 27.

[176] Hawkes, *Retrospect,* 94–97. See also Putnam, comp., *Joshua Hewes,* 353–357. I am grateful to Catherine Wilson of Des Moines, Iowa, a descendant via Solomon, for copies of letters by Virgil Hammond Hewes, George's grandson.

frustrated: he would not have been eligible until the 1832 law required no more than six months' service in any branch.[177] Hewes's application, in the hand of the county clerk to which a local judge and county official attested, gives minute details of his service. A clerk in Washington disallowed three of the months he claimed at sea, listing him for seven months', fifteen days' service as a seaman and nine months in the militia. It added up to sixteen months, fifteen days, or less than the two years required for a full pension; he was therefore prorated down to $60 a year, with $150 in arrears retroactive to 1831. It was, Hawkes thought, a "miserable pittance of a soldier's pension."[178]

Meanwhile, Hewes was winning recognition of a sort. A "venerable lady" whom James Grant Wilson spoke to in 1896 said she first met Hewes in 1820 at a "house raising" where she saw "an alert and little old man with the cocked hat and faded uniform of a continental soldier, who charmed the young people with the account of the destruction of the tea in Boston in December 1773, and his stories of battles on land and sea." Another woman, who attended school in Richfield Springs with one of Hewes's granddaughters, said she was always delighted to listen to the old soldier's stories and to see him on the Fourth of July, "when he would put on his ancient uniform, shoulder his crutch, like Goldsmith's veteran, and show how fields were won."[179] By the late 1820s, possibly earlier, Hewes had become a figure at Fourth of July observances. In 1829 the local paper reported that he "walked three miles on foot to join in the festivities," and "after mingling in the enjoyments of the occasion, with a fine flow of spirits returned in the same manner thro' the wet to home." In 1833 the celebrants toasted him as "the last survivor of the tea party," and he toasted them in turn.[180]

The "venerable lady" also claimed to have seen "the old soldier in conversation with James Fenimore Cooper who invited Hewes to his home in Cooperstown where he was quite a lion at the author's table." This is entirely possible. The novelist, who returned to his family home at intervals, was always mining old timers for the lore of the sea and the Revolution. Later he would invite Ned Meyers, an old salt, to spend five months at Cooperstown while he took down his life. Hewes's tales of the "cowboys and skinners" of Westchester could have added to Cooper's store of information for *The Spy;* his adventures at sea would have confirmed Cooper in his idealization of American privateersmen, a theme in several of his sea novels and his naval history.[181]

[177] Hawkes, *Retrospect,* 94–96, 114. See also Putnam, comp., *Joshua Hewes,* for a story from "a near relative" that Hewes walked 10 miles to visit ex-President John Quincy Adams to ask for help on his pension, possibly a variant of the story about Hewes's walk to ex-President John Adams to get into the navy. For the laws see Resch, "Poverty, the Elderly, and Federal Welfare," 1–7. Resch clarified a number of points for me. See also Robert George Bodenger, "Soldiers' Bonuses: A History of Veterans' Benefits in the United States, 1776–1967" (Ph.D. diss., Pennsylvania State University, 1971), 26–42, and Lemisch, "Life of Andrew Sherburne," secs. XII, XIII, for one veteran's long bitter battle for his pension.

[178] Hawkes, *Retrospect,* 114; Pension Application. The clerk disallowed the three months on the *Diamond,* probably because it was a privateer, but allowed the seven months and fifteen days on the *Defence,* also a privateer but officially a ship of war in the Connecticut navy, under a naval officer.

[179] Wilson, "Last Survivor," 5–6.

[180] *Freeman's Journal* (Cooperstown, N. Y.), July 13, 1829; Hawkes, *Retrospect,* 90.

[181] Cooper's occasional residence in Cooperstown, 1816–1840, may be established from James F. Beard, *Letters and Journals of James Fenimore Cooper* (Cambridge, Mass., 1960–1964), I–IV,

This recognition, it can be argued, had a price. The old man had to dress up in his uniform and tell stories. He was trotted out once a year on Independence Day. He had to play a role; perhaps this may have contributed to his "remembering" himself almost ten years older than he was. And the already-quoted "jesting rhyme," whether Cooper's or not, suggests that if children sat at his feet to hear his tales, they also poked fun at "Old Father Hewes."

Hawkes captured a mood in Hewes that bordered on alienation, especially as he talked about his reactions to Boston in 1821, when he went there to receive his legacy. Hewes spoke of the experience in haunting, poetic language. As he walked around town, he looked for old friends.

> But, alas! I looked in vain. They were gone. Neither were those who once knew them as I did, to be found. The place where I drew my first breath and formed my most endearing attachments, had to me become a land of strangers.

He looked for familiar places.

> Not only had my former companions and friends disappeared, but the places of their habitations were occupied by those who could give no account of them. The house in which I was born was not to be found, and the spot where it stood could not be ascertained by any visible object.

The physical city of 1775 was gone.

> The whole scenery about me seemed like the work of enchantment. Beacon hill was levelled, and a pond on which had stood three mills, was filled up with its contents; over which two spacious streets had been laid and many elegant fabrics erected. The whole street, from Boston Neck to the Long Wharf, had been built up. It was to me almost as a new town, a strange city; I could hardly realize that I was in the place of my nativity.

As he stood in the market, an "aged man" stared at him, then asked,

> Was you not a citizen of Boston at the time the British tea was destroyed in Boston harbour? I replied that I was, and was one of those who aided in throwing it into the water. He then inquired who commanded the division to which I belonged in that affair; I told him one Leonard Pitt. So he did mine, said he; and I had believed there was a man by the name of Hewes aboard the same ship with me, and I think you must be that man.[182]

They had a "social glass," reminisced, parted. "I found he as well as myself had

---

passim. Beard kindly answered my inquiry about Cooper's sources. See Cooper, *The Spy: A Tale of the Neutral Ground* (New York, 1821), and *Ned Meyers; or, a Life Before the Mast* (Philadelphia, 1843); and Thomas Philbrick, *James Fenimore Cooper and the Development of American Sea Fiction* (Cambridge, Mass., 1961), chaps. 2, 4.

[182] Hawkes, *Retrospect,* 77–80.

outlived the associates of his youthful days." Hewes did his legal business, saw his nephews and nieces, and after three days headed home.[183]

Sometime in his declining years Hewes became a Methodist. He was known to the children of the village as "The Old Saturday Man," Wilson reported, because "every Saturday for several years he walked into Richfield Springs for the purpose of being present at the services of the Methodist Church of which he was a member."[184] This lore seems trustworthy. He had become a Bible reader ("he can still read his Bible without glasses," a grandson wrote in 1836), and Hawkes found that he "often expresses his gratitude to a kind providence, for the many favours with which he has been indulged." He was also known for his temperance, a badge of Methodists. It stuck in the memory of the "venerable lady" that at the house-raising Hewes was "perhaps the only man present who did not drink the blackstrap (a mixture of whiskey and molasses) provided for the occasion."[185]

Hewes had not been a member of any other church in Richfield Springs and could hardly have been a Methodist before moving there.[186] But it is not surprising that he became one. Methodism had a growing appeal to poor, hard-working people low in status, whether among shoemakers in Lynn, Massachusetts (a center of Methodist missionaries), textile workers in Samuel Slater's mill in Webster, Massachusetts, or rural folk in the west.[187] Richfield Springs had no fewer than three Methodist chapels scattered around the township, none of which could sustain a minister; circuit riders or laymen served them. Many things about the Methodists would have attracted Hewes: a warm atmosphere of Christian fellowship; a stress on sobriety and industriousness, the Franklinian virtues he had been raised on; the promise of salvation without regard to rank or wealth.[188] This was

[183] Wilson repeated a tale that Hewes had attended the laying of the cornerstone of the Bunker Hill Monument in Boston in 1825 ("Last Survivor," 6). Hewes said nothing of this to Hawkes or Thatcher, and Hawkes said he "had made but one visit," that of 1821 (*Retrospect*, 76). Wilson's tale mixed images of the 1821 and 1835 trips. *Freeman's Jour.*, May 30, June 27, July 11, 1825, and *Cherry Valley Gazette* (N. Y.), June 28, Aug. 9, 1825, say nothing of Hewes in reports of the observance. Benson J. Lossing garbled the story further by claiming that Hewes was at the ceremony for the completion of the monument, June 17, 1843, three years after his death (*Pictorial Field-Book of the Revolution; or, Illustrations by Pen and Pencil . . .* , I [New York, 1851], 501–502).

[184] Wilson, "Last Survivor," 6. Marion Brophy reports that "there are no Methodist church records for the 1830s or 1840s in Richfield unless they are hidden in an attic somewhere. The local officials instituted a search and found nothing" (letter to the author, July 17, 1978).

[185] Wilson, "Last Survivor," 6; Hawkes, *Retrospect*, 93–94. He was not a total abstainer; Hawkes indicated that he used "stimulating liquors" when needed.

[186] The clerk wrote on Hewes's petition for a pension that there was "no clergyman residing in his neighborhood whose testimony he can obtain pursuant to the instructions from the War department" (see above, n. 178).

[187] See Paul Gustaf Faler, "Workingmen, Mechanics and Social Change: Lynn, Massachusetts, 1800–1860" (Ph.D. diss., University of Wisconsin, 1971), chap. 2; Barbara M. Tucker, "Our Good Methodists: The Church, the Factory, and the Working Class in Ante-Bellum Webster, Massachusetts," *Md. Historian*, VIII (1977), 26–37; and Charles G. Steffen, "The Mechanic Community in Transition: The Skilled Workers of Baltimore, 1788–1812" (unpubl. MS), chap. 6.

[188] Bailey, *Richfield Springs*, 148. For the character of early western Methodism see Frank Baker, *From Wesley to Asbury: Studies in Early American Methodism* (Durham, N. C., 1976), chap. 11, esp. 195–197, and George Peck, *Early Methodism within the Bounds of the Old Genesee Conference from 1788 to 1828 . . .* (New York, 1860), passim.

also a church that stressed lay leadership; shoemakers could serve as stewards, "class" leaders, and lay preachers. Hewes's Methodism seems late blooming; he may have found in the fellowship of the chapel the wholehearted acceptance of himself as a person that was missing in the Fourth of July kind of recognition from the village.

IX

For Hewes, the publication of James Hawkes's *Retrospect* in 1834 led to recognition in New England. There is no sign that the book caused a ripple in Richfield Springs or Otsego County, but in Boston it paved the way for the return of one of the "last surviving members" of the Tea Party. Hewes's attraction was his age, supposedly almost one hundred, combined with his role in a symbolic moment of the Revolution. In 1821 Hewes had been ignored. By 1835 a change in historical mood made Boston ready for him. Angry veterans forced from the pension lists in the 1820s helped bring old soldiers into the public eye, leading to the more liberal act of 1832. At the laying of the cornerstone of the Bunker Hill Monument in 1825, Daniel Webster and Lafayette shared the honors with forty veterans of the battle and two hundred other veterans of the Revolution. In the 1830s Ralph Waldo Emerson interviewed survivors of the fight at Concord Bridge, and in 1831 Oliver Wendell Holmes wrote "The Last Leaf," a poem about an aged survivor of the Tea Party.[189]

Workingmen demonstrated a special identification with the artisan republicanism of the Revolution. The Massachusetts Charitable Mechanics Association—masters all—toasted "our revolutionary mechanics" in 1825. On the Fourth of July, 1826, a shoemaker offered a toast to "the *Shoemakers of the Revolution*—they risked their little *all* upon the great *end* and gave short quarters to the foe, in 'the times that tried men's soles.'" Meanwhile Seth Luther, asserting the right of journeymen and factory operatives to combine against masters, asked "was there no *combination* when Bostonians . . . made a dish of tea . . . using Boston harbor for a tea pot?" In May 1835, when Boston journeymen house carpenters, masons, and stone cutters went on strike, they claimed "by the blood of our fathers shed on our battle fields on the War of the Revolution, the rights of American Freeman."[190]

In 1835 Hewes returned to New England on a triumphal tour of sorts accompanied by his youngest son, Fifteen. At Providence he was interviewed by the local newspaper, and the merchant patriarch Moses Brown called on him. On the way to Boston he stopped at Wrentham, perhaps to visit, perhaps to crow a bit. In Boston the papers noted his arrival, printing an excerpt from Hawkes's book. He was a celebrity. He stayed with his nephew Richard Brooke Hewes,

---

[189] Auguste Levasseur, *Lafayette in America in 1824 and 1825,* II (Philadelphia, 1829), 202–206; Kammen, *Season of Youth,* 21, 26, 120; Oliver Wendell Holmes, *Complete Poems* (Boston, 1836).

[190] Joseph Buckingham, *Annals of the Massachusetts Charitable Mechanics Association* (Boston, 1853), 202, reporting a toast at a dinner for Lafayette in 1825; shoemaker toast, 1826, in Kammen, *Season of Youth,* 44–45; Seth Luther, *An Address to the Working-Men of New-England . . . Delivered in Boston . . .* (Boston, 1832), 27. For documents of Boston labor organizations, 1825–1835, see John R. Commons et al., eds., *A Documentary History of American Industrial Society,* VI (Cleveland, Ohio, 1910), 98, 73–100.

Shubael's son, a politician who doubtless made the arrangements for his uncle's visit. Thatcher interviewed him for his biography, reliving his life in Boston. He sat for a portrait by Joseph G. Cole, Boston's rising young painter, which within a month would be on display at the Athenaeum Gallery, entitled "The Centenarian." A group of ladies presented him with a snuff box.[191]

The highlight, of course, was the Fourth of July. He was the featured guest at South Boston's observance. "In a conspicuous part of the procession," according to the newspaper, "was the venerable Mr. Hewes, in a barouche, drawn by four splendid greys," accompanied by the lieutenant governor and his entourage. There was a church service and a dinner. When the orator of the day reached the Tea Party and "alluded to the venerable patriot," Hewes "arose and received the united and enthusiastic congratulations of the audience." He was supported on one side by Major Benjamin Russell, for forty years a leader of the mechanic interest as printer and publisher, and on the other by Colonel Henry Purkitt, who had been a cooper's apprentice and, like Hewes, a Tea Party volunteer. The orator was fulsome in his tribute to Hewes, "formerly a citizen of Boston," now "on the verge of eternity": "Though you come to the land of your childhood, leaning upon a staff and feeling your dependence on the charities of a selfish world, you are surrounded by friends who feel that their prosperity is referable to the privations sacrifices and personal labors of you and your brave associates in arms." At the dinner after the toasts it was Hewes's turn. "Under the influence of strong emotion he gave the following toast, 'Those I leave behind me, May God Bless them.'"[192]

When the celebrations ended, Hewes made his way to Augusta, Maine. Solomon, his eldest, had died there the year before, and his wife had just died, but there were grandchildren to visit. He also went to Portland, perhaps for more family. From Maine, back to Boston, and thence home to Richfield Springs.

Several things struck those who saw Hewes. The first, of course, was his age. Not surprisingly, people came forward from all around—Wrentham, Attleborough, Boston, Maine—to testify, as they had in Richfield Springs, that he was indeed one hundred, if not more. The second was his remarkable physical condition. Third was his wonderful mood. A correspondent of the *Boston Courier* who rode the stagecoach to Augusta was astonished that "he bore the ride of fifty-eight miles with very little apparent fatigue, amusing himself and his fellow passengers occasionally upon the route, with snatches of revolutionary songs, and by the recital of anecdotes of the days which tried mens souls." He was in his glory. And lastly, there was his demeanor. Hewes's Providence interviewer found him "even at this age, a brave, high spirited, warm hearted man, whose tongue was never controlled by ceremony, and whose manners have not been moulded by the fashion of any day. His etiquette may be tea party etiquette, but it was not acquired at tea parties in Beacon Street or Broadway."[193] Hewes, in short, was still not taking his hat off for any man.

---

[191] *Columbian Centinel,* July 1, 9, 1835; *Evening Mercantile Jour.,* July 1, 8, 1835; *American Traveller* (Boston), July 28, 1835. I am indebted to Helen Callahan for making a search of the Boston newspapers for July 1835.

[192] *Evening Mercantile Jour.,* July 8, 1835; *Am. Traveller,* July 7, 1835.

[193] *Boston Courier,* July 22, 1835; *Providence Jour.,* reprinted in *Columbian Centinel,* July 1, 1835.

The remaining five years in Richfield Springs were no different than the previous twenty. Thatcher's biography appeared late in 1835, but there is no sign that it was read any more than Hawkes's. "The Old Saturday Man" continued to walk to church. The veteran continued to be a guest on the Fourth of July. His family was dispersed; there were more than fifty grandchildren, and occasionally one visited him. In 1836 George Whipple, Elizabeth's son, found him "pretty well, and very jovial. He sang for me many old songs and told over all the incidents of the 'scrape' in Boston Harbor. His memory is uncommonly good for one of his age. He jumped about so when I made myself known to him he liked to have lost his drumsticks." The old man clearly was starved for company. A visit from a grandchild only underscored his isolation. In 1836 he sat for a portrait by a local artist, commissioned by a grandson. He looked smaller, shrunken.[194]

On July 4, 1840, as Hewes was getting into a carriage to go to the annual observance, the horses bolted and he was seriously injured. He died on November 5, Pope's Day, once the "grand gala day" of Boston's apprentices. He was buried in what became the Presbyterian cemetery, where his wife already lay. There seem to have been no obituary notices, no public memorial services.

From mid-century on, Hewes began to make an occasional appearance in histories of the nation, the Revolution, Boston, or the Tea Party.[195] Descendants also kept his memory alive. Children and grandchildren named sons after him; one great-grandson bore the distinctive George Twelves Hewes (1861–1921). The generation that matured late in the nineteenth century rediscovered him as some compiled a mammoth genealogy and others applied to patriotic societies.[196] In 1896 his remains were exhumed and reinterred ceremoniously in the Grand Army of the Republic plot in Lakeview Cemetery, Richfield Springs. The inscription on the tombstone reads "George R. T. Hewes, one who helped drown the tea in Boston, 1770, died November 5, 1840, aged 109 years 2 months."[197] If anyone in town knew the truth, no one wanted to destroy the myth. The next year James Grant Wilson published the first article devoted to

285

[194] Putnam, comp., *Joshua Hewes,* 362–363, 439, reported this as an oil by Charles Palmer of Richfield Springs, done Jan. 1836 on a board 2'1" x 2'6," in the possession of David Hewes, Robert Hewes's son. Wilson reprints this, "redrawn from a photograph by Mr. Sidney Waldman" ("Last Survivor," 3). I have been unable to locate painting, photograph, or drawing. Hawkes's *Retrospect* has a drawing in the frontispiece, which could have been made from life, and Thatcher's *Memoir of Hewes* has still another drawing, most likely copied from the Cole portrait. Sometime after Hewes's death there was a second printing of Hawkes's *Retrospect* with a new frontispiece drawing of Hewes and 16 illustrations of events of the Revolution, copied from other engravings.

[195] Lossing, *Pictorial Field-Book,* 499n, 501–502; with numerous inaccuracies repeated in *Appletons' Cyclopedia of American Biography,* ed. James Grant Wilson and John Fiske, III (New York, 1887), 190; William Cullen Bryant and Sidney Howard Gay, *A Popular History of the United States,* III (New York, 1883), 374; Henry C. Watson, *The Yankee Tea Party* (Philadelphia, 1851), Drake, *Tea Leaves,* cxv; Samuel Adams Drake, *Old Landmarks and Historic Personages of Boston* (Boston, 1873), 269–270, 282–283; Bailey, *Richfield Springs,* 98–99. Esther Forbes is the only modern historian to have used the memoirs extensively.

[196] Putnam, comp., *Joshua Hewes,* 353–358, 601–602. I am indebted to the registrar general of the Daughters of the American Revolution for providing me with copies of five applications by Hewes's descendents.

[197] The end of the century had "an obsession with transplanting Revolutionary heroes to more suitable graves" (Kammen, *Season of Youth,* 65).

Hewes, perpetuating the notion that Hewes was the last survivor of the Tea Party.[198]

In 1885 a great-grandson gave the Cole painting to the Bostonian Society, which has displayed it ever since at the Old State House. In the opinion of contemporaries, it was "an admirable likeness."[199] It shows a happy man of ninety-three in his moment of triumph in Boston. He wears Sunday clothes, nineteenth-century style, and leans forward in a chair, his hands firmly gripping a cane. His face is wrinkled but not ravaged; his features are full, his eyes alert. He has most of his hair. There is a twinkle in his eyes, a slightly bemused smile on his lips. The mood is one of pride. It is not a picture of a man as a shoemaker, but we can understand it only if we know the man was a shoemaker. It shows the pride of a man the world had counted as a nobody at a moment in his life when he was a somebody, when he had won recognition from a town that had never granted it before. It is the pride of a citizen, of one who "would not take his hat off to any man." The apprentice who had once deferred to John Hancock lived with the memory that Hancock had toiled side by side with him, throwing tea chests into Boston harbor. The man who had to defer to British officers, royal officials, and colonial gentry had lived to see General Washington, ship captains, and now lieutenant governors, educated lawyers, and writers defer to him.

It is the pride of a survivor. His enemies had all passed on. His "associates," the patriots, had all gone to their graves. He had outlived them all. Fortified by his religion, the old man could rejoice that he would soon join them, but as their equal. "May we meet hereafter," he told his Independence Day well-wishers, "where the wicked will cease from troubling and the true sons of Liberty be forever at rest."[200]

Author's Postscript

I can't for the life of me remember just when I decided to do a study of George Robert Twelves Hughes and his memory of the American Revolution. In the mid-1970s I was well into a larger study now called *In the Streets of Boston: The Common People and the Shaping of the American Revolution* and was exploring different vantage points to get at popular consciousness and groping for a way to trace consciousness over time. Hewes kept popping up in events large and small. At some point it dawned on me that there were not one but two as-told-to biographies of him, published in 1834 and in 1835, and that the portrait "The Centenarian" (1835) hanging in the Old State House in Boston was of the same

---

[198] David Kinneson, who died in Chicago in 1848, seemingly was the last survivor (see Lossing, *Pictorial Field-Book,* 501–502).

[199] *Am. Traveller,* July 28, 1835, wrote of the portrait that "it is an admirable likeness—everything about it—the coloring, expression &c. even to the cane, are true to life." The Bostonian Society acquired the portrait in 1885, according to an article by D.T.V. Hustoon, its secretary (*Boston Weekly Transcript,* Jan. 26, 1886). For Cole (1803–1858) see William Dunlap, *History of the Rise and Progress of the Arts of Design in the United States,* III (New York, 1834), 136, who said that the Hewes portrait was "among the best of his portraits." The dating of the portrait is confirmed by Mary Leen, Librarian, Bostonian Society (letter to the author, Aug. 16, 1977).

[200] Hawkes, *Retrospect,* 91, citing a toast of July 4, 1833.

man. How extraordinary for a shoemaker! After I got going, I wanted to show it was possible to do the life history of a shoemaker, but if memory serves, I did not start out with this goal.

I was inspired by Jesse Lemisch's scholarship, especially his Brecht-like study of Andrew Sherburne, an American prisoner of war who published a bitter memoir. I was also excited by the remarkable display of remembering and disremembering in an African-American sharecropper in his eighties revealed by Theodore Rosengarten's *All God's Dangers: The Life of Nate Shaw*, now a classic of oral history.[201]

I was skeptical about Hewes even after one independent source after another attested to his credibility for events. In my own life I had little experience with the memory of old people; I did not know my grandparents. I did not really acquire confidence in the memory of the elderly until 1978, when I first encountered my eighty-four-year-old Uncle Judah in London for the first time. He was hale; he walked me around London until I dropped. He regaled me with richly detailed stories about himself and my father growing up in London's East End working class three quarters of a century before, which he reconstructed through the lens of his later success. I have a vivid memory of sitting on the floor of his apartment amidst the Young clan constructing my first family genealogy.

After an uninspired first draft failed to move my readers, I realized that my subject was as much the way George Hewes had remembered the Revolution—memory—as the way he had lived it—experience—and that to recover his consciousness I had to unravel the two and then intertwine them anew.

Scholars attempting to do life histories of ordinary people today should encounter fewer griffins guarding the gates than I did. I remember too many counsels of intimidation.

Why do the biography of an insignificant person? Well, why not? Look at what you can learn about the Revolution from Hewes's life.

Can you trust memory in the aged? A mound of scientific literature now attests to the potential accuracy of long-term memory while it establishes remembering as an active process shaped by the present needs of the individual rather than as a matter of mechanical storage and retrieval.

Is the person typical? This griffin still breathes fire. Scholars should not have to do a second article in the footnotes as I did, examining Hewes's representativeness at each phase of his life. One of the potentials of doing life histories of ordinary people is to raise questions that pose entirely new categories of analysis. Let other scholars hypothesize from the particular.

Are the sources there? The griffin should no longer ask this question. For the Revolutionary era, first-person sources—diaries, journals, memoirs, contemporaneous biographies, petitions, letters, veterans' pension applications—are abundant now that our eyes are open to them. And they are rich, now that we are learning to read them. The 20,000-plus pension applications after 1832, in which veterans gave a "full account" of their experiences in the war, remain a largely untapped treasure trove of little autobiographies.

I am currently doing the life history of Deborah Sampson Gannett, a young Massachusetts farm woman and former indentured servant, who disguised herself as a man and fought in the Continental Army, for whom there also are two biog-

[201] New York, 1974.

287

raphers and a score of goggle-eyed contemporary observers. I am searching for a way to let readers in on the critical process the historian goes through that would convey the gaps, uncertainties, and alternative ways of interpreting evidence. I am also searching for a style that would allow the historian to reveal where his own subjectivity enters into the narrative. Getting at Hewes involved peeling off the overlay both his biographers and he had imposed on the memory of his life. I think it's time to peel off the historian as well.

288

Bunker Hill to World War I

Great Battles for Boys

by
Joe Giorello

Note from the Author

Great men make great sacrifices in the battle for freedom.

You'll see that in these battles. These brave warriors teach us about courage and determination, especially when the odds are stacked against them. I hope you'll follow the links at the end of each chapter and discover even more books and movies—although most of the movies were made in Hollywood, so they're not the literal truth. After reading this book, you'll know the difference.

I really like hearing from you. So if you have any questions or want to suggest another battle for a future book, contact me on my web page, www.greatbattlesforboys.com, or check in on the Great Battles page on Facebook: facebook.com/greatbattles. And be sure to check out all the other books in the Great Battles for Boys series.

But above all, remember: "Freedom isn't free."

—Joe Giorello

Table of Contents

The Battle of Bunker Hill

June 17, 1775

"Don't fire until you see the whites of their eyes."

WAY BACK IN the 1770s, America was a colony that belonged to Great Britain. But not everyone liked that arrangement. Basically, Americans had no rights of their own, only what British gave them. Angry colonists started demanding, "No taxation without representation."

What did they mean?

King George III of Great Britain was forcing the American colonists to pay huge taxes, even though these colonists had nobody representing them in British Parliament. So even if these taxes were totally unfair, the colonists had no way to stop the British from taking their money. They had taxation, but no representation in Parliament.

By the summer of 1775, this problem had grown so serious that British soldiers stationed in America had to put down some colonial skirmishes, particularly in the towns of Lexington and Concord, Massachusetts. Those colonists were getting really mad because the taxes were only getting worse and the British army was treating the Americans like servants. The British soldiers were called "Red Coats" because they wore bright red uniforms.

King George believed that his Red Coats could stop these skirmishes, and the American rebellion would go away.

King George III

Just the opposite happened.

Colonists started forming groups so they could fight the British more effectively. On the night of June 16, 1775, under cover of darkness, a man named Israel Putnam and 1,200 other colonists snuck toward Bunker Hill. This hill was the highest point above Boston Harbor, where the British navy anchored its ships. The colonists planned to fire on the Redcoats and drive the British from their city.

Maybe it was because they were creeping through the dark, trying to avoid detection, or maybe somebody got lost, but most of the colonists completely missed Bunker Hill! Instead, they wound up on nearby Breed's Hill. That hill sits in front of Bunker Hill, also facing the water of Boston Harbor. So it wasn't a total disaster.

Throughout the night, these rebel colonists worked under the direction of Colonel William Prescott. They set up military positions and dug a breastwork—that's a fort made of dirt and whatever else might be available. This particular breastwork was made of tree limbs, rocks, and hogsheads—which weren't actually hog's heads, but the nickname for large wooden casks that held wine and beer.

The next morning, when the sun rose in the east, a British officer stationed on the warship *HMS Lively* gazed up at Breed's Hill. There were all those American rebels. The officer sounded the alarm.

Colonial soldiers defending earthworks, Battle of Bunker Hill

The *Lively* fired first, followed by the *HMS Somerset* where an officer ordered all the ship's guns, or cannons, to fire along with all the batteries on nearby Copp's Hill. These first volleys were hit-or-miss, partly because the Americans had staked out the high ground above the harbor.

But chaos came next.

Many of the colonists were part of local militias but didn't have much formal training. Other men were farmers and tradesmen. But here was this rag-tag volunteer force exchanging fire with what was then the world's most powerful army—the Redcoats!

One American private later described their situation:

". . . fatigued by our Labour, having no sleep the night before, very little to eat, no drink but rum, the danger we were in made us think there was treachery, and that we were brought there to be all slain."

But the colonists' passion made up for their lack of discipline—these men *really* wanted the British army out of Boston. As the battle on Breed's Hill raged on, the citizens of Boston climbed onto their roofs to watch the fight. It wasn't pretty. British cannons were literally blowing off limbs and even heads of the rebel fighters.

American Colonel William Prescott saw another problem. The colonial position on Breed's Hill allowed the British to flank them on both sides. So Prescott ordered another breastwork built down the east side of the hill, to the peninsula along the Mystic River. Prescott also sent another regiment with two cannons to build a fort on Bunker Hill, to stop the British advance.

By one o'clock that afternoon, the Redcoats managed to land at the bottom of Breed's Hill. More British troops landed on the banks of the Mystic River. But that second extended breastwork hindered the Red Coats. And around three o'clock, American Colonel John Stark arrived with reinforcements.

Stark told his men to form three separate firing lines. He then walked out fifty yards from the battle's front and drove a stake into the ground. He ordered his men not to fire before the British troops reached that marker. His exact words might have been: "Don't fire until you see the whites of their eyes."

Back then, British soldiers were taught to march forward in three orderly rows. So the first line came, ordered forward by British General Howe.

When the first Redcoats reached that stake in the ground, Stark ordered, "Fire!"

The British line was slaughtered.

Then the second line approached. Stark waited until the soldiers reached that stake in the ground, then called out, "Fire!"

Another slaughter.

The third line of Red Coats marched forward—and met the

same fate.

It didn't help the British that the terrain had tall grass that hid stone walls and ditches. Some of the soldiers were tripping forward. But their worst problem was tactical. The British were using six-pound cannons—but only had twelve-pound shot. That meant, the cannonballs were the wrong size for the cannons!

Meanwhile, the Americans delivered a near-continuous volley of fire.

When British General Howe reorganized his troops for a third assault, he wisely shifted his infantry into deep columns instead of those orderly rows that exposed every man in the line.

The Americans kept firing but soon ran out of ammunition. At that point, the colonists decided to "retreat in order"—that's a military term for when an army keeps firing as it leaves a battlefield, protecting its rear guard and its other troops.

In the end, the British took Breed's Hill.

But what had they gained?

One grassy hill above Boston harbor. Their losses were so much bigger. More than 1,000 British soldiers were killed or wounded in this battle. That was almost a forty percent of their forces in the area.

The Americans suffered, too, with about 450 men killed or wounded. But to the rebels, the Battle of Bunker (Breed's) Hill was a victory. One ragged band of ordinary men had taken on the world's most powerful army—and probably would've won if they hadn't run out of ammunition.

At that point, The Revolutionary War was on. Many more fights lay ahead as American fought for their independence from their British king.

WHO FOUGHT?

The British Army was a big reason why the colonists were paying such high taxes.

Before the Revolutionary War, the British had fought in something called the French and Indian War (1754–1763). In that war, England fought France, mostly in areas around Canada and the New England colonies. Eventually, King George III signed a treaty that ended the French and Indian war, but all that fighting had created massive debts for England. Wars are expensive. King George decided that the American colonists should help pay off that debt with higher taxes and other official acts. The colonists disagreed.

They started boycotting British goods. They also formed groups that opposed all things British. Even colonists who were former British soldiers and who had fought in the French and Indian War didn't agree with King George.

Samuel Whittemore, for instance, was born in England and came to North America in 1745 as a captain in the Dragoons (light cavalry) of the British Army. After the French and Indian War, Whittemore settled in Massachusetts.

But Whittemore didn't pledge life-long loyalty to King

George.

On April 19, 1775, British troops were making their way back to Boston after fighting with American rebels in Lexington and Concord. Whittemore—now 80 years old—hid behind a nearby stone wall and loaded his musket. He ambushed the Redcoats, killing one. He then drew his dueling pistols, killing another soldier and mortally wounding a third. Whittemore fired another shot, but a British detachment reached his position and shot Whittemore in the face as the old man drew his sword.

The British soldiers bayoneted Whittemore thirteen times and left him for dead.

When colonial militiamen found the old man, he was trying to load his musket.

Miraculously, Samuel Whittemore continued to fight for American colonies in the Revolutionary War.

He later died of natural causes, at age 98.

BOOKS

Rush Revere and the First Patriots: Time Travel Adventures with Exceptional Americans by Rush Limbaugh

Woods Runner by Gary Paulsen

Patriots by Gregory T. Edgar

The Battle of Bunker Hill: An Interactive History Adventure by Michael Burgan, a choose-your-adventure story.

INTERNET

History.com offers some re-enactments of Bunker Hill, with information about leaders and heroes of the Revolutionary War: history.com/topics/battle-of-bunker-hill

MOVIES

America: Her People, Her Stories. The Battle of Bunker Hill (DVD)

The Patriot (2000)

The Battle of Saratoga

September 19 – October 7, 1777

Major General John "Gentleman Johnnie" Burgoyne
September 19 and October 7, 1777

THE BATTLE OF Saratoga wasn't one battle—it was a whole series of conflicts. But the battle's final outcome changed the entire Revolutionary War.

General John Burgoyne was among Britain's most influential leaders. He was nicknamed "Gentleman Johnny" because he liked to throw parties between battles. But with the Revolutionary War going on for two years, Burgoyne wasn't having much fun.

He was determined to end this fight—by crushing the rebellious colonists.

Burgoyne's plan was to divide the colonial rebel armies. Britain could gain control of the northern colonies, then Burgoyne believed all the southern colonies would surrender. So Burgoyne and his men planned to advance into the northern colonies from Canada, marching down the Hudson Valley to the city of Albany, New York. From Albany, Burgoyne's forces would join up with more British soldiers and rout the Americans.

Burgoyne also wanted to meet in Albany because that town had a lot of Tories—or colonists who were still loyal to Britain—as well as Iroquois and Mohawk Indians. During the French and Indian War, the Native American tribes had fought alongside the British. Burgoyne expected them to join the British for this battle, too.

The general's first target was Fort Ticonderoga. This fort sat on the banks of Lake Champlain, a gigantic lake in New York state. After scouting the area, the British Army discovered there was an unoccupied mountain that overlooked the fort. Burgoyne ordered his troops to haul cannons up the mountainside. In battle, it's always good to have the high ground—like the colonists on hills above Boston Harbor.

Inside Fort Ticonderoga, the rebel Americans saw these British soldiers moving the guns to high ground. They knew the fort was going to become indefensible, so they abandoned their position and fled into the woods.

Burgoyne took this retreat as a sign of victory.

He wrote to an English lord in London:

"I have the honor to inform your Lordship that the enemy [were] dislodged from Ticonderoga and Mount Independent, on the 6th instant, and . . . left with the loss of 128 pieces of cannon, all their armed vessels and bateaux [boats], the greatest part of their baggage and ammunition, provision and military stores . . ."

Sure sounded impressive, didn't it?

But Burgoyne went on to make a really bad mistake. Instead of using boats to cross Lake Champlain and surprise the Americans on the other side of the water, Burgoyne tried to chase the rebels over land. With 7,500 men, forty-two cannons, and a supply train that included hundreds of carts, the British struggled through thick woods and hilly terrain. Plus, the colonists figured out clever ways to slow the Red Coats even further. For instance, they cut down trees and used them to block the trails. They also initiated skirmishes with Burgoyne's vanguard—the lead soldiers—holding back the rest of the British forces.

Burgoyne's progress slowed to one mile a day. Finally, realizing this enemy was winning, Burgoyne sent some Indians ahead to scout the territory.

The Indians came across a cabin with two women inside: an elderly widow named Mrs. McNeill and a pretty girl named Jane McCrea. The Indians started quarreling with each other. They were arguing over which woman would bring the most money for a ransom—the old woman or the beautiful girl? The Indian who lost that argument shot and scalped Jane McCrea. The rest of them delivered old Mrs. McNeil to the British camp.

The Death of Jane McCrea by John Vanderlyn (1804)

The old woman was, naturally, very upset. She also happened to be the cousin of a powerful British General, Simon Frasier. She told her cousin her terrifying tale. Frasier was outraged. He complained to Burgoyne and demanded justice.

Burgoyne ordered the Indians to be hanged.

The leader of the Indians told Burgoyne that if anything happened to his scouts, the entire tribe would desert the British forces.

Burgoyne was so desperate to wipe out the American rebels, he pardoned the Indians.

That was his second big mistake.

News spread throughout the colonies about Jane McCrea's murder and scalping—and about how the British didn't punish the Indians who committed this terrible crime. But as usually happens with these kinds of retellings, the story grew. Soon people were saying that Burgoyne's plan was to unleash wild

Indians on helpless colonists—they would all be scalped and killed.

That rumor even fired up some Tories. Now they were angry enough at the British army to join the rebel cause. From old men to young boys, Americans started picking up their muskets, swords, and rifles. Soon, the colonial force almost doubled in size, from about 9,000 to 15,000 men.

On the other side, the British army was *losing* men. Troop numbers fell from 7,200 to 6,000 soldiers. And the Red Coats were suffering from severe food shortages. American farmers started destroying their crops and scattering their livestock so that the British wouldn't have anything to eat.

Burgoyne, hoping to replenish his troops and his supplies, sent Lieutenant Colonel Friedrich Baum and 700 soldiers to an area near Lake Champlain. It's a huge lake that sits between the Green Mountains of Vermont and the Adirondack mountains of New York. Baum's force was an odd mix of British soldiers, German mercenaries, Tories, and Indians. To make things even more confusing, Baum didn't speak English. So to talk to his troops, he had to rely on an interpreter.

Baum soon learned that the Americans were planning to chase his forces through the forests around Lake Champlain. Baum asked Burgoyne for reinforcements. The general told him he was sending several hundred German mercenaries to help.

American General John Stark—the same colonist who fought at Bunker Hill—gathered 1,500 men to pursue Baum. And they collected men along the way as news travelled about the scalping of Jane McCrea. The American rebels finally caught up to Baum.

American General John Stark

But Baum was expecting those German reinforcements from Burgoyne—he thought that's who these guys were!

Stark's men surrounded Baum's forces. When the first shots were fired, the Indians took off. They felt no loyalty to the British force. Then Stark made a flanking maneuver that drove Baum's men into a tight center. He launched the main attack. Baum was shot and killed.

The British force fell apart.

But then—guess who showed up?

Those German mercenaries!

These men tried to form ranks and fire volleys at the American. But the colonial Green Mountain Boys—a New Hampshire militia—hid behind trees and picked off the Germans.

Green Mountain Rangers, 1776

The German leader soon realized he was losing men. He asked his drummer boy to beat out a "slow roll," which was the international signal to request a truce. The problem was, amid the thick black smoke of gunpowder, the blasts of gunfire, and the dense forest, the Americans didn't hear the drummer boy. They continued to fight.

In the end, the British lost 207 men. Another 700 were captured, along with four cannons.

The Americans only lost thirty men, although another forty were wounded.

But Burgoyne received even more alarming news. His fellow British officer, General Howe, who fought at Bunker Hill, had captured the American rebel capitol of Philadelphia—but that meant Howe wouldn't come help Burgoyne—he had to hold onto Philadelphia. That left only one other nearby British general—Henry Clinton—but he *also* refused to come help Burgoyne. Clinton was afraid the masterful American General George Washington would retake the New York territory that Clinton had just captured. And Clinton was right.

Washington decided it was time to strike—Burgoyne.

Washington ordered Daniel Morgan, Benedict Arnold, and 1,000 riflemen to join the American troops heading for Saratoga, New York. Led by American General Horatio Gates, these troops began digging earthworks on a Saratoga farm that belonged to a British loyalist named John Freeman.

Artist's drawing of the Battle of Saratoga

The British sent 2,000 soldiers to slip around the Americans' left flank. The Red Coats hoped to seize a hill overlooking the rebel trenches.

American Benedict Arnold wanted to attack the British on open ground. But Gates refused and ordered the colonial troops to wait in the trenches while the British approached.

This situation set up the first battle of Saratoga—also known as The Battle of Freeman's Farm. It took place on September 19, 1777.

As the Red Coats advanced, American Daniel Morgan and 500 sharpshooters began picking off the British officers. The British light infantry used a bayonet charge to push back the Americans. Arnold then ordered out two regiments to stop the British, but the colonists couldn't overcome the powerful Red Coats.

So the British gained control of the field.

But they suffered some 600 casualties, about twice as many as the Americans.

The Americans then moved south and set up defenses at a place called Bemis Heights. More colonial militia men arrived, expanding the colonial force.

On October 7, Burgoyne ordered his troops to advance all along the American line.

Benedict Arnold rode back to Gates and begged for reinforcements. But Gates again refused Arnold's request. He even ordered Arnold confined to headquarters! (Arnold was a bit of a hot-head).

The Red Coats, helped by German mercenaries, managed to push back the Americans. But still, more bad news came to Burgoyne. His communications had been cut off, and most of his supply ships had been captured by American forces on the coast.

Burgoyne refused to surrender. He attacked again.

Gates, however, was slow to retaliate. And now Benedict

Arnold refused to obey any longer. Jumping on his horse, Arnold led a charge straight into the British center.

Benedict Arnold at the Battle of Saratoga

Daniel Morgan called for his best rifleman, Tim Murphy, to shoot the battle's leading field officer, British General Simon Frasier. And in fact, a rifle bullet killed Fraiser, although historians dispute who shot it. As soon as the general went down, the British line broke.

Arnold then led the Americans into the right wing of the British forces. Arnold was shot in the leg, but the Americans forced Burgoyne to retreat. They also pursued the Red Coats for several days, until Burgoyne realized his army was surrounded with nowhere to go.

On October 17, 1777, "Gentleman Johnny" Burgoyne officially surrendered to the Americans.

The Battle of Saratoga was over.

The American rebels had won.

"It was a glorious sight," declared one militiaman, "to see the haughty Brittons march out and surrender their arms to an army which but a little before they despised and called paltroons."

News of the British surrender reached London. It shocked that proud nation. How could a bunch of untrained Americans take down the world's most powerful army?

Even worse for England, now the French wanted to take advantage of this military miracle—France also declared war on England! The French would become a crucial ally in the American Revolution.

And historians would later say that the turning point in this war for independence was the Battle of Saratoga.

Surrender of General Burgoyne by John Trumbull, 1822.
Burgoyne in red, Gates in Blue, Daniel Webster in white.
Do you think the artist was saying something about red, white, and blue?

WHO FOUGHT?

That's where some of the trouble began.

In 1779, Arnold made a secret deal to give the British control of West Point. Yes—he was turning his back on his
country. But Arnold's traitorous plan was exposed before he
could carry it out. Arnold then switched sides—and joined the
British Army as a brigadier general.

Benedict Arnold became a Red Coat.

Today, calling someone "Benedict Arnold" means he's a
traitor.

But if Arnold had never betrayed his fellow Americans, his
courage on the battlefield would've placed him among the
greatest American fighters of all time.

BOOKS

The Notorious Benedict Arnold by Steve Sheinkin

The Battle of Saratoga (We the People) by Don Nardo

INTERNET

In 1864, a minister recorded the words and images of six Revolutionary War soldiers, each veteran more than 100 years old. At that time, the United States was embroiled in the Civil War.

You can read the stories and see pictures of these veterans, some of whom fought in The Battles of Saratoga: earlyamerica.com/review/2012_summer_fall/last-men-of-revolution.html

One man from Daniel Morgan's rifle regiment wrote a first-person account of The Battle of Saratoga: earlyamerica.com/review/2004_summer_fall/saratoga.htm

Check out the original map of the Battle of Saratoga: earlyamerica.com/earlyamerica/maps/saratogamap/enlargement.html

The Alamo

February 23 – March 6, 1836

"The Fall of the Alamo," or "Crockett's Last Stand"
(1903) Texas state archives

TODAY, TEXAS IS among the fifty states within the United States. But back in 1821, Mexico owned the land that we now call Texas, and Mexico itself had just declared its own independence from Spain. (There were a lot of fights for independence during the 1800s).

Because the Mexican government didn't want Spain to get that land back, it offered parcels of land—for free!—to any law-abiding citizen of the United States. That way, Spain couldn't swoop in and steal back the land because so many people would be living on it.

This free land offer started off okay. Farmers, hunters, doctors, and lawyers moved to the territory and started their new life on the wild frontier. These Texas pioneers were nicknamed Texians. Kind of like a combination of "Texan" and "American." Soon there were a lot of Texians. In just five years—from 1823 to 1828—their numbers grew from 500 to 30,000 people.

But now the Mexican government was worried there were *too many* of these immigrants on its land.

So Mexico's Congress passed a law that forbids any more Americans from moving to that land. Mexican General Antonio Santa Anna, who was the real ruler of Mexico, took it one step further. Santa Anna ordered all these "illegal" settlers to leave. Santa Anna also wanted to take all their guns, including any guns that belonged to *Tejanos*—the Hispanic people in the territory who sided with the Texians.

Hoping to keep some peace, Texian leader Stephen Austin rode to Mexico City. Austin asked the Mexican government to declare Texas a state. Independent. Not under Mexico's rule.

The Mexican government threw Austin in jail.

When he was released two years later, Austin returned to the territory of Texas, fully convinced that the only way the Texians and *Tejanos* could keep their land was to fight for it. They basically declared war on the Mexican government.

American Colonel William Travis and twenty-five other men then seized a Mexican fort in the town of Anahuac (pronounced "anna-WHACK"). The year was 1835, and after that fight, the Texians got into another fight with Mexican troops in the town of Gonzales. One hundred Mexican dragoons (cavalry) rode out to capture the Texians' only cannon. But when the dragoons got there, they saw a sign over the cannon's barrel.

It read: "COME AND TAKE IT."

The Texians then fired on the Mexican cavalry.

The dragoons galloped back to San Antonio.

Detail of mural Gonzales, Texas
featuring the *Come and Take It* flag.

Americans came from all over Texas and the western United States to gather in the town of Gonzales. They formed a volunteer army and planned to fight Santa Anna's troops.

In December 1835, Colonel Benjamin Miliam took 300 of these men and attacked the Mexican army in the city of San Antonio. After five days of fighting, Mexican General Martín Perfecto de Cos surrendered to the Texians.

When Cos surrendered, the Texians figured this war with

Mexico was basically over. So people returned to their regular lives as farmers, trappers, merchants, and adventurers. But, as a precaution, the Texians left one garrison—or, small body of soldiers—in a San Antonio mission.

That mission was called as the Alamo.

An enormous Spanish church complex, the Alamo had really thick stone walls that stretched across four *acres*. But the Alamo was never intended to be a military fort. The mission's walls were thick, but they had no bastions or parapets—the catwalks and reinforced beams that normally protect forts. The Alamo also had only about 100 men garrisoned inside. Not nearly enough to protect the whole place.

But the Texians were figuring the war with Mexico was mostly over.

The problem was, Mexican General Santa Anna didn't see things that way. Deeply embarrassed by his losses to the Texians, Santa Anna was determined to boot these people out of the territory and get that land back for Mexico.

In January 1836, Sam Houston, leader of the Texian army, sent a man named Jim Bowie to the Alamo. Bowie was a famous knife fighter (you might've heard somebody talk about a "Bowie knife). Bowie was also a colonel in the Texian volunteer army. Houston wanted Bowie to blow up the Alamo—before Santa Anna could take it.

But when Bowie saw the place, he impressed by all the improvements that had been by the garrison's leader, Colonel J.C Neill. The Alamo now had nineteen cannons, including an 18-pounder. Bowie decided to stay at the Alamo and help these men fight Santa Anna's troops.

Hearing about the fortifications at the Alamo, the governor of the provincial territory of Texas directed Colonel Travis to raise a company of men and bolster the garrison. Travis and thirty men soon joined the force already inside the Alamo.

Then, on February 8, 1836, David "Davy" Crockett arrived with some Tennessee volunteers. Crockett was already considered a frontiersman hero—when he arrived, the men inside the fort threw a party. But Crockett refused to accept any major military rank in the Alamo. Instead, he called himself "a high private."

Davy Crockett

Altogether, this Texian force wasn't large—maybe 150 people, including some ordinary American settlers, some *Tejanos* and their families who supported this fight for independence, and two freed African American slaves. Then, about a week after Crockett arrived, Colonel Neill received word that his family was seriously ill. Neill handed his command over to Colonel Travis and rode for home.

Six days later, Santa Anna's troops marched up to the Alamo.

Thousands of soldiers.

Hoisting the red flag of no quarter—meaning, take no prisoners, kill everyone—the Mexican army gave the garrison one last chance to surrender.

The Texians offered their reply—by firing a shot from that 18-pounder cannon.

The battle of the Alamo was on.

Santa Anna's army attacks the Alamo

Rather than use heavy siege cannons, the Mexican forces worked light-field cannons. But these arms had to be wheeled within a couple hundred yards of the Alamo's walls. That put these men close enough that the Texians could fire on them with their rifles. Mexican soldiers were getting killed right and left. So they started digging entrenchments, hoping for some protection.

On the second day of the siege—February 24—Jim Bowie collapsed. Historians believe he suffered from typhoid pneumonia. As the siege continued, however, most of the wounded were among the Mexican troops, who were still about 200 yards away from the fort's walls.

Davy Crockett and his men took control of the Alamo's weakest link, a low picket barricade between the mission's chapel and its south wall. Skilled marksmen, Crockett and his men could kill at long range. If there was an enemy assault, they planned to use the cannons.

On the night of February 29, some American volunteers arrived to help. These men had survived that earlier battle against General Cos. The men inside the fort cheered—at first. Then they realized only about twenty men had come.

Santa Anna's troops outnumbered them by the thousands.

The gunfire, explosions, screams, and deaths continued. And the Mexican cannons moved closer, close enough that their shots started to crumble the Alamo's stone walls.

On the twelfth day of the siege, March 5, Santa Anna discussed a final assault with his officers. He set the attack for 5:00 a.m., March 6. In the pre-dawn darkness of that chilly morning, the Mexican army silently crept across the open ground.

Inside the Alamo, so few people were available to cover duties that men kept falling asleep at their posts.

Suddenly a cry broke through the dark: *"Viva la Republica!"*

A man named John Baugh heard the shouts. He yelled to Travis: "The Mexicans are coming!"

"Come on, boys!" Travis shouted back. "The Mexicans are upon us and we'll give them hell!"

The Alamo's gunners aimed their rifles and fired the cannons. The morning air filled with black smoke and explosions, and the screams of dying men—on both sides. And now the Mexican Brown Bess Muskets were within killing range. Colonel Travis had just fired both barrels of his shotgun when a bullet drove through his forehead. Travis was among the first men to fall.

But so much deadly fire was coming from the Alamo that part of the Mexican army broke and ran. The only thing stopping them were the officers who ordered them forward again. Then a mass of Mexican troops climbed over the Alamo's north wall. The enemy was inside in the mission.

The Alamo's garrison fell back to the barracks, hoping to make one final defensive position. Crockett's riflemen withdrew to the chapel. But they had no time to spike—or ruin—the cannons, so the Mexican army turned the guns on the building, blasting open doorways and charging through shattered openings.

The battle turned into hand-to-hand combat. "Bowie knives" and bayonets slashed the air. And as promised by that red flag, the Mexicans took no prisoners. They even killed the wounded men who couldn't fight back. Bowie, now too weak to stand from typhoid, fired his pistols from his sick bed. He was bayoneted—and perhaps worse, if later reports were accurate.

Insane with fury and some kind of blood lust, the Mexican troops sliced at everyone in sight, including some of their own comrades.

The last stand came in the chapel. Davy Crockett and six men fought to the end. Crockett most likely died near the Alamo's west wall.

General Santa Anna

When General Santa Anna arrived to inspect the overtaken fort, one of his generals brought forward the few American survivors. These Mexican officers asked that these people be spared because they displayed such bravery under fire. Nearly twenty women and children were spared.

But some Mexican officers who were not involved in the battle hacked other survivors to pieces. Later, a Mexican officer who witnessed the blood-thirsty vengeance said: "these unfortunates died without complaining and without humiliating themselves before their torturers."

Santa Anna told the surviving women to go home and spread the word among the Texians: Unless these people surrendered, his army would slaughter them all.

WHO FOUGHT?

The Alamo was built as a Franciscan mission for Spain during the mid-1700s (remember, Spain owned this land first). The Alamo's chapel walls were twenty-two feet high and four feet thick.

Why would anyone build a church like that? Because Christian missionaries and townspeople needed protection from attacks by the frontier Indians.

The battle of the Alamo didn't end the conflict between America and Mexico. In fact, it started The Mexican War, which lasted from 1846–1848. The United States eventually won that war and gained a vast amount of land that would later include the following states: Texas, Oklahoma, New Mexico, Colorado, Utah, Arizona, Nevada, California, and Wyoming.

Many myths surround the Battle of the Alamo. Because so few people survived the attack, historians are still trying to figure out what happened exactly. In fact, the more you read about the Alamo—and you should, there are some great books out there—you'll find you only have even more questions about this great American battle.

BOOKS

The Boy in the Alamo by Margaret Cousins

The Battle of the Alamo: An Interactive History Adventure by Amie Jane Leavitt

The Battle of the Alamo (Graphic History) by Matt Doeden

Who Was Davy Crockett? by Gail Herman

INTERNET

The Alamo's official website contains everything from details about the building to biographies of the men, women, and children inside during the battle: www.thealamo.org

MOVIE

The Alamo, starring John Wayne (1960)

The Battle of San Jacinto

April 20, 1836

"Sam Houston at The Battle of San Jacinto"
by Henry Arthur McArdle (1836–1908)

SANTA ANNA THREATENED to slaughter the Texians if they didn't surrender.

Do you think that stopped this fight for Independence?

Right.

Instead of surrendering, people started a new battle cry: "Remember the Alamo!"

Sam Houston was one of the Texians' military leaders. But this rebel force didn't look like much of an army. It was less than 400 men. They were poorly trained and had almost no equipment.

However, this was the 1st Regiment Volunteer Army of Texas.

After Santa Anna won the Alamo, he was determined to finish off this revolt.

One week after the Alamo, Santa Anna's forces caught up with Houston and his men. The Texians were short on rations and heavily outnumbered. Rain had been falling almost every day. So Houston's troops were also cold, wet, and struggling through mud. Fortunately, after one four-day march, Houston received some more troops—he now had 600 men.

Meanwhile, Santa Anna had discovered some Texas militiamen. He ordered the execution of all 400 men.

The Mexican general hoped to wipe out the rest of the volunteer army with Houston.

Houston and his men had a strange tactic against Santa Anna's forces. Houston's men would fight, then he would order them to retreat across the vast territory. Fight, then retreat. Over and over. Some of Houston's men got mad—it looked like Houston didn't want to really fight the Mexican forces. Eventually, two companies of Houston's men refused to retreat any further.

Houston decided to turn their decision into an opportunity. He started training these troops. And soon, he received more men for the fight—for a total of 1,500 men.

But Houston's fight-and-retreat plan was actually clever. Every time the Texians retreated, Santa Anna's troops were forced to run after them. That meant the Mexican forces had to detach one garrison after another to guard their military supplies and carry even more supplies to the battlefront. With all the rain and mud, and the large landscape they had to cover, this routine was wearing out the Mexican troops just as much, if not more, than the Texians.

This pursue-and-retreat pattern went on for weeks.

Finally, on April 20, 1836, Santa Anna trapped Houston and his volunteer army in a maze of bayous along the San Jacinto River.

The Texians had nowhere to go.

Mexican General Cos showed up, adding another 500 soldiers to Santa Anna's forces.

Houston had two cannons. His troops were exhausted from running from the Mexican forces. Hungry. Wondering if this would be their last stand.

Realizing the Texians were stuck with their backs against the San Jacinto river, Santa Anna was positive he would kill these men. In fact, he was so sure of it that he told his troops to take a siesta—an afternoon nap.

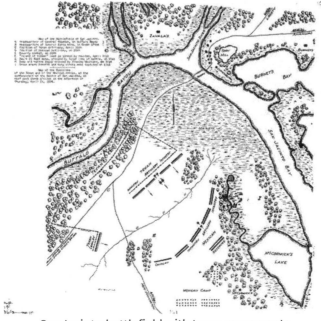

San Jacinto battlefield with troop movements

Seeing the bad situation for what it was, Houston ordered his lead scout, Erastus "Deaf" Smith, to destroy the only bridge that would offer an exit from this battlefield.

Does that sound suicidal?

At 3:30 p.m., in the middle of the Mexican siesta, the Texians snuck through the woods. Hidden from view by the trees, they could see their enemy snoozing away the afternoon.

Now they struck.

They charged out of the woods yelling, "Remember the Alamo!"

The Texian cannons fired double loads of grapeshot—small metal bits—while other men shot rifles and muskets and swung bayonets and swords. Seeing this ambush, some of the Mexican troops dropped their arms and ran.

But Houston had destroyed the only bridge—their only escape.

Mexican soldiers jumped into the San Jacinto river, trying to swim away. The Texians fired on them.

As the battle swirled, Santa Anna took off. He escaped into the woods.

Almost 1,000 Mexican soldiers were killed or wounded. Only eleven Texians died. Another thirty were wounded, including Houston—a bullet had shattered his ankle.

But without the capture of Santa Anna, the victory at the Battle of San Jacinto didn't seem complete.

Two days later, the Texians found the general—only they didn't realize it! Santa Anna had cleverly changed into a regular army uniform. None of the Texian fighters had ever seen the general close-up. And they might never have discovered his true identity except that as the new prisoner was marched back to the Texian camp, all the other Mexican prisoners snapped to attention.

"The General!" they called out. "The General!"

The Texians wanted to hang Santa Anna.

But Houston kept his wits.

He told them that they could kill Santa Anna or they could have Texas. But not both. Killing Santa Anna would only turn the ruthless general into a martyr for the Mexican cause. That would mean this war for independence would go on even longer.

Instead, Houston forced Santa Anna to sign a peace treaty. It gave independence to Texas and ordered the general to withdraw his troops from the territory.

The Battle of San Jacinto is considered one of the most decisive military victories in all of history.

No contest: The Texians beat Santa Anna's powerful army.

It was the battle that ended the Texas revolution of 1836 and freed Texas from Mexican rule. The battle also changed the size and shape of the United States of America.

But you won't believe how long this decisive battle lasted—eighteen minutes.

WHO FOUGHT?

At age sixteen, Sam Houston ran away from home. His dad had died, his family didn't have much money, and Sam didn't like working at his brother's store.

He lived for a time with the Cherokee Indian tribe in Tennessee, even becoming fluent in their language. He later fought against the British in the War of 1812.

One of Houston's most famous battles was the Battle of Horseshoe Bend against the Creek Indians, in the area that's now the state of Alabama. In this battle, Houston was wounded by an arrow in his right thigh and two rifle balls in his right shoulder. His fellow soldiers left Houston for dead. He spent the night on the ground in terrible pain.

The next morning, some men spotted his body moving. They carried him to his home. One rifle ball was removed; one bullet stayed in him.

Houston resigned from the army in March of 1818. He was upset with how the US government was treating the Cherokee Indians. He became an actor for a short time, then studied law and became a lawyer.

In 1827, Houston became governor of Tennessee. He later took control as commander of the Texas forces and was twice elected president of the Texas republic. During the Civil War, however, Houston refused to secede from the Union or to fight for the South.

Many Texas confederates turned on the hero of Texas Independence.

Houston, however, remained loyal to Texas.

His last words, spoken to his wife, were: "Texas, Texas, Margaret."

BOOKS

The Battle of San Jacinto (Fred Rider Cotten Popular History Series) by James W. Pohl

The Texas War of Independence 1835–1836: From Outbreak to the Alamo to San Jacinto by Alan Huffines

Make Way for Sam Houston by Jean Fritz

INTERNET

This website offers more information on the battle and shows the monument commemorating "18 minutes that changed the world." www.sanjacinto-museum.org

Here's a ten-minute video giving a good summary of the battle set to music and images: youtube.com/watch?v=r5PFbQ0vNOo

MOVIES

Texas Forever! The Battle of San Jacinto (1990) A thirty-five-minute
documentary

Texas Rising

The Civil War

April 12, 1861 – May 10, 1865

President Abraham Lincoln

BY THE MIDDLE of the 1800s, the United States was splitting in half over political and economic differences.

The northern states, with large cities such as New York, had factories and good transportation systems with road and railroads. The North also had about twenty-two million white men who were of military age. The Southern states were more rural. Their economy relied on farming. The South also had fewer people, with about nine million men of military age. But the biggest difference between the North and South had to do with rights.

Southerners wanted stronger rights for their individual states. The South relied on slave labor to keep its farming economy going. So most Southerners wanted the right to keep slaves.

Some Northerners owned slaves, too. But they didn't need slaves to keep money flowing through the economy. So most Northerners were against slavery.

In 1860, Abraham Lincoln was elected president of the United States. Lincoln was the nation's first Republican. He also was an abolitionist—a person who wanted to end slavery.

His election worried the South. If Lincoln outlawed slavery, the whole Southern economy would collapse.

One month after Lincoln was elected, the southern state of South Carolina seceded—officially broke away—from the United States. More southern states joined the secession. These states created their own government, called The Confederate States of America.

So the United States was truly divided.

The North was called The Union, or federal, government.

The South was known as the Confederacy.

It wasn't an ideal situation, obviously, but most people didn't think this division would lead to anything like a war.

Southerners believed they had the right to secede under the US Constitution, which does offer that option. Meanwhile, the Union kept trying to convince the southern states to come back to the federal government. First, both sides tried diplomatic talks. When those didn't work, the Union blockaded southern seaports, cutting off all shipping.

The South didn't like that.

On April 12, 1861, Confederates fired on Fort Sumter, South Carolina.

Fort Sumter was inside South Carolina's border, but it was garrisoned by Union soldiers. The Confederates planned to drive all Federal forces out of the south. All diplomatic efforts came to a screeching halt. The Confederacy had declared war on the Union.

This was the start of the American Civil War.

A total of eleven states joined the Confederacy: Virginia, North Carolina, South Carolina, Tennessee, Alabama, Georgia, Florida, Louisiana, Texas, Arkansas, and Mississippi.

The North had twenty-five states that supported the Union.

The South had the better military leaders. Confederate commanders like Robert E. Lee were aggressive and well-trained. The Union leaders were really cautious. And the Confederates were especially formidable on land because most of the rural southern soldiers had grown up hunting—they knew how to use rifles and knives. And since most of the Civil War battles were fought on southern land, the Confederates also knew the territory better than Northerners.

But when the fighting was on water, the North was far and away the better opponent. The Southern navy was pretty much just some small schooners. Plus, after the North blockaded the southern ports, the South couldn't export its main crop—cotton. But the blockade did more than bankrupt southern farmers, it also kept the Confederates from getting arms, ammunition, and other military supplies from supportive allies—friends—in Europe.

From its beginning to its end, the Civil War lasted about four years. There were many significant battles, which are included in *Great Battles for Boys: The Civil War*.

But here are three battles that were major turning points in this war: Antietam, Gettysburg, and Vicksburg.

The Battle of Antietam

Also known as the Battle of Sharpsburg

September 17, 1862

Photo of "Burnside" Bridge at Antietam Creek, taken before the battle

WHEN CONFEDERATE GENERAL Robert E. Lee took command of the Southern forces, he also took command of the war.

In his early victories, Lee humiliated one Union general after another. And when the Union army tried to invade the Confederate capital of Richmond, Virginia, Lee sent them running back to Washington DC.

Eighteen months after the war began, Lee decided it was time for the South to invade the North.

Virginia's farms had been stripped bare by both armies, as soldiers tried to stay alive during the many battles. The Northern farms still had food. With the blockade of its seaports, the Confederacy also needed to get more arms and ammunition. Lee thought they could get those supplies up north, which had plenty of manufacturing factories. On top of all that, Lee believed that a successful invasion of the North would convince the countries of Great Britain and France that the Confederacy was going to win—so those countries would then send some support.

General Lee

But Lee had another reason for the invasion.

Until this point, only Southerners had experienced the real fear and hardship of war. The battles were all taking place in the South. If the average northern person got a taste of war from a brutal invasion, it might be enough to persuade the Union to sue for peace. "Suing for peace" is when an invaded territory surrenders with certain terms for a peaceful ending to the war.

Lee chose Pennsylvania for his invasion, and he wanted to move fast. As he told Confederate President Jefferson Davis, "...we cannot afford to be idle." But this quick movement would lead to the single bloodiest single day of battle in American history—Antietam.

This map shows how both sides were moving troops north during the month of September 1862.

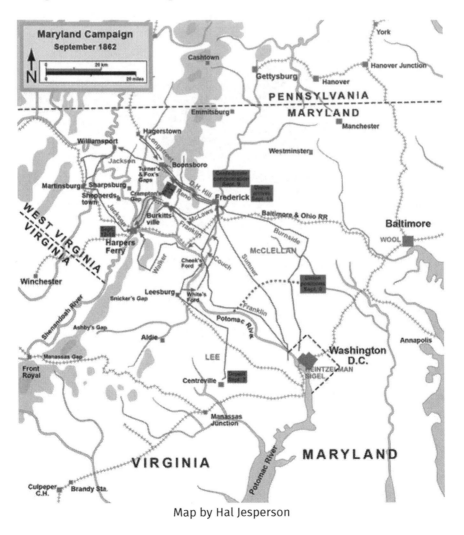

Map by Hal Jesperson

On September 9, Lee issued Special Order 191. This order directed half of his forces to move toward Harrisburg, Pennsylvania—marching through Maryland—to seize control of the regional railroad network. The other half of Lee's force would march to Harper's Ferry, Virginia, and capture that town's gun factory.

By mid-September, the Confederates had penetrated as far north as Sharpsburg, Maryland.

Union General George McClellan and his Army of the Potomac raced from Washington DC to intercept the Confederates—but suddenly, the plan changed.

On September 13, two Union soldiers discovered a copy of Lee's detailed battle plan—that Special Order 191. It was found in a field, with three cigars wrapped around a sheet of paper.

This secret information gave McClellan a chance to isolate both halves of Lee's army and defeat them.

General McClellan

But McClellan hesitated—he was among the super-cautious Northern military leaders. He waited almost an entire day before repositioning his forces to attack Lee's men.

In the meantime, Lee had already arrived at Sharpsburg, Maryland. When McClellan showed up on September 15, he stopped at a place called Antietam Creek. McClellan didn't cross the water. He didn't send out any scouts. And he didn't know this terrain.

The next day, both armies reinforced with troops.

Lee now had about 25,000 more men—for a total of 53,000. Which was great—except that McClellan was also reinforced, keeping a 3-to-1 advantage.

But, once again, instead of attacking with his overwhelming force, McClellan hesitated. He was worried that Lee had more men than anyone realized. And when McClellan delayed his attack, Lee used the time to reorganize his troops.

Gathering his forces on high ground west of Antietam Creek, Lee placed Confederate General James Longstreet's division along a ridge line. General Stonewall Jackson's men filled in on the left, while J.E.B. Stuart positioned his famous cavalry on the right.

McClellan's massive force waited across Antietam Creek.

Tension filled the battlefield air. One soldier later said: " . . . all realized that there was ugly business and plenty of it just ahead."

The next map shows these pre-battle Union and Confederacy positions.

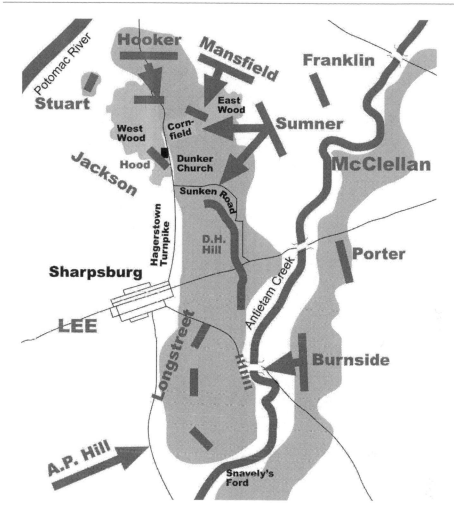

At dawn the next day, September 17, the battle began.

Union General Joseph "Fighting Joe" Hooker attacked down the Hagerstown Turnpike. Hooker's objective was to take the plateau where Dunker Church sat. But when Hooker's 8,600 men marched into the cornfield (see map), they were greeted by almost 8,000 Confederate soldiers who were under the command of Stonewall Jackson.

This artillery duel—in what was later known as Miller's Cornfield—was so intense that one colonel called it "artillery hell." Bullets shot through the autumn air and drilled into men's bodies. Cannonballs and canister shells whistled across the sky and exploded on contact, wiping out dozens in one shot. Soldiers raced from the corn stalks firing their rifles until the weapons overheated and quit working, leaving the men with only the rifle butts and bayonets to beat and stab their enemy. Cavalry officers rode around the confusion on horseback, hollering orders, but there was so much noise from gunfire and confusion from the screaming, the soldiers couldn't hear their orders.

By 7:00 o'clock that morning, Union reinforcements arrived. But their movement was uncoordinated, and there weren't enough men. The Union attack was ineffective. Two hours later, the Confederates had moved into a road that connected the area farms—a road that so worn, it was literally sunken. The southern soldiers decided to use the road as a trench.

Half an hour later, Union troops attacked the left flank of the Confederate lines. They outnumbered the Southerners by about 3,000 men. Despite having far less experience—before today, most of these Union soldiers had never been in combat—they managed to overpower the Confederates.

And then, the Union sent in its Irish Brigade.

These men were recent immigrants to America from Ireland. They were commanded by a fellow Irish-American, Brigadier General Thomas Meagham. To gain headway to the Sunken Road, Meagham asked for volunteers to help clear some fences. The Irish volunteers, waving their green flags, started taking out the fences—while an Irish Catholic priest rode back and forth among them, shouting words of absolution—forgiveness from God—and proclaiming Catholic release from guilt and punishment. In this fight, everyone knew these men would either have to kill or be killed.

Meanwhile, the Confederates felt confident enough to move out of the Sunken Road. But they lay in wait, holding fire until the last possible moment. They killed half of the men in the Irish Brigade's 63rd New York division. Meagham fell from his horse—or his horse was shot out from under him and caused him to fall; or, as some soldiers later claimed, the general was drunk and fell off his horse. But Meagham's absence was a huge problem because now the Union had no commander in this part of the battle.

Confusion covered the cornfield.

Confederate dead near Dunker's church. Photo by Alexander Gardner.

When Union Major General Dick Richardson saw the wounded cornfield soldiers stumbling back from the front line, and that no reinforcements were going forward, he couldn't understand why—the Union had plenty of men in reserve. Then Richardson learned that the officer who was supposed to reinforce those Irish troops was instead hiding behind a haystack—holding back *his* troops while the Irish men got slaughtered.

Richardson ordered the reserve soldiers forward and reinforced the brigade.

The Confederates along the Sunken Road were not being reinforced. Their commander, Brigadier General John B. Gordon, had already been hit four times—two wounds to his right leg, two to his left arm. Now a fifth bullet struck him—in the face. Lying unconscious, face down in his cap, Gordon later said he probably would've drowned in his own blood if it wasn't for the hole the bullet shot into his cap, which drained the blood. Gordon was taken off the battlefield. His replacement, Lieutenant Colonel Lightfoot, decided to pull his troops from the Sunken Road. The Confederates retreated.

Now Lee's center was collapsing. Longstreet tried to turn some of the Union's own cannons on them to stop the onslaught. But the Confederates were on the run. McClellan had another chance to wipe out Lee's army and yet—*again*—he hesitated, choosing to hold his position instead of advancing on the retreating Southerners.

Right there, at 5:30 p.m., the Battle of Antietam stopped.

McClellan called it a victory. But so did Lee—because the Confederacy wasn't forced to retreat, it chose to retreat.

So, after twelve hours of deadly fighting, the Battle of Antietam ended . . . in a stalemate.

More than 23,000 men were dead, wounded, or missing. The Union suffered 12,401 casualties, about one-quarter of its force. Confederate casualties were only slightly less, with 10,318. But that was more than one-third of Lee's force.

Also, six generals were killed—three on the Confederate side, three on the Union side. And twelve generals were wounded—six on the Confederate side, six on the Union side.

But the sad final fact was that on September 17, 1862, more Americans died than on any other day in American military history. Statistically speaking, at Antietam, one man died every two seconds.

That night, both sides collected their dead and wounded. Lee kept up a few skirmishes, but he withdrew his army south, back into Virginia.

So much for the Confederate invasion of the North.

Although Lee declared Antietam a Confederate victory, in reality, the invasion was a total failure. The South had suffered huge casualties, had to leave the area, and with no decisive victory, Europe wasn't going to send war supplies to the Confederacy.

Lincoln and McClellan at Antietam.
The American flag drapes a table outside the tent

On the northern side, the Battle of Antietam convinced President Lincoln to change his objectives. Before the battle, Lincoln's main focus was preserving the United States as one union.

But five days after Antietam, Lincoln signed the Emancipation Proclamation, freeing all American slaves. This proclamation injected fresh passion into the Civil War. Lincoln was going after the entire Southern way of life. Lincoln also relieved General McClellan of command.

Today, historians see many military lessons from Antietam. Among the most poignant is that if McClellan had been aggressive, he could have defeated the South on that battlefield and probably brought an end to the entire Civil War.

Instead, the bloodshed would continue for three more years.

WHO FOUGHT

Catholic chaplains of Union Army Irish Brigade, 1862

When a water fungus wiped out Ireland's potato crop during the 1840s and '50s, an estimated one million people died of starvation and malnutrition. Without crops to sell, food to eat, or money to pay rent, Irish farmers emigrated to other countries.

Millions moved to the United States. Many of them settled in the north, especially in New York City, Boston, and Philadelphia.

But in America, the penniless, jobless, and homeless Irish immigrants faced new challenges. This industrialized country needed skilled factory workers. Irish farmers took jobs as laborers—paving streets, digging canals, and serving as maids. Another big challenge was the widespread distrust that Protestant America felt toward the Irish Catholic foreigners— these people with accents who followed the Pope.

When the Civil War broke out, military recruiters offered bounties for immigrant volunteers. Many new recruits hoped to make enough money to send funds back home to their starving families in Ireland. Others hoped to gain acceptance from their fellow Americans. But their religious faith didn't waiver. During the Civil War, the Irish had Catholic chaplains.

Union Brigadier General Meagher, the Irish immigrant who commanded the Irish Brigade during the Battle of Antietam, insisted on arming his men with Model 1842 smoothbore muskets. Although the weapon was considered obsolete, and later was phased out, Meagher assumed his brigade would fight at close range. These muskets produced a shotgun effect, firing a deadly buck-and-ball shot—a larger musket ball with smaller balls.

At Antietam, the brigade didn't win on the Sunken Road. But its forceful attack gave supporting troops time to flank and break the Confederate position.

In that one battle, the Irish brigade lost as much as sixty percent of its force to casualties.

BOOKS

The Sword of Antietam by Joseph A. Altsheler

Antietam 1862: The Civil War's Bloodiest Day by Norman Stevens

Antietam: The Photographic Legacy of America's Bloodiest Day by William A. Frassanito

From Antietam to Gettysburg: A Civil War Coloring Book by Peter F. Copeland. Forty-five precise black-and-white illustrations document great battles, generals of the War Between the States; Pickett's charge at Cemetery Ridge; Union Army retreat from Fredericksburg; portraits of Lee, Meade, Hood, and other generals. Detailed, informative captions.

Fields of Fury: The American Civil War by James M. McPherson

Dawn Drums by Robert Walton

Soldier's Heart: Being the Story of the Enlistment and Due Service of the Boy Charley Goddard in the First Minnesota Volunteers by Gary Paulsen

Behind the Blue and Gray: The Soldier's Life in the Civil War by Delia Ray

Co. Aytch: A Confederate Memoir of the Civil War by Sam R. Watkins

INTERNET

You will find no better collection of facts and features about The Battle of Antietam than at the website dedicated to saving America's Civil War battlefields: civilwar.org/battlefields/antietam.html

MOVIES

The Civil War, Season 1, by Ken Burns

Lincoln and Lee at Antietam: The Cost of Freedom

Antietam: A Documentary Film

The Battle of Gettysburg

July 1–3, 1863

Dead Confederate sharpshooter in the Devil's Den, Gettysburg, July 1863.
Photograph by Alexander Gardner

HAVE YOU EVER worn shoes that made your feet hurt?

Imagine wearing those shoes every day, walking for miles and miles, over fields and uneven ground. You'd also be carrying a heavy pack, and you hadn't eaten in a long time. If somebody suddenly said they knew where you could get new shoes—free!—you'd jump at the chance, right?

Believe it or not, bad shoes played a big part in the bloodiest battle of the Civil War: The Battle of Gettysburg.

By the spring of 1863, the Confederacy was winning most of

the significant battles, including one at a place called Chancellorsville. But the Southern forces still hadn't managed to invade the North. Even after the failure of Antietam, General Lee wanted to try again.

Lee believed that one successful invasion could end this war. And Lee had a point. Militarily, the Union was on the ropes. President Lincoln had already dismissed *ten* commanders in ten months—imagine having ten different principals in one school year! In some Northern cities, violent riots were breaking out. Taxpayers were sick of paying the high costs of this war—in both money and lives.

In early June 1863, Lee started moving his army north from Virginia, marching across the Potomac River and into southern Pennsylvania. Not long after this movement, Lincoln once again changed military leaders. He removed General Joseph Hooker and appointed General George Meade to lead the Union troops.

General Meade

Meade headed straight for Pennsylvania to intercept the Southern rebels.

Just like with Antietam, Lee had plenty of reasons for picking Pennsylvania for his invasion. Virginia and Washington DC were ravaged by the war, with the area farms running low on food. Lee's men starving. Pennsylvania was still mostly unscathed by the fighting, had really rich farm land, and manufacturing facilities for military needs.

In fact, one Pennsylvania town had a shoe factory. Southern General A.P. Hill's infantry troops needed shoes so badly that soldiers had resorted wrapping rags around their bare feet. When Hill heard about that shoe factory in the town of Gettysburg, Pennsylvania, he and his men headed right for it.

But a Northern cavalry patrol discovered Hill's men near Gettysburg. The Confederates outnumbered this horse patrol, but the Union held the line until Confederate General Richard Ewell arrived with reinforcements. Then the Northerners were forced to take positions in places around Gettysburg such as Cemetery Ridge and Culp's Hill.

Lee's troops were just outside Gettysburg. But the general was without his most reliable cavalry commander. J.E.B. Stuart and his horsemen had left to conduct a raid. Calvary was crucial for gathering reconnaissance or "intelligence." Without Stuart's lightning riders, Lee couldn't know what was happening to his other forces in the area. Lee dispatched a message to Ewell to attack "if practical." Ewell didn't know how many Union troops he was facing. So he decided an attack wasn't practical.

The next day, July 2, Union General Meade gathered 90,000 men. He placed them in a fishhook pattern. This fishhook ran for three miles from Culp's Hill to the north, then along

Cemetery Ridge, and ended at a place called Little Round Top.

Three-quarters of a mile away, Lee's army of 76,000 men stood mostly in an open field. Lee wanted to attack, even though the Union was stationed on higher ground. General James Longstreet advised against this attack. But Lee disagreed. He ordered Longstreet to hit Little Round Top. Lee thought that if Longstreet's men could secure that hill, the Confederate artillery could rain down cannon fire on the Union, turning the enemy's flank.

Longstreet's advance worked—at first.

General James Longstreet

Short on ammunition, the Union artillery was all that stood between the Southerners and the rest of the Union army.

Colonel Joshua Chamberlain ordered his men to fix bayonets. That meant close fighting, hand-to-hand combat. One soldier later recalled Chamberlain's actions.

"With a cheer and a flash of his sword that sent inspiration down the line, full ten paces to the front he sprang . . . 'Come on! Come on, boys!' he shouts. The color sergeant and the brave color guard follow, and with one wild yell of anguish wrung from its tortured heart, the regiment charged.

"The rebels were confounded by the movement. We struck them with a fearful shock. They recoil, stagger, break and run, and like avenging demons our men pursue. The rebels rush towards a stone wall . . . A band of our men leap over the wall and capture at least a hundred prisoners."

In this close and bloody battle, the Union stopped Longstreet's advance.

But Lee didn't seem to understand. He was still convinced that the Confederates just needed to be more aggressive.

He decided to attack Cemetery Ridge.

Longstreet again disagreed.

But for some reason, Lee seemed obsessed with taking Cemetery Ridge. Maybe because he was tired. He was also sick from diarrhea. But instead of trying to outflank Meade, Lee planned a huge artillery bombardment of the ridge, followed by an attack by three divisions, or 15,000 men.

"General Lee," Longstreet told him, "there never was a body of fifteen thousand men who could make that attack successfully."

Lee didn't listen.

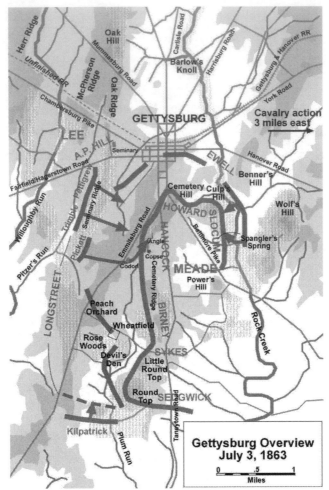

Map of 3rd day. Cemetery Ridge, in center, held by Union.
See the Union's fishhook pattern

On the morning of July 3, Lee ordered Major General George Pickett's division into battle, plus two divisions from General Hill.

Pickett had never led troops into a fight. Pickett also graduated last in his class at the US Military Academy at West Point. He was known more for curling his hair and wearing perfume than for fighting. But his good friend Longstreet had pushed for Pickett's advancement.

Major General George Pickett

After the Confederate artillery's bombardment—which was mostly ineffective—those 15,000 Confederate soldiers began marching across an open field below the Cemetery Ridge. The march was almost a mile long—during which 200 Union artillery guns fired on these men. Hundreds fell dead. The survivors kept marching. When they were about 600 feet from the Union, the Northern infantry opened fire with musket shot. More men fell. In the hailstorm of shells, about half of the Confederate soldiers turned into casualties. Pickett lost 70 percent of his division.

Yet General Lee ordered Pickett to rally his division for another attack.

"Sir," Pickett replied, "I have no division."

The few surviving men—wounded, bleeding, and dying—stumbled back to camp. Lee realized the error of what later was called "Pickett's Charge." On the field below the ridge, thousands of Southern men lay dead. Many of them were combat veterans, soldiers Lee had relied on for his victories over the North.

"It's all my fault," Lee murmured, as the wounded struggled back. "I'm sorry."

Longstreet later said, "That day at Gettysburg was one of the saddest of my life."

Realizing the battle was lost, Lee covered his defensive positions. He expected Meade to attack, and wipe out the vulnerable Confederate forces. But Meade, like so many Union leaders before him, was far too cautious. He allowed Lee and his men to escape.

President Lincoln was furious.

The Battle of Gettysburg was the bloodiest conflict of the Civil War. Lee lost 23,000 men—dead, wounded, captured, or missing. Union General Meade's casualties numbered more than 20,000. As one wounded sergeant later said, during the nights of Gettysburg he heard nothing "but the cries of the wounded and the groans of the dying." Nearby churches, mills, farms, and privates homes were turned into hospitals. With so many dead, the bodies had to be buried in rows inside shallow pits.

The Battle of Gettysburg: Pickett's Charge
by Peter Frederick Rothermel, 1870

The Confederacy, which was supposed to win this battle, was now in deep trouble. Gettysburg had wiped out nearly 40 percent of Lee's force. Without those men, he couldn't launch any more invasions—and that meant Europe definitely wouldn't recognize the South and send much-needed arms and supplies.

Even the most passionate Southerner loyalist understood what this battle meant.

"Yesterday we rode on the pinnacle of success," wrote one Confederate, "today absolute ruin seems our position. The Confederacy totters on destruction."

On November 19, 1863, President Lincoln visited the Gettysburg battlefield. He dedicated it as a memorial cemetery for the men who died there.

In his "Gettysburg Address," Lincoln said:

"Four score and seven years ago, our fathers brought forth upon this continent, a new nation, conceived in Liberty, and dedicated to the proposition that all men are created equal.

"Now we are engaged in a great civil war, testing whether that nation, or any nation so conceived, and so dedicated, can long endure. We are met on a great battlefield of that war. We have come to dedicate a portion of it, as a final resting place for those who here gave their lives that that nation might live . . ."

The Civil War continued for nearly two more years.

WHO FOUGHT?

The Irish riots in New York City,
as shown in a 1863 London newspaper

The Battle of Gettysburg changed the direction of the Civil War.

But it also changed the Irish Brigade. Remember those men—the new Irish immigrants who fought for the Union?

The Brigade was suffering really high casualties. By 1863, many Irish soldiers and their families wondered if the Union Army was throwing them into battle without caring if they lived or died. "Cannon fodder," they called it.

Then in March 1863, Congress passed the National Conscription Act. This law required every unmarried Union man between the ages of twenty-one and forty-five to join a draft lottery—unless that man could hire somebody to take his place. Or pay a $300 fee.

To working-class Irish-Americans who didn't have $3 let

alone $300, this law looked like discrimination—they were poor and being forced to fight in this "rich man's war." The Irish were also angry about slavery—but not for the reasons you might think. Most Irish immigrants didn't care if slavery ended. They didn't particularly like African Americans.

On July 13, 1863, ten days after the Battle of Gettysburg, thousands of Irish immigrants took to the streets of New York City. For five days, they violently protested the draft law and lashed out at the African Americans who they blamed for making this war continue. Mobs assaulted any black person they came across. They ransacked and burned homes in African American neighborhoods. They looted stores owned by blacks and "sympathetic" whites. Even an orphanage for black children was burned to the ground.

When Federal troops arrived in the city, at least 120 people, most of them African American, had died in the riots.

BOOKS

Guinness Book of Decisive Battles by Geoffrey Regan, which provided quotes for this re-telling.

The Battle of Gettysburg by Michael Burgan

What Was the Battle of Gettysburg? by Jim O'Connor

Boys of Wartime: Will at the Battle of Gettysburg by Laurie Calkhoven

This Flag Never Goes Down!: 40 Stories of Confederate Battle Flags and Color Bearers at the Battle of Gettysburg by Michael Dreese

INTERNET

National Parks Service website of Gettysburg Memorial Battlefield: nps.gov/GETT/learn/historyculture/index.htm

US News published interesting historic photos for Gettysburg 150th anniversary: usnews.com/news/articles/2013/07/03/photos-battle-of-gettysburgs-150th-anniversary-relives-civil-war-carnage

Excellent, full-length documentary, produced by Ridley Scott on YouTube: youtube.com/watch?v=UJjwb4eyAyo

MOVIES

Gettysburg

Gods and Generals

Ken Burn's Civil War

The Battle of Vicksburg

May 19 – July 4, 1863

Miles of fortifications dug around
Vicksburg to protect the city

WHILE THE CONFEDERATE army wanted to invade the North, the Union set its sights on the South's main waterway, the Mississippi River.

Wide and powerful, stretching more than 2,000 miles from Minnesota to the Gulf of Mexico, the Mississippi River gave the Confederacy a "highway" to transport supplies from one location to another. The North controlled the river's upper portion, but the South was fiercely guarding its part of the river, especially around the city of Vicksburg, Mississippi.

"Vicksburg is the key!" declared President Abraham Lincoln. "The war can never be brought to a close until that key is in our pocket."

The Confederacy had virtually no navy, so the Union had no trouble blockading the far southern end of the Mississippi River, where it flows into the Gulf of Mexico. But further up the river was another story. The Confederates had placed heavy cannons and small forts along the water. These guns allowed them to dominate the high ground and prevent any Union flotillas from sailing up or down this portion of the river.

The Union, as Lincoln realized, needed an aggressive campaign to take Vicksburg. This fight would need to include both naval and ground forces. To lead the campaign, Lincoln chose General Ulysses S. Grant, naming him commander of the Army of Tennessee.

Grant would be facing the heavy guns on the bluffs of Vicksburg and a Confederate force equal in number to his own troops. Two Southern generals, John Pemberton and Joseph Johnston, used Vicksburg as their headquarters. Between January and March 1863, Grant attempted four assaults on Vicksburg. Each assault failed.

General Grant

Finally, Grant revised his plans. He stepped up his aggression.

On the night of April 16, twelve Union vessels slipped through the dark past the Vicksburg cannons. Just one naval boat was lost to cannon fire. The next day, a Union cavalry division started a sixteen-day raid through central Mississippi. On April 22, a Union supply flotilla also slipped past the Vicksburg guns and joined the rest of the naval fleet just south of the city.

Union vessels passing Vicksburg batteries

One week later, the Union launched a diversionary attack northeast of Vicksburg.

Grant's plan was brilliant.

Every time the Union launched its actions, the Confederates had to deploy units to counter the moves. These counter-moves fragmented the Southern defenses. Grant kept winning these small battles on land, forcing Pemberton and his Southern forces to withdraw westward back to Vicksburg. Pemberton also learned that another aggressive Union general—William T. Sherman—was coming from the north. As the Confederates made their way back to Vicksburg, they burned bridges and removed every edible item in their path—animal and plant.

Grant continued to move the bulk of his army over land. He repaired those burnt bridges. And with the help of the Union navy, Grant managed to transport his army into Mississippi. Then, he prepared his assault on Vicksburg.

But one thing still troubled him: The Confederates had troops stationed in Jackson, Mississippi. That placement meant the enemy could possibly attack Grant's forces from behind. So,

Grant turned around and attacked the city, quickly routing the Rebels.

Then, on May 19, the Union army reached the outskirts of Vicksburg. Grant had about 70,000 men.

General Pemberton's Southern force consisted of about 30,000 soldiers. But Pemberton could claim the advantage of terrain and heavy fortifications. The Southerners had dug about seven miles of defensive trenches around Vicksburg.

During the month of May, Grant tried twice to assault Vicksburg.

Both assaults failed.

Grant once again changed plans. As he later wrote in his memoirs: "I now determined upon a regular siege—to 'out-camp the enemy,' as it were, and to incur no more losses."

Union gunboats on the river were keeping Confederates from being able to resupply. The Union army blocked land access to the city. On top of that, Grant kept up a sustained artillery bombardment.

The Confederates—and the citizens of Vicksburg—were trapped.

Union gunboats fired from the river, allowing the Union land troops to creep closer and closer to the Southern fortifications. Pemberton desperately wanted to hold onto these miles of the Mississippi River. But he needed troops to come help.

As Grant's siege continued, the relentless bombardment killed men and destroyed the city of Vicksburg. And new problems developed.

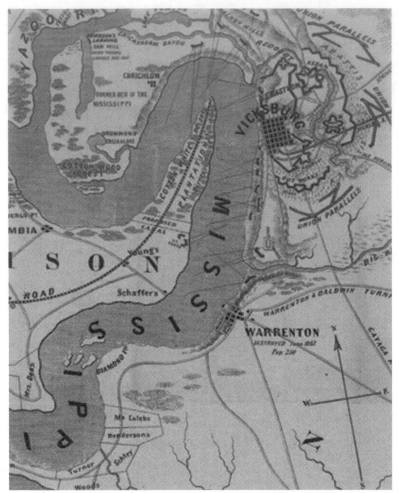

Vicksburg on the Mississippi River and
surrounded by Union forces on land

In summer, Mississippi gets really hot and humid. Grant's constant shelling created a putrid odor that hung in the heavy air—the smell of dead men and animals. Nobody could bury these bodies because of the constant firing from the Union. And the wounded lay there, crying for help and water.

Pemberton approached Grant about a truce. Grant refused. He saw truces as a sign of weakness. But Grant finally allowed a ceasefire so that both sides could recover the dead and wounded. For that short moment, soldiers from both sides walked about as if no war existed between them.

But when the shelling started up again, Pemberton was in even more trouble. Not only were his troops short on food and ammunition, but they were also suffering from malaria, a sometimes fatal mosquito-borne disease. Diarrhea ravaged the ranks, further dehydrating men who were already dying of thirst. As the siege continued, Vicksburg's residents grew so hungry that the town's population of horses, mules, and dogs suddenly dwindled—people needed meat to eat. Other people resorted to eating shoe leather, just to fill their stomachs. Butcher shops sold rats.

Caves dug into the hillsides of Vicksburg during Grant's siege.

Union gunboats kept lobbing shells into the town—some estimates are more than 22,000 shells. Artillery fire grew even heavier. Houses crumbled and burned. People dug holes into the clay ridges around town, carving out some 500 caves to protect themselves. People lived inside these caves for such a long time that they started furnishing them with rugs and chairs and pictures—the caves were now their homes. They learned to time their forages for food outside the caves to avoid the Union cannon fire.

But finally, on July 3, Confederate General Pemberton sent a note to Grant. The Union general had moved to Fort Donelson, Tennessee, a Southern fort he'd captured more than a year earlier. Grant demanded an unconditional surrender from Pemberton. But now Grant decided he didn't want to be responsible for feeding the thousands of sick and hungry Confederate soldiers. Plus, he'd have to spend months shipping all those captured soldiers north to prisons.

So Grant offered to parole all the Confederate soldiers. After all, he decided, these men were too sick to fight again (Grant was wrong; some of these soldiers did fight again).

On July 4, Independence Day, the surrender of Vicksburg was finalized. Pemberton turned over 29,000 soldiers, 172 cannons and 50,000 rifles. As someone raised in the North, Pemberton had picked the Fourth of July on purpose for this surrender. He hoped the Federal holiday would help persuade Grant to offer easier conditions of surrender. That was debatable.

In all, the Vicksburg campaign killed or wounded 10,142 Union and 9,091 Confederate soldiers. Although some skirmishes continued around the area, the fortified city of Vicksburg now belonged to the Union. Five days later, another Southern port on the Mississippi River fell, giving the Union full control of this all-important waterway.

The North had effectively split the Confederacy in half.

"The Father of the Waters," President Lincoln said of the Mississippi River, "again goes unvexed to the sea."

WHO FOUGHT?

Photo of General Ulysses S. Grant,
after he became President of the United States

Most of the Southern soldiers paroled by Grant went right back into the Confederate Army. Some of them were fighting a month later at Mobile Harbor, Alabama. By September, more were fighting in Chattanooga, Tennessee. Others would fight the legendary General Sherman during his invasion of Georgia in May 1864.

It was because of these Vicksburg soldiers who went right

back into battle that Grant ended all further prisoner exchanges during the Civil War.

Grant's full name was Hiram Ulysses Grant. But when he was seventeen, he was nominated to the US Military Academy at West Point by his Congressman, Thomas Hamer. The congressman nominated the young man as "Ulysses S. Grant." Since that name was on the nomination form, West Point wouldn't accept any other name. So, Grant took Ulysses S. Grant as his name.

But as he rose through the ranks in the Civil War, fighting with aggression and showing little mercy for his enemies, people began saying Grant's two initials—*U.S.*—stood for "Unconditional Surrender."

BOOKS

Under Siege! Three Children at the Civil War Battle of Vicksburg by
   Andrea Warren.

Eyewitness Civil War (DK Eyewitness Books) by John Stanchak

INTERNET

The Civil War Trust offers online rendering of the battles and siege of
   Vicksburg: www.civilwar.org/battlefields/vicksburg.html

Here's a photographic tour of "Civil War Vicksburg:"
   oldcourthouse.org/photos/civil-war-tour

Ten Interesting Facts about Ulysses S. Grant:
   republicanpresidents.net/10-interesting-facts-about-ulysses-s-
   grant

MOVIES

The Civil War, documentary by Ken Burns

The Battle of Little Big Horn

Custer's Last Stand

June 25, 1876

"The Custer Fight" by Charles Marion Russell

AFTER THE CIVIL War, gold was discovered in the Black Hills of South Dakota.

"Gold fever" swept across America. People started talking about getting rich quick out West. And, they said, most of the land was "free."

But some of that "free" land was considered sacred by the Sioux Indian Nation. Other parts of the Dakota's Black Hills were given to the Sioux tribe by the federal government after Chief Red Cloud agreed to relocate his tribe there on a reservation.

Some Indians refused to resettle on the reservation. But none of them liked what the white man was doing to their holy places. Among the northern Plain native tribes, the Sioux were probably the most numerous. They also didn't shy away from battle. Angry at the hordes of white settlers and gold miners who were digging into their sacred Black Hills, other tribes joined the Sioux's protests, including a large number of northern Cheyenne and Arapaho Indians who came from eastern Montana and Wyoming.

Two powerful warriors led these tribes: Sitting Bull and Crazy Horse.

Sitting Bull

The tribes started attacking and raiding white settlers. This was a huge problem for newly elected President Ulysses S. Grant—the former Civil War general. His administration couldn't stop the flow of white settlers heading West, and it couldn't get the Indians to stop attacking.

By 1876, Grant decided the US army needed to step in.

General Philip Sheraton devised a plan. He would send out groups of soldiers to surround the Indian tribes on the northern plains. Sheraton ordered General George Crook to lead a column of soldiers from Fort Fetterman, Wyoming to Montana. Each of those columns would have 2,500 men. Colonel John Gibbon would bring a smaller column from Fort Ellis, Montana, while General Alfred Terry would head out from Fort Abraham Lincoln, North Dakota. Terry would also be the overall command

Lastly, Lieutenant Colonel George Armstrong Custer would lead the 7th Cavalry's 600 men.

But Sheraton's plan soon went awry.

On June 17, 1876, Crazy Horse and his Indians attacked General Crook's column in Montana. The Indians pushed the troops into Wyoming. And since there was no communication among the other columns, Terry and Custer didn't realize Crook had retreated. They also only knew the approximate location of the Indian encampment—somewhere between two places called Rosebud Creek and Little Big Horn, Montana.

You can see their movements across the prairie on the map below.

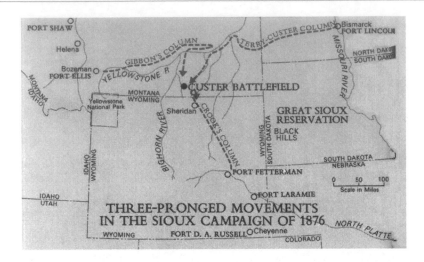

Terry then decided to divide the Indian forces. He sent Custer and the 7th Calvary up the Rosebud trails. Terry took his column, along with Colonel Gibbon's force, to the Little Bighorn. Terry planned to trap the Indians between the two forces. But the plan depended on the assumption that when the Indians were attacked, they would flee.

It wasn't an unreasonable assumption. Up until then, Indians tactics consisted of "hit-and-run."

General Alfred Terry

The real problem was Custer. He had his own ideas. Custer thought that if the Indians scattered, his 7th Calvary wouldn't be able to capture them. Custer wanted a complete and overwhelming victory. Then Custer would get all of the glory.

On June 25, Custer's Indian scouts—members of the Crow and Arikara tribes—warned him that this Indian encampment was the largest they'd ever seen. The scouts counted as many as 2,000 warriors, with thousands more women and children.

But Custer had his own concerns. He suspected his 7th Calvary had been spotted by a group of enemy Indians. So even though his original plan was to attack on June 26, he now feared losing the element of surprise.

So Custer decided to attack that very day, June 25.

Terry's orders had been for the 7th Calvary to swing around the Indian encampment and prevent any warriors from escaping. But Custer pushed his forces far beyond the geographic point where Terry expected to see the 7th Calvary. And now Custer was going to disobey orders even further.

Lt. Colonel George Armstrong Custer.

Custer might've disobeyed for even more glory: by waiting for Terry and Gibbon's forces, he would have to share the victory. Of course, Custer didn't realize that Crook and his men had been pushed back to Wyoming. As a lieutenant colonel, Custer was subordinate to the higher-ranking Crook. So if his superior was around for the fight, Custer would receive even less attention.

At noon, Custer divided his command into four detachments. He led the first with more than 200 men. The second was led by Captain Frederick Benteen with 115 men. The third by Major Marcus Reno with 142 soldiers and about thirty-five scouts. And the fourth detachment, with 135 men, would support a supply train carrying ammunition and food stores.

Benteen was supposed to block the west side of the encampment while Reno charged from the south—a diversionary attack to keep the Indians in place. Then Custer was going to lead the charge straight into the heart of the encampment. It was a bold, risky, and aggressive decision—and it was also egotistical and overconfident.

Looking back with the perspective of time, Custer's plan seemed focused less on military strategy and more on preventing the enemy's escape.

Marcus Reno

Reno and his men first saw the disaster coming. Reno launched his attack three miles from the encampment. Chief Gall then led the Indian warriors forward—but then withdrew back toward the encampment. Reno smelled a trap—he suspected hundreds of warriors were waiting in a nearby ravine. Ordering his men to dismount, Reno set up defensive skirmish lines to the rear. When the Indians set fire to the brush, attempting to smoke the soldiers out, Reno and his troops raced across a river and headed for a high bluff. This retreat killed many of Reno's men.

On the bluff, Reno and his remaining men readied for another attack.

But, surprisingly, aside from some Indians firing on them the enemy didn't attack.

Instead, the Indians galloped back to the encampment.

Thirty minutes later, Reno saw Captain Benteen's column approaching. Benteen had been traveling more than an hour but hadn't seen any Indians. He was searching for the army regiment at Little Big Horn.

Reno ran out, calling, "For God's sake, Benteen, halt your command and help me. I've lost half my men!"

The two men, bogged down in confusion and indecision, suddenly heard the sounds of a great battle, raging somewhere near the encampment. They also saw smoke rising from huge fires and some figures dancing and making triumphant war chants.

But these two men did nothing.

Later, their inaction would lead to a military court martial.

What was happening at this point isn't entirely clear. But the most accepted theory is that Custer led his command to Medicine Tail Coulee, then sent his trumpeter, Giovanni

Martini, to deliver a message to Benteen. As Martini was riding away, he saw Indians attacking Custer.

Martini would be the last man to see Custer alive.

Giovanni Martini

Custer apparently moved toward a central crossing on the Little Bighorn River. Just across the river lay the Indian encampment. Custer's water crossing drew swarms of Indians. Some estimates are that Custer's 200 men faced several thousand native warriors.

Custer—never very concerned about odds—probably charged. Some of his men realized trouble and turned back.

Other historians believe Custer and his command were driven to high ground—that elementary rule of battle—where Custer took an offensive position at the front, ordering two companies to dismount and move backwards, firing as they went, covering the rear.

The Sioux Chief probably heard that gunfire, abandoned his attack on Reno and crossed the river.

What nobody knew—not even the Army's scouts—was that Crazy Horse was inside that Indian encampment. This legendary battle leader, having already turned Crook back at the Rosebud, had hundreds of warriors under his command. And they moved to take Custer head-on.

Photo allegedly of Crazy Horse, circa 1877

Crazy Horse led his warriors up the same hill that Custer was climbing from the other side. Topping the high point just ahead of Custer's retreating forces, the Indians probably struck like hammers. But once again, Custer seemed to rally.

It would be his last stand.

The Sioux chief's warriors were picking off men with bows and arrows. Indian riflemen fired volleys while mounted warriors leaped from their horses, swiftly knifing the soldiers.

Historians believe Custer remained focused until the end, based on the strategic positions in which the troops' bodies were later found. It's also clear the soldiers fought hard. When their carbine (rifle) began overheating, evidence shows they pried out the cartridges with knives—while arrows and bullets would've been flying past them—and men died, horses screamed, and the dust and smoke grew so thick they could barely see. Eventually, Custer's men swung their carbines like clubs. Some soldiers emptied their pistols in the fight, except for one last shot, which they used on themselves.

No man ran away from the fight.

But when the dust settled, every white soldier was dead.

The Battle of Little Big Horn was over. Later it was called Custer's Last Stand.

From the first shot to the last, Custer and his men were wiped out in less than one hour. Among the dead were Custer's two brothers—Captain Thomas Custer and Boston Custer—one nephew, and his brother-in-law, Lt. James Calhoun.

The following day, June 26, the Indian warriors re-engaged Benteen and Reno on the bluff. The fighting lasted until mid-afternoon. Then, without warning, the Indians pulled up their encampment and rode away.

On June 27, General Terry's troops arrived from the north. On the hill, they found Custer among the 197 dead. Custer had two clean wounds, one shot straight to the heart, and the other in the temple. Significantly, Custer was the only man among the dead who was not scalped or mutilated by the Indian warriors. That mercy was a sign of respect. The Indians had considered Custer a fierce warrior. They even had special names for him, including "Long Hair," "Yellow Hair" and "Son of the Morning Star."

Artist's rendering of "Custer's Last Stand."
The general is shown wearing buckskin surrounded by
Lakota Sioux, Crow, Northern, and Cheyenne Indians

WHO FOUGHT?

When George Armstrong Custer graduated from the US Military Academy in 1861, he finished last in his class. Normally that wouldn't earn him any significant role in the military. But the Civil War had just broken out, and the US Army needed soldiers. Commissioned as a second lieutenant, Custer was assigned to the 2nd US Cavalry.

Custer was a terrible student, but he saw action in many important battles and worked his way up the military chain of command, usually by attracting attention to himself. Custer enjoyed flashy uniforms and played military politics with great savvy.

But Custer's men also respected his command in battle. Custer and his brigade played a role in the cavalry battle east of Gettysburg, where Custer had two horses shot out from under him, and still kept fighting.

BOOKS

Remember Little Bighorn: Indians, Soldiers, and Scouts Tell Their Stories by Paul Robert Walke

The Battle of the Little Bighorn by Gary Jeffrey

It Is a Good Day to Die: Indian Eyewitnesses Tell the Story of the Battle of the Little Bighorn by Herman J. Viola

INTERNET

The National Parks Service maintains a memorial at the Battle of Little Big Horn. You can visit in person or online: www.nps.gov/libi/index.htm

The Biography Channel profiles fierce warrior Crazy Horse and his powerful leadership at Little Big Horn: biography.com/people/crazy-horse-9261082/videos/crazy-horse-battle-at-little-big-horn-24512579907

MOVIES

Son of the Morning Star

The American Experience: Last Stand at Little Big Horn

Bury My Heart at Wounded Knee

The Battle of San Juan Hill

"The Rough Riders" of The Spanish-American War

July 1, 1898

Teddy Roosevelt, center, wearing glasses,
with The Rough Riders on San Juan Hill

CUBA IS A tropical island. It sits about ninety miles off the coast of Florida. For a long time, Cuba was a colony of Spain. But just like Mexico, Cuba got tired of being ruled by a country that was thousands of miles away. In the late 1800s, the native Cuban people started to resist Spain's harsh "mother country" rule.

Americans—who beat back England's control in the Revolutionary War—felt a natural sympathy for the Cuban colonists who were being forced to obey Spain. But the Cuban rebellion stretched on for a long time—so long that American businessmen started to worry. Their shipping companies relied on Cuban goods, especially sugar, which can't be grown in the mainland United States. Sugar cane plants do really well in Cuba's hot climate.

Worried about their business interests, many Americans wanted the American military to get involved in the Cuban uprising. American newspapers also started fanning the flames of war, printing emotional stories and harsh editorial cartoons that showed Spain's cruelty to the Cubans—whether those cruelties were real or exaggerated, it probably didn't matter. People started saying something needed to be done for these people whose island was just off the American coast.

President William McKinley tried diplomatic solutions. But on February 15, 1898, the American battleship *USS Maine* mysteriously blew up and sank in Havana Harbor of Cuba.

That story seized the attention of all the major newspapers. The editorials blamed Spain for the attack—even though there wasn't any evidence of sabotage. But, finally, giving in to public pressure, President McKinley declared war on Spain.

The Spanish-American War, as it was officially called, began on April 25, 1898. Several months later, an unusual group of soldiers was sent to Cuba to support the regular US Army. Formally, these men were known as the V Corps.

But newspapers dubbed them "The Rough Riders." That nickname stuck.

These volunteers came from the American frontier—places like New Mexico, Oklahoma, and the Indian territories.

Cowboys, gold prospectors, gamblers, and lawmen, the Rough Riders were definitely not the ordinary military regiment. And their commander, Colonel Leonard Wood, had already won a Medal of Honor for his service fighting Apache Indians in the southwest United States. They were the stuff of legend.

Even more unusual for that time, the Rough Riders included two all-black units—the 9th and 10th Calvary—otherwise known as Buffalo Soldiers. These men were among the most experienced of the V Corps' 17,000 volunteers.

However, the most famous soldier among the Rough Riders was their second-in-command: Theodore Roosevelt.

When President McKinley declared war on Spain, Roosevelt was assistant secretary of the US Navy. Roosevelt resigned that position and volunteered to fight. (Years later, Teddy Roosevelt would become the 26th President of the United States. Many people believe the Spanish American War helped propel him to The White House.)

On June 22, 1898, the V Corps' invasion force landed in the Cuban beach towns of Daiquiri and Siboney before moving toward the Cuban port city of Santiago. About 10,000 Spanish troops were deployed around Santiago and on two hills named San Juan and Kettle.

The Cuban geography proved challenging for the Americans. Not only was this a tropical climate—hot and humid—the terrain was hilly and covered by thick vegetation. There were so few roads that the Americans couldn't even haul their heavy artillery. So soldiers were left with just their outdated black-powder rifles. When ignited, these rifles created a heavy smoke that not only blinded the shooter but exposed his position to the enemy.

Meanwhile, the Spanish soldiers fighting in Cuba had

smokeless German Mauser rifles and brand new machine guns. However, the Spanish soldiers lacked something really important—morale. They weren't thrilled about risking their lives to keep colonial power over a small island thousands of miles from home. And they were fighting the passionate Cubans who desperately wanted independence.

On July 1, the American troops started a frontal assault up San Juan and Kettle Hills. They faced a heavy barrage of artillery. The Spanish fire power sliced into their ranks, sending several units into retreat.

One newspaper reporter on the scene wrote:

"They had no glittering bayonets, they were not massed in regular array. There were a few men in advance, bunched together, and creeping up a steep, sunny hill, the top of which roared and flashed with flame."

Standing in reserve was Lieutenant Colonel Roosevelt, awaiting orders for the Rough Riders. Watching all the mounting casualties, Roosevelt was getting impatient. He decided to lead a charge himself—without orders. But at the last moment before taking off, he was told to "move forward and support the Regulars in the hills in the front."

Calling his regiment out from cover, Roosevelt formed his troops into a column. But Roosevelt had health problems. His heart wasn't strong, and he was exhausted from the tropical heat. He feared that he wouldn't be able to keep up with his men heading up the hill. Most of these soldiers younger and in better shape. So Roosevelt stayed mounted on his horse with the 1st and 9th cavalries—those Buffalo Soldiers—while the 3rd, 6th, and 10th cavalries followed the infantry.

Theodore Roosevelt at Camp in Montauk Point, Long Island, New York,
where the Rough Riders spent time in quarantine
after returning from the fight in Cuba.

Halfway up Kettle Hill, the first line of troops found a road. It dropped behind a depression. What was more surprising was what they found in the trench: Regular Army troops, laying on the ground, trying to avoid the Spanish Mauser rifles.

Back then, camouflage was a fairly new phenomenon in warfare. But the Spanish snipers were using natural camouflage—covering themselves with leaves to disguise their position. The snipers were almost impossible for the Americans to find, adding another deadly element to the fight.

Roosevelt told the captain in command of the hiding soldiers that the troops needed to charge the hill.

The captain refused. He said no such order had been given.

Roosevelt said: "Then I am the ranking officer here, and I give the order to charge."

The captain still refused, saying the order didn't count because it was coming from a volunteer officer.

Roosevelt said, "Then let my men through, sir."

Crossing over the Regulars hidden in the depression, the Rough Riders charged up Kettle Hill. Although lacking military training and protocol, the Rough Riders had plenty of courage and lots of tenacity. When the Regulars saw what was happening, they jumped up and ran with them. Under heavy fire, the all-black cavalry units filled the voids as the Rough Riders attacked the Spanish troops.

Roosevelt continued to lead his men, none of whom retreated. But when he was forty yards from the hilltop, Roosevelt suddenly realized he'd ridden far ahead of his men. He also discovered barbed wire lines strung by the Spanish troops. Dismounting, Roosevelt regrouped the Rough Riders. Then they swarmed Kettle Hill.

Seeing all these gung-ho Americans charging right through the barbed wire, the Spanish troops broke and ran. The Americans took Kettle Hill—and immediately headed for San Juan Hill.

The Spanish had dug more trenches on that hill. But the hill's steep slope meant the Spanish soldiers inside those trenches couldn't see the Americans coming up on them. Some Rough Riders were within thirty feet of their enemy when startled Spanish troops jumped up and fled. The American infantry took the hill all the way to the crest.

A yellow stucco house sat at the top of San Juan Hill. The

Americans guessed there were about forty Spanish troops inside the house, which was made of sturdy block and stone— too strong for the troops to break through the sides or doors. But one American artillery shell tore a hole in the roof. Twenty Americans ran for the house and climbed on the roof. Four men dropped inside. They were immediately killed.

The remaining men all jumped inside at once, fighting their enemy in hand-to-hand combat until the rest of the American troops cleared the yellow house and yanked down the Spanish flag.

The Rough Riders had taken San Juan Hill. The kind of decisive victory that creates legends.

Both American and Spanish sides lost about 1,500 men in this war—dead or wounded. But Spain lost the war and its influence in the Western Hemisphere of the world.

But the victory vaulted the United States into the status of a world power. Soon after, the American military started modernizing its weapons and training. And a liberated Cuba made way for the building of the Panama Canal, which today remains one of the most crucial shipping channels on earth.

But there was another victory on San Juan Hill. The battle showed there was a new way of life in the United States.

Just thirty-five years before this battle, American men living in the North had fought against American men living in the South. Black men in the North were mostly poor and not hired for good jobs. In the South, black men were mostly slaves.

But here was an American force—one fighting unit—that was made up of men from the North and the South, black and white, and all them were working together for the cause of freedom. And winning.

History was made on San Juan Hill, in more ways than one.

WHO FOUGHT?

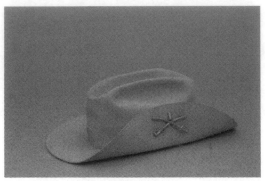

Rough Riders hat

Here's an interesting military history footnote: Two Medal of Honor recipients witnessed Roosevelt's actions at Kettle and San Juan Hills. Both of those men recommended the Rough Riders' intrepid leader for that same medal. But during his lifetime, Roosevelt's political enemies succeeded in denying him that honor.

After Roosevelt's death, his actions in Cuba were debated for decades. Finally, more than 100 years after his famous charge during the Spanish-American War, Congress approved the award. On January 16, 2001, President William Clinton presented Theodore Roosevelt's medal of honor to the leader's great-grandson.

BOOKS

Teddy Roosevelt: American Rough Rider by John Garraty

Bully for You, Teddy Roosevelt! By Jean Fritz

Spanish-American War by Edward Dolan

INTERNET

Teddy Roosevelt's birthplace is now a national park, offering
information the iconic soldier-President-statesman:
nps.gov/thrb/historyculture/tr-rr-spanamwar.htm

MOVIE

The Rough Riders (1997)

The Lost Battalion

October 2–7, 1918

Still photograph from the American war film *The Lost Battalion* (1919), on page 1947 of the June 28, 1919 *Moving Picture World*. Men who fought with the 77th Infantry Division in France acted in the film.

IN 1914, WORLD War I began raging through Europe.

This war pitted Germany against France, Great Britain, and many other countries. The United States, under President Woodrow Wilson, wanted to stay out of this war.

But in January 1917, Germany vowed to begin all-out submarine warfare. Germany said it would attack any ship—even if its home country was neutral in this war—and block all Allied ports. ("Allied" in this case means all the countries banding together to fight Germany).

President Wilson decided American men would have to help stop Germany's brutal aggression.

On April 6, 1917, the United States declared war on Germany. Most Americans greeted the news with enthusiasm. They expected a quick victory—a legendary foreign adventure just like the Spanish-American war.

But it was nothing like that.

In June 1917, the first American troops arrived in France. Called the American Expeditionary Force (AEF), they were led by US General John "Black Jack" Pershing.

Pershing had been part of that charge up San Juan Hill. He led the all-black regiments.

The AEF's first test came in in the Argonne forest of France. It was part of an overall Allied operation headed by a French officer, Marshal Ferdinand Foch. At first, the American soldiers fought well. But eventually, they got bogged down by bad weather, restrictive terrain, and really strong resistance by the Germans. It didn't help that these Americans weren't highly trained soldiers.

Marshal Foch grew impatient with the AEF. They weren't making as much progress as the other troops, and the French commanders thought *they* should be leading the Americans, not Pershing. They also thought the Americans were only good replacements for the more experienced French army.

They had a point: France had been fighting this war for three long years.

General Pershing managed to hold off Foch's plan to scuttle the Americans. But now the Americans felt pressure to prove they could fight. Their first opportunity came in a legendary battle known as "The Lost Battalion."

"Battalion" in this case isn't really accurate because a battalion is made up of four companies, each with 100–200 men. The Lost Battalion was actually seven companies of infantry with one machine gun company. Also, these troops weren't "lost" as in not knowing their location. They knew where they were. They just didn't know where their fellow forces were. They were "lost" as in abandoned.

On October 2, 1918, the unit's 554 men under the command Major Charles Whittlesey were making their way through the dense Argonne Forest. Their objective was to reach a place called Charlevaux Road and another place called Hill 198. Major Whittlesey's men were exhausted, having fought hard for months. He wanted to hold his current position, rest his men, and then move onto the Charlevaux Road.

But General Pershing felt pressure from the French commanders. Pershing gave orders to move out immediately.

For quite some time, the Germans had been defending this area of France. The German soldiers knew this forest like it was their own backyard. They also had established machine gun and mortar positions among the trees.

Major Charles Whittlesey

Major Whittlesey's men managed to slip through an unmanned gap in the German positions on Hill 198. Whittlesey then ordered his men to move down to the road, and take the backside of the hill. His troops set up positions that were about 300 yards in length and 60 yards wide. Machine gun sections were placed on their flanks to the east and west, and runner posts were set up every 100 yards along the route, so the battalion could stay in contact with the main military body to the rear. During WWI, radio wasn't used much for communications. Instead, human runners, dogs, and even carrier pigeons sent information among command posts.

Some patrols going up the hill reported that the surrounding terrain was clear of the enemy. So Whittlesey told his men to dig in for the night. The hillside was hard and rocky, with a muddy brook running along the bottom. Unfortunately, the men had moved so quickly on Charlevaux Road that they left behind their wool blankets and overcoats. Now they were facing a long cold night in the woods.

Then, at daybreak, the American patrols ran into Germans.

WWI soldiers in battle

The Germans had been ordered to move forward and reinforce their defenses on the hill. Seeing no threat from the French, and that their flank looked secure, the Germans returned to their positions on Hill 198—and suddenly they surrounded Whittlesey's unit.

Now these Americans were completely cut off from the rest of the Allied forces.

On the hill, the Germans started bombarding them with trench mortar shells. The Americans had dug into the backside of the slope, so the shells didn't inflict their full damage. But now the runners were coming back with bad news. The rear was completely closed off. The Americans had no way out. And each time they tried to re-establish their link to military command, the Germans opened fire with the heavy machine guns.

"Our mission is to hold this position at all cost," Whittlesey told his officers. "No falling back. Have this understood by every man in your command."

Surrounded, knowing there would be no more ammunition coming and no reinforcements to help, the Americans dug in. The Germans sent a near-constant barrage of machine gun fire, mortar shells, sniper fire, and ground attacks led by flame throwers. The assault continued for days. Stuck on the hillside in the cold French forest, the Americans grew hungry, thirsty, scared, and they were dying—but they resolved not to surrender.

One of the "buck privates" later wrote of his experiences:

> *Oh the stark raving madness of it all,*
> *The wail of the shells large and small,*
> *Sun blotted out by their singing sorrow,*

We waiting here for another tomorrow.

With each passing day, the soldiers dug deeper into what they called "funk holes." Medicine ran so low that men had to remove blood-soaked bandages from the dead and reuse them on the wounded who were still alive. Hardened soldiers wept listening to the wounded who were crying out for help but were just out of reach because of the deadly German guns.

Each morning, Whittlesey arranged burial details.

Carrier pigeon of WWI

But even these burials were dangerous. To keep from being seen by the Germans, soldiers dug graves on their knees or while lying on their sides. If they stood up, they got shot. Even the sound of a shovel could trigger more fire from the German guns. And after burial, mortar and artillery fire sometimes blew dead soldiers from their graves.

Some of the Lost Battalion tried to find an Allied supply drop. The Germans captured several of them. On October 7, the Germans sent back a blindfolded American prisoner-of-war carrying a white flag. The soldier carried this message:

"The suffering of your wounded men can be heard over here in the German lines, and we are appealing to your humane sentiments to stop. A white flag shown by one of your men will tell us that you agree with the conditions. Please treat Private Lowell R. Hollingshead [carrying the note] as an honorable man. He is quite a soldier. We envy you."

Instead, Whittlesey immediately ordered his men to pull down every white sheet that was being used as signals to reach Allied aircraft. He did not want the Germans mistaking these white signal flags for surrender.

Later that same day, seeing no surrender, and after being attacked from the north, the Germans pulled out of the area.

Five days after their ordeal began, an American patrol found The Lost Battalion.

Of the 554 men who were on the hill, 107 had died, and 159 were wounded. The surviving soldiers were incorporated into Allied lines to keep fighting World War I.

Several Distinguished Service Crosses were awarded to soldiers in The Lost Battalion, along with six Medals of Honor, including one for Major Whittlesley.

WHO FOUGHT?

Trench warfare WWI

WWI created new warfare tactics.

One tactic was called "creeping barrage." Soldiers ran ahead while artillery fired just beyond them, destroying any obstacles in their path, including the opposing front line. This barrage allowed troops to "creep" forward.

Another tactic was trench warfare. Opposing armies dug trenches that were separated by territory called No Man's Land. An army would charge from its trench while the other side charged out theirs. Trench warfare was a complete disaster. Men basically got slaughtered.

Other WWI developments included field telephones for communications, runners, homing pigeons, and dogs.

German submarines were known as Undersea Boat, or U-Boats. But the first U-Boats were actually used during the American Civil War as an experimental weapon.

Uniforms also changed during WWI, shifting from the bright, proud colors of the past—those British Red Coats, for instance—to more subtle hues like gray and green that provided some camouflage for troops hiding in woods or fields.

In 1917, when the United States joined WWI, America had one of the world's smallest armies with only 200,000 men. The only modern American weapon was the 1903 Springfield rifle. In 1918, as WWI was ending, the American military had grown to four million men. It also began developing its own modern weapons, such as the Browning light machine gun.

Germany lost WWI. In 1919, the countries that fought in WWI forced Germany to sign a peace treaty. It was called The Treaty of Versailles. Unfortunately, the treaty's conditions were really harsh for Germany and planted seeds of bitterness among the German people. That treaty wound up encouraging a ruthless dictator to take control of Germany. His name was

Adolph Hitler.

Adolph Hitler would lead Germany into World War II.

You can read about that incredible fight in *Great Battles for Boys: WWII in Europe.*

BOOKS

The Lost Battalion, a first-person account by John W. Nell

World War I: An Interactive History Adventure (You Choose: History) by Gwenyth Swain

DK Eyewitness Books: World War I by Simon Adams

INTERNET

History and Rhymes of the Lost Battalion by "Buck Private" McCollum, published in 1919, is available free of charge on the Internet: net.lib.byu.edu/~rdh7/wwi/memoir/Lost/ LostBatTC.htm

Read one of the messages carried by pigeons from the Lost Battalion: slate.com/blogs/the_vault/2013/03/27/ lost_battalion_transcription_of_message_carried_by_ pigeon_from_stranded.html

MOVIES

The Lost Battalion

A Note From Joe

On September 1, 1939, Germany invaded Poland.

It was a brutal invasion. Germany was showing the world a new form of warfare called *Blitzkrieg* or "lightning war."

Within months, Hitler's army would conquer nearly every country in Europe. To stop him, the United States joined forces with England. WWII required many battles and resulted in a lot of bloodshed. Some of the world's most legendary fights—full of heroism, honor, and valor—were fought during WWII.

You can read about WWII's many battles in two *Great Battles for Boys: World War II Europe* and *WWII in the Pacific*.

You can always reach me at my web page, www. greatbattlesforboys.com. And be sure to visit the Facebook page, Great Battles for Boys: facebook.com/greatbattles

Even after many years of reading and studying military battles, I'm still learning more about them. Below are some of the books that helped me put together these battles for you. I hope you'll keep reading about this great history, too.

The Guinness Book of Decisive Battles: Fifty Battles that Changed the World from Salamis to the Gulf War by Geoffrey Reagan

Lee's Lieutenants: A Study in Command (3 Volumes) by Douglas Southall Freeman

Texian Iliad: A Military History of the Texas Revolution, 1835–1836 by Stephen L. Hardin and Gary S. Zaboly

The Sword of San Jacinto: A Life of Sam Houston by Marshall De Bruhl

A Terrible Glory: Custer and the Little Bighorn—the Last Great Battle of the American West by James Donovan

The Last Stand: Custer, Sitting Bull and the Battle of the Little Big Horn by Nathaniel Philbrick

Fifty Battles That Changed the World by William Weir

Great Military Disasters by M. E. Heskew

Military History Quarterly

Military History magazine

About the Author

JOE GIORELLO GREW up in a large Italian family in Queens, New York, hearing firsthand stories from relatives who served in World War II and Vietnam. Those stories sparked his love of history and spurred him into studying military history. He's since acquired a vast library, stretching from ancient battles to modern warfare, and teaches a highly popular middle-grade class called "Great Battles."

As both a teacher and an author, Joe's goal is to remind young people that "freedom isn't free" and that history is anything but boring. When he's not teaching about historic battles, weapons, and warfare, Joe can be found playing blues around the Seattle area with his band, The Fabulous Roof Shakers.

Joe really likes hearing from readers. Contact him at his website, www.greatbattlesforboys.com.

Be sure to sign up for Joe's newsletter so you can be among the first to hear about new battle books in this series. You can also contact Joe on Facebook: www.facebook.com/greatbattles